HOUSEHOLD ACCOUNTS FROM MEDIEVAL ENGLAND

Part 1

RECORDS OF SOCIAL AND ECONOMIC HISTORY
NEW SERIES XVII

HOUSEHOLD ACCOUNTS FROM MEDIEVAL ENGLAND
Part 1

Introduction
Glossary
Diet Accounts (i)

EDITED BY
C. M. WOOLGAR

Published for THE BRITISH ACADEMY
by OXFORD UNIVERSITY PRESS

This book has been printed digitally and produced in a standard specification in order to ensure its continuing availability

OXFORD
UNIVERSITY PRESS

Great Clarendon Street, Oxford OX2 6DP

Oxford University Press is a department of the University of Oxford.
It furthers the University's objective of excellence in research, scholarship,
and education by publishing worldwide in

Oxford New York

Auckland Cape Town Dar es Salaam Hong Kong Karachi
Kuala Lumpur Madrid Melbourne Mexico City Nairobi
New Delhi Shanghai Taipei Toronto
With offices in
Argentina Austria Brazil Chile Czech Republic France Greece
Guatemala Hungary Italy Japan South Korea Poland Portugal
Singapore Switzerland Thailand Turkey Ukraine Vietnam

Oxford is a registered trade mark of Oxford University Press
in the UK and in certain other countries

Published in the United States
by Oxford University Press Inc., New York

Reprinted 2006

ISBN 978-0-19-726112-5

Foreword

For many years economic and social historians have been following the injunction to enter the kitchen but this latest title (being published in two volumes, XVII and XVIII) in the *Records of Social and Economic History* breaks new ground for the series in this respect for the medieval period. It moves from the high ground of charters, cartularies, subsidy rolls, which determined the fate of estates and institutions, to the more intimate documentation of the purchasing accounts for their households. The surviving records remain, for the most part, those of large households – the great nobles and archbishops, monasteries, priories and colleges – but, however eminent the establishment, its functioning rested upon the elemental supplies to its kitchen and their processing; the corn for brewing and baking, bread and ale, the 'ronds' of beef down to the piglets (and their food), chickens, butter, cheese, milk and eggs. Nothing escaped scrutiny or the clerk's pen. Nor was kitchen equipment and other necessary purchasing (such as horses) omitted; while exotics are also meticulously recorded, such as the Countess of Warwick's greyhounds and her bear – yes, she did keep a living symbol of her family's heraldic device.

The volume reveals much about the techniques of such medieval accounting practice, entries being systematically recorded and checked by professional clerks, often examined by the head of the household in person. Such detailed records, kept over time, provide more reliable guides to actual patterns of diet and consumption levels, parameters of nutrition (despite many problems of interpretation), movements of prices and the like, than the extraordinary but unrepresentative instances of occasional gargantuan feasts.

In diverse ways these two volumes provide substantial fare – indeed a feast of sources – for economic and social historians.

June 1992

Peter Mathias
Chairman, Records of Social and Economic History Committee

Contents

Part 2

DIET ACCOUNTS (ii)

Illustrations

Acknowledgements

This study developed, in the first instance, out of an interest in household accounts which arose from discoveries made while cataloguing the archives of Magdalen College, Oxford, in 1979–81. Subsequently, the accounts became the subject of my doctoral thesis and, with the encouragement of Professor P. D. A. Harvey, my supervisor, the project took on its present wider shape. In the preparation of this work, I have incurred a great many debts to owners of manuscripts, archivists and librarians, too numerous to mention by name, who have patiently answered my queries and who have made this study possible. For permission to consult their papers, I am grateful to the College of Arms; the Marquis of Bath; the Master, Fellows and Scholars of Corpus Christi College, Cambridge; the Master, Fellows and Scholars of St John's College, Cambridge; His Grace the Archbishop of Canterbury and the Trustees of Lambeth Palace Library; the President and Fellows of Corpus Christi College, Oxford; the President and Fellows of Magdalen College, Oxford; the Warden and Fellows of Merton College, Oxford; the Dean and Chapter of Westminster Abbey; the Warden and Fellows of Winchester College; the Dean and Canons of St George's Chapel, Windsor; and the Dean and Chapter of Worcester Cathedral. I am grateful to the following for permission to include editions of documents: the Controller of Her Majesty's Stationery Office (**1–4**, **25–26**); the County Archivist of Essex (**5**, **20**); the Trustees of the Earl of Winchilsea (**6**); G. M. T. Foljambe, Esq., and the Principal Archivist of the Nottinghamshire Record Office for material from the Foljambe of Osberton archives (**7**); the President and Fellows of Corpus Christi College, Oxford (**8**); the British Library (**9–10**, **12**, **14**, **24**, **27**); the President and Fellows of Magdalen College, Oxford (**11**); Lord Hampden and the East Sussex Record Office (**13**); the Shakespeare Birthplace Trust (**15**); the Staffordshire Record Office (**16**); Lord Talbot of Malahide (**17–18**); the Earl of Mexborough (**19**); A. J. Massingberd-Mundy (**21**); the Bishop of Carlisle (**22**); the Trustees of the late Captain A. C. Eyton (**23**); and the Dean and Chapter of Westminster Abbey (**28**). The photographs are reproduced by permission of the Controller of Her Majesty's Stationery Office, Basingstoke and Deane District Council and Colonel Sir Joseph Weld.

I owe particular debts to Professor P. D. A. Harvey, whose interest in this study over many years has been invaluable to me; to Dr G. L. Harriss, who offered me encouragement in the early stages; to Dr C. Barron, Dr C. Dyer and Mrs J. Stratford, who have given me advice on various points; and to Dr R. Mortimer and his colleagues at Westminster Abbey, for making my repeated visits a pleasure. Professor R. H. Hilton kindly read the whole work in typescript. I am grateful to the Records of Social and Economic History committee of the British Academy for a grant towards my expenses, which allowed me to pursue household accounts in France and Belgium. I also owe an especial debt to the University of Southampton and to the University Librarian, Mr B. Naylor, for granting me leave of absence from my normal duties to undertake parts of this work; to my immediate colleagues in the Library, whose burden has undoubtedly been greater than they expected; and to the services of the Inter-Library Loan section.

My wife, Sue, has lived with this project and its consequences for more than a decade: its completion would have been unimaginable without her constant support, encouragement and pragmatism; no words of gratitude can repay my debt or adequately describe its extent.

Christopher M. Woolgar
University of Southampton
3 March 1991

Abbreviations

AD Archives départementales
AND *Anglo-Norman dictionary* ed. L. W. Stone, W. Rothwell et al. (Publications of the Modern Humanities Research Association, 8; 1977–)
ANTS Anglo-Norman Text Society
AO Archives office
Arundell MA Manuscripts of R. J. R. Arundell, Lord Talbot of Malahide: Ministers' Accounts (in the Cornwall RO)
Berkeley SR Berkeley Castle Muniments, Select Roll
BIHR *Bulletin of the Institute of Historical Research*
BJRL *Bulletin of the John Rylands Library*
Black Book *The household of Edward IV. The Black Book and the ordinance of 1478* ed. A. R. Myers (Manchester, 1959)
BL British Library, Department of Western Manuscripts
Bodl. Bodleian Library, Oxford
Cal Charter Rolls *Calendar of Charter Rolls*
Cal Close Rolls *Calendar of Close Rolls*
Cal Fine Rolls *Calendar of Fine Rolls*
Cal Inq *Calendar of Inquisitions Miscellaneous*
Cal IPM *Calendar of Inquisitions Post Mortem*
Cal Patent Rolls *Calendar of Patent Rolls*
CCC Corpus Christi College
CP *Complete peerage of England, Scotland, Ireland, Great Britain, and United Kingdom* . . . ed. G. E. Cokayne, revised by Vicary Gibbs et al. (13 vols., London, 1910–59)
CUL Cambridge University Library
Curye on Inglysch *Curye on Inglysch. English culinary manuscripts of the fourteenth century (including the Forme of Cury)* ed. C. B. Hieatt and S. Butler (EETS supplementary series, 8; 1985)
Customs accounts of Hull *The customs accounts of Hull, 1453–1490* ed. W. R. Childs (Yorkshire Archaeological Society Record Series, 146; 1986)
DMLBS *Dictionary of medieval Latin from British sources* ed. R. E. Latham, D. R. Howlett et al. (London, 1975–)
Durham D. and C. Muniments of the Dean and Chapter of Durham, deposited in Durham University Library, Archives and Special Collections
EconHR *Economic History Review*
EDR Ely Diocesan Records
EETS Early English Text Society
EHR *English Historical Review*

History of the King's works *The history of the King's works* ed. H. M. Colvin et al. (6 vols., London, 1963–82)

JSA *Journal of the Society of Archivists*

KMED *Middle English dictionary* ed. H. Kurath and S. M. Kuhn et al. (Ann Arbor, Michigan, 1956–)

LS *A Latin dictionary* ed. C. T. Lewis and C. Short (Oxford, 1879)

Manorial records of Cuxham *Manorial records of Cuxham, Oxfordshire, circa 1200–1359* ed. P. D. A. Harvey (Historical Manuscripts Commission, Joint Publications, 23; 1976)

MCO Magdalen College, Oxford

MFG *A medieval farming glossary of Latin and English words taken mainly from Essex records* ed. J. L. Fisher (London, 1968)

MR Merton College, Oxford, rolls

Northumberland household book *The regulations and establishment of the household of Henry Algernon Percy, the fifth Earl of Northumberland, at his castles of Wresill and Lekinfield in Yorkshire. Begun anno domini MDXII* ed. T. Percy (London, 1770)

OED *Oxford English Dictionary*

OHS Oxford Historical Society

Peterborough D. and C. Muniments of the Dean and Chapter of Peterborough Cathedral

Port book of Southampton 1439–40 *The local port book of Southampton 1439–40* ed. H. S. Cobb (Southampton Records Series, 5; 1961)

PRO Public Record Office, London

PRS Pipe Roll Society

RMLWL *Revised medieval Latin word-list from British and Irish sources* ed. R. E. Latham (London, 1965)

RO Record office

Rose ***Lancastrian navy*** *The navy of the Lancastrian kings. Accounts and inventories of William Soper, Keeper of the King's Ships, 1422–1427* ed. S. Rose (Navy Records Society, 123; 1982)

Rot. Lit. Claus. *Rotuli litterarum clausarum in turri Londinensi asservati, 1204–27* ed. T. D. Hardy (2 vols., Record Commission, London, 1833–44)

RRS *Regesta Regum Scottorum* ed. G. W. S. Barrow et al. (Edinburgh, 1960–)

RS Rolls Series

SJC St John's College, Cambridge, archives

TBGAS *Transactions of the Bristol and Gloucestershire Archaeological Society*

Tout ***Chapters*** T. F. Tout *Chapters in the administrative history of medieval England: the wardrobe, the chamber and the small seals* (6 vols., Manchester, 1920–33)

Treaty Rolls *Treaty Rolls* (2 vols., London, 1956–72)

TRHS *Transactions of the Royal Historical Society*

UL University library

VCH *Victoria County History*

Veale ***Fur trade*** E. M. Veale *The English fur trade in the later middle ages* (Oxford, 1966)

Walter de Wenlok *Documents illustrating the rule of Walter de Wenlok, Abbot of*

Westminster, 1283–1307 ed. B. F. Harvey (Camden Society, 4th series, 2; 1965)

Walter of Henley *Walter of Henley and other treatises on estate management and accounting* ed. D. Oschinsky (Oxford, 1971)

WAM Westminster Abbey Muniments

WCM Winchester College Muniments

Worcester D. and C. Muniments of the Dean and Chapter of Worcester Cathedral

Editorial conventions

Chapter 5 describes many of the conventions used in editing. In addition the following abbreviations and conventions have been used throughout the volumes, for all forms of the words noted below:

bus. *bussellus* or bushel
cest. sester
d. *denarius*
di. *dimidius*, *a*, *um*
esk. abbreviated forms for skep
lag. *lagena*
li. *libra, livre* (sterling)
lib. *libra* (weight)
liv. *livre* (weight)
m. *marca*, mark
ob. *obolus*
pec. peck
pich. pitcher
pint., **pynt.** abbreviated forms of pint
qua. *quadrans*
quart. abbreviated Latin forms for quart
qr. *quarterium*, *quaterona*
s. *solidus*
sex. *sextarius*
virg. *virga*

Insertions in the text are surrounded by oblique strokes \/; deletions are marked by the use of angle brackets < > surrounding the text that has been struck out. The editions preserve the system of underlining employed by each clerk.

Wholly editorial reconstructions of parts of texts that are missing have been placed in square brackets [ ]. Missing areas are represented by three points, where there is a space that would allow up to three letters and abbreviations to be written. Five points have been employed for more extensively damaged passages and where the damaged passage continues onto a further line, the five points have been repeated.

References to counties in England and Wales are to those obtaining immediately prior to the changes made in 1974 under the Local Government Act 1972.

INTRODUCTION

Chapter 1
Introduction

The disappearance of the great aristocratic household in all but a handful of cases by the early years of the present century has cut us off from a tradition of living and lordship that can be traced back directly to early medieval Europe. It is now no longer easy to appreciate the importance and force of the bonds of the household, the impressive scale of its domestic arrangements and the potency of its politics. The difference in status of a yeoman and a groom is not immediately apparent to us, nor could it be of moment to anyone other than a historian. The words valet, butler, steward or marshal conjure before us wholly different images than they would even to our forebears of a century ago. Few of our houses will accommodate more than two or three guests in comfort; fewer still will allow us to entertain two dozen people to dinner; and domestic servants are unlikely to be there to assist us. How can we comprehend the significance of the hospitality offered by Dame Katherine de Norwich on 20 January 1337, the anniversary of the death of her second husband, disbursing a sixth of her annual household expenditure on that day, with probably ninety-two people present in her household; or the expenditure for the many hundreds of people who attended the household of Bishop Richard Mitford of Salisbury on the day of his funeral in June 1407 and who consumed at that time no fewer than 2,746 loaves of bread? As never before we are in danger of misunderstanding and underestimating the role of the household in our history.

The medieval household and its records attracted much attention from historians in the late eighteenth century and the nineteenth century;[1] and they are now again, after a period of fallow, the subject of active historical research. The account is one of the principal classes of record to survive from medieval household administration and it is essential to an

[1] For example, *Liber contrarotulatoris garderobae anno regni regis Edwardi primi vicesimo octavo* . . . ed. J. Nichols (London, 1787); *Compota domestica familiarum de Bukingham et d'Angoulême 1443, 1452, 1462, quibus annexae expensae cujusdam comitis in itinere 1273* ed. W. B. D. D. Turnbull (Abbotsford Club, 1836, with addendum, 1841); C. H. Hartshorne, 'Illustrations of domestic manners during the reign of Edward I', *Journal of the British Archaeological Association* 18 (1862) pp. 66–75, 145–52, 213–20, 318–32.

understanding of the later medieval nobility and monarchy.[2] Accounts have been used in the study of food and diet,[3] living conditions and hospitality,[4] travel,[5] the development of the arts, architecture, music and literature,[6] and they are a unique source for fashion, etiquette, education, politics and much else besides. Little attempt has been made, however, to view the documents as a coherent body of records or to place them in the context of the administrative systems for which they were created. It is the aim of this study to place household accounts in their wider setting, to provide a detailed introduction to their forms and to their development from the earliest surviving examples, in the late twelfth century, to the end of the fifteenth century, when the medieval forms were largely abandoned; the editions are intended to provide a valuable corpus of source material for historians of the medieval gentry, nobility and clergy; and at the same time the work is conceived as a parallel to those on manorial accounting and the financial operations of landed estates, as a contribution to the understanding of medieval finance in general.

In these two volumes are edited all the surviving accounts, once parts of extensive series, for twenty-eight households, which have been selected on the basis of differing size and economic capacity and to give as wide a geographical coverage of the country as possible. They range from aristocratic households, including those of the Earls of Oxford (**5**, **20**), Lincoln (**7**), March (**9**, **12**, **27**), and Salisbury (**26**), and of Thomas of Lancaster, Duke of Clarence (**28**); ecclesiastical households, notably those of a prominent London churchman (**3**), of Richard Mitford, Bishop of Salisbury (**14**), of John Hales, Bishop of Coventry and Lichfield (**16**), and of Richard Bell, Bishop of Carlisle (**22**); to those of knightly families,

[2] *Black Book*; K. B. McFarlane *The nobility of later medieval England* (Oxford, 1973); M. Cherry, 'The Courtenay Earls of Devon: the formation and disintegration of a late medieval aristocratic affinity', *Southern History* 1 (1979) pp. 71–97; *The English court from the Wars of the Roses to the Civil War* ed. D. Starkey (London, 1987); M. G. Underwood, 'Politics and piety in the household of Lady Margaret Beaufort', *Journal of Ecclesiastical History* 38 (1987) pp. 39–52.

[3] C. Dyer, 'English diet in the later middle ages', in *Social relations and ideas: essays in honour of R. H. Hilton* ed. T. H. Aston, P. R. Coss, C. Dyer and J. Thirsk (Cambridge, 1983) pp. 191–216; L. Stouff *Ravitaillement et alimentation en Provence aux xive et xve siècles* (Paris, 1970); M. A. Ladero Quesada, 'La alimentación en la España medieval. Estado de las investigaciones', *Hispania* 159 (1985) pp. 211–19.

[4] C. Dyer *Standards of living in the later Middle Ages. Social change in England c.1200–1520* (Cambridge, 1989); F. Heal *Hospitality in early modern England* (Oxford, 1990).

[5] G. Stretton, 'An earl's voyages in the late fourteenth century from the evidence of his household account books', *Mariner's Mirror* 11 (1925) pp. 307–15.

[6] M. Girouard *Life in the English country house: a social and architectural history* (New Haven and London, 1978); P. R. Coss, 'Aspects of cultural diffusion in medieval England: the early romances, local society and Robin Hood', *Past and Present* 108 (1985) pp. 35–79.

Sir William Waleys of Glynde, Sussex (**13**), and Sir William Mountford of Kingshurst, Warwickshire (**15**). Accounts **1**, **3** and **8** are concerned principally with London; **4** is centred on Bristol; **17** and **18** relate to Devon, **13** to Sussex and **14** to Wiltshire; the focus of **20** is Essex, that of **10** and **24** is East Anglia, while **15** and **16** centre on the Midlands, **23** on Shropshire, **19** near Leeds, **6** in North Yorkshire and **22** largely on Cumbria. **7** and **28** reflect travel to the Continent, **9** is based in Ireland, and **12** includes a journey to Scotland. Other accounts are for households travelling through central and southern England (**2**, **5**). Complete accounts have been chosen wherever possible to allow, for example, the comparison of total expenditures and the examination of seasonal differences. The accounts have also been selected by type of document and to illustrate the development of the forms of account. In so doing it has been possible to publish about five per cent of the surviving accounts for private households in medieval Britain; and all those that are known to survive are listed in the Catalogue included in the second volume.

Written accounts were a feature of the administration of every household of any size in Britain certainly from the beginning of the fourteenth century and probably before then, but, apart from the records of the English royal household, few have survived. There are perhaps three examples from medieval Ireland,[7] and the same number from medieval Scotland or Scots; again there is evidence that they were once more widespread.[8] In comparison with manorial accounts, the other principal form of account employed in private administration in England, the difference in the quantities preserved is very striking. While there are

[7] **9**; *Account roll of the Priory of the Holy Trinity, Dublin 1337–1346* ed. J. Mills (Royal Society of Antiquaries of Ireland, Dublin, 1891) pp. 1–25, 88–105.

[8] N. R. Ker and W. A. Pantin, 'Letters of a Scottish student at Paris and Oxford, *c.*1250', in *Formularies which bear on the history of Oxford c.1204–1420* ed. H. E. Salter, W. A. Pantin and H. G. Richardson (OHS, new series, 4–5; 1942) ii, pp. 471–91; Canterbury Cathedral Chapter Archives, Miscellaneous Accounts 61, Isabel, Countess of Atholl, *c.*1273–4. That household accounts were employed in the Scottish royal household is suggested by the ordinance probably for the household of John Balliol, *c.*1293 (M. Bateson, 'The Scottish king's household and other fragments from a fourteenth century manuscript in the library of Corpus Christi College, Cambridge', in *Miscellany II* (Scottish History Society, 44; 1904) pp. 1–43; R. Nicholson *Scotland in the later Middle Ages* (Edinburgh, 1974) p. 20, n. 77; p. 44); the household entries in the earliest accounts of the treasurer (*Compota thesaurariorum regum Scotorum. Accounts of the lord high treasurer of Scotland* ed. T. Dickson and J. B. Paul (11 vols., Edinburgh, 1877–1916) i); and the accomplished form of the earliest diet accounts to survive, for 1525 (*Excerpta e libris domicilii domini Jacobi quinti regis Scottorum MDXXV–MDXXXIII* ed. [Kilgour] (Bannatyne Club, Edinburgh, 1836), electrotype opposite p. 1).

many thousands of manorial accounts still in existence,[9] the Catalogue of private household accounts for the period to *c.*1500 numbers only some 500 items: although this list is undoubtedly incomplete, it serves to emphasize the disparity. The reasons for this are not hard to seek. There is some evidence that less durable media — wax tablets and paper, as opposed to parchment (invariably the medium employed for manorial accounts) — were used for household accounts and this has had an effect on the pattern of preservation. Further, unlike manorial records, which were evidence of the title to land, there was no legal impetus for the preservation of household documents. Although there was some use of household accounts to plan consumption from year to year, they may not generally have been seen as having a longer term purpose. Some of the accounts of Elizabeth de Burgh must have been preserved within her household for nearly forty years,[10] but it is very unusual in Britain to find household accounts remaining in family archives in company with estate documents. This deficiency contrasts with the rich series of household accounts that have survived on the Continent, for example, for the Counts of Savoy, the Counts of Flanders, the House of Artois, or the more than 10,000 that are still preserved, despite enormous destruction during the French revolutionary wars, for the House of Burgundy:[11] one can but lament the paucity of the material for Britain.

In Britain, the archives of the English royal Exchequer and Chancery are the most prolific source for the accounts of private households, documents that for some extraneous reason, the treason of a later member of the family or a law suit, have been brought into official custody. Elsewhere the accounts are most often found in contexts associated with household use, as pastedowns employed in the binding of books,[12] or, in one instance, possibly as a mirror case;[13] or in other areas where

[9] For example, PRO SC6/740–1088, listed in PRO *List of original ministers' accounts part I* (Lists and Indexes, 5; 1894) pp. 92–289.

[10] PRO E 101/91–5.

[11] Counts of Savoy: M. Chiaudano *La finanza sabauda nel sec. XIII* (Biblioteca della società storica subalpina, Turin, 131–3; 1933–8); Counts of Flanders: below, pp. 50–1; House of Artois, AD Pas de Calais, series A, and AD Nord, B 13587–8; House of Burgundy: W. Paravicini, '"Ordonnances de l'Hôtel" und "Escroes des gaiges". Wege zu einer prosopographischen Erforschung des burgundischen Staats im fünfzehnten Jahrhundert', in *Medieval lives and the historian. Studies in medieval prosopography* ed. N. Bulst and J.-P. Genet (Kalamazoo, Michigan, 1986) pp. 243–66.

[12] **9**; MS Royal 11 B X, ff. 185–8, unidentified household, late 14th or early 15th century; CCC, Oxford, MS 498, fragments 2–4, originally the pastedowns to MS 187, probably for Beatrice, dowager Lady de Roos, late 14th or early 15th century.

[13] Warws. RO CR 2018/1, unidentified household, 1318 or 1329.

parchment could be reused, for other documents[14] or as seal tags.[15] Apart from the Exchequer enrolments and engrossments, the accounts of the English royal household were no less susceptible to this treatment.[16] The consequence is there are very few household accounts that can be described as complete and many are no more than fragments. This has posed considerable problems of identification and dating; unless immediately relevant, however, detailed discussion of these aspects of individual accounts is confined to the Catalogue. There remain many examples which cannot be ascribed to particular households and to which dates can only be attributed on the general grounds of palaeography.

The expression 'household account' encompasses several forms of document which were regularly used for discrete parts of the accounting system. The form to survive most frequently, the diet account, was the one with which members of the medieval household would have been most familiar and which would have formed the most substantial category of household record. It contained the accounts of the household departments, into which medieval households of any size were commonly organised, principally the pantry, buttery, kitchen and marshalsea, with the accounts for each entered day by day, *per dietas*, hence 'diet' (from which, or some closely related usage, 'diet' has come to mean 'food'), or week by week (**1–16**). It was a form that was appropriate to the accounts of all private households, lay and clerical, including the households of bishops, abbots and priors; and, in a modified form, usually without a departmental structure, to corporate institutions, hospitals, abbeys, priories, chantries, colleges and schools. Departments could be added or omitted according to the structure of the household. The diet account was also referred to as an 'itinerant' or 'travelling' account, reflecting the peripatetic nature of the medieval household: there was in general no different form of daily account for a household that remained at a single place and the contrast implied was probably with the manorial account. Daily accounts were sometimes described by contemporaries as 'journals'.

There are accounts for the wardrobe in households in two guises. In its original sense, the wardrobe was a place where clothes were kept and as a

[14] G. H. Fowler, 'A household expense roll, 1328', *EHR* 55 (1940) pp. 630–4, an account later reused as a manorial court roll; **13**, a notarial instrument later reused for a household account.

[15] PRO DL 25/854, unidentified household, late 13th or early 14th century.

[16] BL Add. MS 62998, ff. 1, 130, part of an account of the keeper of the royal wardrobe for August to October in 1360, 1366, 1377, 1383, 1388 or 1394; CCC, Cambridge, MS 132, pasted to the last leaf, a page from a royal wardrobe book, *c.*1405–6; Durham UL, incunable +IVAC.A91P, front pastedown and flyleaf, cut from royal wardrobe accounts, early 15th century; J. C. Holt and Toshiyuki Takamiya, 'A new version of "A rhyme of Robin Hood"', *English manuscript studies 1100–1700* 1 (1989) pp. 213–21.

household department, termed 'the great wardrobe' in the English royal household, it was responsible for certain types of commodity of considerable value, cloth, wax, spices, jewellery. Secondly, it was a financial office, also described as a treasury or chamber, to which the handling and oversight of large sums of cash were entrusted. It was the fulcrum of the medieval accounting system, receiving cash on the one side from the receiver general and manorial accountants, and disbursing it to the household for expenditure on the other. The exact role it assumed varied from household to household: in some smaller households there was no need for a financial reservoir of this sort in the conduit leading from receiver general to household officials; in others, there was a further pool of funds, a 'privy purse', from which the lord spent as he pleased, with a modicum of accounting (**25–28**).

Other forms of household account include departmental accounts, containing separate records of the transactions of individual departments of the household (much in the same way as obedientiary accounts recorded the expenses of each 'obedience' or department of a monastery);[17] cash, corn and stock accounts, in a form resembling the manorial account, usually referring to a static household maintained at a fixed locality (**17–22**); livery accounts, recording the issue of cloth to members of the household;[18] calendars, naming all persons included in the household establishment;[19] and check or checker rolls, listing those entitled to wages and sometimes noting the presence or absence of members of the household, similar to the lists of people present for commons in collegiate institutions.[20]

For all these classes of account there was substantial supporting documentation. Many of the subsidiary records, the warrants, forms of receipt, tallies and vouchers, views of account and inventories, are identical to those employed in manorial administration, which, in the seigneurial economy, was scarcely divisible from the household.[21] There are, however, some items that were peculiar to households. Wax tablets, expressly forbidden in manorial accounting, were employed for rough household accounts.[22] Sections of household accounts, in origin no more

[17] PRO E 101/92/15, kitchen account of Elizabeth de Burgh, 1340–1.
[18] BL Add. Roll 64320, Edward de Courtenay, Earl of Devon, 1384–5.
[19] MCO Fastolf Paper 8, Sir John Fastolf, 1430–1.
[20] East Sussex RO MS GLY 3469 (1)–(17), John of Gaunt, 1381, 1391–4.
[21] *Manorial records of Cuxham* pp. 58–71.
[22] BL MS Harley 4971, ff. 26^{v}–7^{r}; *Manners and meals in olden time* ed. F. J. Furnivall (EETS original series, 32; 1868) p. 316. Household accounts for the Kings of France and the abbey of Cîteaux survive on wax tablets: L. L. Borrelli de Serres *Recherches sur divers services publics du xiiie au xviie siècle* (3 vols., Paris, 1895–1909) i, pp. 141–60; ii, pp. 69–76; *Recueil des historiens . . . de la France* xxi, pp. 226–392; xxii, pp. 430–565; BL Add. MS 33215; É. Lalou, 'Les tablettes de cire médiévales', *Bibliothèque de l'École de Chartes* 147 (1989) pp. 123–40. *Scriptum quoddam* in *Historia et cartularium monasterii Sancti Petri Gloucestriae* ed. W. H. Hart (3 vols., RS, London, 1863–7) iii, p. 216.

than paragraph headings, took on identities of their own, particularly from the mid-fifteenth century. The *preterea* (literally 'beyond this') listed items that fell outside the ordinary departmental structure of the household account (**22**); the 'remaneth', listing stock unexpended, *furniunturs*, *brasyantors* and *necantours*, the records of bakings, brewings and animals slaughtered, and *expendunturs*, probably noting total expenditure each month, were in use in the household of the fifth Earl of Northumberland by the second decade of the sixteenth century.[23]

The household was a body, governed and controlled by its lord, in which its members had defined rights. To belong permanently to a household was a valuable privilege: formal documents grant rights in private households, establishing rates of livery and food, and they even allocate seats at a particular table in the lord's hall, in much the same way as corrodies in religious houses.[24] These arrangements are also reflected in the usually temporary membership of households given in indentures of retinue, frequently encompassing 'bouche of court', the right to eat in the household.[25] Ordinances were employed, especially in the late thirteenth and early fourteenth centuries, and again from the mid-fifteenth century, on the one hand, to define who was a member of the household, effectively limiting the size of the household and its expense, and to provide an exposition of the duties of each office; and on the other, to set out working arrangements and disciplinary procedures, to remedy abuses and to ensure that a well-regulated household functioned 'to the honour and profit of the lord'. To Walter of Wenlok, Abbot of Westminster, at the close of the thirteenth century, accounting was central not only to the injunctions for his own household, but also, by implication, to all whose duty it was to maintain a household.[26]

[23] *Northumberland household book* pp. 3, 60–1, 65, 116, 392–3.

[24] PRO DL 25/929, 2026; MCO Deeds, Multon Hall 122.

[25] M. C. E. Jones, 'An indenture between Robert, Lord Mohaut, and Sir John de Bracebridge for life service in peace and war, 1310', *JSA* 4 (1970–3) pp. 384–94; J. M. W. Bean *From lord to patron. Lordship in late medieval England* (Manchester, 1989) p. 28, n. 118, and *passim*.

[26] *Walter de Wenlok* pp. 241–8; PRO C 47/3/33; *Black Book*.

Chapter 2
The earliest household accounts

Accounting in households was in origin an oral procedure, using a minimum of supporting documentation, perhaps a standard, listing allowances and food farms, against which issues and receipts could be compared. In the English royal household, the *Constitutio domus regis*, modified as allowances and personnel changed to a date after 1135, may represent this phase.[1] Written accounts became the familiar tool of royal administration during the twelfth century; in other establishments, from the end of the century, there can be seen the start of a move away from the most basic of accounting systems, founded on surveys or customaries, designed to verify or establish rights, combined with oral reports, to the formal preparation of written accounts. The speed with which the transition was made must not be exaggerated and it was not until the end of the thirteenth century that the use of written accounts became widespread in private administration; however, not only do the first written household accounts appear in the 1180s (**1**, Plate 1), but also, shortly afterwards, the first written manorial accounts.[2]

About a dozen household accounts have survived from the first half of the thirteenth century, representing the first stage in the development of written accounts in England for this purpose. An important feature is the very early appearance of a 'common form' in households differing greatly in size, regular daily accounts for the departments of the household, frequently in the same order, pantry, buttery, kitchen and marshalsea. The earliest household account from medieval England (**1**) reflects this: it is a fragment from a diet account and it deals with the items that are customarily associated with the individual departments of the medieval household in the order pantry (for example, bread), buttery (ale), kitchen (herring), marshalsea (horseshoes, hay), followed by candles, alms and

[1] C. M. Woolgar, 'The development of accounts for private households in England to *c.*1500 AD' (Univ. of Durham Ph.D. thesis, 1986) pp. 18–23; *Dialogus de scaccario* ed. C. Johnson, revised by F. E. L. Carter and D. E. Greenway (Oxford, 1983) pp. 128–35.

[2] *The pipe roll of the bishopric of Winchester, 1208–9* ed. H. Hall (London, 1903); *Manorial records of Cuxham* pp. 14–15; *The account book of Beaulieu Abbey* ed. S. F. Hockey (Camden Society, 4th series, 16; 1975) pp. 8–9; M. T. Clanchy *From memory to written record: England 1066–1307* (London, 1979) pp. 1–147.

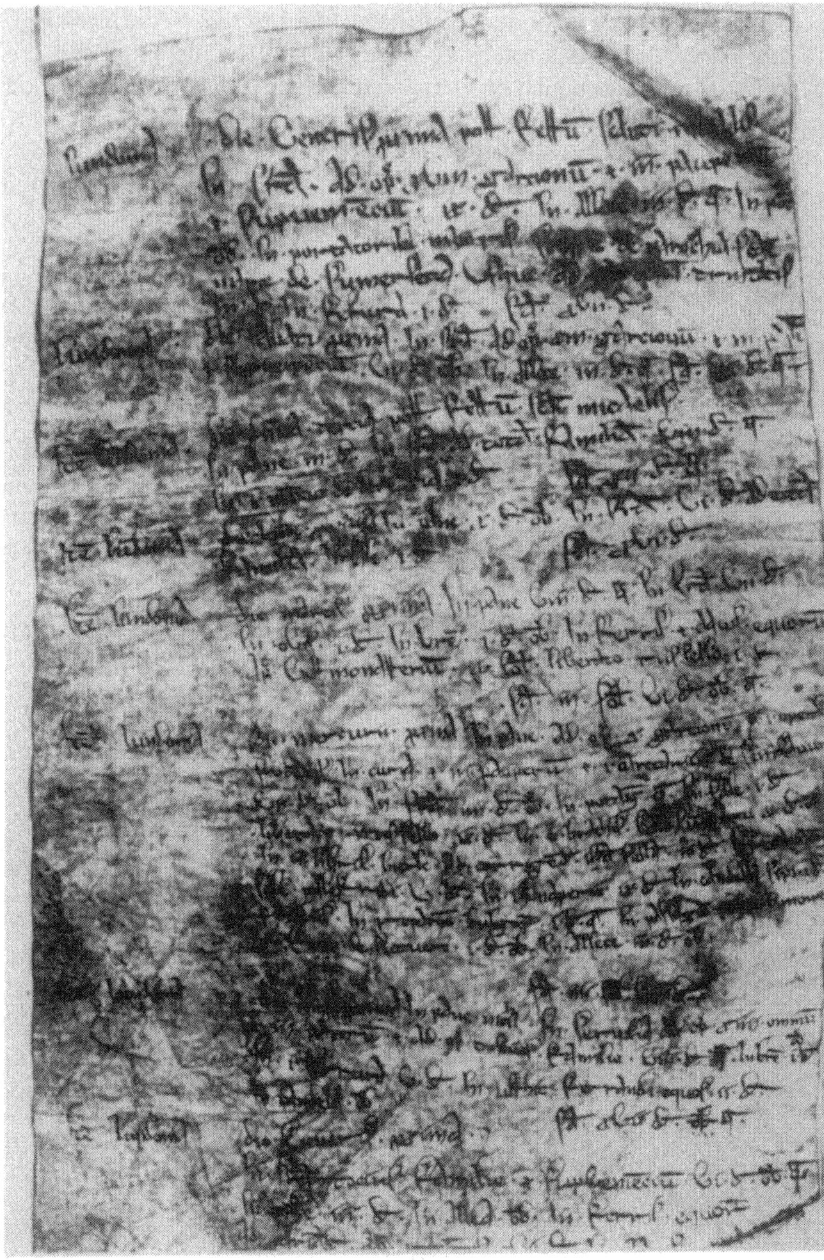

Plate 1 PRO E101/631/1 The earliest household account from medieval England, late twelfth century

miscellaneous items, but without any indication of this departmental responsibility. The correspondence of the account to this pattern throughout is not exact, but it is a tolerably close match. The virtual absence of meat from the account, which encompassed the activities of the kitchen, at a period that was not a season of fasting beyond the three customary days of abstinence in the week (Wednesday, Friday and Saturday),[3] suggests that the account is a record of purchases and cash payments rather than consumption. While it was not written up daily, a systematic check was made on daily purchases.

The primary purpose of all the early accounts was to record cash expenditure, not the consumption of food, although this begins to appear in a haphazard way, with some references to items drawn from stock (*de stauro* or *destor*), that is, goods already in the household's possession, in the kitchen cupboard or freezer, so to speak, as opposed to the entries of cash expenses for the day's shopping (**2**). The account for the household of Eleanor of Brittany, in 1225–6, is concerned wholly with purchases and cash expenses except, after the cash total for the week, are listed items consumed during the week — bread, meat, cheese, oats, wax and spices — in addition to the purchases. This list is in a different sequence of hands to the main text of the account and the consumption of these particular commodities had perhaps been recorded separately (**4**). Another account, a fragment from an unidentified household, *c*.1240–70, indicates consumption from stock but does not specify the quantities consumed.[4]

More than half the accounts surviving from this period are arranged in daily paragraphs. The daily entries all give the day of the week, sometimes referring to a feast day and a place, but never the date in the month. Most follow the departmental order of expenses already outlined, but in only two examples are departments named as headings in the account: the marshalsea appears in this way in the accounts for the household of Eleanor of Brittany (**4**), and a cash amount only is entered for the kitchen in an account for an unidentified household, *c*.1240–70.[5] There are references to the kitchen in the accounts of Hugh de Neville (**2**) and elsewhere, although they are not in a form that indicates the responsibility of a household department at the account. No departmental order, implicit

[3] This pattern of consumption, with fish forming the principal part of the diet on the fast days, continued in England throughout the medieval period and was enshrined in statute after the Reformation, for example, 5 Elizabeth I cap. 5 and subsequent legislation, not repealed until 1863, cited in W. E. Tate *The parish chest: a study of the records of parochial administration in England* (3rd edition, Cambridge, reprinted 1979) p. 156; B. A. Henisch *Fast and feast: food in medieval society* (London, 1976) pp. 28–52.

[4] PRO C 47/3/46/18.

[5] PRO C 47/3/46/18.

or explicit, is discernible in some accounts, such as the accounts of the household at Bristol Castle in 1221–2.[6] Besides the entries of daily expenses, several of the accounts have separate notes of bulk purchases. In the accounts for an unidentified London churchman, there are separate paragraphs for large purchases of corn and prests (**3**). The account for the household of Hugh de Neville includes some subsidiary accounts of purchases and expenses, noting where costs had been incurred by a particular official (**2**); and the accounts for the household at Bristol Castle, 1221–2, have separate paragraphs for large purchases of corn and wine, usually after each Friday's entry, at the end of the week.[7]

It is difficult to generalise about the arrangements for totalling accounts when all are fragments. Apart from the 1221–2 Bristol Castle accounts, the only accounts to exhibit a weekly arrangement and totals are the account for the household of Eleanor of Brittany (**4**) and an account for an unidentified household, *c.*1240–70.[8] On the last mentioned account, the week started on Sunday; on the two Bristol Castle accounts and on that for Eleanor of Brittany, the week started on Saturday. The account for an unidentified London ecclesiastic may have been totalled by membrane, with a grand total at the end (**3**). The remaining accounts have daily totals alone.

Marginal notes appear on several of the accounts. The account for the household of Hugh de Neville gives here some notes about financial responsibility (**2**); accounts for a household at Bristol Castle, 1221, may contain notes in the left margin of guests and visitors in addition to notes about the movements of the keeper of the castle;[9] and the arrival and departure of the lord of an unidentified household appear in the left margin of an account, *c.*1240–70.[10]

In different households varying numbers of clerks were engaged in compiling household accounts, and the records we have were prepared at different stages, from periodic engrossment at short intervals, to fair copies written after the close of the accounting period. Several are written in a single hand throughout, but one is a small fragment from which it would not be appropriate to draw conclusions.[11] The account of Hugh de Neville is in a single hand, possibly written in a single operation, with a few

[6] PRO E 101/349/4, E 101/350/10.

[7] PRO E 101/349/4, E 101/350/10.

[8] PRO C 47/3/46/18.

[9] PRO E 101/349/4.

[10] PRO C 47/3/46/18.

[11] PRO C 47/3/46/15, unidentified household, *c.*1220–50. C 47/3/46/18, unidentified household, *c.*1240–70, is another small fragment with each side written by a different hand throughout.

additional notes in another hand (**2**). The accounts for the household of an unidentified London churchman were written by a number of similar hands, engrossing the roll at fairly short intervals (**3**). The accounts for a household at Bristol Castle, 1221–2, have the text of the daily entries in a single hand, with daily totals at the right hand side in a second hand; weekly totals appear in the left margin in a third hand and grand totals were entered in a fourth hand.[12] The accounts for the household of Eleanor of Brittany are the most elaborate, with the text written up in blocks by one or two hands, including the daily and weekly totals, and the totals for items consumed entered subsequently by another set of clerks (**4**).

The largest households and those closest to the Crown may have already begun the evolution of separate wardrobe accounts. There was a distinction, from a financial point of view, between daily household purchases of consumables and other less frequent purchases, cloth, wine and spices. The latter were usually purchased in bulk and required a considerable amount of money; and the purchase usually took place away from the immediate vicinity of the household, at a market or fair. The value of the purchases, the distance at which they were made, and their comparative infrequency, ensured that the lord's most trusted officials were employed, probably those already engaged in looking after his treasure. Items later associated with wardrobe accounts — cloth, shoe repairs, the purchase of furs, payments to messengers, expenses on buildings and cash payments — are found intermingled with the departmental expenses on **1** and **3**. In contrast these items are excluded from the account for the household of Hugh de Neville, apart from some acquittances for minor accounts and wages, and from the account for Eleanor of Brittany, apart from spices and alms (**2**, **4**). The inference may be that in these two households there were already accounts or financial departments dealing with expenditure of this nature, payments outside the ambit of the principal domestic departments of the household.

It is also from this period that the first written accounts for the English royal household and the monasteries survive.[13] While the first royal household accounts, the *mise* and *prestita* rolls, date from the reign of

[12] PRO E 101/349/4, E 101/350/10.

[13] Earliest monastic accounts: R. A. L. Smith, 'The central financial system of Christ Church, Canterbury, 1186–1512', *EHR* 55 (1940) pp. 368–9; earliest accounts for individual obedientiaries, Bristol UL MSS DM 104/12–13, both printed in translation by V. R. Perkins, 'Documents relating to the monastery of St Mary, Kingswood', *TBGAS* 22 (1899) pp. 193–201.

John,[14] the earliest accounts extant which deal with the domestic departments of the royal household, as opposed to the specialised financial records of the royal chamber, are three fragments of a diet account roll dating from 1225–6.[15] These fragments are particularly important for the information they supply about the size and organisation of the English royal household. The average expenditure during the first week of the first fragment is a little under £6. 15*s*. a day, about eight times the average daily expenditure of Hugh de Neville in 1207 (**2**). The household departments appear in the same order as in many of the other early household accounts. More numerous in the royal household, the departments represent further subdivisions for sections performing tasks associated elsewhere with the principal departments: the care of napery, for example, was customarily the responsibility of the pantry; the scullery, saucery and the hunting larder were all offshoots of the kitchen; the expenses of the marshalsea have been separated into the cost of the stables and expenditure on grooms and horses. The main feature of the accounts — the entry of a cash sum alone for each department day by day — must have been derived from subsidiary records, either separate rolls for each department or perhaps a single, much more detailed roll of which these diet accounts are a breviate, possibly prepared for the chamber. A summary of an account for 8–11 Henry III, recording items of cloth, leather, payments for troops and probably the account for cash expenditure on alms, is the first royal wardrobe account to survive.[16]

Economic changes in the late twelfth and early thirteenth centuries may have hastened the adoption of written accounts. The tendency to the abandonment of food farms and the supply of households from the market, or drawing produce from a demesne agriculture which it was increasingly of value to adopt and control in the advent of the English inflation, may have been of importance, although the appearance of written accounts at this date is not solely an English phenomenon. A similar transition from accounting based on surveys to formal written accounts took place on the Continent without the impetus of inflation;[17] and by the early thirteenth

[14] *Rotuli de liberate ac de misis et praestitis regnante Johanne* ed. T. D. Hardy (London, 1844) pp. 109–253; *Documents illustrative of English history in the thirteenth and fourteenth centuries, selected from the records of the Queen's Remembrancer of the Exchequer* ed. H. Cole (London, 1844) pp. 231–69; J. C. Holt, 'Praestita roll 14–18 John', in *Pipe roll 17 John* ed. R. A. Brown (PRS, new series, 37; 1964) pp. 69–80, 85–100.

[15] PRO C 47/3/43/1–2, C 47/3/46/8, printed in *Roll of divers accounts for the early years of the reign of Henry III* ed. F. A. Cazel, jun. (PRS, new series, 44; 1982) pp. 93–102.

[16] *Roll of divers accounts* pp. 50–4.

[17] *Fiscal accounts of Catalonia under the early Count-Kings (1151–1213)* ed. T. N. Bisson (2 vols., London, 1984) i, p. 155.

century, while they do not survive in great quantity, there are examples of household accounts from all parts of Europe, including some of significantly earlier date. The earliest accounts of domestic expenditure preserved are in the archives of the Count-Kings of Catalonia: from 1156–7 there are accounts for the business of Count Ramon Berenguer IV, for guests and their food at Sant Pere de Vilamajor; and a further series of accounts for the expenditure of his successor, Alfons I, in 1181, 1183 and 1184.[18] While it is not possible to see much structure in the accounts for 1156–7, that for 1181 has begun to take on a regular order of foodstuffs; and there is a more apparent form in another document from this area, the accounts of the household of Guillema de Montcada at the castle of Sentmenat in 1189.[19] The activities of the household of Bishop Wolfger of Passau on a journey to and from Italy in 1204 and subsequently in the same year are represented by a small group of accounts and other examples show a regular pattern of accounting had been established in the French royal household by the early thirteenth century.[20] What is particularly interesting is the evidence that some of these accounts, as well as recording cash expenditure, had developed features that had a utility in household planning and management: the calculation of average cash expenditure per week, on ale, meat, cheese, fuel and other essentials appears in Bishop Wolfger's accounts. This emphasis on planning, estimating the expenses of the household and the provisions required, is also found in the treatise known as the *Rules of St Robert*, probably compiled as statutes for the household of Bishop Grosseteste of Lincoln and revised for the household of the Countess of Lincoln, *c.*1242; and it is likewise implicit in the earliest surviving formulary for a household account in England, possibly originating in the 1220s, which gives specimen entries for two days of a diet account, each of which has a single cash total combining the value of stock and cash expenses.[21] These developments cannot be traced in contemporary English household accounts, few of which mention the consumption of

[18] *Fiscal accounts of Catalonia* i, pp. 13, 18, 49–52, 90; ii, pp. 33–43, 101–3, 118, 120–3.

[19] R. Conde, 'Alimentación y sociedad: las cuentas de Guillema de Montcada (AD1189)', *Medievalia* 3 (1982) pp. 7–21.

[20] *Reiserechnungen Wolfger's von Ellenbrechtskirchen, Bischofs von Passau, Patriarchen von Aquileja* ed. I. V. Zingerle (Heilbronn, 1877), with corrections by A. Höfer, 'Die Reiserechnungen des Bischofs Wolfger von Passau', *Beiträge zur Geschichte der deutschen Sprache und Litteratur* 17 (1893) pp. 441–549; BL Add. Ch. 70697, printed by R. Fawtier, 'Un fragment du compte de l'hôtel du prince Louis de France pour le terme de la purification 1213', *Le Moyen Age* 3rd series, 4 (1933) pp. 225–46, where the document is incorrectly cited as Add. Ch. 70699.; L. L. Borrelli de Serres *Recherches sur divers services publics du xiiie au xviie siècle* (3 vols., Paris, 1895–1909) i, pp. 43–52.

[21] *Walter of Henley* pp. 191–9, 387–415; BL Add. MS 8167, ff. 131^{v}–3^{r}; H. G. Richardson, 'An Oxford teacher of the fifteenth century', *BJRL* 23 (1939) pp. 447–9; *idem*, 'The Oxford law school under John', *Law Quarterly Review* 77 (1941) pp. 319–38.

items from stock that would be necessary to calculate the average expenditure of, or quantities consumed by, the household. Both the *Rules* and the formulary ran some way ahead of contemporary English accounting practice and may have drawn their inspiration ultimately from continental sources; many of the features that develop in later English accounts can be shown to have continental antecedents.[22]

Unlike the first written manorial accounts, which are the product of large, centralised organisations, it is more difficult to see any pattern in the adoption of written accounts in households in medieval England. All came from fairly large establishments; the heads of the households are diverse, ranging from barons to churchmen, all of whom could have been familiar with the practices of the largest monasteries or the royal household, with which there was a close association in nearly half the surviving examples. Nor does the itinerant nature of the medieval household make it easy to discover any geographical basis to their usage. From the second half of the thirteenth century onwards, however, many more accounts survive and it is possible to undertake a more detailed consideration of the process and purpose of accounting.

[22] Below, pp. 50–2.

Chapter 3
Household accounts from the mid-thirteenth century to *c.*1430

The period from the mid-thirteenth century until 1430 is distinguished by the greatly increased number of household accounts that has been preserved. There are twice as many accounts surviving for private households for the second half of the thirteenth century as for the first half. From the next fifty years, there remain at least 175 accounts, and perhaps 160 for the period 1350–1430. This almost certainly reflects the more widespread use of written accounts, attaining a place in every household of substance. Very great quantities are extant for the English royal households, for some of the larger English monasteries, for some colleges and there are significant, if disjointed, runs for private households.

For the first time, from the period after 1250, we have different types of account, not just the diet account. The range of forms and classes employed by each household varied according to its size. For the household of Elizabeth de Burgh, Lady of Clare (*c.*1295–1360), one of the wealthiest women of the age, holding an estate which it has been estimated yielded more than £3000 a year in the 1320s, there remain some 100 accounts, about one-fifth of all the private household accounts that survive from medieval England. These show an elaborate system of financial record-keeping, including accounts of the clerk of her chamber, the clerk of the wardrobe, indentures between them, livery rolls, cash, corn and stock accounts, two forms of diet account, departmental accounts for the marshalsea, kitchen purchases, malt and brewing, and at least two types of counter-roll, summarising expenses.[1] On a lesser scale, the household of Richard, Lord Talbot, which spent about £277 in the year 1393–4, had a domestic accounting system comprising a diet account, a roll giving a

[1] M. Altschul *A baronial family in medieval England: the Clares 1217–1314* (Baltimore, 1965) pp. 166–74; R. E. Archer, 'Rich old ladies: the problem of late medieval dowagers', in *Property and politics: essays in later medieval English history* ed. A. J. Pollard (Gloucester, 1984) pp. 23–4; C. A. Musgrave, 'Household administration in the fourteenth century with special reference to the household of Elizabeth de Burgh, Lady of Clare' (Univ. of London MA thesis, 1923); C. M. Woolgar, 'The development of accounts for private households in England to *c.*1500 AD' (Univ. of Durham Ph.D. thesis, 1986) pp. 96–102.

weekly and monthly summary, and an annual summary account.[2] In further contrast, the wardrobe and diet accounts of John de Multon of Frampton, whose expenses amounted to about £60 in 1343–4, are much less formal, possibly written up by hired clerks rather than by established members of the household (**11a**, **11b**); and there is even less formality in the single diet account that is known for the household of Thomas Bozoun of Woodford next Thrapston, a Northamptonshire squire, for 1348, which shows a weekly cash expenditure a little in excess of 1*s*. 6½*d*.[3]

Both numerically and physically, diet accounts are by far the largest group of documents to survive. During the second half of the thirteenth century, the form of the diet account became more complex, with a new prominence given to information besides purchases that would be of use in household management. Consumption was one of the first areas to attract attention and items drawn from stock appear more frequently in the account (**5**). The household accounts of Eleanor de Montfort, 1265, add a further dimension. As well as the day's purchases, the account includes items from stock (*de stauro*), from manors (*de manerio*) and accounted for previously (*precomputatus*). The account is far from systematic, but it would seem that *de stauro* should refer to household stocks in hand which had probably been purchased some time before, perhaps in bulk, outside the diet account; *de manerio*, to articles drawn directly from manors; and *precomputatus*, to the consumption of items which had recently been entered as purchases in the diet account.[4] Similar notes of consumption of items already purchased or allowed occur in the diet accounts of Roger Leyburn, while combating rebels in 1266–7.[5] At best, however, the system of account was awkward and imprecise, perhaps indicating that its purpose was unclear and still evolving.

By 1290, with further elaboration, the account had taken a more coherent form. On the household roll of Richard de Swinfield, Bishop of Hereford, for 1289–90, the departmental accounts follow a strict order: recent purchases still in hand or stock that had been partly consumed, their consumption and remainder; purchases and gifts, with a note of what was

[2] Shropshire RO, Bridgewater collection, account of Richard, Lord Talbot, 1393–4; Bodl. MS Rolls Hereford 40, account of the same for 1392–3; B. Ross, 'The accounts of the stewards of the Talbot household at Blakemere: an example of medieval accounting practice', *Abacus* 4 (1968) pp. 51–72.

[3] G. H. Fowler, 'A household expense roll, 1328', *EHR* 55 (1940) pp. 630–4. The dating of this account is discussed in the Catalogue.

[4] BL Add. MS 8877, printed in *Manners and household expenses of England in the thirteenth and fifteenth centuries* ed. T. H. Turner (Roxburghe Club, 1841) pp. iv–lvi, 1–86.

[5] PRO E 101/3/9, part printed in A. Lewis, 'Roger Leyburn and the pacification of England 1265–7', *EHR* 54 (1939) pp. 211–14.

consumed and what remained; followed by miscellaneous departmental expenses, for example, for non-comestibles, such as plates, or payments of the expenses of those fetching or purchasing food.[6] Accounts adhering closely to this pattern, with regular details of goods in hand, stock consumed and of the day's remainder, were the exception rather than the rule;[7] but if a record was to be kept of what remained for future consumption, it was essential to note the amount of each purchase and the amount of stock consumed each day. A number of departmental sections in accounts, mainly for larger households, deals with stock before purchases.[8] In the household of Dame Katherine de Norwich, in 1336–7, the order was reversed (**10**). Occasionally there were two separate paragraphs for each day's account, one for purchases, the other for consumption.[9] It was common for stock details to be imprecise: an account such as that for the household of Henry de Overton, Abbot of Peterborough, for 1370–1, which, apart from kitchen purchases, dealt exclusively and elaborately with the movement of stock, was very unusual.[10]

The terminology used for stock and its meaning vary between households. Besides *staurum*, *lestor* and *de precomputato*, a number of accounts uses *de providencia* to refer to items drawn from large quantities of goods — 'gross emptions', bulk purchases or 'provisions' — laid down in store, which are not recorded as purchases in the diet account. It is apparent from the household cash, corn and stock accounts of the mid-fourteenth century onwards that the purchases recorded day by day in the diet accounts, when compared with the 'provisions' or 'gross emptions', represented only a small proportion of the household's overall expenditure. In the household of Margaret Plantagenet, Countess of Norfolk, 1385–6, expenses in the diet accounts amounted to £257. 16*s*. 5½*d*., just over a fifth of the total expenses of the household recorded on the annual roll.[11] The bulk purchases were sometimes recorded with the diet accounts. The accounts for the household of Richard Beauchamp, Earl of Warwick, 1420–1, start

[6] *A roll of the household expenses of Richard de Swinfield, Bishop of Hereford* ed. J. Webb (Camden Society, old series, 59, 62; 1853–4) i, *passim*, especially the note on pp. 87–8.

[7] Durham D. and C. Miscellaneous Charter 214, probably for a Prior of Durham, *c*.1360–90; BL MS Royal 11 B X, ff. 185–8, unidentified household, late 14th or early 15th century.

[8] PRO E 101/365/17, Humphrey de Bohun, 1304; E 101/509/29, attributed to Peter de Mauley, *c*.1320–50; WCM 1, William of Wykeham, Bishop of Winchester, 1393.

[9] BL MS Royal 6 B X, f. 1^{v}, unidentified household, *c*.1320–50; CCC, Oxford, MS 498, fragments 2 and 3, possibly for Beatrice de Roos, late 14th or early 15th century.

[10] Northants. RO Fitzwilliam (Milton) account rolls 266, printed in *Account rolls of the obedientiaries of Peterborough* ed. J. Greatrex (Northamptonshire Record Society, 33; 1984) pp. 56–83.

[11] BL Add. Ch. 17208, printed in *Medieval Framlingham. Select documents 1270–1524* ed. J. Ridgard (Suffolk Records Society, 27; 1985) pp. 86–128.

with a series of sections for large purchases of foodstuffs, arranged by commodity. When these are noted as consumed in the diet account, they are drawn *de providencia*; items purchased in the diet account consumed other than on the day of purchase are described as *de remanentia*.[12] On a number of diet accounts the entries for bulk purchases are intermingled with the daily entries. Paragraphs for the purchase of fish appear in the account of Eleanor de Montfort, 1265; and for the bulk purchases of meat, in November 1289, for the household of Bishop Swinfield of Hereford.[13] The sixth membrane of the accounts of Dame Katherine de Norwich, 1336–7, contains paragraphs for purchases of meat for the larder, for candles and wine, written up on at least two occasions probably close to the end of the account (**10**); stock for the larder and spices for the household of John de Multon, 1343–4, were recorded in a separate paragraph at the end of the account for his household (**11a**); and a paragraph for *instaurum* — oxen, cows and fish for the larder — concludes the diet account of the household of Joan, Lady Dinham, for 1367–8.[14] Similar paragraphs for 'provisions' occur separately on the dorse of the rolls of Thomas Arundel, Bishop of Ely, 1383;[15] and there are separate sections for bulk purchases for the larder in the accounts of Richard Mitford, Bishop of Salisbury, 1406–7 (**14**), and Dame Alice de Bryene, 1412–13.[16]

These developments were not followed in every household. When the household was travelling, there was sometimes little or no mention of items drawn from stock: the accounts represented cash purchases for immediate consumption, the household not wishing to carry stocks.[17] On occasion an itinerant household did draw on the stocks of manors along its route or carry purchases.[18] Some accounts of travelling expenses, on the other hand, do not give anything beyond a cash sum for the day's expenses, without indicating on what it was spent.[19]

In some households, most frequently small households, little attempt

[12] Longleat House MS Misc. IX, discussed by C. D. Ross, 'The household accounts of Elizabeth Berkeley, Countess of Warwick', *TBGAS* 70 (1951) pp. 81–105.
[13] *Manners and household expenses* p. 5; *Swinfield* i, p. 21.
[14] Arundell MA 411.
[15] PRO E 101/510/27, E 101/400/28.
[16] *The household book of Dame Alice de Bryene of Acton Hall, Suffolk, Sept. 1412 – Sept. 1413, with appendices* ed. M. K. Dale and V. B. Redstone (Ipswich, 1931) pp. 103–5.
[17] Berkeley SR 62, Thomas, Lord Berkeley, *c.*1320–50; PRO E 101/506/12, unidentified household, *c.*1320–50; Devon RO CR 1466, Hugh and Edward de Courtenay, 1395–1400.
[18] PRO E 101/507/8, Thomas de Chedworth, 1328; E 101/507/17, Simon de Eye, Abbot of Ramsey, 1337; **12**.
[19] PRO DL 41/10/41, unidentified household, *c.*1325–55; Arundell MA 414, 415, 416, 416a, John, Lord Dinham, 1381.

was made to record anything more than purchases.[20] Other accounts for small households made but a passing attempt to record items from stock or to note consumption from that source. The accounts of Thomas Bozoun of Woodford, Northamptonshire, for 1348,[21] and those of John de Multon of Frampton, 1347–8 (**11b**), record the consumption of stock but do not say what it was. The accounts of Edmund de Stonor, for 1378, are little more informative: bread and ale are distinguished, but no quantities or values are given.[22]

Once details of stock expended were inserted in the account, there were attempts to record the day's total expenses not only in cash, but also in terms of consumption. As a first stage, quantities of stock consumed were listed at the end of the week.[23] An account for William de Rupe, 1322, lists the total quantities consumed in three household departments, the pantry, buttery and kitchen, over the period of the account;[24] a late fourteenth century account for an unidentified household lists each day the amount of goods remaining;[25] and monthly totals of foodstuffs consumed appear in the accounts of Dame Alice de Bryene, 1412–13, and of Richard Beauchamp, Earl of Warwick, 1420–1.[26] These developments are associated very closely with the emergence of an annual stock account for the household in the fourteenth century.

The second step in recording consumption was to establish a valuation of items consumed from stock to produce a daily cash total of all expenses. While an example of this appears in the mid-thirteenth century formulary of William Haseley,[27] the earliest example of a valuation of stock in a British account does not occur before the early fourteenth century (**9**). The household accounts of Ralph of Shrewsbury, Bishop of Bath and Wells, for 1337–8, give the day's total in cash and divide it between purchases and expenses from the coffers (*de coffris*, i.e. cash liveries and payments) on the one hand, and a valuation of the stock consumed (*de instauro*) on the other; and the accounts of John Stratford, Archbishop of Canterbury, for 1347 and 1348, give daily cash totals, made up of purchases, a valuation of

[20] Warws. RO CR 2018/1, unidentified household, 1318 or 1329; PRO C 47/3/53/11, unidentified household, *c*.1320–50.
[21] Fowler, 'A household expense roll', p. 633.
[22] PRO C 47/37/1/25.
[23] Nottingham UL, Middleton MS Mi A1, Henry, Lord de Grey of Codnor, 1304–5; G. H. Holley, 'The earliest roll of household accounts in the muniment room at Hunstanton for the second year of Edward III', *Norfolk Archaeology* 21 (1920–22) pp. 77–96. There are some earlier traces of the system in **4**.
[24] Longleat House MS 4060, mem. 1.
[25] Sheffield City Archives C.D. 436.
[26] *Bryene* pp. 11, 36, etc.; Longleat House MS Misc. IX.
[27] BL Add. MS 8167, ff. 132–3.

stock and a valuation of gifts received.[28] The accounts of Nicholas de Litlington, Abbot of Westminster, for 1371–5, have daily cash totals of purchases (*empciones*) and a valuation of stock (*staurum appreciatum*); a similar feature is found in the accounts of William of Wykeham, Bishop of Winchester, for 1393.[29]

The diet accounts for the period present a more rigorous use of departmental structure and a more elaborate departmental entry within the daily account than earlier examples. Firstly, from the very end of the thirteenth century, following the example of the royal household, the largest households use dating formulae giving the day of the week and the date in the month, rather than referring to the day of the week and occasionally to a feast day.[30] Then, each day, the departmental expenses appear most frequently in the order pantry, buttery, kitchen, marshalsea. Departments were not always named and this order cannot be said to imply that these divisions formed administrative entities in the households where the departmental titles do not appear, or even, although the case is stronger, when the titles are present. The appearance of departmental titles has both a chronological evolution and one based on size of household. In the thirteenth century, outside the royal household, few household departments were named. The accounts of Eleanor de Montfort, 1265, Roger Leyburn, 1266–7, and Bogo de Clare, 1285, mention by name only the kitchen and the marshalsea and these not on every day.[31] From the end of the thirteenth century, there are many more examples and a wider range of departments. The accounts of Joan of Valence, Countess of Pembroke, 1295–7, have sections for the pantry, buttery, kitchen, saucery, ostlery, marshalsea, alms and wages;[32] the accounts of Humphrey de Bohun, 1304, are divided into pantry (*dispensa*), buttery, kitchen, poultry, scullery, chamber, stable and wages; those for the Countess of Hereford, for the same year, have the same divisions, but include the saucery, omitting the chamber.[33] The accounts of Thomas of Lancaster, 1318–19, include the hall;[34] and the hall and chamber appear together as a departmental heading in the account for the household of John Sandale,

[28] J. A. Robinson, 'Household roll of Bishop Ralph of Shrewsbury', in *Collectanea I* ed. T. F. Palmer (Somerset Record Society, 39; 1924) pp. 72–174; WAM 9222–3.

[29] PRO SC 6/1261/6, part 1; WCM 1.

[30] 7; PRO E 101/366/30, Elizabeth de Bohun, Countess of Hereford, 1305; E 101/506/24, household of John Sandale, Bishop of Winchester, after his death, 1319.

[31] BL Add. MS 8877; PRO E 101/3/9; E 101/91/1, mem. 3^{r}.

[32] PRO E 101/505/25–7.

[33] PRO E 101/365/17, 20.

[34] PRO DL 28/1/14.

Bishop of Winchester, after his death in 1319.[35] Other accounts name as departments the chandlery,[36] the cellar (**14**) and the wardrobe.[37] Two thirteenth century Abbots of Westminster, Richard de Ware and Walter de Wenlok, have separate paragraphs most days in their diet accounts for the chamber, covering miscellaneous cash expenses, carriage expenses, workmen, alms and similar items;[38] and Henry de Overton, Abbot of Peterborough, in 1370–1, and Dame Alice de Bryene, in 1412–13, had separate daily sections for kitchen purchases.[39] A daily section for the larder occurs on an account for an unidentified household, *c.*1320–50,[40] and an account, probably for the household of a Prior of Durham, *c.*1360–90, has daily sections for stock, alms, gifts and small expenses.[41]

The areas of activity encompassed by the household departments were not always the same. In the account of Dame Alice de Bryene of Acton Hall, 1412–13, the pantry section of the account embraced those functions usually associated with the buttery; the structure of the account of Bishop Swinfield of Hereford, 1289–90, implies a similar practice.[42] Distinctions are sometimes blurred within the same household, perhaps indicating that personal responsibility was the key to the division, with each department accounting for what those associated with it purchased. On the first membrane of an account for the household of Thomas, Lord Berkeley, *c.*1328–9, cream, butter and cheese all appear in the kitchen section; but on the second membrane, the pantry section includes cream, milk and cheese.[43]

A clearer distinction between departments led to a more detailed departmental account. In the accounts of the household of William de Rupe, 1322–4, the pantry account is elaborated to include the number of loaves in hand at the start of the day, the quantity consumed and the number left at the end of the day; the buttery deals with ale, wine and mead, noting items from stock (*de instauro*); the kitchen section records the number of portions (*fercula*) of each type of meat in hand at the start of the day, what was expended and what remained; and the marshalsea section notes the number of horses present.[44] De Rupe's household was

[35] PRO E 101/506/24.
[36] Hants. RO 148M71/3/1/2, William Edendon, Bishop of Winchester, mid-14th century.
[37] PRO SC 6/1261/6, part 1, Nicholas de Litlington, Abbot of Westminster, 1371–5.
[38] WAM 24489–90.
[39] Northants. RO Fitzwilliam (Milton) account rolls 266; *Bryene* pp. 1–115.
[40] BL MS Royal 6 B X, f. 1^{v}.
[41] Durham D. and C. Misc. Charter 214.
[42] *Bryene* pp. 1–105; *Swinfield* i, *passim.*
[43] Berkeley SR 61.
[44] Longleat House MSS 4050, 4060, 10470.

not particularly large, and it is not surprising, therefore, to find a much more detailed analysis in the accounts of larger establishments. The pantry section of an account probably for Lionel, Earl of Ulster, in the 1350s or 1360s, divides the bread into issues for meals, for breakfast, for rewards, trenchers, the kitchen, predetermined issues, extraordinary issues, the stables, after lunch, and for 'all night' (*tota nocte*); and the sections for wine and ale are divided in a similar way.[45] The allocation of bread appears in the margins of the diet accounts of Richard Beauchamp, Earl of Warwick, 1420–1 and 1431–2, the first of which regularly includes provision of bread for the Countess of Warwick's greyhounds and her bear.[46] No private household account seems to have employed the practice advocated by a fourteenth century treatise, in which the pantry account was to give the number of loaves issued by the pantler and their value, and the amount allowed to the pantler was then to be proportional to the number of meals consumed;[47] but the rolls recording the fines imposed at the nightly audit of accounts in the English royal household of the late thirteenth and early fourteenth centuries show a similar practice, with the careful regulation of rates of issue per portion and the surcharge of the officials responsible for items incorrectly issued (*male expensis*), in most instances representing items used over and above a predetermined allowance per portion of each commodity.[48]

Kitchen sections dealt with food usually in order of size of commodity, in much the same order as stock accounts on the dorse of manorial account rolls. Portions are noted rarely in kitchen sections although it is known that the division of meat was supervised closely: the English royal household provides examples of officials surcharged for meat that had been divided badly.[49] The accounts, however, concentrate on the overall quantities purchased or consumed. Richard Beauchamp's account for 1420–1 is exceptional, recording *ronds* of beef.[50] The functions of the kitchen were sometimes further subdivided into departments, a poultry, scullery, saucery and larder. The poultry dealt not only with domestic fowl, but also with piglets and young animals of all sorts, their food, butter, milk and eggs.[51] Spices were sometimes the province of the kitchen (**13**); sometimes,

45 PRO E 101/94/9. For the later formal ceremony attached to 'all night', *Black Book* pp. 237, n. 47; 259, n. 401; *Northumberland household book* p. 64.

46 Longleat House MS Misc. IX, Warws. RO CR 1618/W19/5.

47 L. Lacour, 'Traité d'économie rurale composé en Angleterre au xiiie siècle', *Bibliothèque de l'École des Chartes* 4th series, 2 (1856) pp. 380–1.

48 PRO E101/353/28; E 101/365/11; E 101/368/9.

49 PRO E 101/353/28, mem. 1[r].

50 Longleat House MS Misc. IX.

51 PRO E 101/506/24, household of John Sandale, Bishop of Winchester, after his death in 1319; Berkeley SR 58, 61, Thomas, Lord Berkeley, 1328–9; Hants. RO 148M71/3/1/2, William Edendon, Bishop of Winchester, mid-14th century.

along with wax and candles, the concern of the wardrobe.[52] Marshalsea sections frequently give the numbers of horses present, sometimes noting a separate number of hackneys,[53] the numbers of grooms and pages, and, on occasion, lists of names of those present for household wages.[54] The departmental order was often followed even when no expense was incurred, *nichil* being entered in the appropriate section.[55] The order in which the departmental accounts were presented varied in some instances from day to day.[56] The day's account was sometimes divided into two, repeating the order of the departmental entries, if the household moved to a second location on the same day (**5**, **12**). Some accounts also made a distinction between purchases for, or consumption at, particular meals.[57]

The departmental framework had become the basis for a very elaborate set of checks on household management. It could be employed as a model even when the household contained no complex internal organisation. The daily accounts of the warden of Merton College, Oxford, on a journey in 1356, follow the order pantry, buttery, kitchen and marshalsea, without naming departments; but the regular diet accounts for his household when at Oxford, for example, for 1378 and 1383–4, are almost exclusively for kitchen expenses, with notes of the expenses of bread, ale, candles and cheese at the end of each week.[58] Other accounts have little or no departmental structure (**10**, **11b**).

More advanced systems of totalling accompanied the developments in departmental structure. Many diet accounts are totalled each day and, besides the daily totals, thirteenth century accounts are often totalled by membrane.[59] Later accounts are often totalled by week and by month and a fourteenth century treatise, concluding the instructions for setting out a diet account, tells the clerk to total the account each day, each week, each month and each year.[60] Weeks usually start on Sundays, but some weekly arrangements start on Saturdays;[61] the accounts of John Stratford,

[52] Longleat House MS Misc. IX, Richard Beauchamp, Earl of Warwick, 1420–1.
[53] Longleat House MS 3772, possibly for an Earl of Stafford, *c*.1350–80; **12**; **14**.
[54] WCM 1, William of Wykeham, Bishop of Winchester, 1393.
[55] PRO E 101/372/4, E 101/505/17, E 101/510/17, Hugh Audley the younger, 1320.
[56] 'Ralph of Shrewsbury'.
[57] PRO C 47/3/35, E 101/506/11, William de Stowe, 1318 or 1329, distinction between *prandium* and *vesper*; *Account roll of the Priory of Holy Trinity, Dublin 1337–1346* ed. J. Mills (Royal Society of Antiquaries of Ireland, Dublin, 1891) pp. 1–15; **12**.
[58] MR 3535, mem. 3; 3545; 3549.
[59] PRO E 101/3/9, Roger Leyburn, 1266–7; E 101/505/25–7, Joan of Valence, Countess of Pembroke, 1295–7.
[60] Lacour, 'Traité d'économie rurale', p. 381.
[61] Fowler, 'A household expense roll'; MR 3532, 3545, 3549, household of the warden of Merton, 1347–8, 1378, 1383–4.

Archbishop of Canterbury, for 1347 and 1348, and the accounts of Nicholas de Litlington, Abbot of Westminster, for 1371–5, have weeks starting on Mondays;[62] those probably for an Earl of Stafford, *c.*1350–80, and those for a Prior of Durham, *c.*1360–90, start on Thursdays.[63] Months could be periods of four weeks[64] or calendar months.[65] Quarterly[66] and annual totals also occur.[67] Some accounts do not have totals;[68] others, mainly for smaller households, have weekly totals but no daily ones.[69] The account of Sir William Waleys of Glynde, Sussex, 1382–3, has no cash totals, but weekly totals of animals killed (**13**). Accounts for some of the larger households give totals of cash expenditure by department.[70] In the accounts for the household of Henry de Lacy, Earl of Lincoln, 1299, in the text of the daily entry there are cash totals for the pantry and buttery combined, the kitchen and the marshalsea (**7**). On other accounts, the departmental totals occur in the margin of each day's entry.[71] These were used to provide grand totals of expenditure by department at the end of the accounting period.

It was customary to enter in the margin the name of a new place of residence on each occasion the household moved (**12**). Brewings and bakings are also recorded in the margin (**5**, **6**, **9**). These notes were made to draw the attention of the auditor to passages in the main text, where, in some accounts at least, the product of each baking or brewing was given.[72] The consumption of wine was also the subject of marginal notes. In the accounts for the household of John Stratford, Archbishop of Canterbury, in 1347 and 1348, the left margin contains notes of wine from stock (*de instauro*): no wine appears in the buttery section of the account. There are also drawings of barrels to mark the start of each new hogshead or pipe.[73] Different shapes of barrel appear in the margins of an account for the household of Richard Beauchamp, Earl of Warwick, 1420–1, to mark the

[62] WAM 9222–3; PRO SC 6/1261/6, part 1.
[63] Longleat House MS 3772; Durham D. and C. Misc. Charter 214.
[64] *Swinfield* i.
[65] CUL EDR D5/2–7, 7a; PRO E 101/400/28, E 101/510/27, Thomas Arundel, Bishop of Ely, 1380–4.
[66] Somerset RO DD/L P37/7, Sir Hugh Luttrell, 1405–6.
[67] Arundell MA 411, Joan, Lady Dinham, 1367–8.
[68] **6**; Longleat House MSS 4050, 4060 mem. 1, 10470, William de Rupe, 1322–4.
[69] **11a**, **11b**; PRO C 47/37/1/25–7, Edmund de Stonor, 1378.
[70] PRO E 101/505/25–7, Joan of Valence, Countess of Pembroke, 1295–7.
[71] PRO E 101/372/4, E 101/505/17, E 101/510/17, Hugh Audley the younger, 1320; Hants. RO 148M71/3/1/2, William Edendon, Bishop of Winchester, mid-14th century.
[72] **9**; Berkeley SR 58, Thomas, Lord Berkeley, 1328, noting the product of beans baked for horse-bread in the marshalsea section; **13**; **14**.
[73] WAM 9222–3.

start of pipes of wine, cades of white or red herring, or salted salmon.[74] Some accounts have marginal entries for the start of carcasses (**6**); others for animals slaughtered for the household (**13**); for partridges from hunting;[75] for venison from the larder and from hunting;[76] for liveries from manors, items from stock or stock started,[77] and possibly for wheat received.[78]

The principal members of the household present and visitors were sometimes listed in the main body of the account (**7**). Some accounts confine their entries to notes of the arrival or departure of the lord or lady from the household establishment (**6**): there is usually no change in the form of the account, although expenditure may decrease during the lord's absence, to be supplemented by purchases in preparation for his return.[79] Visitors, representing an additional charge on the household, were often noted in the margin beside the day's account. Some lists are long and detailed, for example, those for William of Wykeham's household in 1393,[80] or for Bishop Mitford's establishment in 1406–7 (**14**); others, such as an account for the household of Roger de Mortimer, restrict themselves to the most important visitors (**9**). The record of visitors could extend in elaboration to note the meals at which they were present,[81] broken down by name or rank, even as far as recording the entertainment of a late fourteenth or early fifteenth century Abbot of Rievaulx in a household, probably of Beatrice de Roos, for a drink.[82] Other accounts specifically note the number of poor present.[83]

Another development was the recording, frequently in the margin, of the numbers of portions of food or messes (*fercula, mes*) consumed each day. Contemporaries intended a close check to be kept on the issue of all foodstuffs. In the household of Nicholas de Spina, Abbot of St Augustine's, Canterbury, 1273–83, the cook for the hall and his valet were to answer each evening to the cellarer for the portions received;[84] numbers of portions (*mes*) served were to be recorded each night in the household

[74] Longleat House MS Misc. IX.
[75] *Swinfield* i.
[76] WAM 9222–3, John Stratford, Archbishop of Canterbury, 1347 and 1348.
[77] PRO E 101/505/25–7, Joan of Valence, Countess of Pembroke, 1295–7; **10**.
[78] Warws. RO CR 2018/1, unidentified household, 1318 or 1329.
[79] PRO E 101/506/12, unidentified household, *c.*1320–50.
[80] WCM 1.
[81] PRO SC 6/1261/6, part 1, Nicholas de Litlington, Abbot of Westminster, 1371–5; *Bryene*.
[82] CCC, Oxford, MS 498, fragment 3^v.
[83] PRO E 101/505/25–7, Joan of Valence, Countess of Pembroke, 1295–7; **10**; BL MS Royal 11 B X, ff. 185–8, unidentified household, late 14th or early 15th century.
[84] *Customary of the Benedictine monasteries of Saint Augustine, Canterbury, and Saint Peter, Westminster* ed. E. M. Thompson (Henry Bradshaw Society, 23, 28; 1902–4) i, p. 60.

of Walter de Wenlok, Abbot of Westminster, *c.*1295–8;[85] and similar injunctions appear in treatises on household management and accounting.[86] Although numbers of *fercula* are largely absent from the daily household rolls of the English royal household, the household ordinances of 1279 and 1318 confirm that they were to be recorded.[87] It is not, however, until 1320 that numbers of *fercula* appear on a private household account, for Hugh Audley the younger.[88] A single daily figure for *fercula* appears on the accounts of larger households for the remainder of the fourteenth century and early fifteenth century.[89] The figures for *fercula* include halves on an account of Thomas, Lord Berkeley, for 1328–9.[90] A further refinement was to analyse how many *fercula* were consumed at each meal: accounts from the mid-fourteenth century onwards divide the number between two meals, luncheon (*prandium*) and dinner (*cena*),[91] or three meals, including breakfast (*jantaculum*).[92] Other accounts record the number consumed by visitors to the household.[93] Besides visitors, the status of those eating the meals is noted, for example, on three occasions in the household account of Ralph of Shrewsbury, Bishop of Bath and Wells.[94] An account for an unidentified household, *c.*1320–60, divides the daily number of *fercula* between the gentle members of the household (*gentiles*), personnel of the household offices (*officiarii*), and grooms (*garciones*).[95] Three divisions are made for each of the meals noted in the accounts of Nicholas de Litlington, Abbot of Westminster, in 1371–5, but without defining the ranks of those consuming them.[96] On the household account of William of Wykeham, 1393, the total number of *fercula* for each meal is divided between *gentiles*

[85] *Walter de Wenlok* p. 243.

[86] *Fleta* ed. H. G. Richardson and G. O. Sayles (Selden Society, 72; 1955) p. 248; Bodl. MS Fairfax 24, f. 62^{r}: 'Mettaez en remembraunce chascun jour le noumbre des mees qe sont despendus en sale al un manger e al autre'; Lacour, 'Traité d'économie rurale', p. 380.

[87] Tout *Chapters* ii, p. 160; *idem*, *The place of the reign of Edward II in history* (second edition, Manchester, 1936) pp. 253–5.

[88] PRO E 101/372/4, E 101/505/17, E 101/510/17.

[89] PRO E 101/509/29, attributed to Peter de Mauley, *c.*1320–50; E 101/94/10, E 101/95/10, E 101/95/13, Elizabeth de Burgh, Lady of Clare, *c.*1320–50; Northants. RO Westmorland (Apethorpe) 4. xx. 4., Edward Plantagenet, Duke of York, 1409–10; CUL EDR F5/33, ff. 19^{v}–20^{r}, notes from a diet account of Thomas Peverel, Bishop of Worcester, 1413.

[90] Berkeley SR 61.

[91] CUL Add. MS 5963, part 67, unidentified household, late 14th or early 15th century; East Sussex RO MS GLY 3469 (18)–(20), John of Gaunt, 1383.

[92] Northants. RO Fitzwilliam (Milton) account rolls 266, Henry de Overton, Abbot of Peterborough, 1370–1; *Bryene*.

[93] Bodl. MS Rolls Hereford 40, Richard, Lord Talbot, 1392–3.

[94] 'Ralph of Shrewsbury': 5 December 1337, 5 January 1338, 9 March 1338.

[95] PRO E 101/95/6.

[96] PRO SC 6/1261/6, part 1.

and *officiarii*.[97] The record of the consumption of *fercula* was unrelated to the account as a financial instrument and is indicative of the broader role it had come to play in household management.

Underlining, besides highlighting departmental headings, is most frequently used, as it was on manorial accounts, to indicate price per unit — head of cattle, bushel of corn, ell of cloth — or any other cash amount that was not to be included in the total (**11a**, **12**, **15**). The pattern sometimes operated in reverse: in the accounts of Humphrey de Bohun, 1304, and Elizabeth de Bohun, Countess of Hereford, 1305, the total price per purchase is underlined, but not the price per unit.[98] Weights are underlined in the accounts of Henry, Lord de Grey of Codnor, 1304–5, and weights of cheese in an account for Thomas, Lord Berkeley, in 1328.[99] In the accounts of Dame Katherine de Norwich, 1336–7, the appraised values of items drawn directly from manors were underlined and they were subsequently added together to form a separate part of the daily total (**10**). The valuations of gifts in the daily totals of an account of William de Stowe, 1318 or 1329, are underlined, as are the values of items from stock in the accounts of John Stratford, Archbishop of Canterbury, for 1347 and 1348, and in the accounts of Nicholas de Litlington, Abbot of Westminster, 1371–5, in the last example also being combined to form a separate daily total.[100] Numbers of horses at particular rates of livery are underlined in an account probably for an Earl of Stafford, *c*.1350–80.[101] In some accounts no pattern to the underlining can be discerned.[102]

Most diet accounts were made up as Chancery fashion rolls. In some cases there is evidence that additional membranes were sewn to the foot of the roll on an *ad hoc* basis, as more space was required. The household accounts of Eleanor de Montfort, for 1265, were probably made up in this manner, as the membranes are of varying widths, lengths and quality.[103] In broad terms the pattern made by the sewing of those accounts written on Chancery fashion rolls changes during the late thirteenth and early fourteenth centuries from /\/\/\[104] or ///[105] or --- (**5**, **6**) with a fairly

97 WCM 1.
98 PRO E 101/365/17; E 101/366/30.
99 Nottingham UL, Middleton MS Mi A1; Berkeley SR 61, mem. 2.
100 PRO C 47/3/35, E 101/506/11; WAM 9222–3; PRO SC 6/1261/6, part 1.
101 Longleat House MS 3772.
102 PRO E 101/510/27, Thomas Arundel, Bishop of Ely, 1383.
103 BL Add. MS 8877.
104 PRO E 101/505/25–7, Joan of Valence, Countess of Pembroke, 1295–7; E 101/510/5, Genoese visiting England, early 14th century.
105 PRO E 101/91/5, Bogo de Clare, 1284.

wide overlap, to a tight oversew with virtually no overlap.[106] This development in the make up of the diet account is generally similar to the pattern of change in other records of private administration.[107] The membranes were sewn with hemp or linen thread, most frequently now a brownish-white, but occasionally blue (**15**) or green.[108] There are some examples of household accounts made up as Exchequer fashion rolls, but these are markedly fewer in number.[109]

Parchment was frequently prepared for writing by folding it vertically to set out a left margin and the centre of the membrane. Additional folds were made for a right margin or for further subdivisions. The accounts of Humphrey de Bohun, 1304, were laid out with five vertical folds.[110] Lateral folds were occasionally employed to divide off the daily entries (**7**, **8**). Up to the mid-fourteenth century, ruling in lead point or ink wa also used for setting out accounts. On some accounts the ruling is confined to the vertical divisions of the left and right margins;[111] on others a horizontal line was ruled for each line of text.[112] While ruling disappears as a method of laying out accounts, folding continues throughout the medieval period, but is less frequently employed after the late fourteenth century.

Household ordinances and formularies lay stress on the regular hearing of accounts, in many cases nightly, and their engrossment.[113] This nightly account must be imagined as the first hearing or 'auditing' of the accounts. It would be wrong, however, to give the impression that all the surviving diet accounts, as daily accounts, were written up each day: the records are

[106] Nottingham UL, Middleton MS Mi A1, Henry, Lord de Grey of Codnor, 1304–5.

[107] *Manorial records of Cuxham* p. 48.

[108] Longleat House MS 3772, probably for an Earl of Stafford, *c.*1350–80; Arundell MA 420, John, Lord Dinham, 1384–5.

[109] PRO DL 28/1/14, Thomas, Earl of Lancaster, 1318–19, described as a 'Liber hospicii'; C 47/3/35, E 101/506/11, William de Stowe, 1318 or 1329; Norfolk RO NH1, Roger de Holm, 1328; Berkeley SR 61, Thomas, Lord Berkeley, 1328–9; **10**.

[110] PRO E 101/365/17.

[111] PRO E 101/507/17, Simon de Eye, Abbot of Ramsey, 1337–8.

[112] Bodl. MS Lat. hist. d. 1 (R), Bishop Swinfield, 1289–90; PRO DL 28/1/14, Thomas of Lancaster, 1318–19.

[113] *Walter de Wenlok* p. 241; S. J. A. Evans, 'Ely chapter ordinances and visitation records: 1241–1515', in *Camden Miscellany XVII* (Camden Society, 3rd series, 64; 1940) pp. 24–6; *Customary of the Benedictine monasteries of Saint Augustine, Canterbury, and Saint Peter, Westminster* i, p. 55; PRO C 47/3/33, lord and lady of Eresby, 1319 or 1339; *Fleta* p. 243; BL MS Harley 4971, ff. 6^{v}–9^{r}. Daily accounting was also the practice on the Continent: for example, French royal household, 1315 (F. Lot and R. Fawtier *Histoire des institutions françaises au moyen âge* (3 vols., Paris, 1957–62) ii, p. 66); Yolande, Countess of Cassel and Bar, 1352 (AD Nord B 3247 (112185)); Duke of Brabant, 1407 (P. Kauch, 'L'organisation et le contrôle financier de l'hôtel d'Antoine de Bourgogne, duc de Brabant', *Revue belge de philologie et d'histoire* 24 (1945) pp. 180–201); Margaret, Archduchess of Austria, 1516 (AD Nord B 3384 (113883)).

only a part of elaborate accounting systems and represent many methods of compilation from daily engrossment to fair copies written throughout in a single operation. On some diet accounts where periodic engrossment took place, changes in hand and ink coincide with marginal notes indicating a change of accountant. On one of the diet accounts of Bogo de Clare, 1285, there is a change of hand accompanying the heading 'Raymond de Sulye accounted up to here and then W. de Regny began his disbursements.'[114] On Thursday 10 May the new hand wrote its first day's account. A new pen was used on the following Saturday, different ink on Sunday, different again on Monday, and a new pen for the following Thursday. The change in each case occurs at the beginning of the daily entry, suggesting the account was written in short blocks — of two days, one day, one day, three days and two days — rather than variations within a single operation copying out the document. This pattern of entry can be observed on Eleanor de Montfort's account, and on this account there is also a separate sequence of hands that writes the daily totals.[115] The daily text of the accounts of an unidentified late thirteenth century household, residing near Boroughbridge (**6**), the accounts of Hugh Audley the younger, 1320, and those of William de Rupe, 1323, were written several days at a time.[116] The intervals at which other accounts were engrossed varied. The accounts of Joan of Valence, Countess of Pembroke, 1295–7, seem to have been written in periods of irregular length, perhaps ten or twenty days at a time, corresponding to notes that the cash expenses incurred for the period had been paid.[117] The household accounts of Edmund de Stonor, 1378, including weekly totals, were written by different hands in irregular blocks of between two and three weeks' length.[118] Some documents were written a membrane at a time (**11b**).

Accounts on parchment written up at short, if not daily, intervals either date from before about 1340 or belong to small households. One probable reason for this is the spread of paper (or the use of wax tablets) as a medium for recording accounts at an earlier stage of compilation, reserving the use of parchment for revised copies, sometimes engrossed after audit, superseding the drafts and doing away with the need to preserve them. A connected reason for this pattern of survival may have been a change in the emphasis of the procedure for auditing accounts, placing more weight on an annual record in the form of a cash, corn and stock account, supported

[114] PRO E 101/91/1, mem. 3^{r}.
[115] BL Add. MS 8877.
[116] PRO E 101/372/4, E 101/505/17, E 101/510/17; Longleat House MS 4050.
[117] PRO E 101/505/25–7.
[118] PRO C 47/37/1/25–7.

by a fair copy of the diet account, parallel to the estate valors and enrolled manorial accounts of the late fourteenth and fifteenth centuries, to provide a general overview of income and expenditure.[119] Reflecting this is a group of diet accounts which are carefully written fair copies, prepared by a single hand often in one operation. A fragment of the accounts of William Edendon, Bishop of Winchester, from the mid-fourteenth century, falls into this category (Plate 2).[120] The monthly household rolls of John Stratford, Archbishop of Canterbury, for 1347 and 1348, and of Thomas Arundel, Bishop of Ely, 1380–4, are likewise fair copies,[121] as is the household account of William of Wykeham, Bishop of Winchester, for 1393, which is less a practical accounting document than an ornamental engrossment, designed for presentation as a supporting document with a six monthly or annual account.[122] After this date there are very few examples in private households of fair copies of diet accounts on parchment rolls (**15**).

Besides the daily audit or hearing of the departmental accounts of the household, the written account of the clerk of the household was subject to the scrutiny of auditors. Daily totals to accounts are sometimes in a different hand or ink to the text, suggesting that the clerk who wrote the account had a partner (or 'controller') to check or supervise his work.[123] In some instances weekly (**11a**) and monthly totals were added after the text of the account had been written.[124] One of the most common indications of auditing is the use of the word *probatur* ('it is proved' or 'shown to be correct'), or one of its abbreviated forms, placed against totals or on each page of an account book, and written in a different hand to the account and the totals (**11a, 12, 14**). In an account probably for the household of Beatrice de Roos, late fourteenth or early fifteenth century, it also occurs against the list, in the margin, of persons present each day.[125] The word *quit* sometimes appears in the margins to indicate the auditor's approval (**6**). Dots, used in the process of totalling or checking, appear on several documents from the fifteenth century.[126] The examination of these accounts was an important stage in the preparation for the audit of the annual cash, corn and stock account.

[119] P. D. A. Harvey *Manorial records* (London, 1984) pp. 36–8.
[120] Hants. RO 148M71/3/1/2.
[121] WAM 9222–3; CUL EDR D5/2–7, 7a, and PRO E 101/400/28, E 101/510/27.
[122] WCM 1.
[123] PRO E 101/365/20, Countess of Hereford, 1304; Berkeley SR 63, [Thomas], Lord Berkeley, *c.*1330–60; Arundell MA 429, John, Lord Dinham, 1401.
[124] PRO E 101/372/4, E 101/505/17, E 101/510/17, Hugh Audley the younger, 1320.
[125] CCC, Oxford, MS 498, fragments 2 and 3.
[126] **14**; Northants. RO Westmorland (Apethorpe) 4. xx. 4., Edward Plantagenet, Duke of York, 1409–10.

Plate 2 Hants. RO 148M71/3/1/2 A fair copy of a diet account from the mid-fourteenth century, for the household of William Edendon, Bishop of Winchester

In large households, where daily accounts for the whole household would have been extremely lengthy, separate departmental accounts were kept, together with cash journals, which gave only the total cash expenditure of each department. Cash journals are best known from the royal household;[127] they have also been preserved for the household of Thomas, Earl of Lancaster, 1318–19, and for the household of John of Gaunt, 1383.[128] The departmental accounts which should accompany cash journals in this form are extant only on rare occasions outside the royal household. Examples include stable or marshalsea accounts for Gilbert de Clare, 1301–2,[129] Elizabeth de Burgh,[130] and John of Gaunt, 1381 and 1390–4.[131] The last provide, in tabular fashion, for members of the household, its staff and horses, an indication of presence or absence or of allowance received on each day of the week. There are mentions in accounts of other subsidiary documents of this nature: in the account of Edmund Mortimer, Earl of March, 1378, there is a reference to archers whose names are listed in the 'book of the marshalsea' (**12**). These lists would have been based on household check or checker rolls and calendars, setting out the members of the household or those entitled to draw wages, fees or pensions,[132] but little survives today, even from the English royal household, where there was extensive documentation of this nature, to parallel the accounts that remain on the Continent, for example, the daily lists of those paid wages in the household of the Dukes of Burgundy.[133] Butlers' rolls are noted in a mid-fourteenth century treatise on household organisation.[134] A few departmental accounts survive from the fifteenth century, including a fragment of an account of the clerk of the kitchen of Richard Beauchamp, Bishop of Salisbury, 1466–7, and two accounts for officials of the household of Richard, Duke of York.[135]

One class of departmental account for which there are many more examples is the wardrobe account. In the earliest household records, some

[127] *Records of the wardrobe and household 1285–1286* ed. B. F. Byerly and C. R. Byerly (London, 1977) pp. 117–63; *Records of the wardrobe and household 1286–1289* ed. B. F. Byerly and C. R. Byerly (London, 1986) pp. 504–31; A. R. Myers, 'The captivity of a royal witch: the household account of Queen Joan of Navarre, 1419–21', *BJRL* 24 (1940) pp. 263–84; 26 (1941) pp. 82–100.

[128] PRO DL 28/1/14; East Sussex RO MS GLY 3469 (18)–(20).

[129] PRO E 101/91/8.

[130] PRO E 101/93/16; E 101/94/6–7; E 101/95/4–5, 8.

[131] East Sussex RO MS GLY 3469 (1)–(17).

[132] K. B. McFarlane *The nobility of later medieval England* (Oxford, 1973) pp. 109–13.

[133] For a printed example, W. Paravicini, 'Soziale Schichtung and soziale Mobilität am Hof der Herzöge von Burgund', *Francia* 5 (1977) pp. 127–82.

[134] Bodl. MS Fairfax 24, f. 62^{v}.

[135] PRO C 47/3/32/36; BL Egerton Rolls 8786–7.

entries of a wardrobe type — purchases of wine, spices, cloth, jewellery, gifts, expenses of messengers, together with a host of miscellaneous items — were intermingled with the diet account. Wax and spices continue to appear in some diet accounts.[136] Wardrobe entries of all sorts are mixed with the daily purchases of foodstuffs in the accounts of John Catesby, 1392–3 and *temp*. Richard II.[137] Similar entries appear on the annual summary accounts: on the cash, corn and stock account for Edward de Courtenay, Earl of Devon, 1384–5, the paragraph for the wardrobe in the cash discharge section deals solely with wax and spices.[138] Outside the English royal household, the earliest separate wardrobe accounts are found entered on diet account rolls, frequently on the dorse. The household account of Eleanor de Montfort, 1265, has a wardrobe journal on the dorse, entered periodically in the same sequence of hands that wrote the diet account on the front.[139] Wardrobe entries in chronological order appear on the dorse of the diet accounts of Bogo de Clare, 1284–5; John de Multon, 1343–4; and John Stratford, Archbishop of Canterbury, 1347 and 1348.[140] Separate wardrobe or treasurer's journals, interspersing the lord's major financial transactions with purchases of spices and similar wardrobe items, survive, for example, for the households of John Mauduyt, 1312–14 (**25**), William de Montagu, second Earl of Salisbury, 1367–8 (**26**), and Thomas de Stafford, Earl of Stafford, 1391–2.[141]

The information in the wardrobe journal, like the diet account, was the subject of later rearrangement and consolidation. The wardrobe accounts on the dorse of the diet accounts of Richard de Swinfield, Bishop of Hereford, for 1289–90, were rearranged from a journal into subject paragraphs for cloth, wax and spices, fees and stipends and other items.[142] An account probably for Isabel, Countess of Atholl, *c*.1273–4, may also exhibit a sectional arrangement.[143] Bogo de Clare's wardrobe accounts, rearrangements of daily rolls, include receipts from property as well as sections for the expenses of cloths, furs, jewels, cash liveries, expenses of messengers, purchases of horses, spices, wine and gifts.[144] The accounts for the wardrobe of Thomas, Earl of Lancaster, *c*.1319–20, were divided into

136 Nottingham UL, Middleton MS Mi A1, Henry, Lord de Grey of Codnor, 1304–5; **13**.
137 PRO E 101/511/15, E 101/512/5.
138 BL Add. Roll 64803.
139 BL Add. MS 8877.
140 PRO E 101/91/1, 2, 5; **11a**; WAM 9222–3.
141 Longleat House MS Misc. VIII.
142 Bodl. MS Lat. hist. d. 1 (R).
143 Canterbury Cathedral Chapter Archives, Miscellaneous Accounts 61.
144 PRO E 101/91/3, 4, 6, 7, 31; M. S. Giuseppi, 'The wardrobe and household accounts of Bogo de Clare, AD 1284–6', *Archaeologia* 70 (1918–20) pp. 1–56.

sections for the expenses of messengers, purchase of horses, candles and lights, spices, wine, parchment, napery, fees, petty and foreign expenses, liveries, archers, journeys on business, carriage expenses and purchases of wheat and flour.[145] Some of these items, for example, the expenses of messengers and jewels, are reminiscent of the divisions in royal wardrobe accounts.[146] Whether the royal wardrobe and its accounts served as a model can only be a matter of conjecture: the key to the arrangement was probably the need for large sums of cash, restricting the personnel involved to those with access to the lord's coffers. The forms of the accounts themselves are very diverse, but private households of the largest size, from the mid-fourteenth century, follow the royal household in the change from keeping wardrobe accounts on rolls to engrossing them in books.[147]

The elaboration of wardrobe accounts led to the development of specialised accounts for particular parts of the wardrobe's business. Cloth and the issue of livery are noted on most wardrobe accounts and as early as the accounts of Bogo de Clare, 1285–6, there is a form of stock account for cloth and livery.[148] Much more detailed accounts for the purchase and issue of livery occur in the household records of Elizabeth de Burgh. These include a livery roll, listing the names of all the members of the household and noting the livery issued to each.[149] Livery accounts survive for the households of Edward de Courtenay, Earl of Devon, for 1384–5, and for that part of the household of Thomas of Lancaster, Duke of Clarence, which crossed the Channel in the company of his wife in November 1419.[150]

Other households had accounts that dealt in detail with cloth and similar commodities. An account for Roger Mortimer, Earl of March, 1393–4, concerns almost exclusively cloth, goldwork, harness, embroidery and the making of clothes. The account is arranged by purchases made by particular individuals: two documents from the same household for the subsequent accounting year are subsidiary bills of purchases that would

[145] PRO DL 28/1/13.

[146] *Records of the wardrobe and household 1285–1286* pp. 1–116; *Liber quotidianus contrarotulatoris garderobae anno regni regis Edwardi primi vicesimo octavo* ... ed. J. Nichols (London, 1787).

[147] M. T. Clanchy *From memory to written record: England 1066–1307* (London, 1979) pp. 111–12; *Records of the wardrobe and household 1285–1286* pp. ix–xv; BL Add. MS 18632, ff. 2, 101, Elizabeth, Countess of Ulster, 1356–9; M. R. James *A descriptive catalogue of the manuscripts in the library of Peterhouse* (Cambridge, 1899) pp. 61–3; M. Sharp, 'A fragmentary household account of John of Gaunt', *BIHR* 13 (1935–6) pp. 154–60; **28**.

[148] Giuseppi, 'The wardrobe and household accounts of Bogo de Clare', pp. 36–40.

[149] PRO E 101/92/23.

[150] BL Add. Roll 64320; **28**, f. 16^{v} (an inserted leaf); McFarlane *Nobility of later medieval England* pp. 110–13.

have been transcribed to form the annual roll.[151] Some of the late fourteenth century accounts for Henry, Earl of Derby (later King Henry IV), record cash expenditure and a stock account for items of this nature.[152] As well as accounts for purchase and disbursement, constant checks were available on wardrobe items in the form of inventories, containing detailed descriptions.[153]

Like the diet accounts, the surviving wardrobe accounts are representative of different stages in the accounting process. Some are elaborately written fair copies[154] and, of these, some have been audited. The account of Roger Mortimer, Earl of March, 1393–4, has marginal totals and *probatur* written against each paragraph in another hand and ink.[155] Most pages of the account for Thomas of Lancaster, Duke of Clarence, 1418–21, have been marked, in a bottom corner, possibly on two occasions, 'it is examined' (*examinatur*), by an auditor, who also made alterations to the text (**28**). There are also examples of wardrobe accounts which were engrossed periodically, for instance, the account on the dorse of Eleanor de Montfort's household roll, 1265, and the account book of Margaret Plantagenet, Countess of Norfolk, 1394–5.[156] The periodic engrossment and informality of the accounts of Edmund Mortimer, Earl of March, 1413–14, point to the employment of 'privy purse' accounts, for the lord's personal expenditure, his whims and purchases, which almost seem designed to elude a conventional accounting system (**27**).

Receiver's accounts, those listing total cash receipts from manors, lands, etc., collected by bailiffs and handed to a receiver to be transmitted to the centre of the financial system, were sometimes combined with the accounts of the household and wardrobe. The household rolls of John de Multon, 1343–4, John de Catesby, 1392–3 and *temp.* Richard II, and of Sir William Mountford of Kingshurst, Warwickshire, for 1433–4, all include a receiver's account as well as the more usual household accounts, giving a synopsis of the lord's economy in a single document.[157] Other receiver's accounts are the repository of some household expenses: foodstuffs appear in the account of the Lincolnshire receiver of John Gra in 1425–6; cloth and

[151] BL Egerton Roll 8738, printed by W. P. Baildon, 'A wardrobe account of 16–17 Richard II, 1393–4', *Archaeologia* 62, part ii (1911) pp. 497–514, where it is incorrectly identified as a royal wardrobe account; Egerton Charters 7350–1.

[152] PRO DL 28/1/1–6.

[153] e.g. MCO Fastolf Paper 43, Sir John Fastolf, 1448.

[154] Staffs. RO D 641/1/3/1, Gilbert de Clare, Earl of Gloucester, 1307–8; BL Add. MS 18632, ff. 2, 101, Elizabeth, Countess of Ulster, 1356–9.

[155] BL Egerton Roll 8738.

[156] BL Add. MS 8877; College of Arms, London, Arundel MS 49.

[157] **11a**; PRO E 101/511/15, E 101/512/5; **15**.

payments to tradesmen are recorded in the receiver's account for John de Vere, Earl of Oxford, 1442–3; and the expenses of journeys on business are entered in an account probably for the receiver of Joan, Lady Bergavenny, for 1421.[158] In the household of Edward de Courtenay, Earl of Devon, purchases of cloth are noted in the accounts of the receiver general, together with expenses on wine, in search of spices, fees and liveries to the steward of the household.[159]

In the late thirteenth and the fourteenth centuries, the diet account became an immensely detailed record of the household's day by day cash expenditure and consumption. To use the account for the type of planning envisaged by the *Rules of St Robert* in the 1240s, the information had to be digested and presented in a summary form. Summary wardrobe accounts, some using a form of stock account, had been in existence since the late thirteenth century, and it is from this period that systematic records of stock and consumption first appear in diet accounts. The first traces of summaries of accounts for departments of the household other than the wardrobe, however, do not survive from before the second decade of the fourteenth century with the summary cash journal for the household of Thomas, Earl of Lancaster, 1318–19.[160] An account for William de Rupe, 1324, is the earliest to give a statement of the total quantities of commodities used by the pantry, buttery and kitchen in a private household.[161] Total cash expenditure by commodity is recorded in an account for the household of Thomas, Lord Berkeley, for 1346–7, and on the dorse of Berkeley's account are notes of how much more or less of each commodity had been expended than in the preceding year.[162]

A readily available model for the abridged account existed in the form of the manorial account, providing a summary of movements of corn and stock, together with a statement of cash income, expenditure and a balance. The earliest examples in this form are from the household of Elizabeth de Burgh. A view of the accounts of the clerk of the wardrobe in 1325–7 gives a cash account, followed by a corn and stock account.[163] There are cash and corn accounts for 1327–30,[164] and cash, corn and stock accounts from 1331–2, 1336 and later.[165] Cash, corn and stock

[158] MCO Estate Paper 56/13; Essex RO D/DPr 138; PRO C 47/3/32/34.
[159] Devon RO CR 488, CR 500 and BL Add. Ch. 13972, receiver general's accounts, late 14th century, 1388–9 and 1392–3.
[160] PRO DL 28/1/14.
[161] Longleat House MS 4060, mem. 2.
[162] Berkeley SR 64.
[163] PRO E 101/91/11.
[164] PRO E 101/91/17.
[165] PRO E 101/91/26–7, E 101/92/3.

accounts are unlike earlier household accounts in their relationship to particular localities, for example, the account for the household of Richard Turberville, in 1358–9, is for the establishment based at Sampford Peverell, Devon (**17**); and that of John, Lord Dinham, in 1372–3, at Hartland, in the same county (**18**). Indeed one reason for the comparatively late appearance of the household cash, corn and stock accounts may be the less peripatetic existence of substantial non-collegiate households in the fourteenth century, with the development of principal and favoured places of residence: perhaps it was only then that the model of a manorial account was appropriate for summarising household expenses.[166]

The diet account was essentially an account of expenses, not of cash receipts: the cash, corn and stock account was a novelty because it required a cash charge or receipts section as well as a discharge or expenses section. This introduced an element of fiction into the versions employed in household accounts. For the account to balance, produce that was entered as purchased in the discharge section had to be offset in the cash charge. The account for the household of Richard Turberville, 1358–9, has a cash charge account with paragraphs for the sale of corn, sale of malt, sale of stock, sale of cider and salt, and cash receipts. The paragraph headings were probably taken over unaltered from a manorial account, but their purpose is very different. The sale of corn, for example, does not produce cash for the accountant: it is a valuation of corn consumed in the household. Even the cash receipts section contains cash valuations of goods purchased for the household, balanced in the cash discharge by the same sum expended on them. The stock and corn account maintains the pretence that items consumed in the household were sold for the expenses of the lord's household (**17**). The account for the expenses of Robert Waterton of Methley, for 1416–17, has a cash charge account which starts with a series of sections for the sale of corn, stock, capons and fish. These paragraphs do not represent sales at all, but contain cash valuations of all items received from the previous year's stock, from manors, gifts and hunting, in fact, anything that was not purchased during the period of the account. The total of these sections is balanced exactly by a paragraph in the discharge account, *expense hospicii de stauro et alliis* (**19**). Other accounts include not only a statement of the value of goods purchased, but valuations of goods received and gifts.[167]

[166] C. Dyer *Standards of living in the later Middle Ages. Social change in England c.1200–1520* (Cambridge, 1989) pp. 99–101.

[167] Devon RO CR 535, CR 491, Edward de Courtenay, Earl of Devon, 1382–3, 1383–4; PRO E 101/513/2, Margaret Beauchamp, Countess of Warwick, 1405–6; Shropshire RO, Bridgewater collection, accounts for Richard, Lord Talbot, 1393–4, Ankaret, Lady Talbot, 1411–12, and John, Lord Talbot and Furnivall, 1424–5.

All surviving examples of cash, corn and stock accounts employed in households are Chancery fashion rolls and are laid out like most manorial accounts, usually with a cash account on the front and a corn and stock account on the dorse. The accounts were rendered typically by the steward (**20**), keeper[168] or clerk of the household (**17**). As with manorial accounts, the accounting year generally ran from about Michaelmas to the same feast in the year following. This mirrors, insofar as it is possible to tell from the fragmentary nature of the evidence, the pattern of diet accounts. There were exceptions: the cash accounts of Robert Braybrooke, Bishop of London, ran for only parts of the years 1382 and 1399, that for the household of Sir Edward Botiller ran from 1 April 1400 until 12 January 1401, and one for Maud de Vere, Countess of Oxford, from 31 July 1389 to 30 September 1389.[169]

The charge section of cash accounts sometimes starts with arrears, or the discharge with *superplusagium*, *excessus* or *allocacio*. 'Arrears' may be used to represent cash remaining in the hands of the accountant at the close of the previous account[170] or debts outstanding.[171] The *superplusagium* or similar paragraph could also represent the balance in the official's favour from the last account (**19**). The annual cash, corn and stock account uses a paragraph for sales at the audit (*venditiones super compotum*) in exactly the same way as the manorial account, for liabilities incurred at the audit through deficiencies noted by the auditor in the corn and stock account on the dorse and surcharged in the cash charge section.[172]

The surviving cash, corn and stock accounts, like the diet accounts and wardrobe accounts, come from different stages of compilation. On some accounts, the sales at the audit were entered by an auditor in a hand which was markedly different from the remainder of the text of the cash account.[173] On other accounts, the dorse of the roll has been audited and the entries for sales at the audit have been made in a different hand to the text on the dorse, but the entry in the cash charge account was written at the same time and in the same hand as the rest of the charge section.[174] The

[168] WAM 24510–2, Nicholas de Litlington, Abbot of Westminster, 1362–3, 1364–5, 1367–8; BL Add. Ch. 17208, Margaret Plantagenet, Countess of Norfolk, 1385–6.

[169] Guildhall Library MS 25424/3; MS 25431; **23**; Longleat House MS 442.

[170] Shropshire RO, Bridgewater collection, account for John, Lord Talbot and Furnivall, 1424–5.

[171] Shropshire RO, Bridgewater collection, account for Gilbert, Lord Talbot, 1417–18.

[172] J. S. Drew, 'Manorial accounts of St Swithun's Priory, Winchester', *EHR* 62 (1947) pp. 20–41; *Manorial records of Cuxham* pp. 53–4.

[173] BL Add. Ch. 17208, Margaret Plantagenet, Countess of Norfolk, 1385–6; PRO E 101/513/2, Margaret Beauchamp, Countess of Warwick, 1405–6.

[174] BL Add. Roll 64803, Edward de Courtenay, Earl of Devon, 1384–5; MCO Fastolf Paper 8, Sir John Fastolf, 1430–1.

accounts of the keeper of the household of Nicholas de Litlington, Abbot of Westminster, for the 1360s, were written in three operations: the first hand wrote the text and the word *summa* under the paragraphs; the second, in a small hand, the pre-audit total in the margin; and the third, the total for the *summa*.[175] Some accounts are post-audit fair copies.[176] Auditors frequently used the marginal sign ʒ:, in combination with a cash amount, to indicate the surcharge on the corn and stock account.[177] The marginal sign ꝛ, for *respice* or 'look' was used to indicate the need to cross-check a statement with another account.[178] The word *probatur* also appears.[179]

Entries in-the corn and stock accounts on the dorse of the annual rolls were arranged by commodity. Details were given of the stock in hand at the opening of the account, additions and a total, followed by a statement of its expenditure or transfer to another head, with a total and a note of the amount remaining at the end of the account. The exact divisions of stock into paragraphs varied between households, but in general the order was similar to that of manorial accounts. The numerous sections ranged from peacocks' feathers[180] to gannets (**18**), from types of wine[181] and spices, sometimes all grouped together,[182] or in a separate series of paragraphs (**20**), to empty vessels.[183] The product of baking is noted on the account of Edward de Courtenay, Earl of Devon, 1384–5;[184] and the account for bread on the dorse of the roll of Gilbert, Lord Talbot, 1417–18, lists disbursements connected with the issue of bread as recorded in marginal entries for *fercula* in the diet accounts.[185]

A feature of some corn and stock accounts is the cash valuation given to quantities of goods remaining at the end of the accounting period.[186] The valuation was used to calculate net expenditure during the period of the

[175] WAM 24510–12. For pre-audit totals, *Manorial records of Cuxham* p. 50.

[176] BL Egerton Roll 8775, Richard Beauchamp, Earl of Warwick, 1435–6.

[177] BL Add. Roll 64803, Edward de Courtenay, Earl of Devon, 1384–5; **19**; MCO Fastolf Paper 8, Sir John Fastolf, 1430–1. For parallels in manorial accounting, *Manorial records of Cuxham* p. 53.

[178] PRO E 101/512/17, William Molyns, 1401–2; **19**.

[179] Longleat House MS 442, Maud de Vere, Countess of Oxford, 1389; **23**.

[180] MCO Fastolf Paper 8, Sir John Fastolf, 1430–1.

[181] CCC, Oxford, MS 498, fragment 4, possibly for Beatrice de Roos, late 14th or early 15th century; **19**.

[182] Somerset RO DD/L P37/12, Margaret Luttrell, 1431–2.

[183] Devon RO CR 535, CR 491, Edward de Courtenay, Earl of Devon, 1382–3, 1383–4.

[184] BL Add. Roll 64803.

[185] Shropshire RO, Bridgewater collection, account of Gilbert, Lord Talbot, 1417–18.

[186] Devon RO CR 491 and BL Add. Roll 64803, Edward de Courtenay, Earl of Devon, 1383–4 and 1384–5; MCO Fastolf Paper 8, Sir John Fastolf, 1430–1.

account, and it may have served as a check against fraud, providing an inventory of items in hand together with their value. In some accounts, even where no value is stated, a careful note is made of who is responsible for the remainder.[187] When, at the close of some accounts, very little food remains, especially of basic commodities, most of the supplies may have been issued or listed in a separate document as a means of carrying a balance forward.[188]

The cash discharge account was generally arranged in one of two ways. Paragraphs could be ordered by commodity, either in the elaborate layout found in the account for Robert Waterton of Methley, with a separate paragraph for each commodity (**19**), or with some grouping of commodities together, for example, purchases of meat, purchases of fish, as in the accounts of Richard Turberville (**17**), or the keeper of the household of the Abbot of Pershore, 1430–1.[189] Elsewhere commodities were grouped together, sometimes in the same order as the diet account, in paragraphs for each household department.[190] The entries in these paragraphs refer to bulk purchases, distinct from any purchases that occur in the diet account. On the annual account, the purchases made by the main household departments day by day in the diet account were usually entered in a separate section.[191] Other paragraphs in the annual cash account dealt with gifts, cloth for livery, wages, fees and pensions, and miscellaneous expenses.[192]

At the end of the cash account there was usually a balance. Beyond this, or as part of it, were notes of debtors from whom sums were owing. This section is sometimes introduced by the phrase *unde super* ('upon' whom the charge is laid) and it frequently contained entries for items surcharged at the audit. These need not have been the immediate liability of the accounting official: they could be the responsibility of his subordinates. On the account roll of Margaret Plantagenet, Countess of Norfolk, 1385–6,

[187] Somerset RO DD/L P37/10C, Sir Hugh Luttrell, 1425–6; DD/L P37/12, Margaret Luttrell, 1431–2.

[188] PRO E 101/512/17, William Molyns, 1401–2; Somerset RO DD/L P37/11, Sir John Luttrell, 1429–30.

[189] PRO SC 6/1072/22.

[190] Shropshire RO, Bridgewater collection, account for Richard, Lord Talbot, 1393–4.

[191] BL Add. Ch. 17208, Margaret Plantagenet, Countess of Norfolk, 1385–6: the section headed 'expense hospicii' (*Medieval Framlingham* pp. 103–4) excludes major purchases, dealing with items 'prout computatur per dietas in magno papiro dietarum'; PRO E 101/513/2, Margaret Beauchamp, Countess of Warwick, 1405–6, has a list of more than forty paragraphs for the purchase of different commodities and one for 'expense dietarum'.

[192] WAM 24510, Nicholas de Litlington, Abbot of Westminster, 1362–3; **23**; PRO E 101/512/17, William Molyns, 1401–2; Somerset RO DD/L P37/10A–B, Sir Hugh Luttrell, 1422–3, 1423–4.

the cash balance notes a charge against the baker. The account for the steward of the household of Sir John Fastolf, 1430–1, contains items surcharged to Henry the cook and Margary Hoddisson.[193] Other balances note sums which were held over — *respectuantur*[194] — and there are lists of creditors (**23**). The balance also took into account the *remanentia*, the cash value of goods remaining in hand at the end of the account.[195] This was used by the auditor to establish a net or 'clear' (*de claro*) figure for the expenses of the household. The account of the household of Margaret Beauchamp, Countess of Warwick, for 1405–6, after the cash balance has been struck, calculates the year's household expenses *de claro* by taking into consideration the value of the stock remaining from the preceding accounting year and the value of items in hand at the end of the account. From this new balance was derived an average of cash expenditure per day: 'and the daily average is 28*s*. 11*d*., with 10⅝*d*. remaining in all.'[196] A similar average calculation is entered by a new hand in the margin at the end of the account for Margaret Plantagenet, Countess of Norfolk, 1385–6.[197] The average weekly expenses are given after the balance on the cash accounts for the clerk of the household of Robert Braybrooke, Bishop of London, in 1382 and on the cash, corn and stock account for his household of 1399.[198] The calculations at the end of the account for the household of Gilbert, Lord Talbot, for 1417–18, give the total annual cost of the household, the average weekly cost, the total cost by department (presumably derived from daily departmental totals on a diet account) and the average cost of a *ferculum*.[199] Average calculations were not confined to the annual account. The diet account of Sir Hugh Luttrell, 1405–6, as well as purchases, includes a valuation of stock consumed and has a calculation of quarterly, weekly and daily averages, excluding foreign expenses, gifts and stipends.[200] Contemporary notes taken from a diet account of Thomas Peverel, Bishop of Worcester, *c.*1413, include a calculation of average daily expenses.[201]

These calculations would have provided the households with the financial information necessary to control their expenditure, to manage their consumption, or at least to compare it with preceding years: given the

193 *Medieval Framlingham* p. 104; MCO Fastolf Paper 8.

194 Shropshire RO, Bridgewater collection, account for Gilbert, Lord Talbot, 1417–18.

195 BL Add. Roll 64803, Edward de Courtenay, Earl of Devon, 1384–5.

196 PRO E 101/513/2.

197 *Medieval Framlingham* p. 104.

198 Guildhall Library MS 25424/3, mems. 1^r, 3^r; MS 25431, mem. 2^r.

199 Shropshire RO, Bridgewater collection, account for Gilbert, Lord Talbot, 1417–18.

200 Somerset RO DD/L P37/7.

201 CUL EDR F5/33, f. 19^v.

excess of expenditure over income that existed in many medieval households, this would have been of particular importance.[202] What is most noticeable, however, is the late date at which these calculations first appear in the accounts of private households, some 140 years after the *Rules of St Robert*, and there is at least a suspicion that a system of managing expenditure existed during the intervening period. Monasteries and collegiate institutions produced similar calculations at an earlier date: planning of a basic kind must always have taken place in the monasteries, for in the establishment of the system of food and money 'farms', there was surely consideration of the needs of the community in terms of consumption. Estimates of consumption, presumably derived from accounts, were available to the monks of Bury St Edmunds in the late thirteenth century.[203] At Durham Priory, calculations of averages of expenditure and consumption are found in the earliest accounts of the granator and cellarer.[204] At Worcester Cathedral Priory, a weekly cash average was computed in the kitchener's accounts in 1326–7.[205] The average weekly quantity of wheat and oats consumed appears in the subcellarer's account for the same priory in 1326, and similar calculations were made in accounts for this office throughout the fourteenth and fifteenth centuries and, indeed, as late as 1521.[206] The average costs of a *ferculum* were calculated on the diet accounts of the household of St George's Chapel, Windsor, in 1352–4.[207] Calculations of averages appear on a minority, but still a significant quantity, of obedientiary accounts throughout the fourteenth and early fifteenth centuries.[208] Reckonings of average cash expenditure are made fairly frequently in the subcellarer's accounts for the Cistercian

[202] Dyer *Standards of living* pp. 93–8.
[203] BL MS Harley 645, ff. 199^{v}–200^{r}.
[204] Durham D. and C., granator's accounts, ?1295–6, 1305–6; cellarer's accounts, 1307–8(A); 1311–12(A).
[205] Worcester D. and C., C107.
[206] Worcester D. and C., C431, 1326; C441, 1357–8; C448, 1451; *Accounts of the Priory of Worcester for the year 13–14 Henry VIII and a catalogue of the rolls of the obedientiaries* ed. J. M. Wilson, J. H. Bloom and S. C. Hamilton (Worcestershire Historical Society, 21; 1907) p. 7.
[207] Muniments of St George's Chapel, Windsor, XV. 3. 1, mem. 2, rot. 2; mem. 3, rot. 3; mem. 4, rot. 3.
[208] e.g. PRO SC 6/1258/7, household of Maxstoke Priory, weekly average of wheat and malt consumed, *c.*1345–6; SC 6/1259/7, Ramsey Abbey, weekly and daily averages of expenses at London on business, *c.*1339–41; BL Add. Roll 34731, master of the bakehouse, average weekly quantities of wheat and oats expended, 1402–3; Hants. RO 5M50/42, Southwick Priory, kitchener, weekly average of cash expenses, 1358–9; MCO Estate Paper 55/19, Selborne Priory, cellarer and treasurer, weekly averages of wheat baked and malt brewed, 1402–3; G. S. Haslop, 'A Selby kitchener's roll of the early fifteenth century', *Yorkshire Archaeological Journal* 48 (1976) p. 124 and n. 27, average of weekly diet expenses, 1413–14 and 1416–17.

abbey of Boxley, Kent, from 1373 to 1379;[209] and from this house, for Michaelmas 1360, there exists a remarkable document designed to plan the annual budget of the whole monastery. It sets out, manor by manor, the revenues that were anticipated, both in cash and kind, giving precise dates for the liveries throughout the year; and this is followed by a rearrangement of the same information, office by office. From the subcellarer's annual receipts of stock and cash, it was calculated that he could spend 22*s*. per week, or 3*s*. per day and 4*s*. on Sundays.[210] A document similar to this probably lay behind the calculations of averages in other monastic establishments and, conceivably, in private households.

A related method of planning consumption, best known from collegiate institutions, existed in the system of commons and commons allowances, usually money for a fixed allowance of food and drink per person present. On an account roll of the cellarer of Southwick Priory, Hampshire, 1402–3, the expenses were set each week against an allowance, noting remainder, deficit or an exact balance. The allowance seems to have fluctuated in relation to the number of people present, suggesting some form of commons provision, and in relation to subsidies from pittances for various feasts.[211] In the kitchener's account for Worcester Cathedral Priory, probably for 1340–1, the weekly expenses are balanced against an allowance of 80*s*., excluding items drawn from the larder, piggery and weirs.[212] A balance of expenditure against a commons allowance was also made at the establishment of Ralph, Lord Cromwell, at Tattershall in 1447–8.[213] It is just possible that a similar system was in operation in the household of Dame Katherine de Norwich, in 1336–7. Marginal entries give the number of visitors (*extranei*), or a note *eque*, or a figure for *deficientes*, suggesting that as far as the accountant was concerned the household had a set numerical size; but it is no longer possible to understand precisely how the system functioned (**10**).

The accounts of the English royal household supply very little evidence for budgetary planning and control; they are overwhelmingly concerned with cash expenditure, with responsibility for purchases. There is little attempt to record stock in hand and its consumption, except for wax and

[209] PRO SC 6/1254/2, mems. 1^{r}, 2^{r}, 3^{r}; SC 6/1254/4; SC 6/1254/6, mems. 1^{r}, 2^{r} (rot. 2); SC 6/1254/15, mems. 1^{r}, 2^{r}, 3^{r}; SC 6/1254/18; SC 6/1261/15.
[210] PRO SC 6/1253/11.
[211] Hants. RO 5M50/69.
[212] Worcester D. and C., C169.
[213] E. M. Myatt-Price, 'The twelve at Tattershall', *Accounting Review* 35 (1960) p. 681.

wine.[214] Calculations of averages are likewise almost entirely lacking.[215] This might be considered extraordinary in the context of developments in private households as stock in hand would have formed a much more valuable commodity in the royal household simply from the quantities involved; but in fact it parallels the systems of account operated in continental households throughout the fourteenth and fifteenth centuries, which were largely cash based. In the royal household, budgetary control was founded on a predetermined allowance per portion of each commodity, surcharging officials at the nightly audit of accounts within the household when these rates were exceeded, and on controlling the numbers admitted to membership of the household. Planning is evident from other aspects of royal finance, from estimates of Exchequer revenues and expenses, including the share of the royal household, to estimating the king's stable expenses or the quantities of victuals necessary for garrisons;[216] and a fixed financial provision for the king's wardrobe and household expenses, a *certum*, was also proposed as a political device.[217]

One of the most interesting features of household accounts to emerge from this survey is the diversity of the forms and accounting systems. To understand how this arose, it is necessary to look briefly at the clerks who wrote them. Who were these clerks and how were they trained? Typically the medieval household was under the overall charge of one man, the steward of the household, who usually had a clerk, frequently referred to as the 'clerk of the household', responsible for recording the household's financial transactions. Only in the largest households would clerks have been employed solely to write accounts, clerks of the household, kitchen, pantry and buttery; elsewhere clerks would normally have been engaged as well in writing letters, registers and other administrative documents, as the lord's confidential clerks, and they may have had other duties.[218]

214 PRO E 101/373/5, mem. 1^{d}; E 101/383/20.

215 PRO E 101/399/16 is a rare exception.

216 M. H. Mills, 'Exchequer agenda and estimates of revenue, Easter term 1284', *EHR* 40 (1925) pp. 229–34; G. L. Harriss *King, Parliament and public finance in medieval England to 1369* (Oxford, 1975) pp. 466–508; *Henry V: the practice of kingship* ed. G. L. Harriss (Oxford, 1985) pp. 162–3; *Proceedings and ordinances of the Privy Council of England* ed. N. H. Nicolas (7 vols., London, 1834–7) i, pp. 154, 342; ii, p. 14; M. Prestwich, 'An estimate by the Commons of royal revenue in England under Richard II', *Parliamentary History* 3 (1984) pp. 147–55; *idem*, 'Victualling estimates for English garrisons in Scotland during the early fourteenth century', *EHR* 82 (1967) pp. 536–43; PRO E 101/684/84/18, estimate of the king's stable expenses, *c.*1310–50.

217 C. J. Given-Wilson *The royal household and the king's affinity. Service, politics and finance in England 1360–1413* (London, 1986) pp. 128–30.

218 R. A. Griffiths, 'Public and private bureaucracies in England and Wales in the fifteenth century', *TRHS* 5th series, 30 (1980) pp. 109–30; E. Rickert, 'A leaf from a fourteenth century letter book', *Modern Philology* 25 (1927–8) pp. 249–55; PRO C 47/3/33; H. G. Richardson, 'A French treatise on letter writing by Thomas Sampson', in *Formularies which bear on the history of Oxford c.1204–1420* ed. H. E. Salter, W. A. Pantin and H. G. Richardson (OHS, new series, 4 and 5; 1942) ii, pp. 371–2.

Apart from etiquette and cookery books, there was little didactic literature for the medieval household.[219] This deficiency of material on household management and accounts provides a very sharp contrast with works on estate management and manorial accounting: in the absence of any widely disseminated corpus of material, the diversity of form of household accounts is less surprising. Household accounts appear in some of the formularies of the teachers of business methods at Oxford, and compiling these accounts was one of a number of skills they taught to clerks, together with letter writing and the drawing of legal instruments and manorial accounts.[220] The influence of the Oxford teachers on the practices of household accounting cannot be determined precisely, but there is at least an indication that it was not extensive. Their works contain fewer specimen household accounts than, for example, manorial accounts; and the treatment of household accounts is sometimes cursory, barely sketching the form with a specimen account (invariably a diet account), and not discussing its functions or place in the overall scheme of household accounting.[221] While formularies could have supplied some guidance in the layout of the account,[222] it would have been of limited utility: some households, in particular those that had their own permanent clerical establishments, for example, the royal household and that of Elizabeth de Burgh, evolved their own forms and layouts and the clerks working in those households would have been taught especially to prepare their work in a set manner. Perhaps significantly, a specimen account in a formulary, probably originating in the work of Thomas Sampson, and purporting to be a copy of an account of Ralph, Earl of Stafford, in October 1355, is in a different form and language to the only diet account that can be attributed to the Staffords at this period.[223] This may indicate a lack of immediate working familiarity with household accounts.

Where, outside the largest establishments, there was not necessarily any consistency in the form of account in closely succeeding years (**11a**, **11b**), resort may have been had to professional scriveners.[224] Local clerks

[219] *Walter of Henley* pp. 191–9, 387–415; Bodl. MS Fairfax 24, ff. 62–3; *Catalogue of western manuscripts in the old royal and King's collections* ed. G. F. Warner and J. P. Gilson (4 vols., London, 1921) i, p. 343: MS Royal 11 A XVIII; *Walter de Wenlok* pp. 5, 241–8.

[220] H. G. Richardson, 'Business training in medieval Oxford', *American Historical Review* 46 (1940–1) pp. 259–80.

[221] BL Add. MS 8167, ff. 132–3; BL MS Harley 4971, ff. 7, 26^{v}–7^{r}; CUL MS Ee IV 20, f. 144.

[222] Lacour, 'Traité d'économie', pp. 380–1; Bodl. MS Rawlinson C775, p. 126; BL MS Harley 4971, f. 7.

[223] BL MS Harley 4971, ff. 27^{r}–9^{v}; Longleat House MS 3772.

[224] S. Bond, 'The attestation of medieval private charters relating to New Windsor', *JSA* 4 (1970–3) pp. 276–84; J. H. Hodson, 'Medieval charters: the last witness', *JSA* 5 (1974–7) pp. 71–89; A. E. B. Owen, 'A scrivener's notebook from Bury St Edmunds', *Archives* 14 (1979–80) pp. 16–22.

were used by bailiffs and reeves to write manorial accounts from the late thirteenth century onwards.[225] Taught at Oxford, trained from formularies, but most probably learning as apprentices to existing clerks, they produced vast numbers of charters in the thirteenth century and first half of the fourteenth century. Although the field of expertise would have varied between clerks, some undoubtedly wrote household accounts.

Besides the clerks who heard or audited and wrote the daily accounts of the household, we have seen evidence for the work of other auditors examining household accounts. From the fourteenth century, if not earlier, there existed a class of professional auditors to oversee estate administration and the overall financial accounts of the household. Auditors belonged to the permanent staff of the organisation, especially in the largest households, frequently associated with the receiver general's office.[226] There is less evidence for the presence of professional auditors in smaller households, but the personal involvement of the lord is apparent in the accounting. It was not out of the ordinary for a lord to be interested in his accounts;[227] the activities of King Henry V, although unusual for an English monarch, working through financial records, in many ways prefigure the much more active role heads of households were to play in their domestic financial affairs in the second half of the fifteenth century.[228] In 1368, the Earl of Salisbury himself examined and allowed the payments made by his treasurer in his wardrobe account (**26**). In 1384, at the close of the account, Edward de Courtenay, Earl of Devon, pardoned the disallowed expenses of his steward on condition that he conducted himself well in his office up to the following Easter and supervised the expenses of the household better.[229] The audit in the Earl of Devon's household clearly took place within six months of the close of the account (24 September 1384), but the dates when an audit might take place varied greatly. The immediately preceding account for the steward of Courtenay's household, for 8 November 1382 to 27 September 1383, was audited in January 1384.[230] The auditing of the accounts of the English royal household was notoriously in arrears. More typical, perhaps, was the audit of the account

[225] *Manorial records of Cuxham* pp. 37–42.

[226] *Anglo-Norman letters and petitions from All Souls MS 182* ed. M. D. Legge (ANTS, 3; 1941) p. 268; C. J. Given-Wilson *The English nobility in the late Middle Ages: the fourteenth-century political community* (London, 1987) p. 108; *The Marcher lordships of South Wales 1415–1536* ed. T. B. Pugh (Board of Celtic Studies, University of Wales, Cardiff, History and Law Series, 20; 1963) pp. 290, 295, 298–9.

[227] Dyer *Standards of living* p. 94, n. 19.

[228] *Henry V: the practice of kingship* pp. 176–7.

[229] Devon RO CR 491.

[230] Devon RO CR 535, mem. 3^r.

of the household of Margaret Plantagenet, Countess of Norfolk, for the year ending 30 September 1386, for which the accountant's acquittance was dated 1 May 1387.[231]

Just as the period after 1250 sees the survival of many more accounts from Britain, there are also many more preserved on the Continent.[232] It has been suggested that, before 1250, the procedures and forms of household accounting in continental Europe were more advanced than in Britain, and that these accounts could have served as a model for developments here. We have seen how, in England, the diet account evolved to reach its most elaborate form from *c.*1320 onwards: many of the features that have been traced in this chapter appear in accounts on the Continent in the second half of the thirteenth century. Diet accounts for the Count of Savoy, for example, from 1269 and 1271–2, are remarkably similar in form to the later English examples, with departmental headings for every department and appraised values for goods consumed; separate meals — *dignerio* and *cena* — are distinguished in the account; there are marginal notes of *fercula*, giving also the number of grooms, and there are notes of the numbers of horses present.[233] That there were extensive contacts between Savoy and the court of Edward I should not go unremarked; however, the general framework of accounting was widely established on the Continent at this date, as can be seen from about seventy accounts that survive for Guy of Dampierre, Count of Flanders, and his wife, Isabella of Luxemburg, dating from 1260 to the early fourteenth century. The archive of the household of the Counts of Flanders includes four principal types of account. The first contains cash receipts

[231] *Medieval Framlingham* p. 104.

[232] For example, Counts of Savoy, the Popes at Avignon, the Bishops of Grenoble: *Les sources de l'histoire économique et sociale du moyen âge: Provence, Comtat Venaissin, Dauphiné, États de la Maison de Savoie* ed. R. H. Bautier and J. Sornay (2 vols., Paris, 1968–71) i, pp. 91–4, 317–27; ii, p. 795; Counts of Flanders, Counts of Artois, Dukes of Brabant, Counts of Hainault, Counts of Namur: *Les sources de l'histoire économique et sociale du moyen âge: les États de la Maison de Bourgogne I. Archives de principautés territoriales 2. Les principautés du Nord* ed. R. H. Bautier, J. Sornay and F. Muret (Paris, 1984) pp. 57–63, 255–63, 417–21, 556–63, 689–90; Dukes of Burgundy: AD Nord B 3328–B 3514, AD Côte-d'Or B 311–B 341; Guillaume de Murol: *Guillaume de Murol: un petit seigneur auvergnat au début de xve siècle* ed. P. Charbonnier (Publications de l'Institut d' Études du Massif Central, 11, Clermont-Ferrand, 1973); lord of Bioule: E. Forestié *La dépense journalière d'un château quercynois au xive siècle* (Montauban, 1896); Ferdinand of Aragon: E. Sarasa, 'La alimentación de un rey aragonés y su séquito a comienzos del siglo xv', in *Manger et boire au moyen âge* ed. D. Menjot (Publications de la faculté des lettres et sciences humaines de Nice, 1st series, 27–8; 1984) ii, pp. 223–31.

[233] M. Chiaudano *La finanza sabauda nel sec. XIII* (Biblioteca della società storica subalpina, Turin, 131–3; 1933, 1934, 1938) ii (*I 'rotuli' e i 'computi' della corte di Filippo I conte di Savoia e di Borgogna del 1269 al 1285*) pp. ix–xvii, 1, 6–7, 59, 77.

and a journal of wardrobe type payments, described as *grosses parties*.[234] The second group are diet accounts, divided on the front into three columns for each day. After a general statement of the date and where the Count or Countess was for each meal, together with their principal guests, the first column lists the total cash expenditure by department, with each department on a new line. One of the remaining two columns lists *purvance*, items drawn from stock (probably equivalent to *providencia* in England) by each department, with a cash valuation, sometimes also including a note of the number of horses present; and the other lists *parties* or payments outside the normal ambit of the household departments (foreign expenses). On the dorse of the roll, corresponding with each period of account on the front, are long lists of people present within the household and notes of payments to them for wages. The accounts have daily totals, or totals for several days at the same place, on the front, combining the cash expenses of the departments, the total of wages and of *parties*, but not of *purvance*.[235] There is one example of a third type of roll, possibly a counter-roll, which contains the daily totals from the diet account alone,[236] and there are several examples of a fourth type of account, narrow strips of parchment giving more detailed accounts of the daily expenditure, largely of the kitchen, pantry and buttery, but without departmental divisions.[237] There are similarities between the second type of account, the diet account with the arrangement in columns, and other groups of accounts. The first are those for the household of Joan of Valence, Countess of Pembroke, for 1295–7. These accounts start each day with a general statement of the date and where the Countess resided, and then, in a column, is given a brief account, often no more than a cash total, of the departmental expenses, with each department on a new line, the marshalsea giving the number of horses present. The cash totals for the kitchen, marshalsea and wages appear aligned in a second column, sometimes also with a sub-total for the day, followed by another paragraph written across the whole width of the roll, for alms, further wages and miscellaneous expenses, and a centrally placed grand total for the day.[238] Secondly, there is a fragment from an account for the household of the

[234] Rijksarchief, Ghent, Chartes des comtes de Flandre: V.Gaillard *Inventaire analytique des chartes des comtes de Flandre, autrefois déposées au château de Rupelmonde et récemment retrouvées aux archives à l'ancien conseil de Flandre à Gand* (Ghent, 1857) and C. Wyffels *Rijksarchief te Gent. Inventaris van de oorkonden der graven van Vlaanderen. Chronologisch gerangschikt supplement* (Ghent, n.d. 1957). Fonds Gaillard 1, 3–4, 7, 10, 12, 15, 24, 27–9.
[235] Rijksarchief, Ghent: Fonds Gaillard 11, 17, 25, 51; Fonds Wyffels 311, 314[bis].
[236] Rijksarchief, Ghent: Fonds Gaillard 8.
[237] Rijksarchief, Ghent: Fonds Gaillard 38, 41 (front) and 48.
[238] PRO E 101/505/25–7.

Count of Blois, *c.*1320, which is cast in a closely related form, with daily totals for cash expenses, *garnisons* and *parties foreins*.[239] In addition, the monthly totals which appear in the late thirteenth century accounts of the Count of Hainault, for *despens*, *parties* and *waiges*, look as if they may have been derived from an analogous form of account.[240] At this date there were several 'common forms' of layout of diet account in currency in the large households of Europe: the British examples probably imitated earlier and contemporary continental documents.

In the course of the fourteenth century, however, the continental forms of account followed a different path of development. While British households continued to develop elaborate diet accounts, which, with the cash, corn and stock account, could have been used as instruments of domestic management, planning finance and consumption, on the Continent recording purchases and accounting for cash became the overwhelming consideration. That the cash, corn and stock account, derived as it was from the English manorial account, should not appear on the Continent is perhaps to be expected; but the change in the nature of the diet account is more surprising. As early as 1292–4, accounts such as those for the children of Philip of Artois are concerned wholly with cash expenditure;[241] an example derived from an account of Mary of Anjou, Queen of Majorca, for 1340–1, is also solely for cash expenses.[242] This is not to say that there was no record of stock: accounts for Pope Clement V, in 1308–9, give weekly summaries of household expenses that were derived from an account that noted both cash expenses and the use of provisions already purchased in bulk;[243] and the accounts of the Countess of Hainault and her son from 1319 to 1336 include, besides totals of cash expenditure, lists of goods from *pourveances*.[244] The journals of diet expenses for Robert of Cassel, 1326, and for his daughter, Yolande, Countess of Cassel and Bar, for 1349, have notes of items from *proveance*;[245] there are also some entries for total commodities consumed per week in the Countess'

[239] AD Loiret 6 J 13/6.
[240] AD Nord B 3268, f. 16v.
[241] AD Nord B 13587–8.
[242] A. Venturini, 'Un compte de l'hôtel de Marie d'Anjou, reine de Majorque, retirée en Provence', *Bibliothèque de l'École des Chartes* 146 (1988) pp. 69–129.
[243] *Les recettes et les dépenses de la chambre apostolique pour la quatrième année du pontificat de Clément V (1308–1309) (Introitus et exitus 75)* ed. B. Guillemain (Collection de l'École française de Rome, 39; 1978).
[244] AD Nord B 3269–B 3278, printed in *De rekeningen der graven en gravinnen uit het Henegouwsche huis* ed. H. J. Smit (3 vols., Amsterdam and Utrecht, 1924–39) i.
[245] AD Nord B 3245 (112093); B 3247 (112162).

accounts for 1368.[246] Of much greater significance from this archive are the daily accounts of cash expenses, arranged by department, laid out in the account book with a page for each day, as in the account for 1367.[247] In form these are effectively the same as the long series of *escroes* — daily cash accounts, one for the household departments, with usually another for the day's wages, each on a separate membrane, filed as Exchequer fashion rolls, month by month — for the households of the Dukes of Burgundy and their families which appear from the late fourteenth century onwards.[248] Other accounts in which there is comparatively little mention of stock include a diet account for the Duke of Brittany, *c.*1390, and, less unusually, the accounts for the much smaller household of Guillaume de Murol, 1403–20.[249] Where quantities of goods purchased in bulk are noted, for example, in the accounts of the *maistre des garnisons* and the *sommelier* of the buttery of the Duke of Burgundy, 1386–1404, in the accounts of the household of William of Bavaria, Count of Ostravent and Hainault, for 1401–7, or in the butchery and fish accounts for the same household, some for stock, some for cash, the purpose was not so much to allow calculations of the amounts being consumed in the household, but, as marginal annotations and household ordinances make clear, to allow the auditors of the various *chambres des comptes* to follow the movement of each item, to ensure that it did not go astray, and that the right person in the household accounted for it.[250] The daily *escroes*[251] for the Burgundian households are solely for cash expenses and remain so throughout the fifteenth century and into the sixteenth: the households seem to have had no full record of

[246] AD Nord B 3256 (112462).

[247] AD Nord B 3256 (112415).

[248] For the Burgundian system of household accounts, R. Vaughan *Philip the Bold. The formation of the Burgundian state* (London, 1962) pp. 144–6. The whereabouts of the surviving *escroes* is given in W. Paravicini '"Ordonnances de l'Hôtel" und "Escroes des gaiges". Wege zu einer prosopographischen Erforschung des burgundischen Staats im fünfzehnten Jahrhundert', in *Medieval lives and the historian. Studies in medieval prosopography* ed. N. Bulst and J. -P. Genet (Kalamazoo, Michigan, 1986) pp. 243–66. The *escroes* are now kept as separate membranes, but most have filing holes at the head (e.g. AD Nord B 3390 (114273)); contemporary endorsements giving the month and the year suggest a monthly arrangement (e.g. AD Nord B 3438 (119100); B 3455 (120619)).

[249] B. -A. Pocquet du Haut-Jussé, 'L'hôtel de Jean IV. Fragment du compte des dépenses (*c.*1365–1370)', *Bulletin et mémoires de la société archéologique d'Ille-et-Vilaine* 69 (1953) pp. 66–77; for the date, J. Kerhervé *L'état breton aux 14e et 15e siècles. Les ducs, l'argent et les hommes* (2 vols., Paris, 1987) i, p. 244, n. 163; *Guillaume de Murol.*

[250] AD Nord B 3328–9; B 3280–3324; K. Vandermaesen-Vandewoude, 'Een fragment van een hotelordonnantie van Filips de Stoute, hertog van Bourgondië, graaf van Vlaanderen, 23 januari 1389 n.s.', *Bulletin de la commission royale d'histoire* 146 (1980) pp. 15–29.

[251] For example, for 1404, AD Nord B 3390 (114273), household departments; B 3390 (114270), wages.

consumption. The same pattern of accounting appears elsewhere during the fifteenth century: the daily *escroes* are mentioned in the Burgundian inspired household ordinance for the Duke of Brittany of 1404;[252] examples of daily *escroes* survive for the household of Charles, Duke of Orleans, for 1440 and 1442;[253] and there are many more examples for sixteenth century French royal households.[254] The Burgundian pattern of accounting continued in the household of the Habsburg Archduke Maximilian, later the Holy Roman Emperor, and that of his son, Charles V.[255] This reliance on cash accounting is particularly interesting given the changes in the form of account in Britain after 1430 largely in the same direction.

[252] Kerhervé *L'état breton* i, pp. 229, 235–6.
[253] AD Loiret 6 J 9/38, 66, 76.
[254] BL Add. MS 10011.
[255] AD Nord B 3342 (119352), departmental *escroe* for 25 May 1479: 'Et ce jour a commande et ordonne mondit seigneur [Archduke Maximilian] que sa despence soit comptee au bureau des maistres dostel par escroes et mise es contrerolles ainsi et par la maniere que lon a accoustume de faire en la maison de Bourgoigne . . .'

Chapter 4
Household accounts, 1430–1500

The diet account reached the apogee of its complexity in the last years of the fourteenth century and the early years of the fifteenth, recording purchases and consumption, and perhaps serving as the basis for household planning and management in future years, with calculations of average costs per *ferculum* or per day, the careful recording of guests and many other features. In the period after 1430, the form of account is generally abandoned, scarcely surviving in even the largest households, where it had once been firmly established. The departmental order and divisions, numbers of *fercula* and other details, are recorded in only a relatively small group of accounts, including those of Thomas Bourgchier, Archbishop of Canterbury, 1459;[1] two of the accounts of Henry Stafford, 1469–70 and 1470–1;[2] and the account of Edward Stafford, Duke of Buckingham, 1501.[3] More frequently, there is no order within the daily account,[4] although one or two examples maintain a distinction between different parts of the day, noting expenses at night or at breakfast.[5] Bourgchier's accounts for 1459 are without contemporary parallel in devoting themselves exclusively to a record of consumption: few accountants at this period kept any note of this at all. The accounts of John Hales, Bishop of Coventry and Lichfield, 1461, value items *de providencia* (**16**); in the account of the expenses of the great household at Tattershall, immediately after the death of Ralph, Lord Cromwell, in 1456, consumption is divided between 'parcelles of fressh accates' and 'in store expendid';[6] and the account of the funeral expenses of John Waynflete, Dean of Chichester, *c.*1480, has some entries for foodstuffs 'without store'.[7] These features,

[1] Lambeth Palace Library, Estate Document 1973.

[2] WAM 12188, 12190.

[3] PRO E 101/546/18.

[4] BL Add. MS 34213, Anne Stafford, dowager Duchess of Buckingham, 1465–6; WAM 5474, William Smith, archdeacon of Winchester, 1491–2.

[5] PRO C 47/3/53/27, unidentified household, late 15th – early 16th century.

[6] MCO Miscellaneous Deed 422. Consumption from stock is recorded in the accounts of some religious houses, e.g. MCO Estate Paper 137/17, Brackley Hospital, 1445–6; Northants. RO NPL 1103, St Andrew's, Northampton, 1473; PRO E 36/108, Holy Trinity Priory, London, 1513–14.

[7] MCO Estate Paper CP2/55.

although familiar from earlier accounts, are now unusual: the overwhelming majority of accounts for this period records purchases and cash expenses alone, not consumption.

In the smaller households, the accounts effectively record shopping trips to market. The accounts for the Eyre family of Derbyshire, 1472–5, note the expenses of each trip to Chesterfield, Sheffield and Rotherham or to markets elsewhere; and these accounts are also representative in recording a range of cash expenses frequently wider than those associated directly with the provisioning of the household, including wardrobe type expenses — the purchase of cloth, payments for schooling, the wages of servants[8] — and other accounts sometimes include general agricultural expenses as well.[9] The fifteenth century accounts differ from their predecessors in coming from a wider range of households, with more examples surviving from further down the social scale.[10]

The typical account of this period is much less formal in its appearance than earlier documents (Plate 3). Many accounts are written on paper, for the most part in books;[11] and very few diet accounts are preserved on rolls.[12] This pattern is further confirmed by the references to subsidiary documents on the annual cash, corn and stock accounts: none speak of rolls. Many of the diet accounts are written wholly or partly in English.[13] Some of the accounts have little or no form and are really no more than collections of memoranda.[14] This breakdown of the form with the change in language to the vernacular is similar to the transition which occurred in

[8] Bodl. MS DD Weld c. 19/4/2 and 4. PRO C 47/37/2, Alice de Stonor, *c.*1432–3; SC 6/1257/1, Catesby Priory, prioress, 1433–5; BL Add. Roll 74129, schedules 3 and 5, Eleanor, Lady Stafford, *c.*1446–7; H. L. Douch, 'Household accounts at Lanherne', *Journal of the Royal Institution of Cornwall* new series 2, part 1 (1953) pp. 25–32; Bodl. MS Lyell 35, ff. 35–8, William Uvedale, 1478–9; Warws. RO CR 895/45 and 106, Sir Edward Don, 1510–51, are all typical of the form.

[9] A. J. L. Winchester, 'The castle household and demesne farm at Millom in 1513–14', *Transactions of the Cumberland and Westmorland Antiquarian and Archaeological Society* 83 (1983) pp. 85–99.

[10] *A small household of the fifteenth century, being the account book of Munden's Chantry, Bridport* ed. K. L. Wood-Legh (Manchester, 1956): perhaps the smallest household for which we have accounts. With the disappearance of the detailed diet account, there is also a marked absence of 15th century formularies for household accounts. East Sussex RO MS RYE 33/7, ff. 27^{v}–29^{v}, and BL MS Harley 234, ff. 29^{r}–49^{r}, are rare examples.

[11] BL MS Sloane 2128, f. 31, unidentified household, mid to late 15th century; PRO C 47/37/11/6–17, George Cely, 1474–6; Northants. RO, Stopford Sackville MS 3689, William Mordaunt, 1499–1516; BL Add. MS 6668, ff. 375–7, Poles of Derbyshire, 1500.

[12] Lambeth Palace Library, ED 1973.

[13] PRO C 47/37/2, Alice de Stonor, *c.*1432–3; E 101/516/9, account of Simon the cook of Henry Langley, 1473; C 47/37/4/30–1, 33–5, William Stonor, *c.*1478–9; C 47/3/53/27, unidentified household, late 15th – early 16th century.

[14] PRO E 36/107, Abbot of Ramsey, *c.*1505–33.

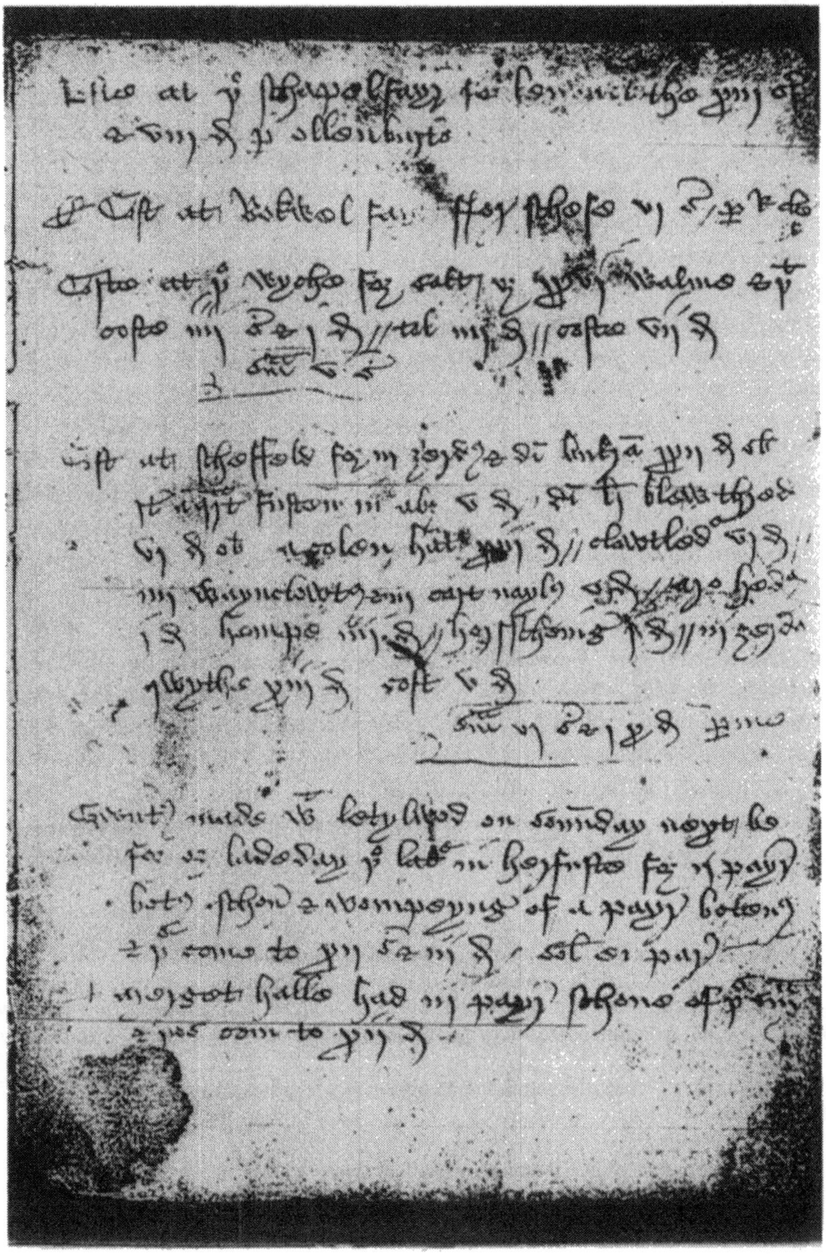

Plate 3 Bodl. MS DD Weld c. 19/4/2, f. 6r Account for household expenses of the Eyre family of Derbyshire, 1473

the accounts of some small households on the Continent in the fourteenth century.[15] The memoranda in some of the English records, however, are grouped more coherently. Some accounts contain separate journals of expenses on different commodities, those for Henry Courtenay, Earl of Devon, 1519, for boat hire, for servants' food, stable expenses, alms and for ribbon; those for Katherine Courtenay, Countess of Devon, 1523–4, for wax, tallow and wicks, wood and coal, stable expenses, foreign expenses, necessary purchases for the Countess, and for wages.[16] Journals are also combined with the annual cash account, with detailed journal entries for some of the classes of expenditure.[17] An account for Netley Abbey, *c.*1455–7, is divided into sections, some for individual servants or creditors, with payments posted into each section as they were made.[18] Some accounts preserve the system of daily totals, weekly, quarterly and annual totals;[19] and some of the accounts had a weekly arrangement.[20]

With the informality of account comes an immediacy of recording. Instead of the elaborately engrossed fair copies that have been preserved from the accounting systems in the larger households in the fourteenth century, many of the accounts preserved for the fifteenth century are documents written up at very short intervals, possibly daily, or on each occasion expenditure was incurred.[21] The accounts of Anne Stafford, dowager Duchess of Buckingham, 1465–6, were written up piecemeal, sometimes several times a day.[22] There was a diminution in the overall formality of the accounting system: a fair copy of the diet expenses was no longer essential at the audit of the overall expenses of the household, the copy compiled day by day would suffice.

It is perhaps necessary to look to external factors to determine the reasons for the change in the pattern of accounting. Throughout the

[15] E. Forestié *La dépense journalière d'un château quercynois au xive siècle* (Montauban, 1896); A. Higounet-Nadal, 'Le journal des dépenses d'un notaire de Périgueux en mission à Paris (janvier – septembre 1337)', *Annales du Midi* 76 (1964) pp. 379–402; BL MS Royal 8 E XI, f. i^v, an unidentified French or Breton household, late 14th or early 15th century.
[16] PRO E 36/218, 223.
[17] PRO SC 6/Hen. VIII/2612, Marham Abbey, *temp.* Henry VIII; SC 6/Hen. VIII/3078, ?Bruton Priory, 1527–8.
[18] PRO SC 6/1258/11.
[19] MCO Estate Paper 137/17, Brackley Hospital, 1445–6; *Munden* (weekly, quarterly and annual); PRO E 36/223, Katherine Courtenay, Countess of Devon, 1523–4.
[20] *Paston letters and papers of the fifteenth century* ed. N. Davis (2 vols., Oxford, 1971–6) i, p. 257.
[21] PRO SC 6/1257/1, Catesby Priory, prioress, 1433–5; *Munden*; PRO SC 6/1258/11, Netley Abbey, *c.*1455–7; Bodl. MS DD Weld c. 19/4/2 and 4, Eyres of Derbyshire, 1472–5; Bodl. MS Lyell 35, ff. 35–8, William Uvedale, 1478–9.
[22] BL Add. MS 34213.

fifteenth century there was a move away from continuous public living towards a more intimate and private domestic life. Greater numbers of private apartments appear in the buildings of the period, and the great hall assumes a reduced prominence.[23] Once the household had become a more intimate institution, less elaborate accounts were required. As in the small households of the fourteenth century, there was no need for complex forms of account. The presence of the lord guaranteed an immediacy of control. This is not to say that the heads of noble households had not always been interested in the accounts of their households; but, from the late fifteenth century in England, there are, for the first time, accounts that are signed by the lord or lady and even written by them. The first English example is an account of 1467 signed by Anne Stafford, dowager Duchess of Buckingham.[24] The accounts of the steward of the household of William Worsley, Dean of St Paul's, were signed by the dean at the discharge of the account, in 1481–2 and 1482–3.[25] The chamber accounts of Henry VII bear his signature; and each page of the privy purse expenses of his wife in 1502 is signed by her.[26] The expense accounts of Lady Margaret Beaufort for 1498–9, 1505–7 and 1507–9 were signed on each page by her, and another account for 1509 was signed on each page by her executors;[27] and the accounts of John de Vere, Earl of Oxford, for 1507–8, were signed by him at the end of each week.[28] There are holograph accounts of Edward Stafford, Duke of Buckingham, for 1518–19, and he had earlier signed his household accounts and worked through them in detail.[29] At another level, in much smaller households, there are also signed accounts or accounts written by the head of the household. In the Stonor household, the accounts for 1478 were signed by both Elizabeth Stonor and William Stonor when noting the payment of all expenses up to a particular point, striking out the earlier accounts at the same time.[30] Informal and scrappy

[23] M. Girouard *Life in the English country house* (London, 1978) p. 30 *et seqq.*; C. Dyer *Standards of living in the later Middle Ages. Social change in England c.1200–1520* (Cambridge, 1989) p. 105; D. Starkey, 'Court and government', in *Revolution reassessed. Revisions in the history of Tudor government and administration* ed. C. Coleman and D. Starkey (Oxford, 1986), especially pp. 30–1.
[24] BL Egerton Roll 2210.
[25] Guildhall Library MSS 25166/3–4.
[26] G. L. Harriss, 'Financial policy', in *Henry V. The practice of kingship* ed. G. L. Harriss (Oxford, 1985) p. 176; *Privy purse expenses of Elizabeth of York* ... ed. N. H. Nicolas (London, 1830) pp. 1–48.
[27] SJC D91.17, D91.21, D91.19; D102.1.
[28] Longleat House MS Misc. XI.
[29] BL MS Royal 7 F XIV, ff. 1–19; C. Rawcliffe *The Staffords, Earls of Stafford and Dukes of Buckingham, 1394–1521* (Cambridge, 1978) p. 89.
[30] PRO C47/37/7.

accounts, sometimes written in the first person, possibly by the lord himself, are the most extreme development of this system of informal reckoning: the accounts of the Eyres of Derbyshire, 1472–5, noting balances struck, debts owed, etc., as the account progresses, are one example of this form;[31] the account written in part by Ralph Pole, for expenses and receipts on behalf of his son, Thomas, in 1500, is another.[32] These documents support a view of fairly widespread personal involvement in accounting. In the largest households, the lord played a part in the formal auditing and approval of the accounts; in the smallest households, there was probably no formal structure for auditing, the head of the household himself keeping the accounts or a running tally of debts and payments outstanding.[33]

The signing of accounts appears much earlier on the Continent, a reflection, in part, of a different tradition of authentication, the use of a signature rather than a seal. In household documents, however, it is usual for the clerk of the expenses or the master of the household to sign, not the lord himself. The accounts of the household of the Dukes of Brabant were frequently signed by the masters of the household.[34] The weekly accounts of *contre-sommes* for the household of Margaret of Bavaria in 1440 were signed by H. Fevre, her *clerc de despens*.[35] A household ordinance of Charles, Duke of Orleans, of March 1449 or 1450, notes that the Duke himself was to sign certain types of household account, for example the account for spices, but not the daily *escroes*.[36] From the mid-1460s, the *escroes* of the household of the Duke of Burgundy are signed by a clerk of the expenses and occasionally by one of the masters of the household. The assertion of Olivier de la Marche, describing the household of Charles the Bold, about 1473–4, that the Duke of Burgundy signed all accounts and rolls, appears from the surviving documents to be wide of the mark, although his description of the compilation of the *escroes*, for the oversight

[31] Bodl. MS DD Weld c. 19/4/2, e.g. ff. 5^v, 6^r, 7^r, etc.

[32] BL Add. MS 6668, ff. 375–7.

[33] The pattern continues through the 16th century, e.g. Warws. RO CR 895/45 and 106, accounts (possibly holograph) of Sir Edward Don, 1510–51; Hants. RO 252M87, household accounts signed by Stephen Gardiner, Bishop of Winchester, 1547–51. The infrequency of the appearance of the signature of the Earl of Northumberland, coupled with the use of signatures of other officials of his household, for example, the controller in 1604–5, marks an interesting change: *The household papers of Henry Percy, ninth Earl of Northumberland (1564–1632)* ed. G. R. Batho (Camden Society, third series, 93; 1962) pp. xxviii, xlii.

[34] A. Uyttebrouck, 'Inventaire des comptes généraux du duché de Brabant antérieurs à l'avènement de Philippe le Bon (1342–1430)', *Acta Historica Bruxellensia* 3 (1974) p. 105.

[35] Weekly account, e.g. AD Nord B 3327 (112921); H. Fevre appears in the list of the Duchess' household as *clerc de despens* in April 1439, AD Nord B 3373 (113502) p. 2.

[36] AD Loiret 6 J 9/104.

of which he was responsible as a master of the household, can be shown to be more accurate.[37] The first continental accounts to have survived that are signed by the head of the household, by Archduchess Margaret of Austria, in 1508, or by Diane de Poitiers, some decades later still, post-date the English examples.[38]

In contrast to the diet account, the annual cash, corn and stock accounts preserve much of their earlier form, remaining almost exclusively as Chancery fashion rolls.[39] Many of these accounts are fair copies, some clearly engrossed after the audit: the *venditio super compotum* entries on the accounts of Richard Beauchamp, Earl of Warwick, in 1435–6, of Anne Stafford, dowager Duchess of Buckingham, in 1462–3,[40] and on the accounts of Sir William Skipwith, in 1467–8, are in the same hand and ink as the rest of the text (**21**). Other accounts exhibit auditing as the second stage in their compilation: on the dorse of the accounts of Humphrey Stafford, Duke of Buckingham, 1443–4 and 1454–5, the corn and stock account on the dorse has been surcharged and the marginal mark ʒ: appears in a second hand and ink.[41] These features are similar to the earlier annual rolls. One notable omission, however, from both the annual cash, corn and stock accounts and the diet accounts, is evidence that they were used for financial planning in the way that earlier accounts, with such features as the calculation of averages, were employed. There is some evidence, largely from Stafford household accounts, that one purpose of the account was a precise statement of the overall financial position of the household, an attempt to calculate the net expenses of the household for the year. An important element in this was the valuation of stock in hand at the beginning and end of the accounting period. The account of Richard Beauchamp, Earl of Warwick, 1435–6, values the remainders of the stock and corn account and the value of the remainder of the previous account is entered in the cash charge.[42] The total cash value of the remainder of the stock of the household in hand is given in the accounts of Humphrey

[37] *Escroes* signed by a clerk of the expenses, e.g. AD Nord B 3431 (118405); B 3433 (118479–80); signed by J. Carondelet, a master of the household, B 3455 (120636). *Mémoires d'Olivier de la Marche* ed. H. Beaune and J. d'Arbaumont (4 vols., Paris, 1883–8) iv, pp. 10–11, 13–15.

[38] AD Nord B 3382 (113850) and (113855); Diane de Poitiers, MS at the Château de Chenonceaux, dép. Indre-et-Loire.

[39] **21**; **22**; Guildhall Library MSS 10307, 25166/1–8, steward of the household and receiver general of William Worsley, Dean of St Paul's, 1479–96; SJC D91.16, Margaret Beaufort, Countess of Richmond, 1506–7. An exception is PRO E 101/518/33, an Exchequer fashion roll, a draft possibly for the Ferrers family, 1522–3.

[40] BL Egerton Roll 8775; Egerton MS 2822.

[41] BL Add. Roll 5962; Egerton Roll 2209.

[42] BL Egerton Roll 8775.

Stafford, Duke of Buckingham, for 1443–4, 1452–3, and 1454–5.[43] In an account for Anne Stafford, dowager Duchess of Buckingham, 1462–3, the remainders in the corn and stock account are not valued, but the value of the remainder of corn and stock of the previous year is entered in the cash charge and somewhat peculiarly is counterbalanced by the same value in the cash discharge, not by the value of the remainder of the current year.[44] The remainders are valued in the corn and stock account of Edward Stafford, Duke of Buckingham, 1503–4.[45] From another of his accounts, for the six months prior to 30 September 1517, comes the clearest attempt to provide a statement of the total household expenses for the period, with the declaration of 'clear expenses' (net expenses) calculated by adding the cash value of the remainder at the start of the account to the cost of provisions for the period of the account, together with a valuation of all gifts received, less the cash value of the remainder at the end of the account.[46]

From the evidence of the accounts, it would be not unreasonable to suppose that their use to plan household consumption and to manage the details of domestic life belonged solely to the period up to 1430. Two closely related groups of evidence, however, show that household management in financial terms was not disregarded. Firstly, household expenses could be known with sufficient precision for agreements to be prepared for financial compensation to the lord of a household for residence in it, acting as 'hotels' in the most literal sense, charging for board and lodging and for the entertainment of 'guests', their friends and visitors. John Rafman, the steward of the household of Sir John Fastolf in 1430–1, was granted an allowance for debts outstanding from Margaret Braunch and Alice Fastolf, who were charged for board and lodging, even though they appear in the calendar of members of the household in the same account;[47] in 1463–4, Isabella, Lady Morley, contributed substantially to the costs of her stay in the household of her son-in-law, John Hastings (**24**); and the cofferer of Lady Margaret Beaufort received two payments in February and March 1502 for the board and lodging of various women in her household, in one instance calculating a weekly rate for a lady and her two servants.[48] Secondly, from the mid-fifteenth century in England, renewed use is made

[43] BL Add. Roll 5962; M. Harris and J. Thurgood, 'The account of the great household of Humphrey, first Duke of Buckingham, for the year 1452–3', *Camden Miscellany XXVIII* (Camden Society, 4th series, 29; 1984) pp. 1–57; BL Egerton Roll 2209.
[44] BL Egerton MS 2822.
[45] BL Add. MS 40859B.
[46] BL MS Royal 14 B XXXV B.
[47] MCO Fastolf Paper 8.
[48] SJC D91.20, p. 5.

of household ordinances. The purpose of these was in part to define the allowances, as well as the duties, of members of the household: they could be used as a foundation for the preparation of estimates of expenditure and, examined in conjunction with a valor, or statement of receipts, to provide an overall view of finances.[49] The Burgundian household ordinances of the fifteenth century had similar aims and served, to a certain extent, as the model for English ones; in Burgundy, in 1470, we find actual expenditure on the household being compared with the estimates.[50] It is no surprise, therefore, to find, accompanying the household regulations of George, Duke of Clarence, 1468–9, a set of estimates of the quantities of various commodities expected to be consumed in the household per day, week, month and year, together with a cash valuation.[51] The Black Book of the household of King Edward IV, *c.*1471–3, contains an estimate for a year's household expenses, calculated from a set rate of expenditure per day;[52] and a similar example survives from the reign of Henry VII.[53] From the period 1516–30, there are tables for the royal household computing the cost of diet expenses, setting out the items consumed in a specimen week.[54] That this sort of analysis was conducted in the households of the aristocracy is shown by model accounting documents included in the Northumberland household book, notably the 'assignemente' for the year 30 September 1511 to 29 September 1512, with its detailed exposition of the provisions required for the year, the quantities and dates when they were to be purchased, and an estimated cash amount for the year for each

[49] P. D. A. Harvey *Manorial records* (London, 1984) p. 38; *The Grey of Ruthin valor. The valor of the English lands of Edmund Grey, Earl of Kent, drawn up from the ministers' accounts of 1467–8* ed. R. I. Jack (Sydney, 1965); *The Marcher lordships of South Wales 1415–1536. Select documents* ed. T. B. Pugh (Board of Celtic Studies, University of Wales, Cardiff, History and Law series, 20; 1963) pp. 154–7.

[50] Many of the ordinances are listed by U. Schwarzkopf, 'La cour de Bourgogne et la Toison d'Or', *Publications du centre européen d'études burgondo-médianes* 5 (1963) pp. 91–104; and by W. Paravicini, 'Expansion et intégration. La noblesse des Pays-Bas à la cour de Philippe le Bon', *Bijdragen en Mededelingen betreffende de Geschiedenis der Nederlanden* 95 (1980) pp. 298–314; and some have now been published: W. Paravicini, 'Die Hofordnungen Herzog Philipps des Guten von Burgund . . .', *Francia* 10 (1982) pp. 131–66; 11 (1983) pp. 257–301; 13 (1985) pp. 191–211; 15 (1987) pp. 183–231. Comparison of household expenses with estimate: AD Nord B 3376 (113548).

[51] *A collection of ordinances and regulations for the government of the royal household, made in divers reigns, from King Edward III to King William and Queen Mary, also receipts in ancient cookery* ed. Anon (Society of Antiquaries, London, 1790) pp. 101–5.

[52] *Black Book* pp. 87–8; R. G. K. A. Mertes, 'The *liber niger* of Edward IV: a new version', *BIHR* 54 (1981) pp. 37–9.

[53] PRO E 101/416/10, printed in *Black Book* pp. 229–30.

[54] PRO E 36/233.

commodity, together with the notes of improvements to be made over the preceding year.[55]

What was the influence of the Continent on household accounting in England in the fifteenth century? The courts of northern Europe set a pattern for English monarchs to emulate: Edward IV had spent time in the Burgundian court and had a description of it presented to him by one of the masters of the household; the Burgundian tradition had an important impact on English art, architecture, literature and pageantry, especially at the court of Henry VII, *c.*1497–1501; and Henry VIII made changes in the structure of his household to liken it the more closely to that of Francis I of France.[56] Despite this, there seems to have been little influence on the administrative procedures and forms of account in the English royal household. No system of daily *escroes* appears. The royal household had always had a system of cash based accounting, not one that encompassed a detailed record of consumption. It is harder to find a reason, beyond the more intimate scale of the operation, for the emergence of a system of cash accounting in private households and the disappearance of the record of consumption. While the cash based accounting systems of the Continent could have provided a model, there is no evidence for a direct link. The centre of the problem, however, is the lack of evidence for accounting procedures in England: proportionately fewer private household accounts have survived for the period from about 1430 to the end of the fifteenth century than for the preceding eighty years; and the quantities for both periods are exceedingly small when compared with the numbers of accounts extant from the sixteenth and seventeenth centuries.[57] It is impossible to say with certainty whether the pattern of accounting in a household, such as that of Henry Stafford in the 1460s and 1470s,[58] is part of a continuing tradition that was employed in many other households for which no evidence is now extant or whether it is an isolated survival. Households in England in the mid to late sixteenth century had elaborate systems of accounting, designed to record information similar to that contained in the accounts of the fourteenth and early fifteenth centuries. Weekly household accounts of Stephen Gardiner, Bishop of Winchester, 1547–51, for example, are fair copies derived from diet accounts and a

[55] *Northumberland household book* pp. 1–29, 57–8.

[56] *Mémoires d'Olivier de la Marche* iv, pp. 1–94; *Black Book* p. 4; G. Kipling *The triumph of honour. Burgundian origins of the Elizabethan renaissance* (The Hague, 1977); D. Starkey, 'Intimacy and innovation: the rise of the Privy Chamber, 1485–1547', in *The English court from the Wars of the Roses to the Civil War* ed. D. Starkey (London, 1987) p. 84.

[57] For references and examples, *Household papers of Henry Percy* pp. xi–xiv; *Black Book* p. 305; *Early Stuart household accounts* ed. L. M. Munby (Hertfordshire Record Publications, 2; 1986).

[58] WAM 12181–90.

book of purchases.[59] The household of Henry Percy, the ninth Earl of Northumberland, had 'books of provisions' (for the bulk purchases) and 'breving books' for daily consumption within the household, noting numbers of the household present from the check rolls, and listing visitors.[60] The balance of probability, however, is against the continuity of the forms of account through the fifteenth century and it is likely that even the largest households at that date depended primarily on a system of cash accounting.

[59] Hants. RO 252M87.
[60] *Household papers of Henry Percy* pp. xxxvi–xlvi.

Chapter 5
Method of editing

In presenting a corpus of texts covering a period of three centuries, employing three languages, written with varying degrees of abbreviation, by clerks with widely differing levels of literacy, three aims have been paramount.[1] The first has been to set out, as clearly as possible, what each clerk wrote, or intended to write, had he extended all his abbreviations, in order that the edition should serve as a base for linguistic as well as for historical research. The second aim has been that the resulting text should be as easy to use as possible, unencumbered by editorial notes. Much of the editorial matter has consequently been gathered together in the Word List and Glossary in the first volume. Thirdly, the intention has been to demonstrate how each document worked, the part of each clerk in its compilation and its significance. Each document is prefaced by a brief introduction which includes a description of the manuscript and an attempt to set it in its historical context. Where it would be too cumbersome to describe in words the part that each clerk played, superscript figures, enclosed in square brackets, have been employed to indicate their work (**8**, **11**).

The exact orthography of the original documents has been preserved with the following exceptions. All capitalisation and punctuation are editorial. The use of *i*, *j*, *u* and *v* has been standardised, *j* and *v* being preferred in all instances where the letter has a consonantal value. In instances where it has been difficult to decide whether a letter is a *c* or a *t* or on questions of word division, for example, whether *incrastino* was intended to be written as one word or two, the case has been resolved by looking at the usage of the manuscript elsewhere. In expanding abbreviations, two rules have been followed. Firstly, all abbreviated words that are not from Latin forms have had their extensions placed in italics. The precise significance of some vernacular contractions and suspensions is uncertain, but rather than overburden the text with editorial matter, the practice in each case, which has been judged word by word, for each clerk,

[1] I have benefited greatly from Professor P. D. A. Harvey's discussion of editorial principles in *Manorial records of Cuxham* pp. 7–11, and from *Paston letters and papers of the fifteenth century* ed. N. Davis (2 vols., Oxford, 1971–6) i, pp. lxxx–lxxxv.

is set out in the Word List and Glossary. Abbreviated forms of place-names have not been extended and retain their final suspensions. Secondly, while there is much less doubt about many of the extensions of the abbreviations employed by clerks when writing Latin, there are equally instances of ambiguity. In extending Latin words, the guide has been the usage of each particular clerk in other instances with regard to the grammatical form, case, gender, number or tense of a word, together with the overall context of the document. Where insufficient evidence exists, the practice adopted is set out in the Word List and Glossary. The rule in these instances has been to follow patterns of classical grammar, unless there is evidence of usage to the contrary. Where ambiguity remains, usually whether a word is to be extended in a singular or a plural form, the extension has been made in italics. Italic type has also been used for all marginal entries. No mention has been made of any entries in a document that date from the sixteenth century or later. Some frequently occurring words, especially weights, measures and currency, have not been extended beyond a standard form: all these appear in the list of abbreviations, together with the conventions for insertions, deletions and editorial reconstructions. Corrections to the text have been made only where there are obvious slips of the pen or where an eccentric spelling might mislead: in all instances the original form has been given in a footnote.

GLOSSARY

Word list and glossary

The purpose of this word list is fourfold. Firstly it sets out to identify and define all words employed in the editions that are not in *LS*, *RMLWL* or *AND*. It only includes words that are in *OED* and *DMLBS* where the usage is different, where the instance here occurs more than thirty years earlier than the first cited use, or where the orthography of the word might lead to confusion about its meaning. Its second purpose has been to make clear some of the potential ambiguities of the documents, by listing words that look the same but have different meanings. Some of these ambiguities can be resolved only by reference to the text itself and a word's position in it; for example, whether *bream* is to be interpreted as a marine fish or a freshwater fish will depend in each instance on its appearance in immediate contiguity with other marine or freshwater fish in the account. The third purpose of the list is editorial, to make clear the assumptions about a word which are inherent in expanding an abbreviated form. To this end, further words have been included, which have otherwise been expanded silently in the editions, or where suspensions have been dropped; and the opportunity has been taken to set out what practices with regard to case, gender and number have been followed where the MSS supply little or no evidence. The fourth aim has been to indicate the conventions that have been followed in the expansion of particular grammatical constructions and to note some, at least, of the principal divergences from classical forms.

Words are given as they appear in the MSS, in their abbreviated form, not in a standardised *nom. sing.* or first person.

Aberdene (5): salted or sun dried cod (*OED* haberdine).
acq' (28): acquittance. Extended to *acquietancia*, except for forms in *acquit-*.
aghtyndelys (19), **eghtyndale (22)**: measure of capacity, literally an eighth part (*OED* eightin-dele).
agist' (23): (*OED* agist). Extended to *agista*, *e*, *f*.
alaud': lark. Extended to forms from *al(l)auda*, *e*, *f.*, in **4**, **10** and **11a**. Also *alowes*, **11a**.
alegr' (20): sour ale, malt vinegar (*OED* alegar 1542). Extended to *alegre*.
all' (19): other. Extended to forms from *allius*, *a*, *um*.

allia (4), **alea (10)**, **alec' (7)**: garlic. Other forms from *allium*, *i*, *n*.
allec: herring. Extended to *allec*, *is*, *n.*, *coll. sing.*, where no other extension on MS; except on **2** where *allecis*, *abl. pl.*, is sometimes used, and on **4**, where it is extended to *allecia*, *e*, *f*.
alloc' (28): allowance. Extended to *allocacio*, *onis*, *f*.
allocacione (7): hiring. Also *ger.*, *allocandis*, **7**.
almary (14): cupboard, chest (*OED* ambry).
alnaz (8): possibly ells (measure of cloth).
amigdal': almonds. Extended throughout to forms in *pl.* from *amigdala*, *e*, *f.*, and variants.
anat': duck. Extended throughout to forms from *anas*, *atis*, *f*.
Andr': Andrew, man's name. Extended throughout to forms from *Andreas*, *Andree*.
anduill' (3): sausage (*RMLWL* andulla 1245). Extended as if from *anduilla*, *e*, *f*.
anguill'; **aguill' (16)**: eel. Extended to *pl.* of *a*(*n*)*guilla*, *e*, *f.*, unless a single eel is explicitly mentioned.
anneys (19): a plant with aromatic seeds (*OED* anise).
anniversar': anniversary (of death). Extended to forms from *anniversarius*, *i*, for *sb.*, and in *-ius*, *-ia*, *-ium* for *adj*.
annuetates, **annuitates (28)**: annuities. All abbreviated forms extended from *annuitas*, *atis*, *f*.
aparile (8): clothing, dress, apparel (*AND* apparail).
aput (1): at (*apud*).
archiediac' (7): archdeacon. Extended as if from *archiediaco*, *onis*, *m*.
arco (11a): chest, box (*LS* arca).
ardei, **ardearum (14)**: heron (*RMLWL* ardea).
arga (14): against (of time) (*RMLWL* erga, variant 1535).
argent' (24): silver. Extended, where an *adj.*, to forms in *-eus*, *-ea*, *-eum*.
larein (11a): brass, bronze (*AND* arein).
armat*urs* (28): armour, military accoutrements (*RMLWL* armatura; *OED* armature 1669).
armener (11a): armourer.
arreragia: arrears. Extended in all accounts to forms from *arreragia*, *orum*, *n. pl.*, unless otherwise written on MS.
arryer (8): possibly to bring (*arriver*) or to prepare (*AND* arraier).
arsnyk' (19): arsenic. Treated as *m*.
ass' (15): [rents of] assize. Extended throughout as *gen.* of *assisa*, *e*, *f*.
astell': piece of firewood. Extended throughout to forms from *astella*, *e*, *f.*, in *pl.* unless a single piece indicated.
atthame, **atthamia (6)**: start of consumption, broaching.
aturnatus est (2): he is acknowledged (*RMLWL* attornamentum).
auc': goose. Extended to forms from *auca*, *e*, *f.*, in *pl.* unless a single goose is indicated. **14** has *nom. pl. auci* and *auce*.
auce*ratis* (18): tethered (*RMLWL* haucera).
aucul' (10): gosling. Extended to forms from *aucula*, *e*, *f*.
aug' (3): tub, trough (*RMLWL* auga). Extended to *auga*, *e*, *f*.
auri de Venys (28): gold thread made in Venice (*OED* gold *sb.*[1]).
avelan' (20): filbert (*RMLWL* abellana). Extended as if from *avelana*, *e*, *f*.

aven': oats. Extended as a *coll. sing.* from *avena, e, f.*, on **2–4**, **6–7**, **9–10**, **12**, **18**, **20**, following the usage of MS; and to *pl.* on **14–17**, **19**, **22–23** and **28**.
aveynus (8): oats.
awmbler (28): ambler (horse).
ax' (20): axle. Extended to forms from *axis, is.*
ayer' (19), aier' (20): a swan, or nesting or nests (of swans) (*RMLWL* aer/ia). Extended to *a(i/y)erium, i, n.*

bacon': preserved pork, probably a side or carcass; a haunch or ham, especially in the phrase *perna baconis*. Extended throughout to forms from *baco, nis, m.*, except in **4** and **14**, where *nom. sing. bacon'* occurs; extended in **4** to *baconus, i, m.*; not extended in **14**.
bacynett' (12), bacenetz (26), basinet (28): type of helmet (*OED* basinet). Not extended and suspension dropped in **12**.
bad' (12): bay (colour). Extended as *adj.* from forms in *-ius, -ia, -ium.*
baile (11a): given, paid, handed over (*AND* bailler).
bailes (28): half hoop supporting cover of wagon (*OED* bail *sb.*[2] 1447).
bal' fructus (11a): bales of fruit, possibly in the sense of packages or of specific quantities (*OED* bale *sb.*[3]). Extended to *balis.*
balinger (28): balinger or ballinger, a small or medium sized boat (Rose *Lancastrian navy* p. 253).
barbell' (4, 12): barbel, freshwater fish of the carp family (*OED*, *RMLWL*). Extended in **4** to *barbellus, i, m.*, as a *coll. sing.*; in **12**, suspension dropped and no extension in *sing.*, extended in *pl.* to *barbellis.*
barber' (10): barbel or barber. Not extended.
barell', barill': barrel. Extended as if from *barellus* or *barillus, i, m.* in **2**, **10**, **12**, **14** and **19**; suspension dropped in *sing.* and treated as *m.* in **15**; extended from *barella, e, f.*, in **20** and also in **28** except where other evidence in a sentence demands *m.* or *n.* forms.
barge (20): barge. Treated as *m.*
barhide (14), barehide (28): barehide, i.e. an undressed skin or one with all the hair removed (*OED* barehide *c.*1450). Treated as *m.*
bars' (4); bars de mari (7); bas', baas (14); base (16): bass, a marine fish (*OED* bass *sb.*[1] 1530). Extended in **4** from *barsa, e, f., coll. sing.*; in **14**, treated as *m.* and extended in *pl.* to *basis.*
Barth': Bartholomew, man's name. Extended throughout to forms from *Bartholomeus, i.*
bas (7): saddle pads or bags (*OED* base *sb.*[3]; *MFG* baaz; *Manorial records of Cuxham* p. 777, baces).
basillard (27): type of dagger (*OED* baselard).
bast' (20): bast, for tying scaffolding (*MFG* basta). Extended where there is a suspension to *basta, e, f.*
bastard' (12): *equus bastard'*, pack-horse (*OED* bast *sb.*[2], pack-saddle; *MFG* basta, saddle pad).
bastard' (24): a sweet wine (*OED* bastard *sb.*).
batell' (3, 28): transport, boat, boat hire. Extended in **3** as if from *batellum, i, n.*; and in **28** from *batella, e, f.*

batellag', batillag' (**7**); **batilag'** (**11a**): transport (by boat), boat hire. Extended in **7** to forms in *-ium*, *-ii*, *n.*; and in **11a** to *batilage*.
baytyng (**28**): giving food to horses (*OED* baiting *c.*1440).
bed (**12**), **bedseche** (**28**): 'bed', part of lower framework of a cart (*RMLWL* beddum).
bem' (**19**): possibly for *brevem*, a writ, although the form of the abbreviation would be unusual.
bendes (**12**): band, strip of metal (*RMLWL* benda).
bendes, bendys (**28**): ribbon, strip of cloth for ornament (*OED* bend *sb.*[2]).
benge (**20**): small, salted ling.
beyvere (**8**): to drink (*AND* beivre).
bill': bill, receipt, voucher. Extended in **28** to *sing.* of *billa*, *e*, *f.*, in *per bill'*.
blaunchepoudr' (**24**): powdered spices, possibly including ginger and sugar (*Curye on Inglysch* p. 172).
blaunderels (**19**): a kind of white apple (*OED* blaundrell).
boilez (**11a**): possibly referring to cloth (*kerchivez*) with a thick nap (*AND* peil).
bokkehorn' (**18**): dried fish, in the seventeenth century, whiting (*OED* buck-horn 1602).
boll': bowl. Extended in **10** as if from *bolla*, *e*, *f.*
bolledisc' (**20**): a deep dish (*MFG*). Extended as if from *bollediscus*, *i*, *m.*
bolstres (**12**): bar over axle of a cart, supporting the bed and raising it from the axle (*MFG* bolstre; *OED* bolster 1686).
bolt worsted (**28**): fine worsted, like muslin.
bonett': bonnet, extra piece of canvas at foot of sail (*RMLWL*). Extended in **28** as if from *bonettus*, *i*, *m.*
bos: ox. Extended throughout to *bos*, *bovis*, *m.* In **4** treated as *coll. sing.*; examples of a possible *nom. sing.* form *bov'* (distinct from forms for *boviculus*) extended to *pl. boves*.
bosco de Caleys (**27**): the name of a ransom for captured soldiers.
botel, botell': pottle (liquid measure, two quarts); 'bottle', vessel for holding liquids; or a small butt. Latin forms in **12** and **20** extended to *botellus*, *i*, *m.*
botellaria: buttery. Extended in **7** from *bo'* to this form in *-a*, *-e*, *f.*
boteris (**3**): boots, footwear (*RMLWL* bota[2]).
botor' (**10**), **botores** (**20**), **butoures** (**11a**): bittern (heron-like bird).
bouge (**25**), **bugge** (**28**): budge, lambskin (Veale *Fur trade* pp. 216–17).
bouges (**28**): bag or saddle bag (*OED* bouge *sb.*[1]; *RMLWL* bulga).
boxyng' (**20**): lining the nave of a wheel or fitting with axle boxes (*MFG* boxo; *RMLWL* boxis; *OED* box *sb.*[2] 1711).
brachis (**1**), **bracis** (**28**): possibly straps.
bra' (**5**): brewing. Extended as if from *braciatura*, *e*, *f.*
bras', brass': malt. Extended to forms from *bras(s)ium*, *i*, *n.*, except in **9–10** and **11b**, where the form *braseum* is preferred, and in **20**, unless written out in the same section of the account as *brasium*.
braum' (**14**): brawn, probably specifically 'boar's flesh' or [one quarter of the carcass of a] boar (*OED*).
braybolt' (**12**): part of a cart's equipment.
bremes: bream. Probably the marine variety in **7** and **14** where they occur listed with sea fish (*OED* bream, as a sea fish, *c.*1460); in **16**, the freshwater fish (also in **16**, *bremett'*, young or small bream).

brennis (4): bream, listed with sea fish in this account. Extended to forms in the *pl.* from *brenna, e, f.*
breoz (11a): malt (*AND* brais).
broch' (12): spit (kitchen equipment). Extended to forms from *brocha, e, f.*
broch', broche (14): 'tortis de broche', candle or taper for placing on a spike (*OED* broach).
brochiand' (12): stretching, staking (*RMLWL* broca, brochio).
Brouneswyk' (28): Brunswick, a type of cloth (*OED* Brunswick 1480).
bruchetos (2): hound, brachet (*DMLBS* brachettus; *OED* brach).
brusket (11b): brisket, joint of meat covering the breast bone (*OED* brisket 1450).
brygaunters (27): body armour, originally for foot soldiers and at first in two halves, made of iron rings or plates sewn to canvas, linen or leather (*OED* brigander, brigandine).
buche (8): firewood (*AND* busche).
buding' (3): pudding (sausage) (*RMLWL* pudingum 1246; *OED* pudding 1305). Extended to *budingum.*
buletell' (4): bolting cloth, sieve. Extended to forms from *buletellum, i, n.*
bultyngcloth' (16, 19): bolting cloth. Treated as *m.*
bundys (19): bundle, items fastened together by a tie (see *OED* bound *ppl. a.*[2]).
burbocz, burboz (10): burbot (freshwater fish) (*OED* burbot 1475).
burle (1): coarse woollen material, burel (*RMLWL* burellus).
butir', buttir', butur': butter. Extended throughout to forms in *-um, -i, n.*
butt (19): a cask for wine, perhaps indicating a specific quantity (*OED*). Treated as *m.*
butt' (10): generic term applied locally to different kinds of flat fish (*OED* butt *sb.*[1]). Extended to *buttis* in *abl. pl.*
bys (28): grey, dark coloured, or brown (*AND* bis[1]).

cad' (10): cade, a measure, usually a barrel of fish, especially of herring. Extended as if from *cadus, i, m.*; in **15**, **19** and **21**, extended to English forms in italics.
calant, calaunt (10): both salted and smoked herring are drawn from this source. Possibly associated in meaning with *AND chalant* or *KMED chalan*, a boat or barge. Suspension dropped in all examples.
calcar' (28): spurs. Extended as if from *calcarium, i, n.*
calfatyng' (28): caulking (*OED* calfret *v.* 1600; Rose *Lancastrian navy* p. 255).
calib' (3): steel (*LS* chalybs).
calid' (10): hot (*calidus, a, um*), but precise meaning of *pane calido* unclear.
camera: chamber. **15** also employs a *n.* or *m.* form with *gen.*, *cameri.*
camis' (28): shirt, smock, 'underwear'. Extended to forms from *camisum, i, n.*
campirnol' (10): possibly oil of camphor.
cand', candel': candle. Extended to *coll. sing.* of *candela, e, f.*, where no evidence to the contrary on MS (**2–3**, **7**, **9–10**, **11b–12**, **15**, **19–20**, and **22–23**); and, following MS, to *pl.* in **13–14**, **16**, **21** and **24**.
candela paris': a tallow candle, not wax as *OED*, as can be seen from, e.g., **19** membrane 3 dorse, *cepum.*
canel (11a), **canell' (14, 19)**: cinnamon. Extended in **14** to forms from *canella, e, f.* **19** uses both *canell'* and *synamoum'* in the same paragraph, perhaps intending casia bark rather than cinnamon for *canell'* (*OED*).

canvace: canvas. Treated as *m.* in **28**.
capist' (3), capistr' (10): halter. Extended to forms from *capistrum, i, n.*
capon': capon. Extended to forms from *capo, nis, m.*, except in **13** and **14**, where the form *caponis, caponis, m.*, is used. **7** uses *calponibus, abl. pl.*
capres (28): capers (*OED* caper *sb.*[1] 1481–90).
capriol' (7, 19): goat. Extended to forms from *capriolus, i, m.*
carayes (2): possibly derived from *capra*, goat, or *carayne*, carcasses.
carbon': coal or charcoal. Extended to forms from *carbo, nis, m.*, in the *pl.* in **15**, **19** and **24**, although no evidence on the MSS. Occurs in **7** and **14** in *pl.* Coal: *carbonum maritimorum* (**14**), *carbonum marinorum* (**19**), ?*carbonum extinctorum* (**24**). Charcoal: *carbonum ligneorum* (**19**).
carc' (12), carcos' (7), cargos' (11b), carcois' (21): carcass. Extended to forms from *car(c/g)o(i)sium, i, n.*
carde (11a, 14): a textile fabric, possibly like muslin, used for curtains, canopies and linings (*RMLWL* carda[1]; *OED* carde). *Ridel de carde*: a curtain of this material.
carn': flesh. Extended from forms of *caro, carnis, f.*, following the usage of MSS, to *sing.* in **2**, **6**, **7** and **10**; in all other instances extended in *pl.* In **16**, MS suggests extension in *pl.* in *in carnibus bovinis*, but in *sing.* in *in i qr. carnis mutuline.* **6** also uses *abl. sing.*, *caro*.
carrew (19): a measure, possibly French, for wine. Treated as *m.* Possibly derived from *carea*, cart-load, or *charre, carrus*, a wagon. See *cue* below.
cas(s)eus (4); caseum (7, 15, 18); casium (14, 21): cheese. Extended to *coll. sing.* in all except **14**.
cass': carcass. Extended to forms from *cassa, e, f.*, in **11b**, **12**, **14** and **20**; and from *cassum, i, n.*, in **16**.
castrimarg' (18): woodcock (*RMLWL* gastrimargia/castrimargus 1430). Extended as if from *castrimargus, i, m.*
cauder' (4), chauder' (7): cauldron, kettle. Extended to forms from *caudera, e, f.*, in **4**; from *chauderium, i, n.*, in **7**.
caulibus (10): a cabbage or some sort of brassica (*OED* caul *sb.*[2]; *LS* caulis).
caumbbrus (8): rooms, chambers.
caumfur' (14): camphor (*OED*).
ceal (11a): saddle.
ceir (11a): wax.
celing' (28): lining of planks inside a ship's bottom (*OED* ceiling *vbl. sb.* 1633; Rose *Lancastrian navy* p. 255).
cell' (27): meaning not clear.
cellar' (4), celar' (14): cellar, storeroom. Extended to forms in *-ium, -ii, n.* **19**, *per selarium*, may mean 'by the cellar account'.
cenap': see *sinap-*.
cendre (8): *peyn cendre*, bread with sanders; or possibly 'cooked', *ceudre*.
cep', sep': onion. Extended in **4**, **7**, **14** and **19** from forms in *-a, -e, f.*
cep', sep': tallow. Extended in **10**, **13**, **15**, **19** and **21** from forms in *-um, -i, n.* **1** has *gen. sing.*, *sipi*; **7** and **18** have *abl. sing.*, *sepe*.
cer': wax. Extended to forms from *cera, e, f.* **23** has *ceri, gen. sing.*, possibly 'wax candle'.
cera pendula (28), ceris (16): padlock (**28**), bolt (**16**) (*RMLWL* sera).

cere frumenti (20): possibly husks (*LS* cera).
cereac' (21): wax (*adj.*). Extended to forms in *-us*, *-a*, *-um*.
cero (14): late hour (*LS* serum).
certo (14): fixed allowance or wage (*RMLWL* certum).
cervisia: see *servis-*.
cesselles (11a): teal or similar ducks (*OED* sarcelle; *RMLWL* cercella).
cest. (16): sester, liquid measure. Treated as *m.*
chaculs (15): shackles.
chanun (8): possibly a canon (ecclesiastic) (*AND* canun).
chara (28): cart.
charbons (8): coal or charcoal (*AND* carbun). See *carbon'*, above.
char de qweyns (10): flesh or pulp of quinces, or a preserve made from them (*OED* chare *sb.*[4] (de quince) *c.*1440).
Chardeyns (19): see *Jardein*.
charemen (28): carters.
charette (25): a cart, possibly a wagon or heavy cart (*AND* charette). See *charietta*.
charietta (14); **chariota (12, 28)**; **chariot (15)**; **chariott' (20)**: wagon, heavy cart (*DLMBS* carriotta). Latin forms in **12**, **14** and **28** extended to *-a*, *-e*, *f.*; in **20**, extended to forms in *-um*, *-i*, *n.*
charjour (19): charger, a large plate or flat dish.
chaump' (25): part of a head-dress (*AND* champ).
Chaumpayn' (28): a cloth from or similar to one from Champagne, France.
chaunce (27): a game of chance, possibly generic rather than specific.
chelynge (20): a form of marine fish, probably a cod (*OED* keeling *sb.*[1]).
chesfattys (19): cheese-vats, moulds for pressing cheese (*OED* vat: cheese-vat 1669).
chevecel (26): a piece of armour, probably for the head.
cheveron' (28): goat (*OED* chevron *sb.*[2]).
cheyveynis (16): chevin, a river fish, the chub (*OED*). Treated as *m.*
chine (11a): a female dog (?) (*AND* chin).
cign', **sign'**: swan. Extended to forms in *-us*, *-i*, *m.*, in **15**, **16** and **19**. **7**, *cinis*, *abl. pl.*, may be the same word. Signets: **10** has *cignott'*, extended to *-us*, *-i*, *m.*; **11a** has *singne*.
cimin' (4); **cymin' (10)**: cumin. Extended to forms in *-um*, *-i*, *n.* **1** has *gen. sing.*, *scimini*.
cinamon' (20), **synamoum' (19)**: cinnamon.
cinap' (11b); **cenap' (19)**; **sinap' (15, 16)**; **synap' (10)**: mustard. Extended to forms in *-ium*, *-ii*, *n.* **15** has *sinapin'*, *adj.*, extended to *-us*, *-a*, *-um*.
cingul': belt, girdle, girth. Extended in *abl. sing.* in **3** to *-o*.
ciph' (4): bowl, goblet, cup. Extended to forms in *-us*, *-i*, *m.*, in *pl.* unless a single item is likely. **2** has *abl. pl.*, *cyfis*; **19** has *gen. pl.*, *siphorum*.
circul' (10): barrel hoop. Extended to forms in *-us*, *-i*, *m.*
cirica (24) (*abl. sing.*): silk (*RMLWL* sericum).
cisar' (17): cider. Extended as if from *cisera*, *e*, *f.*
citronade (28): by analogy with *coynade*, *succade*, etc., probably citron (*OED* 1530) preserved in sugar, either candied or in syrup. *OED* citrinade may be the same substance employed as a cosmetic.
clav' (19): key. Extended to forms from *clavis*, *is*, *f.*, as **15** and **16**.

clav' (13): clove, a measure of weight, 7 or 8 pounds avoirdupoids (*OED* clove *sb.*[3]). Extended to forms from *clavus, i, m.*
clavus, i, m.: nail (e.g. **7**).
clavuris (4) (*abl. pl.*): nails ?
cloche (11a): cloak (*AND*).
clothsak' (28): clothsack. Suspension dropped and treated as *m.* throughout.
cocl' (10, 15); kocl', cocles (10): cockle (shellfish) (*OED* cockle *sb.*[2] 1393). Latin forms in **10** extended to *-ea, -e, f.*; in **15** to *-a, -e, f.*
coco (14) (*abl. sing.*): cock, a spout or short pipe, for liquids, regulating or stopping flow, here, part of a net (*OED* cock *sb.*[1] 1481–90).
codling', codeling', codlyng': codling. Suspension dropped throughout except in **5**. Treated as *coll. sing.* in **10**.
coillour, cuilleur (11a): collector, gatherer (*AND*).
cokschete (16), cokshotys (19): cockshoot, a glade in a wood used as a trap for woodcocks (*OED*, *MFG*).
colar' (12), coler' (28): collar (*RMLWL*). Extended to forms in *-ium, -ii, n.*
Colayn' (28): thread from, or similar to that from, Cologne (*OED* Cologne 1436).
collob' (28): tabard, shirt. Extended to forms in *-ium, -ii, n.*
colops (15): slices of meat, usually bacon, and usually eaten with eggs (*OED*).
color' (23): coloured. Extended to forms in *-atus, -ata, -atum.*
coloures (11a): strained liquid (*AND* culure[1]) or strainer (*RMLWL* colura (*sub* colamentum); *Manorial records of Cuxham* p. 781, colur, culur).
columb' (3, 7): dove or pigeon. Extended to *columba, e, f.*, in *pl.* unless a single bird is intended. **15**, *abl. pl.*, *columbis.*
columbar': dovecot. Extended to forms from *-ium, -ii, n.*
columbell': squab or young pigeon. Extended to *columbella, e, f.*, in *pl.* unless a single bird is intended.
come, cume (3): meaning uncertain.
comes (21): radicle of barley or other corn, developed before malting (*OED* come *sb.*[2]).
compot', comput': account (document or process of audit). Extended to forms in *-us, -i, m.*
con' (28): agreement. In *per con' in grosso* extended as if from *convencio, nis, f.*
conduco: used both in the sense 'to bring' (*conducend' piss'* **15**) and 'to hire' (*xxxix cocis conduct' pur lenterment* **14**).
congr' (4, 10, 14): conger eel. Extended to forms from *-us, -i, m.* Treated as *coll. sing.* in **4. 7** *coungre*; **11b** *cungre*; **15** *congur.*
constab' (4): constable. Extended to *constabularius, i, m.*
Constant': Constant, man's name. Extended throughout to *Constans, Constantis.*
coop' hedes (28): furs made of skins from the heads of animals, squirrel unless others specified (Veale *Fur trade* p. 218, croppes, croupes).
cophous (28): cart-hood or cover (*MFG* cope; *OED* cope *sb.*[4] 1577).
copul' (18), coupull' (15): measure of dried fruits, possibly a variation of *corbell-*, a basket. Extended to forms in *-a, -e, f.*
cor', corr': hide (skin *sb.*). Extended in **10, 19** and **22** to forms in *-ium, -ii, n.* **21**, *correa, n. pl.*
corall' (10): coral. Extended to forms in *-um, -i, n.*

corbell' (**3**, **10**): basket. Extended to forms in *-us*, *-i*, *m.*, in *pl.* unless a single item is intended.
corde (**23**): cord. Treated as *m.*
coreyng' (**28**): dressing of leather or cloth (*OED* curry *sb.*[1]). Suspension dropped.
corkes (**14**): a sandal or slipper made of cork (*OED* cork *sb.*[1] 1462–3).
corpelchon, **corpilchon** (**10**): used to describe red (smoked or kippered) herring, measured by the cade. Possibly related to *corpling* (*KMED*), a type of stockfish.
corpus, oris, n.: **12**, cart-frame or chassis. **28**, *corpus veli*, 'course' (naut.), sail as distinct from bonnets (*RMLWL*).
corsez (**28**): ribbons or bands of silk or other material, a base for ornamentation with metalwork or embroidery, employed as a girdle or garter, etc. (*OED* corse *sb.* *c.*1440).
corteyn' (**24**): curtain.
cost' (**16**): side of mutton. Extended to forms in *-a*, *-e*, *f.*
costag' (**28**): charge, cost, expense. Extended to forms in *-ium*, *-ii*, *n.*
coster' mar*is* (**28**): shore, coast. Extended to forms in *-a*, *-e*, *f.*
costering (**28**): hanging of fabric (*OED* coster).
costrell' (**4**), **costerill'** (**3**): costrel, small keg, especially one suspended from the waist (*RMLWL* costrellus 1236). Extended to forms in *-us*, *-i*, *m.*; treated as *sing.* in **3**; extended in *pl.* in **4** if more than one keg intended. **1**, *costrellorum*, *gen. pl.*
cote: coat, cloak (*AND*).
cotil (**11a**): used on this account to mean both a small coat (membrane 2 dorse), diminutive of *cote*, and a knife (membrane 3 dorse) (*AND* cotil).
coton' (**12**, **14**, **20**); **cotyn** (**13**): cotton, candlewick. Extended in **12** to forms from *-us*, *-i*, *m.* Suspension dropped in **14**.
coule (**14**): a tub or large vessel, used in this account as a measure for ale, of 14 gallons in most instances, although with some of 15 or larger (*OED* cowl *sb.*[2] 1467). Treated as *m.*
courser: a large horse, a charger (*OED*).
coynade (**28**): by analogy with *succade*, etc., quince preserved in sugar, either candied or in syrup (*OED* coyn, coyne *sb.*).
crabb': crab. Treated as *m.* in **14**.
cranag' (**19**): payment for hoisting or unloading. Extended to forms in *-ium*, *-ii*, *n.*
crannoc' (**4**): crannock, a dry measure (*OED*, *RMLWL*). Extended to forms in *-us*, *-i*, *m.*
crass' (**19**): fat, grease. *sb.* extended as if from *crassum*, *i*, *n.*; *adj.* to forms in *-atus*, *-ata*, *-atum*.
crassat (**8**), **crassett'** (**10**): cresset, lamp. Extended in **10** to forms in *-um*, *-i*, *n.*
craticul' (**10**): probably a sieve (*LS*, *RMLWL*). Extended to forms in *-a*, *-e*, *f.*
crem' (**14**): cream. Treated as *m.*
cremes' (**28**): crimson, the colour obtained using the dye of the grain insect (*OED* crimson *c.*1440).
crestes (**14**): a measure of a particular type of linen fabric (*OED* crest *sb.*[3] 1430).
creviciis (**5**); **crevices** (**7**); **crevis** (**14**); **krevycz** (**10**): crayfish (*OED*); originally a general name for larger crustacea, i.e. 'fish with claws', sometimes excluding crabs. **10** and **14** note crab and lobster separately. The modern use of crayfish is

specifically for a freshwater crustacean; its earlier use is for marine crustacea as well.

cribr' (10): sieve. Extended to forms in *-um*, *-i*, *n.*

croc': saffron. Extended in **15** and **18** to forms in *-us*, *-i*, *m.*

cropar' (12): leather strap securing saddle from behind (*OED* crupper). Extended to forms in *-ium*, *-ii*, *n.*

croukepeny (14): possibly a local customary due paid on the death of a bishop.

cruystes (15): a bird, no related word traced.

cruz (8): raw, uncooked.

cues (19): a measure of wine, probably the same as a pipe. Possibly the same word as *carrew*.

cultell': knife. Extended to forms in *-us*, *-i*, *m.*, in **4** as a *sing.* unless more than one clearly indicated. Extended to forms in *-um*, *-i*, *n.*, in **16**.

cumpanag' (3): food eaten with bread. Extended to forms in *-ium*, *-ii*, *n.*, as a *coll. sing.*

cumula (9), **cumul' (21)**: a measure of corn (**9**), probably of 12 pecks. In **21**, a heaped measure.

cural', **curall' (17)**: small corn. Extended to forms in *-um*, *-i*, *n.*

curnekill (11a): possibly a small churn (diminutive of *OED* kirn).

curr' (15): carters, extended to *curramentariis*, *abl. pl.*, membrane 4 recto; and cart, extended to *curramento*, *abl. sing.*, membrane 5 dorse.

cursal': regular, ordinary. Extended to forms in *-is*, *-e*, in **9** and **17**.

curvis (3): curved pieces of wood ?

custamag' (7): customs payment. Extended to *-io*, *abl. sing.*

cust': costs, expense. In **2** extended to forms from *custus*, *i*, *m.*, in *sing.* Other accounts employ the form *custus*, *us*. **28**, *custubus*, *abl. pl.* Treated as *m.* in **28**.

cuva: tub, vat, bowl.

dactal' (28): dates. Extended to *pl.* of *dactalus*, *i*, *m.*

dafis (16): possibly dace (*RMLWL* darsus), a type of freshwater fish.

dam' (14): buck (*damus*) or doe (*dama*). Extended to *-us*, *-i*, *m.*, where no evidence to the contrary.

dealb' (20): white-tawed. Extended to forms in *-atus*, *-ata*, *-atum*.

dec' (15): tithe. Extended as *adj.* to *decimalis*, *e*; as *sb.* to *pl.* of *decima*, *e*, *f.* **18** and **19** use *decima* in *sing.*

dece (12): dice (the same as *talos*).

decrem' (21): decrease. Extended to forms from *-entum*, *-enti*, *n.*

def' (10): lacking. Extended to forms from *deficiens*.

descri' (19): description or distribution (*LS* discriptio). Extended to forms from *descriptio*, *nis*, *f.*

devant (27): a game. Membrane 5 recto has *a le vaunt*.

dewet' (10): brush, scrub, *sb.* (*MFG* dumeta); gorse (*MFG* jampnum, jenectum).

diet': day. Extended to *dieta*, *e*, *f. Liber dietarum*, diet account book.

di.: half. Treated as an *adj.* except where the following *sb.* is given in the MS in *gen.*

dinar' (5): dinner. Extended to forms in *-ium*, *-ii*, *n.*, in *sing.*

discarcac' (7): unloading, discharge. Extended in *abl. sing.* to *discarcacione*.

diss' (19): dish.

dol' (**18**): tun (also liquid measure), cask. Extended to *dolia, e, f.* On other MSS, appears in *n.* in forms in *-ium, -ii,* and *-eum, -ei.*
dolobro, dolobris (**14**): mattock, pick-axe (*LS* dolabra; *RMLWL* dolabrium).
dominabus (**28**): *abl. pl.* form of *domina*, following classical *filia.*
dorre (**7**): dory, a marine fish (*OED* dory).
dorsar' (**12**): cart-saddle. Extended to forms in *-ium, -ii, n.*
dosyn (**15**), **dosens** (**16**): a kind of kersey or coarse woollen cloth (*OED* dozen *sb.* 2 1523).
doublett' (**28**): doublet. Treated as *m.*
doucett', dowcett' (**16**): sweets, desserts.
draff' (**18**): draff, malt dregs. Treated as *m.*
draget' (**10**): dredge, mixed corn of barley and oats. Extended to forms in *-um, -i, n.*
drap': cloth (*AND* drap).
drapez (**21**): sheep fattened for slaughter (*OED* drape *sb.*[2] 1611).
dryhurdil (**18**): a type of hurdle. Treated as *m.*
dublers (**2**): a large plate or dish (*OED* doubler[1] 14th cent.).
duct' (**15**): *unius parvi cameri ducti*, a small passage (*LS* ductus).
duoden' (**23, 28**); **dd'** (**22**): dozen (number). Extended to *duodena, e, f.*
duplicac' (**28**): lining. Extended to forms in *-io, -ionis, f.*

eawros, aqua de roos, aquis deawreis (**28**): rose-water.
ecus, eco: see *equus.*
egres (**3**); **egrecco, eggrecco** (**4**); **egerett'** (**14**): egret, the lesser white heron (*OED* egret 1411).
eghtyndale: see *aghtyndelys.*
electuar' (**14**): electuary, cordial. Extended to forms in *-ium, -ii, n.*
elene campane (**14**): elecampane, a herb with aromatic leaves and root, used medicinally (*OED*).
enchesoun (**11a**): *par enchesoun*, on account of (*AND* achaisun).
eorundem: of them. Abbreviated forms on MSS extended to this rather than *eorumdem.*
epimer (**20**); **ypimer', ypymer'** (**10**): a small marine fish, sold in **20** by the mease containing 1,000; sometimes smoked (*epim' rub'*); caught off the East Anglian coast, but precise identification uncertain. Suspension dropped in **10**; treated as *m.* and *coll. sing.* in **20**.
equus: horse. **6** uses the form *ecus, i, m.*, in the *sing.*, but *equi, orum* in *pl.*
ernement (**14**): a form of horse medicine.
ernest (**15**): sum of money, paid as an instalment (*OED* earnest).
escaeta (**5**): either entrails (as a form of *exitus*) or 'making fit for eating' (from *LS* esca).
esk. (**22**): skep (*OED*), dry measure, here probably 12 bushels.
espleister (**11a**): to accomplish, carry out (*AND* espleiter).
esquels (**11a**): bowls (*AND* escuele).
destaung (**11a**): tin, pewter (*AND* esteim).
estik' (**5**): stick (of eels). Suspension dropped.
est' (**19**): estimate. Extended to *estimacio, nis, f.*
estric (**2**): struck measure, i.e. not heaped.
et: ampersand extended to this wherever it occurs, in Latin and French texts. The

occasional use of *e* rather than *et* for 'and' in French texts has been maintained where it appears.

exen(n)': gift. Extended to forms in *-ium*, *-ii*, *n.*, throughout.

exit': entrails. Extended to *pl.* of *exitus*, *us*, *m.*, unless other evidence in a particular instance demands *sing.*

exp': to spend, disburse. Extended throughout to appropriate parts of *expendo*.

expens': expenses, costs. Extended to forms of *expensa*, *e*, *f.* The *sing.* is used in **2**. Treated as *pl.* in **7** and later accounts.

extra: outside, specifically the outer side or dorse of a roll, as, for example, **19**.

extran': a stranger, one who is not a member of the household, a visitor. Extended to forms in *-ius*, *-i*, or *-eus*, *-ei*, *m.*, according to the usage of MS.

fab': beans. Extended to *pl.* of *faba*, *e*, *f.*, throughout.

fagott' (20); **faggott' (24)**: faggot, firewood. Extended to forms in *-us*, *-i*, *m.*

fam' (7), **famil' (15)**: household. Extended as if from *familia*, *e*, *f.*

fasian' (14): pheasant. Extended to forms in *-us*, *-i*, *m.*

ferdekyns (14); **ferthekyn**, **ferthkyn**: firkin, small cask for liquids, fish etc. (*OED*). Treated as *m.* in **19**.

ferina (4), **ferin' (7)**: flour (*RMLWL* farina). Extended as if from *ferina*, *e*, *f.*

ferine (10), **ferini (16)**: wild, [beast of] the chase. In **10**, treated as *adj.*; in **16**, *sb.*, from *ferinum*, *i*, *n.*, flesh [of deer].

fermailes (28): buckles, clasps, settings (*OED*).

fermes... (14): a place where deer were kept (*OED* fermison *c.*1420).

ferr': horseshoe, ironwork. Extended as if from *ferrum*, *i*, *n.*, in **4**, **7**, **15** and **28**.

ferr', **ferur'**, **ferrur'**: farriery. Extended to forms from *fer(r)ura*, *e*, *f.*, in **3**, **4**, **10** and **20**.

ferreac' (16): shoeing (of horses). Extended to *ferreacione*, *abl. sing.*

fesant' (14), **fesantz (19)**: pheasant(s). Not extended and suspension dropped in *sing.* in **14**; treated as *m.* in **19**.

festuc' (10): straw (*LS*). Treated as *coll. sing.* from *festuca*, *e*, *f.*

festucad' (10): a confection of fistic (pistachio) nuts (*RMLWL* fisticus).

fecitis (7): skilfully made (*RMLWL* factio, feticius).

fetir' serrur' (10): a fetterlock.

ficheo*us* (28): skins of polecat (Veale *Fur trade* p. 219, fitch, ficheux).

ficholer (14): possibly one who keeps a polecat (*OED* fitchew).

fic', **fyc' (10)**; **fix'**, **fixes (3)**; **fygys (19)**: figs. In **10**, *abl. pl.* extended to *-is*.

figuli (24): either [satin] decorated with patterns like a small fig, or [satin] from a particular place.

findendo (14): splitting (*LS* findo).

flokkes (12): refuse wool (*RMLWL*).

flokk' (18); **floc'**, **flocc' (19)**; **flotez (21, 23)**: skimmings of fat (*RMLWL* flota).

flundres (2); **flundr' (4, 5)**; **flunder' (4)**: flounder (fish). Abbreviated forms extended to *-a*, *-e*, *f.*, in *pl.*

flur' (4): flour. Extended to forms in *-a*, *-e*, *f.*

focal': fuel. Extended to forms in *-e*, *-is*, *n.*

fodr' (19): a fother, cart-load (not a specific measure).

forag' (7, 10); **for' (9)**: forage. Extended to *foragium*, *i*, *n.*

forcer' (3): strong-box. Extended to forms in *-um*, *-i*, *n.*

forelokyng' (28): placing forelocks, wedges thrust through a hole in the end of a bolt to keep it in place (*OED* forelock *sb.*[1] 1514).
forett' (10): ferret. Extended to forms in *-us*, *-i*, *m.*
forg' (14): forge. Extended to forms in *-ium*, *-ii*, *n.*
fornac' (10): oven. Extended to forms in *-ium*, *-ii*, *n.*
fourne (11a): oven (*AND* forn).
foynes (28): skins of stone marten (Veale *Fur trade* p. 219, foins).
franco (18): *auceratis in franco*, tethered in the open.
frayel' (20): frail, basket (measure of fruit). Suspension dropped in *sing.*
fresceng' (2), **freschlyng' (13)**: sucking-pig. Extended in **2** to *frescenga.*
freslyng' (13): fresh ling ? (fish, as opposed to 'old ling', or salted ling).
fr' (12): fresh. Extended as if from *friscus*, *a*, *um.*
frisede (15), **frisses (28)**: a kind of coarse woollen cloth, with a nap (*OED* frieze *sb.*[1]), or cloth (in general) with the nap raised.
frontell' (12): a piece of defensive armour, or of harness, coming over the front of a horse's head (*OED* frontal). Extended to forms in *-um*, *-i*, *n.*
fruct', **frut'**: fruit. Extended throughout to forms in *-us*, *-us*, *m.*
frumentum: wheat. All abbreviated forms extended as if from *frumentum*, *i*, *n.*, throughout. In **15** the word also means 'furmenty'.
frumentac' (7): furmenty ? Extended to *frumentacio*, *abl. sing.*
fruturs (11a): fritter, pancake (*AND* friture).
fung' (15), **fungia (16)**: stockfish. Extended as if from *fungia*, *e*, *f.* In **15**, extended in *pl.* unless it refers to a single item.
furchell' (28), **furgell' (12)**: a piece of 'forked' harness for a cart.
furf': bran. Extended throughout as if from *furfur*, *is*, *m.*
furmenti (2): wheat (*frumenti*, *gen. sing.*).
furmag' (7): cheese. Extended as if from *furmagius*, *i*, *m.*
furnag' (7): cooking. Extended as if from *furnagium*, *i*, *n.*
furr' (28): a fur. Extended as if from *furra*, *e*, *f.* Furring, extended as if from *furracio*, *nis*, *f.*
furrures (25): furs (*AND* furrure: lining, cloak, coat).
fustian' (28): a kind of coarse cloth made of cotton and flax (*OED*). Suspension dropped, treated as *m.*
fyol', **fyols (28)**: phial, a vessel for holding liquids (*OED*).

gagus (8): wages (*gages*).
galantyn (10), **galentin (11a)**, **galentyn (11b)**: galantine, a spiced sauce, often associated with ginger (*OED*; *Curye on Inglysch* pp. 190–1).
galyngale (11b), **galingal' (18)**: galingale, a plant with a root which was employed as a spice resembling ginger (*Curye on Inglysch* p. 190).
gall', **gallin'**: chicken. Extended throughout to *gallina*, *e*, *f.*, unless there is evidence to suggest that *gallus*, *i*, *m.*, cock, is intended.
galon' (5, 13): gallon. Extended as if from *galo*, *nis*, *m.*
gardeviantz (28): a travelling trunk (*OED*).
gard' (15, 18): garden. Extended as if from *gardinum*, *i*, *n.*
garenn' (20): warren. Extended to forms in *-a*, *-e*, *f.*
garthez (21): an enclosed piece of ground (*OED* garth[1]).

garth webbes (28); **gerthes, gerth webbes (15)**; **gerthcloth' (20)**: strong cloth for saddle girths (*OED* garth[2]).

gastell' (10): wastel-bread. Extended to forms in *-us*, *-i*, *m.*, in *pl.* unless a single item is intended.

gata (4): bowl, jar (*RMLWL*).

Gaufr': Geoffrey, man's name. Extended throughout to *Gaufridus*, *i.*

gayner' (19): *OED* gainor[1]: tillage. In **19** the *custod' gayner'* looks after the pigs, for fattening, and *gayner'* may be derived from *ganea* (*LS*), an eating house, cook shop.

geet*is* (14): goats (*OED*).

gent (25): people, family. *gens de mestier*, household officials.

gent': see *jant-*.

gere (15): harness for draught animals (*OED* gear).

getynge (15): gating ?

gingebr' (11b), **gingib' (20)**, **gyngibr' (10)**: ginger, or ginger sauce. Extended in **10** and **11b** as if from *g(i/y)ng(e/i)ber*, *bri*; and in **20** as if from *gingiber*, *is*. See also *zinzib'*.

gingebradz, **gingibrad' (10)**: preserved ginger, in a syrup or candied (*OED* gingerbread).

godewytys (19): godwit, a marsh bird, sometimes fattened before eating (*OED*).

granar': granary. Extended to forms in *-ium*, *-ii*, *n.*, throughout.

grang' (9): barn, grange. Extended to forms in *-ia*, *-ie*, *f.*

gran' (15, 16): corn. Extended to forms from *granum*, *i*, *n.*

granopast' (22): corn-mash, including draff. Extended to *granopastu*, *abl. sing.*

grapeis (11a), **graspeys (8)**, **grespays (20)**: the flesh of a dophin or other cetacean.

grenegeys (19): green goose, a young goose or gosling (*OED*).

gresel (10): grey horse (*OED* grizzel *sb.*[1]).

grey (28): winter squirrel skins, with a grey back (Veale *Fur trade* p. 224). **24**, *greye pur'*, pured or trimmed.

greyels (28): graduals, books of antiphons (*OED* grail[1]).

greylyng' (16): grayling, a freshwater fish.

gris' (12): grey. Extended to forms in *-eus*, *-ea*, *-eum*.

gropes (12): iron clamps, especially for cartwheels (*RMLWL* gropa).

grout (20): infusion of malt before and during fermentation; small beer (*OED* grout *sb.*[1]).

gurfus (11a): girths.

gurnard' (4, 14): gurnard, marine fish. Extended in **4** to forms in *-us*, *-i*, *m.*, as a *coll. sing.*; in **14**, suspension dropped and no extension.

guttur' (15): watercourse, channel. Extended to forms in *-us*, *-i*, *m.*

haddoc', **haddog'**, **haddok'**: haddock (fish). Extended to forms in *-us*, *-i*, *m.*, in *pl.* in **2**, and in *coll. sing.* in **3**, **4** and **5**. Suspension dropped in **10**, **12** and **14**. Treated as *m.* in **14**.

hagardo (9): barn, a stack-yard (*RMLWL*, *OED* haggard *sb.*[1]).

hagiz (11b): haggis (*OED c.*1420).

hak' (4, 18); **hakis (2)**; **hake (4)**; **hakes (14)**: hake, a marine fish resembling the cod (*RMLWL* haka 1232; *OED* hake *sb.*[1] 14th cent. ?). In **4**, extended to *hake*; treated as *m. pl.* in **14** and as *m.* in **18**.

hak' (**12**, **20**); **h'** (**12**, **14**); **hakenay** (**7**): hackney, a horse of middle size and quality, used for light loads (*OED*). Latin forms extended to *hakeneus*, *i*, *m*.
hallyng (**28**): tapestry or painted cloth for the walls of a hall (*OED* halling).
hames (**15**): hoop on a horse collar (*OED* hame).
harang' (**8**, **11a**): herring. Not extended and suspension dropped.
harbgeon' (**28**): a sleeveless coat or jacket of mail or scale armour (*OED*).
harnes' (**4**, **14**); **hern'** (**7**); **hernes'** (**12**, **14**, **28**): harness, armour, equipment (*RMLWL*). Extended as if from *h(a/e)rnesium*, *i*, *n*.
harriet' (**15**): heriot. Extended to forms in *-um*, *-i*, *n*.
hastr' (**14**): spit or roasting house (*RMLWL* hasta).
hed' (**4**): kid. Extended to *pl.* of *hedus*, *i*, *m.*, unless a single kid implied by the size of the payment (some entries written out on MS in *sing.*).
henxmen', **henxmann'** (**28**): henchman, a personal servant of a lord or lady (*OED*). Suspension dropped.
heos (**11a**): them (*AND* il).
herb' (**12**): herbs. Extended to forms in *-a*, *-e*, *f.*, as *coll. sing.*
herbag' (**15**): herbage. Extended to forms in *-ium*, *-ii*, *n.*, in *sing.*
herce (**28**): an elaborate frame for candles, especially one used for *tenebrae* or funerals (*OED* hearse).
heron' (**19**): heron. Treated as *m.*
heronsues (**14**), **heronsewys** (**19**), **herunsell'**: small or young herons (*OED* heronsew).
herpstryakes (**27**): harp strings ?
hertnek' (**28**): meaning uncertain. A piece of deerskin ?
hespys (**19**): a hank or skein of yarn or thread (*OED* hasp).
hoggeshede: hogshead, a large flask for liquids. In **16**, contains 45 gallons of ale. Treated as *m.* in **16** and **19**.
hopis (**16**): hoop, dry measure (*RMLWL*). Treated as *m.*
horr' (**15**): barn. Extended to forms in *-eum*, *-ei*, *n.*
hostillar' (**14**): inn keeper. Extended to forms in *-ius*, *-ii*, *m.*
hostr' (**20**): house, home, establishment (*RMLWL*, *MFG* astrum). Extended to forms in *-um*, *-i*, *n.*
huc' (**3**), **houces** (**28**): saddle cloth, housing (*RMLWL*). Extended in **3** to forms from *hucia*, *e*, *f.* Treated as *f.* in **28**.
humbres (**14**): umber (freshwater fish), a grayling (*OED* umber *sb.*[2] 1496; *LS* umbra).
hundr' (**24**): hundred. Extended to forms from *hundredum*, *i*, *n*.
hunt (**11a**): probably 'a man' (*homme*).
hure (**14**): a cap (*OED*).
hurtours (**12**): iron plate to protect axle (*KMED*; *Manorial records of Cuxham* p. 787; *OED* hurter *sb.*[2]).
husbandr' (**21**): husbandry, agriculture. Extended to forms in *-ia*, *-ie*, *f.*
huss' (**14**): huss, the dogfish (*OED* huss *c.*1440).
huyk', **huyke** (**28**): huke, a kind of cape or cloak with a hood (*OED*).

illoeqe (**25**): there (*AND* iluec).
illustro (**28**): distinguished. Some examples written out on MS implying a form *illustrus*, *a*, *um*, rather than *illustris*, *e*.

impersoluc' (**28**): part payment. Extended to forms in *-io*, *-ionis*, *f.* To be distinguished from *in persolucionem*, payment in full.
in: in, into, *prep.* with *acc.* or *abl.* Not always employed consistently, e.g. **1**, *in servisia*, but *in v aulnas panni.*
indent' (**20**): indented. Extended to forms in *-atus*, *-ata*, *-atum*.
Irysshbord' (**28**): a type of large board or plank.

jact' (**9**): kneaded, shaped or made (*RMLWL* jactatio). Extended to forms in *-atus*, *-ata*, *-atum*.
jantant' (**12**); **jantando** (**16**); **gent'** (**7**): breakfast. Extended to forms from *vb. janto* in **12** and **16**; and as a *sb.* in **7**, from *gentaculum*, *i*, *n*.
Jardein (**14**), **Chardeyns** (**19**): a fine variety of almond (*OED* Jordan almond 1440).
jocist' (**15**): jester, entertainer. Extended to forms in *-us*, *-i*, *m*.
joco (**28**): *pro joco suo*, for his pleasure ?
joute (**7**): potherb, vegetable (*RMLWL*, *OED*).
jument' (**23**), **jumente** (**25**): mare. Extended in **23** to forms in *-um*, *-i*, *n*.
junco (**4**): rushes, *sb.*, *coll. sing.* (*LS* juncus); *pl.* form also employed.
jurnal' (**18**); **jornal'** (**20**): journal (daily accounts). Extended in **18** to *-em* in *acc. sing.* Treated as *jornale*, *is*, *n.*, in **20** and **21**.
justic' (**2**, **3**): a justice. Extended to *justiciarius*, *i*, *m*.
juvenc' (**17**), **juvenct'** (**10**): heifer. Extended to forms in *-ia*, *-e*, *f.*
juvencul' (**13**, **21**): young heifer. Extended to forms in *-a*, *-e*, *f.*

karkoys (**10**): carcass. Treated as *n.*
karlell' axes (**22**): a type of axe.
kebbyng' (**18**): *xx ov' matric' de kebbyng'*, ewes whose lambs have been still-born or have died (*RMLWL* kebba; *OED* keb *sb.*[1]).
kellez (**11a**): a fine cloth (*AND* kelle: veil for pyx).
Kendale (**28**): a type of green, woollen cloth.
kersey (**28**): a kind of coarse, narrow cloth, usually woollen (*OED*).
keverchiefs (**28**): *nyght keverchiefs*, possibly night caps (*OED* kerchief).
keying (**28**): fastening (*OED* key *v.*).
korn (**11a**): horn, drinking vessel (*AND* corn).
krevycz: see *crev-*.

lactagium (**21**): yield or ration of milk (*MFG*).
lac, **lact'**, **lacte**: milk. Extended throughout to forms from *lac*, *tis*, *m.*, except where an account has examples of *nom. lacte*, as in **4** and **10**.
lagamine (**14**): a griddle (*RMLWL* laganarium).
lamper' (**3**), **lampered'** (**2**): lamprey. Treated as *coll. sing.* of *lampereda*, *e*, *f.*
lampr' (**4**, **14**); **lamprid'** (**18**): lamprey. Treated as *coll. sing.* of *lampr(e/i)da*, *e*, *f.*
lampreys (**19**): treated as *m.*
lamprons (**8**), **lamperuns** (**2**): lampern, river lamprey.
laner' (**3**): lanner (falcon). Extended to forms in *-ius*, *-ii*, *m*.
langoldus (**15**): langle, hobble, device to constrain the legs of an animal to prevent it straying.
lardar' (**10**, **17**); **larder'** (**13**, **19**): larder. Extended to forms in *-ium*, *-ii*, *n*.
lard' (**4**, **7**); **lardo** (**2**, **3**): lard, the fat of bacon (*LS*). Extended as if from *lardum*, *i*, *n*.

last' (**10**): a last, measure of herring. Extended to forms in *-um*, *-i*, *n.*
lath' (**10**): lath. Suspension dropped.
laton' (**14**), **laton** (**26**): latten or brass. Suspension dropped in **14**, where it is also distinguished from brass (*enia*).
Laur': Lawrence, man's name. Extended, unless written out on MS, to *Laurencius*, *i.*
lavendr' (**7**, **10**): washing. Extended to forms in *-ia*, *-ie*, *f.*
lawnd' (**24**): lawn, a kind of fine linen (*OED*).
layners (**11a**): laces, thongs (*AND* lanere, lanier).
lectuar', **lecuar'** (**3**): litter, bed. Extended to forms in *-ium*, *-ii*, *n.*
lee (**15**): lea, a measure of yarn (*OED*).
lemys (**20**), **lym'** (**12**), **lymours** (**28**): cartshafts (*RMLWL* limo, lemo; *OED* limber). Extended in **12** to *-o*, *-onis*.
leng' (**10**, **14**, **18**); **leyng'** (**18**); **lengys** (**19**); **lyng'** (**16**); **lynge** (**20**): ling, a long, slender, marine fish, often used for food, preserved salted or dried. Suspension dropped in **10**; in **14** in *sing.* Treated as *m.* in **14**, **16** and **18**.
lepes (**11a**): baskets in which to keep fish (*OED* leap *sb.*[2]).
leporar' (**2**): 'levrier', greyhound. Extended to forms in *-ius*, *-ii*, *m.*
leporis (**1**): ? savory (herb) (*RMLWL* herba leporina).
lepros' (**19**): unsound (food). Extended to forms in *-us*, *-a*, *-um*.
levem panem (**12**): puff-bread (*RMLWL* panis levis 1419).
licar' (**18**): liquorice. Extended to *licaricia*, *e*, *f.*
lichuno (**5**), **lichini** (**14**), **lichoni** (**20**): wick. Extended to forms from *lich(i/o/u)nus*, *i*, *m.*, as a *coll. sing.*
lightcorn' (**21**): flour of barley, mixed with oatmeal.
lign' (**19**, **23**): of wood. Extended as *adj.* to forms in *-eus*, *-ea*, *-eum*.
limar' (**3**): leash or band (*RMLWL* liga). Extended as if from *limarium*, *i*, *n.*
limar' (**19**): lights, wicks (*RMLWL* lumen). Extended to *pl.* of *limarium*, *i*, *n.*
limmyng (**28**): illuminating (manuscript) (*OED* limn).
lin' (**20**): linen, *adj.* Extended to forms in *-eus*, *-ea*, *-eum*.
litter' (**3**, **28**); **liter'** (**14**): litter, bedding for animals. Extended in **3** to forms in *-ium*, *-ii*, *n.*; extended in **14** and **28** to *lit(t)era*, *e*, *f.*, *coll. sing.*; in **14** the word also means litter in the sense of a conveyance.
lobbe (**20**), **lobestes** (**12**): lob (fish), the pollack (*OED* lob *sb.*[2]).
lobst' (**14**): lobster. Extended to *lobster(s)*.
loc, **lok** (**27**): a lock, possibly of gold thread.
loc' (**28**): washing. Extended to forms in *-io*, *-ionis*, *f.*
lodis (**16**): loads. Treated as *m.*
lok' (**10**): a farmyard enclosure, specifically for hens (*KMED* lok *n.*(2); *OED* lock *sb.*[2]).
long' (**28**): length. Extended in *abl. sing.* to *longitudine*.
lotur' (**15**): washing. Extended to forms in *-a*, *-e*, *f.*
lower (**11a**): to hire (*AND* loer[2]).
luc' (**3**): pike (fish). Extended to forms in *-eus*, *-ei*, *m.*, as a *coll. sing.* unless a quantity is specified. **4**, *lucio*; **8**, *luz*.
lucrac' (**22**): *lucrac' feni*, hay making (*RMLWL*). Extended to forms in *-io*, *-ionis*, *f.*
lucr' (**3**): otterskin. Extended as if from *lucrus*, *i*, *m.*

lumini' (**3**), **lumin'** (**4**): wick, light. Extended in **3** as *coll. sing.* of *luminium, i, n.* In **4**, treated as if from *lumen, inis, n.*, as a *coll. sing.*; where *nom.*, *lumin'*, appears, it is treated as *pl.*
lut' (**10**): earthenware, *adj.* Extended to forms in *-eus*, *-ea*, *-eum*.
Lyar' (**28**): used as a proper name of a horse, i.e. one spotted with white or silver grey (*OED* lyard).
lyntes (**12**), **lynces** (**28**): linch pin (*OED*; *MFG* lincum).
lyo*ur* (**28**): tape, binding for the edges of fabric (*OED* lear[2]).
Lyre (**28**): cloth of Lire, France.

makerell' (**2, 4, 12, 14**); **makereus** (**7**): mackerel. In **2** and **4**, extended to forms in *-us*, *-i*, *m.*, and treated as *coll. sing.* In **12** and **14**, suspension dropped; treated as *coll. sing.* in **12**; treated as *m.* in **14**.
Malik' (**14**): (raisins from) Malaga (*OED*).
mallard' (**10, 14, 20**); **maulard'** (**14**); **maullard'** (**18**); **maurald'** (**14**): mallard (duck). Not extended in **10**; extended in other accounts to forms in *-us*, *-i*, *m.*
malmaker (**28**): bag or case maker (*RMLWL* mala).
malvesin (**14**), **malvesy** (**14**), **malvesye** (**19**): malmsey, a strong sweet wine (*OED*).
mantellis (**28**): mantle, cloak (*RMLWL*). Extended to forms from *mantellum, i, n.*
man': hand. Extended to forms from *manus, us, f.* In **2** and **3**, *per man'* is extended to *sing.*; in **15**, **21**, **23**, **24** and **28**, it is extended in *pl.*, following the usage of the MSS. In **20**, it is extended in *sing.* (no evidence on MS). **28** uses *per manus*, but *in manu*.
manus Christi (**19**): a cordial, flavoured sugar in a confection (*RMLWL* manus Christi 1514; *OED* manus Christi 1706). Treated as an invariable form.
mar' (**4**); **maresc'** (**6, 12**), **march'** (**7**): marshalsea, stables. Abbreviated forms in **4** extended to *marescaucia, e, f.*; in **7**, to *marchalcia, e, f.*; and in **12** to *mareschalsia, e, f.*
mareschall' (**14**), **marscall'** (**5**): marshal. Extended in **5** to *marscallus, i, m.*; in **14** to *mareschallcius, i, m.*
Margar' (**10**): Margery, woman's name. Extended to forms in *-ia*, *-ie*.
mar' (**15**): marine, *adj.* Extended to forms from *marinus, a, um*.
marterin' (**24**): of the marten. Extended to forms in *-us*, *-a*, *-um*.
mascul' (**28**): male, *adj.* Extended to forms from *masculinus, a, um*.
mastacione (**21**): fattening (of swans) (*OED* mast *sb.*[2], luxurious or fattening food).
masys (**19**): mace (spice).
mat' (**10**), **matt'** (**20**): mat. Extended to forms in *-a*, *-e*, *f.*, in *pl.*
maungeri (**11a**): feast (*AND* mangerie).
mazelard', **mazelarsz** (**10**): duck, mallard (*MFG* madlard, mathelardus). Suspension dropped.
medull' (**10**): marrow (bones). Treated as *adj.*; extended to forms in *-us*, *-a*, *-um*.
mes' (**4**); **meese** (**15**); **mis'** (**18**); **mayse**, **maysys** (**19**); **masez** (**21**): mease, a measure of herrings and sprats. Extended in **4** to forms from *meisa, e, f.*; in **18** to *misis*, *abl. pl.* Treated as *m.* in **15** and **19**.
meles (**15**): *ii meles de present' domine xiii d.*, two apple trees (*OED* mele) or meals (food) ?
melis (**16**): large bowl (*RMLWL* mela).
mell' (**15, 16, 19, 21**): honey (*LS*).

mellvell' (**10**); **melvel** (**11a**); **milwell'** (**12**); **mul'** (**9**); **mulvell'** (**2**, **3**, **5**); **mulewell'** (**4**): cod or similar fish. Latin forms extended to *-us*, *-i*, *m*. **9**, extended as if from *mulvellus*. Treated as *coll. sing.* in **2**, **3** and **4**.
menever' (**24**): minever, dressed squirrel skins (Veale *Fur trade* pp. 228–9). Extended to forms in *-um*, *-i*, *n*.
menus' (**10**): small fry (fish). Extended as *coll. sing.* to forms in *-a*, *-e*, *f*.
merc', **mercur'**: Wednesday. Extended throughout to *mercurii*, except in **6**, the schedule to **11a**, **14** and **15**, where the form *mercurie* is used in MSS.
merleng' (**2**, **3**, **4**); **merling'** (**5**, **7**, **10**, **14**), **merlyng'** (**12**): whiting or similar fish. In **2**, **3**, **4**, **5** and **7** extended as *coll. sing.* to forms in *-us*, *-i*, *m*. Suspension dropped and no extension in **10**, **12** and **14**. Treated as *pl.* in **12** and **14**.
mest' (**8**): *avoeit mester*, to have need.
Mich', **Michael'**: Michael, man's name. Extended throughout to *Michael*, *is*.
mile operat' (**28**): possibly cloth ornamented with stripes (*OED* mile *v.* 1512).
ministrall' (**22**): minstrel. Extended to forms in *-us*, *-i*, *m*.
mixtur' (**10**): mixed corn, maslin. Extended to forms in *-a*, *-e*, *f*.
mod' (**10**): measure for brewhouse. Extended to forms from *modius*, *i*, *m*.
mollend' (**18**): mill. Extended to *mollendinum*, *i*, *n*., in *sing.* unless more than one intended.
morel (**10**): morel, dark brown (horse), sometimes a horse's name.
morter' (**3**); **mortar'** (**12**): small lamp, cresset (*RMLWL* mortarium 1350). Extended to forms in *-ium*, *-ii*, *n*.
moruc' (**6**, **12**); **morues** (**7**); **mur'** (**10**); **murit'** (**11b**): cod or similar fish. In **6** and **12** extended to *-a*, *-e*, *f.*, in **6** as *coll. sing.* In **10** extended to *muruca*, *coll. sing.*; not extended in **11b**. The latter two accounts also include *milvel* etc. and a distinction may be intended between two types of fish.
mottas, **motam** (**2**): pack of hounds, mute.
mules (**12**): nave of wheel (*MFG* muellus; *RMLWL* modius).
mulez (**4**), **mulet** (**7**), **mulett'** (**14**): mullet (fish). Suspension dropped in *sing.* in **14**.
multon': sheep; where distinguished from *bidens*, possibly a wether (e.g. **10**). Extended as if from *multo*, *nis*, *m.*, throughout. Treated as *coll. sing.* in **3**. **5** uses *muto*, *nis*, a form which also occurs in **16**.
multur' (**10**): grinding (of corn), multure. Extended to forms in *-a*, *-e*, *f.*, and to *abl.* in the phrase *in multur'*.
muren' (**20**): lampern (*RMLWL*). Extended to forms from *murenula*, *e*, *f*.
murutts (**2**): possibly cod, or mullet; or mazer bowls (*MFG* murra).
muscul' (**9**), **musculis** (**14**), **musculs** (**15**): mussels (shellfish). Extended in **9** to forms from *musculus*, *i*, *m*.
mustard' (**2**): mustard. Extended to forms in *-um*, *-i*, *n*.
Mustercloth' (**20**), **Musterdevilers** (**28**): a mixed grey woollen cloth (*MFG* Mustre-develres, mustercloth; *OED*); linen in **20**.
my*ur*serne (**19**): a kitchen utensil for grating or crumbling bread (*OED* mye *v.*; *KMED* miour).

nagg' (**10**): nag, a small horse for riding. Suspension dropped.
nakerner (**14**): drummer (*OED* nakerer).
nates (**4**): mats (*RMLWL* natta; *OED* nat *sb.*).
nathe (**12**): *cum coopertur' i nathe*, part of a cart (*OED* nathe: nave of a wheel).

nef (11a), nief' (28): boat (*AND*).
negat' (6): killed, i.e. *necat'*.
negoc' (10, 15): business. Extended to *pl.* of *negocium, i, n.*
neules (7): wafer (*RMLWL* nebula, neula).
Nich': Nicholas, man's name. Extended throughout as if from *Nicholas, Nicholai.*
nisos (5, 27): hawks (*RMLWL* nisus).
noggyng' (15): brickwork between wooden framing (*OED*).
Norman' (28): Normandy. Extended to *Normannia, e, f.*
nouche (27, 28): a clasp, buckle or broach, for holding two sides of a garment together, or as an ornament (*OED* ouch *sb.*).

obba (19): jug (*RMLWL*).
oblatio (4): offering. Extended throughout to forms of *oblatio, nis, f.*
oiwes (28): a measure of wine, possibly French.
olei benedicti (14): a mild laxative (*RMLWL* oleum benedictum; *OED* Benedict *sb.* and *adj.* 1576).
oler' (7, 12): vegetable (*RMLWL* holus). Extended to forms in *-a, -e, f.*
oll': pot (earthenware or of wood or leather). Extended throughout to forms in *-a, -e, f.* Treated as *pl.* unless there is evidence that a single item is intended in **3, 4, 9** and **10**.
ominum (1): men, *gen. pl.* of *homo.*
onyet (15): a form of 'onion' ?
ord' (5, 6, 13, 15, 18): barley. Extended in these accounts, where there is no other evidence in MS, to forms from *ordeum, i, n.* Extension to *ordium* made in other accounts, e.g. **16**, following usage of MS.
ordic' (17): of barley, *adj.* Extended to forms in *-ius, -ia, -ium.*
orengys (19): oranges. Treated as *m.*
orgays (20): a kind of fish, organ ling (*OED* orgays). Divided in membrane 3 dorse into ling and keeling.
ospiciis (7): lodgings.
ostelag' (7): lodging. Extended to *ostelagio, abl. sing.*
ostr': oyster. Extended in Latin forms in **4, 14, 15** and **24** to *ostrium, i,* in *pl.*; and in **9** and **10** to the *pl.* of *ostreum, i, n.*
osttrun (8); **oistres, oystris (2)**: oysters.
osturis (4): goshawk (*RMLWL* austurcus, osturus).
overlop (28): single floor or deck of an early ship, subsequently the lowest deck (*OED* orlop[1] 1467).
oves (11a): birds, for *aves.*
ov': egg. Extended throughout to forms from *ovum, i, n.*
ov': sheep. Extended throughout to forms, as *sb.*, *ovis, is, f.* **6** has *nom. sing. ove.* Sometimes, as in places in **15**, impossible to distinguish from *ov'*, eggs. Form as *adj.* extended throughout to *ovinus, a, um.*
oximell' (14): medicinal drink or syrup made with vinegar and honey (*OED* oxymel).

packthred (23), pakthrede (14): stout thread used for tying bundles (*OED*). Treated as *m.* in **23**.
pag' (7): page (person). Extended to forms from *pagettus, i, m.*

palac' (**15**): fence, palisade. Extended to forms in *-ium*, *-ii*, *n.*
palacio (**14**), **palacia** (**16**): palace.
paleo (**28**): *pro uno sale paleo de rubio albo et virid'*, 'striped vertically' (*OED* pale *sb.*[1] 6; also pale, a fence, a row of vertical stakes).
palefrid' (**7**): palfrey, a (small) saddle horse for ordinary riding (*OED*). Extended to forms in *-us*, *-i*, *m.*
palrons (**28**): meaning uncertain, part of the equipment for arming a knight.
pame (**27**): a form of hand tennis (*OED* palm *sb.*[2] 1440).
pan': bread. Extended throughout to forms from *panis*, *is*, *m.*
paynmayn (**19**): white bread, made of wheat, of superior quality (*OED* pain-demaine). *mayn* perhaps derived from *mesne*, household (see also *Curye on Inglysch* pp. 204–5).
pa', **panetr'**: pantry. Extended throughout to forms from *panetria*, *e*, *f.*, except in most of **14** and **19**, where the MSS suggest a form *panteria*, *e*, *f.*
panier' (**11a**); **pannyer** (**15**); **paner'** (**12**, **18**, **20**): pannier, a large basket for carrying foodstuffs. Extended in **18** and **20** to forms from *panerium*, *i*, *n.*
panns, **panne** (**11a**): pan, cooking utensil, in one instance, of brass.
pannus: cloth.
paperum (**1**): poor, *gen. pl.* of *pauper*.
paper' (**20**), **papir'** (**24**), **papirum** (**19**): paper. Abbreviated forms extended to *-um*, *-i*, *n.*
par': a pair. Extended as if from *par*, *is*, *n.*; *abl. sing.*, *pari*, except in **28**, *pare*. **20** uses *paria*, *e*, *f.*
parcell' (**23**, **28**): parcel, an (itemised) part of an account. Extended in phrase *per parcell'* to *acc. pl.* of *parcella*, *e*, *f.*
pargetynge (**15**): daubing with plaster or parget, a lime-based whitewash (*OED*).
paris' (**7**): money of Paris.
paris: see *candela*.
parmentar' (**3**): a tailor. Extended to forms in *-ius*, *-ii*, *m.*
parmy (**25**): through, by means of (*AND*).
Parrish' (**28**): *serico de Parissh'*, probably Paris.
partitis (**28**): divided (of a shield or coat of arms).
passag' (**7**): transport over water, passage. Extended to forms in *-ium*, *-ii*, *n.*
pastill' (**3**, **4**, **7**); **pastell'** (**10**): pastry, pasty. Extended to forms in *-us*, *-i*, *m.*, in *pl.*, unless a single item is intended.
pastrones (**10**): pastern, hobble, tether.
past' (**17**): a mash, here of oats. Extended as if from *pastus*, *us*, *m.*
patell' (**4**): bowl, pan. Extended to *pl.* of *patella*, *e*, *f.*, unless a single item is intended.
pauteners (**28**): meaning uncertain (*OED* pautener *sb.*[1] and *sb.*[2] do not provide a nautical context). Made by carpenters for a ship.
pavys, **pavyse** (**28**): a large shield (*OED*). Treated as *m.*
paylett', **pailet** (**28**): a piece of armour for the head, usually leather (*OED* pallet *sb.*[1]).
pec.: peck, measure of capacity. Treated as *m.* in **14** and **16**.
pec': piece, item. Extended to forms in *-ia*, *-ie*, *f.*, in **14** and **19**; and to forms in *-ium*, *-ii*, *n.*, in **28**, except where other evidence suggests the word is from *pecia*. **1** has *pesie*, *abl. sing.*

pectinibus (**16**): small flat-fish (*RMLWL* pecten) *or* a type of shellfish, possibly a scallop (*LS* pecten; *OED* pecten).
pelcorn (**17**), **pilcorn** (**18**): pilcorn, a variety of oats (*OED* pilcorn 1578).
pelleccul' (**23**): small skins. Extended to froms from *pelleccula, e, f.*
pelv' (**19**): basin (*Manorial records of Cuxham* p. 791). Extended in *abl. sing.* to *pelve.*
perch' (**4, 14**); **perches** (**16**): perch (fish). Extended in **4** to forms in *-a, -e, f.*, in *pl.* unless a single item is intended. Suspension dropped in **14** and treated as *m.*
perches (**12**): part of the framework of a cart, either rods supporting a canopy (*RMLWL*) or the framework connecting the pairs of wheels in a four or more wheeled cart (*OED* perch *sb.*[2] 1668–9).
perchers (**14**): tall candles of wax (*OED* percher *sb.*[2]).
perdic': partridge. Extended throughout to forms from *perdix, perdicis, m.*, except in **3**, which has *abl. pl.*, *perdicis.* Extensions made in *pl.* unless a single bird intended.
perfourming' (**28**): finishing off, trimming, decorating (*OED* performing *vbl. sb.* 1465).
pergam' (**20**): parchment. Extended to forms from *pergamen, inis, n.*
perkes (**15**): prickets ?
perlisse (**27**): pearls ?
perluria (**24**): parlour.
perquis' (**15**): perquisites. Treated as *n. pl.*, *perquisita, orum.*
Philippo : Philip, man's name. Extended throughout to *Philippus, i.*
picher' (**4**): pitcher, jug. Extended to *pl.* in *-ii, -iorum*, unless a single item intended.
pikerell': small pike. Suspension dropped in **10**, **12** and **14**. Treated as *m.* in **10**.
pilos' (**22**): (hide) with the hair still on. Extended to forms in *-us, -a, -um.*
pingued': fat, grease. Extended to forms from *pinguedo, inis.* Treated as *m.* in **7** and **14**; but as *f.* in **19**, **20** and **23**.
pinitonum (**12**): pine-nuts, *gen. pl.*
pipa, **pipis**: pipe, a quantity of wine or ale, in a large cylindrical container. Latin forms extended as if from *p(i/y)pa, e, f.* **23** uses *pipo, abl. sing.*
pipes (**12**), **pypes** (**15**): part of horse harness, probably leather tubes through which traces were passed, to prevent rubbing (*OED* pipe *sb.*[1] 4a).
pip' (**28**): a roll (of gold thread) (*OED* pipe *sb.*[1] 4c *c.*1440).
pipion' (**16**): squab, young pigeon (*RMLWL*). Extended to forms from *pipio, nis.*
pir' (**15**): pear. Extended to forms from *-um, -i, n.*
pis' (**14, 17, 18, 19**); **piso** (**4**): peas. Except in **4**, extended to forms from *pise, arum, f.* In **4**, treated as is from *pisum, i, n.*
pisc' (**3, 7, 10, 11b, 16, 19**); **piss'** (**13, 15, 21**); **pisse** (**6**): fish. Extended to forms from *piscis* or *pissis, is, m.* Treated as *coll. sing.* in **3** and **7**, and in **10** except where a quantity is given. Treated as *pl.* in **11b** and **15**. **16** has *piscicul'*, small fish.
plaic' (**3, 5**); **plaicis** (**2**); **plaices** (**7**): plaice (fish). In **3** and **5** extended to *plaicis* in *abl. pl.*
plater' (**5**): plates. Extended in *abl. pl.* to *plateris.*
plaustr' (**19**): a wagon load, in general, but also a specific dry measure. Extended to forms in *-um, -i, n.*

plesaunce (28): a textile fabric, possibly in origin from Piacenza, Italy (*OED* pleasance[2]).

plov' (14, 19); **pluver' (3, 18)**; **pluv' (15)**: plover (bird). Extended in **3** to forms in *-us*, *-i*, *m.*, in *pl.* unless a single bird intended.

plyte (24): a specific length or piece of lawn (textile fabric) (*OED* plight *sb.*[2]).

pomade (28): possibly apples candied or preserved in syrup (like *citronade*), rather than a drink akin to cider (*OED* pomade *sb.*[1]).

pomele (26): dappled (*AND*).

pountag' (7): payment for transport or embarkation of horses. Extended in *abl. sing.* to *-io*.

poples (7), **popell' (20)**, **populers (14)**: spoon-bill (bird) (*OED* popeler, poppel).

porchet', **porchett' (3)**: piglet or pork. Extended to forms in *-us*, *-i*, *m.* Treated as *coll. sing.*

porc': pig, or of pigs. Extended as *sb.* to forms in *-us*, *-i*, *m.* Treated in **4** as *coll. sing.* Extended as *adj.* to *porcinus*, *a*, *um*, as in **7** and **13**.

porpais (7), **porpais' (18)**, **purpays (19)**: porpoise. In **18**, treated as *m.* and *coll. sing.*

porrey (8): leek (*AND* poree).

porsed (11a): leek seed ?

portag' (7, 19): carriage, transport. Extended to forms in *-ium*, *-ii*, *n.*

posenet' (19): saucepan, small pot (*MFG*, *OED* posnet).

pot' (14): probably a large wicker basket for carrying fresh fish, possibly a fish trap (*OED* pot *sb.*[1] 5b). Suspension dropped and treated as *m.*

potag' (3, 10, 16, 18, 19): pottage. Extended to forms from *potagium*, *i*, *n.*, in *sing.* In **16** the *pl.* is used and all unextended forms have been made *pl.* in this account.

potella (4): a bowl or pan (*RMLWL* patella).

potello (5); **potell' (7, 24)**; **potel' (14, 16)**: pottle, liquid measure, two quarts. In **5**, **7** and **24** extended to forms in *-um*, *-i*, *n.* Suspension dropped in **14**.

potsugre (19): possibly a moulded form of sugar (i.e. a different shape to a sugar loaf), or ordinary cooking sugar (*Curye on Inglysch* p. 208).

poudre (7), **poudr' (14)**: lightly salted or spiced. In **14** extended to forms in *-us*, *-a*, *-um*.

powes (15): bags (*OED* pough *sb.*), or poles.

prand' (15, 16, 19): lunch. Extended to forms from *prandium*, *i*, *n.*

pranes (10): prawns (*OED* prawn *sb.* 1426).

prebend': fodder. Extended to forms in *-a*, *-e*, *f.*, in **7**, **9**, **10**, **17**, **18** and **21**; and to forms in *-um*, *-i*, *n.*, in **5** and **6**.

prec': value, price. Extended throughout to forms in *-ium*, *-ii*, *n.* In valuations, e.g. *prec' gallin'*, extended to *precium* in all instances except for the hand that wrote the diet entries between 17 and 26 February in **14** and in **16**, where a *gen. sing.* form is used.

precomp' (7, 14); **precomputat' (9)**: (goods) accounted for beforehand. Treated as *adj.*, *precomputatus*, *a*, *um*, in **7** and **9**; and as *sb.*, *precomputatum*, *i*, *n.*, in **14**.

precom' (10): praise, worship. Extended as if from *preconium*, *i*, *n.*

preemp' (10): (goods) purchased beforehand. Extended as *adj.* to forms from *preemptus*, *a*, *um*; and as *sb.* to *preempcio*, *nis*, *f.*

preket (16): a deer (*RMLWL* prikettus, hart or buck of the second year; *OED* sorrel *sb.*[2]).

premer (**11a**): possibly a primer, a devotional manual, but the cost may be too little.
present' (**19**): gift. Extended to forms in *-ia*, *-ie*, *f*.
preterea (**22**): a section of an account listing additional expenses that do not fall within the compass of other sections; a bill of account, starting with the word *preterea*, containing these expenses.
prikett' (**28**): candle or taper.
primage (**28**): a customary allowance to the master and crew of a vessel for loading and looking after cargo (*OED*).
prochou*rs* (**28**): thin, spike-like, wax candles or tapers (*OED* proche *v*.).
promtuar' (**3**): store room. Extended to forms in *-ium*, *-ii*, *n*.
providenc' (**7**, **15**, **19**); **provid'** (**16**): provision, bulk purchase. Extended as if from *providencia*, *e*, *f*., in *sing*. In **21**, the *pl*. is used in MS.
pucell' (**7**): possibly chicks.
pucin' (**3**); **pulcin'** (**7**, **14**); **pulc'** (**10**): chicks. Extended to forms from *pu(l)cinus*, *i*, *m*.
pulaill' (**12**); **pullal'** (**7**, **10**): chicken (**12**) or poultry (**7**, **10**) (*MFG*). Extended to forms in *-us*, *-i*, *m*.
pull' (**10**, **23**); **pullan'** (**10**): a foal. Extended as if from *pullanus*, *i*, *m*.
pull' (**4**, **7**, **15**, **16**, **19**): chicken, pullet. Extended to forms in *-us*, *-i*, *m*.
pulter (**28**): poulterer.
pultr' (**20**): poultry. Extended in *sing*. to forms in *-ia*, *-ie*, *f*.
pulver' (**9**): spice, *albo pulver'*, sugar ground with ginger (blanche powder, blank powder: *Curye on Inglysche* p. 172).
putura (**10**): (allowance of) food (*RMLWL*).
pyghtlyng' (**24**): a textile fabric of a cheap or coarse quality.
pylch*ers* (**14**): pilchard (marine fish) (*OED* pilchard 1530).
pylyng' (**13**): meaning uncertain. Treated as *m. sing*.
pympernoll' (**12**): a small kind of eel (*OED* pimpernol). Suspension dropped.
pynonad' (**10**): a confection made with pine-nuts, candied or in syrup (*OED* pinionade).
pynt (**16**): pint, liquid measure. Treated as *m*.
pysan' (**28**): a piece of armour, protecting the neck and chest.

quarestres (**16**): choristers.
quart. (**16**): quart, liquid measure. Treated as *f*.
q*uer*' (**20**): seeking. Extended as if from *querens*.
quirbippes (**11a**): cubebs, berries from a climbing shrub, resembling pepper, used as a spice.
qwyr' (**28**): leather.

rabett' (**14**, **20**): young rabbit. Extended to forms in *-us*, *-i*, *m*.
racione (**28**): *v huykes virid' coloris brochiat' cum una racione*, a pattern or monogram.
rad' (**10**): a fish, probably freshwater, possibly the rudd (*OED* rudd 1606).
Rad': Ralph, man's name. Extended to forms from *Radulphus*, *i*, unless evidence to the contrary in MS: in **2**, **23** and **24**, extended to *Radulfus*, *i*.
raffel' (**27**): a game of chance played with three dice (*OED* raffle *sb*.[1]).

ragmas (27): a form of cloth of gold (*OED* ragmas).
rak' (10): rack, for feeding animals. Extended to forms in *-a*, *-e*, *f.*
rasen' Correnc' (22), **reysyng' de Coraunse (16)**, **reysynys (19)**: currants (*Correnc'*, etc., for Corinth) (**16, 22**); raisins (**19**).
rasor', **rasours (9, 10)**: shellfish, with a long narrow shell shaped like a razor, common on sandy shores (*OED* razor *c.*1440).
rastell' (3): rake or hoe (*RMLWL*). Extended to forms in *-a*, *-e*, *f.*, in *sing.*
ravell' (20), **ravel clothe (28)**: coarse cloth for straining milk. Extended in **20** to forms in *-um*, *-i*, *n.*
ray (23, 25, 28): striped cloth (*OED* ray *sb.*[4]).
raye, **raiis**, **raies (2)**: ray (marine fish).
rebaunce (27): meaning uncertain: rerebrace (armour) ?; rebus ?; ribbons ?
r*ediundo* (14): coming back. Abbreviated forms extended from *r'* to *rediundo* rather than *redeundo*, as there are many more examples of the former in the MS.
reme (20): ream, measure of paper. Treated as *m.*
remoc' (10): removal (of a horseshoe). Extended to forms of *remocio*, *nis*, *f.*
rerbrace (28): armour for the upper arm (*OED* rerebrace).
reventulac' (22): winnowing again. Extended to forms in *-io*, *-nis*, *f.*
reward' (12, 14); **regard' (15)**: reward, a payment or gift of food or goods acknowledging services rendered or to be rendered. Extended to forms in *-um*, *-i*, *n.* Treated as *sing.*, except in **14**, where it is treated as *pl.*, unless it refers to a single loaf in the bread account. The phrase *in re(w/g)ard'* is treated as implying *abl. sing.* throughout, except in **20**, where *acc. sing.* is intended.
ridel (11a): *ridel de carde*, curtain of carde, a sort of muslin.
ridells (15): a slender rod, twisted or fastened between upright posts, to make a fence or hurdle (*OED* raddle).
rigges (28): ten skins (Veale *Fur trade* p. 222).
Robin': Robin, man's name. Extended as if from *Robinus*, *i.*
roch*es* (10, 14): roach (freshwater fish).
rogett*es* (14): the red gurnard (marine fish) (*OED* rochet *sb.*[2]).
roll*is* (20): a cylindrical piece of wood, or roller, part of the harness of a pair of traces.
rollis, **rolles (28)**: a type of wax candle, or wax rolled into a cylindrical shape (*OED* roll *sb.*[1] 6b 16th cent.).
rond (20): a strip or long slice of fish, especially sturgeon (*OED* rond *sb.*[1] 2b 1572).
rostyngeleys (19): a type of eel, perhaps a large kind for roasting.
rub': red. Extended to *rubeus*, *a*, *um*, in **12** and **16**; extended to *rubius*, *a*, *um* in **10, 14, 18, 19, 20, 21** and **28**.
rub' mell' (14): a type of cloth ?
ruffis (10): the ruff, a small freshwater fish, similar to the perch (*OED* ruff *sb.*[1] 2 1450).
rumnay (19): rumney, a sweet wine, probably from Greece.
rys (19): rice.
ryys (19): a bird of the sandpiper family, the female of the ruff (*OED* ree *sb.*[2] 16th cent.).

sabatouns (28): armour for the foot (*OED*).

saffran' (**4**): saffron. Suspension dropped.
salade (**28**): an armoured headpiece (*OED* sallet, salade *c.*1440).
sale (**28**): hall or large room (*OED* sale *sb.*[1]).
salic' (**13**): salt-water, *adj.* Extended to forms in *-ius*, *-ia*, *-ium.*
saliuncar' (**22**): furze or gorse (*RMLWL*). Extended to *pl.* of *saliunca*, *e*, *f.*
salmon', **salm'**: salmon. Extended throughout to forms of *salmo*, *nis*, *m.* In **19** the form *samo*, *nis*, is used. Treated as *coll. sing.* in **2**, **3**, **6** and **10**. Placed in *sing.* in **7**, **15**, **16** and **19** unless more than one salmon mentioned. In **4**, *salmon'*, *nom.*, extended to *pl.* form, but *salm'* extended to *coll. sing.*
salsamentis (**11b**), **salc'** (**7**): sauce, condiment. In **7** extended as if from *salcamentum*, *i*, *n.*
salsar' (**5**), **saucer'** (**14**): saucer. Extended to forms from *-ium*, *-ii*, *n.*
sals', **salc'**: salted. Extended to *salsus*, *a*, *um*, or *salcius*, *a*, *um*, depending on the usage of MS. In **14**, examples of *sals'* extended to *salsius* where they occur associated with *salc'*, *salcius*.
sanappes (**14**): cloth to protect the tablecloth (*RMLWL* salvatio).
sandres (**10**); **saundres** (**18**, **20**): red sanders, used for colouring in cooking (*Curye on Inglysch* p. 212).
scaged (**28**): damaged ?
scalder (**28**): one who scalds poultry or utensils (*OED* scalder *sb.*[1] 1536).
scalones (**4**): shallot, scallion.
scalpini (**9**), **scalpin'** (**14**): whiting (marine fish) (*OED* scalpin 1400). In **14**, suspension dropped and treated as *pl.*
scanti, **scante**, **scantorum** (**1**): saint, variant forms from *sanctus*, *a*, *um.*
scarbard' (**9**): a large, white-fleshed, marine fish. *OED* has scabbard, scabbard fish, but the late date of the citation, 1836, may mean that a different fish is intended. Extended to forms in *-us*, *-i*, *m.*
schaktrays (**20**): chain traces (*MFG*).
schort game (**27**): a form of backgammon (*OED* table 11).
schoyell', **schoyeld'** (**20**): meaning uncertain, *i carect' cum rot' voc' schoyell'*, *i capistr' de cor' schoyeld'*.
schroudes, **shroude** (**14**): tent covering material (*OED* shroud *sb.*[1] 3).
scice (**7**): thirst (*RMLWL* sitis).
scimini: see *cimin-*.
scopis (**20**): broom or besom. Also *scopett'*, a brush ?
scrempes (**14**): shrimps.
scull' (**10**): a large, shallow basket, often circular or oval, used for farm produce, fish and fishing lines (*OED* skull[2] 1508).
scutell' (**2**, **4**): bowl or dish. Extended to forms in *-a*, *-e*, *f.*, in *pl.* unless a single item intended.
sechiis, **secchiis** (**2**): a fish, possibly a cuttle-fish (*RMLWL* sicca, *Fr.* seiche) or a flat-fish (*Fr.* seiche also means a portion of the sea bottom left uncovered at low tide) or coley (*OED* saithe 1632).
sedul' (**20**): schedule. Extended to forms in *-a*, *-e*, *f.*
seell (**11a**): seal ?
seem' (**22**): a pack-horse load, a specific quantity (of salmon) (*OED* seam *sb.*[2]).
sege (**12**): meaning uncertain. A seat ?
sell' (**12**): saddle. Extended to forms from *sella*, *e*, *f.*

semels (11b): fine wheat flour or a bread made from it (*OED*).
sensours (28): censers, thuribles.
sensyngale, sensale (20): the results of a trial brewing, for tasting ?
separacio (21): weaning.
sep', sip': see *cep-*.
sequestr' (3): sequestration. Extended to forms in *-um*, *-i*, *n.*
servis', cervis': ale. All abbreviated forms extended as if from (*c/s*)*ervisia*, *e*, *f.*
seym (11a): fat, grease (*OED* seam *sb.*[3]).
shafell' (12): a kind of eel, shaft-eel (*OED*).
shynguler' (15): shingler. Suspension dropped.
shyttynglederes (12): a piece of horse harness, connected to the crupper strap.
siel (8): salt ?
sign-: see *cign-*.
sinap': see *cinap-*.
singulorum (28): bands, see *cingul-*.
siph-: see *ciph-*.
situl' (20): bucket. Extended to forms in *-a*, *-e*, *f.*
skitere (16): scullery.
skreyth' (10): a marine fish or shellfish ? Treated as *coll. sing.*, *m.*
skymmer (15): skimmer. Treated as *m.*
skyrewycz (10): skirret, a vegetable, a form of water parsnip (*OED*).
smelt' (10, 15): a small marine fish, the spirling. Extended in **10** to forms in *-us*, *-i*, *m.*
smigmat' (14, 24): soap. Extended in **14** to forms in *-a*, *-e*, *f.*; and in **24** to *-i* in *gen. sing.*
snyt, snytes, snytis (14): snipe, or a species of bird resembling the snipe (*OED* snite *sb.*[1]). **18** has *snyl*, possibly for *snit.*
soil', soill' (4); sol' (10, 14): sole, a flat-fish. Extended in **4** and **10** to *pl.* of forms in *-a*, *-e*, *f.*, unless a single fish intended. Treated as *m.* in **14**.
soldar' (22): soldier. Extended to forms in *-ius*, *-ii*, *m.*
solum (19): site, ground.
somer' (12), somerar' (14), somers (28), sumer' (3): sumpter horse, a pack-horse. Extended in **12** and **14** to forms in *-ius*, *-ii*, *m.* In **28**, extended to *somer*(*s*), suspension dropped. In **3**, treated as an *adj.*, from *sumerius*, *a*, *um* (*RMLWL* sella summaria).
someter (25): sumpterman.
soremulett', soremulet' (14): red mullet (*OED* sore *adj.*[2]; mullet *sb.*[1] 1440).
sort' (20): a 'sort', a measure of fruit, containing three frails (*OED* sort *sb.*[3]; *Customs accounts of Hull* p. 256; *Port book of Southampton 1439–40* p. 125).
sosciorum (1); sosios (28): colleagues, fellows, a form of *socius*.
sourell' (12), sowrell' (16): a deer, sorrel, buck or hart of the third year (*OED*). Extended in **12** to forms in *-us*, *-i*, *m.*
sowre, sowris (16): a deer, buck or hart of the fourth year (*RMLWL* sorus; *OED* sore *sb.*[2]).
specul' (28): spangle, speckle. Extended as if from *speculum*, *i*, *n.*
sperling' (3): spirling, smelt (marine fish). Extended as a *coll. sing.* to forms in *-us*, *-i*, *m.*
spikyngg' (28): spike nail, a large nail with a small head (*OED*).

spinol' (**14**): a linen textile fabric, used for wrapping a corpse (*OED* spinal *sb.*).
sporta (**4**): litter, stretcher, basket or fish trap (*RMLWL*).
sprentt', **sprentes**, **sprentys** (**19**): a young salmon (a more general sense of *OED* sprent *sb.*[1], a young turbot or other flat-fish).
sprot (**11a**), **sprotte** (**19**): sprat, a small marine fish, or a fish resembling a sprat, a smelt (*OED*). Treated as *coll. sing.*, *m.*
spurcattyng' (**28**): spurkets, 'riders' (Rose *Lancastrian navy* p. 259).
squiler' (**14**): scullery.
squirte (**14**): a form of syringe (*OED* squirt *sb.* 2 1530).
stages (**28**): skins from animals taken out of season, i.e. during the summer (Veale *Fur trade* p. 222).
stagyng' (**20**): a temporary platform or structure, scaffolding (*OED*).
stamyn' (**28**): a coarse kind of woollen or worsted cloth (*OED* stamin).
standard' (**28**): a large packing case or chest, a 'safe' for foodstuffs (*OED* standard 23). Suspension dropped.
stapils (**28**): either wooden posts or clasps of metal to assist with securing horses on board ship (*OED* staple *sb.*[1]).
sterling' (7): sterling, money. Extended to forms in *-us*, *-i*, *m.*, as *coll. sing.*
stik' (**12**, **22**); **stykk'** (**19**): stick, a measure of quantity of small eels (*OED* stick *sb.*[2]). Suspension dropped in **12**.
stykhele, **stykeele** (**19**): stick-eel, an eel of small size.
stillatorio (**14**): a still (*RMLWL*).
stintes (**11a**): birds, commonly one of the sandpiper family, especially dunlin (*OED* stint *sb.*[2] 1466).
stipend': stipend, salary. Extended as if from *stipendium*, *i*, *n.*, in *sing.*, except in **14** where the *pl.* is used. In **16**, used to mean 'hire'.
stipite (**15**): a mould for making candles (as opposed to *RMLWL* and *LS* where *stipes* is used for the main stem of a candlestick).
stok' (**14**), **stokf'** (**12**), **stocfys'** (**11b**), **stokfysch'** (**13**), **stocpisc'** (**10**): stockfish, dried fish, typically cod or other large white-fleshed fish. Treated as *m.* in **13**; extended to *-piscis*, *-piscis*, *m.*, *coll. sing.*, in **10**.
stopels (**28**), **stupellis** (**1**): a stopper or bung (*OED* stopple *sb.*[1]).
stott' (**20**): a young ox, steer (*OED* stot *sb.*[1]). Extended as if from *stottus*, *i*, *m.*
stragulat' (**28**): striped or panelled (*RMLWL*).
strak' (**20**), **strakes** (**28**): strakes (*OED* strake *sb.*[1]). In **20**, iron plate connecting felloes on outer rim of wheel; in **28**, lines of continuous planking in the side of a ship, running from stem to stern.
streytours (**12**): meaning uncertain, but part of a cart or needed for its maintenance.
striati (**28**): striped or panelled.
stripes (**28**): scraps of skin sewn together in strips (Veale *Fur trade* p. 222).
stuffur' (**28**): cloth in store. Extended to forms in *-a*, *-e*, *f.*
sturjon' (**14**, **19**, **20**): sturgeon. Suspension dropped.
succade (**28**): fruit preserved in sugar, candied or in syrup (*OED* succade 1463).
sucsagii (**14**): *virid' sucsagii*, verjuice.
sue (**15**, **19**, **20**): a sow. Treated as *f.*
suewet (**16**): suet. Treated as *m.*
suma, **summa** (**3**): seam, horse load. Abbreviated forms extended in this account to *suma*, *e*, *f.*, unless there is a clear abbreviation for *summa*.

super: on, during, *prep.* used variously with *acc.* or *abl.* Extended here in accordance with the usage of each clerk. Followed by *abl.* in **10**. In **28** the usage is not consistent, although the *acc.* is usually employed to denote time, during, and the *abl.*, about, concerning, respecting (a similar distinction is made in **15**). There are exceptions in **28**, however, e.g. f. 22 recto, *de prestito super expensas suas*, *de prestito super vadiis suis*. See also *LS* pp. 1803–4; *Manorial records of Cuxham* pp. 9–10, 797.
superpelic' (**28**): surplice (ecclesiastical vestment). Extended to forms in *-ium*, *-ii*, *n.*
superplus' (**19**): surplus, cash in hand. Extended to forms in *-agium*, *-agii*, *n.*
swepes (**12**): probably part of the outer edge of a cartwheel (related to *OED* sweep *sb.* 25).
synamoun: see *cinam-*.
synap': see *cinap-*.

taberytt' (**24**): a drummer (*OED* tabor).
tablet (**27**): a flat, personal ornament of precious metal or jewellery (*OED* tablet *sb.*).
tackis (**4**), **takkes** (**14**): iron 'tack' on axle of cart (*RMLWL*, *OED* tack *sb.*[1]).
tal' (**14**): possibly a tail of a cart, or a rod or bar (*LS* talea).
talleshide (**28**): wood split for cutting for firewood (*OED* talshide).
tall' (**19**, **23**, **28**), **t'** (**17**): tally. Extended as if from *tallia*, *e*, *f.*, in *sing.* unless MS indicates a *pl.*
tall' (**14**): to cut. Extended to forms of *tallio*.
tallwode (**28**): firewood, often cut to a set length (*OED* talwood).
talos (**12**): dice (*MFG*).
tapet' (**7**), **tapett'** (**28**), **tapit** (**11a**): tapet, ornamented cloth, a hanging. Latin forms in **7** and **28** extended to forms in *-a*, *-e*, *f.*
tapit' (**24**): tapisser, weaver. Extended to forms in *-arius*, *-arii*, *m.*
tappehoses (**20**): strainers (*MFG*, *OED* tap-hose 1480).
tapr' (**10**), **tapyr'** (**24**): taper, a wax candle (*OED* taper *sb.*[1]). Extended in **10** as if from *taper*, *tapri*, *m.*
tartaryn' (**28**): a rich textile fabric, probably of silk (*OED*).
taxham (**14**), **tascc'** (**20**): task work. Extended in **20** to forms in *-a*, *-e*, *f.*
teis (**14**), **teys'** (**20**), **teises** (**26**): measure of length, fathom (*MFG*, *RMLWL*). Extended in **20** to forms in *-a*, *-e*, *f.*
tel' (**14**), **tels** (**19**): teal (bird). Treated as *m.* in **14**.
tench' (**14**, **16**, **20**): tench (freshwater fish). In **14**, suspension dropped in *sing.*
terr' (**19**, **20**): earthen. Extended as if from *terreus*, *a*, *um*.
testers (**25**), **tester** (**28**): a canopy or cover (*OED*).
textrin' (**24**): weaving, *vbl. sb.* Extended to forms in *-a*, *-e*, *f.*
the' (**10**): a brewer's strainer (*OED* thead).
thilhorss' (**28**): shaft-horse or wheeler in a team of horses (*OED*).
thille hamys (**20**): loop, fastened to collar of a draught animal, supporting a cart-shaft (*MFG*, *OED* thill[1], hame[2]).
thornbak' (**14**): the common ray or skate (marine fish). Suspension dropped in *sing.*; treated as *m.*
tintour' (**12**): dyeing.

tisshuz (28): a rich kind of cloth, a belt or girdle made from it (*OED* tissue *sb.*).
tollon' (18): toll. Extended to forms in *-ium*, *-ii*, *n.*
tollyng' eelys (19), **toleyll (22)**: eels, possibly for use as bait (*OED* tolling).
tolman (27): a game.
ton' (20), **tons' (19)**: shearing. Extended to forms from *tonsio*, *nis*, *f.*
torches (15), **torchis (19)**: a light to be carried in the hand, possibly of wax, although sometimes of material soaked in tallow (*OED*). Note also **19**, *torchweyk'*.
torett' (20): a ring, in horse harness, through which the driving reins pass (*OED* terret).
tortes (15); **torteyss'**, **tortayss' (19)**: a large wax candle, usually distinguished from a torch (*OED* tortis).
tostyngyren' (24): toasting iron (*OED* 1596).
tractag' (12): (payment for) haulage (*RMLWL*). Extended to forms in *-ium*, *-ii*, *n.*
tractat' (12): treaty. Extended to forms in *-us*, *-us*, *m.*
traiell' (14): a medicine in a powdered form.
trapper (27), **trappuris (28)**: a form of armour, of leather or metal, for a horse or other animal (*OED* trapper *sb.*[1]).
tr' (14): trencher, thick slice of bread. Extended to *trencherus*, *i*, *m.*
tribul' (20): a tool, especially a shovel, possibly a measure of flour (*RMLWL*). Extended as if from *tribula*, *e*, *f.*
tripudant' (14): dancing, *adj.*
troyt' (12); **trught'**, **trugth' (14)**; **trowtis (16)**: trout (freshwater fish). In **14**, suspension dropped in *sing.*; treated as *m.*
tuell' (14): towel. Extended to forms in *-a*, *-e*, *f.*
tuenge (15): tewing, beating.
tunell' (2), **tonell' (19)**: tun, cask (*RMLWL*). Extended to forms in *-us*, *-i*, *m.*
turb' (2), **turbon' (9)**, **turbar' (10)**: turf, peat. Extended to forms of *turba*, *e*, *f.*, in **2** and **10**; and to forms of *turbonum*, *i*, *n.*, in **9**.
turbutto (4), **turbut' (10)**, **turbot (14)**: turbot, a large flat-fish. In **4**, treated as *coll. sing.* of *turbuttus*, *i*, *m.*; in **10**, suspension dropped; in **14**, treated as *m.*
turibul' (28): thurible. Extended to forms in *-um*, *-i*, *n.*
turtils (28): turtle doves (*OED* turtle *sb.*[1]).
tymbr' (28): a bundle of 40 skins (Veale *Fur trade* p. 223).
tyn (15): *pro ii botells of tyn v d.*, probably not the metal, but earthenware (*OED* tinage).
tynnynge (15): to enclose with a hedge or fence, to repair a hedge or fence (*OED* tine *v.*[1] 2).
tyre (28): dress, clothing, specifically a covering, dress, or ornament for a woman's head, head-dress (*OED* tire *sb.*[1] 1425).

ullag' (17): ullage, the amount required to make good loss by leakage, etc., here from pipes of cider. Extended to forms from *ullagium*, *i*, *n.*
ullen' (28): *v pec' de canabo vocat' boltes de ullen'*, possibly oiled canvas (*OED* ulle).
ultra: beyond. Treated as a preposition with *acc.* unless evidence in MS to the contrary; **28** f.3 verso uses *abl.*
unc' (28): ounce. Extended to forms in *-ia*, *-ie*, *f.*

unco (4): pot hook (*RMLWL* 1440).
ung' (2): grease. Extended as if from *unguentum, i, n.*
un*n*uns (2): onions. Abbreviated forms extended to *unnuns*.
urci (28): a cruet or ewer (*RMLWL*).
urland' (3): bordering, edging.

vas' (10, 14, 19): vessel (pot). Extended to forms in *-um, -i, n.*, in *pl.* unless a single item intended. **14** also has *abl. sing. vasa.*
vaumbrace (28): armour for the fore-arm (*OED*).
veegles (26): namely.
vel' (6): calf, veal.
vermines (11a): ermines.
veter': old. Extended in **10** and **28** in *abl. sing.* to *-i*, not classical *vetere.*
victual' (7, 14): victuals. Extended to *victualia, ium, n. pl.*
vincreke (28): a form of horse medicine.
vinet' (20): vineyard. Extended to forms in *-um, -i, n.*
vino acro (7): vinegar. MS has ending for *adj.* in *-o* in *abl. sing.*, rather than classical *-i.*
virid' (7, 14, 19): green, *adj.*; greenery, *sb.* Extended to forms from *viridis, e*, with *abl. sing.* in *-i.* **14** has one instance, f.36 verso, of *gen. pl., f.*, as *viridarum.*
virid' sicc' (12), virid' succ' (20): verjuice.
volam' (24): sheet, covering (*MFG*). Extended as if from *volamen, inis.*
volat' (23): possibly a place for raising or keeping birds rather than 'a fowling glade' (*RMLWL*). Extended as if from *volata, e, f.*
volatil' (3, 4, 10, 11b, 18, 19): (wild) fowl. Extended as if from *volatile, is, n.*, in *pl.* in all cases except **3**, where it is treated as *coll. sing.*
votell' (14): a bottle or similar vessel.
vord*ours* (28): possibly the batons used for signalling the commencement or cessation of fighting in battle or tournaments (*OED* warder *sb.*[2]).

wadmoll' (12); **wadmole, wademole, wademoll' (28)**: a coarse woollen cloth, often used for covering horse collars (*OED* wadmal).
waferner (16): one who makes wafers.
wafurernys (19): wafer irons.
wambties (14): womb-ties, girths (*OED* womb-tie 1486).
wardecorps (10): an over-garment, short gown (*OED* wardecorps 1440; *RMLWL* sub warda).
wardouns, wardons (19): a variety of pear (*OED* warden *sb.*[2]).
warner (11a): warrener, or keeper of the granary ?
warr' (19), warrant' (28): warrant, voucher. Extended to forms from *warrantum, i, n.*
waynscottes (15), waynskott' (20), waynscott' (28): superior foreign oak, often used for panel work. Treated as *m.* in **28**.
Westfale (20), Westwale (24): a kind of cloth from Westphalia, or similar to cloth from there (*OED* Westvale *sb.*).
whipcord' (12): a type of tough, hempen cord; used to make whip-lashes or similar items (*OED*). Suspension dropped.
whiting' (14): whiting (marine fish). Suspension dropped in *sing.*

winturfizs (**11a**): dried fish, possibly cod; one of the varieties of stockfish (*KMED*, listed sub corpling).
wodecokk' (**14**), **wodcokk'** (**19**): woodcock. Treated as *m.* Suspension dropped in **14** in *sing.*
wombis (**28**): belly (of marten).
wombrop' (**12, 20**): a tie round the girth. Suspension dropped in **12**.
wongtyȝe (**23**): womb-tie, girth.
worsted (**28**): a woollen textile fabric. Treated as *m.*
wrongges (**28**): floor or ground timber of a ship (*OED* wrong *sb.*[1]; Rose *Lancastrian navy* p. 261).
wypys (**19**): probably lapwings (birds), rather than plovers, as plovers occur in the same list (*OED* wype).
wythe (**14**): *pur le wythe in die Pasch'*, a special Easter payment (*OED* wite *sb.*[2]).

ypimer', **ypymer'**: see *epim-*.

zinzib' (**19**): ginger. Extended as if from *zinziber, is.* See also *gingebr'.*
zoukr' (**10**): sugar. Extended as if from *zoukrum, i, n.*

Grammar and syntax

This section sets out those grammatical conventions that have been followed in expanding abbreviated texts, where the precedents of classical practice can be demonstrated to be inappropriate or insufficient, together with the principal divergences in the MSS from classical grammatical forms, where they have not already been described in the word list.

Adjectives

Adjectives directly associated with a place-name, e.g. Ocle Parva, Bentleigh Magna, have been treated as invariable where they are not extended in MSS.

Third declension adjectives have been extended according to classical practice, with forms of the present participle extended in *abl. sing.* in *-i* as an adjective, and in *-e* as a substantive; hence *precedenti* (**10**); *sequenti* (**5**, **7**, **9**, **10**, **13**). The most notable exception is in **28**, where present participles are written out in *-e*, *in anno sequente*, *de anno isto instante*. Comparative forms of adjectives, e.g. *anterior*, *posterior*, have been extended, as in **10**, in *abl. sing.* to forms in *-e* following the classical practice.

vetus has been extended in *abl. sing.* to forms in *-i* rather than classical *-e* (no evidence in MS in **10**; following MS in **28**).

Adjectives following days of the week are usually extended in *abl.*, although some follow a *gen.* form, derived from the case of the second element of the day (*lune*, *martis*, *mercurii*, etc.); hence *die lune proxima* (**1**), *die lune sequentis* (**2**).

Numerals have been treated as adjectives. C is treated thus, except where the MS employs a *gen.* form in the following noun: *in CCCC allecis* (**5**); *in viii pissibus et C allecis* (**6**).

Reflexive pronouns and possessive adjectives

The classical usage of the reflexive pronoun *se* and the possessive adjective *suus* has been largely lost. *sibi* is commonly used for *ei*, *suus* for *eius*.

Gerunds, gerundives

Where a gerundive form follows a noun, it has been extended in the same case, gender and number as the noun; where it precedes the noun, it has been placed in a neuter form, with the following noun in the *acc.* Hence, for example, *pro pane furniendo* (**14**); *ad certificandum indicamentum* (**28**). Ablative constructions with the gerund, for example, *eundo et redeundo*, have been used only where the MS does so explicitly; other examples have been treated adjectivally, in agreement with the noun preceding, for example, *in expensis Davidi eundi*. Where the forms are heavily abbreviated, the rule has been to follow an adjectival form rather than a gerundive; thus in **14**, forms from *capiens* have been preferred to forms from *capiendum*.

DIET ACCOUNTS (i)
(1–14)

1 *Diet account for an unidentified household at London, Westminster and Windsor, late twelfth century*

This account from the late twelfth century is probably the earliest diet account to survive from the British Isles. It was written by a single clerk on several occasions on two narrow membranes, sewn together Chancery fashion. The manuscript has been damaged by damp and it is possibly a fragment of a larger document; although there is now no trace of sewing to attach additional membranes, it lacks a heading and an overall total. The daily account runs for twenty-two days, for Friday 4 October, the Saturday following, and from Sunday 13 October to Friday 1 November inclusive. The hiatus in the daily sequence may result from a slip of the pen, especially as the first four days of the account were written in a single operation: if the account were intended to start on the second Friday after Michaelmas, 11 October, rather than the first, a continuous sequence of days would result. Palaeographically the roll, with its hasty cursive script and irregular Latin, dates from the late twelfth century (Plate 1). The days of the week and the feasts on the roll correspond for the years 1168, 1174, 1185, 1191, 1196 and 1202. The account has been attributed to the household of a nobleman in the king's suite, but this cannot be pressed too closely in the sense that the nobleman and his entourage were with the king at that date. Henry II, Richard I and King John can all be shown to be elsewhere at the period of the account.[1] The personal names on the roll do not assist in the identification of the household, although it may be possible to relate it more closely to one of the establishments resident in the comparatively small London parish of St Mary of Somerset. One candidate may be the household of the Abbot of Bury St Edmunds, who had a London 'hospice' at the end of the twelfth century in this area and who is known from another source to have used household accounts at this date.[2]

PRO E 101/631/1

Membrane 1 recto
Lundonia Die veneris proxima post festum Scanti Micaelis in servisia ad opus xviii garcionum et iii pauperum et superveniencium ix d. In allece

[1] PRO *Supplementary list of accounts, various* (Lists and Indexes, supplementary series, 9, i; 1969) p. 56; R. W. Eyton *Court, household and itinerary of Henry II* (London, 1878) pp. 117, 185, 266; L. Landon *The itinerary of Richard I* (PRS, new series, 13; 1935) pp. 55–8, 115–16; T. D. Hardy, 'Itinerarium Johannis regis Angliae', *Archaeologia* 22 (1829) p. 135.

[2] I am grateful to Dr Caroline Barron for this suggestion; *The chronicle of Jocelin of Brakelond concerning the acts of Samson abbot of the monastery of St Edmund* ed. H. E. Butler (London, 1949) pp. 41–2.

iii d. qua. In pot*agio* ob. In portatoribus majoris sciste de parochia Scante Marie de Sumersetia usque ad parochiam Trinitatis iiii d. In ferura i d.

Summa xvii d.

Lundonia Die sabati proxima in servisia ad opus xiii garcionum et iii pauperum et superveniencium vi d. ob. In allece iii d. qua.

Summa ix d. qua.

Item Lundonia Die dominica tercia post festum Scanti Micaelis in pane iii d. In servisia ad totam familiam viii d. qua. In i nuncio de Doresetia i d.

Summa xii d. qua.

Item Lundonia Die lune proxima in pane x d. ob. In servisia vi d. ad totam familiam. In sale i d.

Summa xvi d.[1]

Item Lundonia Die martis proxima in pane viii d. qua. In servisia vii d. In ovis i d. In bre*nna* i d. ob. In ferris et clavis equorum aput Vestmonasterium ii s. Liberato Russello i d.

Summa iii s. vi d. ob. qua.

Item Lundonia Die mercurii proxima in pane ad opus x garcionum et i operatoris fodientis in curia et iii pauperum et i carecaris de Seint Savur vii d. ob. In servisia iiii d. ob. In potagio qua. In sale i d. Liberato Russello ix d. In ii brachis selle summarii x d. ob. In ii lib. burle ad corrigendam illam sellam ii d. In reparacione selle palefridi v d. In i hanaperio ix d. In candella sipi i d. per iii dies. In reparacione bulgorum i d. qua. In passagio ponti Lunonie cum feno de Sutverc i d. ob. In allece iii d. ob.

Summa iiii s. viii d.

Item Lundonia Die jovis proxima in pane nichil. In servisia ad opus xiiii ominum et iii paperum et ad opus toscius familie viii d. qua. In bre*nna* i d. ob. In i serrura v d. In .....[2] ferrandi equos ii d. In candela ob.

Summa xvii d. <ob.> qua.[3]

Item Lundonia Die veneris proxima in servisia tocius familie et superveniencium vi d. ob. qua. In pisce iii d. In allea ob. In ferris equorum ad cariandum aput Rtinges xvi d. In clavis s*otd*ularum ad cariandum ibidem xvi d. In i lib. piperis vii d. ob. In i lib. scimini i d. In croco x d. In i corda unciatti iiii d.

Summa v s. iiii d.

Membrane 2 recto

Item Lundonia Die sabati proxima in servisia vi d. ob. ad opus xvi ominum et aliorum superveniencium. In pisce iiii d. ob. In v aulnas panni ad coperi*e*ndum equos domini mei xxxii d. <In i corda unc*iati* ... iiii d.>

[1] New pen following this entry.
[2] MS obscure.
[3] New pen following this entry.

Liberato Russello ad emendum carvisium xii d. Liberato Russello sotularibus emendis *v*i d. Johan*n*i de Vincestria v d. ob. Sotularibus emendis v d. Eodham iiii d. ob. In i pesie ferri faciendi barras fenestre ii d. In ferrura equi Jhoa*n*nis Bridel i d. In feno ad omnes equos aput Vestmonasterium ob. In stramine i d. ob.

Summa v s. iii d. <ob.>

Item Lundonia Die dominica quarta post festum predictum in servisia toscius familie et superveniencium viii d.

Summa viii d.

Item Lundonia Die lune proxima in pane *ii* s. In servisia xii d. In vino *v* s. In farrina i d. In pomis i d. In allea i d. In oinnuns ii d. In ovis iiii d. qua. In mustardo i d. In leporis x d. In pi*s*is ii d. qua. In discis v d. In lacte ii d. In v. . . . . *ii d.* ob. In cariacione feni xiii d. ob.

Summa xi s. ix d. ob. qua.

Item Lundonia Die martis proxima in pane viii d. pro familia et pro v garcionibus circa fenum. In servisia ix d. Liberato Grig*or*e iii s. iiii d. ad emendum sal*em*.

Summa iiii s. iii d.

Item Lundonia Die mercurii in pane viii d. In servisia v d. In stupellis costrellorum ii d. In furca ferrea ad emundendam stabulam i d. qua. Liberato Russello i d.

Summa xvii d. qua.

Item Lundonia Die jovis proxima in pane viii d. ob. In servisia vi d. In bre*nna* ob. qua. In candela ob. In lotrice ii d.

Summa xvii d. ob. qua.[4]

Item Lundonia Die veneris proxima in liberacione ad opus meum pro infirmitate mea ob. In lacte ob. In servisia v d. In pisce iii d. In pistore i d. In candela ob.[5]

Summa x d. ob.

Item Lundonia Die sabati proxima in servisia v d. ob. qua. In allece ii d. In di. penula ii s. aput Vestmonasterium. In sucre ad opus domini mei xii d.

Summa iii s. vii d. ob. qua.

Item Lundonia Die dominica quinta post festum Scanti Micaelis in servisia vi d. ob. In candela qua. In prebenda xii d.

Summa xviii d. ob. qua.

Item Lundonia Die lune proxima scilicet die festi Simonis et Jude in servisia vii d. In carne ad opus tercelli qua. In prebenda xii d. <Liberato Rusello di. m.>

Summa xix d. qua.

[4] New pen following this entry.

[5] New pen following this entry.

Vindlesores Die martis proxima in servisia iiii d. ob. In candela ob.
Summa v d.

Item Vindleshores Die mercurii proxima in pane vi d. ad opus garcionum et vi pauperum. In servisia iii d. ob.
Summa ix d. ob.

Vindlesor' Die jovis proxima in pane vi d. In servisia iii d. qua. In allece iii d. In ferrura ob.
Summa xii d. ob. qua.

Item Vindlesores Die Omnium Scantorum in pane iiii d. In servisia iiii d. In allece ii d. ob. In oblsacione domini mei et sosciorum suorum iii d.
Summa xiii d. ob.

2 *Diet account of the household of Hugh de Neville of Essex, March 1207 – April 1207*

Although this fragment of an account lacks a heading, it is possible to attribute it to the household of Hugh de Neville of Essex, the master of the royal hounds, chief justice of the forests and an influential adviser of King John. The account encompasses a series of journeys made by De Neville, from 1 March 1207 to 27 April following, sometimes in the company of the hounds and closely associated with the movements of King John and his queen, Isabella of Angoulême. From the hunting lodge at Geddington, Northamptonshire, drawing on the stock of Rockingham Castle, which De Neville administered for the King, the household went towards Huntingdon and Cambridge, staying on the way with Saher de Quincy, and then moving on, making purchases in preparation for the arrival of King John at Hallingbury. Its next move was to the south west, towards the royal hunting lodge of Freemantle in the manor of Kingsclere, Hampshire, moving on to the royal palace at Clarendon, near Salisbury, whither Hugh de Neville was to escort the queen. From there an excursion was made to the hunting lodge at Cranborne, returning to Clarendon and to the hospitality of the Bishop of Salisbury. After a stay at Marlborough the household returned to Geddington, moving on by way of Aylesbury, High Wycombe and Reading to Windsor. The household then passed on through Newbury and Hungerford for a further brief sojourn at Marlborough, before moving through Gloucester on the way to the castle at St Briavels, another favoured hunting lodge. After two days there, Hugh de Neville returned through Gloucester to Marlborough for Easter. The following Wednesday the household was again on the move, by way of Wherwell, to the royal castle at Portchester.[1]

The account is written on a Chancery fashion roll of two membranes. There are traces of sewing holes at both the head and the foot of the roll, indicating that it was once part of a lengthier document. In its daily entries the account usually notes expenditure in a departmental order of pantry, buttery, kitchen, marshalsea and almonry, but without divisions or headings in the text. The account was written in a single hand, possibly in a single operation, with a few additional notes in another hand; if the roll is a fair copy, some errors in transcription may account for the frequently incorrect totalling of the account, which it is otherwise difficult to reconcile. The roll has been badly stained by damp.

PRO C 47/3/1

Membrane 1 recto

Die jovis apud Gaytontun' pro pane viii s. vi d. et de stauro \ de Gaitydun' / vinum habuimus. .....[1] de stauro de Rokingham' habuimus ad familiam. Pro fresceng*a* iii s. Pro ..... gallin*is* ad aves ii d. Pro avena di. m. Pro feno iii s. Pro litera xii d. Pro ..... ix d. Pro ferramento iiii s. i ob. excepto.

Summa xxvi s. iii d.

Die veneris ibidem pro pane iiii s. Pro cervisia xxiii d. Pro pisce v s. Pro avena v s. iiii d. Summa xvi s. iii d.

Die sabbati ibidem pro pane vii s. excepto i d. Pro cervisia xxxv d. Pro allece xxv d. ..... Pro sale ii d. ob. Pro avena v s. iiii d. Pro cariagio iii d. Pro feno xvi d. Pro garcionibus qui ceperunt hospicium domini apud Sudhon et Humtindun' ix d. ob.

Die dominica fuimus apud Kinebauc' ad custum justiciarii.

Die lune apud Sudh' ad custum Saher*i* de Quincy.

Die martis in capite jejun*ii* apud Huntind' in pane vi s. vi d. Pro cervisia xxviii d. Pro c..... iii s. ix d. Pro fresceng*a* xviii d. Pro chiverill*is* et wodecocis xi d. ob. Pro feno xiiii d. ob. Pro littera xi d. Pro ferrura vi d. Prebendam habuimus de Willelmo Lupo de dono suo. Pro unguento et lardo iii ob. Pro ovis et mustardo ii d. Summa xvii s. iiii d. ob.

Die mercurii apud Cantebrig' in pane iiii s. Pro cervisia xxii d. Pro vino vi d. Pro allece xiiii d. Pro mulvello xviii d. Pro pisce recenti xii d. Pro alleis mustardo sale et vin*o* i s. ii d. Pro busca et turba xiii d. Pro feno xxii d. Pro avena vi s. vi d. Pro littera xi d. Pro ferrura xii d. Summa xx s. vi d.

[1] A. L. Poole *From Domesday Book to Magna Carta 1087–1216* (2nd edition, Oxford, 1954) p. 12, n. 3; *History of the King's works* ii, pp. 815, 821, 910–18, 922, 940–1, 943.

---

[1] Possibly 'acidum'.

Die jovis ibidem in exspensa post dominum quando emebamus piscem xv d. ob. Item eodem die pro cervisia ad opus nostrum et carecariorum apud Neuport' iiii d. Pro feno <iiii> \ v / d. <ob.> Pro avena xxii d. ob. Pro cariagio ii d. Pro candela i s. ob. In exspensa duorum garcionum qui remanserunt ibidem per preceptum domini iiii d. Pro littera ii d.

Summa iiii s. viii d. ob.

Item ibidem pro anguillis salsis contra adventum domini regis apud Halingebir' C s. xv s. Pro unnuns v s. vi d. Pro cariagio anguillarum usque Halingebir' iiii s. \ vi d. / Portitoribus ii d. ob.

Die veneris apud Neuport' pro pane iiii li. xix s. iiii d. Pro cervisia xxiiii s. i d. Pro cariagio ix s. x d. per duos dies. Pro cyfis et scutell*is* vi s. vi d. In exspensa illorum qui misi erant pro pane iii s. iiii d. et totum pacavit Radulfus Clericus.

Item per manum Picoti Coci apud Stertford pro pane xlv s. iiii d. Item pro iiiiM allecis xxii s. viii d. Pro mulvello et raye et cariagio xlviii s. iiii d. Pro cervisia xlvii s. iiii d. Pro unnuns et alleis xxii d. Pro cariagio xx d.

Item per manum Thome de Thotham pro pane xxiiii s. vii d. Pro mustardo xiii d. Pro oystris et welkis et mulvello et haddocis et raiis vii s.

Summa xxxii s. vii d. et totum pacatum est per Radulfum de Nevill' et per receptam suam.

Item per manum Walteri de Everk' pro lampereies ix s. Pro mulvello xxvii s. x d. Pro salmone xiiii d. Pro welkes iiii d. ob. Pro unnuns xxvi d. ob. Pro ciphis et dublers vi s. ii d. Pro sale xii d. Pro cariagio xxxii s. vii d. Pro picheris xvi d.

Item per manum Willelmi Pollard' pro pisce xxv s. Pro cariagio apud Halingebir' et in piscatoribus in insula de R*oc* et in expensa eiusdem Willelmi versus Welle et versus Halingebir' iiii s. ix d.

Summa xxix s. x... d. ... et totum pacatum est per manum et liberacionem Radulfi de Nevill'.

Item per manum Willelmi de Chauk' pro pisce vi s. vi d. et pacatum est per manum eiusdem Radulfi et non per Radulfum Clericum.

Item per manum Galfridi Marescalli xlii s. pro avena et totum pacatum est per eundem Radulfum.

Item v s. qui remanent in debito et aturnatus est ad illos reddendos Willelmus prepositus de Halingebir'.

Item pro pane coquendo in adventu regis et pro busca ad panem coquendum iii s. et ad illos reddendos aturnatus est prepositus.

Item ante adventum regis in d*ominio* expenditi erant iiii s. iii ob. et ad illos reddendos aturnatus est prepositus.

Item diebus sabbati et dominica et lune fuimus apud Halingebir' quando fuit dominus rex.

Item diebus martis et mercurii apud Farnham et Kingestin' xviii s. v d. ob.

per manum Roberti de Wassingel' de denariis quos recepit de Willelmo Wall*ens*.

Die jovis apud Fraitmantell' et veneris et sabbati \ in adventu regis / pro pane xv s. et de stauro iii qr. furmenti et de empcione \ <pro . . . . . qr.> / ii qr. ad panem regis pro ix s. viii d. \ Et remansit tota grossa farina. / Et de stauro cervisie ii tunelli. Item de stauro de allece DC et pro mulvello vi s. et pro menusa vi s. per tres dies. Item de avena de stauro xi qr. et di. et totum pacatum est per manum J. de Sell'.

Die dominica ibidem pro pane iiii s. ii d. Pro cervisia iii s. iii d. Pro mulvello iiii s. et totum pacatum est per J. de Sell'. Pro vino xviii d.

Die lune ibidem pro pane iiii s. vi d. Pro cervisia iii s. iii d. Pro plaicis xii d. Pro menusa ii s. ii d. Pro cariagio xx d. De avena de stauro per duas noctes cum equis Thome Esturm' vii qr. et di. Pro <un> vino viii d. et de allece per duos dies CCCC.

Pacacio Johannis de Sell'[2]

Summa tocius per illos v dies lxii s. x d. et totum pacavit J. de Sell.

xxii equi Die martis apud Wigton' pro pane v s. et di. Pro cervisia xvi d. Pro allece x d. ob. Pro salmone et sechiis xxiii d. Pro busca viii d. Pro feno xii d. Pro avena iii s. xi d. Pro litera xix d. ob. Pro ferrura xi d.

Summa xvii s. ix d.

Item pro exspensa Ade Cisun cum allecis v s. vi d. ob.

Die mercurii pro pane iiii s. vi d. Pro cervisia xi d. Pro feno iiii d. Pro busca iiii d. et fuimus in nocte illa apud Lokerleg'. Pro allece CC xiiii d. Pro raies xviii d. Pro welkes viii d. Pro mustardo et alleis et sale ii d. Pro pisis iii d. Pro ferrura i d. Item eodem die apud Clarendun' quando dominus adduxit reginam de Fraitmantell' pro prebenda xx d. Pro vino apud Winton' xxviii d.

Summa xii s. ix d.

Die jovis apud Clarend' pro pane vi s. Pro cervisia ii s. Pro oistres ii s. Pro allece xiii d. Pro makerello ix d. Pro cariagio viii d. Prebendam habuimus de stauro de Chissebir'. Pro feno et littera ii s.

Summa xiiii s. vi d.

Die veneris ibidem pro vino xvi d. Pro cervisia xxix d. Pro cariagio vi d. Panem et makerellum habuimus de stauro Porecestr' ad totam familiam. Pro feno et littera ii s. Pro clavis ix d. Garcioni qui cepit hospicium domini ibidem ii d.

Summa vii s. ii d.

Membrane 2 recto

Die sabbati in vigilia Concepcionis Beate Marie ibidem pro pane viii s. Pro cervisia ii s. x d. Pro allece ii s. Pro salmone xviii d. Pro lamperuns viii d. ob. Pro vino xvi d. Pro feno per duos dies xxxii d.

Summa xviii s. ii d.

[2] This marginal entry, bracketed against everything since the preceding Thursday, is in another hand.

Die Concepcionis Domini ibidem pro pane xx d. Pro cervisia viii d. Pro makerello xii d. Pro unnuns i d. Pro vino viii d. Summa iiii s. v d.
Die lune sequentis apud Craneburn' pro pane iiii s. x d. ob. Pro cervisia xix d. Pro vino ii s. Pro allece xxxii d. Pro makerello ii s. Pro salmone per duos dies xx d. Pro cariagio vi d. ob. Pro scutell*a* iii d. Pro feno xvi d. Pro avena v s. vii d. ob. Summa xxii s. vi d. ob.
Die martis ibidem quando dominus ivit apud Clarend' pro regina pro pane v s. Pro cervisia xxvii d. ob. Pro vino xvi d. Pro makerello ix d. Pro salmone xx d. Pro avena v s. v d. ob. Pro feno xiii d. Summa xvii s. vii d.
Totum debetur . . . . . iii. s. qui pacantur per Radulfum Clericum et v s. vii d. ob. per Eliam Clericum et superplus restat in debito.[3]
Die mercurii fuimus apud Saresbir' ad custum episcopi.
Diebus jovis et veneris et sabbati fuimus apud Merleb*erg*' et respondebit inde G. de Everk'.
Die dominica fuimus apud Abbend' ad custum abbatis.
Die lune apud Clamdun' \ pro pane / vi s. ix d. Pro cervisia xxix d. Pro allecis xx d. Pro mulvello xxv d. Pro avena iiii s. iiii d. Fenum habuimus de stauro H. de Wylbi. Summa xvii s. iii d.
Die martis fuimus apud Curtonhal' ad custum Roberti de Nevill'.
Willelmus Haket Die mercurii fuimus apud Rikingham pro pane empto xix d. et de stauro ii qr. ibidem. Pro pisce <s> vi s. iii d. ob. De stauro di. tunellus cervisie. Et vinum habuimus ibidem de stauro. Et de avena iiii qr. de empto \ ad precium xvii d. / et respondebit de toto Willelmus Hakett'. Summa viii s. vi d. ob.
Thomas Gikell' Die jovis apud Clyve pro pane viii s. xi d. Pro cervisia ii s. Pro allece ii s. vi d. Pro salmone iii s. <Pro anguillis x d.> Pro mulvello ii s. i d. Pro avena ix s. ii d. Pro feno xxvi d. Pro ferrura xv d.
Summa xxxi s. iiii d. et totum pacatum est per manum Thome Gikell'.
Die veneris apud Gaitend' pro pane viii s. i d. excepto. Pro cervisia xxii d. Pro allece xx d. Pro makerello iii s. Pro salmone iii s. Pro mulvello ii s. Pro alleis et sale iiii d. Pro feno vi d. Pro avena v s. vii d. ob. Pro cariagio ii d. Pro litera i d. Summa xxvi s. iii ob.
Die sabbati sequentis fuimus apud Asse ad domum et custum Roberti de Salsetto.
Die dominica prima Passionis apud Stratford pro pane ix s. Habuimus duas mottas canum. Pro cervisia iii s. Pro anguillis xxvii d. Pro unnuns vii d. ob. Pro mulvello xx d. Summa xvi s. vi d. ob.
Item per manum Rogeri de Salsetto pro pisce empto apud Norhamt' et pro vino xxiiii s. vi d. et idem Rogerus inde respondebit et totum portatum fuit cum domino versus Windesour'.
Item die lune apud Ail*s*ebir' pro pane vii s. i d. Pro cervisia ii s. iii d. Pro

[3] This marginal entry is in another hand to the main text.

vino xx d. quod exspenditum fuit eodem die ibidem. Item pro vino quod portatum fuit cum domino xl d. Pro avena iiii s. ii d. Pro ferrura iii ob. Pro axe ad carecam iii d. Summa xx s. ii d. ob.

Die martis apud Wycumbe in pane v s. Pro cervisia xxi d. Pro vino xx d. Pro murutts expensis in coquina iii d. Pro busca et carbone viii d. ob. \ Pro pisis iii d. / Pro littera x d. Pro feno xviii d. Pro avena iiii s. xi d.
Summa xvi s. x d. ob.

Die mercurii \ apud Radinges / ante diem dominicam in Ramis Palmarum pro pane iii s. iii ob. Pro cervisia xviii d. ob. Pro vino xv d. Pro allece viii d. Pro merlengo ix d. Pro salmone ix d. Pro feno xiii d. Pro litera xiii d. ob. Pro avena xxxi d. ob. Pro busca ii d. ob. Pro carbone iii d. Pro ferrura ix d. Summa xiii s. i ob.

Habuimus xiiii leporarios et ii bruchetos.[4]

Die jovis ibidem in pane iii s. x d. ob. Pro cervisia xviii d. Pro vino ii s. vi d. Pro allece xii d. Pro anguillis vii d. Pro salmone ix d. Pro fabis ii d. Pro unnuns et sale et mustardo iii d. Pro feno xvi d. Pro avena iii s. iiii d. ob. Pro carbone iii ob. Summa xv s. x d. ob.

Eisdem diebus et die veneris sequentis apud Windelesoures pro pane ad opus familie que remansit ibidem post dominum ix s. iii d. Pro cervisia iii s. viii d. Pro vino xv d. Pro mulvello xxix d. Pro raies ii s. Pro minutis expensis coquine per tres dies scilicet in mustardo et barillo et acceto ix d. Pro feno xii d. ob. De stauro de Bedefunt' ix qr. avene. In expensis Galfridi Marescalli qui cepit hospicium domini ibidem ante adventum domini et garcionis qui venit de curia regis xxii d. \ Pro litera vii d. /
Cocam xxxii d.

Summa xxii s. vii d. ob. unde iii s. \ vi d. / adquietati fuerunt in minutis parcellis de iii qr. avene \ de stauro / venditis pro iii s. \ vi d. / Et debentur xviii s. viii d. ob.

Item ibidem pro pane quem servientes apportaverunt apud Merleberg' iiii s. v d. Pro vino x d. et adquietatum fuit totum apud Wycumbe.

Item die sabbati apud Niwebir' in exspensis servientum venientium apud Merleberg' xvii d. ob. Et debentur.

Item eodem die apud Hungerford' quando dominus ivit apud Merleberg' pro pisce xvii d. ob. Eodem die pro feno apud Merleberg' per <duos> \ tres / dies iii s. iii d.

Eodem die et dominica sequenti fuimus apud Merleberg'.

Die lune fuimus apud Musardiam ad custum Radulfi Musard.

Die martis apud Gloverniam in pane xx s. Pro cervisia xiiii d. Pro vino vii s.

[4] Followed by a further marginal note in another hand, now indecipherable.

\ viii /[5] d. et de tota exspensa medietat*es* [6] domine apportate fuerunt apud Sanctum Briavill'. Pro allece viii s. vi d. Pro mulvello et hakis viii s. xi d. Pro salmone vi s. vi d. Pro lampered*a* xxxii d. Pro minutis exspensis coquine iii d. ob. Pro claiis ad carecam que tulit panem cum domino et cord*is* v d. Pro feno vii d. Pro bukelis ad cingulas iiii d. In elemosina i d. Pro scutella ad inponendum elemosinam i d. Portitoribus qui buscam portabant ii d. ob. Pro ciphis vii d. ob. Summa lviii s. ob.

Diebus mercurii \ et jovis / apud Sanctum Briavell' in pane iiii s. i d. Pro cervisia xxiii d. Pro vino vii s. Pro avena x s. v d. Pro clavis v d.

Summa xxiii s. x d.

Die jovis pro cervisia xvi d. Pro feno xii d. ob. Pro avena vii s. Eodem die in exspensa servientum apud Newenham xvi d. Pro ferrura ii d.

Summa x s. x d. ob.

Habuimus magnam motam et omnes leporarios.

In vigilia Pasce apud Gloucestr' in exspensa servientum qui remanserunt post dominum v d. Item a vigilia Pasce usque ad diem mercurii apud Merleberg' in pane empto viii s. x d. et preterea viii s. pro ii qr. furmenti ad faciendum panem dominicum ad opus domini et de stauro xii qr. et di. Item de stauro ii tunelli de cervisia. Item de vino albo Mort*in*' xxxi sex. ad precium x d. et de M*inn*ato iiii sex. ad precium viii d. et summa xxviii s. vi d. Pro pisce iii s. v d. Item pro carne recenti viii s. vi d. Pro ovis xx d. Item de stauro xi bacones et iii boves et xvi carayes. Pro feno ii s. i d. Item de stauro xiiii qr. avene. Pro littera v d. ob.

Summa lxi s. v d. ob. et totum pacandum est per manum Galfridi de Everk'.

Item ibidem per manum Radulfi Clerici pro feno xxvii d.

Item die mercurii apud Weriwoll' in pane iiii s. Pro cervisia xi d. Pro vino xv d. quod fuit portatum de Merleberg'. Pro bacon*ibus* et carne porcina recenti vi s. x d. Pro pullis iiii d. Pro ovis iiii d. ob. Prebendam habuimus de all . . . cia. Summa xiii s. viii d. ob.

et totum pacatur preter viii . . .

Diebus jovis \ et veneris / apud Porecestr' in pane \ empto / iii s. viii d. De stauro ii qr. furmenti mensura estric. Cervisiam habuimus de stauro i tunell*um* parvum.[7] Et vinum habuimus de stauro. De stauro ii bacones et di. Pro carne porcina recenti xxix d. ob. Pro duobus agnis vii d. De stauro \ avene / vi qr. et di. estric. In ferrura viii d. Item pro secchiis xxii d. unde medietas missa fuit apud Merleberg' ad opus domine. Pro flundres xx\ii/ d. Pro menusa iiii d. Item CCCC de ovis de stauro.

Summa xi s. iiii d. ob. et respondebit inde Savaricus.

[5] 'ii' erased.

[6] 'Medietat'' written over 'medietas'.

[7] MS 'parvus'.

3 *Diet account for the household of a London churchman, September to December, 1213, 1219 or 1224*

Although it is no longer possible to identify the ecclesiastic for whose household this is the account, he was almost certainly a prebendary of St Paul's Cathedral, either the holder of the prebend of Willesden or of Harlesden or Twiford in Willesden. The account mentions Willesden on several occasions in contexts which suggest it was a home manor, for example, the expenditure on seed corn, on ironwork for the ploughs, and on the wages of agricultural workers. Also mentioned are Martin of Pattishall, a royal justice in the 1220s and dean of St Paul's 1228–9, other prominent churchmen, including the prior of Westminster and the prior of Durham, and a number of London merchants.[1] The year of the roll is probably 1219 or 1224, although 1213 is possible; the date cannot be 1230 as Martin of Pattishall died the preceding year.[2] Another indication that would support a date in the early 1220s is a reference to William the King's tailor.[3] Of the Jews named in the account, Elias of Lincoln appeared in a plea in 1218, Moses son of Brun and Moses of Colchester in 1219 and 1220, and Sampson son of Abraham in 1220.[4] It may consequently be possible to identify the prebendary with William de Sancte Marie Ecclesia I, archdeacon of London; with William de Sancte Marie Ecclesia II, archdeacon of Middlesex; or with Maurice of Harlow.[5]

The account is written on two small fragments of parchment and continues on a Chancery fashion roll of three membranes. There are remains of sewing holes at the top of the roll. The dorse of the whole of the roll, which has been damaged down one edge of membrane 3, and of the two fragments, is now completely covered with repair parchment. Scribal errors suggest that the account is a fair copy, but one which was written up by a number of similar and barely distinguishable hands at intervals probably of three or four days over the duration of the account. The daily totals are written in the hand that wrote the text for the day. There is a grand total at the end of the roll, and there were probably also totals

[1] For the Bukerel family of merchants, G. A. Williams *Medieval London. From commune to capital* (revised edition, London, 1970) pp. 324–5.
[2] *John Le Neve Fasti ecclesiae anglicanae 1066–1300. I St Paul's, London* ed. D. E. Greenway (London, 1968) p. 6.
[3] *The great roll of the pipe for the fourth year of the reign of King Henry III* ed. B. E. Harris (PRS new series, 47; 1987) pp. 122, 133.
[4] *Select pleas, starrs, and other records from the rolls of the Exchequer of the Jews AD 1200–1284* ed. J. M. Rigg (Selden Society, 15; 1902) pp. 4–5; *Calendar of the plea rolls of the Exchequer of the Jews* ed. J. M. Rigg and H. Jenkinson (4 vols., London, 1905–72) i, pp. 5, 16, 18, 23, 30, 33.
[5] *Fasti 1066–1300. I St Paul's* pp. 51–2, 82, 88.

membrane by membrane throughout the roll (as at the heads of membranes 2 and 3). The daily entries give the expenses in the departmental order pantry, buttery, kitchen, marshalsea, but without headings or divisions. Separate entries are made for large purchases of corn, each with a total, and other 'one-off' items. The diet accounts refer to purchases only, not consumption; bread, for example, is an irregular entry, and the account contains no entries *de stauro*. There are also some items later typical of wardrobe expenditure, for example, the purchase of furs and expenses of messengers.

PRO C 47/3/46/17

Die dominica sequenti in festo Nativitatis Beate Marie apud Knarebure in oblacione vi d. Summa v. . .
Die lune sequenti apud Ebor' in pane vi d. In cervisia iiii d. ob. In pucinis vi d. In lardo i d. In litterio iiii d. ob. In feno ii d. In avena xi d. In bosco i. . . s. In candela i d. ob. In batello i d. Summa vi s. . . .
Die martis ibidem in pane xiii d. In cervisia ix d. In carne bacona v d. In porcheto v d. In assis iii d. ob. In potagio i d. ob. In litterio iii d. ob. In feno iiii d. ob. In avena xvii d. ob. In ii lib. cere xii d. In l. . . . . In denariis ad opus magistri Rogeri iii d. ob. Summa vi s. vii d. ob.
Die mercurii sequenti ibidem in pane xii d. In cervisia iiii d. In alece iiii d. In piscibus vi . . . d. In batello i d. Alano iiii d. ad sotulares. Summa ii s. ix d.
In duobus gladiis emptis apud Ebor' iii s. iiii d. Summa iii s. iiii d.
Die sabbati in festo exaltacionis Sancte Crucis Joppe eunti in nuncium domini ad Lond' xviii d. Summa xviii d.
Die dominica sequenti apud Ham*er*ton' versus Ebor' in cervisia x d. Summa x d.
Die lune sequenti apud Ebor' in pane x d. In cervisia iiii d. ob. In carne vaccina ix d. In porcheto iii d. ob. In assis iii d. ob. In pucinis v d. In lardo i ob. In pipere ob. In potagio i ob. In feno iii d. In avena vii d. ob. In litterio ii d. In batello i d. Summa . . . . .
. . . . . de. . . . . cum domino v d. In vino . . . . . Knareburgh in . . . . .

PRO C 47/3/46/16

. . . . . in alece iii d. In ovis . . . . . ma. . . . . litterio iiii d. In bosco . . . . . In feno . . . . .
Die dominica die Sancti Michaelis . . . d. In pane iii d. In cervisia iiii d. ob. In carne vaccina viii d. D. . . . . iii d. In pucinis iiii d. In . . . . . i d. In aucis v d. In potagio i ob. In ovis i ob. In bosco ii d. In feno iii d. In . . . . . xii d . . . . . s. iiii. . . . .
Eodem die ibidem in pedibus palefri. . . . . rep. . . . .

PRO C 47/3/9

Membrane 1 recto

Die dominica sequenti in cervisia v d. In carne bovina vi d. In multone *vi* d. In porcheto vi d. In aucis vi d. In ovis i ob. In uncto i ob. Summa ii s. vi d

Die lune sequenti in cervisia viii d. In lardo i d. In uncto i ob. In literio vi d. Summa xv d. ob.

<In cordis ad laner*ios* iiii d. quos hospes milit*is* allocare in summa sua.>

Die martis sequenti in cervisia vi d. In carne vi d. In ferura i d. In i come iiii d. In ii lib. cere ix d. ob. In luminio i ob. In batello quando dominus comedit cum domino Willelmo Briwere i d. Summa ii s. iiii d.

In tunica Joppe xxvii d. In tunica eius consuenda iii ob. Summa xxviii d. ob.

Die mercurii sequenti in pane vi d. In cervisia vi d. ob. In vino . . . d. In alece v d. In merlengo vii d. In ovis i d. In batello i d. In expensis cuiusdam hominis iiii d. In una summa avene xvii d. Summa iiii s. ix d. ob.

In una summa frumenti . . . . . una summa mestilonis servient*is* de Willesden' xliiii d. Summa viii s. iii d.

Die jovis sequenti in pane v. . . . . d. In carne bovina vi d. In porcheto v d. ob. In ii doleis . . . . . In batello i d. In companagio servient*is* de Willesden' <iiii d.> iiii d. Summa ii s. vi d. ob.

In iii summis avene iii s. x d. Summa iii s. x d.

Die veneris sequenti in pane vii d. ob. In cervisia v d. In alece iiii d. In merlengo vii d. In ferura iiii d. <In> Summa ii s. iii d. ob.

In ii qr. frumenti ix s. i d. In feno portando xiiii d. In feno cariando ix d. Summa xi s.

Domine Avicie x s. de prestito Summa x s.

Die sabbati in cervisia v d. In vino vi d. In alece iiii d. In butiro iii ob. In ovis i d. In una summa bladi furnienda iii d. ob. In ollis ii d. In ii cuvis portandis de hospicio veneris usque domum i ob. \ In batello i ob. / Summa ii s. ob.

Magistro Laurencio per manum prioris de Westm' xii li. Summa xii li.

Die dominica in cervisia v d. In porcheto xi d. In vacca xii d. In \ ii / aucis vi d. In auca iii ob. In ferura ii d. ob. Summa iii. . . . .

Die lune in cervisia v d. In ovis i ob. In potagio ob. Summa . . . . .

Gaufrido de Parco ii s. Summa . . . . .

Die martis in cervisia v d. In batello i d. In ferura i d. In uncto i ob. In alba candela facienda i d. In luminio i ob. Summa ix d.

In ii qr. avene iii s. i ob. Summa iii s. ob.

Die mercurii in cervisia viii d. In allece v d. ob. In merlengo iii d. In plaicis v d. In ovis i d. Summa xxii d. ob.

Carucariis de Willesden' Gilberto xxi d. Willelmo xix d. Henrico xxiii d. In ferro caruce acquietando a Pascha usque ad festum Sancti Michaelis vii d. ob. Summa v s. x d. ob.

Die jovis sequenti in cervisia vi d. In i tonello vini delato a domo Jacobi iii d. In ollis i ob. In ferura i d. Summa x d. ob.

Willelmo de Norton' di. m. Summa di. m.

Die veneris in cervisia v d. In allece v d. In plai[cis] . . . . . [I]n butiro ii d. In ferura ii d. In ii lib. cere ix d. In luminio i ob. Summa ii s. iii d. ob.

In i suma frumenti <ad> seminanda apud Willesden' iiii s. ix d. In ii summis avene iii s. Item in i suma xvi d. Item in ii sumis avene ii s. x d. Summa xi s. xi d.

Die sabbati sequenti in cervisia v d. In allece iiii d. In merlengo iiii d. In ovis i d. In i suma bladi furnienda iii d. ob. In ferura iii d. In uncta i ob. Summa xxi d.

In lectuario ad opus domini vi d. In batello i d. In \ i / furura ad supertunicam domini xxxiiii d. In vii ulnis de kanevaz ad ventilandum bladum xiiii d. Summa iiii s. vii d.

Die dominica in cervisia v d. In una perna xiiii d. In carne vaccina xii d. In furrura ponenda in tunica domini ii d. In batello i d.
Summa ii s. x d.

Die lune sequenti Gaufrido Aur' ii s. In cervisia vi d. ob.
Summa ii s. vi d. ob.

Die martis in pane v d. In cervisia v d. In lardo i d. ob. In ferura i d. In i *cume* ii d. ob. Summa xv d. ob.

Die mercurii in cervisia v d. In allece iiii d. In ostreis ii d. In haddoco iiii d. In ovis i d. Minutori i d. In pastillis iii d. In ferris et clavis viii d. ob. \ In uncto i ob. / Summa ii s. v d. . . .

In sotularibus et caligis Robini xii d. In lecuario ad opus Rob*ini* vii d. Summa xix d.

In una summa frumenti iiii s. x d. ob. Magistro Ricardo de Garring' xl s. Summa xliiii s. x d. ob.

Die jovis in cervisia v d. In multone vi d. In pucinis iii d. In potagio i ob. In ovis i d. In boteris domini reparandis i ob. <In parietibus stabuli plastrandis iiii d.> Summa xvi d.

Willelmo de Warderoba ii s. Summa ii s.

Membrane 2 recto

xix li. xvii s. vi d. ob.

In cordis iiii d. ad fenestras et limaria. In parietibus stabuli plastrandis iiii d. In gumfis et vertevellis ad fenestram in promtuario ii d. In luto de vico delendo iiii d. In cordis i d. Summa xv d.

Willelmo Tersun viii s. Summa viii s.

Die veneris sequenti in cervisia v d. ob. In allece v d. In merlengo iiii d. In hosis domini reparandis ii d. ob. In uncto i ob. Summa xvii d. ob.

Die sabbati in cervisia v d. In allece iii d. ob. In plaicis ii d. In ovis i d. In ferura i d. In una suma bladi furnienda iii d. ob. Summa xvi d.
Andree Bukerell' pro i tonello vini ii m. et di. Summa ii m. et di.
. . . expensis Gaufridi clerici et magistri apud Dunestapl' iii s. x d. Summa iii s. x d.
Die dominica in cervisia vii d. ob. In carne bovina xvi d. In ii au. . . vii d. In columbis v d. ob. In potagio <v d. ob.> i d. In ovis i d. In batello i d. In cumpanagio servientum de Willesden' iiii d. Summa iii s. vii d.
Die lune in festo apostolorum Simonis et Jude in cervisia v d. In volatili iiii d. In ferura i d. In corbellis ii d. In fixes ii d. ob. In ii lib. cere ix d. ob. In speciebus . . . ob. Summa ii s. iii ob.
In iiii sumis avene v s. xi d. Summa v s. xi d.
Joppe eunti versus Norwic' xii d. \ ad magistrum Hugonem de Beref'. / Summa xii d.
Domino justiciario xl s. de Mosseo filio Brun'. Summa xl s.
Die martis in cervisia v d. In carnibus viii d. In egres i ob. In pane i ob. In ovis i ob. Lotrici ii d. Summa xvi d. ob.
Die mercurii in pane vi d. In cervisia v d. In allece v d. In ovis i d. In butiro iii ob. In ferura i d. Summa xviii d. ob.
In ii sumis frumenti ix s. iii d. Summa ix s. iii d.
Justiciari*o* per manum Gaufridi de Elia de Linc' v m. et de Samesde*n* filio Abrah*am* v m. et de Mosseo de Colecestr' iii m. Summa xiii m.
Die jovis in pane xvi d. In cervisia v d. In allece iii d. In merlengo iii d. In plaicis v d. In batello i d. In elemosina i ob. Hoppessort vi d. Summa iii s. iii d. ob.
Die veneris sequenti in festo Omnium Sanctorum in cervisia ii d. In allece v d. In plaicis iii d. In oblacione iii d. Summa xiii d. ob.
Die sabbatti sequenti in cervisia iii d. In allece iiii d. In plaicis iiii d. In ovis i d. In amigdalis iii d. In ris iii d. In frutu ii d. ob. In oblacione i d. In i rastella ii d. ob. Summa xxiii d.
Die dominica sequenti in pane iiii d. In cervisia iiii d. In carne bovina xiiii d. In i gallina iii ob. In potagio i ob. In[1] Summa ii s.
Die lune in pane xviii d. In cervisia v d. In vino iii s. vii d. In porcheto xviii d. In gallinis vii d. ob. In perdicis x d. ob. In alaudibus vi d. In potagio i d. ob. In lardo i d. In ovis i d. In i morterio ii d. In litterio iii d. In ii lib. cere ix d. In luminio i ob. In i summa et di. bladi furnienda v d. ob. Summa x s. x d. ob.
Die martis in cervisia v d. In assis v d. ob. In ovis i ob. In batello i d. per manum Gaufridi. In uncto i ob. Parmentario i d. In ferura i d. In potagio i ob. Summa xv d.

[1] Followed by a blank space.

Die mercurii in pane i ob. In cervisia v d. In allece iiii d. In ostreis iii ob. In haddogo iiii d. In ovis i d. Summa xvi d.
Die jovis in cervisia vi d. In carne vaccina vii d. In multone et in porco v d. In potagio i ob. In ovis i ob. In alaudibus iii d. In fixes iii d. In litterio portando i d. \ In batello i ob. / Summa ii s. ii d. ob.
Die veneris in pane i ob. In cervisia v d. In allece iiii d. In lampruns iii d. In darsis iii d. Summa xv d. ob.
Die sabbati in cervisia v d. ob. In allece iiii d. ob. In lampereda iiii d. In bar*s* ii d. In ovis i d. In butiro iii ob. Summa xviii d. ob.
In trituracione xiii sumarum et iiii bus. iiii s. ix d. Summa iiii s. ix d.
In ventilacione predictarum sumarum et bus. vi d. Hercarii apud Willesden' per xv dies vii d. ob. In cooperacione orrei iii ob. Summa xv d.
Die <sabbati> \ dominica / in cervisia v d. In multone x d. In carne vaccina viii d. In porchetto iiii d. ob. In potagio . . . . .b. In gallinis iiii d. In volatili iiii d. In ollis ii d. In ov. . . i ob. Summa iii s. ii d. ob.
Thome Bukerell' pro magistro Ricardo de Garring' xxx s. Summa xxx s.
Die lune in festo Sancti Martini in pane viii d. In porcheto ii d. ob. In potagio i ob. In perdicis xi d. In lardo i d. In ferris et clavis iiii d. In cervisia v d. Summa ii s. viii d.
Die martis in cervisia v d. In potagio i ob. In ass. . . . . vii d. In carne bovina viii d. In i \ a*x*a / <aun> ii d. ob. In ferura i d. . . . . . In fexes iii ob. In una summa bladi furnienda iii d. ob. Summa ii s. v d.
In iii sumis avene Summa iiii s. <v. . . d.> \vii d. / ob.
Die mercurii in cervisia v d. In allece iiii d. In ovis i d. In lardo i d. In ferris et clavis vii d. ob. In[2] Summa xviii d.
Die jovis in cervisia v d. In potagio i ob. In multone iiii d. In assis v d. In pastillis faciendis ii d. In[3] Summa xvi d. ob.
Die veneris in cervisia v d. ob. In allece vii d. In haddoco viii d. In ferura ii d. In batello i d. In ii lib. cere ix d. In luminio i ob. Summa ii s. ix d.
In ii sumis frumenti emptis x s. v d. Summa x s. v d.
In una summa avene xviii d. Summa xviii d.
In vi porcis emptis xiiii s. iii ob. Summa xiiii s. iii ob.
Die sabbati in pane i ob. In cervisia v d. In allece v d. In plaicis iii d. In ovis i d. In amigdalis iii d. Minutori i d. In uncto i ob. In clavis i ob. In batello i ob. quando magister Willelmus ivit inde. Vinum in batello ii d. ob. Summa xxii d. ob.
Die dominica in pane viii d. In carnibus xxi d. In volatili ix d. . . . In lardo

[2] Followed by a blank space.
[3] Followed by a blank space.

i d. In potagio i ob. In batello i d. In luminio i d. In sotularibus Joppe v d. In sotularibus Alano vi d. Summa iiii s. iiii d. ob.

Gaufrido Clerico iiii m. ad pacandum ad scaccarium de scutagio abbatis de E. . . . . et ii m. de scutagio abbatis de Abbod*esbir'*. Summa vi m.

Membrane 3 recto

. . . . .[4] li. xxiiii li. xii d.

Die lune sequenti in pane iiii s. v d. In vino ii s. vi d. In cervisia ii s. viii d. ob. In allece xvi d. In luceo ii s. In lampereda xiii d. In ostreis xii d. In darsis viii d. In ovis i d. In potagio i ob. In cimino ii d. In ii lib. cere ix d. In luminio i ob. In discis x d. ob. In litterio xi d. In v sumis avene vi s. viii d. Butevilem' xii d. In una summa bladi furnienda iii d. ob. In batello ii d. ob. Summa xxvi s. ix d.

Die martis in carnibus xii d. Homini Gaufridi Clerici eunti in Dorset' vi d. In batello i d. Summa xix d.

Die mercurii in allece iii d. In merlengo iii d. In pastillis faciendis iii ob. In batello ii d. Summa . . . . .

Die jovis \ in cervisia iii ob. / In carne vaccina viii d. In lardo i d. In batello iii o. . . . .

In vi sumis ordei xvi s. viii d. . . . . .

In avena x s. iii d. pro brasio faciendo . . . . .

Die veneris in pane ix d. In cervisia iiii d. In allece iiii d. In plaicis iiii d. H. . . . . Justiciari*o* vi d. In batello ii d. In ii luceis ad exennium domino P. Wint' faciendum xl. . . . . In una scala ii d. ob. In ollis ii d. . . . . .

In expensis prioris Dunolm' per iiii dies excepto quinto die dum fuit apud Lond' . . . . .

Hoppessort iii s. . . . . .

Die sabbati ante festum Sancti Clementis in pane v d. ob. In cervisia iii d. ob. In allece v d. In . . . . . haddoc*o* v d. In sperlingo ii d. In ovis i d. In butiro iii ob. In ii lib. cere ix d. . . . . . ob. In fixes i d. In una suma bladi furnienda iii d. ob. In ii sumis avene iii s. i d. In batello i d. Summa . . . . .

Die dominica in cervisia v d. In carne bovina xx. . . d. In potagio i ob. In una uncia croci vi d. In pipere i d. <In> Joppe sequenti priorem Dunelm' i d. In elemosina i ob. Summa iii s.

Die lune in pane vi d. In cervisia vii d. In potagio i ob. In cordis i ob. In ovis i ob. Homini Willelmi de Norton' vi d. Summa xx d. ob.

Priori Westm' pro carta prioris \ Dunelm' / C m. apud ipsum deposita in sequestro. <adquietando> Summa C m.

Die martis in pane xii d. In vino ii s. In cervisia viii d. In carne vaccina xii d. In porcheto iiii d. ob. In pluveris ix d. In perdicis xii d. In lardo i d. In potagio i ob. In pipere i d. In ovis i d. In ferura v d. In portacione iiii

[4] Erasure.

summarum frumenti ad brasium faciendum \ iii d. / In ii sumis avene xxxii d. ob. Summa x s. v d. ob.
Die mercurii in pane iii s. i d. In cervisia x d. In vino vi s. ii d. In amigdalis vi d. In mulvello ii s. x d. In salmone vi s. In luceo di. m. In anguillis xviii d. In ostreis vi d. In sperlingo vi d. In ovis i d. In pipere ii s. In ii lib. cere ix d. ob. In ferura iiii d. Waggestaf' istrioni iii d. Coco iiii d.
Summa xxxii s. iii d. ob.
Eodem die In di. suma frumenti xxviii d. ob. Magistro Willelmo eunti in nuncio domini ad wardm*ote* ii s. Summa iiii s. iiii d. ob.
\ Die jovis magistro Waltero eunti apud Luton ad placitum domini iii s. Summa iii s. /
Die jovis in vino vi d. In cervisia iiii d. In carne bovina vii d. In volatili iii d. In potagio i ob. In pastillis faciendis ii d. In una summa ordei xxxiii d. In companagio servientum de Willesden' iiii d. Summa iiii s. xi d. ob.
Die veneris in cervisia iiii d. In allece iiii d. In luceo iiii d. In haddogo vii d. In ollis i ob. In candela i ob. <In> Lotrici ii d. Cuidam femine qui paravit exitus xiiii porcorum iiii d. Summa ii s. ii d.
In iii sumis avene iii s. vii d. Summa iii s. vii d.
Die sabbati \ in festo Sancti Andree / in cervisia v d. In pane iiii d. In allece v d. In haddogo vii d. In ovis i d. Domine Avicie xiiii d. et Sabille xiiii d. Et in ferro et calibe ad caruc*am* de Willesden' vi d. Summa iiii s. vi d.
Die dominica in pane x d. In cervisia v d. In carne vaccina xv d. In porcheto iiii d. In gallinis iii d. ob. In potagio i ob. In ovis i ob. <In>
Summa iii s. ii d. ob.
Domino Martino de Poteshill' pro abbate de Middilton' ii m. Summa ii m.
In cyphis acquietandis pro Willelmo cissore domini regis in judaismo xx s. Summa xx s.
Die lune in cervisia v d. In potagio i ob. In pisce iii d. In ferura iii d. In candela i ob. In uno capistro ii d. ob. In una summa bladi furnienda iii d. ob. In ii lib. cere contra festum Sancti Nicholai ix d. Summa ii s. iii d.
Die martis in cervisia vii d. ob. In vino vi d. In carne vaccina x d. In perdicis v d. In lardo i d. In ovis i d. In potagio i ob. In ferura iii d. In batello ii d. In candela i ob. Summa iii s. <ix d.> ob.
Die mercurii in pane i ob. In cervisia viii d. In vino vi d. In allece v d. ob. In ostreis ii d. In mulvello vii d. ob. In darsis iii d. ob. In ovis i d. In batello ii d. ob. In ii lib. cere ix d. ob. Summa iii s. x d.
Die jovis in cervisia vi d. In potagio i ob. In candela i d. In una auga portanda de hospicio Jacobi i ob. In iiii sumis avene v s. Summa v s. viii d.
Die veneris in festo Sancti Nicholai in pane xviii d. In cervisia viii d. In allece vi d. In vino iii d. In mulvello x d. ob. In sperlingo iiii d. In ostreis iiii d. In oblacione xii d. In candela i ob. Summa v s. vi d.
Die sabbati in pane xi d. In cervisia viii d. In allece v d. In mulvello vii d.

ob. In ovis ii d. In ferura ii d. In candela i d. In una summa bladi furnienda iii d. ob. Lotrici ii d. Summa iii s. vi d.

Die dominica in cervisia v d. In potagio i ob. Summa v d. ob.

Die lune in vino vi d. In cervisia v d. In potagio i ob. In pisce iii d. In ferura ii d. In candela i d. <In> Tidewell' eunti in nuncium domini versus partes boreales viii d. ad expendendum et iiii d. ad sotulares. Homini Elye de Linc' iii d. Summa ii s. viii d. ob.

Die martis in cervisia vi d. In vino iii d. In potagio i ob. In candela i d. In farina ad anduillam faciendam ii d. In ii lib. cere ix d. In i summa avene xiiii d. Summa ii s. xi d. ob.

In i furura ad capam domini viii s. Summa viii s.

Die mercurii in cervisia viii d. In vino iii d. In allece vi d. In mulvello vii d. In lampereda iii d. In candela i d. In ferris et in clavis vi d. Summa ii s. x d.

In iii huciis ii s. ix d. In i auga empta xviii d. Summa iiii s. iii d.

Die jovis in pane iii ob. In cervisia viii d. In ovis ii d. In potagio i ob. In batello i d. In forcero et costerillo reparandis ii d. In cingulo i d. Cuidam qui tulit i augam i ob. In candela i d. In pisce iii ob. Summa xix d.

In xi bobus occidendis et salendis xxii d. In xl multonibus occidendis xx d. In xiiii porcis similiter occidendis vii d. In exitibus eorum preparandis[5] vii d. Summa iiii s. viii d.

Die veneris in pane xii d. In vino iii d. In cervisia v d. In allece v d. In mulvello xii d. In lampereda iii d. In auc*is* ii d. ob. In ii[6] lib. cere xv d. In luminio i ob. In candela i d. Summa iiii s. xi d.

\ In uno bove occidendo et carne removenda de salsacione iiii d. Summa iiii d./

In lucro ad capam domini urlandam xviii d. In iiii sumis frumenti xix s. i d. In sella sumeria reparanda ii s. Summa xxii s. vii d.

Die sabbati in cervisia vii d. In vino iii d. In alleche v d. In haddoco vii d. In butiro iii ob. In ovis i d. In ferris et clavis vi d. In cingulo ad sellam sumariam i d. In curvis ad . . .illum faciendum iii d. In alba candela i d. In i suma frumenti fornienda iii d. ob. Summa iii s. iii d.

[Eo]dem die in xvii ulnis et di. burrelli ad robis garcionum xii s. iiii d. ob. In busca empta de domina Avicia ad brasium siccandum iii s. In iiii paribus cirotecarum ad opus domini iiii d. Summa xv s.[7] viii d. et ob.

Die dominica in pane i ob. In cervisia vi d. In vo\la/tili viii d. In potagio i ob. In candela i d. Summa xvi d.

Weatte eunti usque Dorset' ad Walterum de Segny. Summa vi d.

Die lune in cervisia vii d. In vino iii d. In potagio i ob. In farina ii d. ad

[5] MS 'reparandis'.

[6] Possibly 'iii'.

[7] 'ii' of 'xv<ii>' erased.

budingum faciendum. In pane v d. In sotularibus Grunkil iiii d. In pastillis faciendis i ob. In una summa avene xvi d. In l*i*cor' ii d. Summa iii s. iiii d. Thome Bukerell' pro magistro Ricardo de Garring' xvi s. In una penula ad opus magistri Walteri vi s. Domine Avicie pro uno tonello cervisie v s. *Atero* clerico di. m. Summa xxxiii s. viii d.

Summa iiii^{xx} et <xvi> vii li. xv s. x d.

4 *Expenses of the household of Bristol Castle, including those for the household of Eleanor of Brittany, 7 June 1225 to 6 March 1226*

Bristol Castle was one of the key strategic points in Henry III's kingdom and expenditure on the castle was extensive. A barbican was added in the early 1220s and the keep was considered by contemporaries one of the most impressive fortifications to be seen in England. It was here that Eleanor of Brittany spent many years of her imprisonment. Eleanor was the sister of Arthur of Brittany and the daughter of Constance and Geoffrey, son of Henry II. She was captured by King John after the defeat of her brother, Arthur, at Mirebeau in July 1202, concluding his attempt to control (under Philip Augustus of France) the whole of the Angevin dominions in France. Arthur was murdered in 1203 and Eleanor was taken to England. She remained in custody, at various locations, for the rest of her life; she was at Bristol from 1224 until 1234 and subsequently from 1238 or 1239 until her death in 1241.[1]

The household of the castle was increased to look after her and at the date of the account Eleanor was in the charge of Ralph de Wiliton.[2] Letters close of 9 October 1224 instructed the bailiffs of Bristol and four responsible citizens to visit the castle once or twice a week to ensure her safe custody and, at the end of each week, to hear, in the presence of Ralph de Wiliton, the account for the expenses of Eleanor and others staying in the castle. Ralph was to have one copy of the account roll, the citizens another. Further instructions were given in March 1225.[3] The account for 1225–6 is more elaborate than the two other accounts that survive for the household

[1] *History of the King's works* i, p. 119; ii, p. 578; A. L. Poole *From Domesday Book to Magna Carta* (2nd edition, Oxford, 1955) pp. 378–82; F. M. Powicke *King Henry III and the Lord Edward* (2 vols., Oxford, 1947) i, p. 177, n. 1; *idem*, *The loss of Nomandy 1189–1240* (2nd edition, Manchester, 1961) p. 151; *Accounts of the constables of Bristol Castle in the thirteenth and early fourteenth centuries* ed. M. Sharp (Bristol Record Society, 34; 1982) pp. xxvii-xxix.

[2] *Accounts of the constables of Bristol Castle* p. xxxv.

[3] *Rot. Lit. Claus.* i, p. 649; ii, p. 71.

at Bristol Castle for 1221–2[4] and it provides the most extensive detailed account for household expenses that can be directly related to an identifiable individual at this date. It is a roll of three narrow membranes, sewn Chancery fashion. Sewing holes at the head of the first membrane indicate that it is incomplete, with at least one membrane missing. The roll is a fair copy of the weekly account that would have been heard by the bailiffs and men of Bristol, and it would have been submitted by De Wiliton to support his account at the Exchequer for his expenses on the castle.[5] The surviving part was written in a single operation, rather than piecemeal through the year, principally by two hands, including the daily and weekly cash totals. A further set of totals was added at the end of each week for the quantity of wheat baked for bread, for beef and pigs, for oats for the cart-horses, for cheeses, for wax and for almonds. These totals were added to the roll subsequently, collated from different sources, in some cases by other clerks; all the totals for wax are in the hand of another clerk, those for almonds in the hand of another. The addition on the roll is difficult to reconcile in a number of places and some of this may be the fault of the clerks transcribing the fair copy. There is no sign of auditors working on the roll and the dorse is devoid of contemporary notes.

PRO E 101/350/11

Membrane 1 recto

Die sabbati cervisia xii d. Congrus vi d. In ovis x d. In lacte i d. In farrina i d. In minutione domine ii d. Oblatio i d. In marrescaucia ii s. vi d. Summa v s. iii d.

Die dominica cervisia iiii d. Panis iii d. In bove ii s. In lacte ii d. In serra ad buscam i d. Oblatio i d. In marrescaucia ii s. vi d. Summa v s. v d.

Die lune cervisia iiii d. Panis iiii d. In pullis xi d. ob. Lacte ii d. Vinum acidum iiii d. In multone iii d. In cepo iiii d. Oblatio i d. Marrescaucia ii s. vi d. Summa v s. ii d. ob.

Die martis cervisia vi d. Panis iii d. In bove viii d. In pullis iiii d. ob. In ovis xii d. Lacte ii d. Oblatio i d. Marrescaucia ii s. vi d. Summa v s. vi d. ob.

Die mercurii cervisia xii d. Panis iii d. ob. Salmones et anguille xvi d. Caseus iiii d. Piper vii d. Saffran vii d. Scalones ob. Lacte ii d. Flundre i d. Buttirum iiii d. Oblatio i d. Marrescaucia ii s. vi d. Summa vii s. iiii d.

[4] PRO E101/349/4, E101/350/10.

[5] The enrolment on the Pipe Roll of the account for 1224–5, *Accounts of the constables of Bristol Castle* p. 6, gives the expenses of Eleanor of Brittany as £178. 5*s*. 7*d*., 1*d*. less than the total of the account edited here; there may have been some confusion between the accounts for the two years.

Die jovis cervisia iiii d. Panis iii d. In bove et multone xvii d. In ovis vii d. Pulli vii d. Lacte ii d. ob. Oblatio i d. Marescaucia ii s. vi d. Summa v s. . . . . .
Die veneris cervisia iiii d. Hake xviii d. Salmo xii d. Flundre et anguille iiii d. ob. In vino acido iiii d. In turbutto iiii d. In amigdalis iiii d. In ovis ii s. Oblatio i d. Marrescaucia ii s. vi d. Item in avena ad caretarios xxii d. Fenum ii d. Ferrura ii d. Carbo vi d. Portatoribus cervisie v d. ob. In lumine i d. In saccis emendandis i d. In tribus porcis emptis iii s. viii d. In xii aucis xv d. Summa xvii s.

Summa li s. viii d. ob.

In pane per predictam septimanam vi crannoci frumenti de instauro et i crannocus frumenti de empcione de turri. Item ii boves et di. et i baco. Et ii casei.
Die[1] sabbati cervisia xii d. Farina i d. Congrus xii d. Salmo viii d. In lacte i d. Anguille ii d. Scalones i d. In caseo vii d. ob. In minutione domicelle domine i d. Oblatio i d. In marescaucia ii s. vi d. Summa vi s. iiii d. ob.
Die dominica cervisia iiii d. Panis iii d. In bove xi d. Pulli xix d. ob. In mustardo iii d. In lacte ii d. Oblatio i d. Marescaucia ii s. vi d. Summa vi s. iii ob.
Die lune cervisia vi d. Panis iii d. In bove xviii d. In sagimine iiii d. In ovis x d. Lac ii d. Oblatio i d. Marescaucia ii s. vi d. Summa vi s. . . . d.
Die martis cervisia iiii d. Panis iii d. In vino acido iiii d. In lacte ii d. In piso i d. Oblatio i d. Marescaucia ii s. vi d. Summa iii s. ix d.
Die mercurii cervisia xii d. Panis ii d. ob. Hake xviii d. In ovis x d. Salmo x d. Anguille iii d. Butirum ii d. ob. Scalones i d. In lacte ii d. Oblatio i d. In marescaucia ii s. vi d. Summa vii s. ix d.
Die jovis cervisia iiii d. Panis iii d. In bove x d. In lacte ii d. Scutelle xiiii d. Pulli viii d. In piso i d. In vino acido iiii d. Oblatio i d. Marescaucia ii s. vi d. Summa vi s. v d.
Die veneris cervisia iiii d. Panis i d. Hake xx d. Salmo et turbuttus et soile xviii d. In ovis viii d. ob. Portitoribus cervisie vi d. Oblatio i d. In marescaucia ii s. vi d. Item in feno ad kareccarios v d. Ferrura iii d. Carbo vi d. Auce xv d. Summa ix s. ix d. ob.

Summa xlvi s. iii d. ob.

Item ii boves et di. et i baco. Et ii casei. In pane per predictam septimanam vii crannoci frumenti de instauro. Et i qr. avene ad kareccarios.
Die sabbati cervisia xii d. Panis iii d. Congrus x d. Lac et fabe vi d. Butirum ii d. In vino acido iiii d. In ovis viii d. ob. In i potella emendanda i d. Allia ii d. Scalones i d. Amigdale ii d. Oblatio i d. In marescaucia ii s. vi d. Summa vi s. x d. ob.
Die dominica cervisia iiii d. Panis iii d. \ ob. / Boves xiii d. Porcus i d. Lac

[1] This day's entry, except the total, is in a different hand.

ii d. ob. Pulli xii d. Piper vii d. Picherii iiii d. In piso i d. Oblatio i d. In marescaucia ii s. vi d. Summa vi s. vii d.

Die lune cervisia vi d. Panis i d. Salmo xiii d. Hake xviii d. Amigdale vi d. Flundere et soille iiii d. ob. In ovis xii d. Oblatio i d. In marescaucia ii s. vi d. Summa vii s. vii d. ob.

Die martis cervisia vi d. Panis iiii d. In multone xii d. Fabe iii d. Lac ii d. ob. In vino acido iiii d. Oblatio ii d. In marescaucia ii s. vi d. Summa v s. iii d. ob.

Die mercurii cervisia xii d. Panis iii d. Salmo x d. Caseus v d. Scalones et farina ii d. Lac ii d. In pullis iiii^or d. Butirum ii d. Oblatio i d. Marescaucia ii s. vi d. Summa v s. xi d. ob.

Die jovis cervisia iiii d. Panis iii d. In bove ii s. In multone x d. Pulli v d. Fabe et lac v d. ob. Lardum v d. ob. Item pulli iii d. Oblatio i d. Marescaucia ii s. vi d. Summa vii s. vii d.

Die veneris cervisia iiii d. Panis i d. Hake ii s. iiii d. Salmo xi d. Piper vii d. Safran vii d. In doliis circulandis iii d. ob. Oblatio i d. In marescaucia ii s. vi d. In vino acido iiii d. Ciminum ii d. Amigdale vi d. Fabe v d. In buletello x d. Item in herba ad kareccarios vi d. Ferrura iiii d. In carbone vi d. Portitoribus cervisie v d. ob. In serura medie porte emendanda i d. Summa xi s. x d.

Summa li s. ix d.

In pane per predictam septimanam vii crannoci frumenti de instauro. Item ii boves et i baco de instauro. Et i caseus. Et i qr. avene ad kareccarios.

Die sabbati scilicet vigilia Sanctorum apostolorum Petri et Pauli cervisia x d. Panis i d. Hake ii s. Congrus xviii d. Salmo xii d. Amigdale iiii d. Fabe v d. In ovis ii d. ob. Pastilli ii d. Item in ovis xvi d. ob. Oblatio i d. In marescaucia ii s. vi d. Summa x s. vi d.

Die dominica cervisia vi d. Panis iii d. In multone x d. In caponibus vi d. In xii aucis xv d. Fabe iii d. Lac ii d. ob. Oblatio ii d. In marescaucia ii s. vi d. Summa vi s. v d. ob.

Die lune cervisia vi d. Panis iii d. Pulli vii d. ob. Fabe et lac v d. ob. Olla ob. Sal iii d. ob. In vino acido iiii d. Oblatio i d. In marescaucia ii s. vi d. Summa v s. i d.

Die martis cervisia iiii d. Panis iii d. In bove xiii d. In multone x d. Porcus v d. ob. Fabe iii d. In piso i d. In ovis xvi d. ob. Pulli x d. Oblatio i d. In marescaucia ii s. vi d. Summa viii s. i d.

Die mercurii cervisia xii d. Panis i d. Hake xiiii d. Salmo xi d. Butirum ii d. Scalones ob. Fabe iiii d. ob. In piso i d. Oblatio i d. Marescaucia ii s. vi d. Summa vi s. v d.

Die jovis cervisia iiii d. Panis iiii d. In bove viii d. Pulli iiii d. Porcus v d. Sagimine[2] ii d. Fabe iii d. In vino acido iiii d. In carbone vii d. Oblatio i d. In marescaucia ii s. vi d. Summa vi s.

[2] MS omits 'In'.

Die veneris cervisia iiii d. Panis iiii d. Salmo xiii d. Congrus xiiii d. Hake xii d. Amigdale vi d. Ciphi iii d. Portitoribus cervisie vi d. Oblatio i d. In marescaucia ii s. vi d. Item in herba ad kareccarios vii d. F*errura* i d. In i cuva emendanda i d. In tackis ad kareccas xi d. In i securi ad idem xii d. In sepo ii d. Summa xi s. i d.

Summa liii s. vii d. ob.

In pane per predictam septimanam vii crannoci frumenti de instauro. Item ii boves et i baco. Et ii casei. Et i qr. avene ad kareccarios.

Die sabbati cervisia xii d. Panis ob. Congrus v d. Soile ii d. ob. Butirum iii ob. In ovis xvi d. ob. Oblatio i d. In marescaucia ii s. vi d. \ In plaiccis portatis viii d. / Summa vi s. v d. ob.

Die dominica cervisia iiii d. Panis ii d. In bove vi d. Pulli ix d. In vi multonibus v s. Porcus v d. ob. Piper vii d. In vino acido iiii d. Pastilli iii ob. In oblatione i d. In marescaucia ii s. vi d. Summa x s. x d.

Die lune cervisia vi d. Panis iii d. In bove vi d. Porcus ix d. In junco iii ob. Picherii i d. Oblatio i d. In marescaucia ii s. vi d. Summa iiii s. ix d. ob.

Die martis cervisia vi d. Panis iii d. Porcus iii ob. Pulli iiii d. Oblatio i d. In marescaucia ii s. vi d. Summa iii s. ix d. ob.

Die[3] mercurii cervisia x d. Panis iii d. Hake xii d. Salmo xi d. Sole iiii d. Butirum ii d. Ova viii d. ob. Pisum ii d. In manumolendino iiii d. Oblatione[4] i d. Marescaucia ii s. vi d. Summa vii s. iii ob.

Die jovis cervisia iiii d. Panis ii d. Porcus et lardum iiii d. Pulli iiii d. ob. In ovis iiii d. ob. Caseus viii d. \ ob. / Oblatio i d. Marescaucia ii s. vi d. Summa iiii s. x d.

Die veneris cervisia iiii d. Panis i d. Congrus xiii d. Salmo viii d. Sole iii d. In ovis iiii d. ob. In piso ii d. In vino acido iiii d. In amigdalis vi d. Oblatio i d. Mariscaucia ii s. vi d. Portitoribus cervisie v d. ob. Item in herba ad carecarios vii d. In avena xxi d. In carbone vii d. In lumine i d. In sepo ii d. Summa x s.

Summa xlviii s. iii d.

In pane per predictam septimanam vii crannoci frumenti de instauro. Item i bos[5] et i baco. Et ii casei. Et di. qr. avene ad kareccarios.

Summa lvii li. xiii d.

Die sabbati cervisia xii d. Panis i d. Anguille et sole vii d. Casseus iiii d. Fabe iii d. ob. In ovis ix d. Butirum ii d. Amigdale iiii d. In junco ii d. Oblatio i d. In marescaucia ii s. vi d. Summa vi s. iii d. ob.

[3] The text, but not the totals, of the entries for this day and the following two days, is in another hand.

[4] MS omits 'In'.

[5] MS 'bov''.

Die dominica cervisia vi d. Panis ii d. Pulli xiiii d. ob. In piso i d. In vino acido iiii d. Oblatio i d. In marescaucia ii s. vi d. Summa iiii s. x d. ob.
Die lune cervisia vi d. Panis iii d. In multone xvi d. Porcus x d. Pisum i d. Piper vii d. Safran vii d. Costrelli vii d. In oblatione i d. In marescaucia ii s. vi d. Summa vii s. iiii d.
Die martis cervisia iiii d. Panis iii ob. Porcus iii d. Boves vi d. Pulli ii d. In iiii^or^ multonibus iii s. viii d. In ovis ii d. ob. In oblatione i d. In marescaucia ii s. vi d. Summa vii s. x d.
Die mercurii cervisia xii d. Panis i d. Hake xii d. Sole iii d. In piso iii ob. Butirum iii ob. Amigdale iiii d. Oblatio i d. In marescaucia ii s. vi d. Summa v s. vi d.
Die jovis cervisia iiii d. Panis iii ob. Porcus iii d. In multone xv d. In ovis v d. Auce vi d. In ovis xviii d. Oblatio i d. In marescaucia ii s. vi d. Summa vi s. xi d. ob.
Die veneris cervisia iiii d. Panis iii ob. Congrus xiii d. Salmo et barsa x d. Pisum iii d. In ovis v d. Scalones iii ob. Amigdale iiii d. Oblatio i d. Marescaucia ii s. vi d. Portitoribus cervisie vi d. In avena ad kareccarios ii s. vi d. Herba vii d. Ferrura ii d. Carbo vi d. In doliis vini circulandis v d. ob. Summa x s. ix d. ob.

Summa xlix s. vii d.

In pane per predictam septimanam vii crannoci de instauro. Et ii casei.
Die sabbati cervisia xii d. Panis iii ob. Congrus ix d. Salmo viii d. Sole iiii d. In ovis xi d. ob. Butirum ii d. Amigdale vi d. Caseus i d. In juncis iii ob. Item in amigdalis ii d. Oblatio i d. In marescaucia ii s. vi d. Summa vii s. v d. ob.
Die dominica cervisia iiii d. Panis i d. In bove xix d. In v multonibus iiii s. vi d. Pulli v d. ob. Galline iii d. In ovis vii d. \ ob. / Oblatio i d. Marescaucia ii s. vi d. Summa x s. v d.
Die lune in cervisia vi d. Panis iii ob. In multone ii s. iii d. ob. Pulli xiii d. ob. Columbelle iiii d. Pisum iii d. ob. In ovis iiii d. Oblatio i d. Marescaucia ii s. vi d. Summa vii s. vii d.
Die martis cervisia iiii^or^ d. Panis iii d. ob. In multone xviii d. Pulli iiii d. Boves iii d. ob. In ovis iii d. . . . . . vii d. . . . . . In piso ii d. Item in pane iiii d. In lumine i d. Oblatio iiii d. Marescaucia ii s. vi d. Summa vii s. ii d. ob.
Die mercurii cervisia xiii d. Panis i d. Hake xvi d. Sole et anguille vii d. ob. Salmo vi d. Caseus iii d. In ovis iii ob. In piso i d. Amigdale ii d. Oblatio i d. In marescaucia ii s. vi d. Summa vi s. ix d.
Die jovis cervisia iiii d. Panis i d. In congro et brennis ii s. Allecia xvii d. Amigdale ii d. Pisum i d. In ovis xv d. Oblatio i d. Marescaucia \ ii s. vi d./ Summa vii s. xi . . .
Die veneris scilicet die Sancti Jacobi apostoli cervisia iiii d. Panis iii ob. Allecia xiiii d. Salmo xiii d. Congrus viii d. Amigdale iiii d. Pisum i d. In

vino acido iiii d. Oblatio iii d. In marescaucia ii s. vi d. Portitoribus cervisie vi d. ..... In avena ad kareccarios ii s. x d. In feno ii d. ob. Ferura ii d. Summa x s. x d. ...

lviii s. ii d.

In pane per predictam septimanam vii crannoci frumenti de instauro. Et ii casei.

Die sabbati scilicet in crastino Sancti Jacobi apostoli cervisia xii d. Panis iii ob. Allecia xiiii d. Congrus v d. In ovis v d. Amigdale iiii d. Pisum i d. Scutelle xv d. In dignerio constabularii et sociorum suorum apud Caln' xi d. Oblatio i d. Marescaucia ii s. Summa vii s. ix d. ob.

Die dominica cervisia vi d. Panis iii d. In multone ii s. iii d. Porcus xiiii d. In ovis ix d. ob. Pulli x d. ob. Pisum i d. Lardum i d. Oblatio i d. Marescaucia ii s. Summa viii s. i d.

Die lune cervisia iiii d. Panis i d. In multone ii s. Boves x d. Porcus iii d. ob. In ovis x d. Pulli ix d. Lardum vi d. Pisum i d. Oblatio i d. Marescaucia ii s. Summa vii s. ix d. ob.

Die martis cervisia iiii d. Panis ii d. ob. Porcus x d. Pulli vii d. Pastilli iiii d. In ovis v d. Piper vii d. Pisum i d. Oblatio i d. In marescaucia ii s. Summa v s. v d. ob.

Die mercurii cervisia x d. In pane xiii d. ob. ad opus domine. Allecia xii d. Congrus x d. Salmo x d. In ovis v d. Farina i d. Lac i d. Butirum ii d. In carbone ix d. Amigdale iiii d. In sepo iiii d. Oblatio i d. In marescaucia ii s. Summa viii s. x d. ob.

Die jovis cervisia iiii d. Panis iii ob. In x multonibus viii s. i d. Boves xii d. Porcus vi d. In ovis xv d. Columbelle v d. ob. In ii manutergiis ad opus domine ii s. Oblatio i d. In marescaucia ii s. Summa xv s. x d.

Die veneris cervisia iiii d. Panis iii ob. Congrus xiiii d. Hake viii d. Sole v d. In vino acido iiii d. Oblatio i d. In marescaucia ii s. Item in avena ad kareccarios ii s. iiii d. Fenum iiii d. Ferrura ii d. Portitoribus cervisie v d. ob. Amigdale vi d. In pane v d. ad opus Mathei de Wellop. Summa ix s. iiii d.

Summa lxiii s. ii d.

In pane per predictam septimanam vi crannoci frumenti de instauro. Et ii casei.

Die sabbati scilicet in crastino Sancti Petri ad vincula cervisia x d. Panis iii ob. Congrus viii d. Allecia et sole vii d. Amigdale vi d. Butirum ii d. In piso i d. In ovis xix d. In sepo iii d. ob. Oblatio i d. In marescaucia ii s. Summa vi s. xi d.

Die dominica cervisia iiii d. Panis ii d. In bove xix d. In multone xi d. ob. Porcus v d. Pulli vi d. Item pulli iiii d. ob. In egrecco iii ob. Oblatio i d. Marescaucia ii s. Summa vi s. vi d. ob.

Die lune cervisia vi d. Panis iii d. In multone ix d. Porcus xiii d. Pulli x d.

Pisum ii d. In vino acido iiii d. Oblatio i d. In marescaucia ii s. Summa vi s.
Die martis cervisia iiii d. Panis ii d. Porcus xvii d. Pulli vi d. In ovis v d. Piper vii d. Safran viii d. Sal iii d. ob. Oblatio i d. In marescaucia ii s. Summa vi s. v d. ob.
Die mercurii cervisia x d. Panis iii ob. Allecia xii d. Amigdale iiii d. Sole vii d. Perche vi d. Anguille v d. In ovis x d. Allia ii d. Farina i d. Lac i d. Butirum iii ob. Oblatio i d. In marescaucia ii s. Summa vii s. ii d.

Membrane 2 recto

Die jovis cervisia vi d. Panis ii d. ob. Multones xviii d. Porcus xiii d. Pulli ix d. In vino acido iiii d. Lac et pisum ii d. Carbo vii d. In volatilibus iii ob. Oblatio i d. In marescaucia ii s. Summa vii s. iiii d.
Die veneris cervisia iiii d. Panis iii ob. Congrus xii d. Hake xiiii d. In brennis viii d. Sole ii d. Pisum i d. Pastilli ii d. Oblatio i d. In marescaucia ii s. Item in avena ad kareccarios ii s. xi d. Fenum iiii d. Ferrura iii d. Portitoribus cervisie v d. ob. In expensis Mathei de Wellop infirmi x d. ob. Amigdale vi d. Summa xi s. iii ob.

Summa li s. vi d. ob.

In pane per predictam septimanam vi crannoci frumenti de instauro. Et ii casei.
Die sabbati cervisia x d. Panis iii ob. Congrus vi d. Salmo x d. In ovis ix d. Amigdale iiii d. Lac et farina ii d. In egrecco iii ob. Oblatio i d. In marescaucia ii s. Summa v s. ix d.
Die[6] dominica cervisia iiii d. Panis ii d. ob. Porcus x d. In piris et pomis iii d. Pulli v^{que} d. ob. Lardum i d. In v^{que} multonibus v^{que} s. v^{que} d. Oblatio ii d. Mariscaucia ii s. Summa ix s. ix d.
Die lune cervisia vi d. Panis i d. Porcus iii d. ob. In ovis x d. Lac ob. In melle iii d. Oblatio i d. Marescaucia ii s. Summa iiii s. i d.
Die martis cervisia iiii d. Panis i d. Porcus v d. In sagimine xv d. In ovis x d. Piper vii d. In vino acido iiii d. In egrecco ob. In caseo vii d. ob. Oblatio i d. Marescaucia ii s. Summa vi s. vii d.
Die mercurii cervisia x d. Panis i d. In brennis xiii d. In mulez viii d. Congrus x d. In ovis ix d. In amigdalis vi d. In butiro iii ob. Pastilli iii d. Allia ii d. In uno cribro ad coquinam i d. Oblatio i d. Marescaucia ii s. Summa vii s. v d. ob.
Die jovis cervisia iiii d. Panis i d. Congrus viii d. Allecia xx d. Perche ii d. Fabe et pisum iii d. Oblatio i d. Marescaucia ii s. Summa v s. iii d.
Die veneris cervisia iiii d. Panis ob. Congrus xviii d. Sole iiii d. Amigdale i d. In ovis iii ob. Pisum i d. Sal ii s. i d. In vino acido iiii d. Oblatio ii d. Marescaucia ii s. Item in avena ad karecarios xviii d. Ferrura iii d.

[6] New hand from the start of this day.

Portitoribus cervisie v d. In carbone v d. In axe et harnesio karecarum reparandis ii s. ix d. Summa xii s. vi d.

Summa li s. iiii d. ob.

In pane per predictam septimanam vi crannoci frumenti de instauro. Et ii casei.

Die sabbati scilicet in crastino Assumpcionis Beate Marie cervisia x d. Panis iii ob. Sole iii ob. Amigdale vi d. Butirum ii d. In ovis iiii d. ob. Oblatio \ i / d. Marescaucia ii s. Summa iiii s. ii d. ob.

Die dominica cervisia iiii d. Panis ob. In multone iii s. vi d. Porcus vi d. Pulli xviii d. In ovis v d. Lardum iii d. Oblatio i d. Marescaucia ii s. Summa viii s. vii d. ob.

Die lune cervisia vi d. Panis i d. In bove vii s. iiii d. Porcus vii d. Mel iii d. ob. In vino acido iiii d. Oblatio i d. Marescaucia ii s. Summa xi s. ii d. ob.

Die martis cervisia iiii d. Panis i d. Porcus iii d. In ovis ix d. In egrecco ob. Oblatio i d. Mareschacia ii s. Summa iii s. vi d. ob.

Die mercurii cervisia x d. Panis iii ob. Allecia viii d. Congrus vii d. Sole et anguille v d. Amigdale vi d. In ovis iiii d. ob. Oblatio i d. Marescaucia ii s. Summa v s. vii d.

Die jovis cervisia iiii d. Panis iii ob. Porcus iiii d. ob. In ovis ix d. ob. Piper vii d. Mel iii d. ob. Oblatio i d. Marescaucia ii s. Summa iiii s. vii d.

Die veneris cervisia iiii d. Panis iii ob. Congrus x d. Sole et anguille vii d. Allecia xviii d. Amigdale vi d. Oblatio i d. Marescaucia ii s. Item in avena ad karecarios xxii d. In carbone iiii d. Portitoribus cervisie v d. ob. In picheriis ob. Summa viii s. vii d. ob.

Summa xlvi s. iiii d. ob.

In pane per predictam septimanam vi crannoci frumenti de instauro. Et ii casei.

Die sabbati cervisia x d. Panis iii ob. Salmo ix d. Anguille v d. Pastilli iii d. In ovis ix d. Amigdale vi d. Allia ii d. ob. Oblatio i d. Marescaucia ii s. Summa v s. xi d.

Die dominica cervisia iiii d. Panis i d. In bove xiiii d. Porcus xvii d. In multone xxiii d. Pulli vi d. Mel iii d. In eggrecco i d. Oblatio i d. Marescaucia ii s. Summa vii s. x d.

Die lune cervisia vi d. \ Panis / ob. In multone vii d. ob. Porcus ii d. In ovis ix d. Ciminum ii d. In vino acido iiii d. In clavuris \ ad portam / versus villam iii ob. Oblatio i d. Mariscaucia ii s. Summa iiii s. ix d. ob.

Die martis cervisia iiii d. Panis ii d. ob. In multone xx d. ob. Porcus xii d. In sagimine iiii d. ob. Saffran vii d. Oblatio i d. Marescaucia ii s. Summa vi s. iii d. ob.

Die mercurii cervisia x d. Panis i d. Allecia ix d. In brennis ix d. Solle ii d. ob. In ovis ix d. Caseus iiii d. In lacce i d. In una serrura ad coquinam i d. In i culur iii ob. Oblatio i d. Marescaucia ii s. Summa vi s. i d.

Die jovis cervisia iiii d. Panis i d. Boves viii d. Item in eodem xiii d. Porcus viii d. ob. In ovis iiii d. ob. Oblatio i d. Marescaucia ii s. Summa v s. iiii d.
Die veneris cervisia iiii d. Panis i d. Allecia viii d. Congrus xii d. In brennis ix d. ob. In perche iii ob. Amigdale vi d. In ovis xii d. In egrecco iii d. Oblatio i d. Marescaucia ii s. In avena ad karetarios xxii d. Ferrura vi d. Portitoribus cervisie ii d. ob. In osturis justiciarii iii d.
Summa ix s. vii d. ob.

Summa xlv s. ix d. ob.

Die sabbati in pane per predictam septimanam vi crannoci de instauro. Et ii casei.
Die sabbati cervisia x d. Panis iii ob. Congrus iiii d. Pulli vi d. Piper vii d. Lac et ferina ii d. Solle iii ob. In carbone viii d. In vino acido iiii d. Oblatio i d. Marescaucia ii s. Summa v s. xi d.
Die dominica cervisia iiii d. Panis ob. Boves xiiii d. Porcus xv d. ob. In multone ii s. iii d. Lardum iii d. Pulli vi d. ob. Mel iii d. In sagimine ii d. Oblatio i d. Marescaucia ii s. Summa viii s. iiii d. ob.
Die lune cervisia vi d. Panis i d. In multone xii d. ob. Pulli ix d. ob. In ovis xvii d. In egrecco i d. In sepo iiii d. Oblatio i d. Marescaucia ii s.
Summa vi s. iiii d.
Die martis cervisia iiii d. Panis ob. Boves xiii d. Lardum iii d. In multone xxii d. ob. In egrecco iii ob. Picherii i d. Lumina iii ob. Oblatio i d. Marescaucia ii s. Summa vi s.
Die mercurii cervisia x d. Panis i d. Allecia xviii d. Salmo ix d. In brennis ix d. Butirum ii d. Lac et ferina ii d. Oblatio i d. Marescaucia ii s.
Summa vi s. iiii d.
Die jovis cervisia iiii d. Panis i d. Porcus iii d. ob. Mel iii d. In sagimine iii d. In i tina ad coquinam v d. In carbone vi d. Galline ii d. Oblatio i d. Marescaucia ii s. Summa iiii s. . . . . . d. ob.
Die veneris cervisia iiii d. Panis i d. Congrus x d. In brennis viii d. Solle et anguille v d. ob. Hake ix d. In ovis xvii d. Allecia viii d. In piris i d. Amigdale vi d. Oblatio i d. Marescaucia ii s. Portitoribus cervisie v d. ob. Item in avena ad karecarios xxii d. Fenum et ferrura vii d. Summa x s. ix d.

Summa xlviii s. i d.

In[7] pane per predictam septimanam v crannoci frumenti de instauro. Et ii casei.
Die sabbati cervisia x d. Panis i d. Amigdale iii d. Butirum ii d. Farina et lac ii d. Congrus ii d. Oblatio i d. Marescaucia ii s. Summa iii s. ix d.
Die dominica cervisia iiii d. Panis i d. In multone xxii d. Lardum iii d. ob. In aucis xiiii d. In egrecco iiii d. Pulli vii d. In porco ii s. i d. In sagimine iii d. ob. Oblatio i d. In marescaucia ii s. Summa ix s. i d.

[7] First hand returns.

Die lune cervisia vi d. Panis i d. In multone ii s. vi d. In aucis v d. ob. Porcus ii d. Allia ii d. Item in porco vii d. In minutione domine et domicelle sue ii d. Oblatio i d. In marescaucia ii s. Summa vi s. viii d. ob.
Die martis cervisia iiii d. Panis i d. In bove xix d. In vino accido iiii d. Porcus iii d. Mel iii d. Safran vii d. Piper viii d. In pastillis ii d. In carbone viii d. Oblatio i d. In marescaucia ii s. Summa vi s. xi d.
Die mercurii cervisia x d. Panis ii d. ob. Sole et anguille vi d. In ovis xv d. In lacte ii d. Amigdale iiii d. Oblatio i d. In marescaucia ii s.
Summa v s. iiii d. ob.
Die jovis cervisia iiii d. Panis i d. In multone vii d. Porcus v d. ob. Oblatio i d. In marescaucia ii s. Summa iii s. vi d. ob.
Die veneris cervisia iiii d. Panis i d. Congrus xiiii d. Anguille iii d. Lampreda v d. ob. Amigdale vi d. In egrecco i d. Sole iii d. ob. Oblatio i d. In marescaucia ii s. Item in avena ad kareccarios xxii d. Fenum et ferrura vii d. ob. Summa vii s. viii d. ob.
In i crannoco frumenti ii s. v d.

Summa lv s. vi d.

Et ii casei de instauro.
Die sabbati cervisia x d. Panis i d. Congrus xvi d. Sole et anguille vi d. Amigdale iiii d. In caseo vii d. In ovis iiii d. ob. Oblatio i d. Marescaucia ii s. Summa vi s. iii ob.
Die dominica cervisia iiii d. Panis ob. In bove xix d. In multone ii s. Pulli xv d. Allia i d. In ovis ii d. ob. Mel iii d. Oblatio i d. Marescaucia ii s.
Summa vii s. xi d.
Die lune cervisia iiii d. Panis i d. In multone xiiii d. Lardum et sagimen v d. ob. In egrecco iii ob. Oblatio i d. In marescaucia ii s. Summa iiii s. iii d.
Die martis cervisia iiii d. Panis i d. In multone xvi d. In porco vi d. Mel iii d. In ovis ix d. Oblatio i d. In marescaucia ii s. Summa v s. iiii d.
Die mercurii cervisia x d. Panis i d. Congrus vi d. Lampreda x d. Salmo et sole viii d. ob. Amigdale iiii d. In sepo iiii d. Oblatio i d. Marescaucia ii s. Summa v s. viii d. ob.
Die jovis cervisia iiii d. Panis i d. In multone xiiii d. Lardum iii ob. Vinum acidum iiii d. Sal iii d. ob. Patelle emendande ii d. Oblatio i d. Marescaucia ii s. Summa iiii s. vii d.
Die veneris cervisia vi d. Panis i d. Congrus x d. Hake x d. Amigdale vi d. Oblatio i d. Marescaucia ii s. Item in avena ad kareccarios xxi d. Fenum iiii d. Ferrura iiii d. In scingulis ii d. Carbo viii d. In ponte emendando iii ob. Summa viii s. ii d. ob.
In vi crannocis frumenti xiii s. vi d.

Summa lv s. vii d. ob.

Et ii casei de instauro.
Die sabbati cervisia x d. Panis i d. Hake ix d. Congrus xii d. Amigdale vi d.

In mustardo v d. In D ovis xxii d. ob. In pomis ix d. Anguille v d. Oblatio i d. Marescaucia ii s. Summa viii s. viii d. ob.
Die dominica cervisia iiii d. Panis i d. In bove xxi d. Item in eodem xv d. In sagimine iiii d. Oblatio i d. In marescaucia ii s. Summa v s. x d.
Die lune cervisia vi d. Panis i d. In multone xvi d. Pulli x d. Oblatio i d. In marescaucia ii s. Summa iiii s. x d.
Die martis cervisia iiii d. Panis ob. In multone xiiii d. Piper v d. Allia ii d. ob. In vino acido iiii d. In cultello ob. In lumine i d. In iii lib. cere xvi d. ob. Oblatio i d. In marescaucia ii s. Summa vi s. i d.
Die mercurii cervisia x d. Panis i d. Congrus xi d. Lampreda xii d. Amigdale iiii d. In minutione \ domine / i d. Oblatio i d. In marescaucia ii s. Summa v s. iiii^or d.
Die jovis cervisia iiii d. Panis i d. In bove xiiii d. Porcus iiii d. ob. Pastilli ii d. Oblatio i d. In marescaucia ii s. Summa iiii s. ii d. ob.
Die veneris cervisia iiii d. Panis i d. Ostria et hake xvi d. Anguille ix d. In vi lib. amigdalarum xii d. In lumine i d. Oblatio i d. In marescaucia ii s. Item in avena ad kareccarios xxii d. Fenum iii d. Carbo vii d. Summa viii s. iiii d.
In v crannocis frumenti xi s. iiii d.

Summa liiii s. viii d.

Et ii casei de instauro.
Die sabbati cervisia x d. Hake xiiii d. Congrus xii d. Sal xvi d. ob. Flundre et sole iiii d. ob. In piso i d. In ovis vii d. Piper v d. Oblatio i d. In marescaucia ii s. Summa vii s. xi d.
Die dominica cervisia iiii d. Panis ii d. Pulli ix d. Oblatio i d. In marescaucia ii s. Summa iii s. iiii d.
Die lune cervisia vi d. Panis i d. In carne iii d. Oblatio i d. In marescaucia ii s. Summa ii s. xi d.
Die martis cervisia iiii d. Panis i d. In bove xiii d. Porcus vii d. In balneo domine ii d. ob. Oblatio i d. In marescaucia ii s. Summa iiii s. iiii d. ob.
Die mercurii cervisia vi d. Panis i d. Congrus xii d. Anguille x d. Amigdale vi d. In nucibus i d. In ovis viii d. ob. In iii lib. cere xvi d. ob. Oblatio i d. In marescaucia ii s. Summa vii s. ii d.
Die jovis cervisia x d. Panis i d. In bove xiiii d. Porcus v d. Pulli iiii d. ob. In pomis iii ob. Oblatio i d. In marescaucia ii s. Summa v s. i d.
Die veneris cervisia iiii d. Panis ob. Hake xv d. Lampreda v d. In minuto pisce i d. In ovis iiii d. ob. Safran v d. In panno ad coquinam ii d. Carbo vi d. In vino acido iiii d. Oblatio i d. In marescaucia ii s. Lumina i d. Amigdale iiii d. Summa vi s. v d.
In vi crannocis frumenti xii s. ix d. ob.

Summa l s.

Et ii casei de instauro.
Die sabbati cervisia x d. Panis i d. Congrus xii d. Safran ix d. Lampreda

vi d. Perche ii d. Amigdale iiii d. In piris i d. In ovis ix d. Oblatio i d. In marescaucia ii s. Summa vi s. vii d.
Die dominica cervisia iiii d. Panis i d. In bove ii s. x d. Pulli viii d. ob. Porcus vii d. In pomis ii d. ob. Oblatio i d. In marescaucia ii s. Summa vi s. x d.
Die lune cervisia vi d. Panis i d. Porcus viii d. Oblatio i d. In marescaucia ii s. Summa iii s. iiii d.
Die martis cervisia iiii d. Panis i d. In bove ii s. iiii d. Porcus v d. Pulli vii d. Oblatio i d. In marescaucia ii s. Summa v s. x d.
Die mercurii cervisia x d. Panis i d. Congrus xvii d. Lampreda x d. In ovis v d. Amigdale iiii d. Oblatio i d. Marescaucia ii s. Summa vi s.
Die jovis cervisia vi d. Panis i d. In bove xiiii d. Auce v d. In ovis ii d. Pulli vi d. Carbo v d. Oblatio i d. Marescaucia ii s. Summa v s. iiii d.
Die veneris cervisia iiii d. Panis i d. Congrus xvi d. Makerellus xv d. Lampreda ix d. Amigdale vi d. Piper v d. ob. Oblatio i d. In marescaucia ii s. Item in avena ad kareccarios xviii d. Fenum vi d. ob. Ferrura iii d. In tractibus iii d. In i serura i d. In carbone iiii d. ob. In pane ad opus domine de villa vi d. ob. In iii lib. cere xvi d. ob. In lumine i d. Summa xi s. ix d. ob.
In v crannocis frumenti Summa xi s. iii ob.

Summa lvi s. x d.

Et ii casei de instauro.

In Clii lib. cere	lvii s. x d.
In di. lib. de croco et iiii^{or} lib. de cumino	iii s. vi d.
In xv lib. de pipere	xii s. vi d.
In C et di. et i qr. de amigdalis	xxv s. xi d.
In ii patellis emptis in nundinis Bristoll'	xx d.
In xliiii bobus emptis	viii li. xi s. iii d. ob.
In iiii^{xx} et xviii porcis	vii li. x s. viii d.
In uno dolio vini empto	xxxviii s.

Summa xxiii li. xvi d. ob.
Summa lvii li. viii s. i d.[8]

Die sabbati secunda post festum Sancti Michaelis cervisia x d. Panis iii ob. Congrus xviii d. Salmo et lampreda xxiii d. In ovis ii d. ob. Oblatio i d. Marescaucia ii s. Summa vi s. viii d.
Die dominica cervisia iiii d. Panis i d. Porcus x d. Pulli xiiii d. In vino ad oculos domine iii d. Oblatio i d. In marescaucia ii s. Summa iiii s. ix d.
Die lune cervisia vi d. Panis i d. Boves xiii d. Porcus ix d. In pedibus iii ob. Pulli ix d. In egrecco i d. Oblatio i d. Marescaucia ii s. Summa v s. v d. ob.
Die martis cervisia iiii d. Panis ii d. Porcus xii d. In panno ad piper et

[8] In the same hand as the text, but in a darker ink, i.e. added subsequently.

ciminum reponenda ii d. In ovis iii d. Egrecco iii ob. Oblatio i d. Marescaucia ii s. Summa iiii s. iii ob.
Die mercurii cervisia x d. Panis i d. Congrus xi d. Hake ix d. Salmo vi d. In ovis xvi d. In vino acido iiii d. Oblatio i d. Marescaucia ii s. Summa vi s. x d.
Die jovis cervisia iiii d. Panis ii d. ob. Boves xii d. Porcus xii d. Pulli v d. ob. In egrecco i d. Oblatio i d. In marescaucia ii s. Summa v s. ii d.
Die veneris cervisia vi d. Panis i d. Hake xii d. Raia x d. Lampreda viii d. Anguille viii d. Allia ii d. Oblatio i d. In marescaucia ii s. Item in avena ad kareccarios xiiii d. Fenum ii d. Ferrura iii d. In carbone xiii d. ob. Scutelle xii d. Summa ix s. viii d. ob.
In vi crannocis frumenti xiii s. ix d. ob.

Summa lvi s. vi d.

Et i bos[9] de instauro. Et i porcus. Et ii casei. Et iii lib. cere. Et vii lib. amigdalarum.
Die sabbati scilicet die Luce ewangeliste cervisia x d. Panis ob. Congrus xv d. Lampreda viii d. Allecia v d. ob. In minutione domine ii d. Oblatio i d. Marescaucia ii s. Amigdale vi d. In minutione domine ii d. Summa vi s.
Die dominica cervisia iiii d. Panis i d. In aucis viii d. ob. Pulli x d. In egrecco i d. In lumine i d. Oblatio i d. In marescaucia ii s. Summa iiii s. ii d. ob.
Die lune cervisia vi d. Pulli vi d. In ovis viii d. Sal xvi d. ob. In nates ad turrim ii d. In egrecco ob. Oblatio i d. Marescaucia ii s. Summa v s. iiii d.
Die martis cervisia iiii d. Panis i d. In aucis vii d. In lumine i d. Oblatio i d. In marescaucia ii s. Summa iii s. ii d.
Die mercurii cervisia x d. Panis i d. Hake xii d. Lampreda ix d. Oblatio i d. Marescaucia ii s. Summa iiii s. ix d.
Die jovis cervisia vi d. Panis i d. In aucis v d. Boves xx d. Item iii auce vi d. Porcus iiii d. In ovis vi d. Oblatio i d. Marescaucia ii s. Summa vi s. i d.
Die veneris cervisia iiii d. Panis ob. Hake xx d. Ostria xii d. Lampreda vii d. ob. Sal iiii d. Carbo viii d. Oblatio i d. Marescaucia ii s. Item in avena ad kareccarios xiiii d. Fenum iiii d. Ferrura ii d. In ii circulis ad rotas ii d. Summa viii s. vii d.
In v crannocis frumenti xi s. viii d.

Summa xlix s. ix d. ob.

Et i bos[10] de instauro et i porcus. Et ii casei. Et iii lib. cere. Et vii lib. amigdalarum.
Die sabbati cervisia x d. Panis i d. Lampreda x d. In ovis xviii d. Anguille iii d. Butirum iii d. Pisum ii d. Oblatio i d. Marescaucia ii s. Summa vi s.

[9] MS 'bov''.
[10] MS 'bov''.

Die dominica cervisia iiii d. Panis ob. Allia ii d. In egrecco i d. In aucis xvi d. Pulli iiii d. In vino acido iiii d. Oblatio i d. Marescaucia ii s.
Summa iiii s. viii d. ob.
Die lune cervisia vi d. Panis iii ob. Raia xii d. Ostria xiii d. In ovis vi d. Oblatio i d. Marescaucia ii s. Summa v s. iii d. ob.
Die martis cervisia iiii d. Panis ob. Pulli xiii d. In vino acido iiii d. Oblatio i d. In marescaucia ii s. Summa iii s. x d. ob.
Die mercurii cervisia x d. Panis i d. Hake xx d. Oblatio i d. In marescaucia ii s. Summa iiii s. viii d.
Die jovis cervisia vi d. Panis ob. In ovis xii d. Oblatio i d. In marescaucia ii s. Summa iii s. vii d. ob.
Die veneris cervisia iiii d. Panis i d. Hake iii s. Salmo xv d. Ostria ii s. iiii d. Perche iiii d. Oblatio i d. In marescaucia ii s. Item in avena ad kareccarios ii s. vi d. Fenum iii d. Ferrura i d. In panno ad tinam cervisie cooperiendam iiii d. In carbone viii d. In pastillis ii d. Summa xiii s. v d.
In vi crannocis frumenti Summa xiiii s. xi d.

Summa lvi s. vi d.

Et i bos[11] de instauro. Et i porcus. Et ii casei de instauro. Et iii lib. cere. Et vii lib. amigdalarum.
Die sabbati scilicet die Omnium Sanctorum cervisia x d. Panis ii d. Salmo x d. In piso iii d. Oblatio iii d. Marescaucia ii s. Summa iiii s. iiii^or^ d.
Die dominica cervisia iiii d. Pulli xiiii d. ob. In ovis iii ob. Oblatio i d. In marescaucia ii s. Summa iii s. ix d.
Die lune cervisia vi d. Panis iii ob. Boves vi d. Porcus ix d. In ovis ii d. Oblatio i d. In marescaucia ii s. Summa iiii s. iii ob.
Die martis cervisia vi d. Panis i d. Volatilia vii d. In ovis vi d. ob. Lumina i d. Oblatio i d.[12] In marescaucia ii s. Summa iii s. x d. ob.
Die mercurii cervisia x d. Panis i d. Hake xiii d. Haddocus xiiii d. In minuto pisce i d. Oblatio i d. Marescaucia ii s. Summa v s. iiii d.
Die jovis cervisia iiii d. Panis ob. In ovis xviii d. Volatilia ii d. Pulli vii d. Oblatio i d. Marescaucia ii s. Summa iiii s. viii d. ob.
Die veneris cervisia vi d. Panis i d. Hake xx d. Congrus ii s. Perche iii d. In ollis ii d. ob. In iiii crannocis salis vii s. vi d. Oblatio i d. Marescaucia ii s. In carbone ix d. Item in avena ad kareccarios xiiii d. Fenum v d. Ferrura ii d. In karecca liganda iiii d. ob. Summa xvii s. ii d.
In v crannocis frumenti Summa xi s. xi d. ob.

Summa lv s. iii d.

Et i bos[13] de instauro. Et i porcus. Et ii casei de instauro. Et iii lib. cere. Et vii lib. amigdalarum.

[11] MS 'bov''.
[12] MS omits 'd.'
[13] MS 'bov''.

Die sabbati proxima ante festum Sancti Martini cervisia xx d. Panis ob. In ovis xii d. Vinum acidum iiii d. \ Allia ii d. / Oblatio i d. Marescaucia ii s. Summa v s. iii d. ob.
Die dominica cervisia iiii d. Panis iii ob. Pulli ix d. \ ob. / Anguille ii d. ob. Oblatio i d. In marescaucia ii s. Summa iii s. vi d. ob.
Die lune cervisia vi d. Panis ob. Salmo xii d. In perdicibus v d. Mulewellus ii d. Ostria ii d. \ In vino v d. / In lumine i d. Oblatio i d. Marescaucia ii s. Summa iiii s. x d. ob.
Die martis cervisia iiii d. Panis i d. Hake et haddocus vi d. Pastilli ii d. In vino ad opus domine vii d. ob. Oblatio i d. Mariscaucia ii s.
Summa iii s. ix d. ob.
Die mercurii cervisia x d. Panis i d. Raia et mulewellus xviii d. Hake et makerellus xviii d. Perche iii d. ob. In vino ad opus domine v d. Oblatio i d. In marescaucia ii s. Summa vi s. viii d. ob.
Die jovis cervisia vi d. Panis ob. Pulli iii d. ob. In i apro viii s. In vino v d. Oblatio i d. In marescaucia ii s. Summa xi s. iiii d.
Die veneris cervisia iiii d. Hake ii s. Ostria xii d. Mulewellus ix d. Oblatio i d. Marescaucia ii s. Item in avena ad kareccarios xviii d. Fenum ii d. Ferrura iii d. Carbo xi d. In i crannoco fabarum xii d. ad porcos.
Summa x s.
In vi crannocis frumenti xiiii s. x d.
Summa lx s. iiii d. ob.
Et i bos[14] et di. et i porcus de instauro. Et ii casei. Et iiii lib. cere. Et ix lib. amigdalarum.
Die sabbati proxima post festum Sancti Martini cervisia x d. Panis iii ob. Congrus et plaiz xvi d. Hake vii d. Allia ii d. In cauderis emendandis ii d. In vino ad opus domine vii d. ob. In confessione et minutione domine ii d. Oblatio i d. In marescaucia ii s. Summa vi s. i d.
Die dominica cervisia iiii d. Panis ob. Porcus vii d. Pulli viii d. ob. In vino acido iiii d. In i unco ad coquinam iii ob. In vino ad opus domine vii d. ob. Oblatio i d. In marescaucia ii s. Summa iiii s. x d.
Die lune cervisia vi d. Panis i d. In lucio vi d. In virgis ad coquinam i d. In vino vii d. ob. Oblatio i d. Marescaucia ii s. Summa iii s. x d. ob.
Die martis cervisia iiii d. Panis ob. In ovis xiii d. Volatilia v d. In vino vii d. ob. Oblatio i d. In marescaucia ii s. Summa iiii s. vii d.
Die mercurii cervisia x d. Panis ob. Hake xx d. Merlengus iiii d. In turbutto iii d. In vino vii d. ob. Oblatio i d. Marescaucia ii s. Summa v s. x d.
Die jovis cervisia iiii d. Panis ob. Porcus ii d. ob. Merlengus ii d. In vino v d. Oblatio i d. In marescaucia ii s. Summa iii s. iii d.
Die veneris cervisia vi d. Panis i d. Congrus xvi d. Hake xv d. Ostria xiiii d.

[14] MS 'bov''.

Oblatio i d. Marescaucia ii s. Item in avena ad kareccarios ix d. Fenum iii d. Ferrura ii d. In carbone xi d. Perche ii d. Lumina i d. Summa viii s. ix d.
In v crannocis frumenti xii s. iiii d.

Summa xlix s. vi d. ob.

Summa xvi li. vii s. xi d. ob.

Et i bos[15] et di. et i porcus. Et ii casei de instauro. Et iiii lib. cere. Et ix lib. amigdalarum.

Membrane 3 recto

Die sabbati scilicet die Sancte Cecilie cervisia x d. Panis ob. Pulli x d. Oblatio i d. Marescaucia ii s. Summa iii s. ix d. ob.
Die dominica cervisia iiii d. Panis ob. Congrus iii d. ob. In vino acido iiii d. Oblatio i d. In marescaucia ii s. Summa iii s. i d.
Die lune cervisia vi d. Panis ob. In bove xii d. In mulewello iiii d. In nucibus iiii d. ob. Oblatio i d. Marescaucia ii s. \ In piris viii d. / Summa v s.
Die martis cervisia iiii d. Panis ob. Hake iii d. ob. Pulli iii d. Oblatio i d. In marescaucia ii s. Summa iii s.
Die mercurii cervisia x d. Panis ob. Haddocus et merlengus ii s. Hake xvi d. Oblatio i d. Marescaucia ii s. Summa vi s. iii d. ob.
Die jovis cervisia vi d. Panis ob. Wolkes iii d. Pulli iii d. In minutione domine ii d. In ovis vii d. Perche iii ob. In coclearibus ad oll*as* i d. Oblatio i d. In marescaucia ii s. Summa iiii s. i d.
Die veneris cervisia iiii d. Panis i d. Hake et mulewellus ii s. iiii d. Ostria xviii d. Anguille vii d. Oblatio i d. Marescaucia ii s. Item in avena ad kareccarios xxi d. Fenum et ferrura vii d. In carbone viii d. In ii crannocis salis iii s. v d. Summa xiii s. iiii d.
In vi crannocis frumenti xv s. vi d.

Summa liiii s. i d.

Et iiii lib. cere. Et x lib. amigdalarum. Et i bos[16] et i porcus de instauro. Et ii casei.
Die sabbati cervisia x d. Panis ob. Hake xx d. ob. In nucibus iiii d. ob. Oblatio i d. Marescaucia ii s. Summa v s. ob.
Die dominica cervisia vi d. Panis ob. Anguille ix d. In ovis iii ob. In i gata et ciph*is* v d. Oblatio iii d. Marescaucia ii s. Summa iiii s. i d.
Die lune cervisia vi d. Panis ob. In ovis vii d. Pulli iiii d. Oblatio i d. In marescaucia ii s. Summa iii s. vi d. ob.
Die martis cervisia iiii d. Panis ob. Raia et mulewellus et allecia xiiii d. In ovis x d. ob. Perdices iiii d. In lumine i d. Carbo iiii d. Oblatio i d. In marescaucia ii s. Summa v s. iii d.

[15] MS 'bov''.
[16] MS 'bov''.

Die mercurii cervisia x d. Panis ob. Salmo ii s. v d. Congrus et mulewellus xiii d. Pisum ii d. Oblatio i d. In marescaucia ii s. Summa vi s. vii d. ob.
Die jovis cervisia vi d. Panis i d. Porcus iii d. In pisce ob. In nucibus xvi d. ob. In vino acido iiii d. Oblatio i d. Marescaucia ii s. Summa iiii s. viii d.
Die veneris cervisia iiii d. Panis ob. Hake ii s. vi d. Item in hake et haddoco xx d. Plaiz vii d. Ostria x d. In piso iii d. Oblatio i d. In marescaucia ii s. Item in avena ad kareccarios xx d. Fenum et ferrura v d. In pane ad opus domine iiii d. ob. In ii securibus ad coquinam et kar*eccam* xi d.
Summa xi s. viii d.
In v crannocis frumenti xii s. x d. ob.
Summa liii s. ix d.
Et \ de / instauro i bos[17] et i porcus. Et ii casei de instauro. Et iiii lib. cere. Et ix lib. amigdalarum.
Die sabbati cervisia xii d. Panis i d. Hake xii d. In ovis vii d. Oblatio i d. In marescaucia ii s. Summa iiii s. ix d.
Die dominica cervisia vi d. Panis ob. Hake xii d. Allia iii d. Porcus ii d. ob. Volatilia ii d. Oblatio i d. Marescaucia ii s. Summa iiii s. iii d.
Die lune cervisia viii d. Panis i d. Congrus vi d. Anguille xi d. In mulewello ii d. ob. Oblatio i d. In marescaucia ii s. Summa iiii s. v d. ob.
Die martis cervisia vi d. Panis i d. Pulli iii ob. Congrus vii d. Oblatio i d. In marescaucia ii s. Summa iii s. iiii d. ob.
Die mercurii cervisia x d. Panis i d. Hake ii s. Salmo xvii d. Congrus viii d. In piso ii d. Oblatio i d. In marescaucia ii s. Summa vii s. iii d.
Die jovis cervisia vi d. Panis i d. In lucio et perchis xii d. In piris ix d. ob. In ovis vii d. Gall*ine* iii d. ob. Lumina i d. Oblatio i d. Marescaucia ii s.
Summa v s. v d.
Die veneris cervisia vi d. Panis ob. Haddocus et mulewellus xx d. Ostria xvi d. Hake ii s. ii d. Perche iiii d. In piso ii d. ob. In vino x d. Oblatio i d. In marescaucia ii s. Item in avena ad kareccarios xxii d. Fenum et ferrura x d. Summa xi s. x d.
In vi crannocis frumenti xv s. iii ob.
In xii crannocis salis ad carnes salliendas cum portagio eiusdem xviii s. vi d.
Summa lxxiiii s. xi d. ob.
Et i bos[18] et di. et i porcus de instauro. Et ii casei. Et iiii lib. cere. Et ix lib. amigdalarum.
Die sabbati in cervisia x d. Panis i d. Salmo ii s. Flundre viii d. Merlengus x d. Oblatio i d. In marescaucia ii s. Summa vi s. vi d.
Die dominica cervisia vi d. Panis ob. Hake ii s. iiii d. In carbone viii d. In piso i d. Oblatio i d. In marescaucia ii s. Summa v s. viii d. ob.

[17] MS 'bov''.
[18] MS 'bov''.

Die lune cervisia vi d. Panis ob. Pulli iii d. Porcus iiii d. In alaudis i d. Pastilli iii d. Congrus iii d. Volatilia iii ob. Oblatio iii d. Marescaucia ii s. Summa iiii s. i d.
Die martis cervisia vi d. Raia xviii d. In mulewello iiii d. Volatilia iii ob. Allia ii d. ob. Oblatio i d. Marescaucia ii s. Summa iiii s. ix d.
Die mercurii cervisia x d. Panis ob. Ostria et wolkes x d. Hake et haddocus xviii d. Pisum ii d. In minutione domine i d. Oblatio i d. Marescaucia ii s. Summa v s. vi d. ob.
Die jovis cervisia vi d. Panis i d. Anguille v d. Porcus vi d. Volatilia iiii d. ob. Galline ii d. Literia i d. Lumina ii d. ob. In cepis i d. Oblatio i d. In marescaucia ii s. Summa iiii s. vi d.
Die veneris cervisia iiii d. Panis i d. Congrus iiii d. In mulewello et wolkes viii d. Hake ii s. Anguille v d. Lumina i d. Oblatio i d. In marescaucia ii s. Item in avena ix d. ad kareccarios. Fenum et ferrura viii d. In pane ad opus domine iii d. Carbo iiii d. In tripis faciendis iiii d. Summa viii s. iiii^{or} d.
In vi crannocis frumenti Summa xv s. vi d.

Summa lv s. v d. ob.

Et iiii lib. cere. Et ix lib. amigdalarum. Et de instauro i bos[19] et di. Et i baco. Et ii casei.
Die sabbati in Natali Domini cervisia xii d. Panis i d. Salmo ii s. iiii d. Allecia x d. In vino acido iiii d. Oblatio i d. Marescaucia ii s. Summa vi s. viii d.
Die dominica cervisia xii d. Panis ob. Congrus xiiii d. Volatilia iiii d. Galline vi d. In ovis xiiii d. Haddocus iiii d. In nucibus iiii d. Oblatio i d. In marescaucia ii s. Summa vii s.
Die lune cervisia viii d. Panis ob. Haddocus xiiii d. Hake xii d. Volatilia iii d. Pastilli iii d. Oblatio i d. In marescaucia ii s. Summa v s. v d. ob.
Die martis cervisia xii d. Panis ob. Hake ix d. Haddocus v d. Volatilia iii ob. In mustardo iiii d. Lumina i d. In vino x d. Oblatio i d. In marescaucia ii s. Summa v s. viii d.
Die mercurii cervisia xvi d. Panis iii ob. Haddocus et congrus xx d. Ostria viii d. ob. Barbellus i d. Hake ii s. iii d. In vino x d. In vino acido iiii d. Oblatio i d. In marescaucia ii s. Summa ix s. v d.
Die jovis scilicet die Natalis Domini panis i d. Volatilia ii s. ii d. ob. In ovis xiiii d. Scutelle xv d. In i securi ad coquinam iii ob. In pomis i d. In vi sex. vini v s. In literia v d. In picheriis ii d. In medone iii ob. In i serura ad turrim iiii d. In ciphis vii d. In sale iiii d. Oblatio ix d. In marescaucia ii s. In pastillis faciendis iii d. In oblatione militum et serviencium ii s. i d. Summa xvi s. xi d. ob.
Die veneris panis ob. Haddocus et hake vi d. Salmo viii d. Congrus vi d.

[19] MS 'bov".

Oblatio i d. In marescaucia ii s. In marescaucia kareccariorum ii s. iiii d. Summa vi s. iii ob.
In viii crannocis frumenti xx s. iiii d. ob.
Summa lxxvii s. viii d.
Et viii lib. cere. Et viii lib.[20] amigdalarum. Et ii boves de instauro et ii porci. Et ii casei.
Die sabbati proxima post diem Natallis cervisia x d. Panis ob. Congrus et salmo ii s. In ovis iiii d. ob. Butirum iii d. ob. In lacte i d. In vino die veneris precedente ii s. i d. Item in hoc die sabbati in vino xx d. Oblatio i d. In marescaucia ii s. Summa ix s. v d. ob.
Die dominica cervisia vi d. Panis ob. Galline vi d. ob. In ovis xvii d. ob. Lac i d. In vino xx d. Oblatio iii d. In marescaucia ii s. Summa vi s. vi d. ob.
Die lune cervisia vi d. Galline viii d. Volatilia v d. In vino ii s. i d. Oblatio i d. Marescaucia ii s. Summa v s. ix d.
Die martis cervisia vi d. Panis ob. Porcus iiii d. ob. In gallinis et alaudis vi d. ob. In vino ii s. i d. Allia ob. Oblatio i d. Marescaucia ii s. Summa v s. viii d.
Die mercurii cervisia x d. Panis ob. Salmo vi d. Volatilia xii d. ob. Galline xiiii d. \ ob. / In vino ii s. ii d. Oblatio i d. Marescaucia ii s. Summa vii s. x d. ob.
Die jovis cervisia vi d. In vino xvi d. Oblatio iii d. In marescaucia ii s. Summa iiii s. i d.
Die veneris cervisia iiii d. Panis v d. ad opus domine. Ostria xviii d. Salmo xvi d. Congrus x d. In piso ii d. ob. In vino xvi d. In nucibus v d. Oblatio i d. In marescaucia ii s. Item in avena ad kareccarios x d. Fenum et ferrura v d. Summa ix s. viii d. ob.
In v crannocis frumenti xii s. i d.
Summa lxi s. ii d.
Et iiii lib. cere. Et vii lib. amigdalarum. Et ii boves et i porcus de instauro. Et ii casei.
Die sabbati cervisia x d. Panis i d. Allecia xviii d. Congrus ix d. Anguille iiii d. ob. Butirum iii d. In ovis v d. Oblatio i d. Marescaucia xviii d. Summa v s. ix d. ob.
Die dominica cervisia vi d. Panis ob. Galline x d. In alaudis i d. Oblatio i d. In marescaucia xviii d. Summa iii s. ob.
Die lune cervisia vi d. Panis ob. Galline xvi d. In ovis xv d. ob. Porcus iiii d. Oblatio i d. In marescaucia xviii d. Summa v s. i d.
Die martis cervisia iiii d. Volatilia vii d. Galline ix d. In patellis emendandis

[20] MS omits 'lib.'

i d. In ferura iii ob. In vino acido iiii d. Oblatio iii d. In marescaucia xviii d.
Summa iii s. xi d. ob.

Die mercurii cervisia x d. Panis i d. Allecia xvi d. Hake ix d. Congrus xx d. In lacte i d. Oblatio i d. In marescaucia ii s. iii d. Summa vii s. i d.

Die jovis cervisia vi d. Panis ii d. ob. Porcus xiii d. Literia ii d. Oblatio i d. In marescaucia ii s. iii d. Summa iiii s. iii d. ob.

Die veneris cervisia vi d. Panis iii ob. Salmo ii s. ii d. Ostria xiiii d. Perche iiii d. Allecia ii s. Oblatio i d. In marescaucia ii s. iii d. Item in avena ad kareccarios xxii d. Fenum et ferrura vi d. Literia ii d. ob. In iii doliis vini ponendis in cellario ix d. Summa xi s. xi d.

In vi crannocis frumenti xv s. vii d. ob.

Summa lvi s. ix d. ob.

Et iiii lib. cere. Et vii lib. amigdalarum. Et ii boves et i baconus[21] de instauro. Et ii casei.

Die sabbati cervisia x d. Panis i d. Allecia xiiii d. Ostria et wolkes ix d. In ovis v d. Literia i d. Oblatio i d. Marescaucia ii s. iii d. Summa v s. viii d.

Die dominica cervisia vi d. Panis ii d. Porcus xii d. Farina i d. Oblatio i d. In marescaucia ii s. iii d. Summa iiii s. i d.

Die lune cervisia vi d. Panis ii d. Porcus x d. Galline xix d. In alaudis ii d. Oblatio i d. Marescaucia ii s. iii d. Summa v s. vii d.

Die martis cervisia vi d. Panis ii d. Porcus vii d. ob. Oblatio i d. In marescaucia ii s. iii d. Summa iii s. vii d. ob.

Die mercurii cervisia x d. In luceis et perchis vi d. Allecia ii s. Salmo xi d. Pisum iii d. In ovis xiiii d. Oblatio i d. Marescaucia ii s. iii d. Summa viii s.

Die jovis cervisia vi d. Panis ii d. Porcus iiii d. Volatilia xi d. ob. In vino acido iiii d. Oblatio i d. In marescaucia ii s. iii d. Summa iiii s. vii d. ob.

Die veneris cervisia iiii d. Panis iii ob. Ostria et wolkes xviii d. In luceo v d. Oblatio i d. Marescaucia ii s. iii d. Item avena ad kareccarios xx d. Fenum et ferrura iiii d. In pane ii d. ad opus domine. Allecia[22] ii s.
Summa viii s. x d. ob.

In v crannocis frumenti Summa xii s. viii d. ob.

Summa liii s. ii d.

Et iiii lib. cere. Et vii lib. amigdalarum. Et ii boves de instauro et ii bacones. Et ii casei.

Die sabbati cervisia x d. Allecia xii d. Caseus et in ovis et in butiro xi d. Oblatio i d. In marescaucia ii s. iii d. Summa v s. i d.

Die dominica cervisia vi d. Panis ii d. Porcus xiiii d. Galline xiii d. In ovis iiii d. ob. Volatilia x d. Oblatio i d. In marescaucia ii s. iii d.
Summa vi s. v d. ob.

[21] MS 'bacon''.

[22] MS has 'ii allecia', with the two minims cancelled by subscript dots.

Die lune cervisia vi d. Panis ii d. Galline xvii d. In ovis xv d. In balneo domine ii d. In picheriis iii ob. Oblatio i d. In marescaucia ii s. iii d. Summa v s. xi d. ob.

Die martis cervisia vi d. Panis ob. Galline vi d. Volatilia iiii d. Lumina i d. Oblatio i d. In marescaucia ii s. iii d. Summa iii s. ix d. ob.

Die mercurii cervisia x d. Panis i d. Lampreda xi d. Salmo xiiii d. In ovis xxi d. ob. Oblatio i d. In marescaucia ii s. iii d. Summa vii s. iii ob.

Die jovis cervisia vi d. Panis ii d. Galline x d. In hedo iiii d. Item in gallinis iiii d. ob. Oblatio i d. In marescaucia ii s. iii d. Summa iii s. vi d. ob.

Die veneris cervisia iiii d. Panis iii ob. Ostria et wolkes xix d. Raia x d. In luceis et perchis xii d. Oblatio i d. In marescaucia ii s. iii d. Item in avena ad kareccarios xviii d. Fenum et ferrura vii d. In i coopertorio de pellibus multonum ad pistrinum x d. Summa ix s. iii ob.

In vi crannocis frumenti et di. xvii s. vii d.

Summa lix s. viii d.

Et iiii lib. cere. Et vii lib. amigdalarum. Et ii boves de instauro et ii bacones. Et ii casei.

Die sabbati cervisia x d. Panis i d. Allecia xx d. Haddocus xii d. Allia iii d. In ovis xiii d. ob. Oblatio i d. Marescaucia ii s. iii d. Summa vii s. iii d. ob.

Die dominica cervisia vi d. Panis ob. Galline vii d. In vino acido viii d. Oblatio i d. Marescaucia ii s. iii d. Summa iiii s. iii ob.

Die lune cervisia vi d. Panis ob. Galline xii d. Pisum iii ob. In patillis ligandis xii d. Oblatio i d. In marescaucia ii s. iii d. Summa v s.

Die martis cervisia vi d. Panis ii d. Galline et alaude x d. Porcus v d. In ovis xxi d. ob. Oblatio i d. In marescaucia ii s. iii d. Summa vi s. ob.

Die mercurii cervisia x d. Panis i d. In lucio v d. Raia xiiii d. Menusa iii d. Oblatio i d. Marescaucia ii s. iii d. Summa v s. i d.

Die jovis cervisia vi d. Panis ii d. Porcus x d. In i barillo vi d. Galline ix d. ob. Volatilia vii d. ob. Oblatio i d. Marescaucia ii s. iii d. Summa v s. ix d.

Die veneris cervisia iiii d. Panis iii ob. Gurnardus xiiii d. Ostria xviii d. Perche iiii d. Oblatio i d. Marescaucia ii s. iii d. Item in avena ad kareccarios xv d. Fenum et ferrura v d. Literia ob. In lumine iii d. In carbone vii d. Summa viii s. iiii d.

In v crannocis frumenti xii s. vii d.

Summa liiii s. ii d. ob.

Et xv lib. cere. Et vii lib. amigdalarum. Et ii boves de instauro et iii bacones. Et ii casei.

Die sabbati cervisia ante Purificationem Beate Marie xii d. Panis iii ob. Hake xx d. Congrus xii d. Allecia iii d. Wolkes iii d. ob. In ovis et butiro xi d. In sagimine v d. Oblatio i d. In marescaucia ii s. iii d. Summa viii s.

Die dominica cervisia vi d. Panis i d. Galline xvi d. In vino acido iiii d. Oblatio i d. In marescaucia ii s. iii d. Summa iiii s. vii d.

Die lune cervisia vi d. Panis ii d. Galline xi d. ob. In ovis xiiii d. ob. Oblatio iii d. In marescaucia ii s. iii d. Summa v s. iiii d.
Die martis cervisia iiii d. Panis ii d. Oblatio i d. In marescaucia ii s. iii d. Summa ii s. x d.
Die mercurii cervisia x d. Panis i d. Allecia xix d. Wolkes v d. Oblatio i d. In marescaucia ii s. iii d. Summa v s. iii d.
Die jovis cervisia vi d. Panis ii d. Porcus vi d. ob. Literia iiii d. ob. Galline xiii d. ob. Buket iii ob. In vino acido iiii d. In virgis ad coquinam i d. Oblatio i d. In marescaucia ii s. iii d. Summa v s. vii d.
Die veneris cervisia iiii d. Panis iii ob. Lampreda ix d. Perche v d. In mulewello viii d. Wolkes vi d. Item in pane i d. Oblatio i d. In marescaucia ii s. iii d. Item in avena ad kareccarios xvii d. Fenum et ferrura vi d. In i serura iii d. In tractibus ad kareccam iii d. In carbone vii d. Summa viii s. ii d. ob.
In vi crannocis frumenti xvi s. ii d. ob.

Summa lvi s.

Et iiii lib. cere. Et vii lib. amigdalarum. Et ii boves de instauro et ii bacones. Et ii casei.
Die sabbati cervisia xvi d. Panis ob. In lampreda iii s. vi d. In ovis xiiii d. Butirum iii ob. Oblatio i d. Marescaucia ii s. iii d. Summa viii s. vi d.
Die dominica cervisia vi d. Panis ii d. Porcus ii s. i d. In ovis xvii d. ob. Galline ix d. In vino acido iiii d. Oblatio i d. Marescaucia ii s. iii d. Summa vii s. vii d. ob.
Die lune cervisia vi d. Panis ii d. In hedis xi d. In sagimine ix d. Galline iii d. In ii crannocis salis ii s. i d. Oblatio i d. In marescaucia ii s. iii d. Summa vii s.
Die martis cervisia vi d. Panis ii d. In hedis viii d. Galline iii d. ob. Oblatio i d. In marescaucia ii s. iii d. Summa iii s. xi d. ob.
Die mercurii cervisia viii d. Panis i d. In luceo et perchis xi d. Butirum iiii d. Oblatio i d. In marescaucia ii s. iii d. Summa iiii s. iiii d.
Die jovis cervisia vi d. Panis ii d. Porcus viii d. Galline xiii d. In lumine i d. Oblatio i d. In marescaucia ii s. iii d. Summa iiii s. x d.
Die veneris cervisia iiii d. Panis i d. Ostria et wolkes xv d. Salmo xxii d. Oblatio i d. Marescaucia ii s. iii d. Item in avena ad kareccarios xvii d. Fenum et ferrura vi d. In tackis ad kareccam iiii d. ob. Carbo vii d. Sal ii d. In i barillo ii d. In x doliis vini ponendis in castro ii s. vi d. In circulis ponendis in aliis doliis vi d. Summa xii s. ob.
In C congris xlii s. iii d. In CC hake x s. iiii d. Summa lii s. vii d.
In vi crannocis frumenti xv s. iiii d.

Summa C et xvi s. ii d. ob.

Et iiii lib. cere. Et vi lib. amigdalarum. Et ii boves de instauro et ii bacones. Et ii casei.

Die sabbati cervisia xii d. Panis i d. In ovis xxii d. ob. Oblatio i d. In marescaucia ii s. iii d. Summa v s. iii d. ob.
Die dominica cervisia vi d. Panis ii d. Porcus ii s. ii d. Galline xxii d. Oblatio i d. In marescaucia ii s. iii d. Summa vii s.
Die lune cervisia vi d. Panis ii d. Galline x d. In hedis ix d. In vino acido iiii d. Oblatio i d. In marescaucia ii s. iii d. Summa iiii s. xi d.
Die martis cervisia vi d. Panis ii d. Galline xix d. In ovis xxi d. Oblatio i d. In marescaucia ii s. iii d. Summa vi s. iiii d.
Die mercurii cervisia iiii d. Panis i d. Ostria et wolkes viii d. ob. Butirum iii d. Picherii iiii d. Literia iii ob. Haddocus vii d. Oblatio i d. Marescaucia ii s. iii d. Summa iiii s. ix d.
Die jovis cervisia vi d. Panis ii d. Porcus x d. In pastillis faciendis iiii d. In vino acido iiii d. Oblatio i d. In marescaucia ii s. iii d. Summa iiii s. vi d.
Die veneris cervisia vi d. Panis iii ob. Salmo xx d. In menusa vi d. Oblatio i d. In marescaucia ii s. iii d. Item in avena ad kareccarios xvii d. In ferrura ii d. In carbone vi d. ob. Summa vii s. iii d.
In vi crannocis frumenti xv s. ii d.
In lxvi mulewellis cum portagio xv s. ii d. ob.

Summa lxx s. v d.

Et iiii lib. cere. Et vi lib. amigdalarum. Et ii boves de instauro et ii bacones. Et ii casei.
Die sabbati cervisia xii d. Panis i d. Haddocus vii d. Congrus xiii d. Butirum iiii d. Lac i d. Oblatio i d. Marescaucia ii s. iii d. Summa v s. vi d.
Die dominica cervisia vi d. Panis ii d. Porcus xx d. Oblatio i d. In marescaucia ii s. iii d. Summa iiii s. viii d.
Die lune cervisia vi d. Panis ii d. Galline xix d. Pastilli iii d. ob. In vino acido iiii d. Oblatio i d. In marescaucia ii s. iii d. Summa v s. ii d. ob.
Die martis cervisia vi d. Panis ii d. In ovis xviii d. ob. Galline xix d. ob. In pomis vi d. Oblatio i d. In marescaucia ii s. iii d. Summa vi s. viii d.
Die mercurii cervisia xii d. Raia xiiii d. Wolkes iiii d. Allia ii d. Oblatio i d. In marescaucia ii s. iii d. Summa v s.
Die jovis cervisia vi d. Panis ii d. In sagimine xi d. In hedis ix d. In ovis vi d. In balneo domine ii d. Oblatio i d. Marescaucia ii s. iii d. Summa v s. iiii[or] d.
Die veneris cervisia vi d. Panis i d. Mulewellus xii d. Salmo viii d. In menusa et wolkes xii d. Scutelle vi d. Oblatio i d. In marescaucia ii s. iii d. Fenum ad kareccarios iiii d. In carbone vii d. ob. Summa vii s. ob.
In vi crannocis frumenti xv s. iiii d. ob.
In ii meisis allecie vii s. vi d.

Summa lxii s. iii d. ob.

Et iiii lib. cere. Et v lib. amigdalarum. Et ii casei. Et ii boves et ii bacones. Et i qr. avene ad kareccarios de instauro.

Die sabbati cervisia xii d. Panis ob. Raia xii d. In ovis xi d. Butirum iiii d. In vino acido iiii d. In diminutione domine et domicellarum suarum iii d. Oblatio i d. In marescaucia ii s. iii d. Summa vi s. ii d. ob.
Die dominica cervisia vi d. Panis ii d. In hedis xix d. Galline xiii d. Oblatio i d. In marescaucia ii s. iii d. Summa v s. viii d.
Die lune cervisia vi d. Panis ii d. Galline xix d. ob. Flura iii d. In ovis vi d. ob. Oblatio i d. In marescaucia ii s. iii d. Summa v s. v d.
Die martis cervisia vi d. Panis ii d. Sagimen x d. Pastelli iiii d. Galline x d. Hedi x d. In ovis vii d. Oblatio i d. Marescaucia ii s. iii d. Summa vi s. v d.
Die mercurii cervisia viii d. Panis iii ob. Raia xii d. In turbutto iiii d. Ostria xiii d. Menusa vi d. Oblatio i d. Marescaucia ii s. iii d. Summa vi s. ob.
..... cervisia vi d. Panis iii d. Raia xii d. Lampreda vii d. In oleo ix d. In vino acido iiii d. In i sporta vi d. ..... iii ob. Oblatio i d. In marescaucia ii s. iii d. Summa vi s. iii d.
..... cervisia iiii d. Panis i d. In nucibus xxii d. ob. .....es v d. Oblatio i d. In marescaucia ii s. iii d. Fenum et fe..... kareccar*ios* iiii d. In carbone x d. ob. In piso ii d. Allia iii d. ob. Summa vi s. viii d. ob.

Summa xlii s. viii d. ob.

In pane in predictam septimanam vi crannoci frumenti de instauro. Et i bos[23] et i baco. Et i qr. avene ad kareccarios de instauro. Et iiii lib. cere. Et v lib. amigdalarum. Et ii casei.

Summa xlvii li. viii s. vi d. ob.
Summa Clxxviii li. v s. viii d.

5 *Diet account for the household of a De Vere Earl of Oxford, August to September, c.1245–75*

This fragment of a diet account can be attributed to the household of a De Vere Earl of Oxford on the basis of some of the places at which the household resided, Hedingham, Canfield, Lavenham, Chesham, Whitchurch, Colne, in each of which the De Veres held property, and by references to the 'earl'. The account covers the period 2 August to 26 September in a year around the middle of the thirteenth century or soon after, in 1245, 1251, 1256, 1262 or 1273.[1] There is no heading on the account and the

[23] MS 'bov''.

[1] While 1279, 1284 and 1290 are less likely palaeographically, if the Richard de Chikewell, who supplied fish to the household, is the London fishmonger of the same name, sheriff of the city in 1281–2 and who died in 1306, these dates cannot be ruled out: A. B. Beaven *The aldermen of the city of London, temp. Henry III–1912* (2 vols., London, 1908–13) i, p. 379.

dating can only be given on the general grounds of palaeography; the household could belong to either Hugh de Vere, the fourth Earl of Oxford, or his son, Robert de Vere, the fifth Earl, who succeeded him in 1263. The account provides details of the Earl's stay in Essex, followed by a journey moving with a substantial retinue through Oxfordshire to Tewkesbury and Winchcombe, returning to Essex to the Earl's manor of Colne.

The account was written on the front of a Chancery fashion roll of two membranes in a single hand throughout, although possibly in more than one operation. The first membrane was torn contemporaneously and was sewn back together at the time. The second membrane has been cut away shortly after its start. On the dorse of the roll, inverted, is a short cartulary, probably written towards the end of the thirteenth century, containing agreements between the Earls of Oxford and the priory of Colne. The roll was once attached to two fifteenth century rentals.[2]

Essex RO D/D Pr 136

Membrane 1 recto

Hengham Die mercurii proxima post festum Sancti Petri ad vincula in CCC allecis ii s. iii d. In xii mulettis iiii s. ii d. In plaicis xii d. In soles xx d. In C ovorum vi d.

Summa per prepositum ix s. vii d.

Staurum De frumento in pane i qr. iii bus. De allece C. In prebendo xl[a] equorum i qr. vi bus.

Die jovis sequenti scilicet die invencionis Sancti Stephani in i carcosio et di. boum vi s. vi d. In i carcosio mutonis xvi d. In xvii pullis xv d. In C ovorum vi d. In i potello mellis iiii d. In C allecis vii d.

Summa per prepositum x s. vi d.

Staurum De frumento in pane i qr. et di. Ad coquinam i bus. De allece di. C. De caseo i. De butiro i potellum. In prebendo xlii equorum i qr. vii bus.

Die veneris sequenti in CCCC allecis ii s. vii d. In iiii estik angwillarum ii s. x d. In xiiii galonis aceci xviii d. ob. precium gallonis i d. qua.

Summa per prepositum vi s. iiii d. ob.

Staurum De frumento in pane i qr. ii bus. In prebendo xlvi equorum ii qr.

Die sabbati sequenti scilicet die Sancti Oswaldi in CCCC allecis ii s. ix d. In plaicis et creviciis ii s. iiii d. In vi mulvellis de Aberdene xv d. In C et di. ovorum ix d.

Summa per prepositum vii s. i d.

[2] J. L. Fisher, 'The Probert documents', *Transactions of the Essex Archaeological Society* 23 (1942–5) pp. 263–72; *CP* x, pp. 213–18.

Staurum De frumento in pane i qr. ii bus. De allece C. De caseo i et ad coquinam i. In prebendo xlvi equorum ii qr.

Dominica proxima sequenti in ii carcosiis boum ix s. vi d. In ii carcosiis mutonum ii s. vi d. In escaeta ii mutonum vi d. ob. In lardo v d. In ii caponibus iiii d. ob. In xxiii pullis xvi d. In CC ovorum xii d.

Summa xv s. vii d. ob. per prepositum

Staurum De frumento in pane i qr. v bus. De allece di. C. De caseo i ad coquinam. In prebendo xxxvi equorum i qr. vi bus.

Braciatura Braciatura de ordeo vi qr. et di.

Die lune sequenti in ii carcosiis boum x s. vi d. In ii carcosiis mutonum ii s. v d. In di. porco ii s. vi d. In CC ovorum xii d. In xviii pullis xii d. In i gallina . . . In di. galone mellis iiii d.

Summa xvii s. x d. ob. per prepositum

Staurum De frumento in pane i qr. et di. De porcis di. De gallinis i. De caseis ii. De cepo ii lib. In prebendo xxxviii equorum i qr. ii bus.

Die martis sequenti in i carcosio bovis et di. vi s. vi d. In di. porco ii s. In xviii pullis xii d. ob. qua. In C ovorum vi d.

Summa x s. ob. qua. per prepositum

Staurum De frumento in pane i qr. et di. De porcis di. De gallinis i. De allece di. C. De caseis i. Et ad coquinam i. In prebendo xlvi equorum ii qr. ii bus.

Die mercurii sequenti in vC allecis ii s. viii d. ob. In plaicis et soles iii s. iii d. In v creviciis ix d.

Summa per prepositum vi s. viii d. ob.

Staurum De frumento in pane i qr. i bus. In prebendo l equorum ii qr. i bus.

Die jovis scilicet die Sancti Laurencii in iii carcosiis boum xviii s. v d. In iiii carcosiis mutonum iiii s. viii d. In ii porcis viii s. In escaeta mutonis vii d. In xviii pullis x d. ob. In CC et di. ovorum xv d. In xxx plateris lxx discis et lxvi salsariis ii s. v d. ob.

Summa xxxvi s. ix d. per prepositum

Staurum De frumento in pane ii qr. i bus. De porcis i aper. De caponibus iiii. De gallinis iiii. De allece C. De caseo i. Et ad panetriam ii. In prebendo lx equorum iii qr.

Braciatura Braciatura de ordeo vi qr. et di.

Die veneris in CCC allecis xix d. In iii estik angwillarum ii s. In viii mulvellis ii s. In ligatura iiii barillorum iiii d.

Summa per prepositum v s. xi d.

Staurum De frumento in pane i qr. et di. De caseis i. In prebendo liiii equorum ii qr. ii bus.

Die sabbati sequenti in vC allecis iii s. ii d. In plaicis et soles ii s. vi d. In iiii estik angwillarum ii s. v d. In di. C ovorum iii d.

Summa per prepositum viii s. i d.

Staurum De frumento in pane i qr. ii bus. et ad coquinam i bus. In prebendo l equorum vi bus.
Dominica proxima post festum Sancti Laurencii in i carcosio bovis v s. In xxiiii pullis xv d. In C ovorum vi d.

Summa vii s. vi d. per prepositum

Staurum De frumento in pane i qr. v bus. De allece C. De caseo i. De cepo ii lib. In prebendo l equorum i qr. ii bus.
Braciatura Braceatura de ordeo vi qr. et di.
Die lune sequenti in CCCC allecis ii s. iiii d. In iiii estik angwillarum xvii d.

Summa iii s. ix d. per prepositum

Staurum De frumento in pane i qr. i bus. In prebendo xxxvii equorum i qr.
Die Assumpcionis Beate Marie in i carcosio bovis vi s. In di. carcosio bovis xxii d. In xxvi pullis xvi d.

Summa ix s. ii d. per prepositum

Staurum De frumento in pane i qr. v bus. De allece di. C. De caponibus ii. De caseis i ad panetriam et ad coquinam i. In ponderacione Janekim i. Portantur cum[1] comite apud Canevell' ii. In prebendo xxxv equorum i qr.
Braciatura Braciatura de ordeo vi qr. et di.
Canell' Die mercurii scilicet in crastino Assumpcionis Beate Marie in cervisia iii s. vi d. In CC allecis xiiii d. In vi mulvellis ix d. In salmone vi d. In angwillis x d. ob.

Summa vi s. ix d. ob. per prepositum

Staurum De frumento in pane vi bus. In prebendo xxix equorum i qr. vi bus.
Die jovis sequenti in cervisia iii s. vi d. In i carcosio bovis viii s. In i carcosio mutonis xviii d. In di. porco ii s. In xviii pullis xviii d. In iii pullis ad nisos i d. ob. In C ovorum vi d. In i qr. mellis ii d. In ii bus. salis viii d. In uncto ad carectam ii d. In candela alba[2] ob. In dinario garcionum apud Thele iii d. ob. In emendacione selle panetrie ii d. In ii bus. furfuris ad canes viii d. In ferrura per fabrum ville viii d. ob.

Summa xx s. per prepositum

Staurum De frumento in pane vi bus. De caponibus ii. De pullis columbarum xx. In prebendo xxvii equorum i qr. v bus.
Die veneris sequenti ibidem in cervisia iiii s. ob. In allece xiiii d. In flundris xx d. In soles xvi d. In welekes iii d. ob. In i potello butiri iii d. ob. In cepo i d.

Summa viii s. x d. ob. per prepositum

Staurum De frumento in pane v bus. Ad coquinam i bus. Portantur cum comite iii bus. In prebendo xxxii equorum ii qr.

[1] MS repeats 'cum'.
[2] MS possibly 'abba'.

Campes Die sabbati sequenti apud Campes in cervisia ii s. xi d. In CC et di. allecis ii s. vi d. In salmone xiiii d. In C ovorum v[3] d. ob.

Summa vii s. ob. per prepositum

Staurum De frumento in pane di. qr. De pisce duro x. In prebendo xxxv equorum ii qr. i bus.

Dominica infra octabam Assumpcionis in cervisia iii s. In carne bovis vi s. vi d. In mutone vii d. ob. In di. porco ii s. In vi pullis iii d. In ovis ii d.

Summa xii s. vi d. ob. per prepositum

Staurum De frumento in pane i qr. i bus. De carne bovis i carcois. De gallinis i. De pullis columbarum xliiii. De caseo ii. In prebendo xl equorum ii qr. ii bus.

Die lune ibidem in cervisia iii s. In xviii pullis ix d. In ovis iiii d.

Summa iiii s. \ i d. / per prepositum

Staurum De frumento in pane i qr. De carne bovis di. carcois. De mutonibus i carcois. De caponibus iii. De gallinis ii. In prebendo xl equorum ii qr. ii bus.

Die martis in cervisia iii s. ix d. In di. carcosio bovis iii s. vi d. In i carcosio mutonis xviii d. In lardo ii d. In viii pullis vi d. ob. qua. In ovis iiii d.

Summa ix s. viii d. ob. qua. per prepositum

Staurum De frumento in pane i qr. De pullis columbarum xxiiii. De caseis ii ad coquinam. In prebendo xlvi equorum ii qr. v bus.

Die mercurii sequenti ibidem in cervisia iii s. ix d. In CC et di. allecis ii s. vi d. In iiii estik angwillarum iii s. v d. In ovis iii d. \ ob. / In xii ferris cum clavis iiii d.

Summa x s. iii d. ob. per prepositum

Staurum De frumento in pane vii bus. Portatur cum comite i bus. Ad coquinam i bus. et di. De pisce duro xx. De caseo ad panetriam i et ad coquinam i et portantur cum comite vi. De butiro i galo et di. et i quart. De cepo ad crassattum i lib. In prebendo li equorum ii qr. vi bus.

Hengham Die jovis scilicet die Sancti Bartholomei in pane iii s. iii d. In di. carcosio bovis ii s. vi d. In i porco iii s. vi d. In i carcosio mutonis xiiii d. In xx pullis xv d. ob. qua. In C ovorum vi d. In lichuno v d. ob.

Summa xii s. viii d. qua. per prepositum

Staurum De frumento in pane vi bus. De porcis di. De pullis vi. In prebendo xlvi equorum ii qr. vi bus.

Die veneris sequenti ibidem in CCC allecis ii s. iiii d. In viii mulvellis xx d. In creviciis i d. In i estik et di. angw. . .larum iii s. ii d. In uncto iii d.

Summa vii s. vi d. per prepositum

[3] MS omits ‘v’.

Staurum De frumento in pane i qr. i bus. De allece di. C. De cepo ii lib.
Braciatura Braciatura de ordeo vi qr. et di.
Laveham Eodem die apud Laveham in pane iii d. In cervisia ii s. In prebendo xxxv equorum ii qr. ii bus.
Die sabbati ibidem in cervisia iiii s. In C et di. allecis xviii d. In xii mulvellis ii s. i d. In salmone ii s.

Summa xi s. x d. per prepositum

Staurum De frumento in pane i qr. In prebendo xxxviii equorum ii qr. i bus.
Dominica sequenti ibidem in cervisia v s. In i carcosio et di. boum vi s. ix d. In i porco iiii s. iii d. In i mutone xxii d. In ii bus. . . .lis viii d. In C ovorum vi d. In i lib. cepi i d. ob. In ferris ii d. In C discis xxx plateris xx ciphis et di. C salsariorum ii s. vi d.

Summa xxi s. ix d. ob. per prepositum

Staurum De frumento in pane i qr. et di. De pullis xxii. De pullis columbarum xli. In prebendo xxxii equorum ii qr.
Die lune ibidem in cervisia xxiii d. In viii pullis vi d.

Summa ii s. v d. per prepositum

Hengham Eodem die apud Hengham in pane ii s. vii d. In di. carcosio bovis iii s. iiii d. In i porco iii s. In i carcosio mutonis xiiii d.

Summa x s. i d. per prepositum

Staurum De frumento in pane v bus. De porcis ii et di. De pullis viii. De gallinis i. De cepo i lib. et di. In prebendo xlvi equorum ii qr. et di.
Die martis scilicet die decollacionis Sancti Johannis Baptiste in di. carcosio et i qr. bovis v s. ii d. In x pullis vi d. ob. In di. C ovorum iii d. In dinario carectari*orum* longe carecte apud Gipeswic' querend*orum* vinum ii d. ob. In uncto . . . . .tam longam i d.

Summa vi s. iii d. per prepositum

Staurum De frumento in pane i qr. De porcis ii et di. De allece di. C. In prebendo xliiii equorum ii qr. iii bus.
Canevell' Die mercurii sequenti apud Canevell' in cervisia iii s. v d. ob. In C allecis xiiii d. In di. salmone viii d. In CC ovorum xiiii d. In pull*is* . . . d. In ferris per fabrum ville vi d. In cepo i d. In uncto ad carectam ii d.

Summa vii s. x d. \ ob. / per prepositum

Staurum De frumento in pane vii bus. In prebendo xl equorum ii qr. ii bus.
Wolfhamest' Die jovis sequenti apud Wolfhamest' in cervisia iii s. vii d. ob. In i carcosio bovis vi s. viii d. In di. porco xx d. In i carcosio mutonis . . . d.[4] In x pullis x d. In di. C ovorum iiii d. In sale ii d.

Summa xiiii s. vi d. ob. per prepositum

[4] Under sewing, possibly 'x d.'

Staurum De frumento in pane ii qr. De caseis ii. De butiro di. galo. In prebendo xl equorum ii qr. et di.
Die veneris sequenti ibidem in pisce per manum Ricardi de Chikewell' xiii s.

Summa xiii s. per prepositum

Abanum Eodem die apud Sanctum Alban*um* in literio v d. In feno xii d. In i qr. et vi bus. avene iiii s. i d. precium qr. ii s. iiii d. et dantur ad prebendum . . .xxiii equorum.

Summa per J.Capellanum v s. vi d.

Cestresham Die sabbati apud Cestresham in cervisia ii s. vi d. In i luceo xii d. In angwillis iii s. i d.

Summa vi s. vii d. per prepositum

Staurum De frumento in pane i qr. De caseis iii. In prebendo v bus.
Thame Eodem die apud Thame in vino ii s. In cervisia ix d. In pisce v d. ob. In exsspensis pistoris et hominis sui preeuntis per ii dies iiii d. In i qr. et vi bus. avene et di. bus. iiii s. vii d. ob. precium qr. ii s. viii d. et dantur per marscallum xxv equis ad prebendum.

Summa per J.Capellanum viii s. ii d.

Witteney Dominica sequenti apud Witteney in vino xvi d. In cervisia ii d. In carne bovis xii d. In pullis vi d. In ovis iii d. In menuse ii d. ob. In literio x. . .ii d. In feno xii d. In carbone iiii d. In candela i d. In cepo ad crassatum i d. In i qr. et vii bus. avene v s. et dantur per marscallum xxiiii equis ad prebendum.

Summa xiii s. ii d. per J.Capellanum

Teokesber' Die lune sequenti apud Teokesber' in pane ii s. In vino xviii d. In cervisia xix d. In pullis ii d. ob. In ferris ii d. In candela alba i d. In i qr. avene ii s. viii d. et dantur ad prebendum xviii equorum.

Summa viii s. \ ii d. / per J.Capellanum

Eodem die apud Winchecumbe in exsspensis familie per manum Michaelis Clerici viii s. vi d. ob.

Summa viii s. vi d. ob. per J.Capellanum

Die martis ibidem in exsspensis familie per manum predictam v s.

Summa v s. per manum J.Capellani

Die mercurii in exsspens*is* familie ibidem per manum predictam iiii s.

Summa iiii s. per manum J.Capellani

Die jovis ibidem in exsspensis familie per manum predictam ii s. x d. In exsspensis Scortsrend versus Hengham vi d. In exspensis pistoris et hominis sui versus Witcherche vi d.

Summa iii s. x d. per J. Capellanum

Die veneris ibidem in esspensis familie per manum predictam.
Die sabbati sequenti ibidem scilicet in crastino Nativitatis Beate Marie in exsspensis familie per manum predictam.

Evesham Dominica proxima post festum Nativitatis Beate Marie apud Evesham in pane ii s. vi d. In v lag. vini xvii d. ob. In cervisia ii s. vi d. In carne bovis ii s. vi d. In lardo v d. In sale iii d. In farina avene ii d. ob. In i gallina i d. In feno ad xxiiii equos xii d. In i qr. et vi bus. avene iii s. xi d. In litterio xx d. In busca v d. In candela i d. In alleis ob. In emundacione domus ob. In pull*o* ad falcon*es* i d. In i equo conducto apud Teokesber' iiii d. In ii lib. et di. cere ad mensuram comitis xv d. In elemosina ad fontem ii d.

Summa xviii s. xi d. per J.Capellanum

Bannebir' Die lune sequenti apud Bannebir' in pane iii s. ii d. In vino xvi d. In cervisia ii s. ix d. In iii carcosiis mutonum iiii s. In carne bovis vii d. In carne porcina xii d. In busco ad ignem vi d. In literio vii d. In feno xii d. In candela alba ob. In uncto ad carectam ii d. In cordis ad w. . .pas faciendas i d. In i qr. et vii bus. avene iii s. ix d.

Summa xviii s. xi d. ob. per J.Capellanum

Wytcherche Die martis sequenti apud Witcherche in vino xii d. In cervisia i d. In di. carcosio bovis iiii s. In di. porco xx d. In pullis v d. In di. C ovorum iii d. In di. bus. salis iii d. In cepo ii d. ob. In i qr. frumenti v s. viii d. ob. In i bus. avene iii d.

Summa xiii s. viii d. per prepositum

Cruer' Die jovis sequenti apud Cruer' in exsspensis familie per manum marscalli iii \ s. / v d.

Summa iii s. v d. per J.Capellanum

Campes Die veneris scilicet in crastino exaltacionis Sancte Crucis in cervisia iii s. iiii d. In CC allecis xxiii d. ob. In merlingo ix d.

Summa vi s. i d. per prepositum

Staurum De frumento in pane vi bus. De pisce duro viii. In prebendo xxv equorum i qr. vii bus.

Die sabbati sequenti ibidem in cervisia ii s. vi d. In C et di. allecis xxii d. In angwillis xviii d. In piris i d. In ferris ii d. In emendacione carecte ii d. In uncto ad eamdem i d. In exsspens*is* pistoris et hominis sui preveniencis per ii dies[5] iiii d.

Summa vi s. iiii d. per prepositum

Staurum De frumento in pane di. qr. De aucis iii. De pullis xii portantur cum comite apud Bumsted. De pisce duro viii. De buttiro i galon'. De cepo i lib. In prebendo xxv equorum ii qr.

Colnum Dominica proxima post festum exaltacionis Sancte Crucis in cervisia xx d. In i carcosio bovis vi s. vi d. In di. carcosio mutonis ix d. In

[5] MS 'per ii duos dies'.

carne porcina vi d. In di. C ovorum iii d. In wastello ad coquinam iiii d. In allece i d. In candela alba i d. In cepo ad crassatum i d.

Summa x s. iii d. ob. per J. Capellanum

Staurum De frumento in pane i qr. i bus. Ad coquinam i bus. De carne bovis i qr. De aucis viii. De pullis xxiii. In prebendo xl equorum ii qr. et di.

Die lune sequenti ibidem in cervisia xx d. In di. carcosio et i qr. bovis vii s. vi d. In ii carcosiis mutonum xx d. In xii pullis x d. ob. In C et di. ovorum x d. ob. In sagimine albo ad ungendum palefridum comitis i d.

Summa xii s. viii d. per J. Capellanum

Staurum De frumento in pane i qr. ii bus. In prebendo xxx equorum ii qr.

Die martis sequenti in cervisia xx d. In i carcosio bovis v s. vi d. In i carcosio mutonis x d. ob. In x. . . . .ll' x d. In C ovorum vii d. In cepo i d.

Summa x s. vi d. ob.

Staurum De frumento in pane i qr. ii bus. De aucis viii. De allece C. In prebendo xxxii equorum ii qr.

Die mercurii sequenti in CCCC allecis iii s. In merlingo et in plaicis iii s. i d. In i galone mustardi iiii d.

Summa vi s. iiii d. per J. Capellanum

Staurum De frumento in pane i qr. In prebendo xxvi equorum i qr. v bus.

Die jovis in cervisia ii s. iiii d. In i carcosio bovis v s. In i carcosio mutonis xiiii d. In v pullis v d. ad falcon*es*. In[6] iiii pullis ii d. ob. qua. In cepo ii d. In sale i d.

Summa ix s. iii d. ob. qua. per J. Capellanum

Staurum De frumento in pane i qr. ii bus. De aucis ix. De allece di. C. In prebendo xl equorum ii qr. et di.

Die veneris scilicet in crastino Sancti Mathey in CCC et di. allecis iii s. vii d. In merlingo et flundris xii d. In v galonibus ostriarum xii d.

Summa v s. vii d. per J. Capellanum

Staurum De frumento in pane i qr. ii bus. De allece di. C. In prebendo xl equorum ii qr. ii bus.

Die sabbati sequenti in CCC allecis salsi iii s. iii d. In C allecis recentis xxi d. In C merlingi ii s. In haddoko et codling' v d. ob. In cervisia x d. In C allecis ad fratres minores Colecestr' xiii d. In di. C merlingi ad opus eorum xiii d. In vino ad opus eorum per manum Thome de Laveham ii s. In car. . . . . unius tonelli vini ii d. In ferris per fabrum ville vii d.

xiii s. ii d. ob. per J. Capellanum

Membrane 2 recto

Staurum De frumento in pane i qr. Ad fratres minores i bus. In prebendo xxxiiii equorum[7] ii qr. i bus.

[6] Possibly preceded by 'It''. MS obscure.

[7] MS omits 'equorum'.

Die dominica sequenti in cervisia xx d. In i carcosio bovis v s. vi d. In i carcosio et i qr. mutonum xviii d. In vii pullis vi d. In cepo ad crassattum i d.

Summa ix s. iii d. per J. Capellanum

Staurum De frumento in pane i qr. iii bus. De aucis x. In prebendo xxxix equorum ii qr. ii bus.

Die lune sequenti in cervisia xx d. In i carcosio bovis ix s. In i carcosio mutonis xiiii d. In i porco iiii s. vi d. In xv gallinis xvii d. In C ovorum vi d. In sale ii d. In picheriis ob. qua. In cepo i d.

Summa xviii s. vii d. ob. qua. per J. Capellanum

Staurum De frumento in pane i qr. et di. Ad coquinam i bus. De aucis v. De allece C. In prebendo xlvi equorum ii qr. et di.

Die martis sequenti in cervisia xviii d.[8] In i carcosio et i qr. boum viii s. iii d. In i carcosio mutonis x. . .ii d. In xv pullis xii d. In C ovorum vi d. In sagimine albo . . . . .[9]

6 *Diet account for an unidentified household near Boroughbridge, Yorkshire, July to September, c.1270–90*

This account is written on a Chancery fashion roll of two membranes, with sewing holes at the top of the first, indicating that at least one further membrane was once attached. The diet entries are for the household of an unidentified lord and lady, for the period 27 July to 2 September in 1273, 1279, 1284 or 1290.[1] The account was written up periodically, every two or three days, in a single hand, but with the marginal notes *quit* in another hand. The main accounts represent principally the activities of the kitchen and marshalsea sections of the household, with only marginal notes of the activities of the pantry and buttery. Although it has not been possible to identify the head of the household, it was, to judge by the numbers of horses present, a substantial establishment. It may be possible to identify the Roger Sprenghese who is mentioned with the man of the same name who was sheriff of Shropshire and Staffordshire from October 1278.[2] The Latin of the account is noteworthy for its idiosyncratic grammar and spellings.

[8] MS omits 'd.'
[9] MS cut away at this point.

[1] 1301 and 1307 are also possible years, but less likely.
[2] *List of sheriffs for England and Wales from the earliest times to AD 1831* (PRO Lists and Indexes, 9; 1898); *Accounts of the constables of Bristol Castle in the thirteenth and early fourteenth centuries* ed. M. Sharp (Bristol Record Society, 34; 1982) pp. 16–17, n. 44.

Northamptonshire RO Finch Hatton MS 458

Membrane 1 recto
Die jovis in multone et vel' x d. Liberacio coquine i qr. perne ii aucas iiii pulcinos. Prebendum pro equis supra preter nuncius qui recessit cum i eco. Prebendum i bus. grosse avene iiii^{or} bus. minute avene.
Die veneris in pisse empto per R. de Westone vii d. Liberacio coquine ii pisses. Prebendum pro dictis i bus. grosse iiii^{or} bus. minute.
..... *et domina* Die sabati in allece et tribus piscibus emptis per R. de Westone xviii d. Prebendum pro equis dictis et supervenit dominus et domina cum xiiii equis et dominus J. de Beche cum ii equis. Prebendum pro xxvii equis i bus. grosse avene i qr. et iii bus. minute avene et dy.
...*ane furnito i qr. ... frumenti et ii bus. siliginis* Die dominica in i qr. bovis ii s. In dy. bidente xiii d. In i vitulo xx d. In ovis vi d. Liberacio coquine i qr. bovis i pernam v aucas ix pulcinos. Prebendum pro equis dictis i qr. et iii bus. et dy. minute avene et i bus. grosse.
...*visia braciata i qr. ...dei et ii qr. avene* Die lune in dy. qr. salmonis iii d. In ovis ii d. Liberacio coquine ii pisses. Prebendum pro equis dictis preter dominus J. de Beche qui recessit cum ii equis et Rogerus Sprengehese cum ii equis. Et supervenit summar*i*us Johannis de Quokyn et Phelippus de Beche cum i eco. Prebendum pro xxiiii equis i qr. et iii bus. minute avene et i bus. grosse avene.
Die martis in ovis vi d. Liberacio coquine i qr. bovis i pernam iiii^{or} aucas vi pulcinos dy. vitulum dy. bidentem. Prebendum pro equis dictis iii bus. et dy. grosse avene i qr. minute avene.
Recessit dominus. Lendemeyn de Seynt Pere. Quit Die mercurie in ix pissibus xxxviii d. In allece xi d. In ovis iiii^{or} d. Liberacio coquine iii pisses et dy. Prebendum pro equis dictis exceptis iii equis qui recesserunt cum domino. Prebendum pro xvi equis vi bus. grosse avene et ii bus. minute avene.
Atthamia i qr. bovis Die jovis liberacio coquine i qr. perne i qr. multonis xiiii pulcinos. Prebendum pro dictis vi bus. grosse avene et ii bus. minute.
In pane furnito i qr. et dy. frumenti Die veneris liberacio coquine iii pisses. Prebendum pro equis dictis et supervenit dominus cum iii equis. Prebendum pro xviii equis vi bus. grosse avene et iii bus. minute avene.
Die sabati in salmone et pisse xiii d. per R. de Weston'. Liberacio coquine iiii pisses. Prebendum pro xviii equis vi bus. grosse avene et iii bus. m.....
In pane furnito dy. qr. frumenti pro cibbar..... domini Die dominica in aucis iii d. In ovis iiii^{or} d. Liberacio coquine i qr. bovis i qr. perne i bidentem iii aucas xii pulcinos. Prebendum pro equis dictis vi bus. grosse et ii bus. minute. Et supervenit J. Darcy. Prebendum i bus. grosse avene.

Membrane 2 recto

Die lune in ovis v d. Liberacio coquine i qr. bovis i pernam iiii^{or} aucas i bidentem xv pulcinos. Prebendum pro equis dictis et supervenit T. de Esee cum ii equis et H. de Westone cum i eco. Prebendum pro xxiiii equis vi bus. grosse avene et vi bus. min...

In servisia braciata ii qr. avene et i qr. ordei Die martis in butiro i d. qua. In ovis vi d. Liberacio coquine i qr. bovis dy. pernam[1] iii aucas i bidentem et dy. xiii pulcinos \ i purcellum. / Prebendum pro equis dictis exceptis ii equis domini J. Darci. Prebendum pro xxii equis v bus. minute avene et vi bus. grosse avene.

Die mercurie in ovis x d. In viii pissibus et C allecis \ iii s. / In butiro iii d. In ollis i d. ob. Liberacio coquine iiii^{or} pisses. Prebendum pro equis dictis excepto eco[2] H. de Wistone. Prebendum vi bus. grosse avene et v bus. minute.

Atthame i qr. bovis Die jovis in ovis v d. Liberacio coquine dy. pernam dy. bidentem xiii pulcinos. Prebendum pro equis dictis vi bus. grosse avene et vi bus. minute avene.

Die veneris in pisse empto ad Ponteburgam iiii^{or} s. Liberacio coquine iiii^{or} pisses. Prebendum pro equis dictis et supervenit dominus J. de Beche cum iiii^{or} equis. Prebendum pro xxvii equis vii bus. grosse avene vi bus. et dy. minute avene.

Quit Die sabati in pisse empto ad Ponteburgam xvi d. In butiro i d. qua. Prebendum pro equis dictis exceptis iiii^{or} equis domini J. de Beche. Prebendum pro xxiii equis vi bus. grosse avene v bus. et dy. minute avene.

*In pane furnito i qr. frumenti et dy. qr. siliginis. Negat*i *i ove et i vitulus de stauro* Die dominica in ovis v d. Liberacio i qr. perne i bidentem dy. vitulum iiii^{or} aucas x pulcinos. Prebendum pro equis dictis et supervenit .....[3] domini Emundi Batoun et ecus Rogeri le Sinour. Prebendum pro xxv equis vii bus. grosse avene et v bus. minute avene.

Die lune in ovis iii d. Liberacio coquine i qr. bovis dy. perne i purcellum xiii pulcinos. Prebendum pro equis dictis excepto eco Rogeri le Sinour pro xxiiii^{or} equis vi bus. grosse avene et vi bus. minute avene.

In servisia braciata ii qr. avene et i qr. ordey Die martis in ovis v d. Liberacio coquine dy. qr. bovis dy. perne dy. bidentem ix pulcinos. Prebendum pro equis dictis vi bus. grosse avene et vi bus. minute avene.

Die mercurie in pisse iii s. vi d. \ In i bus. salis vi d. / In butiro iii d. In allece xvii d. In ovis vi d. Liberacio coquine vi pisses. Prebendum pro equis dictis i qr. et dy. minute avene.

Die jovis in ovis iii d. Liberacio coquine i qr. bovis i qr. perne i purcellum i

[1] MS possibly 'i dy. pernas'.

[2] MS obscure, possibly 'exceptus eco'.

[3] MS obscure, 'narinus' or 'harinus'?

bidentem x pulcinos. Prebendum pro equis dictis vi bus. grosse avene et vi bus. minute avene.
In pane furnito i qr. frumenti et dy. qr. mixtilionis Die veneris liberacio coquine iii pisses et dy. Prebendum pro dictis et supervenit Thomas de Esee cum i eco et H*er*bertus de Borhunt' cum i eco et Willelmus de Sceltone cum iii equis. Prebendum pro xxix equis vii bus. et dy. grosse avene et viii bus. minute avene.
Die sabati in salmone et allece emptis ad Ponteburgam.[4] Liberacio coquine iii pisses et dy. Prebendum pro equis dictis vi exceptis Thoma*s* qui recessit cum i eco et H*er*bertus de Borhunt' et Willelmus Sceltone cum iiii^or^ equis. Prebendum pro xxiiii^or^ equis vii bus. grosse avene et vii bus. minute avene.
Die dominica in ovis viii d. \ In carne bovina vii d. / Liberacio i qr. bovis dy. pernam dy. vitulum i bidentem i purcellum i aucam x pulcinos. Prebendum pro equis dictis et supervenit R. Sprengehese cum ii equis pro xxvi equis vii bus. et dy. grosse avene et vii bus. et dy. minute.
Die lune in xx lag. servisie ii s. vi d. En ovis ii d. Liberacio coquine i qr. bovis i qr. perne i bidentem ix pulcinos i aucam. Prebendum pro equis dictis vii bus. et dy. grosse avene et vii bus. et dy. minute avene.
Die martis in pulcinis x d. In ovis v d. \ In caro bovina vii d. et liberacio i qr. bovis i qr. perne xii pulcinos. / In xxviii lag. servisie ii s. iiii d. In pane vi d.[5] Prebendum xii bus. avene grosse.
Recessit dominus Die mercurie in ovis vi d. \ In pane vii d. In pulcinis v d. / In pisse et alece xviii d. Liberacio ii pisses. Prebendum pro equis dictis i qr. et dy. grosse. Et recessit dominus cum viii equis.
Quit Die jovis in pane viii d. In servisia xviii d. In pulcinis xv d. In ovis iiii^or^ d. In caro bovina et dy. vitulo xii d. In allece x d. In pisse ii s. ii d. In i turbot vii d. Liberacio coquine i qr. bovis i qr. perne ii pulcinos. Prebendum pro xvii equis i qr. grosse avene.
In pane furnito i qr. frumenti et dy. qr. siliginis Die veneris in servisia ix d. In butiro i d. qua. Liberacio coquine iiii pisses. Prebendum pro equis dictis et recessit Alexander de Walecote cum ii equis. Prebendum pro xvi equis dy. qr. grosse avene et dy. qr. minute avene.
In servisia braciata ii qr. avene et i qr. ordey Die sabati \ in butiro i d. / Liberacio i pissem. Prebendum dy. qr. grosse avene et vi bus. minute avene pro equis domini Edmundi Hakelut et magistri Hugonis Coci et Henrici de Panetria.
Die dominica in dy. vitulo et dy. multonis xx d. Liberacio i qr. perne i pulcinum. Prebendum pro equis dictis exceptis Edmundi Hakel'. Prebendum dy. qr. grosse et dy. qr. minute.

[4] Followed by a blank space in MS.
[5] 'vi d.' possibly preceded by an erasure.

Membrane 2 dorse
Die lune in pulcinis v d. Liberacio coquine v pulcinos. Prebendum pro dictis et supervenit dominus R. de Sapi cum iii equis. Prebendum pro[6] xix equis i qr.[7] iii bus. minute avene.
Die martis in ovis iii d. In vissero i multonis v d. In pulcinis iiii d. Liberacio coquine ii pulcinos. Prebendum pro dictis i qr. et iii bus. minute avene.
Die mercurie in i qr. vituli iiii d. ob. In i qr. multonis vi d. In C allecis vii d. In dy. C allecis v d. In ovis viii d. In butiro i d. Prebendum pro dictis i qr. ii bus. minute avene.
Die jovis liberacio coquine i qr. vituli et i qr. multonis. Prebendum pro equis dictis i qr. minute avene et ii bus.
In pane furnito i qr. frumenti et dy. qr. siliginis Die veneris liberacio coquine iii pisses. Prebendum pro equis dictis i qr. et ii bus. minute avene et supervenit dominus cum iii equis ii bus. et dy. grosse avene.
Die sabati in ovis iiii^or d. In butiro. In allece x d. In moruca ix d. Prebendum pro dictis.

7 *Diet account for the household of Henry de Lacy, Earl of Lincoln, in Kent and France, 24 May 1299 to 7 June 1299*

In May 1294, the declaration by King Philip IV of France of the confiscation of the duchy of Gascony had led Edward I unwillingly into war. A truce was reached in October 1297, which was subsequently renewed. The position of the duchy was submitted by both kings to the consideration, in a private capacity, of Pope Boniface VIII, who made an award in June 1298. The effect was to support the truce and it was strengthened with proposals for two marriages, between Edward and Philip's sister, Margaret; and between the future Edward II and the French king's daughter, Isabella. Henry de Lacy, the Earl of Lincoln, was one of the experienced diplomats employed by Edward I in the ensuing negotiations, which were concluded in part by the understanding reached at Montreuil-sur-mer in June 1299 and at length by the peace of Paris of 1303.[1]

In May 1299 Henry de Lacy was among those given letters of proxy entrusting them with full powers in the negotiations for the restoration of

[6] MS omits 'pro'.
[7] Probably 'i qr.' written over 'v qr.'

[1] F. M. Powicke *The thirteenth century 1216–1307* (2nd edition, Oxford, 1962) pp. 644–54.

peace between the two countries in accordance with the Pope's award. De Lacy was also given full powers to conclude the marriage contract between the future Edward II and Isabella.[2] This diet account is for De Lacy and his household while he was on his way to conduct the negotiations, leaving England at Dover, crossing the Channel to Wissant, and moving on towards Montreuil-sur-mer.

The accounts are written on a parchment roll of one membrane, laid out with a fold for the left margin and with horizontal folds separating the daily entries. The document is largely in a single hand, with small alterations by a further hand. The account was written in three blocks, the second section starting on the first Thursday, and the third, on the second Sunday.

Nottinghamshire RO DDFJ 8/4/1

Recto

Die dominica xxiiii di Maii apud Hakinton' pro comite et familia in pane x s. viii d. In vino xxx lag. vii s. vi d. In cervisia iiii^{xx} lag.[1] vii s. Summa panetrie et botellarie xxv s. ii d. Coquina In uno carcosio bovis et i qr. xvi s. In una perna iii s. In ii vitulis iiii s. In ii cassis[2] multonum v s. In x aucis v s. x d. In xiiii pullis xx d. In xiii columbis ix d. In pinguedine viii d. In pane pro coquina iiii d. In sale v d. In portagio iiii d. Summa coquine xxxviii s. Marchalcia lxxvii equis. In feno v s. vi d. In prebenda v qr. vii bus. et di. xix s. ix d. ob. In litera viii d. In expensis Willelmi de Holm et magistri W. Coci preeuncium apud Hakinton' non precomputatis x d. In allocacione unius lecti pro Henrico le Converse ii d. In vadiis Inge non precomputatis viii d. ob. In vadiis xxxvii garcionum viii pagettorum v s. iii d. ob. Summa marchalcie xxxii s. xi d. ob. Summa iiii^{xx}xvi s. i d. ob.

Die lune proxima sequenti pro comite et familia in pane viii s. In butiro vi d. In vino xxviii lag. vii s. In cervisia lxx lag. vi s. v d. ob. Summa panetrie et botellarie xxi s. xi d. ob. Coquina In viii morues l makereus poudrees v s. ii d. In merlingo xviii d. In coungre iii s. vi d. In allece et plaices ii s. vi d. In velkes vii d. In CCC ovis ii s. In furmagio et butiro xix d. In flore vi d. In sale iii d. In ferina vi d. In cepis ii d. In persil ob. In portagio ii d. ob. In ii salmonibus v s. vi d. In poudre et furnagio xxii d. In uno hakenay conducto pro illo salmone cariando xvi d. In expensis Thome \ Coci[3] / cum ii equis apud Derteford vi d. Summa coquine xxvii s. viii d. Marchalcia lxxix equis.

[2] *Treaty rolls 1234–1325* pp. 136–9.

[1] MS omits 'lag.'

[2] MS 'caseis'.

[3] MS 'Coco'.

In feno v s. v d. In prebenda v qr. xvi s. viii d. In vadiis xlv garcionum viii pagettorum vi s. iii d. ob. Summa marchalcie xxviii s. iiii d. ob.

Summa emptorum lxxviii s.

Die martis proxima sequenti pro comite et familia in pane v s. et di. qr. frumenti furnito de empcione ut patet inferius. In butiro vii d. In ovis pro wafres iii d. In lavendria i d. In xlvi lag. vini xi s. vi d. In cervisia iiii^{xx} lag. vi s. ix d. ob. Summa panetrie et botellarie xxiiii s. i d. ob. Coquina In xii morues iii s. vi d. In makerel iiii s. x d. In merlingo ii s. iii d. In vii bremes xvi d. In plaices iiii s. ii d. In uno dorre xii d. In welkes xiiii d. In allece ii s. In menues xii d. In ovis xvi d. In furmagio et butiro ii s. In olera pane lacte et sale v d. In vino acro xii d. In portagio iii d. Summa coquine xxvi s. iii d. Marchalcia lxxix equis. In feno vi s. iiii d. ob. In prebenda v qr. i bus. xvii s. i d. In viridi iii d. In correctione de ba*s* pellicibus vi d. In pinguedine i d. ob. In vadiis xliiii garcionum viii pagettorum vi s. iii d. ob. Summa marchalcie xxxi s. vii d. ob. Summa iiii li. ii s.

Die mercurii proxima sequenti pro comite et familia in pane CC panibus de vii bus. frumenti furnitis de <providencia> empcione ut patet inferius. In butiro vii d. In vino xxix lag. et i potello vii s. iiii d. ob. In cervisia lxx lag. vi s. v d. ob. Summa xiiii s. v d. Coquina In morue ii s. vi d. In merlingo xvi d. In allece xv d. In plaices et makerel viii s. In menues x d. In welkes xi d. ob. In ovis ix d. In furmagio et butiro xvii d. In olera et lacte et sale vi d. In mustard et viridi sucto vii d. ob. In portagio ii d. ob. In ovis pro wafres iii d. Summa xviii s. vii d. ob. Marchalcia lxxii equis. In feno vi s. iii d. In prebenda iiii qr. iiii bus. et di. xv s. x d. ob. In coffres em*e*ndandis de coquina vi d. In ferris ii d. In feno <de> \ per Johannem[4] / Clericum i d. In vadiis xlvi garcionum viii pagettorum vi s. vi d. Summa xxix s. iii s. ob. Summa emptorum lxii s. iiii d.

Die jovis proxima sequenti pro comite et familia in festo Assencionis Domini in pane CCxl panibus de i qr. frumenti furnito de empcione ut patet inferius. In vino xxx \ et iiii et di. / lag. vini viii s. vii d. ob. In iiii^{xx} lag. cervisie vii s. v d. Summa panetrie et botellarie xvi s. ob. Coquina In uno carcosio bovis et i qr. xv s. vi d. In iii multonibus vi s. In una perna iii s. In ii vitulis iiii s. In vi aucis iii s. vi d. In v gall*in*is xv d. In xvi pullis xxii d. In xii columbis vi d. In C ovis ix d. In pane et in farina avene pro coquina viii d. \ In sale viii d. / In portagio iii d. Summa coquine xxxvii s. xi d. Marchalcia lxxii equis. In feno vi s. iii d. In prebenda iiii qr. iiii bus. et di. xv s. ii d. ob. In expensis in vadiis xlv garcionum viii pagettorum vi s. iii d. ob. Summa marchalcie xxvii s. ix d. Summa emptorum iiii li. xx d. ob.

Die veneris sequenti pro comite et familia in pane CC panibus de vii bus. frumenti furnitis de empcione ut patet inferius. In lavendria ii d. In vino

[4] MS repeats 'Joh''.

xxx lag. vii s. vi d. In cervisia iiii^{xx}x lag. vii s. x d. qua. Summa panetrie et botellarie xv s. vi d. qua. Coquina In morue ii s. x d. In plaices et coungre vii s. In merlingo xii d. In makerel xvi d. In allece ii s. In uno qr. de porpais ii s. viii d. In bars de mari iii s. vi d. In welkes viii d. In uno dorre iiii d. In menues viii d. In v lib. amigdalarum xii d. ob. In sale iiii d. In pane olera iii d. ob. In portagio ii d. Summa coquine xxiii s. x d. Marchalcia lxxii equis. In feno v s. x d. In prebenda iiii qr. vi bus. et di. xvi s. ob. In viridi pro aula i d. In CCiiiM clavis xviii s. ii d. In albo pinguedine pro equis infirmis iiii d. In vadiis xlv garcionum viii pagettorum vi s. iii d. ob. Summa marchalcie xlvi s. ix d. Summa emptorum iiii li. vi s. i d. qua.

Die sabati sequenti pro comite et familia in pane CCxxii panibus de i qr. frumenti furnito de empcione ut patet inferius. In butiro v d. In vino xx lag. v s. In cervisia iiii^{xx}x lag. vii s. x d. qua. Summa panetrie et botellarie xiii s. iii d. qua. Coquina In morue xx d. In allece xii d. In bars mulet e bremes iii s. In l merlingo vii d. In l makerel xv d. In plaices ii s. vi d. In welkes viii d. In menues iii d. In butiro et furmagio xiiii d. In olera i d. ob. In pane et sale iii d. In portagio ii d. Summa coquine xii s. vii d. ob. Marchalcia lxx equis. In feno v s. ix d. In prebenda iiii qr. vi bus. et di. xvi s. ob. In vadiis xlv garcionum viii pagettorum vi s. iii d. ob. Summa marchalcie xxviii s. i d. Summa emptorum liii s. xi d. ob. qua.

Die dominica proxima sequenti pro comite et familia in pane CCl panibus de i qr. frumenti furnito de empcione ut patet inferius. In vino xxx lag. vii s. vi d. In C lag. cervisie emptis viii s. viii d. Summa panetrie et botellarie xvi s. ii d. ob. Coquina \ In / i carcosio bovis xiiii s. In uno multone et di. iii s. In uno vitulo ii s. In vi aucis iii s. vi d. In iiii calponibus ii s. iiii d. In iii gallinis ix d. In ovis xii d. In pane ii d. In uno bus. salis viii d. In olera i d. In portagio ii d. Summa coquine xxvii s. \ viii d. / Marchalcia lxxiiii equis. In feno vi s. iii d. In prebenda v qr. ii bus. xvii s. vi d. In viridi pro aula iiii d. In vadiis xlvi garcionum vi pagettorum vi s. iii d. Summa marchalcie xxx s. iiii d. Summa emptorum lxxiiii s. ii d. ob.

In expensis Galfridi de Roching' cum iii destraris comitis de Lond' usque Caneford' per vi dies et pro expensis suis retroveniend*o* Lond' mense Maii xvi s. In expensis Edmundi Talbot Nich*ola*i Clerici Edmundi de Elleswrth' de Lond' usque Hakinton' et per unum diem commerant*ium* Lond' post recessum comitis vi s. v d. ob. In expensis Edmundi Clerici de Hakinton' versus Lond' et de Lond' usque Hakinton' et in hakenaus allocandis per viam per iii dies pro argento mutuando iiii s. viii d. In expensis unius garcionis pro fustigacione ii boum de Lond' usque Hakinton' xii d. cum expensis boum. In expensis Thome Ostiar*ii* pro ospiciis capiendis apud Douver xii d. per ii dies. In expensis Lakoc cum uno hakeney conducto de Lond' usque Canterbire pro tapet*is* cariand*is* ii s. Summa xxxi s. i d. ob.[5]

[5] MS 'i d. d.'

In expensis comitis in panetria silicet per viii dies ut patet superius vii qr. frumenti furnitis l s. ii d.[6] precium qr. vii s. ii d. In busca et carbonibus emptis in expensis superius dum comes comoravit apud Hakinton' xxviii s. vi d. Summa lxxviii s. viii d.
In xiiii bobus et vaccis in providencia facienda apud Moustroil emptis apud Hakinton' per Nich*ola*um Clericum mense Maii xv li. xiiii s. In xx baconibus iiii li. In xxiii calponibus xxxiii gall*in*is vi duodenis vi pulcinis \ et / x aucis xxix s. iiii d. In D ovis ii s. xi d. In expensis Nich*olai* Clerici et Thome Coci cum iii equis per ii dies pro illis bobus emendis et pro illo pullalo cariando iii s. xi d. Summa xxi li. x s. ii d.
In uno doleo vini empto per Baskle quod datum fuit archiediaconi Cantuar' de dono comitis xlvi s. viii d. In cariagio predicti vini et in discarcacione predicti dolei apud Hakinton' ix d. In vii bobus \ et vaccis / emptis apud Cantuar' per Thomam Lard*arium* mense Junii in providencia facta versus Moustroil vi li. xii s. i d. In viii multonibus emptis per idem Thomam ibidem pro providencia apud Moustroil xx s. x d. In xxiiii calponibus emptis per eundem pro providencia ibidem x s. x d.
Summa x li. xi s. ii d.

Dorse

Die lune proxima sequenti pro comite et familia in pane CC \ et di. / panibus de i qr. furnito de precomputato. In lavendria i d. ob. In vino xxvi lag. vi s. vi d. In vino de la Rochele vi d. In cervisia iiii^xx lag. vii s. i d. Summa panetrie et botellarie xiiii s. ii d. Coquina In uno carcosio bovis xiiii s. In ii multonibus iiii s. x d. In carne porc*ina* pro pastillis xii d. In uno capriolo ii s. vi d. In uno agno vii d. In x pullis xiii d. In lardo vi d. In flore pro pastillis vi d. In olera et sale v d. In aceco et vino acro et viridi succo xxii d. In portagio ii d. In ii bus.[7] frumenti emptis pro pull*alo* ii s. iii d. In factura iiii cages pro pull*alo* vi d. Summa xxx s. ii d. Marchalcia lxviii equis. In feno v s. vii d. In prebenda iiii qr. vii bus. et di. xvi s. v d. ob. In fustigacione ii animalium usque Douver ii d. In emendacione iiii sigillorum ii s. In emendacione pellium i d. In vadiis xlvi garcionum vi pagettorum vi s. iii d. Summa xxx s. vi d. ob. Summa emptorum lxxiiii s. x d. ob.
Die martis proxima sequenti pro comite et familia in pane CC panibus de vii bus. frumenti furnitis de providencia. In vino xlii lag. et i potello xiiii s. ii d. In una lag. vini vi d. de la Rochele. In cervisia Cvi lag. xii s. iii d. Summa xxvi s. xi d. Coquina In uno carcosio i qr. xvi s. In ii multonibus v s. vi d. In ii vitulis v s. ix d. In xiii aucis vii s. v d. xiii gall*ine* xv pulli Cl ova de providencia. In pisce pro jejunantibus xiiii d. In pane pro coquina et in sep*o* v d. In pinguedine iiii d. In sale et farina viii d. In ii bus. frumenti pro

[6] MS possibly 'iii d.', although the addition is correct with 'ii d.'
[7] MS 'In ii bus. et frumenti'.

sustentacione pullorum xxii d. ob. In portagio coquine i d. ob. In cariagio puletrie ii s. ix d. Summa coquine xlii s. Marchalcia lxxvi equis. Fenum ix s. ix d. ob. In prebenda vi qr. ii bus. xxv s. In litera ix s. viii d. ob. In pane pro palefrid*is* ii d. In viridi xv d. In ferris per viam ii d. In expensis Willelmi Coci et Thome Ostiar*ii* et Henrici le Freremon preeuncium apud Douver iii s. x d. per ii dies. In allocacione unius lecti pro Henrico de Baroun x d. In vadiis xlv garcionum vii pagettorum vi s. ii d. ob. Summa marchalcie lvi s. xi d. ob.

Summa vi li. <iiii s. iiii d. ob.> \ v s. x d. ob. /

Die mercurii proxima sequenti pro comite et familia in pane de empcione iiii s. v d. In xlvii lag. vini xv s. viii d. In cervisia xv d. \ Summa panetrie et botellarie xxi s. iiii d. / Coquina In merlingo xii d. In makerel viii d. ob. In morue vii d. In bremes viii d. In plaices ii s. iiii d. In crevices iii d. In ovis ii d. ob. In sale ii d. ob. <In . . . ii d. ob.> In pane i d. In pane pro cinis vii d. In gall*in*is emptis pro gent*aculo* comitis ii s. vi d. Summa coquine ix s. i d. ob. Marchalcia In feno ii s. In prebenda viii s. In busca vi s. viii d. In candela ii s. vi d. In vadiis xlv garcionum vii pagettorum vi s. ii d. ob. <xxv s. iiii d. ob.>

Summa emptorum lv s. x d.

In passagio pro sex navibus allocandis pro comite et familia de Douver usque Witsand ix li. iiii s. ii d. In portagio \ hern*esii* et in batello / comitis et familie apud Douver xi s. vi d. In batellagio et pountagio unius navis pro equis comitis et familie vi s. iiii d.

Summa passagii de Douver x li. ii s. viii d.

In batillagio portagio cariagio cum pontagio equorum et victualium comitis et familie apud Witsand li s. vi d. ob. qui valent in sterlingo xii s. x d. ii d. ob. de paris. <Item in pountagio et in batillagio unius navis equis et hominibus comitis vi s. iiii d. de sterlingo.>[8] In custumagio apud Witsand vii li. xvii s. vi d. que valent xlv s. sterlingi.

Summa sterlingi lxiiii s. ii d. et ii d. ob. paris.

Die jovis apud Witsand pro comite et familia xxx s. paris. In lavendria viii d.[9] paris. In vino Ciii s. x d. ob. \ paris. / In cervisia iii s. ix d. Summa panetrie et botellarie vi li. xviii s. iii d. ob. Coquina In uno carcosio et i qr. bovis xlviii s. paris. In ii multonibus et di. et i qr. xxv s. paris. Pulli de stauro. In pisce empto pro jejunantibus xxi s. iii d. In sale lardo ovis vino acro et aceco et viridi sucto sepe et blado pro puletria et portagio coquine x s. ii d. In busca et carbon*ibus* xiiii s. vi d. In pastura pro averiis nostris de coquina cum custodia eorundem xvi s. Summa coquine vi li. xiiii s. xi d. Marchalcia lxxi equis. In feno xxxv s. \ paris. / In prebenda Cvii me*n*suris et di. Cvii s. vi d. paris. In vessis pro palefrid*is* x d. paris. In litera xxxii s. vi d. paris. In una sella coquine emendenda viii d. paris. In alba candela iii s.

[8] The 6*s*. 4*d*., although struck through, is included in the total for the paragraph.
[9] MS omits 'd.'

vi d. paris. In viridi pro aula et camera ii s. vi d. paris. In vadiis xlv garcionum vi pagettorum xxiiii s. vi d. Summa marchalcie x li. vii s.

Summa xxiiii li. ii d. ob.

Summa sterlingi vi li. et ii d. ob. paris.

Boloing' Die veneris proxima sequenti pro comite et familia in pane xxiiii s. paris. In nucibus viii d. paris. In neules ii s. paris. In vino lvi s. x d. ob. Summa iiii li. iii s. vi d. ob. paris. Coquina In morue plaices coungre bremes et bars lxi s. x d. In makerel ii s. vi d. paris. In merlingo ii s. viii d. In alec' et percil et aliis erbis pro salc*amento* xi d. In pisis xii d. In sale xviii d. In busca v s. ii d. paris. In cervisia pro scice iiii d. In portagio coquine vi d. In cariagio puletrie cum foragio boum xxxviii s. vi d. In domibus allocandis xvi d. In expensis Thome Lard*arii* xx d. Summa coquine Cxvii s. xi d. paris. Marchalcia lxxi equis. In feno xxiii s. iiii d. In prebenda Cvi s. vi d. In litera xviii s. viii d. In viridi ii s. ix d. In lecto Henrici le Converse xii d. In pane pro palefrid*is* xvi d. In vadiis xlv garcionum vi pagettorum xxiiii s. vi d. Summa marchalcie viii li. xviii s. i d.

Summa xviii li. xix s. v d. que valent in sterlingo
iiii li. xiiii s. x d. sterlingi i d. paris. ob.

Die sabati proxima sequenti ibidem pro comite et familia in pane xxii s. In butiro ii s. iii d. paris. In lavendria v d. In vino lxxviii s. iiii d. Summa Ciii s. paris. Coquina In coungre et makerel xxii s. v d. In plaices xxiiii s. paris. In allece iiii d. In bars xvi s. In bremes vi s. In lacte v d. In ovis iii s. In sale xii d. In pisis xii d. In amigdalis vi d. In busca iiii s. vi d. In sals*amento* viii d. paris In portagio vi d. paris. Summa iiii li. iiii d. paris. Marchalcia lxxii equis. In feno xxiiii s. In prebenda Cxiii mensuris et di. Cxiii s. vi d. In litera viii s. iiii d. In pane pro palefrid*is* xii d. In expensis Lakoc preeuntis apud Neof Chastel vi d. In ferris fecitis viii d. In lecto Henrici le Converse iiii d. In vadiis xlii garcionum vi pagettorum xxiii s. Summa viii li. xi s. iiii d.

Summa emptorum xvii li. xiiii s. viii d.

Manger' Die dominica ibidem in festo Pentecostes pro comite et familia in pane lv s. paris. In vino iiii li. xi s. x d. de paris. Summa panetrie et botellarie vii li. vi s. x d. Coquina In i carcosio bovis et di. et i qr. Cvi s. In vi multonibus lvii s. In una perna baconis x s. In uno vitulo vi s. In xxxvii aucis Ciiii s. In xvii calponibus xxxiii s. In xxx gallinis xxiii s. ix d. In lxxii pucell*is* xx s. v d. In poples et courlues xxiiii s. viii d. In viiC ovis vii s. vi d. In lacte xviii d. In caseo iiii s. In pinguedine ix s. In lardo vi s. In frumento pro frumentac*io* xviii d. In sale iii s. In flore ii s. In pane xii d. In joute xii d. ob. In sals*amento* xv d. In busca et carbon*ibus* xvii s. iiii d. In allocacione unius chauder*ii* xii d. In portagio xii d. Item in pane apud Novum Castrum ad cenam viii s. ii d. In vino xxi s. vi d. In coquina omnibus computis xxiii s. x d. Summa panetrie et botellarie et coquine liii s. vi d. *Summa coquine xxii li. xxiii d. ob.* Marchalcia lxxi equis. Fenum xxix s. viii d. In prebenda

Clxvii mensuris Cix s. iiii d. In viridi ii s. In ostelagio lavendria xx d. In pane pro palefrid*is* vi d. In \ allocacione / lecto Henrici le Converse iiii d. In litera ix s. iii d. In vadiis xl garcionum vi pagettorum xxii s. Summa marchalcie viii li. xiiii s. ix d. paris. Summa xl li. xvii s. ob.

8 *Diet account for part of the household of a great lord coming to Parliament at London, March 1300*

This account records the expenses of John Roges and Henry de Middelton' for the period 6 March to 18 March 1300, in London, with part of the household of a great lord, making purchases there in advance of his arrival for the meeting of Parliament.[1] Although the identity of the lord himself remains unknown, Henry de Middelton' can be identified with the lord of the manor of Milton in Egham, Surrey, among the muniments of which this account has been preserved. The part of the household represented by the account was not insubstantial, with expenditure each day averaging in excess of £1. The document was presumably a subsidiary account to the main household diet account. It was written on a single membrane in two hands, the entries on the front being largely in a single hand as far as that for 16 March, which notes a payment to a clerk for writing the accounts. A second hand, writing an idiosyncratic form of Anglo-Norman French, has completed the document, adding accounts for two further days, then for oats, for expenses of the marshalsea, lodgings and carriage expenses, prior to the lord's arrival, with a concluding paragraph for similar expenses after his arrival.

Corpus Christi College, Oxford, Archives Ga 9/1

Recto

Ces sount les acountes Johan Roges e Henr*i* de Middelton'

Le dymeingne p*ro*chein devant la feste Seint Gregori lan du regne le rey Edward vint e wyt comensa Henr*i* de Middelton' e fust assigne p*ar* moun seingn*ur* a eyder e acatr*e* ensemblement ove Johan Roges secq*em* mon seingn*ur* \ en / aver\eit/ mest*er* a ses despenses

It*em* despendu le dimeinge avantdit en estor payn. C*er*voyse acate xlii galo*ns* prec*ium* galo*n* ii d. P*ayn*[1] cendre acate xviii d. En vin acate v s. iiii d.

[1] Parliament sat from 6 March to about 20 March in 1300.

[1] MS obscured by stain.

Harang en estor e en pessoun *sa*le[2] e en pesson fres vi s. ii d. It*em* en saffran i d. ob. It*em* en welkes iii d. Buche iii s. Portours ii d. Une pipe de iiii^{xx} galo*ns* de ce*r*voyse galo*n* prec*ium* i d. . . . . . vi d. Pur fourner ii q*u*arte*rs* de farine xvi d. Johan de Berklee p*ur* bateaus iii d. Summa xxxi s. v d. ob.
It*em* lundy p*ro*chein sua*nt* payn destor. En peyn cendre xii d. En vin xvi d. Ce*r*voyse destor. En pesson sale xviii d. P*ur* plays v s. iii d. P*ur* luz xxx d. Groses angules ii s. Lamprons C ii s. iiii d. Frut xiiii d. Oystres vi d. En sauce iii d. Peys p*ur* potag*e* ii d. En porrey ii d. En sel i d. Geffrey de Hautevile p*ur* bateaus iiii d. Summa xviii s. vi d.
It*em* mardy p*ro*chein suant peyn destor e en peyn cendre viii d. Ce*r*voyse destor. En vin v s. iiii d. En potag*e* ii d. ob. En sauce iii d. En alemandes ix d. En pesson sale xviii d. En stokfys x d. En plays iiii s. viii d. Luz xxxvii d. En angules xvi d. Lamprons xii d. Sturjon xxxiiii d. En charbons ii d. Harang destor. En oystres ii d. ob. En chandeyle vi d. Portours qe portere*nt* iiii millers de harang a la meson Ada*m* de Fulham iiii d. En un brael p*ur* mon seingn*ur* xxii d. Paye p*ur* un bref a la chancelrie vi d. Geffrey de Hautevile p*ur* bateaus iii d. Summa xxvi s. iii d.
It*em* le mekerdy p*ro*chein suant en peyn destor. En peyn cendr*e* iiii d. Vin xvi d. En ce*r*voyse destor. vi galo*ns* de bone ce*r*voyse ix d. ob. qua. P*ur* pesson sale ii s. Plays ii s. En oystres iii d. En un clerk pur fere les lettres mo*n* seingn*ur* iiii d. En potag*e* iii d. ob. P*ur* un tresse de oynouns i d. En bateaus Joh*a*n de Berkele ii d. Portours qe porterent a loustel une pipe de ce*r*voys*e* vi d. Sire Joh*a*n Bassat p*ur* bateaus i d. ob.
Summa viii s. ii d. ob. qua.
Le judy p*ro*chein suant peyn destor. En peyn cendr*e* xiiii d. E vin iiii s. e viii d. En xl galo*ns* de ce*r*voys*e* v s. Pesson sale xv d. Plays iiii s. Luz ii s. Angules xx d. Lamp*ro*ns iii d. Welkes xii d. Harang destor. Frut*e* xvi d. En oystres vi d. En potag*e* ii d. En charbo*ns* ii d. En alemandes ix d. P*ur* un alnaz aparile a mon seingn*ur* iiii d. P*ur* un crassat novel x d. P*ur* iii brefs a la chancelr*ie* xviii d. e p*ur* escr*i*ve*re* vi d. *Po*rtours[3] ob. Meme le jour vont les \ x / garzons \ e un page / a gages. Paye a les garzons Geffrey de Hautevile iii d. e alere*nt* lendemeyn hors de vile. Summa xxvii s. iiii d. ob.
It*em* vendredy p*ro*chein suant en peyn destor. Peyn cendr*e* xii d. Vin iiii s. Ce*r*voyse de estor. Pesson sale xv d. ob. Plays iiii s. Luz ii s. Oystres xx d. Oystres cruz iiii d. \ ob. / Chaundeyle vi d. En potag*e* iiii d. \ ob. / En alemandes iii d. En saffran ob. En bren pur chevaus x d. It*em* en ix garz*ou*ns en gages. Summa xvi s. iiii d.
It*em* samedy p*ro*chein suant en peyn xviii d. En vin v s. iiii d. Ce*r*voyse destor. Pesso*n* sale xv d. Lampreye iii s. vi d. Welkes ix d. Luz ii s. Sturjon

[2] MS obscured by stain.
[3] Start of word obscure in MS.

ii s. Plays iiii s. En potag*e* iiii d. En oyno*u*ns i d. En sauce ii d. ob. En oystres i d. En ferur*e* des chevaus viii d. ob. En ix garzo*u*ns a gages.
Summa xxi s. ix d.

It*em* dimeingne p*ro*chein suant en peyn xx d. ob. En vin iiii s. En c*er*voys*e* xxviii galo*n*s iii s. vi d. Harang destor. En gurnard v s. vi d. Lus[4] [2]ii s. vi[2] d. Welkes [2]ii s. vii[2] d. En sauce e en siel iiii d. ob. De napes lavez ii d. En ferur*e* des chevaus v d. [2]Osttrun iii d. e ix gersouns a gagus.[2]
Summa xviii s. viii d.

It*em* lundy p*ro*chein sua*n*t en peyn ii s. Vin ii s. viii d. En pesson sale e harang xxiii d. Plays [2]ii s. vi[2] d. En alemandes [2]vi d.[2] Johan le Prest*re* paya en ernes p*ur* les cofres mo*n* seing*nur* xii d. En oystres vi d. En charbons ii d. En potag*e* i d. ob. En ferur*e* des chevaus i d. ob. Waut*er* le Ku vi d. del doun mo*n* seingn*ur*. Sire Johan Bassat p*ur* bateaus i d. ob. [2]Delyver*e* a Jon Rogus pur aveynus ii s. xi d. Delyver*e* a Jon Rogus pur les gagus les gersouns v s. v d. ob. Sounma ixx s. v d.[2]

It*em* mardy p*ro*chein suant en peyn xxvi d. En vin iiii s. En c*er*voyse ix d. \ Un clerk pur escr*i*ver*e* mo*n* seingn*ur* i d. ob. S*ounm*a cink. / Pesson sale e harang xxx d. Graspeys xxi d. Oystres ii s. Lamp*rou*ns e angules ii s. vi d. En saffran ob. En oyno*u*ns i d. En charbo*u*ns ii d. [2]Ferrure de chevaus ii d. ob. En chandel vi d.[2] En oystres vii d. ob. [2]Jon le Prust peyey pu\r/ les coffrus mo*u*n seynour iiii d. e ix gersouns a gagus. <En chaundeylus vi d.> Sounma xxiii s. ix d.[2]

It*em* mekerdy p*ro*chein suant en peyn ii s. En vin iii s. iiii d. En c*er*voyse xxxiii d. En frut vii d. En oystres vi d. En pessoun sale e en harang xxxiii d. Luz iiii s. Floundr*es* xv d. En oystres ii s. vi d. Plays v s. vi d. En potag*e* i d. ob. En alema*n*des vi d. En saffran ob. En charbons iii d. It*em* en un clerk p*ur* escr*i*vere nos acountes iiii d. [2]Jon Gascelyn vii d. p*ur* batteus e x gerssouns a gagus. Sou*n*ma xxvi s. iii d.

Dorse

Le mardy procheyn . . . . .

Le jeudy procheyn suaunt en peyn ixx d. En vin viii d. \ En pessoun sale xii d. En pleys. / In allema*u*ndus xiii d. ob. In pottege i d. In saffran ob. In carbo*u*ns ii d. e x gerssouns a gagus. Fygus iiii d. Jon Gascelyn p*ur* batteus i d. ob.

Le venderdy procheyn suaunt en peyn xviii d. In servicya xxii d. \ ob. / En vyn ii s. viii d. En pessoun salle erreng ixx \v / d. Pleys ii s. xx d. Pottege i d. In sale i d. En chaundeylus vi d. Peye a chanun iiii \ d. / por bautteus p*ar* la meyn Jon Prestre. Osttru*n* iiii d. E*n* feyn peye Geffrey de Parrys par la meyn Jon Rogus xi s. durra*u*nt vi jours. Peye en aveyne*s* ixx s. \ viii d. / pour iiii q*uarterus* viii boussel p*ar* v jours lyver*e* a cheyvas xvii cheyvaus.

[4] 's' of 'lus' in the second hand.

Pour ferrure de cheyvas xviii d. ob. e x gerssouns a gagus. Peye a Geffrey de Parrys pour buche iii s. Peye a gersouns pour iiii jours iiii s. x d. ob. Jon Rogus peye pour feyn a un autre omme de key il laveyt le jour avantditte xiii d. Pour caumbbrus e marchausye v s. e serveyze ke nous avum acatte pour beyvere iiii d. ob.
De la porveyaunc*e* moun seynour ke il mey couma*u*nd p*ar* sa lettre e mey ma*u*nd encerent p*ar* sa lettre ke Allessaundre mey portey p*ar* moun seynour ke je feyze sce ke Allesaundre mey dyrreyt de bouche e ke je pourveyc*e* a countre le \ vennue mo*u*n seynour au / p*ar*lemen*t* de feyn e des aveynus e de lytere e de busche e mey maunda vi li. de pollers sce veyllount estre iiii mars e demiey.
De feyn acatte xxiiii s. a Pouttunhu*he* e de . . .rem[5] accate in charrecc*s* viii s. vi d. P*our* carriag*e* \ e portours / v s. iii \ d. / Pour feyn ke Allysaundre \ Brokenore / e Henr*i* de Middelt' akatteroun en Lo*u*ndrus xii s. e des aveynus acatte x q*u*arter*us* \ e vi bousseus / prys quaurter iii s. \ x d. / e pour le carryag*e* ii s. vi d. Touce est de Pottu*n*huȝe e pour sent de talvodde iiii s. e a feyrre carryer deus pypus de servoyze xvi d. de la meyssoun Joenne de Lambourn' e en mes despensus pour moy pour deus cheyvas viii s. vi d. Cette pourveyaunc*e* surro*u*n fet acountre sa vennue.
Les despe*n*sus apres sa vennue pour iiii quarter*s* de aveynus payey xv s. \ vi d. / E pour treys quarterus xi s. vi d. E pour ii quarterus le semadi vii s. vii d. \ E pour cariag*e* ii s. vii d. ob. / Chaumbrus e maurchausye v s.
E de sette porveyaunce cy sount peye iiii li. xiii s.[2]

9 *Diet accounts of the household of Roger de Mortimer, probably 1308 x 1311*

The two fragments of diet accounts edited here form the flyleaves to a volume including a renowned collection of Middle English lyric poetry, British Library MS Harley 2253. The accounts date from the early years of the fourteenth century, some thirty years earlier than the Middle English lyrics; and, unlike the lyrics, which are believed to have originated in the West Midlands, the accounts are a rare survival from Ireland. N. R. Ker has identified the accounts as belonging to the household of Roger de Mortimer, subsequently Earl of March, and his wife, Joan, at Ardmulghan, near Skrine, County Meath; and he has dated them to the period 1308 x

5 The first two or three letters are indistinct in the MS.

1311.[1] On his retirement to the Dominican friary at Trim, at the end of 1307, the liberty of Trim was resigned by Geoffrey de Geneville to his granddaughter, Joan, Mortimer's wife.[2] Ker suggested that these fragments are consecutive parts of an account, with the second preceding the first. There is a gap between the accounts, however, and it is not clear that more can be said than that the first fragment is for part of March, during Lent; and that the second fragment is also from Lent. The weekly cash total close to the start of the first fragment would not preclude the second fragment forming part of the week's account concluded on the first.

The daily accounts, recording both purchase and consumption, are arranged by household department in the order the pantry, buttery, kitchen, marshalsea, without departmental headings, followed by sections for alms and miscellaneous items. Each section carefully notes all receipts and liveries, their source and destination, and goods are listed in a regular order within each section. Each day concludes with two cash totals: the *summa in denariis* represents payments in cash; the *summa instauri* represents the appraised value (*precium*) of goods drawn from local estates.

The two fragments were both written in a single hand, probably in one operation, with the sole exception of the cash amounts of the weekly total. It is just possible that the cash amounts in the daily totals were entered by the principal hand on a subsequent occasion.

British Library MS Harley 2253, ff.ir, 142v

[*f.ir*] ..... equ*is* precium xix d. In prebenda eorundem i cumula v pec. avene \ empt*e* / iiii s. viii d. In cariagio literie xviii d. In iiii lib. candele paris emptis vii d. In oblacione ad Sanctum Patricium v d. per Chaundos. Item in xxxvii anguillis emptis de T*ris*t*in*athg iii s. i d. Item xxx lib. amigdalarum et v lib. de ris de garderoba.

Summa in denariis ix li. xii d. ob. Summa instauri iii s. iii d.

Summa totalis in denariis xv li. iii d. ob.

Summa totalis instauri iiii li. vi s. viii d. ob.

Ardmol' Die dominica proxima ante festum Sancti Patricii in pane furnito i cumula frumenti de T*ru*m iiii s. <Item di. cumula de molendino ibidem empta.> Item di. cumula de Lochton' precium ii s. et respondit de CC et xl

[1] *Facsimile of British Museum MS Harley 2253* ed. N. R. Ker (EETS, 255; 1965) pp. ix, xxii-xxiii, sets aside their ascription to Thomas Charlton, Bishop of Hereford: *Anglo-Norman political songs* ed. I. S. T. Aspin (ANTS, 11; 1953) pp. 24–5; *The Harley lyrics* ed. G. L. Brook (Manchester, 1956) p. 3.

[2] H. Wood, 'The muniments of Edmund de Mortimer', *Proceedings of the Royal Irish Academy* 40, section C (1931–2) p. 320.

jactatis panibus. Vinum et cervisia precomputata. iiiiC et di. allec precomputatum. x mulvelli precomputati. iiii salmones de gurgite expen*diti*. Item i missus domino G. de G. In welkis et rasours emptis Dubln' xx d. Item in iiiM ostreis emptis ibidem iii s. Foragium de instauro loci pro lxiii equis precium xxi d. In prebenda eorundem i cumula iiii pec. avene de Lochton' precium iii s. x d. Item di. C panes de panetria. In oblacione ii d. In litteris portatis ii d.

Summa in denariis ix s. Summa instauri <vi s. ix d.> vii s. vii d. Fuit canc*ellarius* et thes*aurarius* Hyb*ernie*.

Ibidem Die lune sequenti in pane furnito i cumula frumenti de Lochton' precium iiii s. Item i cumula frumenti de hagardo de Ardm' precium xl d. et respondit de CCC et xxx jactatis panibus. Inde lib*erati* pro canibus xx panes. Vinum et cervisia precomputata. iiiiC et di. allec precomputatum. vi mulvelli precomputati. ii salmones de gurgite. Item i missus domino H. de Lacy. viii scalpini precomputati. Foragium de instauro loci pro xlvii equis precium xv d. ob. In prebenda eorundem vi pec. avene de Lochton' precium xvi d. ob. Item viii pec. de hagardo loci precium xx d. ob. x ferra equi precomputata. In oblacione i d.

Summa in denariis i d. Summa instauri xi s. viii d. ob.

Ibidem Die martis sequenti in pane furnito i cumula frumenti de Lochton precium iiii s. Item di. cumula de hagardo loci precium xx d. et respondit et lib*erati* ut prius. Vinum et cervisia precomputata. iiiiC allec precomputatum. vi mulvelli et x scalpini precomputati. i salmo et di. de gurgite. Foragium de instauro loci pro l equis precium xvii d. In prebenda eorundem i cumula de grangia loci precium iii s. In oblacione i d. Str. . .

Summa in denariis i d. Summa instauri <vi> x s. i d.

*i dolium vini attami*atur *Ibidem* Die mercurii sequenti in pane furnito i cumula frumenti de Lochton' precium iiii s. et respondit de CC panibus. Vinum et cervisia precomputata. iiiiC allec precomputatum. <iiii allec> iiii mulvelli precomputati. ii scalpini precomputati. ii salmones precomputati. Item i salmo missus domino S. de G. Foragium de instauro loci pro xliiii equis precium xiiii d. <In oblacione i d.> In prebenda eorundem i cumula avene de grangia loci precium iii s. In oblacione i d.

Summa in denariis i d. Summa instauri viii s. ii d.

Ibidem Die jovis sequenti in pane furnito i cumula et di. frumenti de Lochton' precium vi s. et respondit de CC et xxx jactatis panibus et lib*erati* pro canibus xx panes. Vinum et cervisia precomputata. iiiiC allec precomputatum. iii mulvelli expen*diti*. Item in xv mulvellis emptis de Balir' vi s. vi d. cum \ cariagio / inde. iii exp*enditi*. Item ii scalpini precomputati. ii salmones precomputati. Foragium de instauro pro li . . . . .[1] precium xviii d. . . . . .

[1] Probably 'equis'.

[*f.142v*] . . . . . precium vi s. x d. xv ferra equi precomputata expen*dita*. In oblacione i d. In expensis Fort apud T*rum* iii d. In incausto ii d. In oll*is* pro camera domini i d.

Summa in denariis v s. xi d. Summa instauri xvi s. i d.

*Frumentum de Lochton attami*atur *Ibidem* Die martis sequenti in pane furnito i cumula frumenti de Lochton' precium iiii s. iiii d. Item di. cumula de grangia loci precium xx d. et respondet de C et di. panibus. Vinum precomputatum. *Brasiatur* In cervisia brasciata vi pec. capitalis brasei de Kilcoli precium iiii s. Item v cumula brasei cursalis de grangia rectoris de Ardmol' precium xx s. et respondit de xxxii sex. cervisie. CC et di. allec precomputatum. v mulvelli precomputati. i salmo et di. de gurgite. Item i dat*us* domino G. de G. In eodem port*ando* i d. Foragium de instauro manerii pro xxvi equis precium ix d. In prebenda eorundem di. cumula avene de Lochton' precium xviii d. Item di. C panes de panetria. In oblacione i d. <Postea apud Moyrath> Item in oblacione pro Rogero Bokke xii d. per Fort. *Et Moyrath* Postea apud Moyrath in pane empto apud Trum x s. ix d. Vinum de instauro de T*rum*. In cervisia empta apud T*rum* xii s. v d. C allec precomputatum expen*ditum*. Item CC de dono rectoris. In xi mulvellis et di. emptis apud T*rum* de Ricardo Molahide et David Ros cum cariagio vii s. vii d. unde vi mulvelli expen*diti*. i salmo di. de gurgite de Ardmol'. In allea i d. per W. Cocum. Fenum avena et turbonum de dono rectoris ibidem.

Summa in denariis xxxii s. Summa instauri xxxi s. xi d.

Ibidem Die mercurii sequenti panes vinum et cervisia precomputata. CC et di. allec precomputatum. Item in di. C alle*cis* albi empt*a* de quodam de Magd' v d. Expen*dita*. v mulvelli et di. precomputati. Expen*diti*. Di. salmo de gurgite de Ardmol'. Item in i salmone empto de Hugone de Nova Villa iii s. Expen*ditus*. In viiC musculis de quodam de Donachkerny x d. ob. Expen*diti*. Fenum et turbonum de dono rectoris pro xlvi equis. In prebenda eorundem xv pec. avene empt*a* de Talebot iii s. vi d. In oblacione ii d. In albo pulvere port*ato* apud Moyrath i d. x ferra equi precomputata.

Summa in denariis viii s. ob. Summa instauri nichil.

Ardmolchan Die jovis sequenti venit dominus ad prandium apud Ardmol'. In pane furnito i cumula et di. frumenti de Lochton' precium vi s. et respondit de CC panibus et xxx jactatis et lib*erati* pro canibus ut supra. Vinum et cervisia precomputata. iiiiC allec precomputatum. In xii mulvellis v scarbardis emptis de Schorthals ix s. \ ii d. / cum cariagio. Inde viii expen*diti* et iii scarbardi. i salmo de gurgite. In vC et di. ostreis emptis de Patricio le Saltar' xiiii d. In M cepis emptis de quodam homine de Dubln' xx d. \ per Strange. / In welkis emptis de Sc*rin* v d. \ per Strange. / In senapio per Strange xiii d. ob. In expensis suis i d. In vino acro de T*rum* xii d. per Fort. Foragium de instauro manerii pro xliiii equis precium xv d. In prebenda eorundem i cumula avene de Lochton' precium iii s. Item di. C panes de panetria. In oblacione i d. *Trum* Item fenum apud T*rum* pro xiii equis precium iiii d. In prebenda eorundem iii pec. avene empt*a* prope T*rum* ix d. per W.

Summa in denariis xv s. v d. ob. Summa instauri x s. vii d.

Ibidem· et Trum Die veneris sequenti in pane furnito i cumula et di. frumenti de Lochton precium vi s. et respondit et lib*erati* pro canibus ut supra. Vinum precomputatum. In xvi sex. vi lag. cervisie emptis de Sc*rin* xii s. iiii d. Item in xxii sex. xi lag. de Novan' xvii s. iii d. qua. CCC allec precomputatum. vi mulvelli ii scarbardi precomputati. i salmo et di. de gurgite. ii lib. amigdalarum et i lib. de ris de garderoba. Foragium de instauro loci pro xxvi equis precium viii d. ob. In prebenda eorun. . . v pec. avene de Lochton' precium xii d. ob. Item C panes de panetria. In oblacione i d. In expensis Fort apud Dondalk querentis allec ibidem et pro i dolio allecis carectando ibidem xiii d. *Trum* Postea apud T*rum* sero fenum pro xlvi equis precium xv d. ob. In prebenda eorundem i cumula iii pec. avene empt*a* prope T*rum* . . . . .[2]

Summa . . . . .[3]

10 *Accounts for the household of Katherine de Norwich, September 1336 to September 1337*

Katherine de Norwich (d. 1341 x 1343), the daughter of Sir John de Hethersett, was the widow of Walter de Norwich, who died 20 January 1329. After a career in royal service, most notably at the Exchequer, Walter de Norwich was treasurer of the Exchequer from 1314 to 1317 and was keeper of the same office at various times between 1319 and 1324. He was Katherine's second husband, whom she had married by February 1305. Her first husband, Piers Braunche, had died by March 1296. In 1336 Katherine had rights of dower in a number of manors in Norfolk and Suffolk, which had been held jointly with her second husband, and to which her eldest son, John de Norwich, was the heir. One group of properties lay about 10 miles west of Lowestoft, centred on Mettingham and Shipmeadow, Suffolk, and Kirby Cane, nearby in Norfolk, across the River Waveney. About 10 miles to the north west, close to Norwich, were the manors of Blackworth in Stoke Holy Cross and Howe. Another pair of

[2] Under repair. Possibly 'iiii s. i d. per W.'

[3] Under repair. Possibly 'in denariis xxxiiii s. <iiii d. qua.> \ x d. qua. / '

manors, Dallinghoo and Bredfield, were situated in Suffolk about 15 miles to the south of Mettingham, close to Woodbridge and Wickham Market; two other properties were further afield, in Suffolk, the manor of Dalham, between Bury St Edmunds and Newmarket, and in Norfolk, the manor of Sculthorpe, near Fakenham. In addition there may have been a town house in Norwich, and goods were also supplied from the manor of Cookley, Suffolk, adjacent to Huntingfield. The second of Katherine's daughters, Cicely, had married Sir Roger de Huntingfield. Her other daughter, Margaret, had married as her second husband Robert de Ufford, Earl of Suffolk. In addition Katherine had two other sons, Roger de Norwich and Thomas de Norwich, from her marriage to Walter de Norwich.[1]

At the end of September 1336, Katherine de Norwich was at Blackworth, travelling to Mettingham on 16 October, where she stayed until 13 January 1337. She then went to Norwich, by way of Blackworth, and remained in the city until at least the end of April 1337. The account roll provides a record of the daily expenses of the household for 214 days, from 29 September 1336 to 30 April 1337. There is also an account for bulk purchases of stock (oxen, pigs, geese and herring), spices, wine, candles and herbage for the whole year from Michaelmas 1336. Taken together these provide an average daily expense of about 7*s.* 5*d.*; however on a single day, 20 January 1337, the anniversary of the death of her second husband, the household spent £10. 18*s.* 8*d.*, just under one-sixth of the total daily expenses recorded on the roll (£65. 16*s.* 7¼*d.*), dwarfing, for example, the expenditure of the Christmas season.

The account is written on an Exchequer fashion roll of six parchment membranes, fastened by a parchment thong filed through two holes at the top of each membrane. The first five membranes contain the diet accounts, the sixth the stock account. The diet accounts for each day start with items entailing cash payments, and corn and stock drawn from demesne manors at an appraised value (which is underlined on the account). There follow other items described as *de stauro* or *de preempto*, which are drawn from the store of the household, items purchased in bulk for the household (and accounted for in membrane 6 or in a similar, earlier account) or the continued consumption of items that had recently been entered as purchases in the diet account. After this usually comes the account for the thirteen paupers whose presence is a regular feature of this household, and then the account for provender for the horses. Each day has a daily cash total, divided between purchases and stock. The total for purchases covers all items for which cash payments were made during the day. The total for

[1] *CP* ix, pp. 762–3; *Cal IPM* 7, pp. 169–70.

stock does not refer to the items in the account described as *de stauro* or *de preempto*, but to the appraised value for items drawn from manors, a value for gifts received during the day and for hens drawn from the enclosures (*lok*) on demesne manors. The diet accounts were written up largely by a single hand, probably on several occasions. The daily cash totals appear in the same hand, sometimes in a darker ink, suggesting that in some instances at least they were subsequent additions; but the overall impression is that the daily accounts were a fair copy. There are also grand cash totals, and, in one instance, a total of corn and stock, for each membrane of the daily accounts, at the foot of the dorse of each roll, where, on an Exchequer fashion roll, they would have been easily visible. The daily accounts have some marginal notes of the number of visitors (*extranei*), or a note *eque*, or a figure for *deficientes*. This suggests that in accounting terms at least the household was an establishment of a set numerical size, *extranei* denoting the presence of supernumeraries, *eque* a balance, and *deficientes* a shortfall. Although now difficult to comprehend its precise operation, this was probably a means of keeping a control on the progress of expenditure. The roll lacks the membranes of the daily accounts which would have carried it to the close of the accounting year at Michaelmas 1337, where further calculations may have made the purpose of the marginal entries apparent. The only trace of auditing is in the notes of cash totals at the foot of membranes 1^r, 2^d and 4^d. Membrane 6 contains an annual account of stock and other consumables purchased in bulk for the household. It was written on at least two occasions, probably close to the end of the accounting year (Michaelmas 1337), and it also seems designed to transfer the balance of stock remaining to the account for the following year.

Besides its incompleteness, the account roll is now in part very faded and has also been stained and damaged by water.

British Library Additional Roll 63207

Membrane 1 recto

Primus rotulus pro expensis domus domine \ Katerine de Norwyc' / tenendis a festo Sancti Michaelis anno Edwardi tercii x^o

Extranei xiiii Die dominica in festo Sancti Michaelis apud Blacworth'. Eodem die in oblacione ii d. Item in carne bovis empta xviii d. Item in carne multonis xvi d. Item in carne porci vii d. Item ii auce de stauro preempto. Item iii pulcini de preempto. Item xiiii ova de preempto. In putura xiii pauperum panis de stauro et xiii allec de preempto. In prebenda v equorum domine et domini Rogeri di. bus. i mensura di. avene de preempto et tantum furfuris.

Summa Empcionis iii s. vii d.
Stauri nichil.

Extranei iiii Die lune sequenti in cervisia empta xii d. ob. Item iii pulcini de preempto. Item vi ova de preempto. In putura pauperum ut die precedenti. In prebenda iiii equorum domine ii mensure avene de preempto et tantum furfuris.

Summa Empcionis xii d. ob.
Stauri nichil.

Extranei v Die martis sequenti de empcione nichil. Item i auca de stauro preempto. Item i pulcinus de preempto. Item vi ova de preempto. In putura xiii pauperum panis de stauro et allec de preempto. In prebenda iiii equorum domine ii mensure avene et tantum furfuris.

Summa Empcionis nichil.
Stauri nichil. Nichil.

Extranei v Die mercurii in iiii^xx^vi allece empto vii d. In xl ovis emptis ii d. Item iii ferrure gresel de Lek' cum ii ferris anterioribus iii d. Item in ovis ob. In iiii bus. avene emptis pro prebenda x d. ob. Item i muruca et i mellvellus de stauro. Item xii ova de preempto. In putura pauperum ut supra. In prebenda iiii equorum domine ii de Thoma de Brigham i bus. avene de preempto et tantum furfuris.

Summa Empcionis xxiii d.
Stauri nichil.

Extraneus i Die jovis in cervisia empta xii d. In carne bovis empta ii s. \ ii d. / In carne multonis viii d. In carne porci ii d. Item i auca de stauro preempto. Item i pulcinus de preempto. In putura pauperum panis de stauro et allec de preempto. In prebenda iiii equorum domine ii mensure avene de preempto et tantum furfuris.

Summa Empcionis iiii s.
Stauri nichil.

Extranei v Frumentum de B' Die veneris sequenti in pane furnito i qr. frumenti de veteri grano de manerio de Blacworth' precium vi s. unde xiiii^xx^ panes. In multura eiusdem iii d. Item in allece empto iii d. Item i mellvellus de stauro preempto. In putura pauperum panis de stauro et allec de preempto. In prebenda iiii equorum domine ii mensure avene de preempto et tantum furfuris.

Summa Empcionis vi d.
Stauri vi s.

Extraneus i Braseum de[1] *Anguille pro stauro* Die sabati in oblacione i d. Eodem die in cervisia braciata vi bus. brasei de veteri de manerio de Blacworth' precium iiii s. vi d. unde lvi lag. cervisie. In pane pro coquina

[1] Followed by a blank space.

i d. Item in CCCxxxvi anguillis pro stauro remanendo ii s. vi d. Item in synapio ii d. Item i mellvellus de stauro preempto. Item lx anguille de stauro preempto. In putura pauperum ut supra. In prebenda iiii equorum domine et ii de Kyneburle di. bus. i mensura di. avene et tantum furfuris.

Summa Empcionis ii s. ix d.
Stauri iiii s. vi d.

Extranei xvii Bidentes de B' Die dominica in festo Sancte Fidis virginis in oblacione i d. Item in carne bovis empta xv d. In carne multonis x d. In carne porci vii d. In carne vituli v d. In xii columbellis v d. In pomis i d. Item ii auce de stauro preempto. Item i pulcinus de exhennio M. de Denton'. Item in occisione i bidens matrix de manerio de Blacworth' precium viii d. Item xxiiii ova de preempto. In putura pauperum panis et carnes de stauro. In prebenda vi equorum domine et vi de domino Constant*e* Mortim*er* sic de avena ii bus. i mensura avene de preempto et tantum furfuris.

Summa Empcionis iii s. viii d.
Stauri ix d.

Extranei ix Vacca de B' Bidentes de B' Die lune sequenti in farina ii d. ob. In vi columbellis ii d. ob. Item i lag. cervisie i d. ob. In i remocione pro le nagg ob. Item in occisione i juvencta de manerio de Blacworth' precium v s. Item in occisione i multo et i bidens matrix de manerio de Blacworth' precium utriusque xviii d. Item i auca de stauro preempto et i pulcinus de exhennio Denton'. Item vi ova de preempto. In putura xiii pauperum panis de stauro et allec de preempto. In prebenda vi equorum domine i pec. avene et i bus. di. et ii mensure furfuris.

Summa Empcionis vii d.
Stauri vi s. vi d.

Extranei vii Die martis sequenti de empcione nichil. Item ii pulcini de exhennio Denton'. Item x ova de preempto. In putura xiii pauperum panis de stauro et xiii allec de preempto. In prebenda iiii equorum domine i pec. i mensura di. avene de preempto et tantum furfuris.

Summa Empcionis nichil.
Stauri i d. ob.

Extranei v Die mercurii sequenti in Cxvi de allece empto xiii d. Item in codling et merling vi d. In solis ii d. In pomis iiii d. Item in i lag. mellis empta vii d. In aleis emptis i d. In ferrura equi domini Rogeri cum i ferro posteriore i d. Item i mellvellus de stauro preempto. Item vii ova de preempto. Item putura pauperum nichil. In prebenda vi equorum domine i bus. et di. pec. avene de preempto et tantum furfuris.

Summa Empcionis ii s. x d.
Stauri[2]

[2] Followed by a blank space.

Extranei iiii Frumentum de B' Bidentes de B' Die jovis sequenti in pane furnito i qr. frumenti de manerio de Blacworth' precium vi s. unde xiiii^{xx}iiii panes. In multura eiusdem iii d. Item in ovis iii d. In carne vituli v d. In expensis Johannis Capellani versus Sculthorp ii d. Item in lacte pro pueris i d. Item i bidens matrix de manerio de Blacworth' precium x d. Item i auca de stauro preempto. Item ix columbelle de exhennio Ricardi Hacon. Item in putura pauperum panis de empcione et allec de preempto. Item in prebenda vi equorum domine i pec. et ii mensure di. avene et tantum furfuris.

Summa Empcionis xiiii d.
Stauri vii s. i d.

Eque Die veneris sequenti in C de allece empto x d. Item in pane pro pauperibus xv d. In merling et codling vi d. In synapio iiii d. Item in putura pauperum panis de preempto et xiii allec de preempto. In prebenda vi equorum domine di. bus. ii mensure avene de preempto et tantum furfuris.

Summa Empcionis ii s. xi d.
Stauri nichil.

Extranei iii Die sabati in oblacione i d. Item in allece empto v d. Item in merling et codling iiii d. Item in buttis iii d. Item in ii lib. de amigdalis iii d. Item in i pari de pastrones pro pullano domine vi d. Item in i ferro anteriore pro le nagg et i remocione pro morel ii d. Item in i qr. avene pro prebenda equorum xxiii d. In reparacione vasorum pistrine et coquine viii d. Item in putura pauperum ut die precedenti. Item in prebenda viii equorum domine et Jacobi de Metingham i bus. i pec. avene de preempto et tantum furfuris. Item in cignottis di. bus. i pec. avene et tantum furfuris.

Summa Empcionis iiii s. vii d.
Stauri[3]

Extranei ix Bidentes de B' Die dominica sequenti in oblacione i d. Item in ii lag. cervisie et xii lag. mediocris cervisie emptis xv d. In carne bovis xv d. In carne vituli v d. In carne porci iiii d. In columbellis iiii d. In lx ovis iii d. In lacte pro coquina ob. Item in pane pro coquina ii d. \ In ferrura Fryk' apud Heringlond' ii d. / Item in expensis pro gresel Fysymion ad nundinas Sancte Fidis viii d. Item in occisione ii multones et i bidens matrix de manerio de Blacworth' precium omnium ii s. vi d. Item ii auce de stauro preempto. Item xix ova de preempto. Item in putura pauperum ut supra panis et allec de preempto. Item in prebenda vi equorum domine ii de Ricardo Hacon' et Jacobo de Metingham iii pec. ii mensure di. avene de preempto et tantum furfuris.

Summa Empcionis iiii s. xi d. ob.
Stauri ii s. vi d.

[3] Followed by a blank space.

Extranei ix Die lune de empcione nichil. Item ii pulcini de preempto. Item in putura pauperum panis de preempto et allec. Item in prebenda vi equorum domine ii de Sculthorp et Ricard*o* Hacon i bus. di. avene de preempto et tantum furfuris.

Summa Empcionis nichil.
Stauri nichil.

Extranei xii Memorandum quod domina venit hic de Blacworth' usque Metingham' Die martis sequenti in cervisia empta vi d. Item in ix pulcinis emptis vi d. Item in iiii qr. avene pro prebenda emptis vi s. viii d. In lacte pro pueris i d. ob. Item i auca de stauro preempto. Item xii columbelle de exhennio Ricardi Hacon. Item xii ova de preempto. Item in putura pauperum ut supra. In prebenda vi equorum domine ii de magistro . . .ng' i bus. i mensura et di. pec. avene de preempto et tantum furfuris.

Summa Empcionis vii s. ix d.
Stauri v d.

Extranei viii Frumentum de M' Braseum de M' Die mercurii in festo Sancti Michaelis in Monte Tumba. Eodem die domina removit de Blacworth' usque Metingham ad cenam cum tota familia. In pane furnito i qr. frumenti de manerio de Metingham precium vi s. unde xiiii^{xx}vi panes. In multura eiusdem iii d. Item in cervisia braciata i qr. bracei de manerio de Metingham de veteri precium vi s. unde iiii^{xx}iiii lag. cervisie. Item in elemosina iii d. qua. In pane ii d. In cervisia iii d. ob. qua. Item in xi^{xx}ii allece novi empcionis xv d. ob. In codling et merling xi d. In ovis pro foretto ob. In cor*io* empt*o* iii d. In campirnol' i d. ob. In vadiis Johannis Pistoris per vii dies et garcionis sui per ix dies braciandorum contra adventum domine xxiii d. Item i bolla et i thed' et v circuli pro mod*io* et vi craticuli pro cuvis pistrine ix d. ob. qua. Item liiii allec de preempto. In putura pauperum nichil. In prebenda x equorum domine iii bus. ii pec. furfuris et avene.

Summa Empcionis vi s. iiii d. qua.
Stauri xii s.

Extranei viii Mixtura de Schepmed' Die jovis sequenti in pane furnito pro pauperibus iiii bus. mixture de manerio de Schepmed precium xx d. unde ix^{xx}x panes. Item i auca de exhennio Jacobi de Metingham. Item ii pulcini de exhennio de eodem. In putura pauperum panis de stauro et allec de preempto. In prebenda vii equorum domine ii bus. di. et i mensura avene et furfuris de preempto.

Summa Empcionis nichil.
Stauri[4]

[4] 'ii s. ob.' erased.

Extranei xvi Die veneris in allece empto iii d. In codling et merling iiii d. In candela pro pistrina i d. Item lx allec de ultima preemp*cione*. In putura pauperum panis de stauro et xiii allec de preempto. In prebenda vi equorum domine v de T. de Brigham et ii clericorum prepositorum de Bredef' et Dalyngho iii bus. di. et i mensura i pec. avene et furfuris.

Summa Empcionis viii d.
Stauri nichil.

Extranei xii Die sabati sequenti in oblacione i d. Item in lxvi de allece empto v d. In codling et merling vii d. Item in buttis iii d. In pranes <iii> \ v / d. Item iiii^{xx} allec de preempto. In putura pauperum ut die precedenti. In prebenda vi equorum domine iii de Thoma de Brigham et clericorum iiii de Cecil*ia* de Hedirset . . . . . iiii bus. ii pec. avene et furfuris de preempto et tantum furfuris.

Summa Empcionis xxi d.
Stauri nichil.

Extranei xv i boviculus de B' iiii bidentes de M' Die dominica sequenti in carne bovis empta viii d. In carne multonis v d. In carne porci iiii d. In occisione i boviculus de manerio de Blacworth' precium v s. Item in occisione iiii bidentes matrices de manerio de Metingham precium ii s. viii d. Item i perna baconis veteris incipitur de stauro de Metingham. Item i qr. carnis bovis incipitur de eadem. In ii aucis de exhennio Jacobi de Metingham. Item iii pulcini de eodem. In putura xiii pauperum panis de stauro et xiii allec de preempto. In prebenda v equorum domine iiii de Cecil*ia* de Hedirset' iii bus. ii mensure avene et furfuris de preempto.[5]

Summa Empcionis xvii d.
Stauri viii s. vi d.

Extranei vi Die lune sequenti in xlviii ovis emptis ii d. Item i[6] pulcinus de exhennio et ii pulcini de preempto. In putura . . . . . pauperum ut die precedenti. In prebenda v equorum domine i bus. di. ii mensure avene et furfuris.

Summa Empcionis ii d.
Stauri iiii d.

iiii li. . . .x s. ob.
iiii li. iii s. . . . . .
Membrane 1 dorse

Rotulus primus de anno x^{o}

Extranei iiii Frumentum de M' iii bidentes de M' Die martis apud Metingham in pane furnito i qr. frumenti de manerio de Metingham precium vi s. unde xiiii^{xx}x panes. In multura eiusdem iii d. Item in dono i garcioni eundo apud

[5] MS adds 'Item' followed by a blank space.
[6] MS faded.

Bredef' ii d. In occisione iii bidentes matrices de manerio de Metingham precium omnium ii s. iii d. Item iii pulcini de preempto. Item xx ova de preempto. In putura pauperum ut supra. In prebenda iiii equorum domine i bus. di. et i mensura avene et furfuris.

Summa Empcionis v d.
Stauri viii s. iii d.

Extranei iiii Die mercurii in ix^{xx}xviii de allece empto xiii d. In merling et codling <vii d.> \ x d. / Item lx allec de preempto. In putura xiii pauperum panis de stauro et xiii allec de preempto. In prebenda v equorum domine i bus. di. ii mensure avene et furfuris.

Summa Empcionis xxiii d.
Stauri nichil.

Extranei ix Braseum de M' Bidentes de M' Die jovis in cervisia braciata ii qr. brasei de manerio de Metingham precium qr. vi s. unde vii^{xx}xvi lag. cervisie. Item in carne porci ii d. ob. Item in lavendria iii d. Item ii bidentes matrices de manerio de Metingham precium xviii d. Item i auca de stauro preempto. Item iii pulcini de manerio de Metingham. Item i qr. carnis bovis veteris incipitur de manerio de Metingham. Item in putura pauperum panis de stauro et allec de preempto. In prebenda iiii equorum domine ii de Margaria Weylond' ii bus. ii mensure avene et furfuris.

Summa Empcionis v d. ob.
Stauri xx d.

Extranei iiii Die veneris in \ di. / C de alece empt*a* v d. Item in codling et merling vi d. Item in pane pro coquina i d. Item xl allec de preempto. Item in putura pauperum ut supra. In prebenda v equorum domine i bus. iii pec. avene et furfuris.

Summa Empcionis xii d.
Stauri nichil.

Extranei v Die sabati in oblacione i d. Item in C de allece empt*a* ix d. Item in codling vi d. In expensis Johannis Capellani et Barfot' iiii d. In i supercinggulo ii d. In i cribro ii d. In vadiis Johannis Tyler' cum ii garcionibus suis per ii dies viii d. Item lx allec de preempto. In putura xiii pauperum panis de stauro et allec de preempto. In prebenda v equorum domine ii bus. i pec. avene et furfuris.

Summa Empcionis ii s. viii d.
Stauri nichil.

Extranei iii ii bidentes de M' ii bus. avene de M' Die dominica in vigilia appostolorum Symonis et Jude in oblacione i d. Item in carne bovis xiii d. Item in carne multonis vi d. In carne porci v d. In occisione ii bidentes matrices de manerio de Metingham precium xviii d. Item ii auce de stauro preempto. Item i pulcinus de manerio de Metingham. Item in farina facta pro coquina ii bus. avene de manerio de Metingham precium viii d. In putura pauperum ut supra. In prebenda v equorum domine ii bus. avene et furfuris.

Summa Empcionis ii s. i d.
Stauri ii s. ii d.

Extranei vii Frumentum de M' Die lune sequenti in pane furnito i qr. frumenti de manerio de Metingham precium vi s. unde xiiii^{xx}vi panes. In multura eiusdem iii d. Item in expensis Rudde veniend*o* de Bredef' i d. ob. Item ii pulcini de manerio de Metingham. In putura xiii pauperum panis de stauro et allec de preempto. In prebenda vi equorum domine ii bus. avene et furfuris.

Summa Empcionis iiii d. ob.
Stauri vi s. i d. ob.

Extranei x ii bidentes de M' Mixtura de S' Die martis in ovis ii d. In ferrura gresel de Lek' cum ii ferris posterioribus et ii remocionibus iii d. Item in occisione ii bidentes de manerio de Metingham precium xx d. Item i auca de stauro preempto. Item iiii pulcini de exhennio de Kokele hic primo. Item[7] xix ova de preempto. Item x ova pro foretto. Item in pane furnito pro pauperibus iiii bus. mixture de manerio de Schepmed' precium xx d. unde ix^{xx}xvi panes unde in putura xiii pauperum panis de stauro et xiii allec de preempto. Item in prebenda iiii equorum domine et <iiii> \ v / de domino ii de domino Rogero v bus. ii mensure avene et furfuris.

Summa Empcionis <iiii d.> \ v d. /
Stauri iii s. viii d.

Extranei xx Die mercurii sequenti in C de allece empt*a* ix d. In codling et merling xii d. Item in anguillis iiii d. Item in synapio ii d. Item C de allece de stauro de preempto. Item xlv ova de preempto. Item in putura pauperum ut die precedenti. Item in prebenda iiii equorum domine iii de domino i de domino Rogero ii de Emma de Lek' ii de Thoma de Brigham v bus. avene et furfuris.

Summa Empcionis ii s. iii d.
Stauri nichil.

Extranei xiii Die jovis in vigilia Omnium Sanctorum in CC de allece nove empcionis xvi d. In rubio allece ii d. In codling et haddok emptis xxi d. In merling iiii d. Item in schrympes et smeltis vi d. In anguillis vi d. In gyngibr*o* et galantyn i d. In oleo de oliva vii d. In cepo iii d. In ferrura ii ferrorum anteriorum et ii ferrorum posteriorum pro morel. Item in i ferro anteriore et i remocione pro gresel de Norwyc' vii d. \ In iiii bus. furfuris viii d. / In lacte pro coquina ob. qua. In lacte pro pueris i d. Item lx allec de preempto. In putura pauperum panis et allec de preempto. In prebenda iiii equorum iiii de domino et ii de domino Rogero et ii de Thoma de Brigham

[7] MS repeats 'item'.

et i de serviente de Sculthorp et iii equorum carectariorum de Blacworth' vi bus. i mensura i pec. avene et furfuris.

Summa Empcionis vi s. x d. ob. qua.
Stauri nichil.

Die veneris in festo Omnium Sanctorum in oblacione iiii d. Item C et v allec de preempto. In putura pauperum ut supra. In prebenda v equorum domine v de domino ii de domino Rogero iii bus. iii pec. avene et furfuris.

Summa Empcionis iiii d.
Stauri nichil.

Extranei xxxii Frumentum de Kok' Die sabati in die Animarum in oblacione iii d. Item in pane furnito i qr. frumenti de manerio de Cokele precium vi s. et hic primo hoc anno unde xiiii^{xx} panes. In multura eiusdem iii d. In allece rubio ii d. In ostreis v d. In anguillis v d. In schrympis i d. In cymino iii d. In pane pro coquina i d. In merling ii d. In expensis i garcionis versus Sculth' ii d. Item iiii^{xx} allec de preempto. In putura pauperum ut supra. In prebenda v equorum domine v de domino iii bus. iii pec. avene et furfuris.

Summa Empcionis ii s. iii d.
Stauri vi s.

Extranei xvi iiii bidentes de M' Memorandum quod incipitur hic ad expendendum de xii pernis remanentibus in lardario apud Metingham de anno precedenti Die dominica proxima post festum Omnium Sanctorum in oblacione i d. Item in carne porci vi d. In pomis ii d. In pane pro coquina i d. Item in lx de ovis iii d. Item in ii gallinis emptis iii d. Item in occisione pro hospicio iiii bidentes matrices de manerio de Metingham precium omnium iii s. iiii d. Item ii auce de stauro preempto. Item ii capones de stauro manerii de Metingham. Item ii pulcini de exhennio de Kokele. Item i perna baconis incipitur de stauro anni precedentis. Et memorandum quod incipitur hic primo ad expendendum de vi baconibus de factura anni precedentis. Item i qr. carnis bovis incipitur de stauro de Metingham. Item xv ova de preempto. In putura pauperum panis et allec de . . . . . In prebenda iiii equorum domine vi de domino i de Willelmo de Carlton' iiii bus. avene et furfuris.

Summa Empcionis xv d.
Stauri iii s. x d.

Extranei vii Die lune sequenti in carne porci empta iiii d. In carne multonis vi d. Item in trypis vi d. Item in iii ventribus boum xii pedibus boum emptis xi d. \ In iii bus. furfuris viii d. / Item in dono garcioni domine de Uff' ii d. Item i pulcinus de exhennio. Item vi ova de preempto et iiii pro foretto. In putura pauperum ut supra. In prebenda iii equorum domine i de Ricardo Hacon ii mensure iii pec. avene et furfuris.

Summa Empcionis iii s. i d.
Stauri i d.

Deficientes iiii Braseum de[8] Die martis sequenti in cervisia braciata ii qr. brasei de manerio de Blacworth' precium qr. vi s. unde vii^{xx}iiii lag. cervisie. Item i auca de stauro preempto. Item i pulcinus de exhennio de Kokele. Item vi ova de preempto. In putura xiii pauperum panis de stauro et allec de preempto. In prebenda ii equorum domine di. bus. i mensura avene et furfuris.

Summa Empcionis nichil.
Stauri xii s. i d.

Extranei iiii Memorandum quod incipiuntur hic ii cadi allecis rubii et corpelchun et hic primo hoc anno Die mercurii in codling et merling emptis xi d. Item in lx de allece novo empto iiii d. In buttis iiii d. Item lxvi allec rubium de stauro. Et memorandum quod incipitur hic ad expendendum de i lasto allecis empto apud Jernemut' de empcione istius anni. Item in putura pauperum ut supra. In prebenda iii equorum domine de domino de Ufford' ii de domino Constant*e* Mortym*er* vi de domino Rogero ii sic de avena et furfure v bus. ii mensure.

Summa Empcionis xix d.
Stauri[9]

Extranei viii Frumentum de[10] *ii bidentes de M'* Die jovis sequenti in pane furnito i qr. frumenti de manerio de Kokele precium vi s. unde xiiii^{xx} panes. In .....[11] eiusdem iii d. Item in occisione ii bidentes matrices de manerio de Metingham precium ii s. Item ii auce de stauro preempto...... i capo de manerio de Metingham et iii pulcini de exhennio de Kokele. Item xx ova de preempto. In putura pauperum ut supra. In prebenda ii equorum domine ii de domino de Uff' i bus. di. et i mensura avene et furfuris.

Summa Empcionis iii d.
Stauri viii s. iii d. ob.

Deficientes iiii Die veneris in merling et haddok emptis vi d. Item in synapio iiii d. Item in cervisia pro garcione veniendo de Ufford' et clavis ferri pro pullano ob. qua. Item de stauro nichil. Item putura pauperum ut supra de pane et allece. In prebenda iii equorum domine i bus. avene et furfuris.

Summa Empcionis x d. ob. qua.
Stauri nichil.

Deficiens i Die sabbati in oblacione i d. Item in codling empto iii d. In buttis ii d. In pane pro coquina i d. In cariagio unius dolii vini ex dono domini Johannis Norwyc' ex Teppeystathe usque Stonhale x d. Item xxxiii

[8] Followed by a blank space.
[9] Followed by a blank space.
[10] Followed by a blank space.
[11] Possibly 'multura'.

allec rubium de stauro. In putura pauperum ut supra de allece albo et pane. Item in prebenda i equi domini iii equorum domine i bus. ii mensure avene et furfuris.

Summa Empcionis xvii d.
Stauri nichil.

Eque Mixtura de S' ii bidentes de M' Die dominica in oblacione ii d. In pane furnito pro pauperibus iiii bus. mixture de manerio de Schepmedwe precium xx d. unde ix^{xx}xvi panes. In carne bovis xiii d. Item in carne porci iiii d. In occisione ii[12] bidentes matrices de manerio de Metingham precium omnium ii s. vi d. Item i auca de stauro preempto. In putura xiii pauperum panis de stauro et xiii allec album de preempto. In prebenda iiii equorum domine ii mensure ii pec. avene et furfuris.

Summa Empcionis xix d.
Stauri iiii s. vi d.

. . . . . Die lune sequenti in festo Sancti Martini in oblacione i d. Item in iiii gallinis et iiii pulcinis emptis xi d. Item in iiii bus. furfuris emptis viii d. Item ii pulcini de ultima preempcione. Item ix allec rubium de stauro. Item in putura xiii pauperum panis de stauro et xiii allec rubium de stauro et hic primo hoc anno. Item in prebenda iii equorum domine ii mensure i pec. avene et furfuris.

Summa Empcionis xx d.
Stauri nichil.

Summa Empcionis istius rotuli iiii li. v s. iiii d. ob. qua.
Stauri istius rotuli Cvii s. v d.
ix li. xii s. . . . . .

Staurum istius rotuli De Blacworth' ii qr. frumenti ii qr. vi bus. \ brasei / i boviculus et i juvenca iii multones iiii bidentes.
De Metingham iii qr. frumenti et v qr. brasei ii bus. avene pro farina et xxi . . . . .
De Schepmed' i qr. iiii bus. mixture.
De Kokele ii qr. frumenti.

Solutum Laurencio . . . . . pro cof. . . . . xxi d. Item Waltero Coco pro oleo pro Quadragesima . . . xiii d.

Membrane 2 recto

Secundus rotulus de anno x^{mo}

Deficientes ii Die martis proxima post festum Sancti Martini apud Metingham de empcione nichil. Item ii pulcini de preempto. Item xxiii ova de preempto. In putura xiii pauperum panis de stauro et xiii allec rubium de stauro. In prebenda ii equorum domine ii mensure i pek. avene et furfuris.

Summa Empcionis
Stauri Nichil.

[12] MS 'iii'.

Deficientes iiii Die mercurii in codling et merling viii d. In lx ovis emptis iii d. In ferrura gresol Fysymon vi d. Item xlvii allec rubium de stauro. Item vii ova de preempto. In putura pauperum ut die precedenti. In prebenda ii equorum domine ii mensure i pec. avene et furfuris.

Summa Empcionis xvii d.
Stauri nichil.

Deficientes ii i bidens de M' Die jovis sequenti de empcione nichil. Item in occisione i bidens matrix de manerio de Metingham precium x d. Item ii auce de stauro preempto. Item ii pulcini de preempto. In putura xiii pauperum panis de stauro et allec rubium de stauro.[13] In prebenda ii equorum domine i mensura et i pec. avene et furfuris.

Summa Empcionis
Stauri Nichil.

Deficientes iii Frumentum de K' Memorandum quod i barellus allecis albi incipitur hic ex dono domini et domini Rogeri Die veneris sequenti in pane furnito i qr. frumenti de manerio de Kokele precium vi s. unde xiiii^{xx}vi panes. In multura eiusdem iii d. Item in allece \ novo / empto viii d. Item in codling et merling vi d. In pane pro equis querentibus lib*eraturam* domine de Norwyc' ii d. In elemosina iii d. In vii reticulis pro cuniculis capiendis iii d. Item xii allec rubium de stauro. Item i barellus de allece albo \ precium ix s. / incipitur hic de dono domini Johannis de Norwyc' et domini Rogeri unde xxx lib*erata* coquine et hic primo. In putura pauperum ut die precedenti de pane et allece rubio. In prebenda iii equorum domine ii mensure i pec. avene et furfuris.

Summa Empcionis ii s. i d.
Stauri xv s.

Deficientes iiii Die sabbati in oblacione i d. Item in C de allece novo empto vii d. In codling et merling ii d. Item xii allec rubium de stauro. Item viii allec album de barello. In putura xiii pauperum panis de stauro et de[14] allec*e* novo de preempto. In prebenda iii equorum domine ii mensure et i pec. avene et furfuris.

Summa Empcionis x d.
Stauri nichil.

Extranei ix Braseum de B' ii bidentes de M' Die dominica proxima post festum Sancti Martini in oblacione ii d. Eodem die in cervisia braciata ii qr. brasei de veteri de manerio[15] de Blacworth' precium xii s. unde vii^{xx}xvii lag. cervisie. Item in carne bovis xviii d. In carne porci v d. Item in xvii gallinis emptis xx d. Item in lx ovis emptis iii d. In pane pro coquina i d. In

[13] MS 'allec de rub' st''.
[14] MS omits 'de'.
[15] MS 'de man' de vet' de man''.

occisione ii bidentes de manerio de Metingham precium xx d. Item i perna baconis de anno precedenti. Item i qr. carnis bovis incipitur de veteri. Item viii galline de preempto. Item xii ova de preempto. In putura pauperum ut die precedenti. In prebenda <iiii> \ v / equorum domine et viii veniencium cum domina Margeria de Sculton' v bus. i mensura i pec. avene et furfuris.

Summa Empcionis iiii s. i d.
Stauri xiii s. viii d.

Eque Die lune sequenti de empcione nichil. Item i gallina de preempto. Item vi ova de preempto. In putura pauperum ut die precedenti. In prebenda iiii equorum domine iii pec. i mensura avene et <tantum> furfuris.

Summa Empcionis
Stauri Nichil.

Extranei iii Die martis de empcione nichil. Item i auca de stauro preempto. Item viii ova de preempto. In putura pauperum ut supra de pane et allece novo. In prebenda iiii equorum domine iii pec. i mensura avene et furfuris.

Summa Empcionis
Stauri Nichil.

Extraneus i Die mercurii in festo Sancti Edmundi regis in oblacione i d. Item in codling et merling vi d. In schrympes i d. Item pane pro equo Johannis Capellani i d. \ Item carectar*io* domini de Hunt' ii d. / In lacte pro pueris ii d. Item in Dlx de allece novo empto ii s. i d. Item in xi qr. avene pro prebenda equorum emptis xx s. ix d. Item xx allec rubium de stauro et viii allec de[16] barello. In putura pauperum ut supra de pane et allece novo. In prebenda v equorum domine i bus. ii mensure i pec. avene et furfuris.

Summa Empcionis xxiii s. xi d.
Stauri nichil.

Extranei iiii Frumentum de K' ii bidentes de M' Die jovis in pane furnito i qr. frumenti de manerio de Kokele precium vi s. unde xiiii^{xx}v panes. In multura eiusdem iii d. Item in carne porci v d. In occisione ii bidentes matrices de manerio de Metingham precium xx d. Item i auca de stauro preempto. In putura xiii pauperum panis de stauro et allec novum de preempto. In prebenda iiii equorum domine i bus. i mensura et i pec. avene et furfuris.

Summa Empcionis viii d.
Stauri vii s. viii d.

Extranei ii Die veneris sequenti in codling et merling vi d. In pomis ii d. In i strenyour[17] ii d. In expensis pro Warde versus Blacworth' i d. Item xii allec rubium de stauro et vi allec de barello. In putura xiii pauperum panis de

[16] MS omits 'de'.
[17] MS 'srenyour'.

stauro et xiii allec novum de preempto. In prebenda ix equorum domine et domini Rogeri iii bus. ii mensure et i pec. avene et furfuris.

Summa Empcionis xi d.
Stauri nichil.

Extranei ii Multura de S' Die sabbati in oblacione ii d. Eodem die in pane furnito pro pauperibus iiii bus. multure de manerio de Schepmedwe precium xx d. unde ix^{xx}xiiii panes. In ostreis iii d. In haddok i d. In codling xiiii d. In schrympes i d. In merling i d. In pacacione fabr*i* de Bungeye pro ferrura equi Bryset' pro anno precedenti vi d. Item xx allec rubium de stauro et viii allec de barello. Item xxiiii allec novum. In putura pauperum ut die precedenti. In prebenda vii equorum domine i de Dalham ii bus. di. et ii mensure avene et furfuris.

Summa Empcionis ii s. iiii d.
Stauri xx d.

Extranei viii Die dominica \ in festo Sancte Kateryne / in oblacione ii d. In farina ii d. qua. In carne bovis xviii d. In carne porci i d. qua. In i capite apri xviii d. ob. In iiii gallinis vi d. Item iii galline de preempto. In putura xiii pauperum panis de stauro et allec novum de preempto. In prebenda v equorum domine i bus. ii mensure i pec. avene et furfuris.

Summa Empcionis iiii s.
Stauri nichil.

Extranei viii Die lune sequenti in ollis luteis i d. Item ii galline de preempto et xi columbelle de exhennio Ricardi Hacon. In putura pauperum ut die precedenti. In prebenda iiii equorum domine et vi de domino ii de Ricardo Hacon et domino Ricardo Dun v bus. avene et furfuris.

Summa Empcionis i d.
Stauri iii d.

Extranei xii i porcellus de M' i multo de K' Die martis in carne porci empta iiii d. In ferrura pullani in singulis pedibus v d. In ferrura Frik' cum i ferro anteriore et i ferro posteriore ii d. ob. Item i porcellus de manerio de Metingham'. Item i auca de preempto. Item i gallina de preempto. Item xii ova de preempto. In occisione i multo de manerio de Kirkeby precium xii d. In putura pauperum ut supra. In prebenda iiii equorum domine v de domino et i de domino Waltero de Thorp iiii bus. et i mensura avene et furfuris.

Summa Empcionis xi d. ob.
Stauri xiii d.

Extranei xiii Frumentum de Kok' Die mercurii in pane furnito i qr. frumenti de manerio de Kokele precium vi s. unde xiiii^{xx} panes. In multura eiusdem iii d. Item in ostreis i d. Item in haddok codling et merling x d. Item in lx ovis iii d. In lacte pro coquina i d. Item xl allec rubium de stauro et xvi allec de barello. Item xx ova de preempto. In putura pauperum panis de stauro et xiii allec album de preempto. In prebenda iii equorum domine vii de domino i de Ricardo Hacon iiii bus. i pec. avene et furfuris.

Summa Empcionis xviii d.
Stauri vi s.

Extranei xv i multo de K' Die jovis sequenti in carne porci empta iiii d. Item in occisione i multo de manerio de Kirkeby precium xii d. Item i auca de stauro preempto. Item iiii galline de preempto. In putura pauperum ut die precedenti. In prebenda vi equorum domine et domini Rogeri et vi de domino v bus. avene et furfuris.

Summa Empcionis iiii d.
Stauri xii d.

Extranei xix Die veneris sequenti in codling et merling ix d. Item in lacte pro pueris i d. In lavendria i d. In . . . . . pro . . . . . Willelmi de Hunting. . . i d. Item in synapio iiii d. In pane pro coquina i d. Item xx allec rubium de stauro viii de barello. Item lxxii allec album de preempto. In putura pauperum ut supra de pane et allece albo. In prebenda vi equorum domine et domini Rogeri i de Rob*erto* . . .rtym*er* ii bus. di. avene et furfuris.

Summa Empcionis xvii d.
Stauri nichil.

Extranei ix Braseum de B' Die sabbati in festo Sancti Andree appostoli in oblacione ii d. Item eodem die in cervisia braciata ii qr. brasei de veteri de manerio de Blacworth' precium xii s. unde vii^{xx} et x lag. cervisie. Item in codling ii d. Item xxiiii allec rubium de stauro et viii allec de[18] barello. Item xxvi allec novum de preempto. In putura pauperum ut supra de allece novo. In prebenda vii equorum domine et domini Rogeri iii bus. avene et furfuris.

Summa Empcionis iiii d.
Stauri xii s.

Extranei xvi i multo de K' Die dominica sequenti in oblacione ii d. In carne bovis empta xvi d. In carne porci empta v d. In carne vituli xii d. In uno capite apri empto xx d. Item in xiii gallinis emptis xxii d. ob. qua. Item in iiii bus. furfuris . . . . . In occisione i multo de manerio de Kirkeby precium xii d. Item iii galline de preempto. In putura pauperum panis de stauro . . . . . de preempto. In prebenda vi equorum domine et domini Rogeri ii bus. i mensura et i pec. avene et furfuris.

Summa Empcionis vi s. xi d. ob. qua.
Stauri xii d.

Extranei viii Die lune de empcione nichil. Item i gallina de preempto. In putura pauperum ut supra. In prebenda iiii equorum domine i bus. i mensura avene . . . . .

[18] MS omits 'de'.

Summa Empcionis
Stauri Nichil.

Extranei viii ..... Die martis in pane furnito i qr. frumenti de manerio de Kokele precium vi s. unde xiiii^{xx}iii panes. In multura eiusdem iii d. Item i qr. carnis bovis de veteri incipitur. Item ii galline de preempto. In putura pauperum ut supra. In prebenda vi equorum domine et iiii de domino iii bus. iii pec. avene et furfuris.

Summa Empcionis iii d.
Stauri v. . .

Extranei xii Die mercurii in ostreis ii d. In codling et haddo. . . vii d. In emend*acione* unius olle panetrie ob. Item x. . . allec . . . de stauro. Item viii allec de barello. Item xl allec album de preempto. In putura pauperum ut supra ..... In prebenda i pull*ani* domine i de Chandeler' i bus. avene et furfuris.

Summa Empcionis ix d. ob.
Stauri .....

Extranei Eque i bidens de M' Die jovis de empcione nichil. In occisione i bidens matrix de manerio de Metingham precium x d. Item i auca de preempto. Item i gallina de preempto. In putura pauperum ut supra. In prebenda iii equorum domine iii pec. avene et furfuris.

Summa Empcionis nichil.
Stauri x d.

Deficientes ii Mixtura de S' Die veneris in pane furnito pro pauperibus iiii bus. mixture precium xx d. unde x^{xx} panes. Item datum clerico Sancti Nichol*ai* et in oblacione vii d. In merling ..... craticul*is* et vas*is* lardarii et coquine emendend*is* ix d. Item xvi allec rubium de stauro. Item vi allec de ba. .... allec alb*um* de preempto. In putura xiii pauperum panis de stauro et xiii allec rubium. In prebenda iii equorum ..... et furfuris.

Summa Empcionis ii s.
Stauri xx d.

Membrane 2 dorse

Secundus rotulus de anno x^{o}

Extranei iiii Die sabbati in crastino Sancti Nichol*ai* apud Metingham in oblacione i d. In pisce marino empto iii d. In lacte pro pueris i d. In ii ferris anterioribus pro Frik' et le nagg ii d. In i capistro ob. Item vi allec rubium de stauro. In putura xiii pauperum panis de stauro et xiii allec rubium de stauro. In prebenda vi equorum domine et domini Rogeri ii bus. i mensura avene et furfuris.

Summa Empcionis vii d. ob.
Stauri nichil.

Extranei xi ii multones de K' Die dominica in festo Concepcionis Beate Marie in oblacione vii d. In carne bovis empta xvi d. In carne porci v d.

Item in v gallinis emptis viii d. ob. qua. Item in i gall*o* i d. ob. Item in xl ovis emptis ii d. Item in carne vituli vi d. Item in occisione ii multones de manerio de Kirkeby precium ii s. Item ii galline de preempto. Item xliiii ova de preempto. In putura xiii pauperum ut die precedenti. In prebenda v equorum domine et domini Rogeri i bus. iii pec. avene et furfuris.

Summa Empcionis iiii s. x d. qua.
Stauri ii s.

Extranei vii Frumentum de Kok' Die lune sequenti in pane furnito i qr. frumenti de manerio de Kokele precium vi s. unde xiiii^{xx} et iiii panes. In multura eiusdem iii d. In pane pro coquina i d. In vino aceto i d. In tonsione vi... wardecorps i d. Item i gallina de preempto. In putura pauperum panis de stauro et xiii allec album. In prebenda v equorum domine ii bus. et i pec. avene et furfuris.

Summa Empcionis vi d.
Stauri vi s.

Eque ii bidentes de M' Die martis sequenti in cervisia empta iii d. In lacte qua. Item in occisione ii bidentes de manerio de Metingham precium xx d. Item ii galline de preempto. In putura pauperum panis de stauro et rubium allec. Item in prebenda vi equorum domine i de Ricardo Hacon ii bus. di. avene et furfuris.

Summa Empcionis iii d. qua.
Stauri xx d.

Eque Die mercurii in ostreis i d. In cervisia iii d. In codling merling et haddok viii d. In schrympes i d. In rad' i d. qua. In barber' iii d. In lavendria i d. Item xxxi allec rubium de stauro. Item vi allec de barello. Item xx allec album de preempto. In putura panis de stauro et allec rubium de stauro. In prebenda iiii equorum domine i bus. avene et furfuris.

Summa Empcionis xviii d. qua.
Stauri nichil.

Extraneus i Die jovis in carne porci empta iii d. Item in i mazelard ii d. \ ob. / In ovis iii d. Item i auca de stauro preempto. Item i gallina de preempto. In putura pauperum ut die precedenti.

Summa Empcionis viii d. ob.
Stauri nichil.

Extranei viii Braseum de B' Die veneris sequenti in cervisia braciata ii qr. brasei de manerio de Blacworth' de veteri precium xii s. unde vii^{xx}x lag. cervisie. Item in ostreis iii d. In ypimer iii d. ob. In codling viii d. In schrympes i d. Item xxxvi allec rubium de stauro. Item xii de barello. Item xx allec album de preempto. In putura pauperum panis de stauro et allec rubium de stauro. In prebenda v equorum domine pro ista nocte et nocte precedenti et v equorum domini iiii bus. i mensura i pec. avene et furfuris.

Summa Empcionis xv d. ob.
Stauri xii s.

Extranei xiiii Die sabati in oblacione i d. In ypimer i d. Item xl allec rubium de stauro. Item x de barello. Item xvi allec album de preempto. In putura pauperum ut die precedenti. In prebenda iii equorum domine v de domino iii bus. di. avene et furfuris.

Summa Empcionis ii d.
Stauri nichil.

Extranei xiiii Frumentum de Kok' et Kyrkeby iii bidentes de M' Die dominica in oblacione i d. Eodem die in pane furnito vi bus. de Kokele et ii bus. de Kyrkeby frumenti precium vi s. unde xiiii^{xx}vi panes. In multura eiusdem iii d. In carne bovis empta xv d. In carne porci v d. In viii gallinis xvi d. In ii mazelarsz emptis iiii d. In occisione iii bidentes de Metingham precium ii s. vi d. Item i auca de stauro preempto. Item iii galline de preempto. Item xv ova de preempto. In putura xiii pauperum panis de stauro et xiii allec rubium de stauro. In prebenda iii equorum domine iiii de domino ii bus. di. avene et furfuris.

Summa Empcionis iii s. viii d.
Stauri viii s. vi d.

Extranei iiii Die lune sequenti de empcione nichil. Item i auca de stauro preempto. Item ii galline de preempto. In putura pauperum ut die precedenti. In prebenda iii equorum domine v de domino iii bus. di. avene et furfuris.

Summa Empcionis
Stauri Nichil.

Extranei xii Avena pro farina Die martis in farina facta pro potagio iii bus. avene de manerio de Metingham precium xi d. In factura eiusdem i d. In pane pro coquina i d. In carne porci empta ii d. Item iii galline de preempto. Item xii ova de preempto. In putura xiii pauperum ut supra de pane et allece rubio. In prebenda iii equorum domine vi de domino iii bus. iii pec. avene et furfuris.

Summa Empcionis iiii d.
Stauri xi d.

Extranei vii Die mercurii in ostreis emptis iiii d. In codling vi d. Item ypimer ii d. In schrympes ii d. In lacte pro pueris i d. In putura pauperum ut supra de pane et allece rubio. In prebenda iii equorum domine i bus. avene et furfuris.

Summa Empcionis xv d.
Stauri nichil.

Extranei xiii Mixtura de S' Die jovis in pane furnito pro pauperibus iiii bus. multure de manerio de Schepmed' precium xx d. unde ix^{xx} panes. Item iii galline de preempto. In putura xiii pauperum panis de stauro et nichil de allece. In prebenda iii equorum domine ii de domino Philippo de Norwyc' i bus. di. et i mensura avene et furfuris.

Summa Empcionis nichil.
Stauri xx d.

Extranei iiii Frumentum de Kyr' Die veneris sequenti in pane furnito i qr. frumenti de manerio de Kyrkeby precium vi s. unde xiiii^{xx}vi panes. In multura eiusdem iii d. In codling x d. In ypymer ii d. In synapio iiii d. In lavendria ii d. Item xxviii allec rubium de stauro. Item vi allec de barello. Item xiiii allec album de preempto. In putura xiii pauperum panis de stauro et xiii allec rubium de stauro. In prebenda iii equorum domine i bus. avene et furfuris.

Summa Empcionis xxi d.
Stauri vi s.

Extranei iii Die sabati in festo Sancti Thome appostoli in oblacione ii d. In pisce empto xiiii d. In cepo i d. In iiii bus. avene pro prebenda emptis xiii d. Item datum carectar*io* domine de Huntingf' iii d. Item xxxvi allec rubium de stauro. Item viii allec de barello. Item xvi allec album de preempto. In putura pauperum ut die precedenti. In prebenda iii equorum domine et equorum de Huntingf' i bus. di. avene et furfuris.

Summa Empcionis ii s. ix d.
Stauri nichil.

Extranei xxii ii bidentes de M' Memorandum quod ii qr. avene incipiuntur ad expendendum de exhennio domini Johannis de Norwyc' Die dominica in oblacione i d. In \ i karkoys et di. / carnis bovis empt*is* ix s. qua. In carne porci vi d. In ix gallinis xviii d. In i qr. croci xx d. In gyngibr*o* iiii d. In zoukro xii d. In semine i d. ob. In CC de ovis emptis xii d. In vi craticulis pro modi*is* lardarii faciend*is* v d. ob. Item in occisione ii bidentes de manerio de Metingham precium xx d. Item v galline de preempto. Item xii ova de preempto. In putura pauperum ut supra. In prebenda iiii equorum domine ix de domino i de Tyteshale iiii bus. iii pec. avene et furfuris.

Summa Empcionis xv s. viii d. qua.
Stauri iiii s.

Extranei xvi Die lune sequenti in carne bovis empta x d. In carne porci vi d. In di. bus. albarum pisarum pro potagio iiii d. I. . . . . i auc*a* de stauro preempto. \ In pane pro coquina . . . . . / Item ii galline de preempto. In putura pauperum panis de stauro et allec rubium de stauro. In . . . . . v equorum domine et v de domino iiii bus. iii pec. avene et furfuris.

Summa Empcionis xxii d.
Stauri nichil.

Extranei xl Braseum Die martis in vigilia Natalis Domini. Eodem die in cervisia braciata ii qr. brasei de veteri de manerio de Blacworth' precium qr. vi s. unde vii^{xx}[19] lag. cervisie. In pisce marino empto xvii d. In buttis iiii d. In smeltis iii d. Item in galantyn et gingibr*o* iii d. In cepo i d. Item in i qr. furfuris empto xvi d. In factura candele de cera viii d. Item lviii

[19] MS adds 'et' but no further figure.

allec rubium de stauro. Item xx allec de barello et x de allece albo. In putura pauperum ut supra de allece rubio de stauro. In prebenda vii equorum domine xi de domino iiii extraneorum vi bus. ii mensure avene et furfuris.

Summa Empcionis iiii s. iiii d.
Stauri xii s.

. . . . . *lxii*[20] Die mercurii in Natali Domini in oblacione xx d. Eodem die in pane furnito ii qr. frumenti de manerio de Kyrkeby precium qr. vi s. unde xxviii^{xx}xi panes. In multura eiusdem vi d. In carne bovis viii d. In carne porci viii d. In carne vituli empta xx d. Item carn*es* multonis xvi d. In volatilibus iiii d. ob. qua. In uno porcello vii d. Item i cingnettus de exhennio. Item ii auce de stauro preempto. Item x galline de exhennio Ricardi Capellani et iii galline de lok de Schepmed' et i gall*ina* de preempto. Item vii perdices de exhennio. Item in frumento furnito pro pastellis et pro coquina ii bus. frumenti de manerio de Kirkeby precium xviii d. Item xxxvi ova de preempto. In putura pauperum panis de stauro et allec album de preempto. In prebenda equorum domine viii et xii de domino et iii de R. Hacon' Markant et Bryset' vi bus. di. et ii mensure avene et furfuris.

Summa Empcionis viii s. v d. ob. qua.
Stauri xviii s. x d.

Extranei xxxviii Die jovis in festo Sancti Stephani in oblacione v d. In ii ferris pro Frik' et i ferro anteriore pro palefrido domini Rogeri et i ferro pro le nagg iiii d. In pomis i d. In expensis i garcionis versus Bredef' iii d. Item ii auce de stauro de preempto. Item v galline de lok de Schepmed'. Item v perdices de exhennio. Item xl ova de preempto. In putura panis de stauro et xiii allec rubium de stauro. In prebenda vii equorum domine x de domino \ ix extraneorum / vi bus. ii mensure et i pec. avene et furfuris.

Summa Empcionis xiii d.
Stauri xii d.

Extranei xxxvii Memorandum quod ii cadi allecis rubii incipiuntur hic Die veneris in festo Sancti Johannis in oblacione iii d. In pisce iiii d. Item ii cadi incipiuntur hic de rubio allece et corpelch*u*n unde iiii^{xx}ix allec et xx allec de barello. Item xii ova de preempto. In putura pauperum ut die precedenti. In prebenda vii equorum domine viii de domino i de Ricardo Hacon' v bus. i mensura et i pec. avene et furfuris.

Summa Empcionis vi d.
Stauri nichil.

. . . . .

[20] MS faded: possibly also 'Farina pro coquina' in the margin.

Summa Empcionis istius rotuli Cv s. vi d.
Stauri istius rotuli vii li. ii s. xi d.
Summa tocius xii li. viii s. v d.[21]

Membrane 3 recto

Tercius rotulus de anno x^mo^

Extranei xlvi Braseum Die sabbati in festo Sanctorum Innocencium adhuc apud Metingham in oblacione i d. Eodem die in cervisia braciata ii qr. brasei \ de veteri / de manerio de Blacworth' precium xii s. unde vii^{xx}xiii lag. cervisie. In pisce empto vii d. Item viii^{xx}ix allec rubium de stauro. Item xxx allec de barello. In putura xiii pauperum panis de stauro et xiii allec de stauro. In prebenda vi equorum domine et vii de domino iiii bus. i mensura i pec. avene et furfuris.

Summa Empcionis viii d.
Stauri xii s.

Extranei xxxv Die dominica in festo Sancti Thome martiris in oblacione vi d. In carne vituli empta xix d. In carne porci empta xii d. Item in carne multonis empta xviii d. In volatilibus vii d. In pane pro coquina i d. In lacte pro coquina ob. qua. In i porcello empta v d. Item ii auce de stauro preempto. Item ix galline de lok de Bredef' et hic primo hoc anno. Item xl ova de preempto. In putura xiii pauperum panis de stauro et xiii allec rubium de stauro. In prebenda iiii equorum domine et iiii de domino ii bus. i pec. et i mensura avene et furfuris.

Summa Empcionis v s. x d. ob. qua.
Stauri xiii d. ob.

Extranei xxxi ii multones de Kyrkeby Die lune sequenti in . . . . . de stauro. In occisione ii multones de manerio de Kirkeby precium ii s. Item vi galline de lok de Bredef'. Item ii perdices de stauro. Item xii ova de preempto. In putura pauperum ut die precedenti. In prebenda iii equorum domine iii de domino et i de magistro Jacobo de Birlingham et ii extraneorum ii bus. avene et furfuris.

Summa Empcionis nichil.
Stauri ii s. xi d.

Extranei xi Frumentum de Kyrk' Die martis sequenti in pane furnito i qr. frumenti de manerio de Kirkeby precium vi s. unde xiiii^{xx}x panes. In multura eiusdem iii d. Item i auca de stauro preempto. Item ii galline de manerio de Bredef' de lok. Item ii perdices de stauro. Item vi ova de preempto. In putura pauperum panis de stauro et allec rubium.[22] In

[21] MS has two lines of figures, written in a small hand, probably cash sums (as on membrane 1 recto), which are now too faded to be read.

[22] MS 'allec de rub''.

prebenda iii equorum domine et iii de domino i bus. et ii mensure avene et furfuris.

Summa Empcionis iii d.
Stauri vi s. v d.

Extranei xxi Mixtura de S' Die mercurii in festo Circumcisionis Domini in pane furnito pro pauperibus iiii bus. mixture de manerio de Schepmed' precium xx d. unde x^{xx} panes. \ In oblacione i d. / Item in haddok et codling xviii d. In ypimer i d. In i congro xii d. Item in smeltis ii d. Item in lx ovis emptis iii d. \ In alece pro coquina ob. / Item v^{xx} et v allec rubium de stauro. Item xxx allec de barello. Item xv ova de preempto. In putura pauperum ut die precedenti. In prebenda ii equorum domine vi de domino i bus. di. et ii mensure avene et furfuris.

Summa Empcionis iii s. ob.
Stauri xx d.

Extranei xiii Memorandum de i qr. avene de M' pro prebenda Die jovis in carne bovis empta xii d. Item in iiii bus. furfuris emptis viii d. Item i auca de stauro de preempto. Item ii galline de lok de Bredef'. In putura pauperum ut supra de allece rubio. Item receptum de Metingham ad lib*erandum* pro prebenda i qr. avene de manerio de Metingham. In prebenda ii equorum domine et iii de domino ii mensure et iii pec. avene et furfuris.

Summa Empcionis xx d.
Stauri ii s. ix d.

Extranei xii Die veneris de empcione nichil. Item xl allec rubium de stauro. Item viii de barello et vii de allece albo. In putura pauperum ut die precedenti de pane et allece rubio. In prebenda i equi domine iiii de domino i bus. et di. avene et furfuris.

Summa Empcionis
Stauri Nichil.

Extranei xv Die sabbati in oblacione i d. Item in codling[23] merling et buttis ix d. In pane pro coquina i d. In synapio ii d. In gyngibr*o* i d. In melle ii d. Item xli allec rubium de stauro. Item xvi allec de barallo et iiii allec album. In putura xiii pauperum panis de stauro et allec rubium. In prebenda ii equorum domine et iii de domino et iii de domino Johanne Nogon ii de Waltero de Norwyc' i de Barsham iii bus. di. et i mensura avene et furfuris.

Summa Empcionis xvi d.
Stauri nichil.

Extranei xliiii Frumentum de K' Braseum de B' Die dominica in vigilia Epiphanie in oblacione i d. Eodem die in pane furnito i qr. frumenti de manerio de <Schepmed> \ Kokele / precium vi s. unde $xiiii^{xx}x$ panes. In

[23] MS 'colling'.

multura eiusdem iii d. In carne bovis empta xvi d. In carne porci viii d. In carne multonis empta ii s. iiii d. In carne vituli xx d. In volatilibus v d. In allaudis ii d. In vino aceto ii d. In gyngibr*o* i d. Eodem die in cervisia braciata i qr. iiii bus. brasei de veteri de manerio de Blacworth' precium ix s. unde vi^{xx}vi lag. cervisie. Item ii auce de stauro de preempto. Item viii galline de Bredefeld' de lok. Item xxviii ova de preempto. In putura pauperum ut die precedenti. In prebenda iiii equorum domine viii de domino i de Barsham i de Ricardo Hacon iii bus. et iii pec. avene et furfuris.

Summa Empcionis vii s. viii d.
Stauri xvi s.

Extranei liii Die lune in festo Epiphanie in oblacione iiii d. In ii porcellis emptis xiii d. In lacte i d. In skyrewycz i d. Item i cingnettus de exhennio. Item ii auce de stauro preempto. Item xi galline de lok de Bredef'. Item xxiiii ova de preempto. In putura pauperum ut supra de pane et allece rubio. In prebenda iiii equorum domine viii de domino et iiii de domino Rogero v bus. iii pec. avene et furfuris.

Summa Empcionis xix d.
Stauri iiii s. ix d. ob.

Extranei xviii Die martis de empcione nichil. Item vi galline de lok de Bredefeld'. Item i auca de stauro preempto. Item xxi ova de preempto. In putura pauperum ut supra de allece et pane. In prebenda vi equorum domine et domini Rogeri ii bus. i mensura avene et furfuris.

Summa Empcionis nichil.
Stauri ix d.

Extraneus i Die mercurii in p. . . . . empt*o* viii d. In expensis i garcionis eund*o* usque Sculthorp' i d. Item l allec rubium de stauro. Item xxxviii allec de barello. In putura xiii pauperum panis de stauro et allec rubium de stauro. In prebenda iiii equorum domine i bus. et i mensura avene et furfuris.

Summa Empcionis ix d.
Stauri nichil.

Extranei iiii Frumentum Die jovis sequenti in oblacione apud Bungeye iii d. Eodem die in pane furnito i qr. et di. frumenti de manerio de Kirkeby precium ix s. unde xxii^{xx}vi panes. In multura eiusdem iiii d. ob. In carne bovis empta xvi d. In carne porci iiii d. ob. In xxii ovis emptis i d. In pane pro coquina i d. In synapio iiii d. In lavendria i d. In expensis i garcionis super negociis domine usque Dalham v d. Item ii auce de stauro preempto. Item iii galline de lok de Howe hic primo hoc anno. Item xvi ova de preempto. In putura pauperum ut supra. In prebenda ii equorum domine i de Ricardo Lek' iii pec. avene.

Summa Empcionis iii s. iiii d.
Stauri ix s. iiii d. ob.

Extranei vii Die veneris sequenti in pisce empto vi d. In xxxiii allece rubio de stauro. Item xx allec de barello. In putura pauperum ut supra de pane et allece rubio. In prebenda iii equorum domine di. bus. i mensura avene.

Summa Empcionis vi d.
Stauri nichil.

W. Cocus debet hic domine v s.

Extranei ii Die sabati in oblacione iiii d. In ostreis emptis ii d. In pisce empto vi d. In pipere iii d. In factura v^{xx} et iiii lib. candele de parys viii d. In . . . . . iiii d. In lacte pro pueris i d. Item in xxiiii discis xxiiii salsariis xviii platellis et vi ciphis emptis xv d. . . . . . Fysymon iii d. In xxxiiii . . . . . alb*o* de barello. In putura pauperum ut die precedenti. In prebenda ii . . . . . ii mensure i pec. avene

Summa Empcionis iii s. ix d.
Stauri nichil.

iiii bus. avene de Metingham Die dominica sequenti in oblacione i d. Eodem die in carne bovis empta ii s. Item in carne porci empta v d. In carne vituli vi d. In volatilibus ii d. qua. Item ii bidentes matrices de Metingham precium xv d. Item ii auce de stauro preempto. Item i gallina de lok de Howe. Item xvi ova de preempto. In putura xiii pauperum panis de stauro et allec rubium de stauro. In prebenda equorum domine iiii bus. avene de manerio de Metingham et ii bus. furfuris de preempto.

Summa Empcionis iii s. ii d. qua.
Stauri xvi d. ob.

Memorandum quod domina removit hic de Metingham Die lune in festo Sancti Illarii domina removit de Metingham invenienda versus Norwic'. Sero ad cenam apud Blacworth'. Eodem die in iii lag. cervisie et xii[24] lag. mediocris cervisie emptis xvi d. ob. \ In sale xii d. / In pane pro equis carectari*is* apud Brok' et apud Norwyc' v d. Item i gall*ina* de Schepmed'. Item ii galline de lok de Howe et ii galline de stauro preempto. In putura pauperum ut die precedenti. In prebenda equorum veniencium cum domina.

Summa Empcionis ii s. ix d. ob.
Stauri iiii d.

Die martis sequenti apud Blacworth' in carne bovis et mutilina xviii d. ob. In carne vituli v d. Item iii galline de lok de manerio de Blacworth' et iii gall*i* de lok de eodem.[25] In putura pauperum ut supra. In prebenda ii equorum domine i de Wacelyn.

Summa Empcionis xxiii d. ob.
Stauri vii d. ob.

[24] MS possibly 'xvi'.
[25] MS 'eadem'.

Et venit hic cum familia usque Norwic' Die mercurii sequenti in i lag. cervisie et iii lag. cervisie mediocris ..... In pisce vi d. In ypimer i d. qua. In .....

Die jovis ..... pro pullan*o* v d. In ..... cum i ferro anteriore et i remocione i d. In feno et ..... equis venientibus ad villam cum ..... i d. In vadiis Johannis Pistoris et garcionis per ix dies ii s. iii d. In vadiis ..... coci per iiii dies ..... panetria empt*o* ii d. In candela pro pistrina i d. In expensis carectar*ii* de .....ham venien*tis* cum vit..... i d. In lavendria iii d. Item i porcellus de exhennio. ..... Item v ..... Item iii gall*ine* de lok de Blacworth'. Item in putura pauperum ut die prec..... In prebenda xiiii equorum domine veniencium de Norwyc' ... i bus. et i pec. furfuris.

Summa Empcionis iiii s. x d. ob. qua.
Stauri iiii s. viii d. ob.

Membrane 3 dorse

Tercius rotulus de anno x^{mo}

Frumentum de Howe Memorandum quod ii cadi allecis rubii incipiuntur hic. Mixtura Die veneris proxima post festum Sancti Illarii apud Norwyc'. Eodem die in pane furnito i qr. frumenti de manerio de Howe precium vi s. hic primo hoc anno unde xiiii^{xx} panes. In multura et pistura eiusdem vii d. In ostreis i d. qua. In pisce vii d. In ypymer empt*o* i d. ob. In fycis et racemis i d. In astellis pro aula iii d. In i qr. avene pro prebenda ii s. i d. Item ii cadi allecis rubii incipiuntur hic unde xliiii expend*untur*. Item xx allec de calant. In pane furnito pro pauperibus iiii bus. mixture de manerio de Blacworth' precium xx d. unde x^{xx} panes. In pistura eiusdem ii d. In putura pauperum panis et allec rubium de stauro. In prebenda viii equorum domine et domini Rogeri iii bus. i pec. avene et furfuris.

Summa Empcionis iii s. xi d. ob. qua.
Stauri vii s. viii d.

Die sabbati in oblacione i d. In pisce empto x d. In ypimer i d. Item in salmone empto xviii d. In cocleis emptis qua. In lacte pro pueris qua. In sale pro panetria qua. Item lxii allec rubium de stauro. Item xxx allec de calaunt. In putura pauperum ut die precedenti. In prebenda vii equorum domine et domini Rogeri i de rectore de Redynhale ii bus. di. et ii mensure avene et furfuris.

Summa Empcionis ii s. vi d. ob. qua.
Stauri nichil.

Avena pro farina Die dominica sequenti in oblacione ii d. \ In carne vituli xiiii d. / In carne multonis vi d. Item in carne porci xii d. Item in farina facta pro coquina iiii bus. avene de manerio de Blacworth' precium xv d. Item i qr. carnis bovis incipitur hic primo de stauro istius anni. Item i perna veteris baconis incipitur. Item iii galline de lok de Blacworth' et vi galline de exhennio Nichol*a*i Palmer'. Item xiiii ova de preempto. In putura xiii pauperum panis de stauro et xiii allec rubium de stauro. In prebenda viii equorum domine et domini Rogeri ii bus. di. et ii mensure avene et furfuris.

Summa Empcionis ii s. x d.
Stauri ii s. v d. ob.

Fercula iiii^{xx}xii Frumentum Braseum Anniversarius domini Die lune sequenti in festo Sanctorum Fabiani et Sebastiani in anniversario domini Walteri de Norwyc' in oblacione viii d. In elemosina ii d. qua. In CC de gastellis pro pauperibus iiii s. Eodem die in pane furnito i qr. di. frumenti de manerio de Howe precium ix s. xxi^{xx} panes. In multura eiusdem xi d. ob. In frumento furnito pro pastellis ii bus. de Howe <.....> precium xviii d. In frumento furnito pro pane calido \ i bus. frumenti / de eodem[26] precium ix d. Item in potagio di. bus. frumenti de eodem[27] precium iiii d. ob. Item in dono precon*io* iiii d. In cervisia braciata ii qr. brasei de manerio de Blacworth' unde medietas de novo grano hic primo hoc anno precium xii s. unde vii^{xx}iiii lag. cervisie. In focali pro brac*iatura* eiusdem x d. In sale pro panetria i d. In i qr. carnis bovis empto ii s. ii d. Item in i karkoys porci empto iii s. In i karkoys multonis empto xviii d. Item in iii vitulis emptis vi s. x d. Item in v porcellis emptis ii s. vi d. Item in v mallard x d. Item in i heron et i botor emptis ii s. viii d. Item i heron de exhennio precium xvi d. Item in x plovers et iiii wodekockis emptis ii s. vi d. Item iii plovers de exhennio precium vi d. Item in iiii decenis allaudarum et v^{xx}vii de minutis avibus emptis xii d. Item MCC de ovis emptis xii d. In flore pro coquina vi d. In pane pro coquina i d. Item in i qr. de sandr*es* xii d. Item iiii lib. de pulvere de rys vi d. Item in i lag. vini aceti vi d. Item in di. lag. mellis empta iii d. ob. In synapio ii d. In di. lag. gyngibr*i* iiii d. Item in x lib. de ..... emptis x d. In skyrewycz ii d. In alb*a* pingguedine iiii d. \ ob. / Item in xxiiii gallinis furnitis et vii^{xx}xvii de pyes iiii d. In C de astellis empt*a* pro camera et aula empt*a* xv d. In di. lasto turbarum pro coquina iiii s. ii d. In lacte iii d. qua. In ostreis i d. \ Item xx lib. cere pro iii tap*eris* de stauro precium x s. In factura eorundem x d. / Item in dono pro anima domini priori et conventui Sancte Trinitatis lx s. Item fratribus minoribus x s. Item fratribus carmel*itis* predicatoribus et Sancti Augustini xx s. Item ii bestie ferine di. precium v s. Item iiii cingnotti precium xii s. Item iii auce precium xii d. Item xxvii galline de lok de Schulthorp' precium iii s. iiii d. ob. Item xx galline de lok de Howe \ precium / ii s. vi d. Item xi cuniculi de manerio de Blacworth' et vi cuniculi de Ling' precium v s. viii d. Item i capud apri de exhennio precium xviii d. Item xviii perdices de Metingham et viii de exhennio precium iiii s. iiii d. Item xxiiii lag. vini de stauro precium viii s.

[26] MS 'eadem'.
[27] MS 'eadem'.

Item xxiiii lib. de amigdalis de stauro precium iiii s. Item iii lib. de rys de stauro precium vi d. Item i lib. de zoukro de Cafatyn et ii lib. de zoukro de Cyp... de stauro. Item di. qr. de saffran de stauro. Item di. qr de clowes ..... In putura pauperum ..... In prebenda vii equorum domine i de rectore de Redynhale ii bus. ii mensure et i pec. avene et furfuris.[28]

Summa Empcionis vi li. xii s. ix d.
Stauri iiii li. v s. xi d. x li. xviii s. viii d.

Frumentum Memorandum de ii qr. avene de exhennio Johannis Skilman
Die martis sequenti in pane furnito iiii bus. frumenti de manerio de Howe precium iii s. unde v^{xx} panes. In multura eiusdem i d. ob. \ In pistura eiusdem ii d. / In carne vituli empta vi d. In i porcello empto vii d. Item in CCCC de ovis emptis xxiii d. Item i qr. carnis bovis incipitur de stauro lardarii. Item i perna incipitur veteris baconis. Item ii galline de lok de Blacworth'. Item viii ova de preempto. Item in putura xxvi pauperum xxvi panes et totidem allec rubium de stauro. In prebenda vii equorum domine ii de rectore de Redynhale ii bus. ii mensure et i pec. avene et furfuris.

Summa Empcionis iii s. iii d. ob.
Stauri iii s. iiii d. ob.

Die mercurii in pisce empto vi d. In i pikerell empto vi d. Item xlix de allece rubio et xxxi de allece albo. In putura pauperum panis de stauro et xiii allec rubium de stauro. In prebenda vii equorum domine et i de rectore de Redynhal' ii bus. ii mensure et i pec. avene et furfuris.

Summa Empcionis xii d.
Stauri nichil.

Die jovis sequenti de empcione nichil. Item i cingnottus de exhennio precium ii s. Item i gallina de lok de Blacworth ..... de stauro. Item in putura pauperum ut die precedenti. In prebenda v equorum domine i bus. ii mensure avene et furfuris.

Summa Empcionis nichil.
Stauri ii s. ii d.

Die veneris sequenti in .....[29] vii d. ob. In pisce empto viii d. Item ..... ii d. In ferrura gresel Fysymion v d. In feno iiii d. Item xxvi allec rubium de stauro. Item lvi allec album de calant. In putura pauperum ut supra de allece rubio. In prebenda vi equorum domine i bus. ii mensure et i pec. avene et furfuris.

Summa Empcionis ii s. iiii d. ob. ...
Stauri nichil.

Die sabati in conversione Sancti Pauli in oblacione ii d. In cervisia iiii d. Item piscis ..... d. In roches emptis i d. \ In ypimer i d. ob. / In pane pro

[28] Possibly 'xii s. x d.' running in from the margin at this point.
[29] Possibly 'cervisia empta'.

coquina i d. Item in expensis i garcionis usque Redynhale ii d. Item xxvi de allece rubio de stauro. In putura xiii pauperum panis et allec rubium de stauro. In prebenda vi equorum domine i de magistro Jacobo ii bus. et i pec. avene et furfuris.

Summa Empcionis xviii d. ob.
Stauri nichil.

Extranei x Braseum Die dominica sequenti in oblacione i d. Eodem die in cervisia braciata ii qr. brasei de manerio de Blacworth' unde medietas de veteri precium xii s. \ unde vii^{xx}x lag. cervisie. / In focali pro eadem bracianda ii d. Item in carne multonis empta x d. Item in carne vituli empta xx d. In carne porci empta vii d. Item ii galline de lok de Blacworth' et ii gall*i* de eadem. Item iii galline de exhennio Alicie de Formeset' hic primo. Item ii perdices de stauro. In putura pauperum ut supra. In prebenda vi equorum domine i de magistro Jacobo ii bus. i pec. avene et furfuris.

Summa Empcionis iii s. iiii d.
Stauri x. . . ix d.

Extraneus i Frumentum Die lune . . . . . Eodem die in pane furnito . . . . . frumenti de . . . . . In putura pauperum . . . . .

Summa Empcionis xviii . . . . .
Stauri v. . . . .

Extranei iiii Die martis sequenti de empcione nichil. Item ii galline de lok de Howe. In putura pauperum ut die precedenti. In prebenda iii equorum domine i bus. avene et furfuris.

Summa Empcionis nichil.
Stauri iiii d. ob.

Extranei v Mixtura Die mercurii in pisce empto viii d. In pisce marino vi d. In ypimer i d. ob. In pane pro coquina i d. In expensis i garcionis versus Bredef' i d. Item lx allec rubium de stauro. Item xxx allec album de calant. Eodem die in pane furnito pro pauperibus iiii bus. mixture de manerio de Blacworth' precium xx d. unde ix^{xx} panes . . . . .[30] eiusdem ii d. In putura pauperum ut die precedenti. In prebenda iii equorum domine i bus. avene et furfuris. Item in cingnottis inpingguendis ii bus. avene de manerio de Blacworth' precium vii d.

Summa Empcionis xviii d. ob.
Stauri ii s. iii d.

Extranei vi Die jovis sequenti in i qr. carnis vituli et i qr. carnis mutuline xii d. In carne porci ii d. ob. Item i qr. carnis . . . . . incipitur. Item i perna veteris baconis incipitur. Item iii galline de lok de Howe. Item iiii perdices de stauro. Item i . . . . . de exhennio. Item in putura pauperum ut supra de allece rubio. In prebenda iii equorum domine i bus. avene et furfuris.

Summa Empcionis xiiii d. ob.
Stauri vii d.

[30] Possibly 'In multura'.

Extranei . . . . . Die veneris . . . . . stauro empto v d. In roch*es* i d. In i lath pro hostio aule qua. Item xxxii allec rubium . . . . . In putura pauperum ut supra. In prebenda iiii equorum domine i bus. i pec. avene et furfuris.

Summa Empcionis vi d. . . .
Stauri . . . . .

Die sab*ati* in oblacione ii d. In pisce empto vii d. In pikerell ii d. Item x allec rubium de stauro. . . . . . pauperum panis et allec rubium de stauro. In prebenda iiii equorum domine et domini Rogeri i bus. i pec. avene et furfuris.

Summa Empcionis . . . . .
Stauri . . . . .

Summa Empcionis istius rotuli x li. iiii s. iii d. ob.
Stauri istius rotuli ix li. viii s. xi d.
Summa tocius xix li. xiii s. ii d. ob. . . .

Membrane 4 recto

Quartus rotulus de anno Edwardi tercii x^{mo}

Extranei xxi Frumentum Die dominica in festo Purificacionis Beate Marie apud Norwyc'. Eodem die in pane furnito i qr. frumenti de manerio de Howe precium vi s. unde xiiii^{xx} panes. In multura et pistura eiusdem vii d. In oblacione v d. \ In cera pro cereis vii lib. stauri. / Item in carne bovis empta vii d. In carne porci vii d. In carne multonis empta xxi d. In i ossa medulla ii d. In carne vituli xiiii d. \ In i porcello vii d. / In volatilibus iiii d. In gingibr*o* ob. In galantyn iiii d. Item i qr. carnis bovis incipitur. Item i cingnottus de exhennio precium ii s. Item vii galline de lok de Sculthorp. Item lvi ova de preempto. In putura pauperum panis de stauro et xiii allec rubium de stauro. In prebenda iiii equorum domine et domini Rogeri i bus. i pec. avene et furfuris.

Summa Empcionis vi s. vi d. ob.
Stauri viii s. x d. ob.

Extranei xiiii Die lune sequenti in oblacione vii d. In carne bovis ix d. In carne porci iiii d. In flore vi d. In focali pro pastellis ii d. In pane pro coquina i d. Item vi galline de lok de Sculthorp. In putura pauperum ut die precedenti. In prebenda iiii equorum domine i bus. i pec. avene et furfuris.

Summa Empcionis ii s. iiii d.
Stauri x d. ob.

Extranei xii Die martis sequenti in carne porci empta v d. Item iiii galline de lok de Sculthorp. Item ix ova de preempto. In putura pauperum panis de stauro et allec rubium de stauro. In prebenda iiii equorum domine i de magistro Jacobo i bus. i mensura et i pec. avene et furfuris.

Summa Empcionis v d.
Stauri vi d.

Extranei xiiii Braseum Die mercurii sequenti in cervisia braciata ii qr.

brasei de manerio de Blacworth' unde medietas de veteri grano precium xii s. unde vii^{xx}x lag. cervisie. In focali ii d. In pisce empto v d. In pisce marino ii d. ob. In scull' ii d. In ypimer i d. ob. In i corbello panetrie emendendo i d. In iii circulis pro mod*io* et i cuva emend*endis* ii d. In i barello reparando pro panetria ii d. Item in dono garcioni domini Constantis Mortymer portando farinam iii d. Item lx allec rubium de stauro et xl de allece albo de calant. Item <xvii> \ xxi / ova de preempto. In putura pauperum ut die precedenti. In prebenda iiii equorum domine i de magistro Jacobo i bus. i mensura i pec. avene et furfuris.

Summa Empcionis xxi d.
Stauri xii s.

Extranei xv Frumentum Die jovis sequenti in pane furnito i qr. frumenti de manerio de Howe precium vi s. unde xiiii^{xx} panes. In multura eiusdem et pistura vii d. In carne bovis empta ii s. In carne multonis x d. In carne vituli vi d. In carne porci v d. Item vii galline de lok de Dalyngho hic primo hoc anno. Item vii ova de preempto. In putura pauperum ut supra de pane et allece rubio de stauro. In prebenda iiii equorum domine i de Ufford i bus. i mensura et i pec. avene et furfuris.

Summa Empcionis iiii s. iiii d.
Stauri vi s. x d. ob.

Extranei ix Memorandum quod unus barellus allecis de calant incipitur hic Die veneris in pisce empto viii d. In raso*rs* iii d. In pisce marino ii d. In rys et racemis et ficis iii d. In lacte pro coquina qua. In lavendria iii d. In lacte pro pueris i d. In pane pro coquina i d. Item xxiiii allec rubium de stauro. Item i barellus de allece de calant incipitur hic precium vii s. unde xxvi allec. In putura pauperum panis de stauro et allec rubium de stauro. In prebenda iiii equorum domine i bus. avene et furfuris.

Summa Empcionis xxi d. qua.
Stauri vii s.

Extranei xii Die sabati in oblacione ii d. In ostreis emptis i d. ob. In muruca empta iii d. In cepo i d. Item xxxvi allec rubium de stauro. Item xl allec album de calant. Item i muruca et ii mellvelli de stauro de Blacworth' et hic primo post festum Omnium Sanctorum. Item ix ova de preempto. In putura pauperum panis de stauro et allec rubium de stauro. In prebenda iiii equorum domine i bus. i pec. avene et furfuris.

Summa Empcionis vii d. ob.
Stauri nichil.

Extranei xix Die dominica in oblacione iiii d. In carne bovis empta xvi d. In carne multonis xx d. In carne porci vii d. In carne vituli xv d. In astellis pro aula et camera ii s. vii d. In turbis pro coquina iiii d. In i qr. avene pro prebenda empto ii s. ob. In dono garcioni sacriste portando ceram die Purificacionis Beate Marie vi d. Item i auca de stauro preempto. Item iiii galline de lok de Dalyngho. Item vii ova de preempto. In putura pauperum ut die precedenti. In prebenda iiii equorum domine i bus. i pec. avene et furfuris.

Summa Empcionis x s. vii d. ob.
Stauri vi d.

Extranei xvi Die lune sequenti in carne bovis empta vi d. In carne porci vii d. In focali pro fornacio coquine i d. In turbis pro coquina iii d. In flore pro pastellis iii d. In zoukro roseto zoukro plato viii d. In galant*yn* ii d. In dat*is* ii d. In sale pro panetria i d. Item i perna veteris baconis de Metingham incipitur. Item vi galline de lok de Dalyngho. Item x ova de preempto. In putura pauperum ut supra de pane et allece rubio de stauro. In prebenda v equorum domine i bus. ii mensure i pec. avene et furfuris.

Summa Empcionis ii s. ix d.
Stauri ix d.

Extranei xvii Die martis in caulibus ob. In volatilibus iiii d. ob. In turbis pro coquina v d. In reparacione porte coquine videlicet in bordis i d. ob. In clavis ferris serrur*is* hespys et i fetir*o* serrur*arum* v d. In stipendio i carpentarii faciendi dictam portam et i rakam stabuli v d. Item i qr. carnis bovis incipitur de stauro de Metingham. Item iii galline de lok de Dalyngho. Item i auca de stauro de Blacworth'. Item ii capones de exhennio Nichol*a*i Palmer'. Item vi ova de preempto. In putura pauperum ut die precedenti. In prebenda v equorum domine i de magistro Jacobo i bus. di. ii mensure avene et furfuris.

Summa Empcionis xxi d. ob.
Stauri xiii d. ob.

Extranei vi Frumentum de B' Mixtura Die mercurii in pane furnito i qr. frumenti de manerio de Blacworth' precium vi s. unde xiiii^{xx}v panes. In multura eiusdem et pistura vii d. Item in pane furnito pro pauperibus iiii bus. mixture de manerio de Blacworth' precium xx d. unde ix^{xx}x panes. Item in pistura eiusdem ii d. Item in pisce marino iii d. In pane pro coquina i d. Item lxxvi allec rubium de stauro. Item lv allec de calant. Item xix ova de preempto. In putura pauperum panis de stauro et allec rubium de stauro. In prebenda v equorum domine i bus. i mensura et i pec. avene et furfuris.

Summa Empcionis xiii d.
Stauri vii s. viii d.

Extranei . . . Die jovis sequenti in carne porci empta v d. In carne vituli vii d. In oleo et uncto pro gresel Fysymon emptis iii d. ob. In caulibus ob. . . . . . Item vi galline de lok de Howe. Item in putura pauperum . . . . .

Summa Empcionis xx d.
Stauri ix d.

Extranei iiii Die veneris in festo Sancti Valentini in codling viii d. In ficis et racemis i d. In pisce ..... ii d. In DC de turbis vi d. Item in expensis i garcionis super negociis domine versus Sculthorp \ ii d. / Item xxvii allec rubium de stauro et xx allec de calant. Item ii mellvelli de stauro de Blacworth'. In putura pauperum ut die precedenti. In prebenda v equorum domine i bus. i mensura et i pec. avene et furfuris.

Summa Empcionis xix d.
Stauri nichil.

Extranei x Memorandum quod i cadus de corpelchon incipitur hic Die sabati sequenti in oblacione i d. In ostreis ii d. In pisce grosso vi d. In pikerell burbocz et roch*es* i d. ob. In smeltis et kocleis i d. Item xx allec rubium de stauro. Item xl allec album de calant. Item vii ova de preempto. In putura pauperum ut supra. In prebenda v equorum domine i bus. i mensura et i pec. avene et furfuris.

Summa Empcionis xi d. ob.
Stauri nichil.

Extranei xxx Braseum de B' Die dominica \ in oblacione ii d. / In cervisia braciata ii qr. brasei de manerio de Blacworth' unde medietas de novo precium tocius xii s. unde vii^{xx}xi lag. cervisie. In focali preter focale de stauro ii d. In barell*o* emendand*o* ii d. In carne bovis empta ii s. v d. In carne porci xiii d. In i qr. carnis multonis v d. In carne vituli empta xv d. In volatilibus viii d. In flore pro coquina i d. In synapio iiii d. Item vii galline de lok de Howe. Item i perna baconis \ veteris / incipitur de stauro. Item xiiii ova de preempto. In putura pauperum ut supra de allece rubio et pane de stauro. In prebenda v equorum domine i bus. i mensura et i pec. avene et furfuris.

Summa Empcionis vi s. ix d.
Stauri xii s. xi d. ob.

Extranei xviii Frumentum Die lune sequenti in pane furnito i qr. frumenti de manerio de Blacworth' precium vi s. unde xiiii^{xx}iiii panes. In multura eiusdem et pistura vii d. In flore pro pastellis iiii d. In astellis i d. ..... pro coquina iiii d. Item in lacte pro pueris i d. In lavendria iii d. Item i qr. carnis bovis incipitur de stauro de Metingham. Item vi galline de lok de Howe. Item xiiii ova de preempto. In putura pauperum ut supra. In prebenda ...[31] equorum domine i bus. i mensura et i pec. avene et furfuris.

Summa Empcionis xix d.
Stauri vi s. ix d.

Extranei ix Die martis in carne bovis empta xvi d. In carne porci ii d. In carne vituli empta viii d. In pane pro coquina i d. Item in CC de turbis emptis ii d. In dewet' pro gresel Fysymon ii d. In i capistro i d. In piris i d. Item in iiii remocionibus pullani ii d. In i ferro posteriore pro palefrido

[31] Possibly 'v'.

domini Rogeri i d. Item in marchella*cia* gresel Fysymon i d. Item i auca de stauro preempto. Item iiii galline de lok de Howe. In putura pauperum ut supra de pane et allece de stauro. In prebenda v equorum domine i bus. i mensura et i pec. avene et furfuris.

Summa Empcionis iii s. i d.
Stauri vi d.

Extranei xv Die mercurii in pisce empto viii d. In playcz iii d. In raso*rs* iiii d. In di. lag. mellis iiii d. Item lii allec rubium de stauro. Item lxiii allec album de calant. Item xxiii ova de preempto. In putura pauperum ut supra. In prebenda v equorum domine i bus. i mensura et i pec. avene et furfuris.

Summa Empcionis xix d.
Stauri nichil.

Extranei v Die jovis sequenti in carne porci empta ii d. In carne vituli vii d. In vi gallinis xii d. \ et expenduntur. / In CC de turbis ii d. In matis pro aula . . . iiii d. In putura pauperum panis de stauro et allec rubium de stauro. In prebenda v equorum domine i de magistro Jacobo de M' i bus. i mensura i pec. avene et furfuris.

Summa Empcionis ii s. iii d.
Stauri nichil.

Membrane 4 dorse

Adhuc quartus rotulus de anno x^{mo}

Extranei iiii Memorandum quod i cadus allecis rubii incipitur hic Die veneris proxima ante festum cathedre Sancti Petri apud Norwyc' in pisce grosso empto ix d. In playcz iii d. In rys ii d. Item in fructu i d. Item in flore empto iiii d. ob. qua. In CCC de turbis iii d. Item i cadus allecis rubii incipitur hic unde xxi allec rubium de stauro. Item xlvii allec rubium de calant. In putura xiii pauperum panis et allec rubium de stauro. In prebenda iii equorum domine i bus. avene et furfuris.

Summa Empcionis xxii d. ob. qua.
Stauri nichil.

Extranei iiii Die sabbati sequenti in playcz iiii d. In burbocz ob. In viiC de turbis emptis vii d. In i qr. avene pro prebenda ii s. ii d. In flore ii d. qua. Item xxxii allec rubium de stauro. In putura pauperum ut die precedenti. In prebenda iiii equorum domine et domini R. i bus. i mensura avene et furfuris.

Summa Empcionis iii s. iii d. ob. qua.
Stauri[32]

Extranei xviii Frumentum i porcelus de Howe Die dominica in pane furnito i qr. frumenti de manerio de Howe <u>precium vi s.</u> unde xiiii^{xx}vi panes. In multura eiusdem et pistura vii d. In oblacione iii d. In carne bovis empta

[32] Followed by a blank space.

x d. In carne vituli xiiii d. In carne porci iii d. Item in i auca iiii d. Item in iii gallinis emptis vi d. \ et expend*untur*. / In volatilibus iii d. In caulibus ob. In pane pro coquina i d. In flore empto i d. Item in occisione i porcelus de manerio de Howe precium iii s. iiii d. Item i cingnottus de exhennio precium ii s. Item xv ova de preempto. In putura pauperum panis de stauro et allec rubium de stauro. In prebenda iiii equorum domine i bus. i mensura avene et furfuris de preempto.

Summa Empcionis iiii s. iiii d. ob.
Stauri xi s. iiii d.

Extranei vi Die lune in festo Sancti Mathie in oblacione i d. In iii gallinis emptis vi d. In ii pulcinis emptis ii d. In burbocz i d. In percameno pro rotul*is* faciend*is* v d. Item ii galline de lok de Howe et iii galline de preempto. In putura pauperum ut die precedenti. In prebenda iiii equorum domine i bus. i mensura avene et furfuris.

Summa Empcionis xv d.
Stauri iii d.

Extranei xvii Die martis sequenti in carne vituli empta vii d. In ii pulcinis emptis iii d. In CC de turbis emptis ii d. Item i auca de stauro preempto. Item iii galline de lok de Howe. Item vi ova de preempto. In putura pauperum ut die precedenti. In prebenda iiii equorum domine i bus. et i mensura avene et furfuris.

Summa Empcionis xii d.
Stauri iiii d. ob.

Extranei xviii Mixtura Die mercurii sequenti in pane furnito pro pauperibus iiii bus. mixture de manerio de Blacworth' precium xx d. unde ix^{xx}xiii panes. \ In pistura ii d. / Item in pisce grosso empto vii d. In playcz v d. In burbocz i d. Item in leng et playcz ex empcione Derby vi d. In rasouns[33] i d. ob. \ In lacte pro pueris iii d. / Item xl allec rubium de stauro. Item xxxviii allec album de calant. Item xv ova de preempto. In putura pauperum ut supra. In prebenda ii equorum domine ii mensure avene et furfuris.

Summa Empcionis ii s. i d. ob.
Stauri xx d.

Extranei iii Die jovis sequenti in carne bovis empta xvi d. In carne porci iii d. ob. In uncto pro crassetto implendo <i d.> ob. Item in i gallina empta et expend*itur* ii d. In turbis iii d. In i remocione palefridi domini Rogeri ob. In uncto et cord*is* pro gresel Fysimon ii d. In expensis Rudd ad domum Cecili*i* atte Hil ob. Item i gallina de lok de Howe et iii galline de preempto. In putura pauperum panis et allec rubium de stauro. In prebenda gresel Fysymon i mensura avene et furfuris.

Summa Empcionis ii s. iii d. ob.
Stauri i d. ob.

[33] MS obscure. Possibly 'rasours'.

Extranei vi Die veneris \ in cervisia vii d. / In pisce grosso empto vi d. In plaicz v d. Item in di. salmone xvii d. In ficis et racemis i d. Item xx allec rubium et xvi allec album de stauro. In putura pauperum panis et allec rubium de stauro. In prebenda iiii equorum domine i bus. iii pec. avene et furfuris.

Summa Empcionis iii s.
Stauri nichil.

Deficientes v Frumentum Braseum Die sabbati in pane furnito i qr. frumenti de manerio de Howe precium vi s. unde xiiii^{xx}vi panes. In multura et pistura eiusdem vii d. Item in cervisia braciata ii qr. brasei de manerio de Blacworth' unde medietas de veteri precium tocius xii s. unde vii^{xx}x lag. cervisie. Item in focali preter staurum ii d. Item in pisce grosso empto vii d. In plaicz iiii d. In anguillis iii d. Item in vino empto vi d. Item in turbis emptis v d. In ii bus. furfuris emptis ii d. In feno empto viii d. ob. qua. In cepo i d. Item xxxiiii allec rubium et xiiii allec album de stauro. In putura pauperum ut supra. In prebenda ii equorum domine ii mensure avene et furfuris.

Summa Empcionis iii s. ix d. ob. qua.
Stauri xviii s.

Extranei xix Die dominica in oblacione iii d. Item in carne bovis empta xiii d. In carne porci iii d. Item in carne vituli ii s. i d. Item in i porcello v d. ob. Item in iiii gallinis et i gallo ix d. ob. In volatilibus iii d. In ii pulcinis ii d. ob. In pane pro coquina i d. In vino aceto ii d. Item i auca de preempto. Item iii galline de lok de Howe et hic ultimo hoc anno. Item iiii galline de preempto. Item xl ova de preempto. In putura pauperum panis et allec rubium de stauro. In prebenda iiii equorum domine i bus. et i mensura avene et furfuris.

Summa Empcionis v s. vii d. ob.
Stauri iiii d. ob.

Extranei xvi Die lune in oblacione pro anniversario Petri Branch' et matris domine iii d. In flore pro coquina iii d. Item in turbis ii d. Item i qr. carnis bovis incipitur et i perna veteris baconis incipitur de stauro de Metingham hic. Item viii galline de lok de Sculthorp'. Item xx ova de preempto. In putura pauperum ut die precedenti. In prebenda iii equorum domine i bus. avene et furfuris.

Summa Empcionis viii d.
Stauri xii d.

Extranei xxi Die martis in i porcello empto vi d. In carne vituli ix d. Item in iii gallinis emptis vi d. In volatilibus ii d. In caulibus i d. ob. Item in i gallina ii d. In lacte pro coquina ob. In i auca iii d. Item vi cuniculi de stauro de Blacworth'. Item iii galline de lok de Sculthorp'. Item iiii galline de preempto. Item lx ova de preempto. In putura pauperum ut supra. In prebenda iii equorum domine iii mensure avene et furfuris.

Summa Empcionis ii s. vi d.
Stauri ii s.

Extranei vii Memorandum de xii piscibus computatis Die mercurii in capite jejunii in ostreis emptis i d. ob. In skreyth' empto vi d. In playcz vi d. Item in C de welk*is* empt*a* v d. ob. In roch*es* emptis iii d. In anguillis iiii d. In cymino iii d. In ficis et racemis ii d. In grano ii d. Item panis pro equis i d. In feno empto v d. In turbis vi d. In lavendria ii d. In galant*yn* ob. In expensis i garcionis versus Kyneburle ii d. Item liiii allec rubium de stauro. Item xviii allec album de calant. Item i muruca et i mellvellus de stauro. In putura pauperum ut supra. In prebenda iii equorum domine i bus. avene et furfuris.

Summa Empcionis iiii s. vi d. ob.
Stauri[34]

Extranei vi Frumentum Die jovis in pane furnito i qr. frumenti de manerio de Howe precium vi s. unde xiiii^{xx}ii panes. In multura eiusdem vii d. In playcz ii d. In ostreis iiii d. Item xl allec rubium de stauro. Item xx allec album. Item i melvellus de stauro. In putura pauperum ut supra. In prebenda iiii equorum domine iiii mensure furfuris.

Summa Empcionis xiii d.
Stauri vi s.

Extraneus i Die veneris in playcz vi d. In burbocz et roch*es* i d. In rys ii d. In turbis iii d. In lacte pro pueris i d. In vii bus. avene pro prebenda emptis xxiii d. In <haben> \ i freno / pro gresel Fysymon v d. In pane pro equis ii d. ob. Item xxiiii allec rubium de stauro. Item xvi allec album de stauro. In putura pauperum ut supra. In prebenda v equorum domine i bus. ii mensure avene et furfuris.

Summa Empcionis iii s. v d. ob.
Stauri nichil.

Extranei iii Die sabbati in oblacione i d. In i salmone empto ii s. ii d. In welk*is* iiii d. Item in feno empto iiii d. ob. Item xxx allec rubium de stauro. Item xvi allec album de stauro. Item i mellvellus de stauro. In putura pauperum ut supra. Item in prebenda iii equorum domine i bus. avene et furfuris.

Summa Empcionis ii s. xi d. ob.
Stauri nichil.

Extranei xiii Die dominica videlicet prima dominica xl^{e} in oblacione iii d. Item in playc*z* vii d. Item in roch*es* i d. In kocleis i d. ob. In oleo iiii d. Item

34 Followed by a blank space.

in fructu iii d. In elemosina iii d. In pane pro coquina i d. Item lx allec rubium de stauro. Item xxiiii allec de calant. Item i mellvelus de stauro. Item in putura pauperum ut supra. In prebenda iii equorum domine i bus. avene et furfuris.

Summa Empcionis xxiii d. ob.
Stauri nichil.

Extranei vii Die lune in skreyth' empto iii d. In pisce marino viii d. In lacte pro pueris i d. In turbis iii d. Item xxvi allec rubium de stauro. Item xxii allec album de stauro. Item i muruca et i mellvellus de stauro. Item in putura pauperum ut supra. In prebenda v equorum domine i bus. ii mensure avene et furfuris.

Summa Empcionis xv d.
Stauri nichil.

Extranei v Die martis in playcz emptis vi d. Item in krevycz iii d. \ In datis ii d. / Item in turbis iii d. Item xxx allec rubium de stauro. Item xx allec album. Item i mellvellus de stauro. In putura[35] pauperum ut supra. In prebenda v equorum domine i bus. ii mensure avene et furfuris.

Summa Empcionis xiiii d.
Stauri nichil.

Extranei iii Frumentum . . . . . Die mercurii in festo Sancti Gregorii pape in oblacione i d. Eodem die in pane furnito i qr. frumenti de manerio de Howe precium vi s. unde xiiii^{xx}iiii panes. In multura eiusdem et pistura vii d. Item in pane furnito pro pauperibus iiii bus. mixture de manerio de Blacworth' precium xx d. In pistura eiusdem ii d. unde viii^{xx}x panes. In playcz v d. Item in roch*es* et smeltis iii d. In ruffis et burboz i d. In krevycz i d. In stocpisce iii d. In ferrura ii equorum domini Rogeri et pullani domine xv d. Item solutum Roberto le Ferour pro antiqua ferrura equorum domini Rogeri x d. Item in synapio iiii d. Item xxx allec rubium de stauro. Item xviii de calant. Item i mellvellus de stauro. In putura pauperum ut supra de pane et allece rubio. In prebenda iii equorum domine et domini Rogeri i bus. et . . .[36] mensur*e* avene et furfuris.

Summa Empcionis iiii s. iiii d.
Stauri vii s. viii d.

Summa Empcionis istius rotuli Cvi s. i d.
Stauri istius rotuli Cxv s. xi d.

Summa tocius xi li. ii s.[37]

[35] MS repeats 'putura'.

[36] Possibly 'ii'.

[37] Some further figures, now illegible, follow in the left margin.

Membrane 5 recto

Quintus rotulus de anno x^{mo}

Extranei vi Die jovis in crastino Sancti Gregorii pape apud Norwyc' in vino empto iii d. In cervisia iiii d. ob. In ostreis i d. ob. Item in pikerell et roch*es* viii d. In anguillis vi d. In playcz iiii d. Item lxvi allec rubium de stauro et xxiiii allec album de stauro. Item i mellvellus de stauro. In putura xiii pauperum panis de stauro et allec rubium. In prebenda iii equorum domini Rogeri de N' i bus. avene et furfuris de preempto.

Summa Empcionis ii s. iii d.
Stauri nichil.

Extranei iii Die veneris in cervisia empta v d. ob. In playcz vi d. Item in oleo pro coquina i d. Item xviii allec rubium de stauro et xvi allec album de stauro. In putura pauperum ut die precedenti. In prebenda iii equorum domini Rogeri i bus. avene et furfuris.

Summa Empcionis xii d. ob.
Stauri nichil.

Extranei iii ***Braseum*** Die sabbati in oblacione i d. Eodem die in cervisia braciata ii qr. brasei de manerio de Blacworth' precium xii s. unde medietas de veteri et memorandum quod nichil rem*anet* amplius de veteri braseo unde $vii^{xx}x$ lag. cervisie. In focali pro dicta cervisia brac*ianda* preter focale de stauro ii d. In filo pro sacc*is* i d. In ostreis i d. ob. In vino i d. ob. In pikerell vii d. In smeltis i d. In i salmone empto xix d. In menusa ii d. In pane pro coquina i d. In turbis pro coquina vi d. Item xxx allec rubium de stauro et xxvi allec album de stauro. Item i muruca de stauro. In putura pauperum ut die precedenti. In prebenda iii equorum domini Rogeri i bus. avene et furfuris.

Summa Empcionis iii s. vii d.
Stauri xii s.

Extranei xvi Memorandum quod ii cadi allecis incipiuntur hic Die dominica in oblacione iiii d. In playcz emptis iii d. In anguillis iii d. In vino aceto ii d. In oleo pro gresel Fysimon ii d. In lacte pro pueris ii d. In i serrura pro hostio coquine i d. ob. Item in expensis Derby versus Metingham i d. Item lx allec rubium de stauro et xxvi allec album de stauro. Item i mellvellus de stauro. In putura pauperum ut supra. In prebenda iii equorum domini Rogeri i bus. avene et furfuris.

Summa Empcionis xviii d. ob.
Stauri nichil.

Extranei v Die lune sequenti in muruca empta ii d. Item in stocpisce ii d. In cocleis i d. In oleo pro coquina iiii d. In wilk*is* iiii d. In playcz iiii d. In buttis ii d. In smeltis ob. In roch*es* i d. \ In festuca pro aula viii d. / In sanguine domine et domini Rogeri minuendo iiii d. Item xxx allec rubium de stauro. Et xxiiii allec album de stauro. Item i muruca et ii mellvelli de stauro. In putura pauperum ut supra de allece rubio et pane de stauro. In prebenda iii equorum domini Rogeri i bus. avene et furfuris.

Summa Empcionis ii s. viii d. ob.
Stauri nichil.

Extranei iii Frumentum Die martis in pane furnito i qr. frumenti de manerio de Howe precium v s. x d. unde xiiii^{xx}iiii[38] panes. In multura eiusdem et pistura vii d. In ostreis vii d. In playcz iiii d. In i pikerell i d. In turbis iii d. In candela iii d. In cepo ii d. In expensis i garcionis versus Sculthorp' i d. In i qr. avene pro prebenda ii s. ii d. Item xl allec rubium et xxii allec album de stauro. Item i muruca et i mellvellus de stauro. In putura pauperum panis et allec rubium de stauro. In prebenda iii equorum domini Rogeri i bus. avene et furfuris.

Summa Empcionis iiii s. vi d.
Stauri v s. x d.

Extranei v Die mercurii \ in vino v d. qua. / In muruca empta ii d. In pikerell iiii d. In playcz et solis iii d. In rasours iiii d. In lacte pro pueris i d. Item xxxvii allec rubium de stauro et xx allec album de stauro. Item xxxviii anguille salse de stauro hic primo apud Norwyc'. In putura pauperum ut die precedenti. In prebenda iii equorum domini R. i bus. avene et furfuris.

Summa Empcionis xix d.
Stauri nichil.

Eque Memorandum quod i barellus allecis albi incipitur hic Die jovis in i lag. i pynt. vini emptis ix d. In ostreis i d. ob. In roch*es* i d. ob. In cocles ob. In playcz i d. ob. In solis ii d. Item[39] xxxvi allec rubium de stauro. Item i barellus allecis albi de calant incipitur hic de stauro ex dono domini Rogeri de Norwyc' precium viii s. unde expend*untur* vii. Item i mellvellus de stauro. In putura pauperum panis et allec rubium de stauro. In prebenda iii equorum domini Rogeri i bus. avene et furfuris.

Summa Empcionis xvi d.
Stauri viii s.

Extranei iiii Die veneris in playcz emptis iiii d. ob. In solis iiii d. \ In flore ii d. / In CCC de turbis iii d. Item xviii allec rubium. Item vii allec album de stauro. Item i mellvellus de stauro. In putura pauperum ut die precedenti. In prebenda iii equorum domini Rogeri i bus. avene et furfuris.

Summa Empcionis xiii d. ob.
Stauri nichil.

Deficiens i Die sabbati in oblacione i d. In playcz vi d. In roch*es* i d. Item xxx allec rubium de stauro et xii allec album. In putura pauperum ut

[38] MS omits 'xx'.
[39] MS repeats 'item'.

supra de allece rubio. In prebenda iii equorum domini R. i bus. avene et furfuris.

Summa Empcionis viii d.
Stauri nichil.

Extranei xii Mixtura Die dominica sequenti \ in oblacione iii d. / In pane furnito pro pauperibus iiii bus. mixture de manerio de Blacworth' precium xx d. unde ix^{xx}x panes. In pistura eiusdem ii d. In anguillis v d. In playcz ii d. In pikerell v d. In wilk*is* et rasours vii d. In turbar*io* iii d. In lacte pro pueris i d. In pane pro coquina i d. In expensis Johannis Capellani et garcionis sui versus Sculthorp' i d. ob. Item lxvi allec rubium de stauro. Item xii allec album. Item xxii anguille salse de stauro. Item i mellvellus de stauro. In putura pauperum ut supra. In prebenda iiii equorum domine i bus. i mensura avene et furfuris.

Summa Empcionis ii s. vi d. ob.
Stauri xx d.

Extranei iiii Die lune sequenti in merling ob. Item xix allec rubium de stauro. Item i mellvellus de stauro. In putura pauperum ut die precedenti. In prebenda iiii equorum domine et domini Rogeri i bus. i mensura avene et furfuris.

Summa Empcionis ob.
Stauri nichil.

Extranei xii Frumentum Die martis sequenti in festo Annunciacionis Beate Marie in oblacione vi d. Eodem die in pane furnito i qr. frumenti de manerio de Howe precium v s. x d. unde xiiii^{xx}v panes. In multura eiusdem et pistura vii d. In anguillis emptis v d. In pikerell et roch*es* vii d. In stocpisce ii d. Item lxxii allec rubium de stauro. Item xii album allec. Item i muruca et i mellvellus de stauro. In putura xv pauperum panis et allec rubium de stauro. In prebenda iii equorum domini Rogeri i bus. avene et furfuris.

Summa Empcionis ii s. iii d.
Stauri v s. x d.

Extranei iiii Die mercurii sequenti in pikerell et roch*es* vii d. In stramine empto iiii d. qua. In turbis i d. In ii carectatis argilli pro \ plumbo / pistrini pendendo iiii d. In clavis ferri pro eodem ob. In stipendio Peming' pendentis plumbum i d. In ii circulis pro i barello panetrie i d. Item liiii allec rubium et xii album de stauro. Item i mellvellus de stauro. In putura pauperum panis et allec rubium de stauro. In prebenda iii equorum domine i bus. avene et furfuris.

Summa Empcionis xviii d. ob. qua.
Stauri nichil.

Extraneus i Die jovis in playcz et solis viii d. In turbis emptis iii d. In feno per vices x d. ob. In di. lag. vini empta v d. Item xl allec rubium de stauro et xii allec album. \ Item xxxii anguille salse de stauro. / Item i mellvellus de stauro. In putura pauperum ut supra de pane et allece rubio. In prebenda iii equorum domini Rogeri i bus. avene et furfuris.

Summa Empcionis ii s. ii d. ob.
Stauri nichil.

Extranei iii Die veneris sequenti in playcz et solis emptis vii d. ob. Item in stocpisce ii d. ob. In lacte pro pueris i d. In feno i d. ob. In iii bus. avene pro prebenda emptis xiiii d. Item xxv allec rubium de stauro. Item i muruca incipitur de stauro. In putura pauperum panis et allec rubium de stauro. Item in prebenda iiii equorum domine et domini Rogeri i bus. i mensura avene et furfuris.

Summa Empcionis ii s. ii d. ob.
Stauri nichil.

Extranei ii Die sabbati in oblacione i d. In oleo empto iii d. In flore pro coquina i d. In feno empto iiii d. ob. qua. In lavendria i d. Item in xlix allece rubio de stauro et xii allece albo de stauro. Item i mellvellus de stauro. In putura pauperum panis et allec rubium de stauro. In prebenda iii equorum domini Rogeri et i de cam*erario* domine de Ufford' i bus. avene et furfuris.

Summa Empcionis x d. ob. qua.
Stauri nichil.

Extranei xi Braseum Die dominica in media xl^{a} in oblacione iii d. Eodem die in cervisia braciata ii qr. brasei de manerio de Blacworth' precium xii s. unde vi^{xx}xi lag. cervisie. In focali pro brac*iatura* eiusdem preter staurum ii d. In playcz et solis vii d. ob. In anguillis emptis vii d. In cocles i d. ob. qua. In iiii bus. furfuris emptis vii d. In synapio ii d. In caulibus ob. In turbar*io* iii d. In stocpisce i d. Item in char de qweyns et di. lib. ad restaurandum cum seminibus[40] et iii albis corallis et in i qr. de zoukro rosetto empto . . . . . domini Rogeri de Norwyc' per manus Tyneteshale xviii d. Item i muruca et i mellvellus de stauro. Item iiii^{xx} allec rubium de stauro et xii allec album de stauro. In putura pauperum panis et allec rubium de stauro. In prebenda iii equorum domini R. i bus. avene et furfuris.

Summa Empcionis iiii s. iiii d. ob. qua.
Stauri xii s.

Extranei x Frumentum Die lune sequenti in pane furnito i qr. frumenti de manerio de Howe precium v s. x d. unde xiiii^{xx}iii panes. Item in multura eiusdem et pistura vii d. \ In vino iiii d. / In playcz ii d. In stocpisce i d. In galant*yn* ob. In cocleis i d. In lacte pro pueris i d. In candela iiii d. ob. In feno iiii d. \ In pane et stramine pro gresel Fysymon vi d. / Item xxx allec rubium de stauro et x allec album. Item xxiiii anguille de stauro. In putura

[40] MS 'siei'bus'.

pauperum ut supra. In prebenda iii equorum domini Rogeri i bus. avene et furfuris.

Summa Empcionis ii s. iiii d.
Stauri v s. x d.

Extranei x Die martis sequenti \ in sale empto i d. / In caulibus ob. In vino empto iiii d. In i pikerell vi d. In stocpisce empto i d. ob. In plaicz et solis vii d. Item in turbar*io* iii d. qua. Item lxxvi allec rubium de stauro et xviii allec album. Item xvi anguille salse de stauro. Item[41] i muruca et i mellvellus de stauro. In putura pauperum ut supra. In prebenda iii equorum domini Rogeri et gresel de Fysimon i bus. di. avene et furfuris.

Summa Empcionis xxiii d. qua.
Stauri nichil.

Extranei xii Memorandum quod ii cadi allecis rubii incipiuntur hic Die mercurii in vino empto vi d. In plaicz emptis iiii d. Item in solis i d. Item in pane pro coquina i d. <Item in lacte pro pueris i d.> Item ii cadi allecis rubii incipiuntur hic de stauro unde medietas de corpilch*un* unde expenduntur lxiiii. Item xviii allec album de stauro. Item i mellvellus de stauro. In putura pauperum ut supra. In prebenda i equi domine i mensura avene et furfuris.

Summa Empcionis xii d.
Stauri nichil.

Extranei x Die jovis in caulibus emptis ob. In stocpisce empto i d. In feno empto iii d. In lacte pro pueris i d. Item iiii^{xx}x allec rubium de stauro et xx allec album. Item i muruca et i mellvellus de stauro. In putura pauperum ut supra. In prebenda ii equorum domine i mensura ii pec. avene et furfuris.

Summa Empcionis v d. ob.
Stauri nichil.

Extranei vii Die veneris in turbis iii d. Item xxvi allec rubium de stauro et vi allec album. Item xx anguille salse de stauro. Item i mellvellus de stauro. In putura pauperum ut supra de pane et allece rubio de stauro. In prebenda ii equorum domine di. bus. i mensura furfuris et avene.

Summa Empcionis iii d.
Stauri nichil.

Extranei ..... *Frumentum* Die sabbati in oblacione ..... Eodem die in pane furnito i qr. frumenti de manerio de Howe precium v s. x d. unde xiiii^{xx}v panes ..... multur*a* ..... empt*o* viii d. In caulibus ob. In plaicz et solis v d. In anguillis vi d. Item in ..... In oleo et uncto pro equis iii d. In galantyn ii d. In ferrura gresel de ..... v d. ..... Item in x... allece rubio ..... de stauro. In putura pauperum ut supra. In prebenda ii equorum .....

Summa Empcionis iii s. vi d.
Stauri v s. x d.

[41] MS repeats 'item'.

Extranei xx Mixtura . . . . . Eodem die in pane furnito pro pauperibus iiii bus. mixture de manerio de Blacworth' precium . . . . . unde . . . . . <In anguillis vi d. In sale pro panetria i d.> In lacte pro pueris i d. Item iiii^{xx}xiiii allec rubium . . . . . Item xx. . . . . de stauro. Item i muruca et i mellvellus de stauro. In putura pauperum ut supra. In prebenda ii equorum . . . . . ii mensure . . . . .

Summa Empcionis v d.
Stauri xx d.

Extranei xv Braseum . . . . . Die lune sequenti in cervisia braciata ii. . . . . maneri*o* de Blacworth' precium tocius xii s. unde vi^{xx}xvi lag. cervisie. In focali pro dicta cervisia bracianda viii d. In krevycz . . . raso*rs* viii d. In caulibus ob. In synapio ii d. In turbis iii d. In pane pro gresel Fysymon iii d. Item lvi allec rubium . . . . . Item xvi album de stauro. Item i muruca et i mellvellus de stauro. In putura pauperum ut supra. In prebenda i equi domine i mensura avene et furfuris.

Summa Empcionis ii s. iiii d. . . .
Stauri xii s.

Membrane 5 dorse

Adhuc quintus[42] rotulus de anno decimo

Extranei xii Avena pro farina Die martis sequenti proxima post festum Sancti Ambrosii apud Norwyc'. Eodem die in farina facta pro potagio iiii bus. avene de manerio de Blacworth' precium xiiii d. In factura eiusdem iiii d. Item in vino empto iiii d. Item in playcz et solis vii d. ob. In stocpisce i d. <In oleo de oliva iii d.> In roch*es* iiii d. In pistura pastellorum de turbut i d. Item in iiii bus. avene pro prebenda xiiii d. Item in feno iii d. ob. qua. Item lxiii allec rubium de stauro et xii allec album. Item xxvi anguille salse de stauro. Item i mellvellus de stauro. Item i congrus et i turbut de exhennio Johannis B*un*sted' precium ix s. Item i salmo de exhennio Jacobi de Causton' precium iii s. In putura pauperum panis et allec rubium de stauro. In prebenda i equi domine i mensura avene et furfuris.

Summa Empcionis iii s. iii d. qua.
Stauri xiii s. ii d.

Extranei xv Die mercurii \ in elemosina ii d. In pane pro coquina i d. / In potagio empto ob. In solis et plaicz v d. In welk*is* vi d. In anguillis vi d. In stocpisce ii d. In stramine i d. ob. In feno i d. In lacte pro pueris i d. Item iiii^{xx}xvi allec rubium et xviii allec album. In putura pauperum ut supra. Item in prebenda iii equorum domine et domini R. de N' i bus. avene et furfuris.

Summa Empcionis ii s. ii d.
Stauri nichil.

Extranei xi Die jovis in vino empto vi d. Item in potagio empto ob. In

[42] MS 'quartus'.

playcz x d. Item in feno empto v d. In foragio ii d. ob. In dono garcioni domini Rogeri de Norwyc' iiii d. Item lxii allec rubium de stauro. Item xix allec album. Item xxiiii anguille salse de stauro. Item i muruca et ii mellvelli de stauro. In putura pauperum ut supra de pane et allece de stauro. In prebenda iii equorum domine et domini Rogeri i bus. di. avene et furfuris.

Summa Empcionis ii s. iiii d.
Stauri nichil.

Extranei xv Frumentum Die veneris sequenti in pane furnito i qr. frumenti de manerio de Howe precium v s. viii d. unde xiiii^{xx} panes. In multura eiusdem et pistura vii d. In plaicz ii d. In datis xii d. In turbis iii d. Item xxxvi allec rubium de stauro et viii allec album de stauro. Item i muruca de stauro. In putura pauperum ut supra. In prebenda i equi domine di. bus. avene et furfuris.

Summa Empcionis ii s.
Stauri v s. viii d.

Extranei vii Die sabbati in oblacione i d. Item in vino iiii d. Item in plaicz ii d. Item in krevycz iiii d. In synapio ii d. In stocpisce i d. ob. In lacte pro pueris i d. In oleo pro coquina iii d. Item lv allec rubium et xv allec album de stauro. Item xx anguille salse de stauro. Item i mellvellus de stauro. In putura pauperum ut supra de allece rubio et pane de stauro. In prebenda i equi domine di. bus. avene et furfuris.

Summa Empcionis xviii d. ob.
Stauri nichil.

Extranei xxv Die dominica in Ramis Palmarum in oblacione ii d. In vino viii d. In potagio ob. In solis vi d. In roch*es* iii d. In krevycz vi d. In galant*yn* i d. In pistura de turbut i d. In flore pro coquina i d. Item in ii ferris anterioribus palefridi domini R. de N' et in ii ferris posterioribus gresel de Lek' et ii remocionibus pro eodem vi d. In pane pro gresel Fysimon iii d. ob. Item iiii^{xx}x allec rubium et xxx allec album de stauro. Item i muruca et i mellvellus de stauro. In putura xiii pauperum panis et allec rubium de stauro. In prebenda gresel Fysimon di. bus. furfuris.

Summa Empcionis iii s. ii d.
Stauri nichil.

Extranei xiiii Die lune sequenti in pikerell x d. In plaicz v d. In anguillis v d. In vino aceto ii d. In datis iiii d. Item in turbis iii d. In iii circulis pro i modio et in factura unius barelli de novo iiii d. Item xlii allec rubium de stauro et xx allec album. Item i muruca et i mellvellus de stauro. Item i turbut de exhennio rectoris et C de welk*is* precium xl d. In putura pauperum ut die precedenti. In prebenda i equi domine di. bus. furfuris.

Summa Empcionis ii s. ix d.
Stauri xl d.

Extranei iii Die martis sequenti in potagio ob. In vino iiii d. In stocpisce i d. In krevicz vi d. In lacte pro pueris i d. In turbar*io* iii d. Item xix allec rubium et xxii allec album de stauro. Item xx anguille salse de stauro. Item i mellvellus de stauro. In putura pauperum ut supra. In prebenda i equi domine di. bus. furfuris.

Summa Empcionis xv d.
Stauri nichil.

Extranei iii Frumentum Die mercurii sequenti in pane furnito i qr. frumenti de manerio de Howe precium v s. viii d. unde xiiii^{xx} et i panes.[43] Item in multura eiusdem et pistura vii d. In vino empto iiii d. In stocpisce ii d. In krevicz vi d. In roch*es* v d. In solis iiii d. In lavendria i d. In pane pro gresel Fysimon i d. Item xxx allec rubium et xiiii allec album de stauro. Item i mellvellus de stauro. In putura pauperum ut supra. In prebenda ut nocte precedenti di. bus. furfuris.

Summa Empcionis ii s. vi d.
Stauri v s. viii d.

<Memorandum quod W.Cocus debit hic domine pro albo allece iiii s.>

Extranei ix Huc Die jovis in cervisia empta i d. Item in i pikerell empto x d. In plaicz vii d. In datis ii d. In festuca iii d. Item xl allec \ rubium / et xxviii allec album de stauro. Item xx anguille salse de stauro. Item i muruca et i mellvellus de stauro. In putura pauperum ut supra de allece rubio de stauro. In prebenda i equi domine di. bus. furfuris.

Summa Empcionis xxiii d.
Stauri nichil.

Extranei x Die veneris in festo Parasceves in oblacione v d. ob. Item in gastellis pro pauperibus iiii s. In putura pauperum nichil. In prebenda equorum nichil.

Summa Empcionis iiii s. v d. ob.
Stauri nichil.

Extranei xv Die sabbati in vigilia Pasche in oblacione et elemosina iii d. In vino iiii d. Item in plaicz et solis viii d. In anguillis v d. In welk*is* et rasor*s* x d. In turbar*io* viii d. In i qr. avene pro prebenda ii s. ii d. In feno vi d. In lacte pro pueris i d. Item in cepo et alea emptis i d. Item xxx\vi/ allec rubium et xx allec album de stauro. Item i mellvellus de stauro. In putura xiii pauperum panis et allec rubium de stauro. In prebenda iii equorum domine i bus. i pec. avene et furfuris.

Summa Empcionis vi s.
Stauri nichil.

Extranei xxxviii Braseum Frumentum pro coquina i bus. Die dominica in festo Pasche in oblacione xxii d. ob. Eodem die in cervisia braciata ii qr.

[43] MS 'panis'.

brasei de manerio de Blacworth' precium xii s. unde iiii bus. de brasei drageti unde vii^{xx} lag. cervisie. Item in focali pro dicta cervisia bracianda viii d. Item[44] in carne bovis xvi d. In carne porci x d. In carne vituli xviii d. In i porcello vi d. In i angnello vii d. Item in iiii auculis emptis xxiii d. et expend*untur*. Item in xxiiii pulcinis emptis xviii d. In synapio ii d. In gingibr*o* i d. In pane pro coquina i d. Item lib*eratur* pro coquina i bus. frumenti de manerio de Blacworth' precium ix d. Item i perna baconis veteris et i perna novi baconis de stauro de Metingham incipiuntur hic. Et memorandum quod novus baco incipitur hic primo hoc anno. Item ii qr. carnis bovis incipiuntur hic de stauro. Item iiii capones de manerio de Sculthorp' hoc anno primo. Item xii pulcini de exhennio Ricardi Orlham. Item xvii columbelle de exhennio Ricardi Hacon et uxoris Ricardi Orlham. Item viii^{xx}vii ova de manerio de Howe et v^{xx} ova de Blacworth'. In putura pauperum ut die precedenti. In prebenda iiii equorum domine et domini Rogeri i bus. i mensura avene et furfuris.

Summa Empcionis xi s. ob.
Stauri xv s. vii d.

Extranei xviii Frumentum Die lune sequenti in oblacione i d. Item in pane furnito eodem die i qr. frumenti de manerio de Blacworth' precium v s. vii d. unde xiii^{xx}x panes. In multura et pistura eiusdem vii d. In carne bovis empto xvi d. Item in turbis pro coquina v d. In pane pro coquina i d. \ In feno v d. / Item in CCCxlvii ovis emptis ii s. \ ix d. ob. / Item i qr. carnis bovis incipitur de stauro de Metingham. Item ii capones de Sculthorp'. Item de exhennio Palmer' iiii pulcini. Item xlvi ova de stauro preempto. In putura pauperum panis et allec rubium de stauro. In prebenda iiii equorum domine i bus. i mensura avene et furfuris.

Summa Empcionis v s. viii d. ob.
Stauri vi s. iiii d.

Extranei xvii Mixtura Die martis sequenti in pane furnito pro pauperibus iiii bus. mixture de manerio de Blacworth' precium xx d. unde ix^{xx} panes. In pistura eiusdem ii d. Item in carne porci empta ii d. ob. In potagio ob. In feno empto v d. In turbis pro coquina iii d. Item ii capones de stauro de Sculthorp'. Item viii pulcini de exhennio Palmer'. Item xxiiii columbelle de stauro manerii de Sculthorp'. Item lvi ova de preempto. In putura pauperum panis et allec rubium de stauro. In prebenda iii equorum domine i bus. avene et furfuris.

Summa Empcionis xiii d.
Stauri ii s. x d.

Extranei xi Memorandum quod ii cadi allecis rubii incipiuntur hic Die mercurii in roch*es* iiii d. In butiro empto i d. ob. qua. In lacte pro coquina

[44] MS repeats 'item'.

i d. ob. In feno empto v d. Item ii cadi allecis rubii incipiuntur hic \ unde i de corpelch*un* / unde xxxvi allec rubium expenduntur. Item xx allec album de . . . . . Item lxx ova de preempto. Item iii mellvelli de stauro. Item in putura pauperum ut die precedenti. In prebenda iii equorum domine i bus. avene et furfuris.

Summa Empcionis xii d. qua.
Stauri nichil.

Extranei xi Die jovis sequenti in potagio qua. \ In carne porci empta iiii d. / In carne vituli empta v d. Item in feno empto v d. In turbis pro coquina iiii d. Item i perna veteris baconis incipitur hic de stauro de Metingham. Item ii capones de Sculthorp'. Item xxxiii ova de preempto. In putura pauperum ut supra. In prebenda iiii equorum domine i bus. i mensura avene et furfuris.

Summa Empcionis xviii d. qua.
Stauri v d.

Extranei xiiii ***Frumentum*** Die veneris sequenti in pane furnito i qr. frumenti unde medietas de manerio de Howe et altera medietas de manerio de Blacworth' precium v s. \ viii d. / unde xiii^{xx}xii panes. In multura et pistura eiusdem vii d. In plaicz et solis emptis x d. In krevicz et crabb*is* emptis vi d. Item in roch*es* ii d. In turbar*io* iii d. <In pane pro coquina i d.> Item in di. bus. ordei empto pro pullalo iii d. Item in ii bus. avene pro pullalo inpingguendo vii d. ob. In clavis ferri pro clausura domus pullali i d. Item xlviii allec rubium de stauro et xvi album. Item i mellvellus de stauro. In putura pauperum ut supra. In prebenda iii equorum domine et domini Rogeri i bus. avene et furfuris.

Summa Empcionis iii s. iii d.
Stauri v s. viii d.

Extranei v Die sabbati in elemosina et oblacione ii d. \ In lacte pro pueris i d. / Item in grosso pisce empto vii d. Item xxxiiii allec rubium et xviii allec album de stauro. In putura pauperum ut supra de allece rubio. In prebenda iii equorum domine i bus. avene et furfuris.

Summa Empcionis x d.
Stauri nichil.

Extranei ix Die dominica sequenti in oblacione iii d. Item in potagio qua. Item in carne bovis empta xiii d. Item in carne vituli empta xi d. In carne porci v d. Item in i auca vi d. et expenditur. Item in vi columbellis iii d. qua. \ et expend*untur*. / Item in feno empto x d. Item i qr. carnis bovis incipitur et i perna veteris baconis de Metingham. Item ii capones de Sculthorp'. Item viii pulcini de preempto. Item lxxvi ova de preempto. In putura pauperum ut supra. In prebenda iii equorum domine i bus. avene et furfuris.

Summa Empcionis iiii s. iii d. ob.
Stauri v d.

Extranei vi Die lune sequenti in cervisia empta v d. ob. Item in i gallina empta i d. ob. Item in pane pro coquina i d. Item in xvi auculis emptis ii s. iii d. Item i capo de manerio de Sculthorp'. Item vi pulcini de preempto. Item v columbelle de Sculthorp'. Item liii ova de preempto. In putura pauperum panis et allec rubium de stauro. In prebenda i equi domine i mensura avene et furfuris.

Summa Empcionis ii s. xi d.
Stauri v d.

Extranei ix Braseum Die martis in cervisia braciata ii qr. brasei de manerio de Blacworth' . . . . . unde iiii bus. de bra. . . . . vii^{xx}iiii lag. cervisie. In focali pro dicta cervisia bracianda viii d. . . . . . qua. In . . . . . xiii d. In carne vituli vi d. Item . . . . . xxx ova de preempto. In putura pauperum ut . . . . .

Summa Empcionis . . . . .
Stauri . . . . . viii d.

. . . . . Die mercurii sequenti in butiro empto ii d. In lacte pro coquina i d. ob. Item . . . . . empt*o* x d. In p. . . . . empt*o* vi d. In galantyn ob. Item lxvii de all. . . . . xl all. . . . . pauperum panis de stauro et allec rubium. In prebenda iiii equorum domine . . . . .

Summa Empcionis . . . . .
Stauri nichil.

Summa Empcionis istius rotuli Cxvii s. iiii d. . . . . .
Stauri istius rotuli vii li. ii s. x. . . . .
Tocius xiii li. ii d.

Membrane 6 recto

Minute neccessarie tam de empcione quam de stauro pro hospicio domine anno x^{mo}

Boves et vacce pro lardario In occisione pro lardario pro stauro remanendo videlicet iii boves de manerio de Metingham precium xlii s.
Item ii boves de manerio de Howe precium amborum xx s.
Item i bos de manerio de Kirkeby precium viii s.
Item ii vacce de Metingham precium xvii s.

Summa lxx s.

<Item ii vacce empte pro lardario de Ranulpho Har' xvii s.>
Item in ii karkoys emptis xvi s. ix d.

Summa xvi s. ix d.

Porci pro lardario Item in occisione pro lardario x porci de manerio de Metingham <precium xl s.> precium xl s. de quibus ix remanent in lardario apud Metingham et i remanet in lardario apud Norwyc' pro stauro remanendo.

Summa xl s.

Auce In v^{xx}xiii aucis emptis pro stauro remanendo pro anno futuro xix s. x d.

Summa xix s. x d.

De quibus expend*untur* hoc anno xvi. Et remanent pro anno futuro videlicet die Sancti Michaelis iiii^{xx}xvii auce ut patet in capite primi rotuli anni proximi sequentis.

Allec rubium In i lasto de allece rubio empto de Waltero de Fenne unde medietas de corpelch*un* lxiiii s. x d.

In expensis circa cariagium eiusdem de Jernemut' usque Metingham ix d.

Summa lxv s. vii d.

*Specer*ia In ii pixidibus de gingebradz et pynonad' de Rad*ulph*o de Salle iii s. ii d.

Item in C lib. cere de Lubyk' emptis de eodem xlviii s. In C de amigdalis xvi s. Et in iiii lib. de gingibr*o* x s. iiii d. Et in iiii lib. de ganinghal' x s. Et in i lib. de canele xiii d. Et in di. lib. de clowys iii s. ii d. Et in di. lib. de mazes xx d. Et in ii lib. de saffran xi s. viii d. Et in iiii lib. de pipere iii s. vii d. Et in uno pane de zoukro Caphatyn ponderanti viii lib. iii qr. viii s. Et in iii lib. de zoukro de Cypre xviii d. Et in ii lib. de coton xxii d. Et in ii pixidibus quorum i vocatur festucad' et altera de alb*o* gingibrad' iiii s. vi d.

Item in lx lib. de rys emptis de Galfrido Salle vii s. Et in i copula de ficis et racemis empta de Johanne de Beggheton' ponderanti ix^{xx} lib. viii s. ob. sic in universo

Summa vi li. xix s. vi d. ob.

...dela de parys In C lib. de candela de parys emptis de Hamone Mustarder vii s. vi d.

Vinum Item de exhennio domini Johannis de Norwyc' i dolium vini precium xl s. Item de dono Willelmi de la Pole i dolium vini precium lx s. C s.

Herbagium In herbagio empto apud Castr' pro equis in estate x s. viii d.

Summa Cxviii s. ii d.

Summa tocius istius rotuli xxiii li. ix s. x d. ob.

11 *Accounts of the household of John de Multon of Frampton, Lincolnshire, September 1343 to March 1344 and September 1347 to March 1348*

The Multons of Frampton were a cadet branch of the Multon and Lucy families that held the barony of Egremont.[1] Most of their property was concentrated in three areas in Lincolnshire, in and around Frampton and Boston; on the coast close to Saltfleetby and Somercotes; and in Heapham, Sturton by Stow, Stow and Ingleby, between Gainsborough and Lincoln;

[1] W. O. Massingberd, 'Notes on the pedigree of Multon of Frampton, co. Lincoln', *The Ancestor* 2 (1902) pp. 205–7.

with some property at Hoby in Leicestershire. In 1343–4, John de Multon's agent, Nicholas de Twycrosse, received about £40 from rents, possibly only for a half year, and from other sources. In the same period household expenses on food came to about £24, and on 'necessary and foreign' expenses, to about £36.

Two household accounts have survived for this family. The earlier account (**11a**), for 1343–4, is a Chancery fashion roll of three membranes, sewn with white thread in a tight oversew, with one, much narrower membrane, attached to the foot of the roll by a parchment tie. The front of the roll contains a diet account; the dorse, the account of a receiver and wardrobe type expenses. The membrane attached to the foot of the roll contains a list of hen rents and continues the diet account from the front of the roll. Nine clerks worked on the roll at different stages in its compilation. Hands 1, 3 and 5 wrote most of the text, both front and dorse, probably engrossing blocks of diet expenses, receipts and wardrobe expenses at the same time. Hand 2 supplied the totals and hand 4, that of an auditor, marked them *probatur*. Hand 6 wrote the list of hen rents, and hands 7, 8 and 9 wrote very small sections, occasional receipts or totals. The account was written up piecemeal on a number of occasions, from mid-October 1343, when a certain amount of material (diet expenses, receipts and wardrobe expenses) was in hand — the sequence of hands in both expense sections is the same — and the account was subsequently totalled and audited about Easter 1344.

The second roll (**11b**), a diet account covering the period 30 September 1347 to 5 March 1348, consists of two membranes, sewn together Chancery fashion with white thread, using a tight oversew. Each membrane was written by a single hand throughout in one operation, including all totals.

The two accounts are unusual in surviving in association with deeds and estate papers for the family, and it is possible to trace the work of the clerks in other records in the archive. Hand 1 of the 1343–4 account wrote the second membrane of the 1347–8 account; this clerk also wrote a number of charters for the Multons of Frampton between 1344 and 1348,[2] as well as a collector's account as early as 1331.[3] The clerk who wrote the second block of text of the 1343–4 diet account (hand 3) was also responsible for a rental of the same date.[4] These clerks were either directly connected with the household or were available for hire to write the documents. The variation in the form of the household account over four years is particularly marked in comparison with, for example, the regularity of the Clare household

[2] MCO Deeds: Saltfleetby 10a, 13a, 25a, 30a; Multon Hall 15, 35.

[3] MCO Additional Charter 9.

[4] MCO Additional Charter 7.

forms. It perhaps suggests that there was no permanent bureaucracy within the household of John de Multon; it would be more difficult to establish patterns and forms of account if the clerks were hired from outside to write the documents.

11a Magdalen College, Oxford, Deeds: Multon Hall 160

Membrane 1 recto
[3]Expense domus domini Johannis de Multon' a festo Sancti Michaelis anno regni regis Edwardi tercii octavo desimo incipiente usque ad annum revolutum[3]
[1]En p*ri*mes le lundy en la fest Seint Michel en vin pur le seignur a Engleby ix d. En un quart*er* de char de boef xviii d. En un carcois de motoun xx d. En offrand pur le seignur ii d. En ii liv. de chaundail ii d. ob. Le vendredy en pesso*u*n achate a Fraunkton' xiii d. En pulcins chaundail chars et pesso*u*n achatez pur la dame a Frampton' mesme la simaingne xxi d. Le samady achatez pur le seignur a Fraunkton' en sturjo*u*n xiiii d. En pleices viii d. En anguilles viii d. En oistres iiii d. En wilkes iiii d. En vin xii d. En pikerels xii d. En blaunk pesso*u*n vi d.[1]
[2]*Summa istius septimane xii s. ix d. ob.*[2]
[1]Item le dimeinge p*ro*chein ap*re*s la fest Seint Michel en char de boef xxiii d. En char de moto*u*n xii d. En blaunk seym pur fruturs i d. En oefs i d. Le meskredy en oistres ii d. En harang iii d. En pleices vi d. En alowes i d. Le joefdy en moto*u*n achate ix d. En iiii liv. de chaundail v d. Le vendredy en harang vii d. En harang fresch i d. En melvel vii d.[1]
[2]*Summa istius septimane vi s. vi d.*[2]
[1]Le dimeinge p*ro*chein ap*re*s la fest Seint Dionis en char de boef ii s. vii d. En char de moto*u*n xvi d. En ii liv. de chaundail ii d. ob. Le meskredy en char de moto*u*n iiii d. En dur pesso*u*n viii d. En oefs i d. En pleices iiii d. En codeling ii d. En harang iiii d. Le samady en la fest Seint Luke a Engleby en pain xiii d. En cervoise xiiii d. En vin ii s. En dur pesso*u*n x d. En harang vi d. En alemands et zucre v d. ob. En pikerels xvi d. En roches et p*er*ches v d. En anguilles viii d. En laump*er*uns vi d. En oistres et wilkes vi d. En sausse i d. ob. En la portage de ditz vitailles ii d. En pain pur un chival portant les ditz vitailles de Nichole a Engleby i d. En iiii liv. de chaundail v d. ob.[1]
[2]*Summa istius xvi s. iiii d.*[2]
[1]Le dimeinge ap*re*s la fest Seint Luke a Engleby en pain iiii d. En chars xiiii d. A Frampton' en char de boef ii s. iiii d. En char de moto*u*n xvi d. En i liv. de chaundail i d. qua. En oefs ii d. Le meskedy en harang ii d. En codeling et altre pesso*u*n iii d. En pleices ii d. Le joefdy en char de moto*u*n iiii d. En ii liv. de chaundail ii d. ob. Le vendredy en harang vi d. En

pesso*u*n salee ix d. En sturjo*u*n ix d. En samo*u*n iii d. En oistres iii d. En pleices iii d. En wilkes iii d. Le samady en pesso*u*n salee ii d. En oistres ii d. En pleices et codeling vi d. En harang stor et fresch v d.[1] [3]En harang frez le jeuedi et le vendurdi ix d. En vin vi d. En dur*e* pessoun viii d. pur stor.[3]

[2]*Summa istius xii s. viii d. ob. qua.*

Summa xlviii s. iiii d. qua.[2]

[4]*Probatur*[4]

[3]Le dimeinge dewant le fest*e* de les aposteles Seynt Simon et Judee en char de boef iiii s. En chars de moto*u*n xvi d. En vin iii d. Le lundy apres en la veile de les aposteles en harang frez iii d. En codeling iii d. En pesso*u*n sale et en dure pesso*u*n vi d. En oef*s* ii d. En vC de rouge harang pur stor xl d. En iiii liv. de chaundel iii d. ob. qua. Le mekerdi apres en pesso*u*n sale iiii d. En chars de moto*u*n iiii d. En harang frez i d. En vin vi d. En ii liv. de sucre xvi d. Le vendurdi ap*re*s en la veil*e* de Touz Seynz \ en harang iii d. En plais iii d. En dur*e* pesso*u*n vii d. / En saferoun ix d. En vin iii d. Et le jour mesmes en vin iii d. En codeling iii d. En plays v d. En harang blang iii d. En angu*i*ll*es* iii d. En oistr*es* ii d. En oef*s* iii d. En bure i d.[3]

[2]*Summa xvi s. xi d. ob. qua.*[2]

[3]Le dimeingne prochein ap*re*s[1] en volatil achate iii d. En iiii liv. de chaundel v d. En char de beof iiii s. En chars de moto*u*n viii d. Le lundy ap*re*s en payn vi d. Le mekerdy pur char de beof iii s. En volatil v \ d. / Pur vin iii d. En char de moto*u*n iiii d. En pesso*u*n frez vii d. En ferur*e* al chaivalx Nichol de Twicros ii d. Le jeuedi en volatil ii d. En iiii liv. de chaundel v d. Le vendurdi en pesso*u*n sale viii d. En dure pesso*u*n ii d. En plais ii d. En codeling ii d. Le samadi en i pik v d. En codeling ii d.[3]

[2]*Summa xii s. xi d.*[2]

[3]Le dimeigne dewaunt le fest*e* de Seynt Martin en chars de moto*u*n iiii d. En volatil ii d. En oef*s* i d. Le lundy ap*re*s en pain achate pur defaut de vent vi d. En volatil i d. En iiii liv. de chaundel v d. Le jour de Seint Martin en pain achate pur defaut de vent xii d. <En iii quar*ters* de breoz achate a Nichol pur xii s. iiii d.> Le mekerdi ap*re*s en plais ii d. Le vendurdi en dur*e* pesso*u*n et blanc pesso*u*n xiii d. En harang blang ii d. En ii pikerell*es* vii d. En anguill*es* v d. En oister*es* ii d. <En codeling> En i liv. de almaunds ii d. En i liv. de gynger xiii d.[3]

[2]*Summa vi s. v d.*

Summa xxxvi s. iii d. ob. qua.[2]

[4]*Probatur*[4]

[3]Le dimeigne ap*re*s la feste Seynt Martyn en oisel achate iii d. Le mardi ap*re*s en oisel iiii d. Le mekerdi ap*re*s en codeling et en plais iiii d. En chaundel v d. En vin iiii d. ob. Le jeuedi en chaundel v d. En vin iii d. et

[1] MS 'ap*re*s prochein ap*re*s'.

pur oisel iii d. En pesoun frez viii d. En xl liv. de almaunds vi s. viii d. En ceir achate v s. i d. pur xiii liv. En vi liv. de ging*er* vi s. vi d. En volatil iii d. En oef*s* iii d. Et paie pur deversez colour*es* al koeu iiii s. En x liv. de rys viii d. En di. i liv. de safferoun xviii d. Le vendurdi ap*res* en plais et en codeling vii d. En pesso*un* sale viii d. En dur*e* pesso*un* iiii d. En vin iii d. Le samadi ap*res* iii codeling e en plais vii d. En ii liv. de chaundel ii d. ob. En oef*s* iii d. Pur peirs a ma dame iiii d. et paie pur ii lepes pur demetter*e* \ pesso*un* / en le ewe entour le man*er* iiii d.[3]
[2]*Summa xxxi s. ix d.*[2]
[3]Le dimeigne en le jour de Seint Clement en offerand i d. En volatil iii d. Le mekerdi ap*res* pur iiii liv. de chaundel v d. Le vendurdi <en pesso*un*> en codeling \ et / haddoc vii d. En plais ii d. En sprot ii d. En pesso*un* frez viii d. En pesso*un* sale xxi d. En vin pur les desspenc*es* mo*un* seignur a le mesoun Joh*an* Reignald pur divers p*ar*cels en la simeigne xvi d. Pur lez chivax mo*un* seignur a meme le meso*un* iiii d. Pur vin vi d. E paie pur iC de dur*e* pesso*un* q*e* est appele winturfizs xiii s. iiii d. En muskeles i d. Le samadi en plais et codeling iiii d.[3]
[2]*Summa xx s.*[2]
[3]Le dimeigne en la fest*e* de Seint Andreu en volatil ii d. Le lundi en plais et en codeling iiii d. En oef*s* iii d. En iiii liv. de chaundel v d. Le merkerdi en plais ii d. En codeling ii d. En un rai ii d. Le vendurdi ap*res* en pesso*un* frez xiii d. et paie pur vii oves xxi d. En vin vi d. et pur iiii liv. de chaundel v d.[3]
[2]*Summa v s. vi d.*[2]
[3]Le dimeinge ap*res* la feste de Seint Nicholas paie pur volatil iii d. Le lundi ap*res* en vin vi d. Et paie pur un diner a lez gens la dame le Ros viii \ d. / p*ar* comaundeme*n*t le seignur et pur lour chivalx en pain et en foin iiii d. Le mardi en vin xii d. En iiii liv. de chaundel v d. Le vendurdi en pesso*un* frez xii d.[3]
[2]*Summa iiii s. ii d.*
Summa lvi s. v d.[2]
Membrane 2 recto
[4]*Probatur*[4]
[3]Le dimeinge \ ap*res* le jour de Nostre Dame en offer*and* iiii d. / Paie pur volatil ii d. et pur oef*s* ii d. Le mardi ap*res* pur pesso*un* a ma dame ii d. Le mekerdi pur pesso*un* frez iiii d. Pur un di. liv. de canel viii d. Et pur les chivalx mo*un* seignur et pur lez chivalxs q*e* fur*e*nt oveq*e* li vi d. Pur un botel de venegr*e* iii d.[3]
[2]*Summa istius ii s. vii d.*[2]
[3]Le dimeingne en la feste Seint Thomas le apostel en offer*and* i d. Le lundi ap*res* en volatil achate en countr*e* le Nowel ii s. Le mardi ap*res* paie pur volatil viii d. Et paie pur ii purcelles en countr*e* le jour de Nowel x d. Et

v purcelles <en> echate en countr*e* le ma\u/nger*i* le seignur ii s. i d. Et pur lendemeing ap*res* le maungeri iii purcell*es* achate pur xiii d. Et iii velles echate en countr*e* le Nowell et en countr*e* le maungeri vii s. viii d. Et en fil achate pur torches et tortis et autr*e* chaundel ii d. Et pur vessel achate pur le maungeri ii s. Et paie pur vi plov*ers* la veille de Nowel xii d. Et mesme ceo jour en oister*es* plais codeling ii s. vi d. Et paie pur stintes vi d. Et paie pur un peir*e* de tenailes pur le sale vi d. En i quar*ter* de bof ii s. En i quar*ter* de pork ix d.[3]
[2]*Summa istius xxiii s. x d.*[2]
[3]Le jour de Nowel en offerend la dame et le meine ii s. vii d. Le vendurdi ap*res* paie pur pess*ou*n frez xiiii d. En vin a Seint Botulf' pur le seignur vi d. Et xi aves achate xiiii \ d. / en countr*e* le maungeri. Le samadi ap*res* en codeling plais et anguilles xiiii d. En ii boltingclothes iiii d. En i liv. de sucre de plate xvi d. Et paie pur ii butour*es* et i heroun viii s. x d. Et paie pur plovers le jour del maungeri et le jour ap*res* viii s. vi d. Et mesme ceo jour paie pur cessell*es* iiii s. x d. Et pur ix poucines ix d. Et pur i couple de maulars vi d. Et pur stintes vi d. Et paie pur oefs pur le maungeri x d.[3]
[2]*Summa istius xxxiii s. <vi d.>*[2]
[3]Le dimeingne ap*res* le Nowel en offerend i \ d. / Et paie pur pess*ou*n le vendurdi et le samadi ap*res* xvi d. Et paie pur i teist et di. un senguler vii s.[3]
[2]*Summa viii s. v d.*[2]
[3]Le dimeingne dewaunt Lepufphaine paie pur vi plov*ers* xv d. et \ pur / vi cesselles viii d. Le jour del Epiphaine en offerend ii d. Le vendurdi ap*res* en bur*e* ii d. En offerand p*ar* devers p*ar*celez iiii d. En i ma\u/lard i d. ob. Et paie pur ging*er* sauz et pur moustart et galentin al feste Seint Mich*e*ls deqe a le Epyphaine iii s.[3]
[2]*Summa istius v s. viii d. ob.*
Summa iii li. xiii s. vi d. ob.[2]
[4]*Probatur*[4]
Membrane 3 recto
[3]Le mekerdi devaunt la feste Seint Hillar*i* en oister*es* ii d. Le vendurdi ap*res* en codeling iii d. En oister*es* ii d. Le samadi en oister*es* ii d.
Le mekerdi ap*res* la feste Seint Hillar*i* en oister*es* ii d. Le vendurdi ap*res* en oister*es* ii d.[2] Le samadi ap*res* en oister*es* ii d. Item le lundi et le mardi devaunt en oistr*es* iii d. Et en plais codeling et muskeles ii d. ob. En offerend pur ma dame a Framton' le jour de lez joustes de Windesouer iii d.[3]
[2]*Summa xxiii d. ob.*[2]
[3]Le dimeingne en la feste le conv*er*sioun de Seint Poule en oister*es* iii d.

[2] 'ii' not clear on MS.

En bur*e* pur la dame ii d. Le lundi et le mardi en oisteres vi d. Le mekerdi en bur*e* i d. Le vendurdi apres en pessoun frez x d.[3]
[2]*Summa xxii d.*[2]
[3]Le dimeingne ap*re*s en char frez achate pur le \S/chaundelour iii s. vi d. En volatil x d. Le lundi apres en oisteres iii d. En batilag*e* pur vi quar*ters* de brez a Kirkebi deke a Frampton' ix d. Le mekerdi apres en oister*es* iii d. Le vendurdi apres en pessoun frez vi d.[3]
[2]*Summa istius vi s. i d.*[2]
[3]Le dimeigne ap*re*s en oef*s* v d. Le lundi en gelines ii s. En oister*es* vi d. Le vendurdi ap*re*s en pessoun vi d. En oister*es*. En gelines xxiii d.[3]
[2]*Summa istius v s. iiii d.*
Summa xviii s. vi d. ob.[2]
[4]*Probatur*[4]
[3]Le dimeingne ap*re*s la feste de Seinte Valantil iii s. ii d.[3] [5]en vele pork et boef. En offerend ii d.
Le jouedy ap*re*s en pesson iiii d. Mesme cest*i* jour en batilligage mon seyngnur dev*er*s Ingelby xx d. Item en s*er*veys*e* vi d. En fyges et rayzines iii d. Mesmes cest*i* neut pur les chyvaux mon seyngnur en p*ro*vandr*e* viii d. Et mesmes le jouedy a Seynt Botul*p*' pur les garsons et les chyvaux iii d. ob. Et mesmes le neut en custage mon s*eyngnur* en payn vyn et pessoun ix d. ob. et pur un diner a Joh*a*n de Lodlow al Seynt Botul*p*' iiii d.
Le meskerdy de Cendrez p*ar* enchesou*n* de hostes en pesso*un* iii s.
Dymeynge en la fest de Seynt Pyer in chathedra en offerand i d.[5]
[2]*Summa vii s. iii d.*[2] 3
[5]In iiii^{or} bobus emptis ad lardarium contra festum Sancti Martini xlvi s. Item in xl bidentibus lxxiii s. iiii d. precium cuiuslibet xxii d. Item in xii porcis xxix s. precium cuiuslibet ii s. v d. Item iiii^{xx} \ xiiii / lib. candele paris emptis ix s. ix d. ob. precium lib. i d. qua. Preterea mactantur ad lardarium de stauro i bos et xii porci. Item in iiiiM allece xxviii s. Item in pisc*ibus* sals*is* xxiiii s. Item Johanni lez Spic*er* in clavis ii s. In maces ii s. In flore de canel ii s. In quirbippes ii s. In i lib. de suker de platz contra Natalem xvi d. In ii lib. feniculi vi d. In ii bal*is* fructus ix s. vi d. In oleo oliv*ero* iiii d. Item in i lag. olei xviii d.[5]
[2]*Summa xi li. xi. s. iii d. ob.*[2]
[4]*Probatur*[4]
[3]<Item paie pur schandel de paris ix s. ix d. ceo est asavoir pur iiii^{xx} liv. xiii liv. et di. precium de lib. i d. qua.>[3]
[4]*Quia superius.*[4]
[2]*Summa totalis xxiiii li. ix s. v d. ob.*[2]

3 MS unclear; the total does not equate with the amounts in the text.

[3]Summa totalis expensarum domus cum quadam billa enexa istius rotuli xxiiii li. xiiii s. v d. ob.[3]

Recto of parchment schedule tied to the foot of Multon Hall 160

[1]Rec*epta* de collectore[1]

[3]Exspence \ die jovis / per Stephanum Cocum in i parvo arco empto pro lardario ix d. Die veneris in oister*es* i d. ob. \ In plais iii d. In codeling v d. In sepo i d. /

Die sabbati in oister*es* i d. ob. Die dominica in i cithara empta pro domina vi d. Die lune in oister*es* i d. ob. Die martis in oister*es* i d. ob.

Die mercurie in festo Sancti Mattehee in codeling et plais viii d. In laumprouns iiii d. In velkes iii d. Die veneris in oisteres iii d. In plais iii d. Die sabbati in plais et codeling vi d.

Die dominica postea in oisteres iii d. Die lune in plais et codeling vi d. En wilkes ii d. Die martis in plais iiii d. In oisteres iii d. Die jovis in oisteres ii d. Die veneris in plays et haddog iiii d. Summa vi s. ix d.

Die dominica ante festum Sancti G\r/eorgii in oisteres ii d. In plais ii d. Die lune in plays iii d. Die veneris in festo Sancti Gregorii in plais iii d. Item lib*eravit* Roberto del P*a*rk' pro eunte in negoci*is* domini iiii d.

Die dominica proxima post festum Sancti Gregorii in rai vi d. In turbot viii d. In codeling v d. In sturjoun vii d. Item dat*um* carpent*ario* Rogeri Hert ii d. Die lune in plais i d. Item in i panier \ empt*o* / i d. Die lune in codeling empt*o* pro stauro xxi d. In porpeys vi d. In salmone iii d. Die veneris in plais codeling v d. In salmone iiii d. In welkes iii d. In oister*es* i d. In i pik vi d. Summa vii s. ix d.

Die dominica in Passione in oister*es* iii d. In plais et codeling iiii d.

Die sabbati ante Passionem in exspensis Thome de Multon' et Nich*ola*i de Twicrosse apud Linc' xiiii d. Item lib*eravit* fratribus domini vi d. Die lune postea in plais et codeling vii d. Item Johanni le Spiser ii s. in porsed. Item in expensis Walteri Bavent apud Sanctum Botulf' ii d.[3]

Dorse of the schedule

[6]Walter filius Willelmi portavit i gallum et i gallinam.
Robertus le Garden*er* portavit ii gallos et ii gallinas.
Willelmus del Grene i gallum et i gallinam.
Johannes del Grene ii gallos[4] et ii gallinas.
Robertus de Coquina i gallum et ii gallinas.
Agnes le Mulner i gallum et i gallinam. Non portavit.
Riche del Park' ii gallos et ii gallinas.
Alicia Eliot ii gallinas.
Eliot Cullul ii gallinas.
Reginald Loveles ii gallos et ii gallinas.

[4] MS 'gallu*m*'.

Ricardus Loveles ii gallos et ii gallinas. Non adhuc.
Margeria Bischop i gallinam.
Johannes ad Pontem i gallum et i gallinam.
Walterus frater eius i gallum et i gallinam. <Non pa*cavit.*>
Robertus Henr' Nicholas frater eius et Jo*hanne*s frater eorum i gallum et i gallinam.
Heredes Thome Rondulf' i gallum et i gallinam.
Thomas Henr' et Nicholas frater eius i gallum et i gallinam.
Agtha uxor Johannis Prepositi Basilia Bischop i gallum et i gallinam.
Heredes Alani Cullul i gallum et i gallinam.
Robertus Rondulf i gallum et i gallinam.
Johannes filius Roberti Garden*er* ii gallinas.
Robertus le Cok' et Thomas le Koc et Alicia filia Alani le Cok' iiii gallos et iiii gallinas.
Memorandum quod Robertus filius Alani de Culbuldik' deberet portare iiii^{or} gallos et iiii^{or} gallinas et nativi dicunt quod dominus Thomas de Multon' qui mortuus est mutavit predictos gallos et gallinas in argento scilicet x d.
Rogerus Thormound i gallum.
Alanus Thurmound unam gallinam.
Hugo filius Thome unum gallum et unam gallinam.
Nicholas filius Roberti Henr' unum gallum et unam gallinam.
Reginaldus P*ar*ker unam gallinam.
Adelard Benet unam gallinam.[6]
[3]Item dat*um* camerario domini Hugonis Hasting*s* ix d. Item in oblacione apud Screvelesbi die Annunciacionis Beate Marie iii d. Item \ dat*um* / in hernes super i doleum vini xiiii d. Item die Annunciacionis Beate Marie in grapeis vi d. In oister*e*s et plais iiii d. Die veneris postea in rai iiii d. In codeling plais vi d. Die dominica postea in pisc*ibus* salsat*is* xviii d. Die lune in oisteres[5] ii d.[3]
[2]Summa x s. vi d.
Summa totalis istius rotuli xxv s.[2]
Membrane 1 dorse
[1]Compotus Nich*ola*i de Twycrosse a festo Sancti Michaelis archangeli anno regni regis Edwardi a conquestu septimodecimo finiente
<De xxxiiii s. viii d. qua. de arreragiis ultimi anni.>[6]
Resceyt De xiii s. iiii d. resceu de Amabile de Cobeldyk'. Et de viii s. resceu del coillour de la rente de Engleby. Et de xx s. resceu de la rente de Bayard

[5] MS 'in oisteres in oister*e*s ii d.'
[6] The arrears were included in the total written by hand 7; they were subsequently struck out by hand 9.

en Seint Botholf'. Et de x s. resceu de la rente Rog*er* de Biry \ per Nich*ola*um de Salmo*n*bi / de Seint Botholf'. Et de xvi s. viii d. resceu de William Asser de fynes. Et de iiii s. resceu de Nichol de Salmanby sauntz taille.[1] [3]Et de iiii li. resceu de mo*u*n seignur. Et de xl s. resceu de les coffer*e*s mo*u*n seignur le jour de Seint Andreu. Et de xl s. resceu de mo*u*n seignur. Et resceu de William Hawleie xxv s. Et iiii li. resceu del rente de Ingulbi de la rente Seinte Andreu. ii s. de mesme ceo rente. Et de lv s. resceu de Nichol de Salmonbi. Et resceu del p*ro*vot de Henningbi xxx s. Et resceu del warn*er* de Ingulbi x s. Et resceu de s*ire* Alain Wrangul xi s.[7] Et resceu del rente de Ingulbi vii li.[3] [1]Et de lx s. resceu de William Attegrene cuilleur de Fraunkton'.[1] [3]Et resceu de Nichol de Salmonbi xxiii s. de la rente de <Henningbi> \ Enderby. / Et xxi d. de gelines. Et resceu de Jon del Meres de la rente de Pauske anno xviii° l s. Et resceu de Jon Bose carponter de Kirketon' v s.[8] Et de xviii s. resceu de Reignald le Greive Frampton'.[3] [5]Et de v s. resceu p*ar* la mayn Nich*ol* de Salmanby de la rent de Endreby. Et de le coillyur de Frampton' iii s.[5]

[2]*xxxvii li. x s. ix d.*[2]

[9]Item de lxvi s. viii d. resceu de Amavill*e* de Cobeldik' p*ur* tot lan p*ur* Neuvand. Item de vi s. resceu de mesme ceste Amavile p*ur* pastur*e* yemayl*e*.

Summa xl li. vi s. vi d.[9] [9]

[5]De xiiii s. de coriis v boum mactatorum ad lardarium venditis. Item \ de / xxv s. de xl pellibus bidentium mactatarum ad lardarium precium cuiuslibet vii d. ob. Et de ix s. ix d. de ix petris sepi de exitibus dictorum boum et bidentium venditis precium petre xiii d. Et de iii s. vii d. ob. qua. de exitibus xxxv bidentium venditis precium cuiuslibet i d. qua.[5]

[7]*Lii s. iiii d. ob. qua.*

Summa totalis xli li. xvii s. x d.[7]

[8]Item de lxx s. resceu de x li. les queux la p*ar*sone de Saltfletby avoit en garde pur labbe de Lagnet'.[8]

[9]*Summa totalis recepte xlvi li. viii s. v d. ob. qua.*[9] [10]

[1]*Despenses necessaries et foreins* Des queux il acompte livere a Steven le Ku pur les despens William et Thomas les frer*e*s le seignur vers Nichole a la escole ove la lower de une nef ii s. ovesq*e* les despens*es* le dit Steven en revenaunt. Et livere a Joh*a*n de Basingham p*ar* le comandeme*n*t le seignur pur ses despens*es* a Hepham x d. Et en offrand le seignur a Stowe le jour de Seint Michel ii d. Et en p*ar*chemyn achate a Nichole iii d. Et en la seell le

[7] MS unclear.

[8] MS unclear.

[9] The total has been altered and the amounts to which it refers are unclear.

[10] The total has been altered and the amounts to which it refers are unclear.

seignur amender a Nichol' ii d. En offrand le seignur a Nichol' le marsdy apr*e*s la fest*e* Seint Michel ii d. En vyn achate pur le seignur le meskredy vi d. Et mesme le jour en payn achate pur les chivaux le seignur a Kirkeby iiii d. ob. Et en vyn vi d. Et en cervoise mesme le jour vi d. Et livere a Robert le Chaumberlayn a Frankton' p*ar* le comandeme*n*t le seignur vi s. viii d. le vendredy p*ro*chein apr*e*s la fest Seint Michel. Et mesme le jour en vin achate pur le seingnur a Seint Botholf' vii d. ob. Et en lx bord achate v s. vi d. Et livere a Joh*a*n Oliver carpent*er* de Fraunkton' xiii d. Et livere a Rog*er* Hert p*ar* le comandeme*n*t le seignur vi s. viii d. Et en les despens*es* Nicholas de Twicrosse vers sir*e* Rog*er* Illary ovesq*e* un garscon Joh*a*n de Twicrosse ii s. vi d. Et en pain chars et chaundaile achatez a Engleby le meskredy devant la feste Seint Luke xix d. qua. Et en vin et pesso*u*n achate pur le seignur a Engleby la veille de Seint Luke ii s. vii d. Et en les despens*es* Joh*a*n de Twicrosse et Nichole son frer*e* ovesq*e*s un facouner et deux garcons vers Engleby le joefdy p*ro*chein devant la fest*e* Seint Luke ii s. vi d. Et en layners pur le seignur iii d. Et livere a Thom*as* Marchaunt de Seint Botholf' pur div*er*ses choses de lui achatez p*ar* heos xvii s. ii d. Et a Rog*er* de Farnham pur soulers al seignur et a la dame xii d. Et done a un mestr*e* pur feare un chymene x s.[11] Et en batellage de meryme a Nichole tantq*e* a Seint Botholf' iiii d. En les despens*es* le seignur a Nichole le marsdy apr*e*s la fest Seint Luke ii s. iii d. Et done al mestr*e* des escoles pur les comuns les frer*e*s le seignur iiii s. viii d. En deux pairs de esporouns pur le seignur ii s. viii d. Et done a povers p*ar* le comandeme*n*t le seignur ii d. En offrand le seignur ii d. Et mesme le jour en les despens*es* le seignur a Kirkeby xvi d. Et en Swynesheved en vin achate iiii d. Et livere a la dame v s. vi d. Et en soulers pur les enfauntz iii d. Et livere a Rog*er* le Drapur xl s. Et a sir*e* Nichole le Chapelein xii d. Le dimeinge apr*e*s la fest Seint Luke en offrand le seignur a Engleby i d. En le lundy ensuant en les despens*es* le seignur[12] illoq*e*s xvi d. Et done al serjant de Hepham ii d. Et done al garco*u*n Nichol de Salmanby a Alington' i d. Et done al bercher de Engleby pur despens*es* ii d. En cervoise achate illoq*e*s pur le seignur et sir*e* Gefrey de Cotes iiii s. iii d. En vin pur sir*e* Gefrey de Cotes xviii d. En esquels destaung xi d. En drap al oeps le facouner ii s. En drap al oeps le seignur iii s. Et liver*e* a Thom*as* de Multon' vi d. En une ciste pur la dame iiii s. vi d. En pain pur chivaux iii d. En argent dieu iii d. En sey pur la dame xii d. En vin iiii d. ob. Et livere a Joh*a*n le Armourer x s. Done al hunt le seignur Daubeney p*ar* le comandeme*n*t le seignur vi d. Et paie a la Seint Botholf' pur i ridel de carde al oeps le seignur ii s. vii d. Et liver*e* a Joh*a*n le Carpent*er* pur ses gages a Seint Botholf' p*ar* Steven le Cu ix d.[1]

[11] MS unclear; possibly 'xx s.'

[12] MS 'le se seignur'.

[3]En canvas pur lez tables en la sale xvi d. En peutur vessel achate a Seint Botulf' vi s. En sope et brumston iiii d. Et paie al orfever*e* pur le oever*e* mo*un* seignur xii d. <Delivere a lez freres mo*un* seignur et lour compaine a Seint Botulf' deqe a Nichol pur lour espence*s* xvi d.>[3] [2]*Vacatur quia N. de Salmanby dicit quod ipse solvit.*[2] [3]En \ i / peire de gauns pur mo*un* seygnur viii d. A Symme le garso*un* mo*un* seignur ii d. Et pur ii peire*s* de gaunz a les enfaunz i d. ob. et i d. a lez povres. En xxv auns de canvas achatez pur le moleine iiii s. ii d. En vi tapite*s* echatez pur garsons v s. En ii tapite*s* pur gens de meister iii s. iiii d. En i pot*e* de larein ix s.[3]

[2]*Summa ix li. vii s. vii d. qua.*[2]

Membrane 2 dorse

[4]*Probatur*[4]

[3]En i basyn et i lavor ii s. vi d. En ii panns de bras iii s. vi d. En i petit panne iiii d. Et paie a Thom*as* de Molton' le frer*e* mo*un* seignur xii s. p*ar* comaundement de ly. En payn et en ferur*e* pur vi chivalx moun seygnur qant il fust a Seynt Botulf' pur de achatr*e* so*un* liver*e* vi d. En batelag*e* a Nichol deqe a Frampton' pur vi quar*ters* et di. de brez et iiii quar*ters* de aveines xx d. et paie al armener de Linne v s. Baile a Anable de Colbeldik' pur bosoines ma dame v s. Et baile a Alain le filz Rob*ert* pur so*un* travail vere Som*er*kotes et Kirkeby iii d. Pur un petyt premer a mo*un* seygnur vii d. Et pur i spade al garden*er* viii d. Paie a petit Kitte q*e* fust oveqe ma dame pur sa travail xii d. Et paie xvi d. a cesti Kitte pur ces despence*s* a Framton' deke en Arderne oveqe un homme et un chivalx.

Le lundy dewaunt le fest*e* \ Seynt Martin / en offerend pur mo*un* seygnur i d. Et paie a Rog*er* Herd p*ar* comaundeme*n*t de seignur xiii s. iiii d. et a mo*unsire* Henr*i* Hillari xl s. Et paie a les masounes pur le chimene xl d. En i jaloun de tar pur les berbiz iiii d. En i peire de gauns a mo*un* seignur ii d. En amendeme*n*t les liveres del chapell iiii s. Et livere a mo*un* seygnur xx d. En canvas achate pur les tables en la sale et pur liz garsouns[13] xlii auns pur vii s. ii d. En gu\r/fus et en sursengl*es* pur lez chivalx vii d. En i peir*e* de botes a mo*un* seignur ii s. En i hache pur le garden*er* x d. \ et / a petit Watte le Mercer pur drap de lin et pur drap de sai et pur pepur v s. En kercheve*z* flemez vi s. vi d. En kellez xv d. En kerchivez boilez vii s. iii d. Et paie pur tourberie xviii s.[3] [2]*Quire*[2] [3]Et paie a la p*ar*sone de Frampton' iii li. pur dette de mo*un* seignur. Et paie pur ii peire*s* de souler*es* a mo*un* seignur xii d. Et liver*e* a Thom*as* Denbi par coma*und*eme*n*t mo*un* seignur ii s. viii d.[3] [2]*Quire*[2] [3]Et a Joh*an* le Carpo*un*ter ii s. En iii auns de drap achate pur i cloche a ma dame v s. En drap pur i cote a Nichol le Chapell*ein* qil usse de covena*un*t iii s. x d. Et pur i cotil al seignur xviii d. Baile al orfever*e* de Seynt Botulf' pur le opvereigne le seignur vii d. E paie al scherm*oun* de

[13] MS 'liz g garsouns'.

Seint Botulf' pur dev*er*se p*ar*celes xxii d. Le jour de Seint Cleme*n*t paie a lez maso*un*s \ pur le chimene / xiii s. iiii d. P\a/ie pur xii qissins iiii s. vi d. En iii auns de drap pur un lini*ng*e a le cloche ma dame iiii s. viii d.[3]
[2]*Summa xii li. vi s. ix d.*[2]
[4]*Probatur*[4]
[3]Paie pur [*Membrane 3 dorse*] iiii peles de p*ar*chemi*n* iiii d. et done a le garso*u*n la p*ar*sone de Frampton' vi d. pur ceo q*e* il fust oveq*e* ma dame a Screvelesbi. Et xii d. q*ant* mo*u*n seignur iva illeke oveq*e* mo*un*s*ire* Henr*i* Hillari. Et paie a Alain le filz Rob*er*t pur ses despe*n*cez a Frampton' deqe a Henningbi ii d. Deliv*er*e a ma dame vi d. Et paie pur i \ pipe / de vin xxvii s. Et al armen*er* de Line vii s. pur i pisaine. Et paie pur vi auns drap echate pur Joni la damisel ma dame ix s. Et a Rob*er*t del Park ver*s* Nichol pur so*u*n travail iii d. Et paie pur un di. drap echate pur les frer*es* mo*u*n seignur et pur Alain Wrangul xviii s. i d. Et a Walt*er* le Clerc de Seint Botulf' pur les bosoins mo*u*n seignur xl d. Et al orfever*e* de Seint Botulf' pur le seintur*e* mo*u*n seignur xxx d. Et a Jon de Basingham pur ses despencz ver*s* Ingulbi vi d. \ et / pur ii potes de peutr*e* xii d. Et pur iii bosongns al seignur iii d. Et paie al pelter Jon de Ewer*e*wik' iii li. Et paie pur batilag*e* a Ingulbi deqe a Frampton' et arer*e* a Ingulbi pur Jon de Basingham et le coilour de Ingulbi et autr*es* xii d. Et a Alain le filz Rob*er*t pur ses gajes ver*s* Som*er*cotes iii d. Baile al seignur pur les di*m*es iii d. Et pur iii gurzes achate al ceal le seignur iii d. Et pur i chine echate pur lez chens v d. Et baile a iii b\er/cheres pur de achaser le berbis de Frampton' v*er*s Ingulbi xiiii d. Et pur batilage a Kerkebi deke a Frampton' pur bres*e* xiiii d. Et pur i pel de he\r/min al over*e* mo*u*n seignur vi d. Pur i korn al seignur xii d.
Et ii s. q*ant* le seingnur iva al hasard. Et paie al pelter de Kirketon' iiii s. pur iii vermines. Et paie pur un diner a Seint Botolf' pur le seignur et so*u*n compainie xv d. Et paie en hernes pur drap al seignur iii s. Et pur batilage pur le frer*es* mo*u*n seignur et lour compainie et pur lour despencez a Frampton' deke a Nichole xviii d. Et delivere a Thom*as* le frer*e* le seignur q*i* est oveq*e* Rog*er* de Cobbuldik' ii s. le lundi devaunt le Nowel et ii s. a mesme cesti Thom*as* le jour del Epiphaine ap*re*s. Et al armerer de Line xii d. Et ii s. a Jon le Carponter q*i* est oveqe le seignur en p*ar*ti de soun salar*e*. Et paie pur le seintur*e* le seingnur al orfever*e* de Seint Botulf' x s. Et paie pur un forur*e* a Jon le Carponter xvi d. le quel il usse de covenaunt. En batilage pur iii seales le seingnur a Nichol deke a Frampton' iii d. Et a William Godeson' ii s. Et a Alain le filz Rob*er*t ix d. lez quex le seignur ly dona pur travail q*e* il usse oveq*e* ly. Et paie a Jon Driffeld' de Seint Botulf' iii s. ii d. pur hermin. Et paie pur batilage de merime a Ingulbi deqe a Frampton' iii s. vi d. Et paie pur i cotil et i boidekin al oeps le seignur ii d.[3]
[2]*Summa viii li. xvii s. iiii d.*[2]
[4]*Probatur*[4]

[3]Le samadi p*ro*chein ap*re*s la fest*e* del Epyphaine paie pur ii cotelles a le cusine xl d. Et baile a Jon le Carponter ii s. en p*ar*tie de so*un* salar*e*. Et deliver*e* a William le garso*un* Nichol de Twicros iiii d. pur cez despe*n*cez ver*s* Ingulbi et ar*e*re. Et baile v d. a v portours pur ceo q*e* ils aider*u*nt le charet le seingnur q*e* fust en perel ver*s* la dame le Ros oveq*e* un p*re*sent. En i carkois de bof achate pur i p*re*sent a la dame le Ros xii s. En ii veles achate pur mesme ceo p*re*sent vi s. Et ii pors et ii singne de estor pur mesme ceo p*re*sent. Et done a le garso*un* le bailif le roi vi d. pur de porter i bref a Nichol. En despence*s* feste a Seint Botulf' le mekerdi ap*re*s la feste Seint Hillari pur les bosoines espleister p*ar* le bailif le roi xix d. En oinounes et aille echate pur de plaunter en le gardine iiii s. En xx et iii aunz de drap de lin echate pur la dame iii s. vi d. En les despencez Nichol le Chappelein ver*s* s*ire* Seril de Recheford pur lez bosoingnes le seingnur \ p*ar* iii jour*s* / ix d. En lez despencez Nichol de Twicros a Wode Endurbi et a Ingulbi et arer*e* a Frampton' ii s. Et paie a le pelter de Seint Botulf' p*ar* comaundeme*n*t le seingnur viii d. Et paie al orfever*e* de Seint Botulf' en p*ar*ti de xiiii s. vi d. pur le seintour le seingnur v s. Et paie a la p*ar*sone de Frampton' pur dette ma dame et Margarete qe fust oveq*e* ma dame xxxii s. ix d. Et paie pur ail a le gardeine de Ingulbi ii s. Et paie pur sope a ma dame iii d. Et baile a Robert del Park' vere Windesou*er* xviii \ d. / Et xii d. paie illekes pur le cote Wade. Et a mesme cesti Robert del P*ar*k' iiii d. ver*s* Nichol a Walt*er* de Basigham. Et a Jon de Cobbuldik' iii s. pur deste le seingnur. Et done a Gige le Harpour ii s. Et paie pur pinnes a ma dame v d. Et paie a Adam le Baker p*ar* comaundeme*n*t ma dame iiii d. ob. Et ii d. pur i seintur*e* de quir a mo*un* seingnur. Et pur i peire de gaunz a mo*un* seingnur xii d. Et vi d. done a Adam le garsoun Walt*er* de Basingham q*e* porta un robe al seingnur. E pur un tonaile achate pur le chappelle vi d. Et deliver*e* a Jon del Mer*e*s \ pur / leet de berbiz vi s. viii d. Et paie Robert Maning' pur bordes de ly achate v s. vi d. Et paie a William Godessone iiii d. Et pur i pouche al seingnur xv d. Et paie pur i harpe q*e* ma dame dona a William Hardi iiii d. Et paie pur i scheine a ma dame pur lez leverer*es* v \ d. / Et pur ii peire*s* souler*es* pur mo*un* sei\n/gnur et pur la dame xii d. Et deliver*e* a William le garso*un* Nichol de Twicrosse pur ses gages ver*s* Twicrosse et arer*e* viii d.[3]

[2]*Summa v li. iii s. xi d. ob.*[2]

[4]*Probatur*[4]

[2]<*Summa xxxvi li. xv s. vii d. ob. qua.*>[2]

[5]Bayllye al mestre del estowe a Karrem p*ar*vaunt pur les kokes de les enfaunz ii d. Al warn*er* de Skeldynghop' p*ar* comaundment mons*ire* ii d. Al corveyser de Kyrcton' pur solers pur les enfauns xiiii d. Bayllye a Thom*as* de Denby a Seynt Botul*p*' p*ar* comandme*n*t mons*ire* i d. ob. Baillie a Henr*i* Courserman' vers Wyndesour xii d. Paye pur t*er*re achate pur la fourne a Frampton' ix d.[5]

[9]*Summa iii s. iiii d. ob.*[9]
[4]*Probatur*[4]
[3]Item luvor*e* al p*ro*pvot p*ur* let as agnels p*ar* le main de berch*er* pur le issuez de xxxv berbiz a li vendus \ iii s. vii d. ob. qua. / Item liver*e* a Anable de Cobbuldik' xxv s. dez xl pell*es* a li venduz.[3]
[2]*Summa totalis xxxvi li. xix s. ii d.*
xxviii s. vii d. ob.[2]
[4]*Probatur*[4]
[2]*ix li. viii s. ix d. qua.*[2]
[3]Summa totalis xxxvii li. vii s. vii d. ob. qua.[3]

11b Magdalen College, Oxford, Estate Paper 85/2

Membrane 1 recto
[10]Expense domus domini Johannis de Multon' ab incrastino Sancti Michaelis anno regni regis Edwardi tercii a conquestu xxi^{mo}
Die dominica in crastino Sancti Michaelis in carne bovina porcina et mutulina iiii s. vi d. Die lune in ovis iii d. Die martis in allece iii d. Die mercurii de stauro. Die jovis in piscibus recentibus ii d. Die veneris in piscibus salsis et recentibus xi d. Die sabbati in cervisia empta pro defectu brasei v s. ix d.

Summa xi s. x d.

Die dominica sequenti in carne bovina porcina et mutulina iiii s. v d. In ovis i d. Die lune in volatilibus ii d. Die martis in allece ii d. Die mercurii omnia de stauro. Die jovis in ovis ii d. Die veneris in piscibus duris et salsis viii d. In roches et pikes iiii d. In allece iii d. In allece recenti et aliis piscibus recentibus iiii d. ob. In wylkes i d. Die sabbati in allece iiii d. In salsamentis i d. Item in vino empto per diversas vices xi s. ix d. Item in candela empta per vices ii s. i d.

Summa xx s. x d. ob.

Die dominica proxima ante festum Luce[14] ewangeliste in carne porcina et mutulina xiiii d. In columbellis ii d. ob. Die lune de stauro. Die martis in allece recenti ii d. In piscibus duris i d. In ovis i d. Die mercurii de stauro. Die jovis de stauro. Die veneris in piscibus duris et salsis vii d. In vii bus. Lond' salis emptis ii s. iiii d. In pleices i d. In allece et roches iiii d. Die sabbati in allece iii d.

Summa v s. iii d.

Die dominica post festum Sancti Luce[15] in carne bovina porcina et mutulina xviii d. In ovis i d. Item in i porcello iii d. Die lune de stauro. Die

[14] MS 'Lucie'.
[15] MS 'Lucie'.

martis in ovis i d. Item lib*eratum* domine per Stephanum Cocum i d. Diebus mercurii et jovis de stauro. Die veneris in piscibus salsis ix d. In allece v d. In pleices i d. Die sabbati in piscibus recentibus i d.

Summa iii s. iii d.

Die dominica in festo apostolorum Simonis et Jude in i porcello iii d. ob. In carne porcina et mutulina iiii d. ob. Die lune in ovis i d. Die martis in ovis i d. In cinapio ii d. In iiii lib. candele v d. Die mercurii in piscibus et allece vi d. Die jovis in i porcello iii d. ob. Die veneris in allece iii d. In piscibus salsis et duris vi d. In roches et plaices ii d. Die sabbati in allece ii d. In piscibus duris ii d.

Summa iii s. v d.

Die dominica proxima post festum Omnium Sanctorum in i porcello iii d. ob. Die lune de stauro. Die martis in ovis i d. Die mercurii in iiii lib. candele v d. Die jovis de stauro. Die veneris in allece iiii d. In piscibus duris et salsis viii d. In i pike et roches iiii d. In pleices ii d. Die sabbati in i pike iii d. ob. In allece et pleices ii d.

Summa ii s. ix d.

Die dominica in festo Sancti Martini omnia de stauro. Die lune in ovis ii d. Die martis in cinapio ii d. In allece i d. In iiii lib. candelarum v d. Die mercurii de stauro. Die jovis de stauro. Die veneris in piscibus duris et salsis x d. In allece v d. In pleices ii d. In i pike iiii d. In lamprons i d. In salsamentis ix d. Die sabbati in allece ii d. In lampr*ons* i d. In ovis i d. In galentyn ob.

Summa iii s. ix d. ob.

Die dominica in octabis Sancti Martini et die lune de stauro. Die martis in allece ii d. In melvel i d. In di. lib. piperis xii d. In croco xii d. Die mercurii et die jovis omnia de stauro. Die veneris in piscibus duris et salsis ix d. In allece ix d. In ost*er*s i d. In sprotte i d. In lampr*ons* ii d. In pleices i d. In xxiii lib. candele ii s. i d. Die sabbati in sprotte i d. In lampr*ons* i d.

Summa iiii s. iiii d.

Die dominica sequenti omnia de stauro. Die lune in carne vitulina iii d. In ovis ii d. Die martis in sprotte et milvel ii d. Die mercurii de stauro. Die jovis in vigilia Sancti Andree apostoli in piscibus duris et salsis x d. In allece vi d. In sprotte ii d. In cinapio ii d. In lampr*ons* i d. Die veneris in piscibus duris et salsis ii d. In i pike iii d. In allece ii d. Die sabbati in allece iii d. In sprotte et lamprons ii d.

Summa iii s. iiii d.

Die dominica in i qr. vituli iiii d. In ovis i d. Die lune de stauro. Die martis in sprotte et milvel i d. In cinapio ii d. Die mercurii de stauro. Die jovis et die veneris omnia de stauro. Die sabbati in piscibus duris et salsis vi d. In allece iiii d. In sprotte et pleices ii d. In i pike ii d. ob. In gingebr*o* ob.

Summa xxiii d.

Die dominica proxima ante festum Sancte Lucie[16] in carne vitulina et porcina viii d. In ovis ii d. Die lune de stauro. Die martis in sprotte et milvel ii d. Die mercurii et die jovis omnia de stauro. Die veneris in piscibus duris et salsis x d. In allece vi d. In sprotte ii d. In i pike et lamprons iii d. In ost*er*s ii d. Die sabbati in allece ii d. In sprotte i d. In piscibus duris i d.

Summa iii s. iii d.

Die dominica proxima post festum Sancte Lucie[17] in carne porcina et vitulina viii d. In carne bovina ii d. In ovis i d. In gingebr*o* vi d. In galyngale iii d. In semels i d. In xx lib. candele ii s. i d. Die lune in ii mille allece xx s. In sexaginta stocfys' xii s. In xii murit iiii s. Die martis in ost*er*s et sprotte i d. ob. Die mercurii in i murit iii d. ob. In ost*er*s i d. ob. In sprotte ii d. qua. In cinapio ii d. In ovis i d. Die jovis in ost*er*s ii d. In vino empto per vices v s. Die veneris in piscibus recentibus vi d. Die sabbati de stauro.

Summa xlvi s. v d. ob. qua.

Die dominica proxima ante Natale Domini in di. cargosio carnis vituline x d. Die lune in vigilia Natal*is* in codelyng vi d. In lamprons et anguillis x d. In sturj*ou*n x d. In galentyn et vino acro vi d. In sprotte ii d. ob. In ii lib. amigdolarum et i lib. de rys vii d. In croco iii d. In vino vii d. Die Natal*i* Domini in vino vii d. In ovis vi d. In ii porcellis viii d. In i plover iii d. In carne bovina ii d.[18] Die mercurii de stauro. Die jovis in volatilibus i d. ob. Die veneris in piscibus salsis iii d. ob. In sprotte iii d. In lamprons i d. In buturo i d. Die sabbati in ix ciphis iii d. In iiii ciphis cum i curnekill i d. ob.

Summa viii s. vi d.

Die dominica sequenti in carne vitulina v d. In carne porcina ii d. In i lib. candele i d. qua. In vino v d. Die lune de stauro. Die martis in cinapio ii d. In piscibus salsis i d. In x lib. candele xii d. ob. Die mercurii et die jovis omnia de stauro. Die veneris in milvel ii d. In ost*er*s ii d. In lamprons i d. In sprotte i d. Die sabbati omnia de stauro. In buturo ii d.

Summa iii s. <x s.> ob. qua.

Die dominica in festo Epiphanie in carne vitulina xi d. In carne porcina ii d. In ovis i d. Die lune de stauro. Die martis de stauro. Die mercurii et die jovis omnia de stauro. Die veneris in mulvel ii d. In lampr*ons* ii d. In salmone ii d. Die sabbati omnia de stauro. In iiii lib. candele v d. In i lib. candele i d. qua.

Summa ii s. ii d.[10]

[16] MS 'Sancti Luce'.

[17] MS 'Sancti Luce'.

[18] MS adds 'de' followed by a blank space.

Membrane 2 recto

[1]Die dominica in festo Sancti Illari in vino v d. In i porcello v d. In carne vitulina iiii d. In carne porcina i d. In ovis i d. Die lune omnia de stauro. Die martis in ovis i d. In xx lib. candele ii s. i d. Die mercurii in carne vitulina v d. In carne porcina i d. In butiro i d. Die jovis omnia de stauro. Die veneris in sinapio ii d. In salmone ii d. In lamprons i d. Die sabbati omnia de stauro.

Summa istius septimane iiii s. vi d.

Die dominica in festo Sanctorum Fabiani et Sebastiani in carne vitulina xi d. Die lune omnia de stauro. Die martis in butiro et ovis ii d. In piscibus recentibus ii d. Die mercurii et jovis de stauro. Die veneris in piscibus recentibus ii d. Die sabbati in piscibus recentibus i d.

Summa istius septimane xviii d.

Die dominica proxima post festum conversionis Sancti Pauli in carne vitulina vii d. In allaudis i d. Die lune in ovis i d. Die martis in butiro i d. Item in volatilibus i d. Die mercurii in ovis i d. Diebus jovis et veneris de stauro. Die sabbati in festo Purificacionis in pleices et cungr*e* iiii d. In i lag. vini vi d. Item in x lib. candele xii d. ob.

Summa istius septimane ii s. x d. ob.

Die dominica in crastino Purificacionis in carne mutilina xii d. In carne vitulina vi d. In carne porcina et capite i vituli vi d. In exitu i bidentis iii d. Die lune in ovis i d. Die martis in butiro i d. Item in vino v d. Die mercurii omnia de stauro. Die jovis in i perna xviii d. In i cassa multonis xv d. Die veneris in ostriis ii d. In salmone ii d. Item in lamprons i d. In melvel i d.

Summa istius septimane vi s. i d.

Die dominica sequente in di. carcosio carnis bovine iiii s. viii d. Item in ii cassis multonum ii s. vi d. In carne vitulina vii d. In vino vi d. In ovis i d. Die lune et die martis omnia de stauro. Die mercurii in butiro i d. Die jovis de stauro. Die veneris in ostriis ii d. In salmone ii d. In pleices i d. Die sabbati de stauro.

Summa viii s. x d.

Die dominica proxima post festum Sancti Valentini in i perna xv d. In i hagiz ii d. In carne vitulina viii d. In i brusket ii d. Die lune in ii cassis multonum ii s. In ovis iii d. In butiro i d. In candela xiiii d. Diebus martis mercurii et jovis omnia de stauro. Die veneris in piscibus recentibus vi d. Die sabbati in piscibus recentibus ii d. ob. Item in i qr. carnis bovine xx d.

Summa viii s. i d. ob.

Die dominica sequente in carne bovina et mutilina v s. ii d. Diebus lune et martis omnia de stauro. Die mercurii in carne mutilina ii s. vi d. In carne vitulina iiii d. Die jovis de stauro. Die veneris in salmone wilkes et pleices iii d. Die sabbati omnia de stauro.

Summa viii s. iii d.

Die dominica in Carniprivio in vino pro domino Furnivall' et aliis ad hastilud*os* vi s. ix d. In carne bovina xviii d. In carne vitulina iii s. iiii d. In xviii gallinis iii s. In iii gallis iiii d. ob. In i perna ii s. iiii d. In carne porcina recenti iii d. In iiii curlues ii s. iiii d. In aliis volatilibus x d. In croco iiii d. In pipere vi d. In sinapio ii d. In zinzib*ere* i d. In galantyn iii d. In vinegr*e* iii d. In x lib. candele xii d. ob. In ficubus et racemis iii d. In x lib. amigdalarum xv d. In di. lib. zucur' viii d. In ovis iii d. Die lune de stauro. Die martis in butiro i d. In codeling i d. Die mercurii in piscibus iiii d. In oleo iii d.
Summa xxvi s.
Hic omnia talliantur cum domina preter xxxvi s.[1]
Membrane 1 dorse
[10]Iste die dominica \ in festo Sancti Hillari / est ad tall*iandum* cum domina lvi s. vii d. ob. qua.[10]

12 *Diet accounts of Edmund Mortimer, Earl of March, on a journey from Hertfordshire to Scotland, May 1378 to June 1378*

The context of this account is the continuing series of disturbances on the Scottish border through the 1370s and 1380s, leading to open warfare and culminating in John of Gaunt's Scottish expedition of 1385. Edmund Mortimer, Earl of March (1352–81), was the husband of Philippa, the daughter of Lionel, Duke of Clarence, and a granddaughter of Edward III. From 1368–9, Mortimer held, in right of his wife, the lands of the honour of Clare and he had extensive possessions in Ireland as lord of Ulster and Connaught. In May 1373, he had been made chief guardian of the truce with Scotland. Under Richard II his energies were again directed towards Scotland, in January 1378, to resolve breaches of the truce and to inspect fortresses on the border. Later the same year, in May and June, he travelled to Scotland, to Jedburgh, as one of the commissioners who treated with the Scots over the question of the Marches, and it is this journey that the account records. The following February, he was a commissioner for a peace treaty with Scotland; and in the same year, he was appointed the King's lieutenant in Ireland, arriving there in May 1380, where he died at the end of 1381.[1]

The account is written on a single parchment membrane. A tear at the top centre of the roll suggests that it may once have formed part of an

[1] *CP* viii, pp. 445–8; R. L. Storey, 'The wardens of the Marches of England towards Scotland, 1377–1489', *EHR* 72 (1957) pp. 593–615; M. McKisack *The fourteenth century 1307–1399* (Oxford, 1959) pp. 438–40.

Exchequer fashion roll. The text and cash totals were written by a single hand, in a single operation. Further notes to the cash totals were added in a second hand; and an auditor has marked the totals *probatur* in a third hand.

British Library Egerton Roll 8728

Recto

Custus et expense domini cum familia sua itinerantis versus partes Scocie pro tractatu ibidem habendo cum Scoticis ex parte regis et regni

Empcio equi et reparacio chariotarum In i palefrido badio empto pro domino per Johannem Reyne xii li. Item in reparacione ii chariotarum domini videlicet per manus Willelmi Whelere ut in emendacione ii rotarum ligni viii s. In factura unius corporis ligni cum bolstres et perches novis xx s. In iiii axiltres emptis et factis iiii s. In i pari lymonum ii s. iiii d. In i chariota brochianda ii s. viii d. In iiii streyt*our*s iiii d. In emendacione ii parium furgell' iiii d. In largicione des mules viii rotarum viii d. Et in diversis necessariis factis pro dict*is* chariot*is* per Henricum Aleyn fabrum videlicet in Cvi clavis viii s. x d. In bendes et plates pro i perch' xiiii d. In ii capitibus de iiii bendes viii d. In vii hurt*our*s xiiii d. In emendacione iiii lyntes vi d. In emendacione i braybolt' ii d. In i sege cum v bendes x d. In ii bendes pro ali*o* sege iiii d. In i plate pro i bed iii d. In emendacione i plate pro corpore iii d. In i pari gropes cum clavis xvi d. In di. pari gropes pro alia chariota viii d. In emendacione ii swepes viii d. In ferracione iii rotarum antiquarum de ferro domini ii s. vi d. Item in i novo colario empto xxii d. In i novo dorsario iii s. In emendacione i selle chariote cum coopertura i nathe ii s. viii d. In ii novis cropariis pro chariota v s. iiii d. In ii novis pipes v d. In iii novis shyttynglederes vi d. In i novo frontello pro i capistro iii d. In i novo wombrop iii d. Et in emendacione vii colariorum veterum iii s. In xii virg. wadmoll emptis pro colari*is* cooperiend*is* iii s. In tintour eiusdem ii s. In C cloutnaill*es* iiii s. In ii baskettes emptis pro chariot*is* iii s. vi d. In whipcord empt*o* viii d. In ii cordis emptis pro chariot*is* ligand*is* iii s. In ii paner*es* emptis pro victualibus cariandis in officio coquine ii s. vi d. In i pari botellorum de ii lag. et i pari botellorum de i lag. emptis x s. In emendacione ali*i* botell*i* veter*is* xii d.

Probatur Summa xvii li. iiii s. vii d. Totum de i equo et aliis necessariis emptis et reparacione chariotarum.

Empcio necessariorum et vadia familie In iii lib. croci emptis London' xlviii s. In xvi lib. pulveris zinzeber*i* ad xx d. xxvi s. viii d. In viii lib. pulveris piperis ad xviii d. xii s. In vadiis Hugonis Corr*our* euntis de London' in diversis partibus cum litteris domini pro retinencia sua munienda a xiii die Maii usque xxvi diem eiusdem per xiiii dies capiendi per diem iii d. iii s.

vi d. In expensis Ricardi Chariot' ducentis ii equos de chariota domini usque Clare et reducentis de ibidem iii equos de manerio ibidem et reducentis usque Clare ii equos de manerio ibidem per ix dies a xx die Maii incipienti cum expensis eorundem equorum ii s. ix d. Et in rewardo facto clericis regis in officio Willelmi Walworth' liberantibus ad opus domini pro viagio Scocie CClxvi li. xiii s. iiii d. de prestitis super vadiis domini vi s. viii d.
Probatur Summa iiii li. xix s. vii d. <Unde vi s. iii d. in expensis forinsecis> Et in denariis vi s. viii d.
Ware Die sabbati xxix die Maii domino cum familia sua prandenti apud Ware Panetria In albo pane empto ii s. iii d. Buttellaria Vinum In i sex. ii pich. vini rubei emptis ad x d. v s. Cervisia In xxv lag. cervisie emptis ad i d. ob. iii s. i d. ob. Coquina Expenduntur iiii pisces salsi di. C makerell sals*us* Cxl merlyng ii salmones salsi xiii allec makerell xx crabb*es* et i turbut de remanentia. Et in menuses emptis xiiii d. In xxi shafell*es* ii s. In butiro vi d. In ovis iiii d. In olera ii d. In herba ii d. In sale iii d. In focali xi d. Mareschalsia In feno empto xix d. ob. In di. bus. avene ii d. ob. Et in pane equino vi s. iii d. ob. Et in expensis Johannis Brag' Johannis Stoke Johannis North' cum equis suis et cum iiii sommariis domini pernoctancium apud Ware die veneris precedenti iiii s. iii d. *Royston* Eodem die domino pernoctanti apud Royston' Panetria In albo pane empto iiii d. Buttellaria In iii pich. di. vini rubei iii s. vi d. Cervisia In xvii lag. cervisie ii s. x d. Coquina De precomputato. Mareschalsia In feno empto pro li equis et xxi hakeneis v s. vii d. ob. In iiii qr. avene xiii s. i d. ob. In pane equino iii s. i d. In litera empta x d. In iii lib. candele vi d. In carbone xii d. In lecto xxii d. In portagio cervisie de villa in prioratu ii d. In expensis Johannis Stoke Edwardi Bire et Melett' preeuncium isto die in prandio apud Royston xiii d. Et in expensis sommariorum per viam computatis per manus Willelmi Abyngdon' cum ferura apud Bontyngford' xi d. Et in expensis equ*i* Thome Fooll' hac nocte iiii d. Et in expensis equorum et hominum itinerancium per manus Willelmi Mallyng' ix d. ob. Et per manus Ricardi Lavyngton' vi d. ob. Et in expensis ii palefridorum domini apud Waltham et Ware per manus Johannis Ferro*ur* vi d. ob.
Probatur Summa lxv s. iii d. ob.
Die dominica xxx die Maii jantanti apud Royston in albo pane empto ii s. In iii pich. vini iii s. In xxxi lag. cervisie v s. ii d. Coquina In di. carcosio bovis empto ix s. In i cassa multonis ii s. iiii d. In ii vitulis v s. In viii columbellis viii d. In di. C ovis iiii d. et totum expenditur. Item in oblacione domini ad sommum altare in prioratu de Royston vi s. viii d. Et ad crucem ibidem iiii d. Et liberantur domino Johanni Kepston' pro elemosina domini facienda pauperibus per vices xii s. *Huntyngdon'* Eodem die pernoctanti apud Huntyndon' in albo pane empto ii s. ii d. In ii sex. ii pich. vini x s. In xxxii lag. cervisie v s. iiii d. Coquina In di. carcosio bovis

vi s. viii d. In ii vitulis vii s. vi d. In i cassa multonis ii s. x d. In ii caponibus xii d. In xii pulcinis ii s. In sale et farina avene iiii d. In i qr. porci baconis x d. In herba i d. In focali iii s. iiii d. Mareschalsia In feno empto pro lvi equis xxi hakeneis vii s. iiii d. ob. In iiii qr. i bus. di. avene xiii s. xi d. ob. In pane equino xix d. In litera xvi d. In ferura ii s. In lecto ii s. iiii d. Item in dono facto cuidam nuncio vicecomitis[1] Northumb' obvianti domino prope Huntyngdon' per manus domini Johannis Kepston' xx d. In oblacione domini in prioratu de Huntyngdon' iiii d. et ad missam ibidem i d. In expensis Johannis Stoke Johannis Brag' Ricardi Squiller' et aliorum apud Huntyngdon' in prandio ante adventum domini vii d. ob. In i freno empto pro fratre Johanne Shelyng' per manus Melett' xii d. In emendacione sellarum vii d. In i equo car*iagii* conducto cum i homine de Royston' usque Huntyngdon' pro hernesio camere domini iiii d.

Probatur Summa vi li. xxi d. ob. unde in elemosina domini xii s. In oblacione <v d.> vii s. v d. In dono xx d. In <empcione necessariorum> et cariagio xxiii d.

Steelton' Die lune[2] ultimo die Maii domino jantanti apud Stelton' in albo pane empto xii d. In ii pich. i quart. vini ii s. iii d. In x lag. cervisie xx d. Coquina In i qr. bovis iii s. vi d. In iii caponibus xviii d. In ii pulcinis vi d. ob. In focali ii d. In feno et pane equino iiii s. xi d. *Staunford* Eodem die pernoctanti Staunford in albo pane ii s. ii d. In ii sex. ii pich. vini x s. In xli lag. cervisie vi s. x d. Coquina In ii qr. di. bovis emptis xi s. In ii vitulis di. vi s. iii d. In di. cassa multonis xii d. In di. porco bacone xii d. In i auca v d. In vi caponibus ii s. vi d. In xvi pulcinis ii s. In sale iii d. In farina avene i d. In sauce i d. In focali xx d. In i qr. carbonum xx d. In sepis et allea iiii d. Mareschalsia In feno empto pro iiii^{xx}ii equis xx hakeneis x s. x d. ob. In v qr. iiii bus. iii pec. avene xviii s. vii d. ob. In pane equino ii s. vi d. In litera xxii d. In lecto xxi d. Item in expensis officiariorum preeuncium ante dominum apud Staunford' xiiii d. In ferura iii d. In expensis hominum cum sommariis et equis cariagiorum inter Huntyngdon' et Staunford' videlicet per manus Johannis Ferro*ur* i d. Willelmi Mallyng' ii d. Willelmi Abyngdon' iiii d. Willelmi Page x d. Willelmi Lovesay ii d. Davidi de Coquina vi d. In cepo empto pro tibiis equorum domini v d. Et in pane equino empto apud Huntyngdon' mane ante recessum x d. Et in expensis Willelmi Claye commorantis London' et euntis illuc usque Staunford' cum sigill*o* domini per ii dies di. ii s. vi d. Et in vadiis Willelmi Hakele missi usque London' per dominum et redeuntis usque Staunford' per iii dies ii s.

Probatur Summa Cvii s. vii d. ob.

[1] MS 'vicem''.

[2] MS repeats 'lune'.

Grantham Die martis primo die Junii jantanti apud Grantham in albo pane ii s. vi d. In iii pich. di. vini iii s. vi d. In xv lag. cervisie ad ii d. et xiii lag. cervisie ad i d. ob. iiii s. i d. ob. Coquina In iii vitulis emptis ix s. In i cassa di. multonis iiii s. vi d. In di. porco bacone xx d. In iiii aucis xvi d. ob. In ii porcellis xii d. In xxiiii pulcinis iii s. In sale et farina avene iiii d. In focali ii s. ix d. In feno xiii d. In pane equino vii s. x d. Et in expensis Johannis Brag' Johannis Stoke et Willelmi Lovesay apud Grantham die lune precedenti de nocte preeuncium ante dominum ii s. *Newerk* Eodem die pernoctanti apud Newerk Panetria In ii bus. frumenti emptis et furnitis apud Staunford' pro domino xvi d. Et in albo pane empto xix d. In ii sex. iii pich. \ di. / vini rubei xi s. v d. In xxxiiii lag. di. cervisie v s. ix d. Coquina In di. carcosio bovis vi s. viii d. In ii vitulis vi s. In i cassa multonis ii s. viii d. In i pikerell vi d. In herba sale et farina avene vi d. In focali xii d. In iiii bus. carbonum xvi d. Mareschalsia In feno empto pro iiii^{xx}ii equis xxi hakeneis viii s. v d. ob. In v qr. iii bus. pec. avene pro eisdem xiiii s. v d. In pane equino xxiii d. ob. In litera ii s. In lecto ii s. vi d. Et in expensis hodie per viam videlicet per manus Walteri Egerton' i d. et per Abyngdon' iii d. et per Willelmum Page iii d. In xv ferris equinis ad ii d. et xxiiii remocionibus ad ob. et ferratis iii s. vi d.

Probatur Summa Cxvi s. x d.

Tuxford Die mercurii ii die Junii jantanti apud Tuxford in albo pane xvii d. In iii pich. iii quart. vini iii s. ix d. In xxiii lag. cervisie iii s. x d. Coquina In i cassa multonis ii s. vi d. In iiii caponibus xx d. In iiii stokf*ish* ii s. iiii d. In i salmone ii s. viii d. In viii anguillis ii s. iiii d. In floundres vi d. In ovis vi d. In caseo ii d. In sale i d. In focali ii d. In feno ix d. In pane equino vii s. ii d. ob. In i homine cum equo suo conducto pro victualibus cariandis de Newerk' usque huc v d. Et in iiii duodenis pinitonum[3] emptis pro domino per manus Rogeri Hugges xvi d. In filo viii d. Et liberantur domino Johanni Kepston' pro elemosina domini per viam vi s. viii d. *Blithe* Eodem die pernoctanti apud Blithe Panetria In pane albo empto ii s. In ii sex. iii quart. vini viii s. ix d. In xl lag. cervisie vi s. viii d. Coquina In di. carcosio bovis empto vi s. In i cassa multonis ii s. viii d. In i vitulo ii s. vi d. In iii aucis xii d. In focali xxiii d. In sale et farina avene v d. In viii pulcinis xii d. In bacone iiii d. Item in i stik di. pympernoll ix d. In menuses vi d. In ovis viii d. In butiro ii d. In flore frumenti ii d. ob. In i barbell xii d. Mareschalsia In feno empto pro iiii^{xx}v equis et xvii hakeneis vii s. viii d. In v qr. i bus. avene xiiii s. vi d. In pane equino v s. iiii d. In litera ii s. vi d. In lecto ii s. iii d. In ferura ii s. iii d. ob. Et in expensis Johannis Stoke et Willelmi Lovesaye preeuncium dominum apud Tuxford' die martis precedenti ad noctem vi d. ob. Et in expensis sommariorum per viam videlicet per manus Johannis

[3] Reading uncertain.

Paulyn iii d. Item per manus Willelmi Mallyng' iiii d. Et in lusu domini ad talos cum Willelmo Kirkeby vi s. viii d.
Probatur Summa Cxvii s. x d. unde in elemosina domini vi s. viii d. In lusu domini ad dec*e* vi s. viii d.
Dancastre Die jovis iii die Junii jantanti apud Dancastr' Panetria In pane albo empto xix d. In ii pich. vini ii s. In xx lag. cervisie iii s. iiii d. Coquina In iii caponibus emptis xx d. In ii cassis multonum v s. iii d. In vitul*o* ii s. iiii d. In focali ii d. In feno xiiii d. In pane equino vii s. viii d. ob. In ferura iiii d. In elemosina domini iii d. Et in expensis Willelmi Claye Johannis Brag' Edwardi Bire et Willelmi Lovesay preeuncium domini videlicet die mercurii predicto apud Dancastr' in nocte et isto die apud Pountfreyt in prandio ii s. iiii d. ob. *Pountfreyt'* Eodem die pernoctanti apud Pountfreyt' Panetria In pane albo iiii s. ii d. In iii sex. iii quart. vini xii s. ix d. In lxviii lag. di. cervisie xi s. v d. Coquina In iii qr. bovis xi s. iiii d. In ii vitulis vi s. viii d. In iii cassis di. multonum ix s. iiii d. In vi aucis ii s. vi d. ob. In xvi pulcinis ii s. In salmone frisco vi d. In sale vii d. In farina avene iiii d. In allea i d. In sauce xviii d. In focali ii s. In i qr. ii bus. carbonum xx d. In cariagio aque iii d. Mareschalsia In feno empto pro Cxviii equis et xxxviii hakeneis xiii s. xi d. ob. In viii qr. i bus. pec. avene xxi s. xi d. In pane equino iiii s. vii d. In litera v s. iiii d. In lecto iii s. xi d. Et in i virg. canevac*e* empta pro mortario cere cariando in clothsak camere domini vi d. In don*is* fact*is* cementari*is* et carpentari*is* operantibus in castro de Pountfreyt per manus Johannis James xiii s. iiii d. In iii virg. i qr. panni nigri ad ii s. viii d. et dat*um* Thome Fooll' per manus Johannis Royne viii s. viii d. In emendacione sellarum xv d. In cepo vii d. In xxvii ferris ad ii d. et ix remocionibus ad ob. iiii s. x d. ob. In expensis sommariorum per viam per manus Willelmi Mallyng' iiii d. et per manus Hoell' i d. ob. et per manus Willelmi Abyngdon' iii d.
Probatur Summa viii li. xi d. unde <in neccessariis emptis et reparatis xxi d.> \ in elemosina iii d. / In donis xxii s.
Wetherby Die veneris iiii die Junii commoranti apud Wetherby in pane albo cervisia feno pane equino et avena xii s. viii d. ob. Et in expensis Willelmi Claye Edwardi Bire Johannis Brag' preeuncium dominum die jovis precedenti apud Wetherby et pernoctancium apud Burghbrigge iii s. ob. *Burghbrigge* Eodem die prandenti et cenanti apud Burghbrigge Panetria In pane albo empto iiii s. x d. In iiii sex. i quart. et i gille vini rubei xviii s. vii d. In iiii^{xx}viii lag. cervisie ad i d. ob. lag. xi s. Coquina In iiii piscibus poudr*is* emptis vi s. In iiii halibut*es* xi s. In x salmonibus et iii qr. salmonis xxiii s. iiii d. In vi^{xx} merlyng poudr*is* ii s. In xii anguillis iii s. vi d. In iiii barbell*is* x d. In menuses vi d. In butiro x d. In ovis x d. In lacte i d. In sale ii d. In herba ii d. In focali xii d. Mareschalsia In feno empto pro Cxvii equis et xxxviii hakeneis xiii s. ob. In viii qr. iii bus. pec. avene xxiii s. ix d. In pane equino ii s. xi d. In litera iii s. iii d. In xxiii ferris et vi remocionibus

iiii s. i d. In lecto iiii s. vi d. In emendacione sell*e* per manus Paulyn iii d. Et liberantur domino Johanni Kepston' pro elemosina domini distribuenda pauperibus xiii s. iiii d.

Probatur Summa viii li. v s. vi d. ob. unde in elemosina xiii s. iiii d.

Northallerton' Vacat dominus mane Die sabbati v die Junii domino cum domino Ricardo Lescrop' apud Sanctam Agatham et familia prandenti apud Northallerton in albo pane empto iii s. iii d. In lvii lag. di. cervisie ad i d. ob. vii s. i d. ob. Coquina In viii salmonibus emptis xviii s. In vi halibutt*es* et ii morucis xxi s. In vii anguillis ii s. iii d. In cariagio dictorum victualium de Burghbrig' usque Allerton' pro ii equis conductis xvi d. In farina avene i d. In sale iii d. In focali xx d. Mareschalsia In feno empto iii s. v d. In i qr. ii bus. avene ii s. vi d. ob. In pane equino xi s. ob. In feriagio ultra Swale ii d. In elemosina iii d. In expensis Willelmi Claye et aliorum officiariorum precedencium die veneris precedenti apud Allerton' ad noctem xxii d. *Derlyngton'* Eodem die pernoctanti apud Derlyngton' Panetria In albo pane empto ii d. In xii lag. cervisie xviii d. Coquina Nichil. Mareschalsia In feno empto pro Cxi equis et xliiii hakeneis xiii s. ix d. In viii qr. vi bus. iii pec. avene xvii s. x d. In litera vi s. i d. In pane equino xxiii d. In lecto iii s. ii d. In expensis hominum per viam computatis per manus diversas xxiii d. ob. In cepo pro equ*is* iii d.

Probatur Summa vi li. x d. unde <in passagio ii d.> in elemosina ii d.

In expensis i equi bastard i *cur*sor et xii equorum chariotarum domini Willelmi Ferthyng' Roberti Arm*ur*er et Rogeri Squiller cum iii hakeneis suis cum expensis iiii hominum chariotarum domini inter London' et Derlyngton' cum diversis cariagiis armorum et aliorum necessariorum domini videlicet die mercurii xxvi die Maii apud Chesthunt' et Ware in omnibus computatis ix s. vi d. Item xxvii die Maii apud Arlyngton' ix s. viii d. Item xxviii die Maii apud Weston' under Wold viii s. ix d. ob. Item xxix die Maii apud Stanford[4] viii s. viii d. Item xxx die Maii apud Grantham vii s. vii d. Item ultimo die Maii apud Tuxford' vii s. Item primo die Junii apud Dancastre viii s. iii d. Item ii die Junii apud Pountfreyt' v s. x d. Item iii die Junii apud Abrefford' vii s. viii d. Item iiii die Junii apud Topclef' Swale vi s. viii d. Et v die Junii pernoctantitus in hospicio apud Derlyngton'. Et in xii clout*es* et C clavis emptis pro chariotis per viam iiii s. iiii d. In cepo pro equis xii d. ob.

Probatur Summa iiii li. v s. unde in reparacione chariotarum iiii s. iiii d.

Verte

[4] MS 'Stanfor', possibly torn away at the end.

Dorse

Derlyngton' Festum Pentecostes Die dominica vi die Junii familia domini tota die apud Derlyngton' Panetria In albo pane iiii s. ix d. In ii sex. i pich. iii quart. vini emptis apud Rychemond' ad xiiii d. pich. xi s. iiii d. ob. In cariagio eiusdem xvi d. In iiii^{xx} lag. cervisie x s. Coquina In i carcosio bovis empto xix s. In v cassis multonum x s. In iii vitulis vi s. In di. porco xx d. In vi porcellis iii s. xi d. In iiii caponibus xiii d. ob. In ii pulcinis iii d. In xii pulcinis xii d. In CC ovis xii d. In lacte v d. ob. In ii bus. salis xvi d. In farina avene i d. ob. In herba iiii d. ob. In focali iiii s. In iii qr. carbonum xviii d. Mareschalsia In feno empto pro Cxi equis et xliiii hakeneis xi s. x d. In vii qr. vii bus. di. avene xv s. xi d. In pane equino iiii s. vii d. In lecto iii s. vii d. In litera iiii s. ii d.

Probatur Summa Cxix s. iii d. ob.

Derlyngton' Die lune vii die Junii ibidem tota die in albo pane empto iiii s. x d. In iiii^{xx}i lag. cervisie ad i d. ob. x s. i d. ob. Coquina In iii qr. bovis emptis xvi s. In vi cassis multonum xii s. In ii vitulis iiii s. In xvii caponibus iiii s. v d. In xxxiiii pulcinis ii s. x d. In CC ovis xii d. In lacte ii d. ob. In allea et herba v d. Mareschalsia In feno empto pro[5] Cix equis et xxxviii hakeneis iii s. x d. ob. In viii qr. v bus. avene xiii s. vi d. ob. In pane equino ii s. i d. ob. In iiii^{xx}iii ferris equinis ad ii d. et lxvi remocionibus ad ob. xvi s. vii d. In lecto iii s. xi d.

Probatur Summa iiii li. xv s. x d. ob.

Durham Venit dominus ad cenam Die martis viii die Junii prandenti et cenanti apud Durham Panetria In albo pane empto iiii s. viii d. In i sex. iii pich. di. vini rubei viii s. ix d. In Ci lag. cervisie ad i d. ob. xii s. vii d. ob. Coquina In i carcosio bovis xxiiii s. In viii cassis multonum xvi s. In ii vitulis iiii s. viii d. In vii aucis ii s. In xxiiii pulcinis ii s. Mareschalsia In feno empto pro Cxlii equis et xl hakeneis xiiii s. x d. In vii qr. i bus. di. avene emptis ultra iii qr. avene expensis de stauro prioris ibidem xviii s. In pane equino iiii s. i d. In litera viii s. vii d. In lecto iii s. iii d. Et in \ expensis / equ*orum* domini et partis familie apud Lemyng' et Pontem Percy euncium de Burghbrig' usque Sanctam Agatham et illinc usque Akeland' ad episcopum Duneln' per manus Meletti ii s. vi d. In oblacione domini apud Sanctam Agatham die Pentecostes iiii d. et die lune proximo sequenti apud Akeland' iiii d. In ii nunciis conductis cum litteris domini de Akeland' usque Derlyngton' per ii vices xvi d. In oblacione domini ad tumbam Sancti Cutberti vi s. viii d. Et ad missam ibidem iiii d. In expensis Willelmi Hornby Edwardi Bire et Willelmi Lovesay apud Durham die lune precedenti cum expensis Willelmi Claye et Johannis Brag' et equorum suorum iii s. viii d. ob. In stabul*o* mundand*o* apud Durham i d. In i equo griseo

[5] MS omits 'pro'.

empto pro officio coquine cariando eo quod sommarius eiusdem officii moritur xxvi s. viii d. In sapone empto pro naperia ii d. In expensis \ hominum et / equ*orum* chariot*arum* inter Derlyngton' et Durham isto die ii s.

Probatur Summa viii li. vii s. vii d. unde in oblacione vii s. viii d. In expensis forinsecis xvi d. In equo cariagii xxvi s. viii d.

Novum Castrum super Tynam Presentibus episcopo Hereford' et aliis hominibus ville in prandio Die mercurii ix die Junii prandenti apud Novum Castrum super Tynam Panetria In albo pane empto ultra levem panem datum per homines ville iii s. vi d. In iii sex. iii quart. vini ultra ii sex. de exhennio ville xii s. ix d. In iiii^{xx} lag. cervisie emptis ad i d. ob. x s. Coquina In iii piscibus salsis emptis iiii s. In vi salmonibus friscis viii s. In ii salmonibus pist*atis* ii s. iii d. In iiii salmonibus salsis iiii s. vi d. In C codlyng \ parvis / poudr*is* vi s. viii d. In i halibut xviii d. In C lobest*es* ii s. x d. In iiiiC ovis ii s. In i pec. salis ii d. In farina avene ii d. In di. lag. vini acri vi d. In butiro x d. In xiiii lag. lactis xxi d. In portagio vi d. Mareschalsia In feno empto pro Cxlii equis et xl hakeneis xv s. In vii qr. v bus. di. avene ultra iiii qr. de exhennio ville xiii s. iiii d. In litera vi s. ii d. In pane equino iii s. i d. ob. In lxxiii ferris ad ii d. et lxi remocionibus ad ob. emptis et ferratis xiiii s. viii d. ob. Et in ferura per viam xix d. ob. In cepo pro ped*ibus* equ*orum* iii d. In flokkes pro sell*is* ii d. In pot*u* sometari*i* per viam iii d. In expensis Willelmi Claye E. Bire Johannis Brag' et Willelmi Lovesay nocte precedenti apud Novum Castrum ii s. iiii d. In don*is* fact*is* ministrall*is* hominum ville obvianc*ium* domino per viam xx s. In don*is* fact*is* iiii^{or} gentilibus mendicantibus per viam per manus domini Johannis Kepston' vi s. viii d. In expensis equ*orum* chariot*arum* per viam isto die ix d. Et in lecto empto iiii s. ii d.

Probatur Summa vii li. x s. v d. ob. unde in donis xxvi s. viii d.

Morpath' Vacat dominus post prandium Die jovis x die Junii apud Morpath' domino cum tota familia sua ad prandium ibidem et cum parte familie sue apud Werkeworth' in cena cum comite Northumbr' ceteris de familia remanentibus apud Morpath' Panetria In albo pane empto[6] v s. vi d. In vii sex. iii pich. vini emptis apud Novum Castrum et cariatis xxxi s. Inde expenduntur ii sex. In Cx lag. cervisie ad i d. ix s. ii d. Coquina In i carcosio di. bovis xxiii s. In vii cassis multonum xiiii s. x d. In ii vitulis v s. viii d. In vi porcellis iiii s. In viii aucis ii s. x d. In xxii pulcinis xxii d. In i pec. salis iii d. In i qr. porci baconis xv d. In i pec. farine avene iii d. In herba ob. In focali ii s. vi d. In vi lag. di. vini acri v s. v d. In i lag. viridis sicci viii d. In i lag. senapii iiii d. Mareschalsia In feno empto pro Cxvi equis xli hakeneis xiiii s. In ix qr. iii bus. di. avene xviii s. x d. ob. In pane equino

[6] MS 'eq''.

iiii s. viii d. In litera v s. ix d. ob. In lecto conducto iii s. iii d. In xxxiiii ferris et xxxii remocionibus vii s. In lx ferris equinis emptis pro stauro habendo ix s. In M clavis equinis pro stauro iiii s. Et in expensis equorum chariot*arum* per viam isto die ii d. Et in expensis sommari*i* et garcion*is* i d. ob. Et in elemosina domini facta hominibus facientibus pontem de Morpath' xiii s. iiii d. Et in expensis Willelmi Claye Edwardi Bire Johannis Brag' et Willelmi Lovesay pernoctancium apud Morpath' nocte precedenti vii d. ob. In portagio victualium de villa in abbathiam viii d.

Probatur Summa ix li. ix s. xi d. ob. unde in elemosina xiii s. iiii d.

Morpath' Die veneris xi die Junii ibidem Panetria In albo pane empto iii s. iii d. Et expenditur i sex. vini de precomputato. In xlviii lag. cervisie iiii s. Coquina In iii paner*es* diversorum piscium videlicet merlyng codlyng haddok salmonum et lobest*es* et troyt*es* simul emptorum xi s. iiii d. In butiro ovis et lacte xii d. In focali xviii d. Mareschalsia In feno empto pro Cii equis et xx hakeneis x s. iiii d. In vii qr. i bus. di. avene xiiii s. iiii d. ob. In pane equino xxi d. In litera ii s. iiii d. In lecto ii s. iii d. Et in portagio panis et cervisie de villa ad abbathiam iiii d. Et in expensis diversorum officiariorum preeuncium cum cariagi*is* usque Bolton' et illinc usque Alnewyk' cum expensis diversorum sagittariorum pro salva custodia hernesii domini ut patet per librum mareschalsie de eorum nominibus cum expensis equorum chariot*arum* et hominum earundem computatis per manus diversas xiii s. iii d. ob. In i gydo conducto pro chariot*is* ducend*is* eodem tempore xii d. In expensis equ*orum* domini inter Morpath' et Werkeworth' et illinc usque Alnewyk' per manus Melett' xiii d. Et in expensis per manus Philippi Medik' v d. ob. In i equo conducto pro Edwardo Bire in negociis domini de Morpath' usque Werkeworth' die precedenti et red*eundo* xii d. In expensis per manus Davidi de Coquina per vices xii d. In cepo empto pro chariot*is* per manus Willelmi Ferthyng' x d. In cepo pro sommari*is* ii d. ob. In reparacione selle sommarii Johannis Paulyn iiii d. Et in reparacione coffrorum de armis domini cum i clavi de novo facta pro eisdem et cum mundacione bacynett domini per manus Roberti Arm*ur*er x d.

Probatur Summa lxxii s. vi d. unde <in expensis forinsecis ii s. In reparacione hernesii domini xiiii d.>

Alnewyk' Venit dominus ad prandium Presentibus episcopo Hereford' et decano Sancti Pauli Die sabbati xii die Junii prandenti domino cum tota familia sua apud Alnewik' Panetria In albo pane empto iiii s. In ii sex. iii pich. vini xi s. In Ciiii lag. cervisie ad i d. viii s. viii d. Coquina In viii milwellis emptis xii s. In C parvis codlyng poudr*is* viii s. iiii d. In iiii^{xx} lobest*es* xx d. In viiC haddok et merlyng xxi s. In xxxvi codlyng parvis friscis iii s. In ii hominibus cum iiii equis conductis cum piscibus cariandis de Newebyggyng' usque Felton' et illinc usque Morpath' x s. In iiii equis conductis pro piscibus cariandis de Morpath' usque Alnewyk' v s. viii d. In expensis Willelmi Claye in patria pro piscibus providendis per ii dies precedentes xii d. In ferura equi sui iii d. In cariagio piscium de abbathia de Alnewyk' usque castrum ibidem iiii d. Mareschalsia In feno empto pro Cli equis xlii hakeneis xix s. ii d. ob. In x qr. vi bus. avene xxi s. vi d. In litera iiii s. x d. In lecto iii s. v d. In pane equino ii s. vi d. ob. In cariagio feni x d. In expensis per manus Abyngdon' ii d. In locione naper*ou*ns de coquina i d. In dono facto cuidam scutifero comitis Northumbr' presentanti domino i palefridum et i jumentum ex parte dicti comitis xl s. Et garcioni suo vi s. viii d. In stramine empto pro lecto in castro ii s. In mundacione domus ibidem x d.

Probatur Summa ix li. ix s. unde in cariagi*o* conduct*o* <xv s. viii d.> in dono facto xlvi s. viii d.

Presentibus Ricardo Scrop' et decano Sancti Pauli D~~ie~~ dominica xiii die Junii prandenti apud Alnewik' Panetria In albo pane empto iii s. In i sex. vini rubei iiii s. In lxx lag. cervisie v s. x d. Coquina In ii carcosiis boum xxiii s. Inde expenditur i. In ix cassis multonum xix s. iiii d. Inde expenduntur vi. In xii agnis x s. Inde expenduntur vi. In i vitulo empto iii s. In xii porcellis viii s. Inde expenduntur viii. In v aucis xx d. In vi caponibus ii s. In xix pulcinis ii s. In i bus. salis x d. In i pec. frumenti i d. ob. In viii lag. lactis viii d. In CC ovis xii d. ob. In i qr. porci xvi d. In focali vi d. Et in pane equino ii s. iiii d. *Buwik'* Eodem die cenanti apud Buwik' Panetria In albo pane empto iiii s. In Cxx lag. cervisie ad i d. x s. In portagio eiusdem de diversis locis xx d. Coquina Expenduntur i carcosium bovis iii casse multonum vi agni iiii porcelli de remanentia. In viii cassis multonum emptis xiii s. iiii d. In vi agnis v s. In xxviii pulcinis xxi d. ob. In sale viii d. In i capone iii d. In herba et farina avene vii d. In focal~~i~~ xiiii d. In flore frumenti v d. Mareschalsia In feno empto pro Clxxvii equis et xliiii hakeneis xiii s. iiii d. In xi qr. avene xxvi s. viii d. In litera empta vi s. viii d. ob. In lecto ii s. iii d. In expensis Edwardi Bire Johannis Brag' et Willelmi Lovesay preeuncium nocte precedenti x d. In expensis Willelmi Hakele euntis de Alnewik' usque Bamb*ur*gh pro vino querendo et euntis illinc usque Buwik' vi d. In i homine cum i equo conducto de Alnewik' usque Bamburgh' et illinc usque Buwik' pro dicto vino cariando xii d. In i gydo conducto per viam v d. In portagio et tractagio diversorum victualium apud Buwik' ix d. In ii hominibus cum ii equis conductis pro cariagio victualium de Buwik' usque Killom xii d. In cariagio panis et carnis de Alnewik' usque Buwik' ii s. Et in dono facto cuidam famulo comitis Northumbr' presentanti domino i sourellum iii s. iiii d. Et in i gydo conducto pro equ*is* chariot*arum* per viam x d. In expensis sommari*orum* domini per manus Mallyng' v d. In ferura per manus Johannis Ferro*ur* apud Alnewik' et hoc de iiii s. iiii d. In i sacco empto pro ferris equinis cariandis iiii d. In v lib. saponis emptis pro camera domini per manus Rogeri Hugges xix d. In locione pannorum lineorum per manus eiusdem vi d.

Probatur Summa ix li. xiiii s. v d. unde <in expensis forinsecis et gydorum v s. iii d.> In dono iii s. iiii d. <In empcionibus necessariorum iiii d.>

Providencia victualium In ix qr. frumenti emptis ad vi s. viii d. in partibus Scocie pro hospicio apud Gedworth lx s. In cariagio eiusdem iii s. ii d. In i pipa vini rubei empta apud Novum Castrum Cxiii s. iiii d. Et recipiuntur de dono domini de Nevyll' de stauro suo apud Bamburgh' viii barelli ferrers vini continentes xx sex. In expensis Willelmi Hakele missi pro vi barellis predictis usque Gedworth' querendis per i diem di. xii d. In iii equis et i homine conductis pro eisdem cariandis v s. vi d. In CCCiiii^{xx}x lag. cervisie emptis ad ii d. et xxx lag. cervisie ad iii d. facientibus viiiCxl lag. anglicas lxxii s. vi d. In xx lib. candel*e* coton*i* iii s. iiii d. In iiii vaccis emptis xliiii s. iiii d. In v carcosiis boum xlv s. iiii d. In xx cassis multonum xxx s. i d. In ii porcis x s. In sagimine albo pro coquina x d. In iii capriolis ii s. In lx aucis x s. In lii caponibus xiii s. x d. In xxx gallinis v s. In CCiiii^{xx}x pulcinis xxiiii s. ii d. In MDxx ovis vii s. vii d. In ii qr. salis albi xiii s. vi d. In i bus. farine avene xii d. In iiii porcellis ii s. viii d. In \ i qr. / i bus. ordei pro pulaillis v s. x d. In ii bus. frumenti emptis pro pitura aucarum xviii d. In ii bus. avene pro pitura pulaillorum viii d. In iiii^{xx}v oneribus eq*ui* de focali empto ad ii d. cum cariagio xiiii s. ii d. In vi qr. vi bus. carbonum emptis et cariatis vi s. In xlvi truss*es* feni emptis lxiii s. ii d. In CCiiii^{xx}vi thraves straminis emptis tam pro foragio quam pro lecto et stabulo xxxii s. In xlvii qr. ii bus. avene vi li. ix s. x d. ob. In xxiiii piscibus salsis xxiiii s. In i salmone xx d. In factura broche pro coquina ii d. In ii hominibus conductis pro iiii vaccis mactandis ix d. In hominibus conductis per Johannem Whithed' in officio pistrine pro flore faciendo et cariando per vices iii s. i d. In cariagio cervisie de villa in castrum de Gedworth' per manus eiusdem ii s. vii d. In ii barellis conductis pro cervisia inponenda viii d. In emendacione ii barellorum iiii d. In emendacione ostii boterie ii d. In mulier*e* conduct*a* pro pultria querenda per vices xiiii d. In x oneribus cirporum x d.

Probatur Summa xxxvii li. xvii s. ix d. ob.

Geddeworth' Fercula cena Cii Inde gentiles xxii fercula Furnitur Attameatur Die lune xiiii die Junii jantanti per viam in pane albo ii s. Buttellaria Vinum Expenduntur iii pich. de remanentia. Et expenditur de officio coquine de preempto. In feno et pane equino emptis per manus Walteri Holter' ii s. Item per manus Willelmi Page vii d. In expensis equ*orum* chariot*arum* per manus Willelmi Ferth' vi d. Et in ferura ii d. ob. Eodem die cenanti et pernoctanti apud Geddeworth' Panetria Furniuntur iiii qr. frumenti. Respondentur MC panes et expenduntur Cxxxviii panes videlicet in ferculis Cii reward*is* xi trencher*is* vii coquina ii liberacionibus certis iii liberacionibus incertis viii post prandium ii et tota nocte iii. Buttellaria Attameatur i pipa vini rubei continens xxvi sex. i pich. Inde expenduntur iiii sex. i pich. di. videlicet in ferculis i sex. ii pich. potacionibus in cameri*s* i sex. i pich. tota nocte ii pich. di. et potacionibus ad ostium i sex. Cervisia Expenduntur lxxiiii lag. di. de remanentia videlicet in ferculis xlviii lag. coquina iii lag. liberacionibus certis i lag. di. liberacionibus incertis iiii lag. cameris viii lag. et potacionibus x lag. Garderoba Expenduntur cera et species de precomputato et ii lib. candel*e* coton*i* de remanentia. Coquina Expenduntur i carcosium iii qr. boum vi casse i qr. multonum i capriolus xxvi pulcini de remanentia. Mareschalsia Foragium pro Cli equis et xlvi hakeneis de precomputato. Avena pro eisdem cum[7] vi bus. de r*ewardo* pro equis chariot*arum* et aliis equis domini xi qr. v bus. de remanentia.

Probatur Summa v s. iii d. ob.

Fercula CCxi Prandium Cxvi Cena iiii^{xx}xv Inde gentiles lii fercula Presentibus ad cenam comite Northumbr' et aliis Die martis xv die Junii ibidem Panetria Expenduntur CCCxii panes de remanentia videlicet in ferculis CCxi jant*aculo* vii reward*is* xxxiii trencher*is* xviii coquina x pro candellaria x liberacionibus certis iii liberacionibus incertis xii post prandium iiii et tota nocte iiii. Buttellaria Vinum Expenduntur vii sex. ii pich. di. de remanentia videlicet in ferculis iiii sex. ii pich. coquina ii pich. di. potacionibus in cameri*s* i sex. tota nocte iii pich. et potacionibus ad ostium iii pich. Cervisia Expenduntur Cxxx lag. di. de remanentia videlicet in ferculis C lag. coquine v lag. liberacionibus certis i lag. di. liberacionibus incertis vi lag. cameris viii lag. et potacionibus x lag. Garderoba Expenduntur cera et species de precomputato et iiii lib. candel*e* coton*i* de remanentia. Coquina Expenduntur ii carcosia iii qr. boum ix casse iii qr. multonum ii caprioli iii porcelli xvi auce i porcus xlvii pulcini iiiiC ova xxiii capones de remanentia. Mareschalsia Foragium pro Cli equis et xlv hakeneis de precomputato. Avena pro eisdem cum vi bus. de r*ewardo* xi qr. iiii bus. iii pec. de remanentia.

Summa nichil

In carpentari*o* conduct*o* per Johannem Waren*er* pro necessariis faciendis in officio pultrie per vices xv d. In carpentari*is* et aliis hominibus conductis pro diversis necessariis reparandis in officio avenarie per manus Ricardi Horton' cum portagio straminis mundacione domu*m* in castro reparacione formul*arum* et trestell*es* in aula et cameri*s* . . . . . cum iii seruris emptis in officio avenarie ix s. ii d. Et in expensis Willelmi Stotevill' Ricardi Horton' Johannis Waren*er* Johannis Whithed' cum v equis et i garcione euncium de London' usque Geddeworth' pro diversis providenciis et reparacionibus officiorum faciendis contra adventum domini a xv die Maii incipienti usque xiiii diem Junii per xxx dies ut patet per particulas compoti per Willelmum

[7] MS repeats 'cum'.

Stotevill' lxxv s. iiii d. ob. In vadiis Johannis Wynkels missi de Novo Castro usque Gedworth' x die Junii ix d.

Probatur Summa iiii li. vi s. vi d. ob. unde in reparacionibus necessariorum x s. v d.

Summa totalis infra et extra Clxxvii li. viii s. vi d. Probatur.

13 *Diet account for the household of Sir William Waleys at Glynde, Sussex, 2 November 1382 to 17 January 1383*

At the date of this account, Sir William Waleys held manors in Glynde, Hawkesden, and Patching, and the sub-manor of Bainden in Mayfield, all in Sussex, with interests in property at Thanington and Newenden, in Kent. Glynde was very much a home manor, probably still farmed by its lord in demesne in the 1380s, and it must be imagined that as well as the produce and animals noted as consumed in the household account, further goods were supplied directly from the estate or purchased by the bailiff for the household. The bailiff's accounts for the manor, of which four survive from the period 1368–73, show cheese, butter, milk, wheat, goslings, sea-fish, oysters, boars, pigs and barley, besides unspecified victuals, purchased by the bailiff and delivered to the household of Sir John Waleys, Sir William's father, when it resided at Glynde and elsewhere. Sir William Waleys acted as sheriff for Sussex in 1383 and on one subsequent occasion, also being returned as a Member of Parliament on five occasions and holding various other commissions.[1]

This account is written on the dorse of a single membrane containing a notarial instrument of 7 March 1349, exemplifying the sentence of the dean of Chichester in a case brought by the vicar and parishioners of Arlington, Sussex, against the executors of Master Richard de Sefford, a canon of Chichester, relating to a claim for a portion of the residue of the canon's estate for repairs to the fabric of the church of Arlington; together with an exemplification of letters of procuration, dated 15 November 1348, relating to the same case. The household account contains the diet entries for eleven weeks and was written in a single hand in at least four operations, probably writing the first three weeks, then the next two weeks, followed by a further block containing the next two weeks, and concluding with the four remaining weeks of the account. The expenses are set out in weekly

[1] N. Saul *Scenes from provincial life. Knightly families in Sussex 1280–1400* (Oxford, 1986) *passim*, but especially pp. 18–20, 161–2; R. F. Dell *The Glynde Place archives. A catalogue* (Lewes, 1964); for the estates, East Sussex RO MS GLY 19, GLY 1139; account rolls, MS GLY 1073–6.

paragraphs, starting on Sundays, with an entry for each day of the week. Items are usually entered in the order pantry, buttery, kitchen. There is no mention of stable expenses, although candles, associated elsewhere with stable accounts, do occur; and while some spices are purchased, there is no mention of a separate wardrobe. The account has no cash totals and there is no trace of auditing; but each week has marginal totals of the animals and poultry killed during the week for the household, and notes of corn expended in baking and brewing. The Latin of the accountant is striking for its irregular grammar, particularly the use of passive forms of verbs in an active sense, effectively as deponent verbs.[2]

East Sussex RO MS GLY 4B[1]

Expense domus domini Willelmi Waleys militis apud Glynde die dominica proxima post festum Simonis et Jude anno regni regis Ricardi secundi sexto
Furnitur v bus. frumenti. Brasiatur i qr. vi bus. brasii. Necat i juvenculam et i . . . . .ellum de stauro. Die dominica proxima post festum Simonis et Jude furnitur v bus. frumenti qui respondet vii^{xx} panes. Brasiatur i qr. vi bus. brasii ordei qui respondet $\text{iiii}^{\text{xx}}\text{x}$ galones servicie. Item in xxi lib. cere emptis ix s. vii d. ob. precium lib. v d. ob. Item in ii pissibus salsis emptis ii s. iiii d. Item in C allece empto xvii d. \ Item xx stokfysch[2] empti ii s. ix d.[3] / Die lune i porcellus necatus de stauro. Item in carnibus bovinis et ovinis emptis xvi d. Die martis totum de stauro. Die mercurii in pisse empto v d. Die jovis totum de stauro. Die veneris de stauro. Die sabati in pisse empto ii d. Item necat i juvenculam etatis iii annorum[4] de stauro.
. . . . . qr. frumenti. . . . . . qr. vi bus. brasii. Die dominica sequenti totum de stauro. Die lune \ furnitur i qr. frumenti qui respondet iiCxl panes. / i caponis necatus de stauro. Die martis necat i aucam de stauro. Die mercurii totum de stauro. Die jovis necat i aucam de exennio. Die veneris et die sabati in pisse empto v d. Item in xv clavis et i lib. de cepo pro candelis x s. precium clavi viii d. Item i qr. de cotyn iiii d. Brasiatur i qr. vi bus. brasii qui respondet C galones servicie.
Necat aprum[5] *iii porcos. Furnitur vi bus. frumenti.* Die dominica sequenti totum de stauro. Die lune necat pro lardario domini iii porcos. Item i multo necatus de empcione. Die martis furnitur vi bus. frumenti qui respondet

[2] I am grateful to Christopher Whittick for a discussion of the notarial instrument.

---

[1] Renumbered from 4A.
[2] MS 'sokfysch'.
[3] MS omits 'd.'
[4] MS obscure.
[5] MS 'aper'.

iiC et xi panes. Die mercurii de stauro. Die jovis de stauro. Die veneris in pisse empto viii d. Die sabati in pisse i d. ob. Item ante istum diem iii stokfysch expendiebatur et ii pisses salic*i*i de stauro incepti.
. . . . . aprum[6] *et iii porcos . . . . . i qr. frumenti. Brasiatur i qr. vi bus. brasii.* Die dominica proxima ante festum Katerine virginis i auca necata de stauro \ et i caponis. / Die lune totum de stauro. Die martis i caponis de stauro. Die mercurii in pisse empto v d. Et necat eodem die iii porcos de stauro ad lardarium. Die jovis furnitur i qr. frumenti qui respondet iiCxlvii panes. Necat i caponem. Die veneris in pisse empto iii d. ob. Die veneris in pepir et saffran emptis vi d. Et necat i aprum[7] de stauro. Item necat ii matrices de empcione. Brasiatur i qr. vi bus. brasii ordei qui respondet C<x> galones servicie.
Necat vi porcos et ii matrices ad lardarium et i porcellum fresclyng'. Furnitur i qr. frumenti. Die dominica sequenti i auca necata de stauro. Die lune totum de stauro. Die martis i caponis de stauro. Item in v bus. salis emptis iiii s. ii d. Die mercurii de stauro. Et necat iiii porcos ad lardarium. Die jovis necat i ca. . . . . de stauro. Die veneris i bos necatus ad lardarium. Die sabati necat ii porcos ad lardarium et i porcellum fresclyng'. Furnitur i qr. qui respondet iiClviii panes. Item necat ii matrices ad lardarium.
Necat iii matrices. Brasiatur i qr. vi bus. brasii. Die dominica sequenti necat i aucam de stauro. Die lune i caponis necatus de stauro. Die martis i caponis. Item necat iii matrices ad lardarium. Die mercurii de stauro. Die jovis ii \ capones / et i gall*ina* necati casa domina Sencler. Die veneris totum de stauro preter i stokfysch. Die sabati in pisse empto iii d. ob. Brasiatur i qr. vi bus. brasii qui respondet iiii^{xx} et x galones servicie.
Furnitur i qr. frumenti. Matrices necate iii. Brasiatur i qr. vi bus. brasii. Aucas[8] *v. Capones xi et i gallinam ante istum diem et necat ante istum diem xii matrices unde per . . . . .* Die dominica sequenti i auca necata de stauro. Die lune i caponis de stauro. Item i matrix necata de empcione. Die martis de stauro. Furnitur i qr. frumenti qui respondet iiClii panes. Die mercurii i stoffych de stauro. Item in pisse empto iii d. ob. Item in ovis i d. Die jovis in carnibus porcinis emptis i d. ob. Die veneris et die sabati i stokfych'. Item . . . . . piss*e* empt*o* vii d. ob. contra Quatuor Tempora. Brasiatur i qr. vi bus. brasii contra Natalem Domini qui respondet iiii^{xx}x galones servicie. Et necat ii matrices de empcione.
*Furnitur i qr. frumenti. Brasiatur i qr. vi bus. brasii. Porcellum i freschly*ng. *Matrices*[9] *ii. Aucas iii. Capones iii.* Die dominica proxima ante festum

[6] MS 'aper'.
[7] MS 'aper'.
[8] 'Aucas' etc. in right margin.
[9] 'Matrices' etc. in right margin.

Natalis Domini necat i aucam de stauro. Die lune necat i bidentem de stauro et i caponem. Die martis furnitur i qr. frumenti qui respondet iiClx panes. Brasiatur i qr. vi bus. brasii ordei qui respondet iiii^{xx}x galones[10] servicie. Die mercurii in vigilia Natalis Domini in pisse empto ix d. Necat i porcellum freschlyng' et i matricem de empcione. Item in ovis emptis ii d. Die jovis in festo Natalis Domini necat ii aucas et ii capones de stauro. Die veneris et die sabati ii stokfysch'.

Brasiatur i qr. vi bus. ordei. Furnitur i qr. frumenti. Porcellum i. Bidentem[11] *i. Aucam i. Capones ii. Gall*inam *i.* Die dominica sequenti necat i aucam de stauro. Die lune ii capones necati de stauro. Die martis necat i bidentem de empcione. Die mercurii de stauro. Die jovis totum de stauro preter i gall*inam*. Brasiatur i qr. vi bus. brasii ordei qui respondet iiii^{xx}xii galones servicie. Die veneris i stokfysch' de stauro. Die sabati in pisse empto iii d. Furnitur i qr. frumenti qui respondet iiClviii panes. Item necat i porcellum freschlyng' de stauro.

Bidentem[12] *i. Aucam i. Gallinas iiii.* Die dominica sequenti in pylyng' empto ii d. Item i auca de stauro. Die lune[13] i gallina de stauro. Die martis i gallina de stauro. Die mercurii totum de stauro. Die jovis i auca de stauro. Item ad sen*escallum* ii galline. Die veneris et die sabati i stokfysch' de stauro. Item pisse empt*o* freslyng' vi d. Item in sale i d. Item eodem die sabati necat i matricem de stauro.

Porcellum i. Furnitur i qr. frumenti. Porcellum[14] *i. Matricem i. Aucas ii. Gallinas* . . . Die dominica sequenti i auca de stauro. Die lune totum de stauro. Die martis i auca necata de stauro. Item necat i porcellum de stauro. Item i gallina de stauro. Die mercurii totum de stauro. Die jovis necat i aucam et i gallinam de stauro. Furnitur i qr. frumenti qui respondet iiClx panes. Die veneris et die sabati totum de stauro. Item in . . . . . empt*is* ii d. Item necat i matricem de stauro. Item in uno cade allecis rubii[15] empto per dominum precium vi s. viii d.

14 *Accounts for the household of Richard Mitford, Bishop of Salisbury, October 1406 to June 1407*

Richard Mitford had entered royal service as a clerk of the household under Edward III as early 1366, and rose to become one of the more senior

[10] MS omits 'galones'.
[11] 'Bidentem' etc. in right margin.
[12] In right margin.
[13] MS omits 'lune'.
[14] 'Porcellum' etc. in right margin.
[15] MS 'rubia'.

of the establishment under Richard II, acting as the King's secretary between 1385 and 1388, and suffering imprisonment at the hands of the Appellants in 1388. Richard II was initially unsuccessful in obtaining for him promotion to the episcopate, to the see of Bath and Wells in 1386, where Mitford was passed over in favour of Walter Skirlaw. With the King's assistance Mitford obtained the election to St David's in 1389, but the election was subsequently declared void by the pope. He secured the see of Chichester in 1390 and was translated to Salisbury in 1395, retaining an active connection with the government to the end of the reign. He remained Bishop of Salisbury until his death late in May 1407.[1]

The account that has survived for the final eight months of his life is one of the longest and most detailed extant for a medieval English bishop. His annual income was in excess of £1,000 and during the period of the account more than £600 was spent.[2] The document provides a detailed description of his expenditure and of the maintenance of his household, his visitors and guests, the conduct of business in his diocese and his relationship with the chapter of Salisbury,[3] his interests and pastimes, together with the ministrations of his physicians and the expenses of his funeral. The manuscript has the merit not only of including a lengthy diet account, recording the bishop's residence at his Wiltshire manors of Woodford and Potterne, with parts of the establishment maintained at Ramsbury, and in the palace at Salisbury; but also of containing an extensive, if incomplete, account of bulk purchases and wardrobe expenditure. These two elements, which were once probably separate documents, are now bound together in one volume.

The volume contains 80 large paper folios. It has no original cover and the whole account has been conserved, mounted and bound. Some of the leaves were missing prior to this work and others have become disorganised. Folios 1–8 and 10–67 contain diet accounts for the period 1 October 1406 to 11 June 1407, when Bishop Mitford's household was broken up, immediately after his funeral, and the remainder of its goods and administration subsumed within the household of Master Walter Mitford. Folios 9 and 68–80 contain the accounts for bulk purchases and wardrobe expenditure.

[1] E. F. Jacob *The fifteenth century 1399–1485* (Oxford, 1961) p. 271; C. Given-Wilson *The royal household and the king's affinity. Service, politics and finance in England 1360–1413* (London, 1986) pp. 175–83; *The Westminster Chronicle 1381–1394* ed. L. C. Hector and B. F. Harvey (Oxford, 1982) pp. 382, 412–13.

[2] C. C. Dyer, 'The consumer and the market in the later middle ages', *EconHR* 2nd series, 42 (1989) p. 306; *idem*, *Standards of living in the later middle ages. Social change in England c.1200–1520* (Cambridge, 1989) pp. 74–5.

[3] For the view from the side of the Dean and Chapter, *The register of John Chandler, Dean of Salisbury, 1404–17* ed. T. C. B. Timmins (Wiltshire Record Society, 39; 1984).

The order of the folios of this second part of the account is uncertain, although folios 75–9 must form a sequence.

The accounts were copied up from a number of sources and were written by a series of clerks, working on both the diet account and the section for bulk purchases simultaneously throughout the eight months. The original intention was that it should be an impressive document, and the first clerk wrote an elaborate heading to start the diet accounts and similar headings for some of the sections (e.g. *empciones frumenti* and *empciones boum*) of the account for bulk purchases. The first clerk was responsible for the first section of the diet account, including the marginal entries for *fercula* and visitors, up to and including 1 November. This clerk also wrote the daily summary paragraphs of cash expenditure by department that occur at the end of each day's entry, but these he wrote throughout the whole account; the summary paragraphs were clearly written on a different occasion to the text of the day's account and a markedly different ink was employed on some occasions. It was also quite common for another part of the daily account, the last section of the stable account, for hay and oats for horses away from the main place of residence, to be entered either subsequently by the clerk who was writing the text (for example, on 27 and 28 October), or by another clerk. One hand in particular occurs very frequently making this entry and it appears for the first time on 20–21 and 24–26 October. The impression is that this material was collated into the account often on a subsequent occasion. The large number of blank entries for the quantities of wine and candles throughout the account suggest that these sections, too, were also collated from another source that was not always available at the time the main text of the day's account was written. A third clerk wrote the diet entries from 2 November to 5 December. These three clerks wrote the remainder of the document, with the exception of entries between 17 February and 26 February in both the diet account and the account for bulk and wardrobe purchases, which are in the hand of another clerk.[4] At the end of the account an auditor examined the volume. His work can be seen in the *probatur* that is written against the total of cash expenditure each day, and in the presence of dots for calculation written in the margins of the account

[4] The sequence of clerks for the remainder of the account is: clerk 1, 6 Dec to 10 Dec; clerk 3, wages after 10 Dec to 20 Dec; clerk 1, 21 Dec to 10 Jan; clerk 3, 15 Jan to 7 Feb (clerk 1 wrote the wages after 20 Jan); clerk 1, 8 Feb (just after the start of the day) to 14 Feb; clerk 3, 15 and 16 Feb; clerk 4, 17 Feb to 26 Feb; clerk 3, 27 Feb to 9 Mar; clerk 1, 17 Mar to 5 Apr; clerk 3, 6 Apr to 17 Apr; clerk 1, 18 Apr to part way through 12 May; clerk 3, part of 12 May to part way through the pantry account for 2 Jun, with the exception of the kitchen, chandlery and stable entries on 27 May to 1 Jun, which are by clerk 1; clerk 1 from mid-way through the pantry account for 2 Jun to the end of the diet account and *preteria*.

for bulk purchases and wardrobe expenses. The work of writing up this latter account, however, although carried out in tandem with the diet account, was left incomplete.

British Library MS Harley 3755

[*f.2r*][1] Compotus hospicii domini Ricardi Sarum episcopi a primo die Octobris anno regni regis Henrici quarti post conquestum octavo usque eundem primum diem Octobris anno dicti regis nono et translacionis dicti domini episcopi anno undecimo
Wodeford' Fercula Gentiles xiii Valecti garciones xxx Summa ferculorum xliii
Extranii Daungen cum ii filiis suis magister W. Metford se viii° magister G. Creke se iii° magister J. Pedwelly se iiii° ii fratres cum famulo et alii xxiii
Die veneris primo Octobris Panteria Furniuntur per i talliam i qr. iiii bus. frumenti que respondent ad CCCvii panes. Et expenduntur lxviii panes unde pro ferculis xliii panes trencheris iiii liberacionibus v coquina vi canibus iii panes rewardis vii panes. Et remanent CCxxxix panes. Celarium Expenduntur iiii lag. vini de remanentia. Butillaria Expenduntur xxviii lag. cervisie de remanentia. Et remanent xvii lag. cervisie. Coquina Expenduntur l allec album de remanentia. Item iiii congri salcii de remanentia. In CC ostriis emptis et expensis iii d. In i congro recenti empto et i sole vi s. vi d. In ii soles ii soremulett*es* i codeling i gurnard et ii lopsters emptis et expensis vi s. In scrempes iiii d. In menues vii d. In lacte iii d. et expenditur. Item in expensis emptoris i d. Candelaria In xxvi lib. candelarum emptis iii s. et expenduntur ii lib. Stabulum Fenum pro iiii equis iii hakeneis de stauro. In prebenda eorundem ii bus. avenarum. Item fenum apud Sarum pro x equis i hakeneo de stauro. In prebenda eorundem v bus. avenarum de stauro ibidem.

Summa empcionum xiiii s. unde

Panteria Furniuntur i qr. iiii bus. frumenti que respondent ad CCCvii panes. Celarium Vinum de remanentia. Butillaria De remanentia. Coquina Empciones xiiii s. Candelaria De empcione. Stabulum Fenum avene de[2]
[*f.2v*] *Wodeford' Fercula Gentiles xxi Valecti garciones xxxix Summa ferculorum lx*

[1] The cover, f. 1, is a singleton, probably not now in its original place, although the outside is dirty as if it has been the cover for some time. There is one contemporary note, which is part of the account: '<Memorandum de xxxii \ li. / vi s. unde [blank] receptis de magistro Waltero Metford de burs*a* domini. Et de> Et de xx s. receptis de eodem per manus Nicholai Cap*e*ron'.'
[2] Followed by a blank space in MS.

Extranii magister W. Metford se viii^{o} Wynslow se iiii^{o} Laurencius Dru se vi^{o} dominus J. Lincoln se vi^{o} vicarius ville se ii^{o} et alii xxiii

Die sabbati secundo Octobris Panteria Expenduntur C panes unde pro ferculis xl panes trencheris vi liberacionibus iiii coquina ii canibus iii rewardis xxvi panes. Et remanent Cxxxix panes. Celarium Expenduntur v lag. vini de remanentia. Butillaria In vii coules emptis de Levesham continentibus Cii lag. cervisie precium cuiuslibet coule xviii d. x s. vi d. In xiii lag. cervisie emptis de eodem x d. In ii coules cervisie emptis de Milbury continentibus xxviii lag. cervisie precium coule xviii d. iii s. In ii coules emptis de eodem continentibus xxviii lag. cervisie precium coule xii d. ii s. In ii coules cervisie emptis de Johanne Broune continentibus xxviii lag. cervisie precium coule xviii d. iii s. In ix coules cervisie emptis de Ricardo Smyth' de Wodeford continentibus Cxxvi lag. cervisie precium cuiuslibet coule xviii d. xiii s. vi d. In vii lag. cervisie emptis de eodem iii d. Et expenduntur xxxviii lag. cervisie. Et remanent CCiiii^{xx}xiiii lag. cervisie. Coquina Expenduntur l scalpin de remanentia. In C allece albo empto et expenso ii s. Item expenduntur v pisces salcii de remanentia. In vii plais iiii soles ii mulett*es* ii bas*is* ii gurnard vi bremes et i soremulet emptis et expensis xi s. iiii d. In CC ostriis emptis et expensis iii d. In i trugth empt*o* et expens*o* iiii d. In menues emptis et expensis vi d. In expensis emptoris \ ii d. / Candelaria Expenduntur ii lib. candelarum de precomputato. Stabulum Fenum pro vii equis iii hakeneis de stauro. In prebenda eorundem iii bus. di. avenarum de stauro. Item fenum apud Sarum pro xviii equis iii hakeneis de stauro. In prebenda eorundem i qr. iii bus. avenarum de stauro.

Probatur Summa empcionum xlvii s. viii d. unde

Panteria De precomputato. Celarium Vinum de remanentia. Butillaria In CCCiiii lag. cervisie emptis xxxiii s. i d. Coquina Empciones xiiii s. vii d. Candelaria De precomputato. Stabulum Fenum de stauro. Avene de stauro.

Gentiles xvi Valecti garciones xl Summa ferculorum lvi

Extranii magister W. Metford se viii^{o} dominus R. Bussh' se vi^{o} rector de Alington se iii^{o} vicarius <W> ville se ii^{o} et alii xiiii. Necatur i bos. ii multones de stauro.[3]

Die dominica tercio Octobris Panteria Expenduntur C panes unde pro ferculis lvi panes trencheris iiii liberacionibus iiii coquina ii canibus vi rewardis xxvii panes. Et remanent xxxvi panes. Celarium Expenduntur iiii lag. vini de remanentia. Butillaria Expenduntur xl lag. cervisie. Coquina Expenduntur i qr. bovis de stauro remanenti ii casse multonum de remanentia. Item expenduntur iiii capones de remanentia. Item i qr. porci de remanentia. In i porco empto iii s. iiii d. et expenditur i qr. In i porcello

[3] 'Necatur' etc. in right margin.

empto et expenso vi d. In vii cuniculis emptis xxii d. et expenduntur iiii. In iiii pulcinis emptis vi d. et expenduntur iii. In i lag. vini acerbi empta et expensa viii d. In i lag. verjuc*e* empta[4] et expensa vi d. In i lag. cenapii empta ix d. In expensis emptoris i d. Itm expenduntur C ova de remanentia. Candelaria Expenduntur iii lib. candelarum de precomputato. Stabulum Fenum pro v equis ii hakeneis de stauro. In prebenda eorundem ii bus. avenarum de stauro. Item fenum apud Sarum pro xix equis iiii hakeneis de stauro. In prebenda eorundem i qr. ii bus. avenarum.

Probatur Summa empcionum viii s. ii d.

Panteria De precomputato. Celarium De remanentia. Butillaria De precomputato. Coquina Empciones viii s. ii d. Candelaria De precomputato. Stabulum Fenum de stauro. Avene de stauro.

[*f.3r*] *Gentiles xiiii Valecti garciones xxxiiii Summa ferculorum xlviii*
Extranii magister W. Metford se viii^{o} dominus R. Bussh' se iiii^{o} Becot se iii^{o} vicarius ville se ii^{o} et alii xiiii

Die lune iiii Octobris Panteria Furniuntur per i talliam i qr. iiii bus. frumenti que respondent ad CCCxviii panes. Et expenduntur iiii^{xx}x panes unde pro ferculis xlviii panes[5] trencheris v liberacionibus iiii coquina iii canibus viii panes rewardis xxii panes. Et remanent CClxii panes. Celarium Expenduntur iii lag. vini de remanentia. Butillaria Expenduntur xxxii lag. cervisie. Et remanent CCxxii lag. cervisie. Coquina Expenduntur i qr. bovis i cassa di. multonum de stauro. Item expenditur di. porcus de precomputato. In xxv columbellis emptis xi d. et expenduntur xx. In expensis emptoris i d. ob. Item expenduntur iii capones de remanentia ii pulcini de precomputato. \ In cep*is* iiii d. / Candelaria Expenduntur ii lib. candelarum de precomputato. Stabulum Fenum pro vii equis iiii hakeneis de stauro. In prebenda eorundem iii bus. pec. avenarum de stauro. Item fenum apud Sarum pro xviii equis iii hakeneis de stauro. In prebenda eorundem i qr. ii bus. avenarum de stauro.

Probatur Summa empcionum xvi d. ob.

Panteria Furniuntur i qr. iiii bus. frumenti que respondent ad CCCxviii panes. Celarium Vinum de remanentia. Butillaria De precomputato. Coquina Empciones xvi d. ob. Candelaria De precomputato. Stabulum Fenum de stauro. Avene de stauro.

Fercula Gentiles xiiii Valecti garciones xxx Summa ferculorum xliiii
Extranii magister W. Metford se vi^{o} ii fratres cum famulo et alii xiiii

Die martis v^{o} Octobris Panteria Expenduntur iiii^{xx} panes unde pro ferculis xliiii panes trencheris iiii liberacionibus v coquina iii canibus vi panes rewardis xviii panes. Et remanent Ciiii^{xx}ii panes. Celarium Expenduntur iii

[4] MS 'emta'.
[5] MS 'lag. cervisie'.

lag. vini de remanentia. Butillaria Expenduntur xxxii lag. cervisie. Et remanent Ciiii^{xx} lag. cervisie. Coquina Expenduntur i qr. bovis i cassa multonis de stauro. Item expenditur di. porcus de stauro. Item ii capones de remanentia xii columbelle v cuniculi iii auce de precomputato. Candelaria Expenduntur iii lib. candelarum de stauro precomputato. Stabulum Fenum pro ix equis v hakeneis de stauro. In prebenda eorundem iii bus. avenarum. Item fenum apud Sarum pro xviii equis iii hakeneis de stauro. In avenis pro eisdem i qr. ii bus.

Summa empcionum nichil

Panteria De precomputato. Celarium De remanentia. Butillaria De precomputato. Coquina De precomputato. Candelaria De precomputato. Stabulum Fenum de stauro. Avene de stauro.

[*f.3v*] *Wodeford Fercula Gentiles xviii Valecti garciones xxxvi Summa ferculorum liiii*

Extranii magister W.Metford se viii^{o} Bonham se iiii^{o} Prentis se vi^{o} dominus Andreas Acton' se vii^{o} i armiger ducis Ebor' se ii^{o} vicarius ville se iii^{o} et alii viii

Die mercurie vi^{o} Octobris Panteria Expenduntur C panes unde pro ferculis liiii panes trencheris iiii liberacionibus v coquina iiii canibus vi rewardis xxvii panes. Et remanent iiii^{xx}ii panes. Celarium Expenduntur iiii lag. vini de remanentia. Butillaria Expenduntur xl lag. cervisie. Et remanent Cxl lag. cervisie. Coquina Expenduntur l allec album de precomputato iii pisces salcii i salmon' salc*ius* de remanentia. In CC allece albo empto iiii s. et expenduntur l. In i salmone salcio empto et expenso xv d. In ii hakes salciis emptis viii d. In iii trught*es* emptis xii d. In ii humbres vi d. In menues x d. In lacte iiii d. et expenso. Candelaria Expenduntur iii lib. candelarum de stauro. Stabulum Fenum pro xxv equis v hakeneis de stauro. In prebenda eorundem i qr. ii bus. avenarum de stauro.

Probatur Summa empcionum viii s. vii d.

Panteria De precomputato. Celarium De remanentia. Butillaria De precomputato. Coquina Empciones viii s. vii d. Candelaria De precomputato. Stabulum Fenum avene de stauro.

Fercula Gentiles xxiiii Valecti garciones lv Summa ferculorum lxxix

Extranii magister W. Metford se viii^{o} dominus W. Langford se ix^{o} dominus W. Stormy se ix^{o} Laurencius Dru se vi^{o} Calston' se iiii^{o} magister Edward Prent' se vi^{o} J. Maundevile se iii^{o} rector de Alingt' se iii^{o} et alii xxii

Die jovis vii^{o} Octobris Panteria Furniuntur per i talliam i qr. vi bus. frumenti que respondent ad CCClv panes. Et expenduntur Cxx panes unde pro ferculis lxxix panes trencheris viii liberacionibus v coquina iiii canibus vi rewardis xviii panes. Et remanent CCCxvii panes. Celarium Expenduntur vii lag. cervisie de remanentia. Butillaria Expenduntur xlii lag. cervisie. Et remanent Cxviii lag. cervisie. Coquina Expenduntur i qr. bovis ii casse multonum de stauro. Item expenditur i porcus de stauro. Item vii capones <empti> de remanentia. Item iii auce de stauro. Item i signus de exennio. In iii qr. porci emptis ii s. ii d. et expensis. In ii porcellis emptis et expensis xiii d. In ii cuniculis emptis viii d. et expensis. In xxvii columbellis emptis et expensis xii d. Candelaria Expenduntur iiii lib. candelarum de precomputato. Stabulum Fenum pro xiiii equis iiii hakeneis de stauro. In prebenda eorundem v bus. di. avenarum de stauro.

Probatur Summa empcionum iiii s. xi d.

Panteria Furniuntur i qr. vi bus. frumenti que respondent ad[6] iiiClvi panes. Celarium Vinum de remanentia. Butillaria De precomputato. Coquina Empciones iiii s. xi d. Candelaria De precomputato. Stabulum Fenum de stauro. Avene de stauro.

[*f.4r*] *Fercula Gentiles x Valecti garciones xxv Summa ferculorum xxxv*
Extranii magister W. Metford se viii^{o} et alii x

Die veneris viii^{o} Octobris Panteria Expenduntur lx panes unde pro ferculis xxxv panes trencheris iiii liberacionibus[7] iii coquina iiii canibus viii rewardis vi panes. Et remanent CClvii panes. Celarium Expenduntur iiii lag. vini de remanentia. Butillaria Expenduntur xxviii lag. cervisie. Et remanent iiii^{xx}x lag. cervisie. Coquina Expenduntur l allec album de precomputato ii congri salcii de remanentia i trught de stauro. In iii congris salciis emptis iii s. v d. In C allece albo recenti empto et expenso ii s. In CCCC ostriis emptis et expensis vi d. In lacte iii d. In casio empto v d. In i trught empto xii d. \ et expenso. / In CCC allece albo empto vi s. In Ciiii^{xx}ii anguillis parvis ii s. xi d. et expensis. Candelaria Expenduntur iii lib. candelarum de stauro. Stabulum Fenum pro xiii equis v hakeneis de stauro. In prebenda eorundem v bus. avenarum de stauro.

Probatur Summa empcionum xvi s. vi d.

Panteria De precomputato. Celarium De remanentia. Butillaria De precomputato. Coquina Empciones xvi s. vi d. Candelaria De precomputato. Stabulum Fenum avene de stauro.

Apud Sarum

In vadiis Thome Ferro*ur* a primo die Octobris usque viii diem eiusdem utroque computato capientis per diem iii d. xxi d.

Item in vadiis Ferey pagetti senescalli a primo die Octobris usque viii diem eiusdem capientis inter se per diem iii d. ii s.

Item in vadiis Girkin' pagetti magistri Walteri Metford per iiii dies capientis per diem ii d. ob. viii d.

Item in vadiis pagetti cancellarii per iiii dies capientis per diem i d. ob. vi d.

6 MS omits 'ad'.
7 MS repeats 'lib.'

Item in vadiis Harding per vii <dies> primos dies Octobris capientis per diem i d. ob. x d. ob.

Probatur Summa vadiorum v s. ix d. ob.

Fercula Gentiles xiii Valecti garciones xxxi Summa ferculorum xliiii
Extranii uxor Bisle se iiii^{o} vicarius ville se ii^{o} et alii xii

Die sabbati ix^{o} Octobris Panteria Expenduntur lxxii panes unde pro ferculis xliiii panes trencheris iiii liberacionibus iiii coquina iii canibus vi rewardis viii panes. Et remanent Ciiii^{xx}v panes. Celarium Expenduntur iiii lag. vini de remanentia. Butillaria Expenduntur xxx lag. cervisie. Et remanent lx lag. cervisie. Coquina Expenduntur iiii^{xx} allec album ii congri di. salcii ii hakes salcii i salmon' salcius de precomputato. In ii congris salciis emptis ii s. viii d. In i lopster et i crabb' emptis xx d. et expensis. In iii trught*es* emptis et expensis xv d. In iii humbres emptis et expensis xi d. In menues iiii d. In lacte ii d. In ii hakes \ expensis / salciis emptis viii d. Item in expensis emptoris apud Sarum per iii vices iii d. Candelaria Expenduntur iii lib. candelarum de <re> precomputato. Stabulum Fenum pro xii equis iiii hakeneis de stauro. In prebenda eorundem iiii bus. avenarum de stauro.

Probatur Summa empcionum vii s. xi d.

Panteria De precomputato. Celarium Vinum de remanentia. Butillaria De precomputato. Coquina Empciones vii s. xi d. Candelaria De precomputato. Stabulum Fenum avene de stauro.

[*f.4v*] *Wodeford Fercula Gentiles xx Valecti garciones liiii Summa ferculorum lxxiiii*
Extranii priorissa de Ambisbur' se x^{o} Bonham se iiii^{o} prior de Ederose se vi^{o} rector de Alingt' se iii^{o} rector de Ufton' se iii^{o} rector de Pole se iii^{o} uxor Bisle se iii^{o} et alii extranii xxxi. Necantur i bos vii multones.[8]

Die dominica x^{mo} Octobris Panteria Expenduntur Cxxviii panes unde pro ferculis lxxiiii panes trencheris xi liberacionibus iiii coquina iiii canibus iiii rewardis xxxi panes. Et remanent lvii panes. Celarium Expenduntur vi lag. vini de remanentia. Butillaria Expenduntur l lag. cervisie de precomputato. Et remanent x lag. cervisie. Coquina Expenduntur i qr. \ di. / bovis i cassa multonis i porcus di. ii cigni de stauro. Item expenduntur ix capones de remanentia iiii auce de stauro. In di. carcosio vituli empto et expenso xviii d. In iii porcellis emptis et expensis xxii d. In xi caponibus emptis iiii s. v d. In vi pulcinis emptis viii d. In iii maribons emptis iii d. In x cuniculis emptis ii s. viii d. ob. et expenduntur vi. In i perdice empto et expenso ii d. In xvi larkes emptis et expensis iii d. In ii lib. dat*es* emptis vii d. In CCC ovis emptis xviii d. ob. et expenduntur C ova. In iiii lib. albe pinguedinis emptis iiii d. In xxiiii columbellis emptis et expensis xii d. In i lag. mellis empta x d. Candelaria In xxx lib. candelarum emptis iii s. ix d. et expenduntur v lib.

[8] 'Necantur' etc. in right margin.

Stabulum Fenum pro xii equis iiii hakeneis de stauro. In avenis pro eisdem vi bus. avenarum.

Probatur Summa empcionum xix s.[9] <. . .>[10] \ x / d.

Panteria De precomputato. Celarium Vinum de remanentia. Butillaria De precomputato. Coquina Empciones xvi s. i d. Candelaria Empciones iii s. ix d. Stabulum Fenum avene de stauro.

Fercula Gentiles xv Valecti garciones xxiii Summa ferculorum xxxviii Extranii viii

Die lune xi^{o} Octobris Panteria Furniuntur per i talliam i qr. iiii bus. frumenti que respondent ad CCCxviii panes. Et expenduntur iiii^{xx} panes unde pro ferculis xxxviii panes trencheris iiii liberacionibus iiii coquina iiii canibus iiii rewardis xxvi panes. Et remanent CCiiii^{xx}xv panes. Celarium Expenduntur iii lag. vini de remanentia. Butillaria In Cx lag. cervisie emptis de Croston' de Ambesbur' precium lag. i d. ob. deductis ix lag. cervisie de avantagio xii s. vii d. ob. In xxviii lag. cervisie emptis de eodem precium lag. i d. deductis inde ii lag. de avantagio ii s. ii d. In iiii coules cervisie emptis de Levesham continentibus lvi lag. cervisie precium coule xviii d. vi s. In ii coles emptis de eodem continentibus xxviii lag. cervisie precium coule x d. xx d. Et expenduntur xxvii lag. cervisie. Et remanent Ciiii^{xx}vi[11] lag. cervisie. Coquina Expenduntur di. qr. bovis di. porcus i cassa multonis de stauro. Item i caponis xii columbelle de precomputato. Candelaria Expenduntur iiii lib. candelarum de stauro. Stabulum Fenum pro xii equis iiii hakeneis de stauro. In avenis pro eisdem iiii bus. di.

Probatur Summa xxii s. v d. ob.

Panteria Furniuntur per i talliam i qr. iiii bus. frumenti que respondent ad iiiCxviii panes. Celarium Vinum de remanentia. Butillaria In CCxxii lag. cervisie emptis xxii s. v d. ob. Coquina Empciones[12] Candelaria De precomputato. Stabulum Fenum avene de stauro.

[*f.5r*] *Fercula Gentiles xiii Valecti garciones xxiiii Summa ferculorum xxxvii Extranii magister W. Metford se viii^{o} Latton' se iiii^{o} et alii extranii ix*

Die martis xii^{o} Octobris Panteria Expenduntur lxx panes unde pro ferculis xxxvii panes trencheris iiii liberacionibus iiii coquina ii canibus iiii rewardis xiiii panes. Et remanent CCxxv panes. Celarium Expenduntur iii lag. vini de stauro. Butillaria Expenduntur xxx lag. cervisie. Et remanent Clvi lag. cervisie. Coquina Expenduntur di. qr. bovis i cassa multonis i porcus de stauro. Item i caponis i auca de precomputato. In i lag. vini acerbi empta

9 Altered from 'xii s.'

10 'i' altered to 'x' and subsequently struck out.

11 Possibly 'Ciiii^{xx}vii'.

12 Followed by a blank space in MS.

vii d. Candelaria Expenduntur iiii lib. candelarum de stauro. Stabulum Fenum pro xiiii equis vi hakeneis de stauro. In avenis pro eisdem v bus. pec. avenarum de stauro.

Probatur Summa empcionum vii d.

Panteria De precomputato. Celarium Vinum de remanentia. Butillaria De precomputato. Coquina Empciones vii d. Candelaria De precomputato. Stabulum Fenum de stauro. Avene de stauro.

Fercula Gentiles xxii Valecti garciones xliii Summa ferculorum lxv
Extranii magister J. Haket se iiii° J.Metford se ii° Metford junior se ii° Latton' se iii° Goolde se iii° Schupton' se ii° et alii extranii xvi

Die mercurie xiii° Octobris Panteria Expenduntur iiii^{xx}xiiii panes unde pro ferculis lxv trencheris v liberacionibus iiii coquina v canibus vii panes rewardis viii panes. Et remanent Cxxxi panes. Celarium Expenduntur iiii lag. vini de remanentia. Butillaria Expenduntur xxxv lag. cervisie. Et remanent Cxxi lag. cervisie. Coquina Expenduntur C allec album de precomputato i piscis salcius de precomputato C scalpin de remanentia. Item i congrus salcius de remanentia. In CC ostriis emptis et expensis iii d. In ii thornebak*es* emptis et expensis xii d. In xiii floundres emptis et expensis ii s. ii d. In ii solis <emptis> et iiii mulett*es* et ii basis emptis et expensis ii s. In i congro recenti empto et expenso ii s. ii d. In v lag. lactis emptis v d. et expensis. In expensis emptoris i d. Candelaria Expenduntur iiii lib. candelarum de precomputato. Stabulum Fenum pro xxi equis iii hakeneis de stauro. In avenis pro eisdem v bus. di.

In vadiis Thome Ferro*ur* a xi° die Octobris illo die computato per iii dies sequentes xii d.

Item Forey a viii° die Octobris per vii dies capienti per diem i d. ob. x d. ob.

Item in vadiis pagetti senescalli hospicii per v dies pagetti Tydeme*r*ssh' per vii dies capiencium per diem inter se iii d. xviii d. ob.

Item in vadiis garcionis cancellarii per vii dies capientis per diem ii d. xiiii d.

Item in vadiis Thome Norman per iii dies capientis per diem ii d. vi d.

Probatur Summa empcionum xiii s. ii d. unde

Panteria De precomputato. Celarium Vinum de remanentia. Butillaria De precomputato. Coquina Empciones viii s. i d. Candelaria De precomputato. Stabulum Fenum de stauro. Avene de stauro. Vadia <iiii> \ v / s. i. . .

[*f.5v*] *Wodeford Gentiles xxi Valecti garciones xxxix Summa ferculorum lx*
Extranii magister J.Haket se iiii° More se ii° Metford se ii° Latton' se ii° rector de Alingt' se ii° Gore se ii° Schipton' se ii° et alii xiiii

Die jovis xiiii° Octobris Panteria Expenduntur iiii^{xx}ix panes. Et remanent xlii panes. Celarium Expenduntur iiii lag. vini de remanentia. Butillaria Expenduntur xxxiii lag. cervisie de precomputato. Et remanent iiii^{xx}viii lag. cervisie. Coquina Expenduntur di. qr. bovis i cassa di. multonum ii capones i pulcinus ii cuniculi i perdix xii columbelle de precomputato. In di. porco empto et expenso xx d. In i porcello empto et expenso vi d. In i gallo empto iiii d. In ii pulcinis emptis iii d. Item expenduntur l ova de precomputato. Candelaria Expenduntur iii lib. candelarum de precomputato. Stabulum Fenum pro xx equis de stauro. In prebenda eorundem v bus. avenarum de stauro.

Probatur Summa empcionum ii s. ix d.

Panteria De precomputato. Celarium Vinum de remanentia. Butillaria De precomputato. Coquina Empciones ii s. ix d. Candelaria De stauro. Stabulum Fenum avene de stauro.

Gentiles viii Valecti garciones xxiiii Summa ferculorum xxxii

Extranii rector de Alington' se iii^{o} Johannes Draper se ii^{o} et alii v

Die veneris xv Octobris Panteria Furniuntur i qr. iiii bus. frumenti que respondent ad CCCxiii panes. Et expenduntur lxx panes unde pro ferculis xxxii panes trencheris iii coquina ii canibus vii panes rewardis xxiiii panes. Et remanent CCiiii^{xx}v panes. Celarium Expenduntur iii lag. vini de remanentia. Butillaria Expenduntur xxvi lag. cervisie de remanentia. Coquina Expenduntur l allec album i congrus salcius iii hakes salcii de precomputato. Item l scalpin de remanentia. In CC ostriis emptis et expensis iii d. In ii mulett*es* ii basis et expensis iii s. ii d. In soles <emptis> ii plais i congro ii lopsters emptis iiii s. iiii d. et expenduntur ii solis ii lopsters. Et remanent i congrus i lopster. In C allece recenti empto ii s. et expenduntur l. Et remanent l allec recens. In v lag. lactis emptis et expensis v d. In casio empto v d. et expenso. In expensis emptoris <i d.> ob. Candelaria Expenduntur ii lib. candelarum de stauro. Stabulum Fenum pro viii equis iiii hakeneis de stauro. In prebenda eorundem[13] iii bus. di. de precomputato.

Probatur Summa empcionum x s. vii d. ob.

Panteria Furniuntur i qr. iiii bus. frumenti que respondent ad CCCxiii panes. Celarium Vinum de remanentia. Butillaria De precomputato. Coquina Empciones x s. vii d. ob. Candelaria De precomputato. Stabulum Fenum de stauro. Avene de stauro.

[*f.6r*] *Wodeford Fercula Gentiles xii Valecti garciones xxx Summa ferculorum xlii*

Extranii xiiii

Die sabbati xvi^{o} Octobris Panteria Expenduntur lxxv panes unde pro ferculis xlii panes trencheris iii liberacionibus iiii coquina iii canibus vii rewardis xx panes. Et remanent CCx panes. Celarium Expenduntur iiii lag. vini de remanentia. Butillaria Expenduntur xxxii lag. cervisie. Et remanent

[13] MS ‘eod”.

xxx lag. cervisie. Coquina Expenduntur l allec album de precomputato i congrus salcius C scalpin de remanentia xxv allec recens i stike anguillarum de precomputato. Item expenduntur de exhennio maioris Sarum viii bas*is* vi whiting*es* i sole iiii <ba> plais et ii lopsters. Item expenduntur l ova de precomputato. Item in C ostriis emptis et expensis i d. ob. In l allece recenti empto et expenso xii d. In ii lag. lactis ii d. In i lag. di. i pint cenapii emptis et expensis x d. ob. In i lag. verjuc*e* empta vi d. In ii lag. iii quart. i pynt vini acerby emptis xx d. Candelaria Expenduntur iii lib. candelarum de stauro precomputato. Stabulum Fenum pro xi equis xi hakeneis de stauro. In avenis pro eisdem iiii bus. di.

Probatur Summa empcionum iiii s. iiii d.

Panteria De precomputato. Celarium Vinum de remanentia. Butillaria De precomputato. Coquina Empciones iiii s. iiii d. Candelaria De precomputato. Stabulum Fenum avene de stauro.

Fercula Gentiles xvi Valecti garciones xxxv Summa ferculorum li

Extranii rector de Alingt' se iiii^{o} Wilmyngt' se ii^{o} magister Simon Best se ii^{o} et alii xiiii

Die dominica xvii^{o} Octobris Panteria Expenduntur Cx panes unde pro ferculis li trencheris v liberacionibus iiii coquina iii canibus vii rewardis xxxv panes. Et remanent C panes. Celarium Expenduntur iiii lag. vini de remanentia. Butillaria Expenduntur xxx lag. cervisie. Et nichil remanet. Coquina Expenduntur di. qr. bovis i cassa di. multonum de stauro. Item expenditur i qr. porci de precomputato. In i qr. bovis empto iii s. iiii d. In di. porco empto xx d. In iiii porcellis emptis xx d. et expenduntur ii. In vi caponibus emptis ii s. In vi pulcinis emptis viii d. In iiii cuniculis emptis xi d. et expenduntur ii. In xxvi columbellis emptis et expensis xi d. In expensis emptoris ob. Item expenduntur iiii capones viii pulcini l ova de precomputato. Item expenduntur iii auce de precomputato. Candelaria Expenduntur iiii lib. candelarum de precomputato. Stabulum Fenum pro xii equis iiii hakeneis de stauro. In avenis pro eisdem v bus.

Probatur Summa empcionum xi s. ii d. ob.

Panteria De precomputato. Celarium Vinum de remanentia. Butillaria De precomputato. Coquina Empciones xi s. ii d. ob. Candelaria De precomputato. Stabulum Fenum avene[14]

[*f.6v*] *Wodeford Fercula Gentiles xii Valecti garciones xxx Summa ferculorum xliii*

Extranii xiiii

Die lune xviii^{o} Octobris Panteria Expenduntur lxx panes unde pro ferculis xliiii panes trencheris iiii liberacionibus iiii coquina iii canibus vii rewardis viii panes. Et remanent xxx panes. Celarium Expenduntur iii lag. vini de

[14] Followed by a blank space in MS.

remanentia. Butillaria In vii coules cervisie emptis de Cooke continentibus Cxxxii lag. cervisie precium cuiuslibet coule xviii d. x s. vi d. In i coule empto de eodem continenti xiiii lag. cervisie xii d. Et expenduntur xxx lag. cervisie. Et remanent Cxvi lag. cervisie. Coquina Expenduntur i qr. bovis i cassa di. multonum de stauro. Item di. porcus de precomputato. Item expenduntur ii capones xii columbelle i cuniculus iii perdices iiii qualis iiii pulcini l ova de precomputato. Candelaria Expenduntur iiii lib. candelarum de precomputato. Stabulum Fenum pro xvi equis iiii hakeneis de stauro. In prebenda eorundem i qr. avenarum.

Probatur Summa empcionum xi s. vi d.

Panteria De precomputato. Celarium Vinum de remanentia. Butillaria In Cxlvi lag. cervisie emptis xi s. vi d. Coquina De precomputato. Candelaria De precomputato. Stabulum Fenum avene de stauro.

Gentiles xiii Valecti garciones xxxiii Summa ferculorum xlvi

Extranii rector de Alingt' se vii^{o} vicarius ville se iii^{o} et alii xviii

Die martis xix Octobris Panteria Furniuntur per i talliam ii qr. frumenti que respondent ad CCCCxxx panes. Et expenduntur iiii^{xx}vi panes unde pro ferculis xlvi panes trencheris iiii liberacionibus iiii coquina iii canibus iii rewardis xxvi panes. Et remanent CCClxxiiii panes. Celarium Expenduntur v lag. vini de remanentia. Butillaria Expenduntur xxxvi lag. cervisie. Et remanent iiii^{xx} lag. cervisie. Coquina Expenduntur di. qr. bovis i cassa di. multonum de stauro i porcus ii capones iiii pulcini de precomputato. Item l ova de precomputato. In i qr. bovis empto iiii s. In ii caponibus emptis viii d. In ii cuniculis emptis et expensis viii d.[15] In vii pullettis emptis xvi d. In expensis i d. Candelaria Expenduntur iii lib. candelarum de remanentia. Stabulum Fenum pro xvi equis iiii hakeneis de stauro. In prebenda eorundem i qr. avenarum. Item fenum apud Sarum pro x equis ii hakeneis de stauro. In prebenda eorundem iiii bus. avenarum de stauro.

Probatur Summa empcionum vi s. ix d.

Panteria Furniuntur ii qr. frumenti que respondent ad iiiiCxxx panes. Celarium Vinum de remanentia. Butillaria De precomputato. Coquina Empciones vi s. ix d. Candelaria De precomputato. Stabulum Fenum avene de stauro.

[*f.7r*] *Fercula Gentiles xx Valecti garciones xl Summa ferculorum lx*

Extranii magister W.Metford se viii^{o} magister J.Haket se vii^{o} magister J.Kymbell' se iiii^{o} magister J.Best se ii^{o} rector de Alingt' se ii^{o} vicarius ville se ii^{o} et alii xiiii

Die mercurie xx^{o} Octobris Panteria Expenduntur C panes unde pro ferculis lx trencheris vi liberacionibus v coquina v canibus iiii rewardis xx panes. Et remanent CClxxiiii panes. Celarium Expenduntur vi lag. vini de

[15] MS 'viiii d.' 8*d*. is required for correct addition.

remanentia. Butillaria Expenduntur xl lag. cervisie. Et remanent xl lag. cervisie. Coquina Expenduntur C allec album de precomputato. Item expenditur i piscis salcius de remanentia. Item iii congri salcii l scalpin de remanentia. In menues emptis et expensis xi d. In i lag. verjuc*e* empta vi d. et expensa. In expensis emptoris i d. In D ostre emptis et expensis vii d. ob. In lacte empto et expenso iiii d. In xxvi lib. candelarum emptis iii s. et expenduntur iiii lib. candelarum. Stabulum Fenum pro xx equis iiii hakeneis de stauro. In avenis pro eisdem i qr. iii bus. avenarum. Item fenum apud Sarum pro xii equis ii hakeneis de stauro. In prebenda eorundem v bus. avenarum de stauro. Item fenum pro xxx equis de cariagi*is* domini venientibus de Shirbo*ur*ne usque Pot*er*ne ante adventum domini. In prebenda ii qr. v bus.

Probatur Summa empcionum v s. v d. ob.

Panteria De precomputato. Celarium Vinum de remanentia. Butillaria De precomputato. Coquina Empciones v s. v d. ob. Candelaria De precomputato. Stabulum Fenum avene de stauro.

Fercula Gentiles xxviii Valecti garciones xliiii Summa ferculorum lxx

*Extranii decanus Sarum se ix^{o} magister H.Harburgh' se iiii^{o} W.Spens*er *se iii^{o} W.Warin se iii^{o} W.Walters se iii^{o} Wilmyngton' se ii^{o} Colingborne se ii^{o} Item iiii rectores extranii Item alii extranii xx*

Die jovis xxi Octobris Panteria Expenduntur Cxxx panes unde pro ferculis lxxi panes trencheris x[16] liberacionibus vii coquina vi panes canibus vi rewardis xxx panes. Et remanent Cxliiii panes. Celarium Expenduntur x lag. vini de remanentia. Butillaria In Cviii lag. cervisie emptis de Cruston de Aumbesbur' deductis inde viii lag. di. cervisie de avantagio precium lag. i d. ob. ix s. viii d. ob. In xxvii lag. cervisie emptis de eodem ii lag. de avantagio precium lag. i d. ii s. i d. In iiii coules cervisie emptis de Cooke continentibus lvii lag. cervisie precium cuiuslibet coule xviii d. vi s. <In> Et expenduntur lx lag. cervisie. Et remanent Clxxii lag. cervisie. Coquina Expenduntur i qr. bovis ii casse di. multonum di. porcus de precomputato. Item expenduntur ix capones de precomputato x pulcini i porcellus de precomputato. Item expenduntur ii cigni de remanentia. Item ix cuniculi de precomputato. In di. porco empto et expenso xviii d. In maribons emptis et expensis vi d. In xxii aucis emptis viii s. ii d. et expenduntur vi. In vi pullettis xiiii d. In iiii porcellis emptis et expensis xxii d. In v caponibus emptis ii s. In xxiiii columbellis emptis xii d. In expensis emptoris i d. ob. Item expenduntur viii perdices xxiiii columbelle Cl ova de precomputato. Candelaria Expenduntur iiii lib. candelarum de stauro. Stabulum Fenum pro xxxvi equis iiii hakeneis de stauro. In avenis pro eisdem ii qr. Item fenum apud Wodeford pro xi equis iii hakeneis de stauro. In avenis iiii bus.

[16] MS possibly 'ix', but 'x' is required for correct addition.

Item fenum pro vii equis ibidem. In prebenda iii bus. avenarum de precomputato.

Probatur Summa empcionum xxxiiii s. i d. unde

Panteria De precomputato. Celarium Vinum de remanentia. Butillaria In Ciiii^{xx}xii lag. cervisie xvii s. ix d. ob. Coquina Empciones xvi s. iii d. ob. Candelaria De precomputato. Stabulum Fenum avene de stauro.

[f.7v] Wodeford' Gentiles vii Valecti garciones xxiii Summa ferculorum xxx
Extranii R. Hunt se iii^{o} Tauke se ii^{o} et alii iiii

Die veneris xxii^{o}[17] Octobris Panteria Expenduntur lxiiii panes unde pro ferculis xxx panes trencheris iiii liberacionibus v coquina iii canibus viii rewardis xiiii panes. Et remanent iiii^{xx} panes. Celarium Expenduntur iiii lag. vini de remanentia. Butillaria Expenduntur xxviii lag. cervisie. Et remanent Cxxxiiii lag. cervisie. Coquina Expenduntur l scalpin iii congri salcii de remanentia. Item l allec album de precomputato. In xi plais i sole iiii mullett*es* iiii lopsteres et ii thornebak*es* emptis viii s. et expensis. In CCCC ostriis emptis et expensis vi d. In lacte iii d. In expensis i d. In i salmone salcio empto et expenso xv d. Candelaria Expenduntur iii lib. candelarum de stauro. Stabulum Fenum pro xii equis iiii hakeneis de stauro. In avenis pro eisdem vii bus. avenarum. Item fenum apud Sarum pro xxi equis iiii hakeneis de stauro. In prebenda eorundem <vi> \ ix / bus. avenarum de stauro.

Probatur Summa empcionum x s. i d.

Panteria De precomputato. Celarium Vinum de remanentia. Butillaria De precomputato. Coquina Empciones x s. i d. Candelaria De precomputato. Stabulum Fenum avene de stauro.

Gentiles xvii Valecti garciones xl Summa ferculorum lvii
Extranii Montacu se iii^{o} R. Hunt se vi^{o} Best cum socio suo et alii xiiii

Die sabbati xxiii^{o}[18] Octobris Panteria Expenduntur iiii^{xx} panes unde pro ferculis lvii panes trencheris v liberacionibus iiii coquina iiii canibus vii rewardis iii panes. Et nichil remanet. Celarium Expenduntur v lag. vini de remanentia. Butillaria Expenduntur xl \v / lag. cervisie. Et remanent iiii^{xx}ix lag. cervisie. Coquina Expenduntur l allec album de precomputato l scalpin de remanentia l merling de precomputato iii congri salcii de remanentia. In v bremes v mullet*es* ii basis et i whiting emptis et expensis vi s. vi d. In l allece recenti empto et expenso xii d. In cepis emptis et expensis iiii d. In farina avenarum vi d. In ii gurnard vi d. In lacte i d. In expensis emptoris ii d. et expenduntur. Candelaria Expenduntur iii lib. candelarum. Stabulum Fenum pro xii equis iii hakeneis de stauro. In avenis pro eisdem v bus. Item

[17] MS 'xxiii^{o}'.
[18] MS 'xxiiii^{o}'.

fenum apud Sarum pro xxi equis ii hakeneis de stauro. In avenis pro eisdem <vi> \ ix / bus. avenarum de stauro.

Probatur Summa empcionum ix s. i d.

Panteria De precomputato. Celarium Vinum de remanentia. Butillaria De precomputato. Coquina Empciones ix s. i d. Candelaria De precomputato. Stabulum Fenum avene de stauro.

[*f.8r*] *Wodeford Gentiles xxii Valecti garciones li Summa ferculorum lxxiii Extranii dominus Andreas Accon' chivaler se viii*^{o} *magister J. Shirbourne se ii*^{o} *et alii xxviii*

Die dominica xxiiii^{o} Octobris Panteria Furniuntur per i talliam i qr. vii bus. frumenti que respondent ad CCClxxiiii panes. Et expenduntur Cxxx panes unde pro ferculis lxxiiii panes trencheris vii liberacionibus iiii coquina vii canibus vii rewardis xxvii panes. Et remanent CCxliiii panes. Celarium Expenduntur viii lag. vini de remanentia. Butillaria In iiii coules cervisie emptis de Cooke continentibus lvi lag. cervisie precium coule xviii d. vi s. In ii coules cervisie emptis de eodem continentibus xxviii lag. cervisie precium coule xii d. ii s. In ii coules cervisie emptis[19] de Mulbury continentibus xxviii lag. cervisie precium coule xviii d. iii s. In xxviii lag. cervisie emptis apud Wodeford de filio prepositi de Wodeford iii s. Et expenduntur lxvi lag. cervisie. Et \ remanent / Clxiii lag. cervisie. Coquina In iii qr. bovis emptis xv s. <x> \ iii / d. Et expenduntur \ i qr. / di. iii casse multonum iiii capones vi pulcini vi auce de precomputato. In i porco empto iii s. iiii d. et expenditur di. In iiii porcellis emptis et expensis ii s. iiii d. In ii aucis xii d. In viii cuniculis emptis xx d. et expenduntur ii. In xii gallinis emptis ii s. vi d. In xxx columbellis emptis xiiii d. et expenduntur xii. In expensis emptoris ii d. Item expenduntur l ova de precomputato. Candelaria Expenduntur iiii lib. candelarum de stauro. Stabulum Fenum pro xviii equis apud Wodeford de stauro. In prebenda eorundem x bus. avenarum de stauro. Item fenum pro[20] xx equis apud Sarum et Pot*er*ne de stauro. In prebenda v bus. avenarum de stauro.

Probatur Summa empcionum xli s. v d. unde

Panteria Furniuntur i qr. vii bus. frumenti que respondent ad[21] iiiClxxiii. Celarium Vinum de remanentia. Butillaria In Cxl lag. cervisie xiiii s. Coquina Empciones xxvii s. v d.[22] Candelaria De precomputato. Stabulum Fenum avene de stauro.

Gentiles xvii Valecti garciones xxxv Summa ferculorum lii
Extranii Loring se vii^{o} *Wilesdon se vi*^{o} *Kymbell' se ii*^{o} *et alii xiiii*

[19] MS repeats 'In ii coules cervisie emptis'.
[20] MS omits 'pro'.
[21] MS omits 'ad'.
[22] MS altered from 'xxiii s.'

Die lune xxv Octobris Panteria Expenduntur C panes unde pro ferculis lii panes trencheris v liberacionibus iiii coquina iiii canibus vii panes rewardis xxviii panes.[23] Et remanent Cxliiii panes. Celarium \ In i lag. de malvesin empta apud Sarum xvi d. / Expenduntur vii lag. vini de remanentia. Butillaria Expenduntur xlviii lag. cervisie. Et remanent Cxv lag. cervisie. Coquina Expenduntur i qr. bovis ii casse di. multonum di. porcus de precomputato vi pulcini iii capones iiii cuniculi Cl ova \ de / precomputato xii columbelle de precomputato. Candelaria Expenduntur iiii lib. candelarum de stauro. Stabulum Fenum pro xxviii equis apud Wodeford de stauro. In prebenda ibidem ii qr. iiii bus. avenarum de stauro. Item fenum pro xl equis apud Sarum et Pot*er*ne de stauro. In prebenda ii qr. ii bus. avenarum de stauro.

Probatur Summa empcionum xvi d.

Panteria De precomputato. Celarium Vinum emptum xvi d. Butillaria De precomputato. Coquina Empciones[24] Candelaria De precomputato. Stabulum Fenum avene de stauro.

In vadiis Thome Ferrour apud Sarum a xv^{o} die Octobris usque xxvi diem eiusdem utroque computato capientis per diem iii d. ii s. ix d.

Item in vadiis Forey pagetti senescalli pagetti Tidemerssh' per idem[25] tempus capiens quilibet eorum per diem i d. ob. iiii s. i d. ob.

Item in vadiis Bathe garcionis T. Ferrour per idem tempus capientis per diem ii d. xxii d.

Item in vadiis pagetti cancellarii per viii dies capientis per diem i d. ob. xii d.

Item in vadiis Thome Norman per xii dies di. capientis per diem ii d. ii s. i d.

Item in vadiis pagetti Hulcot per xiii dies capientis per diem i d. ob. xx d.

Item in vadiis Thome Norman per ii dies cum equo suo in negociis domini xii d.

Item in vadiis Rogeri Baker apud Wodeford et alibi per <ix> \ xiii / dies pro providencia facienda pro adventu domini ii s. ii d.

In vadiis pagetti Nicholai Cap*er*on' apud Sarum per ii dies capientis per diem i d. ob. iii d.

Probatur Summa vadiorum xvi s. x d. ob.

[*f.8v*] *Gentiles xxii Valecti garciones <lxiii> \ xlii / Summa ferculorum lxiiii Extranii R. Hunt se iii^{o} rector de Alingt' se ii^{o} rector de Horston' se ii^{o} Daubeney se ii^{o} Kymbel' se ii^{o} Wilmyngt' se ii^{o} et alii xiiii*

Die martis xxvi^{o} Octobris domino existenti apud Wodeford in prandio et

[23] MS 'lag. cervisie'.

[24] Followed by a blank space in MS.

[25] MS 'eid''.

Horston' in cena Panteria Expenduntur Cxliiii panes de remanentia apud Wodeford' unde pro ferculis lxiiii panes trencheris iiii liberacionibus vii coquina vii rewardis xlii panes. Item in pane empto et expenso iii d. Celarium Expenduntur viii lag. vini de remanentia. Butillaria Expenduntur iiii^{xx} lag. cervisie de remanentia apud Wodeford. Et in rewardo facto famulis de Wodeford per senescallum xxxv lag. Item in cervisia empta apud Horston' ii s. viii d. Coquina Expenduntur i qr. di. bovis iii casse di. multonum de precomputato. Item expenduntur v cuniculi de precomputato. In xl columbellis emptis et expensis xx d. Item in focali empto apud Horston' \ per senescallum / ii s. iiii d. Camera In lect*is* conduct*is* vii d. Candelaria In candelis emptis et expensis vi d. Stabulum In feno et litera emptis apud Horston' pro liiii equis v s. iii d. In ii qr. avenarum emptis ibidem et expensis iiii s. ii d. Item fenum pro xxiii equis et iii cum iii carectis preter hospicium cum harnesio domini. In prebenda eorundem v bus. avenarum de precomputato.

Probatur Summa empcionum xvii s. v d. unde

Panteria In pane empto iii d. Celarium Vinum de remanentia. Butillaria In cervisia empta ii s. viii d. Coquina Empciones iiii s. Candelaria In candelis emptis vi d. Camera In lect*is* conduct*is* vii d. Stabulum Feno et litera v s. iii d. Avenis iiii s. ii d.

Poterne Gentiles xii Valecti garciones xxxiiii Summa ferculorum xlvi
Extranii R.Hunt se iii^{o} Daubeney se iiii^{o} et alii xxiiii

Die mercurie xxvii^{o} Octobris Panteria Furniuntur per i talliam i qr. vii bus. frumenti que respondent ad CCClxx panes. Expenduntur Cxx panes unde pro ferculis xlvi trencheris viii liberacionibus vii coquina x canibus xiiii panes rewardis xxxv panes. Et remanent CCl panes. Celarium Expenduntur v lag. vini de remanentia. Butillaria In Cxxiiii lag. cervisie emptis de Warener precium lag. i d. ob. deductis inde de avantagio x lag. cervisie xiiii s. iii d. In xxiiii lag. cervisie emptis de eodem precium lag. i d. ob. deductis inde de avantagio[26] ii lag. cervisie xxii d. In Cxvii lag. cervisie emptis de Shepherd precium lag. i d. ob. deductis inde ix lag. di. de avantagio xiii s. vi d. In l lag. cervisie emptis de eadem[27] precium lag. i d. deductis inde iiii lag. de avantagio iii s. x d. Et expenduntur xl lag. cervisie. Et remanent CClxxiiii lag. cervisie. Coquina Expenduntur C allec album i piscis[28] salcius de precomputato. Item expenduntur[29] ix congri salcii de remanentia. Item i salmon' salcius de precomputato. Item Cl scalpin de remanentia. Item xxv anguille salcie de stauro. In D ostriis emptis et expensis xiii d. In

[26] MS 'avvantagio'.
[27] MS 'eodem'.
[28] MS 'pic''.
[29] MS repeats 'Item exp''.

lacte iii d. et expenso. Item C ova de precomputato. Candelaria Expenduntur iiii lib. candelarum de precomputato. Stabulum Fenum pro liii equis de stauro. In avenis pro eisdem ii qr. v bus. avenarum de stauro.

Probatur Summa empcionum xxxiiii s. ix d. unde

Panteria Furniuntur i qr. vii bus. frumenti que respondent ad[30] CCClxx. Celarium Vinum de remanentia. Butillaria In CCCxv lag. cervisie xxxiii s. v d. Coquina Empciones xvi d. Candelaria De stauro. Stabulum Fenum avene de stauro.

[*f.11r*][31] *Poterne Gentiles xxi Valecti garciones lx Summa ferculorum lxi*
*Extranii Robertus Hunt se vi*º *et alii de custumariis domini de Poterne xxii*
Die jovis xxviiiº Octobris Panteria Expenduntur Cxx panes unde pro ferculis lxi panes trencheris v liberacionibus iiii coquina v canibus x rewardis xxxv panes. Et remanent Cxxx panes. Celarium Expenduntur iiii lag. vini de remanentia. Butillaria Expenduntur liiii lag. cervisie. Et remanent CCxx lag. cervisie. Coquina Expenditur i qr. bovis de precomputato. Item iiii casse di. multonum de stauro. Item expenduntur iiii capones vi galline de precomputato. In di. carcosio bovis empto vi s. et expenditur di. qr. In i apro empto xii s. viii d. et expenditur i qr. In iii porcellis emptis et expensis ii s. In iiii aucis emptis et expensis xvi d. In x gallinis[32] emptis xx d. In iiii caponibus emptis xvi d. In v pulcinis emptis vi d. In di. porco empto et expenso xviii d. In expensis emptoris ii d. In xxiiii columbellis emptis ix d. Candelaria Expenduntur iii lib. candelarum de precomputato. Stabulum Fenum pro xxxiiii equis v hakeneis de stauro. In avenis pro eisdem i qr. di. avenarum de stauro.

Probatur Summa empcionum xxvii s. xi d.

Panteria De precomputato. Celarium Vinum de remanentia. Butillaria De precomputato. Coquina Empciones xxvii s. xi d. Candelaria De stauro. Stabulum Fenum avene de stauro.

Gentiles xi Valecti garciones xxviii Summa ferculorum xxxix
Extranii R. Hunt et alii xiii
Die veneris xxixº Octobris Panteria Expenduntur iiii^xx panes unde pro ferculis xxxix panes trencheris iiii liberacionibus v coquina iii canibus x rewardis xix panes. Et remanent l panes. Celarium Expenduntur iiii lag. vini de remanentia. Butillaria Expenduntur xxxi lag. cervisie. Et remanent Ciiii^xxix lag. cervisie. Coquina Expenduntur \ de / scalpin Ciii. Congr*us* salci*us* de remanentia. In iii lag. lactis emptis et expensis iii d. In D ovis

[30] MS omits 'ad'.

[31] Folios 9 and 10 are two singletons, now bound out of sequence; f. 9 belongs with the bulk purchases at the end of the volume and in this edition appears before f. 68, while f. 10 contains diet entries for 3–6 November and has been appropriately placed in the chronological sequence.

[32] MS 'gall' and four minims.

emptis ii s. i d. In iiiiC allece albo empto vii s. In i pot de bremes et gurnard empto vii s. viii d. et expenditur di. In ii thornebak*es* emptis et expensis xviii d. In iiii casiis emptis et expensis ix d. Candelaria Expenduntur ii lib. candelarum de stauro precomputato. Stabulum Fenum pro xxvi equis vi hakeneis de stauro. In avenis pro eisdem i qr. ii bus. de stauro.

Probatur Summa empcionum xix s. iii d.

Panteria De precomputato. Celarium Vinum de remanentia Butillaria De precomputato. Coquina Empciones xix s. iii d. Candelaria De stauro. Stabulum Fenum avene de stauro.

[*f.11v*] *Poterne Gentiles x Valecti garciones xxv Summa ferculorum xxxv*
Extranii R. Hunt se iiii^{o} et alii ix

Die sabbati xxx Octobris Panteria Furniuntur per i talliam ii qr. frumenti que respondent ad CCCCi panes. Et expenduntur lxxv unde pro ferculis xxxv trencheris iii liberacionibus iiii coquina iiii canibus vi rewardis xxvi panes. Et remanent CCiiii^{xx}xvi panes. Celarium Expenduntur vi lag. vini de remanentia. Butillaria Expenduntur xxviii lag. cervisie. Et remanent Clxi lag. cervisie. Coquina Expenduntur C allec album l scalpin ii congri salcii de remanentia di. salmon' salcius de precomputato. Item expenditur di. pot piscis recentis de precomputato. In l allece recenti empto et expenso xv d. In i congro recenti ii s. et expenditur di. In cepis emptis et expensis viii d. In ii lag. cenapii emptis et expensis viii d. ob. Candelaria In lv lib. candelarum emptis vi s. x d. et expenduntur iii lib. Stabulum Fenum pro xxvii equis vi hakeneis de stauro. In avenis pro eisdem i qr. ii bus. de stauro.

Probatur Summa empcionum xi s. v d. ob. unde

Panteria Furniuntur ii qr. frumenti que respondent ad CCCCi panes. Celarium Vinum de remanentia. Butillaria De precomputato. Coquina Empciones iiii s. vii d. ob. Candelaria De stauro empto vi s. x d. Stabulum Fenum avene de stauro.

Gentiles xix Valecti garciones lii Summa ferculorum lxxi
Extranii R. Hunt se ii^{o} et alii de tenentibus domini xx

Die dominica ultimo die Octobris Panteria Expenduntur Cx panes unde pro ferculis lxxi panes trencheris vi liberacionibus v coquina v canibus vi rewardis xvii panes. Et remanent Ciiii^{xx}vi panes. Celarium Expenduntur xi lag. vini de remanentia. Butillaria Expenduntur lv lag. cervisie. Et remanent Cvi lag. cervisie. Coquina Expenduntur i qr. bovis iii casse di. multonum de stauro. Item expenditur i porcus de stauro. Item ii capones iiii galline de precomputato. In vi porcellis ii s. vi d. et expenduntur iii. In iiii aucis emptis et expensis xvi d. In iii gallinis emptis vi d. ob. In v pullettis emptis vii d. In DC ovis emptis ii s. vi d. In lx columbellis emptis xx d. et expenduntur xxiiii. In expensis emptoris i d. Item expenduntur iii perdices de stauro. Item expenduntur iii maulard*i* de rivera. Item CC ova de precomputato. Candelaria Expenduntur iii lib. candelarum de precomputato. Stabulum Fenum pro xxx equis iiii hakeneis de stauro. In avenis pro eisdem i qr. di. de stauro. In ferrura equorum apud Poterne in absencia Thome Ferour iiii d.

Probatur Summa empcionum ix s. <ii> \ vi / d. ob.

Panteria De precomputato. Celarium Vinum de remanentia. Butillaria De precomputato. Coquina Empciones ix s. ii d. ob. Candelaria De precomputato. Stabulum Fenum avene de stauro. Ferrura equorum iiii d.

[f.12r] Poterne

In vadiis domini David Nicholai Cap*er*on' per vii[33] dies apud Wodeford capiencium inter se per diem vi d. iii s. vi d.

In vadiis Roberti Baker et Javener de Coquina ibidem per idem tempus xvi d.

In vadiis Roberti Gale apud Shirbo*ur*ne et Pot*er*ne in absencia hospicii per xxvi dies capientis per diem i d. ob. iii s. iii d.

In vadiis Willelmi de Butill*aria* ibidem per idem tempus capientis per diem i d. ob. iii s. iii d.

Item in vadiis Galfridi Catour per ix dies di. apud Bristoll' Schirbo*ur*ne Pot*er*ne Canyng' et alibi in negociis domini capientis per diem vi d. iiii s. ix d.

In vadiis Johannis Brigge existentis apud Shirbo*ur*ne extra hospicium per xxi dies capientis per diem ii d. iii s. vi d.

In expensis Johannis Charet*er* garcionis sui cum chariett*a* domini et vii equis de Wodeford usque Shirbo*ur*ne pro harnesio hospicii ibidem querendo et rediundo cum carecta mane*rii* de Shirbo*ur*n usque Pot*er*ne eundo et rediundo per iiii dies x s. i d.

In expensis eiusdem cum chariett*a* et ii carectis de Pot*er*ne usque Shirbo*ur*ne et red*i*undo versus Pot*er*ne cum dictis ii carectis et equis una cum expensis carect*e* de Shirbo*ur*ne in red*i*undo per iii dies xx s. viii d.

Item in expensis eiusdem alia vice cum chariett*a* et equis usque Shirbo*ur*ne pro diversis neccessariis domini ibidem querendis et ducendis usque Pot*er*ne eundo et rediundo per iii dies vii s. iiii d.

Item in expensis eiusdem cum chariett*a* de Pot*er*ne usque Shirbo*ur*ne pro vino ibidem querendo eundo et rediundo per iii dies v s. ii d.

Item in expensis eiusdem cum charett*a* ibidem ult*ima* vice pro neccessariis hospicii ibidem querendis eundo et rediundo per iii dies iii s. viii d.

Item in ferrura equorum per eundem ad diversas vices ii s. vi d.

Item in xiiii charett*e* nal*es* emptis cum stipendiis fabri pro imposicione eorundem xiii d.

Item in i tal' empt*o* pro charietta ii d.

[33] MS 'ix'.

Item in pane equino et avenis emptis apud Shirbo*ur*ne per dictum Johannem ii s. i d.
Item in i homine conducto ad conducendum chariett*am* usque Pot*er*ne tempore infirmitatis dicti Johannis xii d.

Probatur Summa vadiorum et expensarum predictarum lxxiii s. iiii d.

Summa empcionum istius mensis cum vadiis et aliis expensis xxvi li. x s. i d. ob.

[*f.12v*] *Poterne*

Festum Omnium Sanctorum

Gentiles xxv Valecti garciones lxi Summa ferculorum iiii^{xx}*vi*
Extranii Rouse se vii^{o} *et alii xxxiii*

Die lune primo Novembris Panteria Expenduntur Cxl panes unde pro ferculis iiii^{xx}vi trencheris ix liberacionibus v coquina viii rewardis xxxii panes. Et remanent xlvi panes. Celarium Expenduntur x lag. vini de remanentia. Butillaria Expenduntur lxvi lag. cervisie. Et remanent xl lag. cervisie. Coquina In i carcosio bovis xx s. Expenduntur i qr. di. apri de stauro \ iiii casse multonum de stauro.[34] / Item i porcus de stauro. Item vii capones iiii galline de precomputato. Item i damus salcius de stauro. Item expenduntur iiii pulletti iiii pulcini de precomputato. In i carcosio vituli empto iii s. iiii d. In iii porcellis emptis xviii d. In ix caponibus emptis ii s. vii d. ob. In ix pullettis emptis xiii d. ob. In ii gallinis emptis iiii d. In alli*i*s emptis vi d. et expensis. Candelaria Expenduntur[35] lib. candelarum de precomputato. Stabulum Fenum pro xxxv equis de stauro. In prebenda i qr. i bus. avenarum de stauro.

Probatur Summa empcionum xxix s. v d.

Panteria De precomputato. Celarium Vinum de remanentia. Butillaria De precomputato. Coquina Empciones xxix s. v d. Candelaria De precomputato. Stabulum Fenum avene de stauro.

Gentiles xx Valecti garciones iiii^{xx} *Summa ferculorum C*
*Extranii ii capellani extranii et de tenentibus domini de Pot*er*ne Worton' et M*er*ston' cariantibus buscum de prece lii*

Die martis secundo Novembris Panteria Furniuntur per i talliam ii qr. frumenti de stauro que respondent de CCCCiiii panibus. Et expenduntur Ciiii^{xx} panes unde pro ferculis C trencheris v liberacionibus iiii coquine iiii canibus vi rewardis lx. Et remanent CClxx panes. Celarium Expenduntur ix lag. vini de stauro. Butillaria <Expenduntur> In Cxxiiii lag. cervisie emptis de Shepherde precium lag. i d. ob. deductis inde x lag. de avantagio xiii s. ix d. In xl lag. cervisie emptis de eadem precium lag. i d. deductis iii

[34] MS omits 'stauro'.
[35] Followed by a blank space in MS.

lag. de avantagio iii s. i d. In xlviii lag. cervisie emptis de Axford precium lag. i d. ob. deductis iiii lag. de avantagio v s. \ vi d. / In xx lag. cervisie emptis de eadem precium lag. i d. deductis <d> i lag. di. de avantagio xviii d. ob. In lix lag. cervisie emptis de Johanne Nassh' precium lag. i d. ob. deductis v lag. de avantagio vi s. ix d. In xxxviii lag. cervisie emptis de eodem precium lag. i d. deductis iii lag. de avantagio ii s. xi d. Et expenduntur iiii^{xx}x lag. cervisie. Et remanent CClxxix lag. cervisie. Coquina Expenduntur di. carcosium bovis viii casse multonum de stauro. Item ii capones i gallina xviii columbelle de precomputato. Candelaria Expend*i*tur[36] lib. candelarum de stauro. Stabulum Fenum pro xxxii equis de stauro. In prebenda i qr. avenarum de stauro.

Probatur Summa empcionum xxxiii s. vi d. ob.

Panteria Furniuntur ii qr. frumenti que respondent ad CCCCiiii panes. Celarium Vinum de remanentia. Butillaria In CCCxxix lag. cervisie xxxiii s. vi d. ob. Coquina Empciones[37] Candelaria De precomputato. Stabulum Fenum avene de stauro.

[f.10r][38] *Poterne Gentiles xix Valecti garciones xxxviii Summa ferculorum lvii*

Extranii Benton' Willelmus Roches uxor Merssh dominus Willelmus Elys et alii extranii vii

Die mercurie tercio Novembris Panteria Expenduntur Cvii panes unde pro ferculis lvii panes trencheris v liberacionibus iiii coquine[39] iii canibus vi rewardis xxxii. Et remanent Clxiii panes. Celarium Expenduntur v lag. vini de stauro. Butillaria Expenduntur xl lag. cervisie. Et remanent CCxxxix lag. cervisie. Coquina Expenduntur C allec album ii congri salcii C scalpyn ii pecie st*ur*jen de stauro. Item expenduntur viii brem*es* iiii gurnard de precomputato. \ In i pot piscis recentis x s. et expenso. / Item expenduntur C ova de precomputato. Candelaria Expenduntur iii lib. candelarum de precomputato. Stabulum Fenum pro xxvi equis de stauro. In prebenda eorundem <v h. . .> i qr. avenarum de stauro.

Probatur Summa empcionum x s.

Panteria De precomputato. Celarium De remanentia. Butillaria De precomputato. Coquina Empciones x s. Candelaria De precomputato. Stabulum Fenum de stauro. Avene de stauro.

Gentiles xix Valecti garciones lxxv Summa ferculorum iiii^{xx}xiiii

Extranii lxv de tenentibus domini <ven> de Canyng' Lavynton' et Chitue cariantibus buscum de prece

[36] Followed by a blank space in MS.

[37] Followed by a blank space in MS.

[38] f. 10 out of place in original.

[39] This hand sometimes uses a dative, rather than an ablative, following from 'pro'.

Die jovis iiii^{to} Novembris Panteria Expenduntur Cxl panes unde pro ferculis iiii^{xx}xiiii trencheris iiii liberacionibus v coquina[40] iii canibus vi rewardis xxviii panes. Et remanent xxiii panes. Celarium Expenduntur x lag. vini de stauro. Butillaria Expenduntur lxix lag. cervisie. Et remanent Clxx lag. cervisie. Coquina Expenduntur di. carcosium bovis <...> viii casse multonum i porcus de stauro. Item i caponis ii galline iiii auce ii porcelli de precomputato. In i car*cosio* bovis empto viii s. viii d. In i porco empto iii s. viii d. In ii caponibus emptis vii d. In ii gallinis emptis iiii d. In v wodecokk*es* emptis vii d. ob. In ii plovers emptis et expensis iii d. In alba piguedine empta iii d. Item expenduntur xviii columbelle de precomputato. Candelaria Expenduntur iiii lib. candelarum. Stabulum Fenum pro xviii equis v hakeneis de stauro. In prebenda eorundem i qr. i bus. avenarum de stauro.

Probatur Summa empcionum xiiii s. iiii d. ob.

Panteria De precomputato. Celarium De remanentia. Butillaria De precomputato. Coquina Empciones xiiii s. iiii d. ob. Candelaria De stauro. Stabulum Fenum avene de stauro.

[*f.10v*] *Poterne Gentiles ix Valecti garciones xxv Summa ferculorum xxxiiii Uxor Merssh' et alii extranii xii*

Die veneris v Novembris Panteria Furniuntur per i talliam ii qr. frumenti de stauro que respondent de CCCCxiiii panibus. Et expenduntur lxvi panes unde pro ferculis xxxiiii panes trencheris iii liberacionibus iiii coquine iii canibus vi rewardis xvi. Et remanent CCClxxi panes. Celarium Expenduntur iii lag. vini de stauro. Butillaria Expenduntur xxviii lag. cervisie. Et remanent Cxlii lag. cervisie. Coquina Expenduntur iii qr. allecis albi i congrus salcius iC scalpyn de stauro. In DCC ostriis emptis xiiii d. et expensis. In xviii piscibus salciis emptis xiii s. iiii d. In expensis emptoris apud le Wuys' per ii vices ii d. In i bus. farine avenarum xi d. In i bus. pisarum viridum empto viii d. Candelaria Expenduntur iii lib. candelarum de precomputato. Stabulum Fenum pro xii equis iiii hakeneis de stauro. In prebenda ibidem vi bus. avenarum.

Probatur Summa empcionum xvi s. iii d.

Panteria Furniuntur ii qr. frumenti que respondent ad iiiiCxiiii panes. Celare*r*' Vinum de remanentia. Butillaria De precomputato. Coquina Empciones xvi s. iii d. Candelaria De precomputato. Stabulum Fenum de stauro. Avene de stauro.

Gentiles xviii Valecti garciones xxxviii Summa ferculorum lvi
Extranii Metford Manger' et alii extranii viii

Die sabbati vi Novembris Panteria Expenduntur iiii^{xx}x panes unde pro ferculis lvi panes trencheris iiii liberacionibus iiii coquina iiii canibus vi

[40] Underlined in MS.

rewardis xvi panes. Et remanent CCiiii^{xx}i panes. Celarium Expenduntur iiii lag. vini de stauro. Butillaria Expenduntur xxxviii lag. cervisie. Et remanent Ciiii lag. cervisie. Coquina Expenduntur C allec album iii congri salcii C scalpyn i salmo salcius xxx roch*es* de stauro. In <i> \ iii / salmonibus <recentibus> \ salciis / vi s. In xx brem*es* v s. viii d. <iiii d.> et expensis. Candelaria Expenduntur iii <di. lib.> \ lib. di. / candelarum de precomputato. Stabulum Fenum pro xiiii equis iii hakeneis de stauro. In prebenda vii bus. avenarum de stauro.

Probatur Summa empcionum x s. viii d.

Panteria De precomputato. Celarium De remanentia. Butillaria De precomputato. Coquina Empciones x s. viii d. Candelaria De precomputato. Stabulum Fenum avene de stauro.

[*f.13r*] *Poterne Gentiles xxi Valecti garciones xlix Summa ferculorum lxxi*[41]
*Extranii magister Johannes Pedwell' Hauber*v*yle Metford Johannes Piers Castelton' et alii extranii xix*

Die dominica vii^{o} Novembris Panteria Expenduntur iiii^{xx}v panes unde pro ferculis lxxi panes trencheris v liberacionibus iiii coquine iiii canibus vi rewardis.[42] Et remanent Ciiii^{xx}xvi panes. Celarium Expenduntur vi lag. vini. Butillaria Expenduntur xliiii lag. cervisie. Et remanent lx lag. cervisie de precomputato. Coquina Expenduntur i qr. bovis v casse multonum di. porcus de stauro. Item ii capones ii galline iiii wodecokk*es* ii plovers de precomputato. In v porcellis emptis ii s. vi d. et expenduntur iii. In xxxvi caponibus emptis x s. ii d. et expenduntur iii. In iii plovers emptis iiii d. ob. In ii gallinis emptis v d. In DCC ovis emptis ii s. xi d. In i lag. cinapii empta vi d. In columbell*is* xii d. et expens*is*. Candelaria Expenduntur v lib. candelarum de precomputato. Stabulum Fenum pro xi equis iiii hakeneis de stauro. In prebenda ibidem vi bus. avenarum de stauro.

Probatur Summa empcionum xvii s. x d. ob.

Panteria De precomputato. Celarium Vinum de remanentia. Butillaria De precomputato. Coquina Empciones xvii s. x d. ob. Candelaria De precomputato. Stabulum Fenum avene de stauro.

Gentiles xxvii Valecti garciones <xx> lvi Summa ferculorum iiii^{xx}iii
*Extranii Hauber*v*yle Metford magister Johannes Pedwell' Johannes Piers et alii extranii xx*

Die lune viii Novembris Panteria Expenduntur Cxii panes unde pro ferculis iiii^{xx}iii trencheris vi liberacionibus iiii coquine iii canibus vi rewardis x. Et remanent iiii^{xx}iiii panes. Celarium Expenduntur iiii lag. vini de stauro. Butillaria Expenduntur lii lag. cervisie. Et remanent viii lag. cervisie. Coquina Expenduntur di. qr. bovis iiii casse multonum de stauro. Item ii

[41] MS totals 70, but 71 loaves were disbursed for *fercula* in the pantry account.
[42] MS blank; 5 loaves needed to total 90.

capones ii galline xviii columbelle ii plovers i wodecok iiii pulcini de precomputato. Candelaria Expenduntur iiii lib. di. candelarum de precomputato. Stabulum Fenum pro x equis iii hakeneis de stauro. In prebenda ibidem v bus. avenarum de stauro.

Summa empcionum nichil quia de precomputato

Panteria De precomputato. Celarium Vinum de remanentia. Butillaria Coquina Candelaria De precomputato. Stabulum Fenum avene de stauro.

[*f.13v*] *Poterne Gentiles xxii Valecti garciones xlvii Summa ferculorum lxix*
Magister Johannes Pedwell' se ii^{o} *et alii extranii xviii*

Die martis ix^{o} Novembris Panteria Furniuntur per i talliam i qr. vii bus. frumenti de stauro que respondent de CCCiiii^{xx}ii panibus. \ Et expenduntur Cx / unde pro ferculis lxix panes trencheris vi liberacionibus v coquine v canibus vi rewardis xix. Et remanent CCClvi panes. Celarium Expenduntur iiii lag. vini de stauro. Butillaria <Expenduntur> In Cxlii lag. cervisie emptis de Shepherde precium lag. i d. ob. deductis inde xii lag. cervisie xvi s. iii d. In xlvi lag. cervisie emptis de eadem precium lag. i d. deductis iiii lag. de avantagio iii s. vi d. In iiii^{xx}iiii lag. cervisie emptis de Warner precium lag. i d. ob. deductis inde vii lag. cervisie ix s. vii d. ob. In xxiiii lag. cervisie emptis de eodem precium lag. i d. deductis ii lag. de avantagio xxii d. In xxiii lag. cervisie emptis de Felicia Aas precium lag. i d. ob. deductis ii lag. de avantagio <xx d.> \ ii s. vii d. ob. / In xvii lag. cervisie emptis de Walssh' precium lag. i d. ob. ii s. i d. ob. In xl lag. cervisie emptis de Lucia Lavynton' precium lag. i d. ob. deductis iii lag. di. de avantagio iiii s. <xi d.> \ vii d. / In x lag. cervisie emptis de eadem precium lag. i d. ix d. <iii s. viii d.> Et expenduntur xl lag. cervisie. Et remanent CCClxxvii lag. cervisie. Coquina Expenduntur i qr. bovis iii casse di. multonum di. porcus de stauro. Item i caponis ii galline iii auce ii cuniculi de precomputato. In ii porcellis emptis et expensis xii d. Item expenduntur l ova de precomputato. Candelaria Expenduntur iiii lib. candelarum de stauro. In xl lib. candelarum emptis per Galfridum Catour v s. Stabulum Fenum pro xiiii equis iiii hakeneis. In prebenda ibidem i qr. i bus. avenarum de stauro.

Probatur Summa empcionum xlvii s. iii d. ob. unde

Panteria Furniuntur i qr. vii bus. frumenti que respondent ad iiiCiiii^{xx}ii panes. Celarium Vinum de remanentia. Butillaria In CCCiiii^{xx}vi lag. cervisie xli s. iii d. ob. Coquina Empciones xii d. Candelaria <De precomputato> De empcione v s. Stabulum Fenum avene de stauro.

Gentiles xviii Valecti garciones xxxix Summa ferculorum lvii
Extranii xiiii

Die mercurie x^{o} Novembris Panteria Expenduntur iiii^{xx}viii panes unde pro ferculis lvii panes trencheris vi liberacionibus v coquine ii canibus xii rewardis iiii. Et remanent CClxviii panes. Celarium Expenduntur iiii lag. vini de stauro. Butillaria Expenduntur xxxviii lag. cervisie. Et remanent

CCCxxxix lag. cervisie. Coquina Expenduntur C allec album iii congri salcii C scalpyn ii pecie st*ur*jon i salmo salcius xxx roches i perch de stauro. Item iiC <a> ova de precomputato. In v lag. lactis emptis v d. et expensis. Candelaria Expenduntur iiii lib. candelarum de precomputato. Stabulum Fenum pro xxvi equis ii hakeneis de stauro. In prebenda ibidem i qr. iiii bus. avenarum de stauro.

Probatur Summa empcionum v d. unde

Panteria De precomputato. Celarium Vinum de remanentia. Butillaria De precomputato. Coquina Empciones v d. Candelaria De stauro. Stabulum Fenum de stauro. Avene de stauro.

[*f.14r*] *Poterne Gentiles xix Valecti garciones xlviii Summa ferculorum lxvii Extranii xvii*

Die jovis xi Novembris Panteria Expenduntur Cxx panes unde pro ferculis lxvii trencheris vi liberacionibus v coquine iiii canibus xx panes rewardis xviii panes. Et remanent Cxlviii panes. Celarium Expenduntur iiii lag. vini de stauro. Butillaria Expenduntur xl lag. cervisie. Et remanent CCiiii^{xx}xix lag. cervisie. Coquina Expenduntur i qr. bovis iiii casse multonum iii qr. porci i exitus porci de stauro. Item i caponis ii galline iii auce de precomputato. In i porco empto ii s. x d. In ii porcellis emptis et expensis xi d. In iiii aucis emptis iiii s. iiii d. In v gallinis emptis xii d. In v woddcok*es* emptis et expensis vi d. ob. Candelaria Expenduntur iiii lib. candelarum de precomputato. Stabulum Fenum pro xx equis iiii hakeneis de stauro. In prebenda i qr. ii bus. avenarum de precomputato.

Probatur Summa empcionum ix s. vii d. ob.

Panteria De precomputato. Celarium Vinum de remanentia. Butillaria De precomputato. Coquina Empciones ix s. vii d. ob. Candelaria De precomputato. Stabulum Fenum de stauro. Avene de stauro.

Gentiles x Valecti garciones xxii Summa ferculorum xxxii Extranii xii

Die veneris xii Novembris Panteria Expenduntur lxvi panes unde pro ferculis xxxii trencheris ii liberacionibus iiii coquine[43] <exp> ii canibus xvi rewardis x. Et remanent iiii^{xx}ii panes. Celarium Expenduntur iiii lag. vini de stauro. Butillaria Expenduntur xxix lag. cervisie. Et remanent CClxx lag. cervisie. Coquina Expenduntur iii qr. allecis albi iii congri salcii l scalpyn di. salmo salcius i stok' de stauro. In CCxl allece albo empto iii s. vi d. In i pot piscis recentis empto continenti xiiii brem*es* viii gurnard et iii merlyng vii s. vi d. Et expenduntur vii brem*es* ii gurnard et ii merlyng. In viii lag. di. vini acerbi emptis iiii s. xi d. ob. In i lag. di. viridis sucsagii emptis x d. In i lag. di. mellis emptis xvi d. In expensis emptoris ii d. ob. In D ostriis emptis et expensis xii d. ob. Candelaria Expenduntur iiii lib.

[43] Underlined in MS.

candelarum de precomputato. Stabulum Fenum pro xxxiii equis iiii hakeneis de stauro. In prebenda ibidem ii qr. avenarum de precomputato.

Probatur Summa empcionum xix s. iiii d. ob.

Panteria De precomputato. Celarium Vinum de remanentia. Butillaria de recomputato. Coquina Empciones xix s. iiii d. ob. Candelaria De precomputato. Stabulum Fenum de stauro. Avene de stauro.

[*f.14v*] *Poterne Gentiles xviii Valecti garciones l Summa ferculorum lxviii Extranii Gawayn' se iiii*^{o} *magister Johannes Preston' se iii*^{o} *rector de Upton Robard' se ii*^{o} *et alii extranii xii*

Die sabbati xiii^{o} Novembris Panteria Furniuntur per i talliam ii qr. frumenti de stauro que respondent de CCClxvi panibus. Et expenduntur Cxx panes unde pro ferculis lxviii panes trencheris iiii liberacionibus v coquine iii canibus xx rewardis xx panes. Et remanent CCCxxviii panes. Celarium Expenduntur iiii lag. vini de stauro. Butillaria Expenduntur xliiii lag. cervisie. Et remanent CCxxvi lag. cervisie. Coquina Expenduntur C allec album iii congri salcii l scalpyn de stauro. Item expenduntur vii brem*es* vi gurnard et i merlyng de precomputato. In v lag. lactis emptis v d. In i lag. cinapii vi d. Candelaria Expenduntur v lib. candelarum de precomputato. Stabulum Fenum pro xxvi equis iiii hakeneis de stauro. In prebenda i qr. iiii bus. avenarum.

In vadiis Thome Ferro*ur* apud Remesbur' per xi dies precedentes capientis per diem iii d. ii s. ix d.

In vadiis Thome Norma*in* et Bath' ibidem per idem tempus capiens quilibet eorum per diem ii d. iii s. viii d.

In vadiis pagetti somerarii pagetti Tidemerssh' pagetti Cap*er*on' et Forrey pagetti domini per idem tempus v s. vi d.

Probatur Summa empcionum xii s. x d.

Panteria Furniuntur per i talliam ii qr. frumenti que respondent ad[44] CCClxvi. Celarium Vinum de remanentia. Butillaria De precomputato. Coquina Empciones xi d. Candelaria De precomputato. Stabulum Fenum de stauro. Avene de stauro. Vadia xi s. xi d.

. . .ntiles xxiii . . .lecti . . .rciones lx . . .ma ferculorum iiii^{xx}*iii*
. . . Wylmynton' se ii^{o} *. . .rle se ii*^{o} *. . .hannes Piers cum uxore se iiii*^{o} *. . .lrond' cum uxore se iiii*^{o} *. . . de Ufton' Robard' . . . . . alii extranii xxii*

Die dominica xiiii^{o} Novembris Panteria Expenduntur Cxxiiii panes unde pro ferculis iiii^{xx}iiii panes trencheris v liberacionibus iiii coquine iiii <coquine> canibus xvi rewardis xi. Et remanent CCiiii panes. Celarium Expenduntur vi lag. vini de stauro. Butillaria Expenduntur lii lag. cervisie. Et remanent Clxxiiii lag. cervisie. Coquina Expenduntur i qr. bovis iiii casse di. multonum iiii capones di. porcus de stauro. Item i qr. braum' de

[44] MS omits 'ad'.

stauro. In x multonibus emptis xvi s. viii d. et expenduntur iii. In x pullettis emptis xx d. In ii porcellis emptis[45] et expensis xi d. In ii cuniculis emptis et expensis v d. In xi wodecok*es* emptis xiii d. ob. et expensis. Candelaria Expenduntur v lib. candelarum de precomputato. Stabulum Fenum pro xxvi equis iiii hakeneis de stauro. In prebenda i qr. iiii bus. avenarum.

Probatur Summa empcionum xx s. ix d. ob.[46]

Panteria De precomputato. Celarium Vinum de remanentia. Butillaria De precomputato. Coquina Empciones xx s. <x> \ ix / d. ob. Candelaria De stauro. Stabulum Fenum de stauro. Avene de stauro.

[f.15r] Poterne Gentiles xix Valecti garciones xlv Summa ferculorum lxiiii
Extranii Parle se ii^{o} ii fratres Johannes Piers se iiii^{o} et alii extranii xvi

Die lune xv^{o} Novembris Panteria Expenduntur C panes unde pro ferculis lxiiii trencheris iiii liberacionibus iiii coquine iii canibus xv rewardis xiii. Et remanent Ciiii panes. Celarium Expenduntur iii lag. vini de stauro. Butillaria Expenduntur xxxviii lag. cervisie. Et remanent Cxxxvi lag. cervisie. Coquina Expenduntur[47] di. qr. bovis iii casse multonum di. porcus de stauro. Item i caponis ii galline de precomputato. Candelaria Expenduntur iiii lib. candelarum de precomputato. Stabulum Fenum pro vii equis iiii hakeneis de stauro. In prebenda iii bus. avenarum de precomputato.

Summa nichil quia de precomputato

Panteria De precomputato. Celarium Vinum de remanentia. Butillaria De precomputato. Coquina Empciones[48] Candelaria De stauro. Stabulum Fenum avene de stauro.

Gentiles xiiii Valecti garciones xxxviii Summa ferculorum lii
Extranii ix

Die martis xvi^{o} Novembris Panteria Expenduntur iiii^{xx}xii panes unde pro ferculis lii trencheris iiii liberacionibus iiii coquine ii canibus xv rewardis xv. Et remanent xii panes. Celarium Expenduntur ii lag. vini de stauro. Butillaria Expenduntur xxx lag. cervisie. Et remanent Cvi lag. cervisie. Coquina Expenduntur i qr. bovis iii casse di. multonum di. porcus de stauro. Item i caponis ii galline ii auce ii wodecok*es* vi columbelle de precomputato. \ In ii porcellis emptis et expensis xii d. In di. carcosio vituli xx d. et expenso. / Candelaria Expenduntur iii lib. \ di. / candelarum de precomputato. Stabulum Fenum pro vi equis iiii hakeneis de stauro. In prebenda iiii bus. avenarum de precomputato. Item fenum apud Remesbur'

[45] MS repeats 'empt''.
[46] MS amended; the arithmetic of the addition is obscure.
[47] MS repeats 'Expen''.
[48] Followed by a blank space in MS.

pro xviii equis iiii hakeneis de stauro. In avenis pro eisdem i qr. iii bus. avenarum de stauro.

Probatur Summa empcionum ii s. viii d.

Panteria De precomputato. Celarium Vinum de remanentia. Butillaria De precomputato. Coquina Empciones ii s. viii d. Candelaria De precomputato. Stabulum Fenum avene de stauro.

[*f.15v*] *Poterne Gentiles xiii Valecti garciones xxxviii Summa ferculorum li*
Extranii ii fratres et alii extranii viii

Die mercurie xvii° Novembris Panteria Per i talliam i qr. vii bus. frumenti de stauro que respondent de CCCli panibus. Et expenduntur C panes unde pro ferculis li panes trencheris iiii liberacionibus iiii coquine ii canibus xiiii panes rewardis xxv panes. Et remanent CClxiii panes. Celarium Expenduntur iii lag. vini de stauro. Butillaria Expenduntur xl lag. cervisie. Et remanent lxvi lag. cervisie. Coquina Expenduntur C allec album l allec <album> rubium i piscis salcius et di. ii congri salcii v stok' de stauro. Item viii roch*es* de stauro. Item C ova de precomputato. In D ostriis emptis ii s. i d. In iiii lag. lactis iiii d. In iii casiis emptis vi d. Candelaria Expenduntur iiii lib. candelarum de stauro. Stabulum Fenum pro vii equis iiii hakeneis de stauro. In prebenda iii bus. avenarum de precomputato. Item fenum apud Remesbur' pro xii equis i hakeneo de stauro. In prebenda eorundem v bus. avenarum de stauro.

Probatur Summa empcionum ii s. xi d.

Panteria Furniuntur i qr. vi bus. frumenti que respondent ad[49] CCCli panes. Celarium Vinum de remanentia. Butillaria De precomputato. Coquina Empciones ii s. xi d. Candelaria De precomputato. Stabulum Fenum avene de stauro.

Gentiles xiiii Valecti garciones xl Summa ferculorum liiii
Extranii viii

Die jovis xviii° Novembris Panteria Expenduntur Ciiii panes unde pro ferculis liiii panes trencheris iiii liberacionibus v coquine ii canibus xiiii panes.[50] Et remanent Clix panes. Celarium Expenduntur ii lag. vini de stauro. Butillaria Expenduntur xl lag. cervisie. Et remanent xxvi lag. cervisie de precomputato. Coquina Expenduntur di. qr. bovis iiii casse multonum iii qr. porci de stauro. Item iii auce v wodecok*es* ii plover*s* de precomputato. In ii porcellis emptis et expensis xii d. In iii gallinis emptis vi d. In iii wodecok*es* emptis iii d. In xii columbellis emptis et expensis iiii d. In expensis emptoris ii d. Candelaria Expenduntur iiii lib. candelarum de stauro. Stabulum Fenum pro iiii equis iiii hakeneis de stauro. In prebenda

49 MS omits 'ad'.
50 MS omits 25 loaves, possibly for rewards.

eorundem iii bus. avenarum de precomputato. Item fenum apud Remesbur' pro xiii equis i hakeneo de stauro. In avenis pro eisdem v bus. de stauro.

Probatur Summa empcionum ii s. iii d.

Panteria De precomputato. Celarium Vinum de remanentia. Butillaria De precomputato. Coquina Empciones ii s. iii d. Candelaria De stauro. Stabulum Fenum avene de stauro.

[*f.16r*] *Poterne Gentiles ix Valecti garciones xxxviii Summa ferculorum xlvii Extranii xii*

Die veneris xix Novembris Panteria Expenduntur iiii^{xx}ii panes unde pro ferculis xlvii panes trencheris iii liberacionibus v coquine ii panes canibus xiiii rewardis xi panes. Et remanent lxxvii panes. Celarium Expenduntur ii lag. vini de stauro. Butillaria Expenduntur xxvi lag. cervisie. Et nichil remanet. Coquina Expenduntur iii qr. allecis albi et l allec album i piscis salcius et di. i congrus salcius de stauro. In pisce recenti empto et expenso xi d. In DCC ostriis emptis xiiii d. et expenduntur iiiiC ostria. In iiii lag. lactis emptis iiii d. In i lag. crem' empta et expensa viii d. Candelaria Expenduntur iii lib. candelarum de stauro. Stabulum Fenum pro v[51] equis iiii hakeneis de stauro. In prebenda ibidem ii bus. di. avenarum de precomputato. Item fenum apud Remesbur' pro xiii equis i hakeneo de stauro. In avenis pro eisdem v bus. di. pec.

Probatur Summa empcionum iii s. i d.

Panteria De precomputato. Celarium De remanentia. Butillaria De precomputato. Coquina Empciones iii s. i d. Candelaria De stauro. Stabulum Fenum avene de stauro.

Gentiles xvi Valecti garciones xl Summa ferculorum lvi
Extranii domina de Cary se viii^{o} Paynell' se vi^{o} et alii extranii x

Die sabbati xx Novembris Panteria \ Furniuntur per i talliam i qr. iiii bus. frumenti de stauro que respondent ad[52] CCCxi panes. / Expenduntur Cxiiii panes unde pro ferculis lvi panes trencheris viii liberacionibus viii coquine ii canibus xii panes rewardis xxviii panes. Et remanent CClxxiiii panes. Celarium Expenduntur iii lag. vini de stauro. Butillaria In Cliiii lag. cervisie emptis de Shepherde precium lag. i d. ob. deductis inde xii lag. di. de avantagio xvii s. viii d. In xli lag. cervisie emptis de eadem[53] precium lag. i d. deductis inde iii lag. di. cervisie iii s. i d. ob. In xlix lag. cervisie emptis de Axford precium lag. i d. ob. deductis inde iiii lag. de avantagio v s. vi d. In xxiiii lag. cervisie emptis de eadem precium lag. i d. deductis inde ii lag. de avantagio xxii d. In l lag. cervisie emptis de Cardmaker' precium lag. i d. ob. deductis inde iiii lag. cervisie de avantagio v s. ix d. In xxiiii lag.

[51] MS 'iiiii'.
[52] MS omits 'ad'.
[53] MS 'eamdem'.

cervisie emptis de e*a*dem precium lag. i d. deductis inde ii lag. de avantagio xxii d. In xxxii lag. cervisie emptis de[54] Carlet' precium lag. i d. ob. deductis inde ii lag. di. cervisie iii s. <ii d.> \ viii d. / In xiiii lag. cervisie emptis de eadem precium lag. i d. deducta inde i lag. cervisie xiii d. Et expenduntur xlviii lag. cervisie. Et remanent CCCxl lag. cervisie. Coquina Expenduntur C allec album C rubium ii pisces salcii i congrus salcius iii stok' de stauro. In iiii brem*es* vii gurnard et vi merlyng emptis et expensis ii s. xi d. In iii congris recentibus emptis et i crabb' vi s. x d. In CCCCl welk*es* emptis et expensis xi d. In i bus. farine avenarum empto xi d. In i lag. i quart. cenapii emptis vii d. ob. In xiii allece recenti empto et expenso iii d. Candelaria Expenduntur v lib. candelarum de stauro. Stabulum Fenum pro xx equis iiii hakeneis de stauro. In prebenda ibidem i qr. ii bus. avenarum de precomputato. Item fenum apud Remesbur' de stauro pro xiii equis i hakeneo de stauro. In avenis v bus. di. pec.

In vadiis Thome Ferro*ur* apud Remesbur' per v dies precedentes capientis per diem iii d. xv d.

In[55] vadiis pagetti Tydemerssh' Forrey et pagetti Nicholai Cap*er*on' apud Rem*m*esbyry per v dies precedentes quilibet capiens per diem i d. ob. xxi d. ob.

Probatur Summa empcionum lv s. xi d. ob. unde

Panteria Furniuntur per i talliam <ii qr.> i qr. iiii bus. que respondent ad[56] iiiCxi panes. Celarium Vinum de remanentia. Butillaria In CCCiiii^{xx}viii lag. cervisie xl s. <x> \ v / d. ob. Coquina Empciones xii s. v d. ob. Candelaria De stauro. Stabulum Fenum de stauro. Avene de stauro. Vadia . . .ii s. ob.

[*f.16v*] *Poterne Gentiles xx Valecti garciones lii Summa ferculorum lxxii Extranii domina de Cary se viii^{o} et alii extranii xiiii*

Die dominica xxi Novembris Panteria Expenduntur Cxx panes unde pro ferculis lxxii trencheris viii liberacionibus vi coquine iiii canibus xiiii rewardis xvi. Et remanent Cliiii panes. Celarium Expenduntur iiii lag. vini de stauro. Butillaria Expenduntur l lag. cervisie. Et remanent CCiiii^{xx}x lag. cervisie. Coquina Expenduntur i qr. bovis i cassa di. multonum de stauro. Item i caponis i gallina iii auce i mallard*us* de precomputato. Item C ova de precomputato. Item ii exitus porcorum de stauro. In iiii porcellis emptis xxii d. et expenduntur ii. In ii gallinis emptis iiii d. In iiii wodecok*es* emptis iiii d. In xxxvi lark*es* emptis iiii d. Candelaria Expenduntur iiii lib. candelarum de stauro. Stabulum Fenum pro xxvi equis iiii hakeneis de stauro. In prebenda ibidem i qr. iiii bus. avenarum de stauro. Item fenum

[54] MS omits 'de'.

[55] Marginal note: 'P' N'' — ?'Per Nicholaum'.

[56] MS omits 'ad'.

apud Remesbur' pro xii equis i hakeneo de stauro. In prebenda eorundem v bus. di. pec. avenarum de stauro.

Probatur Summa empcionum ii s. x d.

Panteria De precomputato. Celarium Vinum de remanentia. Butillaria De precomputato. Coquina Empciones ii s. x d. Candelaria De stauro. Stabulum Fenum avene de stauro.

Gentiles xxii Valecti garciones xxxix Summa ferculorum lxi

Extranii domina de Cary se viii^{o} Johannes Piers cum uxore se iiii^{o} et alii extranii ix

Die lune xxii^{o} Novembris Panteria Expenduntur Cxxiiii panes unde pro ferculis lxi panes trencheris viii liberacionibus vii coquine iiii canibus xiiii rewardis xxx panes. Et remanent xxx panes. Celarium Expenduntur v lag. vini de stauro. Butillaria Expenduntur xliiii lag. cervisie. Et remanent CCxlvi lag. cervisie. Coquina Expenduntur i qr. bovis i cassa multonis i exitus porci de stauro. Item expenduntur i caponis ii pulcini xxxvi lark*es* de precomputato. Candelaria Expenduntur iiii lib. candelarum de stauro. Stabulum Fenum pro xxiii equis iiii hakeneis de stauro. In prebenda ibidem i qr. iii bus. avenarum de precomputato. Item fenum apud Remesbur' pro xiii equis i hakeneo de stauro. In avenis pro eisdem iiii bus. di. pec. de stauro.

Summa nichil

Panteria De precomputato. Celarium Vinum de remanentia. Butillaria De precomputato. Coquina Empciones[57] Candelaria De stauro. Stabulum Fenum de stauro. Avene de stauro.

[*f.17r*] *Poterne Gentiles xxvi Valecti garciones xlix Summa ferculorum lxxv*

Extranii domina de Cary se viii^{o} Johannes Piers se iiii^{o} et alii extranii xvi

Die martis xxiii^{o} Novembris Panteria Furniuntur per i talliam ii qr. v bus. frumenti de stauro que respondent de Dxxx panibus. Et expenduntur Cxl panes[58] unde pro ferculis lxxv trencheris x liberacionibus vii coquine v canibus xiiii panes <Et remanent> rewardis xxvii panes. Et remanent CCCCxx panes. Celarium Expenduntur iiii lag. vini de stauro. Butillaria Expenduntur xlviii lag. cervisie. Et remanent Ciiii^{xx}xviii lag. cervisie. Coquina Expenduntur di. qr. bovis i cassa di. multonum. Item ii capones ii pulcini iii auce ii porcelli de precomputato. Candelaria Expenduntur v lib. candelarum de stauro. Stabulum Fenum pro xxiii equis iiii hakeneis de stauro. In prebenda i qr. ii bus. avenarum de precomputato. Item fenum apud Remesbur' pro xiii equis i hakeneo de stauro. In prebenda eorundem v bus. di. pec. de stauro.

Panteria Furniuntur ii qr. v bus. frumenti que respondent ad Dxxx panes.

[57] Followed by a blank space in MS.

[58] 138 loaves disbursed.

Celarium Vinum de remanentia. Butillaria De precomputato. Coquina Empciones nichil. Candelaria De stauro. Stabulum Fenum de stauro. Avene de stauro.

Gentiles xx Valecti garciones xliii Summa ferculorum lxiii

Extranii domina Cary se viii^{o} Johannes Piers cum uxore se iiii^{o} rector de Alynton' se ii^{o} Castelton' et alii extranii xiii

Die mercurie xxiiii^{o} Novembris Panteria Expenduntur Cxxii panes unde pro ferculis lxiii trencheris x liberacionibus vii coquine iii canibus xiiii rewardis xxv panes. Et remanent CCiiii^{xx}xviii panes. Celarium Expenduntur v lag. vini de stauro. Butillaria Expenduntur xliiii lag. cervisie. Et remanent Cliiii lag. cervisie. Coquina Expenduntur Cl allec album l rubium ii pisces salcii et di. de stauro. Item Cl ova de precomputato. Item expenduntur i congrus recens de precomputato et vi roch*es* de stauro. In iiii lag. lactis emptis et expensis iiii d. In iii casiis emptis vi d. In DCCC ovis emptis iii s. iiii d. In vii ollis luteis emptis pro alba pinguedine imponenda ix d. Candelaria Expenduntur iiii lib. candelarum de stauro. Stabulum Fenum pro ix equis v hakeneis de stauro. In prebenda eorundem vi bus. avenarum de precomputato. Item fenum apud Remesbur' pro xiii equis i hakeneo de stauro. In avenis pro eisdem v bus. di. pec. avenarum de stauro.

Probatur Summa empcionum iiii s. xi d.

Panteria De precomputato. Celarium Vinum de remanentia. Butillaria De precomputato. Coquina Empciones iiii s. xi d. Candelaria De stauro. Stabulum Fenum avene de stauro.

[*f.17v*] *Poterne Gentiles xxvii Valecti garciones lv Summa ferculorum iiii^{xx}ii*

Extranii decanus Sarum se xii^{o} domina de Cary se viii^{o} Blakbourne cum i clerico regis se iiii^{o} rector de Alyngton' rector de Ufton' Robard et alii extranii xii

Die jovis xxv Novembris Panteria Expenduntur Cxlviii panes unde pro ferculis iiii^{xx}ii panes trencheris xii liberacionibus x coquine v canibus xxii rewardis xvii panes. Et remanent Cl panes. Celarium Expenduntur viii lag. vini de stauro. Butillaria Expenduntur lx lag. cervisie. Et remanent iiii^{xx}xiiii lag. cervisie. Coquina Expenduntur i qr. bovis iii casse di. multonum de stauro. Item ii capones i gallina vi pulcini iii auce de precomputato. Item expenduntur C ova de precomputato. In ii aucis emptis vii d. In iii porcellis emptis et expensis xiiii d. In iiii caponibus emptis xvi d. In xi gallinis emptis xx d. In v wodecok*es* emptis et expensis v d. In vi cuniculis emptis xviii d. et expenduntur iiii <d.> cuniculi. In xvi lark*es* emptis et expensis ii d. In expensis emptoris ii d. Candelaria Expenduntur v lib. candelarum de stauro. Stabulum Fenum pro xxv equis v hakeneis de stauro. In prebenda eorundem i qr. iiii bus. avenarum de precomputato. Item fenum apud Remesbur' pro xiii equis i hakeneo de stauro. In avenis pro eisdem v bus. di. avenarum de stauro.

Probatur Summa empcionum vii s.
Panteria De precomputato. Celarium Vinum de remanentia. Butillaria De precomputato. Coquina Empciones vii s. Stabulum Fenum avene de stauro.
Gentiles xi Valecti garciones xxiii Summa ferculorum xxxiii
Extranii viii
Die veneris xxvi Novembris Panteria Expenduntur lxx panes[59] unde pro ferculis xxxiii trencheris iiii liberacionibus vi coquine ii canibus xvi rewardis xv panes. Et remanent iiii^{xx} panes. Celarium Expenduntur iii lag. vini de stauro. Butillaria Expenduntur xxiiii lag. cervisie. Et remanent lxx lag. cervisie. Coquina Expenduntur C allec album l rubium ii pisces salcii i congrus salcius de stauro. In di. congro recenti empto xvi d. In viiC ostriis emptis xiiii d. et expenduntur iiiC ostria. In CCCC welk*es* emptis x d. In iii lag. lactis emptis et expensis iii d. In ii bus. pisarum viridum emptis xvi d. In i bus. farine avenarum empto xi d. Candelaria Expenduntur iiii lib. candelarum de stauro. Stabulum Fenum pro[60] xvi equis iiii hakeneis de stauro. In prebenda eorundem i qr. <ii bus.> avenarum de precomputato. Item fenum apud Remesbur' pro xiii equis ii hakeneis de stauro. In prebenda eorundem v bus. di. pec.
Probatur Summa empcionum v s. x d.
Panteria De precomputato. Celarium Vinum de remanentia. Butillaria De precomputato. Coquina Empciones v s. x d. Candelaria De stauro. Stabulum Fenum de stauro. Avene de stauro.
[*f.18r*] *Poterne Gentiles xx Valecti garciones xliii Summa ferculorum lx<x>iii*
Extranii Johannes Pyll' Johannes Metford extranii xiiii
Die sabbati xxvii^{o} Novembris Panteria Furniuntur per i talliam ii qr. frumenti de stauro que respondent de CCCCi panibus. Et expenduntur Cxx panes <Et remanent> unde pro ferculis lxiii trencheris iiii liberacionibus vi coquine iii canibus xvi panes rewardis xxvi panes. Et remanent CCClxii panes.[61] Celarium Expenduntur iii lag. vini de stauro. Butillaria Expenduntur xl lag. cervisie. Et remanent xxx lag. cervisie. Coquina Expenduntur C allec album l rubium ii pisces salcii vi stok' Cl ova de precomputato. Item di. congrus recens CCCC ostria CC welk*es* de precomputato. Candelaria Expenduntur v lib. candelarum de stauro. Stabulum Fenum pro xxiiii equis v hakeneis de stauro. In prebenda i qr. ii bus. avenarum de precomputato.

[59] 76 loaves disbursed; overall remainder correct for 70.
[60] MS omits 'pro'.
[61] The addition cannot be followed.

Item fenum apud Remesbur' pro xiii equis ii hakeneis de stauro. In avenis pro eisdem v bus.

Summa[62]

Panteria Furniuntur ii qr. frumenti que respondent ad CCCCi panes. Celarium Vinum de stauro. Butillaria De precomputato. Coquina Empciones[63] Candelaria De stauro. Stabulum Fenum de stauro. Avene de stauro.

Gentiles xxii Valecti garciones xlviii Summa ferculorum lxx
Extranii xx

Die dominica xxviii° Novembris Panteria Expenduntur C<xl>\xx/viii panes[64] unde pro ferculis lxx panes trencheris vi liberacionibus iiii coquine iii canibus xiiii rewardis xxix panes. Et remanent CCxxxiiii panes. Celarium Expenduntur v lag. vini de stauro. Butillaria <Expend*un*tur> In iiii^{xx} lag. cervisie emptis de Warn*er* precium lag. i d. ob. deductis inde vi lag. di. ix s. iii d. In xx lag. cervisie emptis de eodem deducta i lag. de cervisia precium lag. i d. xix d. Et expenduntur lv lag. cervisie. Et remanent lxxiiii lag. cervisie. Coquina Expenduntur i qr. bovis i cassa di. multonum iiii exitus porcorum de stauro. Item expenduntur iii auce i caponis i gallina l ova de precomputato. Item ii cuniculi de precomputato. In iiii porcellis emptis et <expen*sis*> xxi d. et expenduntur ii. In di. porco empto et expenso xx d. In iii wodecok*es* emptis et expensis iii d. Candelaria Expenduntur iiii lib. candelarum de stauro. Stabulum Fenum pro xviii equis v hakeneis de stauro. In prebenda eorundem i qr. avenarum de precomputato. Item liberantur chariett*e* domini versus Vell' vi bus. avenarum. Item liberantur pro i equo senili existenti apud le Devys' ad medicandum iiii bus. avenarum. Item fenum apud Remesbur' pro xiii equis i hakeneo de stauro. In avenis pro eisdem v bus. di. pec. avenarum de stauro.

Probatur Summa empcionum xiiii s. vi d. unde

Panteria De precomputato. Celarium Vinum de remanentia. Butillaria In Clvi lag. cervisie emptis x s. x d. Coquina Empciones iii s. viii d. Candelaria De precomputato. Stabulum Fenum avene de stauro.

[*f.18v*] *Poterne Vigilia Sancti Andree Gentiles xii Valecti garciones xxx Summa ferculorum xlii*
Extranii mareschallcius domini de Lovell' se ii° Johannes Connolde ii fratres minores et alii extranii x

Die lune xxix Novembris Panteria Expenduntur iiii^{xx}xii panes unde pro ferculis xlii panes trencheris iii liberacionibus vi coquine ii canibus xvi \ rewardis xxiii. / Et remanent Cxlii panes. Celarium Expenduntur iii lag.

62 Followed by a blank space in MS. No cash expenses this day.

63 Followed by a blank space in MS.

64 Details are given only of the disbursement of 126 loaves.

vini de stauro. Butillaria Expenduntur xxxiiii lag. cervisie. Et remanent xl lag. cervisie. Coquina Expenduntur C allec album l allec rubium ii pisces salcii viii stok' de stauro. Item CC ova de precomputato. Candelaria Expenduntur v lib. candelarum de stauro. Stabulum Fenum pro xvi equis iiii hakeneis de stauro. In prebenda i qr. avenarum de precomputato. Item fenum apud Remesbur' pro xiiii equis i hakeneo de stauro. In avenis pro eisdem v bus. di. avenarum de stauro.
Panteria De precomputato. Celarium Vinum de remanentia. Butillaria De precomputato. Coquina De precomputato. Candelaria De stauro. Stabulum Fenum avene de stauro.
Gentiles xxii Valecti garciones xliiii Summa ferculorum lxvi
Extranii xviii
Die martis ultimo Novembris Panteria Expenduntur Cxx panes[65] unde pro ferculis lxvi trencheris vi liberacionibus vi coquine iiii canibus xvi <Et remanent> rewardis xxix. Et remanent xxii panes. Celarium Expenduntur iiii lag. vini de stauro. Butillaria Expenduntur xl lag. cervisie de[66] precomputato. Coquina Expenduntur i qr. bovis i cassa di. multonum i qr. porci iiii exitus porcorum de stauro. Item i caponis i gallina ii cuniculi et iii wodecok*es* de precomputato. Candelaria Expenduntur iiii lib. candelarum de stauro. Stabulum Fenum pro xiiii equis iiii hakeneis de stauro. In prebenda eorundem vi bus. avenarum de precomputato. Item fenum apud Remesbur' pro xiiii equis i hakeneo de stauro. In avenis pro eisdem v bus. avenarum de stauro.
Panteria De precomputato. Celarium Vinum de remanentia. Butillaria De precomputato. Coquina Empciones nichil. Candelaria De stauro. Stabulum Fenum avene de stauro.

Summa empcionum istius mensis xvii li. iiii s. v d.

[*f.19r*] *Poterne Gentiles xvi Valecti garciones xxxv Summa ferculorum li*
Extranii xiiii
Die mercurii primo Decembris Panteria Furniuntur per i talliam ii qr. frumenti de stauro que respondent de CCCiiii^{xx}xii panibus. Et expenduntur Cviii panes unde pro ferculis li trencheris iiii liberacionibus v coquine ii canibus xvi rewardis xxx. Et remanent CCCvi panes. Celarium Expenduntur iiii lag. vini de stauro. Butillaria <Expend*un*tur> In Cxlii lag. cervisie emptis de Sheph*er*d' precium lag. i d. ob deductis inde xii lag. cervisie xiii s. <xi> \ viii / d. In xxv lag. cervisie emptis de eadem precium lag. i d. deductis inde ii lag. de avantagio xxiii d. In l lag. cervisie emptis de Nassh' precium lag. i d. ob. deductis inde iiii lag. de avantagio v s. ix d. In x lag. cervisie emptis de eodem ix d. In xxvi lag. cervisie emptis de Ryle precium

[65] 127 loaves disbursed.
[66] MS repeats 'de'.

lag. i d. ob. deductis inde ii lag. de avantagio iii s. In xii lag. cervisie emptis de eodem xi d. In li lag. cervisie emptis de Axford precium lag. i d. ob. deductis inde iiii lag. de avantagio v s. iiii d. ob. Inde expenduntur xxxvi lag. cervisie. Et remanent CCiiii^{xx} lag. cervisie. Coquina Expenduntur C allec album l rubium ii pisces salcii vi stok' l welk*es* Cl ova de stauro et precomputato. In iiii lag. lactis emptis et expensis iiii d. In CC ovis emptis et expensis x d. Candelaria Expenduntur iiii lib. candelarum de stauro. Stabulum Fenum pro xii equis iii hakeneis de stauro. In prebenda eorundem vii bus. avenarum de precomputato. Item fenum apud Remesbur' pro xiiii equis i hakeneo de stauro. In avenis pro eisdem v bus. di.

Probatur Summa empcionum xxxii s. vi d. \ ob. / unde

Panteria Furniuntur ii qr. frumenti que respondent ad CCCiiii^{xx}xii panes. Celarium Vinum de remanentia. Butillaria In CCCxvi lag. cervisie emptis xxxi s. iiii d. ob. Coquina Empciones xiiii d. Candelaria De stauro. Stabulum Fenum avene de stauro.

[f.19v] Poterne Gentiles xx Valecti garciones xxxvi Summa ferculorum lvi
Extranii ii fratres et alii xii

Die jovis secundo Decembris Panteria Expenduntur Cxxiiii panes unde pro ferculis lvi trencheris v liberacionibus vi coquine iiii canibus xiiii rewardis xxxix panes. Et remanent Ciiii^{xx}ii panes. Celarium Expenduntur iiii lag. vini de stauro. Butillaria Expenduntur xlv lag. cervisie. Et remanent Clxi lag. cervisie.[67] Coquina Expenduntur i qr. bovis ii casse multonum iiii exitus porcorum de stauro. Item expenduntur i caponis ii galline i mallard*us* ii cuniculi ii wodecok*es*. In ii porcellis emptis et expensis xii d. In iiii aucis emptis xvi d. et expenduntur iii auce. In v caponibus emptis xx d. In vi pulcinis emptis vi d. In iiii gallinis emptis viii d. In ii wodecok*es* emptis ii d. In expensis emptoris ii d. ob. Candelaria Expenduntur v lib. candelarum de stauro. Stabulum Fenum pro x equis v hakeneis de stauro. In prebenda eorundem vii bus. avenarum de precomputato. Item fenum apud Remesbur' pro xiiii equis iii hakeneis de stauro. In avenis v bus. di.

Probatur Summa empcionum v s. vi d. ob.

Panteria De precomputato. Celarium Vinum de remanentia. Butillaria De precomputato. Coquina Empciones v s. vi d. ob. Candelaria De stauro. Stabulum Fenum avene de stauro.

Gentiles xi Valecti garciones xxi Summa ferculorum xxxii
Extranii xiiii

Die veneris tercio Decembris Panteria Expenduntur iiii^{xx}iiii panes unde pro ferculis xxxii <l> trencheris iii liberacionibus iiii coquine iii canibus xiiii rewardis xxviii panes. Et remanent iiii^{xx}viii panes.[68] Celarium

67 The arithmetic cannot be followed.
68 The arithmetic cannot be followed.

Expenduntur ii lag. vini de stauro. Butillaria Expenduntur xxviii lag. cervisie. Et remanent Cxxxiii lag. cervisie. Coquina Expenduntur C allec album l rubium i piscis salcius et di. vii stok' l welk*es* x roch*es* de stauro. In iiii lag. lactis emptis iiii d. In xxvi leng*es* et mul*ettes* emptis xiii s. iiii d. Candelaria Expenduntur iiii lib. candelarum de stauro. Stabulum Fenum pro xii equis iiii hakeneis de stauro. In prebenda eorundem i qr. avenarum de precomputato. Item fenum apud Remesbur' pro xiiii equis i hakeneo de stauro. In avenis pro eisdem[69] v bus.

Probatur Summa empcionum xiii s. viii d.

Panteria De precomputato. Celarium Vinum de remanentia. Butillaria De precomputato. Coquina Empciones xiii s. viii d. Candelaria De stauro. Stabulum Fenum avene de stauro.

[f.20r] Poterne Gentiles xx Valecti garciones xli Summa ferculorum lxi
Extranii Willelmus Stok' se iiii^o parcarius de Hamstede et alii xii

Die sabbati iiii° Decembris Panteria <Expend*un*tur> Furniuntur per i talliam ii qr. frumenti de stauro que respondent de CCCCvi panibus. Et expenduntur Cxx panes unde pro ferculis lxi panes trencheris v liberacionibus vi coquine ii canibus xiiii rewardis xxxii. Et remanent CCClxxiiii panes. Celarium Expenduntur iiii lag. vini de stauro. Butillaria Expenduntur xlii lag. cervisie. Et remanent iiii^xx^xi lag. cervisie. Coquina Expenduntur l allec album C rubium i piscis salcius et di. viii stok' de stauro. Item C ova de precomputato. Item vi roch*es* de stauro. Candelaria Expenduntur v lib. candelarum de stauro. Stabulum Fenum pro x equis iii hakeneis de stauro. In prebenda eorundem vii bus. avenarum de precomputato. Item fenum apud Remesbur' pro xiii equis iii hakeneis de stauro. In avenis pro eisdem v bus. avenarum de stauro.

Summa nichil quia de precomputato

Panteria Furniuntur ii qr. frumenti de stauro. Celarium Vinum de remanentia. Butillaria De precomputato. Coquina Empciones[70] Candelaria De stauro. Stabulum Fenum avene de stauro.

Gentiles xxi Valecti garciones xlv Summa ferculorum lxvi
Extranii Johannes Piers cum uxore se iiii° et alii xiiii

Die dominica v Decembris Panteria Expenduntur Cxx<x> panes unde pro ferculis lxvi panes trencheris vi liberacionibus vi coquine ii canibus ix rewardis xxxi. Et remanent CCliiii panes. Celarium Expenduntur iiii lag. vini de stauro. Butillaria Expenduntur xliiii lag. cervisie. Et remanent xlvii lag. cervisie. Coquina Expenduntur i qr. bovis ii casse di. multonum iiii exitus porcorum de stauro. Item iii auce de precomputato. In di. carcosio bovis empto v s. v d. In ii porcellis emptis et expensis xi d. In iiii pullettis

[69] MS 'eidem'.
[70] Followed by a blank space in MS.

emptis vi d. In iii wodecok*es* emptis iii d. In vii snytis et iii grossis avibus emptis iiii d. In xxvii parvis avibus emptis ii d. Et expenduntur ii capones iii auce ii wodecok*es* xxiiii parve aves de precomputato. Item di. damus recens de stauro. Candelaria Expenduntur v lib. candelarum de stauro. Stabulum Fenum pro xii equis de stauro. In prebenda eorundem <iiii qr.> vi bus. avenarum de precomputato. Item fenum apud Remesbur' pro xvi equis ii hakeneis de stauro. In avenis pro eisdem v bus. de stauro.

Probatur Summa empcionum vii s. vii d.

Panteria De precomputato. Celarium Vinum de remanentia. Butillaria De precomputato. Coquina Empciones vii s. vii d. Candelaria De stauro. Stabulum Fenum avene de stauro.

[*f.20v*] *Gentiles xxi Valecti garciones xlii Summa ferculorum lxiii*
Extranii Golde se iiii^{o} magister Thomas Fisic' se ii^{o} et alii xiiii

Die lune vi^{o} Decembris Panteria Expenduntur Cxx panes unde pro ferculis lxiii panes trencheris viii liberacionibus vi coquina v canibus xii rewardis xxvi panes. Et remanent Cxxxiiii panes. Celarium Expenduntur vi lag. vini de remanentia. Butillaria Expenduntur xl lag. cervisie. Et remanent vii lag. cervisie. Coquina Expenduntur i qr. bovis ii casse di. multonum de stauro. Item di. porcus de stauro. Item i caponis ii galline de precomputato. Item expenduntur ii wodecok*es* ii cuniculi de precomputato. Candelaria Expenduntur iiii lib. candelarum de stauro. Stabulum Fenum pro xxi equis iiii hakeneis de stauro. In avenis pro eisdem i qr. ii bus. Item fenum apud Remesbur' pro xiiii equis i hakeneo de stauro. In avenis v bus. de stauro.

Summa[71]

Panteria De precomputato. Celarium Vinum de remanentia. Butillaria De precomputato. Coquina Empciones nichil. Candelaria De stauro. Stabulum Fenum avene de stauro.

Gentiles xi Valecti garciones xxv Summa ferculorum xxxvi
Extranii magister T. de Redyng' se iii^{o} et alii iiii

Die martis vii^{o} Decembris Panteria Expenduntur iiii^{xx} panes unde pro ferculis xxxvi panes trencheris iiii liberacionibus v coquina iii canibus xii panes rewardis xx panes. Et remanent liiii panes. Celarium Expenduntur v lag. vini de remanentia. Butillaria In iiii^{xx}vi lag. cervisie emptis de Warenar precium lag. i d. ob. deductis inde vii lag. de avantagio ix s. x d. ob. In xxvii lag. cervisie emptis de eodem precium lag. i d. deductis inde ii lag. de avantagio ii s. i d. In Clv lag. cervisie emptis de Schepherd precium lag. i d. ob. deductis inde xiii lag. cervisie de avantagio xvii s. ix d. In l lag. cervisie emptis de eadem[72] precium lag. i d. deductis inde iiii lag. de avantagio iii s. x d. In lxxii lag. cervisie emptis de Axford precium lag. i d. ob. deductis

[71] Followed by a blank space in MS.
[72] MS 'eodem'.

inde vi lag. de avantagio viii s. iii d. In xxv lag. cervisie emptis de eadem[73] precium lag. i d. deductis inde ii lag. de avantagio xxiii d. In xlv lag. cervisie emptis de Petro Lavyngton' precium lag. i d. ob. deductis inde iii lag. di. de avantagio v s. ii d. In xvi lag. cervisie emptis de eodem precium lag. i d. deducta inde i lag. de avantagio xv d. Et expenduntur xxviii lag. cervisie. Et remanent CCCClv lag. cervisie. Coquina Expenduntur i piscis salcius l allec rubium l allec album de stauro. Stabulum Fenum pro xxvii equis v hakeneis de stauro. In avenis pro eisdem i qr. iii bus. avenarum de stauro. Item fenum apud Remesbur' pro xiiii equis i hakeneo de stauro. In avenis pro eisdem iiii bus. avenarum de stauro.

Probatur Summa li s. i d. ob.

Panteria De precomputato. Celarium Vinum de remanentia. Butillaria In <xvi> CCCCiiii^{xx}x lag. cervisie <xl> l s. i d. ob. Coquina Empciones nichil. Candelaria De precomputato. Stabulum Fenum avene de stauro.

[f.21r] Poterne Gentiles xxiii Valecti garciones xlviii Summa ferculorum lxxi
Extranii magister T. ut supra rector de Alington' se ii^{o} Osberne se iii^{o} et alii xxiii

Die mercurie[74] viii^{o} Decembris Panteria Furniuntur per i talliam ii qr. frumenti que respondent ad CCCCiii panes. Et expenduntur Cxl panes unde pro ferculis lxxi panes trencheris x liberacionibus v coquina vi canibus ix rewardis xxxix panes. Et remanent CCCxvii panes. Celarium Expenduntur x lag. vini de remanentia. Butillaria Expenduntur l lag. cervisie. Et remanent CCCCv lag. cervisie. Coquina Expenduntur C allec album C allec rubium iii pisces salcii iii stok' de stauro. Item expenduntur CCC ova de precomputato. Item expenduntur iii pecie storjon' de stauro. Item iii salmones salcii de stauro. \ In lacte v d. crem ii d. / <S> Candelaria Expenduntur iiii lib. candelarum de stauro. Stabulum Fenum pro xx equis v hakeneis de stauro. In avenis pro eisdem i qr. i bus. avenarum de stauro. Item fenum apud Remesbur' pro xiiii equis i hakeneo de stauro. In avenis pro eisdem v bus. de stauro.

Probatur Summa empcionum vii d.

Panteria Furniuntur ii qr. frumenti que respondent ad CCCCiii panes. Celarium Vinum de remanentia. Butillaria De precomputato. Coquina De precomputato empto vii d. Candelaria De stauro. Stabulum Fenum avene de stauro.

Gentiles xxix Valecti garciones xlviii Summa ferculorum lxxvii
Extranii magister Henricus <h> Harburgh' se viii^{o} G.Louthorp se vi^{o} magister Thomas Lech' se ii^{o} rector de Alingt' se ii^{o} et alii xiiii

[73] MS 'eodem'.
[74] MS 'mart''.

Die jovis ix^{o} Decembris Panteria Expenduntur Cxxx panes[75] unde pro ferculis lxxvii panes trencheris xii liberacionibus x coquina vi canibus viii rewardis xxii panes. Et remanent Ciiii^{xx}vii panes. Celarium Expenduntur x lag. vini de remanentia. Butillaria Expenduntur l lag. cervisie. Et remanent CCClv lag. cervisie. Coquina Expenduntur i qr. bovis iii casse \ di. / multonum iii qr. porci de stauro. Item expenduntur iii auce. Item expenduntur iii capones vii galline de precomputato. Item expenditur i damus recens de stauro. In ii porcellis emptis et expensis xi d. In x aucis emptis iii s. vi d. In ii caponibus emptis viii d. In ii gallinis emptis vii d. In vii wodecok*es* emptis vii d. In v snites emptis[76] et expensis ii d. Item iii wodecok*es* de precomputato. In iii grossis avibus emptis i d. In xxii parvis avibus emptis ii d. In expensis emptoris iii d. et expenduntur. <In expensis emptoris iii d.> Candelaria Expenduntur v lib. candelarum de stauro. Stabulum Fenum pro xxi equis v hakeneis de stauro. In avenis i qr. iiii bus. de stauro. Item fenum apud Remesbur' pro xiiii equis v hakeneis de stauro. In avenis pro eisdem v bus. avenarum de stauro.

Probatur Summa empcionum vi s. xi d.

Panteria De precomputato. Celarium Vinum de remanentia. Butillaria De precomputato. Coquina Empciones vi s. xi d. Candelaria De precomputato. Stabulum Fenum avene de stauro.

[f.21v] Poterne Gentiles xiii Valecti garciones xxviii Summa ferculorum xli Extranii Henricus Harburgh' se viii^{o} et alii xiiii

Die veneris x^{o} Decembris Panteria Expenduntur iiii^{xx}x panes unde pro ferculis xli panes trencheris vi liberacionibus iiii coquina iiii canibus vi rewardis xxix panes. Et remanent iiii^{xx}xvii panes. Celarium Expenduntur iiii lag. vini de remanentia. Butillaria Expenduntur xxxii lag. cervisie. Et remanent CCCxxiii lag. cervisie. Coquina Expenduntur l allec rubium C allec album ii pisces di. salcii xvi roches i perche de stauro. Item expenduntur ii casii de precomputato. In iii salmonibus salciis emptis iii s. In ii lag. lactis ii d. In i lag. mellis xiiii d. et expensa. \ In iiii casiis emptis et expensis xiii d. / Candelaria Expenduntur iii lib. candelarum de stauro. Stabulum Fenum pro <xxii> \ xxvi / equis v hakeneis de stauro. In avenis[77] pro eisdem i qr. iiii bus. de stauro. Item fenum apud Remesbur' pro xiiii equis iii hakeneis de stauro. In avenis pro eisdem v bus. de stauro.

Probatur Summa empcionum v s. v d.

Panteria De precomputato. Celarium Vinum de remanentia. Butillaria De precomputato. Coquina Empciones v s. v d. Candelaria De stauro. Stabulum Fenum avene de stauro.

[75] 135 loaves disbursed.

[76] MS 'emt''.

[77] MS 'avene*us*'.

In vadiis Thome Ferour apud Remesbyry cum equis domini a xxi die Novembris usque xi Decembris videlicet per iii septimanas capientis per septimanam xxi d. v s. iii d.
In[78] vadiis Johannis Bath' garcionis forgii ibidem a vii die Novembris usque xi Decembris videlicet per v septimanas cum vadiis eiusdem apud Sarum per i septimanam capientis per septimanam xiiii d. vii s.
In vadiis \ iiii / pagettorum ibidem per <idem tempus> \ iii septimanas / videlicet Forrey pagetti senescalli pagetti Tydem*er*ssh' pagetti Cap*er*on' x s. vi d.
In vadiis pagetti Lovell' ibidem a xxv die Novembris usque xi Decembris utroque computato videlicet per ii septimanas et iii dies ii s. i d. ob.
In vadiis Javen*er* ibidem per i septimanam capientis per diem ii d. xiiii d.
In vadiis garcionis cancellarii ibidem per viii dies per diem ii d. xvi d.
In vadiis Thome Norman ibidem per vi dies capientis per diem ii d. xii d.
In vadiis pagetti Holcote ibidem per septimanam capientis per diem i d. ob. x d. ob.
In vadiis Thome Chariett' ibidem per ix dies capientis per diem ii d. xviii d.

Probatur Summa xxx s. ix d.

[*f.22r*] *Gentiles xviii Valecti garciones xxxix Summa ferculorum lvii Extranii xiii*

Die sabbati xi^{o} Decembris Panteria Furniuntur per i talliam ii qr. frumenti de stauro que respondent de CCCCxiii panibus. Et expenduntur Cxx panes unde pro ferculis lvii trencheris vi liberacionibus vi coquine iii canibus viii rewardis xl panes. Et remanent CCCiiii^{xx}x panes. Celarium Expenduntur iii lag. vini de stauro. Butillaria Expenduntur xliii lag. cervisie. Et remanent CCiiii^{xx} lag. cervisie. Coquina Expenduntur l allec[79] rubium C album ii pisces salcii viii stok' Cl ova de stauro et precomputato. In xxii gurnard et ix merlyng \ i brem / et iii thornbakk*es* emptis vi s. iii d. In expensis emptoris apud Wermystr' cum somerario vi d. In CCCC ostriis emptis et expensis viii d. In CC welk*es* emptis et expensis v d. <I> Et expenduntur xvii gurnard ix merlyng i brem et iii thornbak*es*. Candelaria Expenduntur iii lib. candelarum de stauro. Stabulum Fenum pro xvi equis iiii hakeneis de stauro. In prebenda eorundem i qr. avenarum de precomputato. Item fenum apud Remesbur' pro xiiii equis iiii hakeneis de stauro. In avenis pro eisdem v bus. de stauro.

Probatur Summa empcionum vii s. x d.

Panteria Furniuntur ii qr. que respondent ad[80] CCCCxiii. Celarium Vinum

[78] Marginal note: 'P' N'' — ?'Per Nicholaum'.
[79] MS 'l alb' rub''.
[80] MS omits 'ad'.

de remanentia. Butillaria De precomputato. Coquina Empciones vii s. x d. Candelaria De stauro. Stabulum Fenum avene de stauro.
Gentiles xxiii Valecti garciones xlix Summa ferculorum iiii^{xx}ii[81]
Extranii xxii
Die dominica xii^{o} Decembris Panteria Expenduntur Cxxxix panes[82] unde pro ferculis iiii^{xx}ii trencheris vi liberacionibus vi coquine iiii canibus viii rewardis xxiii. Et remanent CCli panes. Celarium Expenduntur vi lag. vini de stauro. Butillaria Expenduntur lii lag. cervisie. Et remanent CCxxviii lag. cervisie. Coquina Expenduntur i qr. bovis iii qr. multonis i qr. apri de stauro. Item iii capones i gallina iii auce de precomputato. In ii porcellis emptis[83] et expensis xi d. In i wodecok empto i d. In xxiiii snyt*es* emptis ix d. In vi grossis avibus emptis ii d. In iiii cuniculis emptis xii d. In MCCC ovis emptis v s. v d. Et expenduntur ii porcelli iiii wodecok*es* xii snyt*es* et parve aves. Item i cuniculus de precomputato. Candelaria Expenduntur iiii lib. candelarum de stauro. Stabulum Fenum pro xiiii equis iii hakeneis de stauro. In prebenda eorundem i qr. avenarum de precomputato. Item fenum apud Remesbur' pro xiiii equis ii hakeneis de stauro. In avenis pro eisdem iiii bus. avenarum de stauro.

Probatur Summa viii s. iiii d.

Panteria De precomputato. Celarium Vinum de remanentia. Butillaria De precomputato. Coquina Empciones viii s. iiii d. Candelaria De stauro. Stabulum Fenum avene[84]
[*f*.22*v*] *Poterne Gentiles xxi Valecti garciones <xxvi> \ xlvii / Summa ferculorum lxvii*
Extranii Gowayn se iiii^{o} et alii xii
Die lune xiii^{o} Decembris Panteria Expenduntur Cxxx panes unde pro ferculis lxvii panes <Et remanent> trencheris vi liberacionibus vi coquine ii canibus x rewardis xxxix panes. Et remanent Cxxi panes. Celarium Expenduntur vi lag. vini de stauro. Butillaria Expenduntur xl lag. cervisie. Et remanent Ciiii^{xx}viii lag. cervisie. Coquina Expenduntur i qr. bovis di. cassa multonis de stauro. Item iiii exitus porcorum de stauro. Item ii capones xxiiii parve aves de precomputato. Candelaria[85] Expenduntur v lib. candelarum de stauro. Stabulum Fenum pro xvii equis vii hakeneis de stauro. In prebenda i qr. <ii bus.> avenarum. Item fenum apud Remesbur' pro xiiii equis i hakeneo de stauro. In avenis pro eisdem v bus. avenarum de stauro.

Summa nichil

[81] MS totals 72.
[82] 129 loaves disbursed; 139 are needed for the remainder to be correct.
[83] MS repeats 'emp''.
[84] Followed by a blank space in MS.
[85] MS 'Coquina'.

Panteria De precomputato. Celarium Vinum de remanentia. Butillaria De precomputato. Coquina Empciones[86] Candelaria De stauro. Stabulum Fenum avene de stauro.

Gentiles xiiii Valecti garciones iiii^{xx}xviii Summa ferculorum Cxii

Extranii de tenentibus domini de Poterne Worton' et Merston' iiii^{xx} cariantibus buscum pro hospicio de prece

Die martis xiiii° Decembris Panteria Furniuntur per ii tallias iiii qr. frumenti de stauro que respondent de DCCCvi panibus. Et expenduntur CCxl panes unde pro ferculis Cxii trencheris vi liberacionibus vi coquine iiii canibus viii rewardis Ciiii. Et remanent DCiiii^{xx}vii panes. Celarium Expenduntur viii lag. vini de stauro. Butillaria Expenduntur C lag. cervisie. Et remanent iiii^{xx}viii lag. cervisie. Coquina Expenduntur di. carcosium bovis ii casse multonum di. baco de stauro vi exitus porcorum de stauro. Item ii capones iiii auce i perdix ii wodecok*es* de precomputato. In porcellis emptis et expensis x d. Candelaria Expenduntur iiii lib. candelarum de stauro. Stabulum Fenum pro xiii equis iiii hakeneis de stauro. In prebenda eorundem v bus. avenarum de precomputato. Item fenum apud Remesbur' pro xiiii equis iiii hakeneis de stauro. In avenis pro eisdem iiii bus. avenarum de stauro.

Probatur Summa empcionum x d.

Panteria Furniuntur iiii qr. frumenti que respondent ad viiiCvi. Celarium Vinum De remanentia. Butillaria De precomputato. Coquina Empciones x d. Candelaria De stauro. Stabulum Fenum avene de stauro.

[*f.23r*] *Poterne Gentiles xi Valecti garciones xxii Summa ferculorum xxxiii Extranii*[87]

Die mercurie xv Decembris Panteria Expenduntur iiii^{xx} panes unde pro ferculis xxxiii trencheris iiii liberacionibus vi coquine ii canibus viii rewardis xxvii panes. Et remanent DCvii panes. Celarium Expenduntur iiii lag. vini de stauro. Butillaria Expenduntur xxviii lag. cervisie. Et remanent \ lx / lag. cervisie. Coquina Expenduntur C allec album l rubium i piscis salcius et di. di. salmo salcius viii roch*es* de stauro. In xvii congris salciis et viii hakes recentibus emptis xxii s. i d. In CCCC ostriis emptis et expensis x d. In ii lag. lactis emptis ii d. Et expenduntur ii hakes recentes. Candelaria Expenduntur v lib. candelarum de stauro. Stabulum Fenum pro xii equis iiii hakeneis de stauro. In prebenda eorundem iiii bus. di. avenarum de precomputato. Item fenum apud Remesbur' pro xiiii equis ii hakeneis de stauro. In avenis pro eisdem iiii bus.

Probatur Summa xxiii s. i d.

Panteria De precomputato. Celarium Vinum de remanentia. Butillaria De

[86] Followed by a blank space in MS.

[87] Followed by a blank space in MS.

precomputato. Coquina Empciones xxiii s. i d. Candelaria De stauro. Stabulum Fenum avene de stauro.

Gentiles xxiii Valecti garciones xliiii Summa ferculorum lxvii

Extranii magister Johannes Maydenhythe se viii^{o}[88] *rector de Alyngton' se ii*^{do} *rector de Berwyk et alii extranii xii*

Die jovis xvi Decembris Panteria Expenduntur Cxx panes unde pro ferculis lxvii trencheris vi liberacionibus vi coquine ii canibus viii rewardis xxxi panes. Et remanent CCCCiiii^{xx}vii panes. Celarium Expenduntur vi lag. vini de stauro. Butillaria Expenduntur xl lag. cervisie. Et remanent xx lag. cervisie. Coquina Expenduntur i qr. bovis ii casse multonum \ de stauro / i caponis iiii pulcini iii auce iii cuniculi ii mallard*i* de precomputato. In ii porcellis emptis et expensis xi d. In vi aucis emptis ii s. i d. In xiiii caponibus iii s. viii d. In viii gallinis xvi d. In xxv grossis avibus emptis \ et expensis / iiii d. In viii snyt*es* iii d. In iii wodecok*es* iii d. \ et expensis. / In ii bus. farine avenarum emptis xxii d. In expensis emptoris cum somerario apud Wermystr' iii d. Candelaria Expenduntur iiii lib. candelarum de stauro. Stabulum Fenum pro xvi equis v hakeneis de stauro. In prebenda eorundem vii bus. avenarum de precomputato. Item fenum apud Remesbur' pro xiiii equis iii hakeneis de stauro. In avenis[89] pro eisdem iii bus. avenarum de stauro.

Probatur Summa empcionum x s. xi d.

Panteria De precomputato. Celarium Vinum de remanentia. Butillaria De precomputato. Coquina Empciones x s. xi d. Candelaria De stauro. Stabulum Fenum avene de stauro.

[*f.23v*] *Pot*erne *Gentiles viii Valecti garciones xxiiii Summa ferculorum xxxii Extranii vi*

Die veneris xvii^{o} Decembris Panteria <Furn*i*tur i> Expenduntur lxiiii panes unde pro ferculis xxxii trencheris iii liberacionibus v coquine ii canibus viii rewardis xiiii. Et remanent CCCCxxiii panes. Celarium Expenduntur ii lag. vini de stauro. Butillaria Expenduntur xx lag. cervisie de precomputato. Coquina Expenduntur l allec rubium iii qr. allecis albi ii pisces salcii ii stok' ii hakes recentes di. salmo salcius de precomputato. In MCC ostriis emptis ii s. In C welk*es* emptis iii d. In iii lag. lactis emptis et expensis iii d. Et expenduntur CC ostria. Candelaria Expenduntur iiii lib. candelarum de stauro. Stabulum Fenum pro x equis ii hakeneis de stauro. In prebenda eorundem iiii bus. avenarum de precomputato. Item fenum apud Remesbur' pro xii equis iii hakeneis de stauro. In avenis iiii bus. avenarum de stauro.

Probatur Summa empcionum ii s. vi d.

[88] MS 'viiii^{o}'.

[89] MS 'aveneois'.

Panteria De precomputato. Celarium Vinum de remanentia. Butillaria De precomputato. Coquina Empciones ii s. vi d. Candelaria De stauro. Stabulum Fenum avene de stauro.

Gentiles xi Valecti garciones xxix Summa ferculorum xl

Extranii Gore se ii^{o} Wylmyngton' se ii^{o} Walrond se ii^{o} et alii vi

Die sabbati xviii^{o} Decembris Panteria Expenduntur iiii^{xx} panes unde pro ferculis xl trencheris iiii liberacionibus v coquine iii canibus viii rewardis xx. Et remanent CCCxliii panes. Celarium Expenduntur[90] lag. vini de stauro. Butillaria <Expend*un*tur> In Dii lag.[91] cervisie emptis de Shepherde precium lag. i d. ob. deductis inde xlii lag. lvii s. vi d. In Ciii lag. cervisie emptis de eadem[92] precium lag. i d. deductis inde viii lag. di. cervisie vii s. vii d. ob. In xliiii lag. cervisie emptis de Ryle precium lag. i d. ob. deductis inde iii lag. di. de avantagio v s. i d. In xiii lag. cervisie emptis de eodem precium lag. i d. xii d. Et expenduntur xxx lag. cervisie. Et remanent DCxxxi lag. cervisie. Coquina Expenduntur iii qr. allecis rubii C album i piscis salcius i congrus salcius iii hakes poudri de stauro. In xliii merlyng xxxii gurnard iiii brem*es* et i haddok et i parvo congro recenti empto viii s. Et expenduntur xvi merlyng viii gurnard. Item expenduntur CC ostria de precomputato. In expensis emptoris apud Wermystr' cum somerario v d. In xxvii lag. mellis emptis precium lag. viii d. xviii s. Candelaria Expenduntur v lib. candelarum de stauro. Stabulum Fenum pro xi equis iii hakeneis de stauro. In prebenda eorundem iiii bus. avenarum de precomputato. Item fenum apud Remesbur' pro <x> vi equis i hakeneo de stauro. In avenis ii bus. pec.

Probatur Summa empcionum iiii li. xvii s. vii d. ob. unde Panteria De precomputato. Celarium Vinum de remanentia. Butillaria In DClxii lag. cervisie lxxi s. ii d. ob. Coquina Empciones xxvi s. v d. Candelaria De stauro. Stabulum Fenum avene de stauro.

[*f.24r*] *Poterne Gentiles xxi Valecti garciones xlix Summa ferculorum lxx*

Extranii Johannes Walrond se ii^{o} extranii alii x

Die dominica xix^{o} Decembris Panteria Expenduntur Cxxx panes unde pro ferculis lxx trencheris vi liberacionibus vi coquine[93] ii canibus viii rewardis xxxviii. Et remanent CCxiii panes. Celarium Expend*un*tur[94] lag. vini de stauro. Butillaria Expenduntur xlii lag. cervisie. Et remanent Diiii^{xx}ix lag. cervisie. Coquina Expenduntur i qr. bovis ii casse multonum de stauro.

[90] Followed by a blank space in MS.

[91] MS repeats 'lag.'

[92] MS 'eodem'.

[93] Underlined in MS.

[94] Followed by a blank space in MS.

Item ii galline ii pulcini iii wodecok*es* xxiiii parve <...> aves de precomputato. Item expenduntur iii auce de precomputato. In iiii porcellis emptis xxii d. et expenduntur ii. In i wodecok i d. In xviii snyt*es* vi d. In xxv grossis avibus v d. In xxx parvis avibus emptis iiii d. Candelaria Expenduntur v lib. candelarum de stauro. Stabulum Fenum pro xiiii equis ii hakeneis de stauro. In prebenda eorundem iiii bus. di. avenarum de precomputato. Item fenum apud Remesbur' pro v equis ii hakeneis de stauro. In avenis ii bus. de stauro.

Probatur Summa empcionum iii s. ii d.

Panteria De precomputato. Celarium Vinum de remanentia. Butillaria De precomputato. Coquina Empciones iii s. ii d. Candelaria De[95] stauro. Stabulum Fenum avene[96] de stauro.

Gentiles xv Valecti garciones xxvii Summa ferculorum xlii

*Extranii <r> vicarius ville rector de Busshoppesthrow Johannes Piers Thomas Auncell' Johannes Walrond se ii^o Medford Man*ger *et alii extranii xii*

Die lune xx° Decembris Panteria Expenduntur iiii^{xx} panes unde pro ferculis xlii trencheris ii liberacionibus iiii coquine ii canibus viii rewardis xxii. Et remanent Cxxxiii panes.[97] Celarium Expend*un*tur[98] lag. <cervisie> vini de stauro. Butillaria Expenduntur xxx lag. cervisie. Et remanent Dlviii lag. cervisie.[99] Coquina Expenduntur C allec album l rubium i piscis salcius i congrus salcius de stauro. Item i hake poudrus xvi merlyng xviii gurnard i congrus recens de precomputato. Item expenduntur CCCl ostria de precomputato. Candelaria Expenduntur iiii lib. candelarum de stauro. Stabulum Fenum pro xv equis ii hakeneis de stauro. In prebenda eorundem v bus. di. avenarum de precomputato. Item pro viii equis iii hakeneis de stauro. In avenis pro eisdem iii bus. di. avenarum de stauro.

Probatur Summa empcionum nichil

Panteria De precomputato. Celarium Vinum de remanentia. Butillaria De precomputato. Coquina Empciones nichil. Candelaria De stauro. Stabulum Fenum avene de stauro.

[*f.24v*] *Poterne Gentiles xxiii Valecti garciones lxii Summa ferculorum iiii^{xx}vii*

Extranii vicarius ville se iii° Floure se iiii° et alii capellani extranii xii

95 MS 'Del <de>'.
96 MS 'avenen'.
97 MS repeats 'pan''.
98 Followed by a blank space in MS.
99 Totals 559 gallons.

Die martis xxi^{o} Decembris Panteria Expenduntur Cxxx[100] panes unde pro ferculis iiii^{xx}vii panes trencheris v liberacionibus vi coquina v canibus ix rewardis xvii panes. Et remanent iii panes. Celarium Expenduntur v lag. vini de stauro remanenti. Butillaria Expenduntur liiii lag. cervisie. Et remanent Diiii lag. cervisie. Coquina Expenduntur i qr. bovis i cassa di. multonum de stauro. Item expenduntur i qr. porci i capo iii auce de precomputato. In ii porcellis emptis et expensis viii d. <In> Item expenduntur ii perdices xxiiii aves de precomputato. Candelaria Expenduntur v lib. candelarum de stauro. Stabulum Fenum pro[101] xxi equis iiii hakeneis de stauro. In avenis pro eisdem i qr. ii bus. avenarum de stauro. Item fenum apud Remesbur' pro xi equis ii hakeneis de stauro. In avenis iiii bus. di.

Probatur Summa empcionum viii d.

Panteria De precomputato. Celarium Vinum de remanentia. Butillaria De precomputato. Coquina Empciones viii d. Candelaria De stauro. Stabulum Fenum avene[102]

Gentiles xx Valecti garciones lxi Summa ferculorum iiii^{xx}i

Extranii magister J. Shirbourne se v^{o} vicarius ville se ii^{o} ii clerici extranii et alii de tenentibus domini cariantibus boscum xii

Die mercurie xxii^{o} Decembris Panteria Furniuntur per i talliam ii qr. frumenti que respondent ad CCCCv panes. Et expenduntur Cxxiiii panes unde pro ferculis iiii^{xx}i panes trencheris iiii liberacionibus v coquina iiii canibus vi rewardis xxiiii panes. Et remanent CCiiii^{xx}iiii panes. Celarium Expenduntur iiii lag. vini de remanentia. Butillaria Expenduntur l lag. cervisie. Et remanent CCCCliiii lag. cervisie. Coquina Cl allec album l allec rubium iiii congri salcii de stauro. In viii congris recentibus emptis xi s. et expenduntur ii. In lacte empto et expenso ii d. ob. Item expenduntur Cl ova de precomputato. Candelaria Expenduntur vi <lag.> lib. candelarum de stauro. Stabulum Fenum pro xxx equis vi hakeneis de stauro. In avenis pro eisdem ii qr. Item fenum apud Remesbur' pro x equis iii hakeneis de stauro. In avenis pro eisdem iiii bus. di.

Probatur Summa empcionum xi s. ii d. ob.

Panteria Furniuntur ii qr. frumenti que respondent ad iiiiCv panes. Celarium Vinum de remanentia. Butillaria De precomputato. Coquina Empciones xi s. ii d. ob. Candelaria De stauro. Stabulum Fenum avene de stauro.

[*f.25r*] *Poterne Gentiles xxxii Valecti garciones lii Summa ferculorum iiii^{xx}iiii*

[100] 129 loaves disbursed.

[101] MS omits 'pro'.

[102] Followed by a blank space in MS.

Extranii suffraganus domini se viii^{o} Walront se iii^{o} vicarius ville se ii^{o} et alii xii

Die jovis xxiii^{o} Decembris Panteria Expenduntur Cxl panes unde pro ferculis iiii^{xx}iiii panes trencheris viii liberacionibus vii <trencheris> coquina vii canibus x rewardis xxiiii panes. Et remanent <CCCxiiii> \ Cxliiii / panes. Celarium Expenduntur vi lag. vini de remanentia. Butillaria Expenduntur lii lag. cervisie. Et remanent CCCCii lag. cervisie. Coquina Expenduntur i qr. bovis ii casse di. multonum de stauro. Item expenduntur iii qr. porci de stauro. Item expenduntur ii capones iii auce de precomputato. In i cassa multonis empta xviii d. In ii porcellis emptis et expensis xi d. In xiii aucis emptis iiii s. vi d. In x caponibus emptis ii s. ix d. In viii gallinis emptis xvii d. In ii wodecok*es* emptis ii d. In xx snites vii d. In xxxv grossis avibus emptis vii d. In ii cuniculis emptis vi d. In expensis emptoris ii d. Candelaria Expenduntur v lib. candelarum de stauro. Stabulum Fenum pro xv equis v hakeneis de stauro. In prebenda eorundem v bus. avenarum de stauro. Item fenum apud Remesbur' pro xiii equis iii hakeneis de stauro. In avenis v bus.

Probatur Summa empcionum xiii s. i d.

Panteria De precomputato. Celarium Vinum de remanentia. Butillaria De precomputato. Coquina Empciones xiii s. i d. Candelaria De stauro. Stabulum Fenum avene[103]

Gentiles xvii Valecti garciones xxxi Summa ferculorum xlviii

*Extranii suffraganus domini ut supra magister Walt*erus *Metford se viii^{o} magister J. Wotton'*[104] *se ii^{o} magister T. de Redyng' se iii^{o} et alii xiiii*

Die veneris xxiiii^{o} Decembris Panteria Expenduntur C panes unde pro ferculis xlviii trencheris vii liberacionibus viii coquina iiii canibus viii rewardis xxv panes. Et remanent xliiii panes. Celarium Expenduntur viii lag. vini de stauro remanenti. Butillaria Expenduntur xl lag. cervisie. Et remanent CCClxii lag. cervisie. Coquina Expenduntur Cl allec album Cl allec rubium iiii congri salcii de stauro. Item expenduntur iiii congri recentes de precomputato. Item expenditur i hake poudrus de precomputato. Item expenduntur CC ova de precomputato. In CCC allece albo empto v s. ii d. In xxvi merling et ii thornebak*es* emptis iiii s. et expenduntur xii merling et ii thornebak*es* de precomputato. In viiiC <s.> ostriis emptis xvi d. In CCC welkes emptis vii d. \ In lacte iii d. / In i bus. seminis cenapii empto iii s. Et expenduntur CCC ostria CC welkes de precomputato. Candelaria Expenduntur v lib. candelarum de stauro. Stabulum Fenum pro xx equis iii hakeneis de stauro. In prebenda

[103] Followed by a blank space in MS.
[104] MS 'Sotton''.

eorundem i qr. avenarum de stauro. Item fenum apud Remesbur' pro xv equis ii hakeneis de stauro. In avenis pro eisdem iii bus. di. pec.
Item in vadiis Thome Ferro*ur* apud Remesbur' a xi die Decembris usque xxv die eiusdem utroque computato iii s. vi d.
Item in vadiis Forrey pagetti Nicholai per idem tempus iii s. vi d.
Item in vadiis Thome Norman ibidem a xv die Decembris usque xxv eiusdem utroque computato xxii d.
Item in vadiis Lang' a xx die Decembris usque eundem diem capientis per diem i d. ob. ix d.
Item in vadiis Bathe ibidem per viii dies capientis per diem ii d. <viii d.> xvi d.

Probatur Summa empcionum xxv s. iii d.

Panteria De precomputato. Celarium Vinum de remanentia. Butillaria De precomputato. Coquina Empciones xiiii s. iiii d. Candelaria De stauro. Stabulum Fenum avene de stauro. Vadia x s. xi d.

[*f.25v*] *Poterne*

Festum Natalis Domini

Gentiles xxxii Valecti garciones lxv Summa ferculorum iiii^{xx}*xvii*

Extranii suffraganus se iii^{o} *magister W. Metford se vii*^{o} *magister J. Wotton' se ii*^{o} *Becot se ii*^{o} *J. Me\t/ford se ii*^{o} *magister Thomas de Redyng se ii*^{o} *et alii xxviii*

Die sabbati xxv Decembris Panteria Furniuntur per iii tallias vi qr. iiii bus. frumenti que respondent ad MCCCxvi panes. Et expenduntur CC panes[105] unde pro ferculis iiii^{xx}xvii panes trencheris xvi liberacionibus viii coquina v canibus xviii rewardis lvii panes. Et remanent MClx panes. Celarium Expenduntur xii lag. vini de remanentia. Butillaria Expenduntur iiii^{xx} lag. cervisie. Et remanent CCiiii^{xx}ii lag. cervisie. Coquina Expenduntur di. carcosium bovis iii casse multonum i bacon'. Item expenduntur ii cigni de stauro. Item expenduntur x capones viii galline v auce de precomputato. In ii carcosiis vitulorum emptorum viii s. et expenditur i. In i apro empto xiiii s. ii d. et expenditur di. In xxiiii cuniculis emptis vi s. et expenduntur vi. In vii porcellis emptis iii s. vi d. et expenduntur iiii porcelli. In viii caponibus emptis ii s. In lacte iii d. et expenso. In DCCCC ovis emptis iii s. ix d. et expenduntur CC. Item expenduntur ii wodecok*es* xx snites xxxv grosse aves et ii cuniculi de precomputato. Item expenduntur iiii maulard*i* iii teles de stauro. Item expenduntur l allec album l allec rubium ii congri salcii de stauro. Item expenditur i congrus recens de precomputato. Item expenduntur CC ostria C welkes de precomputato. Candelaria Expenduntur viii lib. candelarum de stauro. Stabulum Fenum pro xx equis iii hakeneis de stauro. In prebenda eorundem i qr. i bus. avenarum de stauro. Item fenum

[105] 201 loaves disbursed.

apud Remesbur' pro xviii equis iii hakeneis de stauro. In avenis pro eisdem i qr. de stauro.

Probatur Summa empcionum xxxvii s. viii d.

Panteria Furniuntur vi qr. iiii bus. frumenti que respondent ad MCCCxvi. Celarium Vinum de remanentia. Butillaria De precomputato. Coquina Empciones xxxvii s. viii d. Candelaria De stauro. Stabulum Fenum avene de stauro.

Gentiles xxxiii Valecti garciones lxviii Summa ferculorum Ci

Extranii suffraganus se iii^{o} magister W. Metford se vii^{o} magister J. Wotton' se ii^{o} magister T. Reding' se ii^{o} Becot se ii^{o} Metford se ii^{o} magister J. Murrey se ii^{o} vicarius ville se ii^{o} et alii xxviii

Die dominica xxvi^{o} Decembris Panteria Expenduntur Cl panes unde pro ferculis Ci panes trencheris viii liberacionibus viii coquina iii canibus x rewardis xx panes. Et remanent Mx panes. Celarium Expenduntur x lag. vini de stauro remanenti. Butillaria Expenduntur lxiiii lag. cervisie. Et remanent CCxvii lag. cervisie.[106] Coquina Expenduntur i qr. bovis ii casse multonum di. porcus i cignus de stauro. Item expenditur i qr. apri de precomputato. Item expenduntur i capo x galline de precomputato. Item expenduntur v auce iii porcelli de precomputato. Item expenduntur viii cuniculi CC ova de precomputato. Item ii dami salcii de stauro i damus recens de stauro. Candelaria Expenduntur vi lib. candelarum. Stabulum Fenum pro xxiii equis iiii hakeneis de stauro. In prebenda eorundem i qr. i bus. di. avenarum de stauro. Item fenum apud Remesbur' pro xx equis iii hakeneis de stauro. In avenis pro eisdem i qr. avenarum de stauro.

Panteria De precomputato. Celarium Vinum de remanentia. Butillaria De precomputato. Coquina Empciones nichil. Candelaria De stauro. Stabulum Fenum avene de stauro.

[*f.*26*r*] *Poterne Gentiles xxxv Valecti garciones lvii Summa ferculorum iiii^{xx}xii*

*Extranii suffraganus domini magister W*alt*erus* *Metford se vi^{o} Dionis*ia *Peris se iiii^{o} Becot se ii^{o} Metford se ii^{o} et alii xxx*

Die lune xxvii^{o} Decembris Panteria Expenduntur Clxviii panes unde pro ferculis iiii^{xx}xii panes trencheris x liberacionibus x coquina viii canibus xv rewardis xxxiii panes. Et remanent viiiCxlii panes. Celarium Expenduntur viii lag. vini de stauro. Butillaria Expenduntur lxviii lag. cervisie. Et remanent Cxlix lag. cervisie. Coquina Expenduntur i qr. di. bovis ii casse di. multonum de stauro. Item expenditur i bacon' de stauro. Item expenduntur i capo iiii galline iiii cuniculi i damus recens de stauro. Item expenditur di. carcosium vituli de precomputato. Candelaria

[106] 218 gallons should remain.

Expend*un*tur[107] lib. candelarum de stauro. Stabulum Fenum pro xxiiii equis iii hakeneis de stauro. In avenis pro eisdem i qr. ii bus. de stauro. Item fenum apud Remesbur' pro xx equis iii hakeneis de stauro. In avenis i qr. di. bus.

Summa empcionum[108]

Panteria De precomputato. Celarium Vinum de remanentia. Butillaria De precomputato. Coquina Empciones nichil. Candelaria De stauro. Stabulum Fenum avene de stauro.

Gentiles C Valecti garciones lxxi Summa ferculorum Clxxi

Extranii suffraganus ut supra Becot se iii^o Metford se ii^o J. Peris se iiii^o vicarius ville cum iii capellanis et aliis de tenentibus domini de Poterne et Merston Clx

Die martis xxviii° Decembris Panteria Expenduntur CCCxx[109] unde pro ferculis Clxxi panes trencheris xvi liberacionibus x coquina vi canibus xvi rewardis Cx panes. Et remanent Dxxii panes. Celarium Expenduntur xx lag. vini de remanentia. Butillaria Expenduntur Cxlix lag. cervisie. Et nichil remanet. Coquina Expenditur iii qr. bovis. Item iii casse multonum i aper ii capones xii galline ii cigni xiiii auce di. carcosium bovis CCC ova de precomputato. Item expenduntur iii dami salcii ii dami recentes de stauro. Item expenduntur viii cuniculi de precomputato. In x cassis multonum emptis xiii s. vi d. et expenduntur iiii casse multonum. In ii carcosiis vitulorum emptis vii s. x d. et expensis. In xi porcellis emptis et expensis iiii s. vii d. In v pulcinis emptis vi d. et expensis. In x lag. lactis x d. et expensis. In xxiiii cuniculis emptis vi s. et expenduntur xx cuniculi. Candelaria Expenduntur vi lib. candelarum de stauro. Stabulum Fenum pro xxiiii equis iiii hakeneis de stauro. In avenis pro eisdem i qr. ii bus. avenarum de stauro. Item fenum apud Remesbur' pro xxiiii equis iii hakeneis de stauro. In avenis pro eisdem i qr. iii bus. avenarum de stauro.

Probatur Summa empcionum xxxiii s. iii d.

Panteria De precomputato. Celarium Vinum de remanentia. Butillaria De precomputato. Coquina Empciones xxxiii s. iii d. Candelaria De stauro. Stabulum Fenum avene de stauro.

[*f.26v*] *Poterne Gentiles xliii Valecti garciones lxxiiii Summa ferculorum Cxvii*

Extranii suffraganus domini Rousse se iii^o Becot se ii^o Metford se ii^o J.Wilscoumbe se iii^o J.Peris cum uxore et aliis x Et alii xxxii

Die mercurie xxix Decembris Panteria Expenduntur Clx panes unde pro ferculis Cxvii panes trencheris xiiii liberacionibus vi coquina vi canibus xiiii

[107] Followed by a blank space in MS.

[108] Followed by a blank space in MS.

[109] 329 loaves disbursed.

panes rewardis iii panes. Et remanent CCClxii panes. Celarium Expenduntur xii lag. vini de remanentia. Butillaria In Cxl lag. cervisie emptis de Shepherd' precium lag. i d. ob. deductis inde xi lag. \ di. / de avantagio xvi s. <ii d.> \ ob. / In l lag. cervisie emptis de eadem precium lag. i d. deductis inde iiii lag. de avantagio iii s. x d. In Cii lag. cervisie emptis de Axford precium lag. i d. ob. deductis inde \ iii lag. / xi s. ix d. In xliiii lag. cervisie emptis de eadem[110] precium lag. i d. deductis inde iii lag. di. de avantagio iii s. iiii d. ob. In C lag. cervisie emptis de Waren*er* precium lag. i d. ob. deductis inde viii lag. di. de avantagio xi s. v d. In xl lag. cervisie emptis de eodem precium lag. i d. deductis iii lag. de avantagio iii s. i d. In lxii lag. cervisie emptis de Willelmo Lange precium lag. i d. ob. deductis inde[111] vii s. i d. <ob.> In xii lag. cervisie emptis de eodem deducta inde i lag. de avantagio xi d. In iiii^{xx} lag. cervisie emptis de Johanne atte Asshe precium lag. i d. ob. deductis inde de avantagio vi lag. di. ix s. ii d. In xx lag. cervisie emptis de eodem precium lag. i d. deductis inde i lag. di. de avantagio xviii d. ob. In lxxiii lag. cervisie emptis de Lavyngton' precium lag. i d. ob. deductis inde vi lag. de avantagio viii s. iiii d. ob. In xl lag. cervisie emptis de eodem precium lag. i d. deductis inde iii lag. de avantagio iii s. i d. Et expenduntur iiii^{xx} lag. cervisie. Et remanent DCiiii^{xx}\iii/ lag. cervisie. Coquina Expenduntur i qr. di. bovis ii casse multonum i bacon' ii capones iiii galline ii pulcini di. carcosium vituli iiii cuniculi C ova de precomputato. Item expenduntur C allec album l allec rubium i congrus salcius iiii stok' i congrus recens de precomputato. Candelaria Expenduntur vi lib. candelarum de stauro. Stabulum Fenum pro xxvi equis iii hakeneis de stauro. In avenis pro eisdem i qr. iii bus. avenarum de stauro. Item fenum apud Remesbur' pro xx equis ii hakeneis de stauro. In avenis pro eisdem vii bus. de stauro.

Probatur Summa empcionum lxxix s. viii d.

Panteria De precomputato. Celarium Vinum de remanentia. Butillaria In viiClxiii lag. cervisie lxxix s. viii d.[112] Coquina Empciones nichil. Candelaria De stauro. Stabulum Fenum avene de stauro.

Gentiles xxxviii Valecti garciones lx Summa ferculorum iiii^{xx}xviii

Extranii suffraganus domini se iiii^{o} Rousse se iiii^{o} J.Peris se iiii^{o} Metford se iii^{o} J.Becot se iii^{o} et alii xlii

Die jovis xxx Decembris Panteria Expenduntur Clx panes unde pro ferculis iiii^{xx}xviii trencheris xii liberacionibus viii coquina iiii canibus xv rewardis xxiii panes. Et remanent CCii panes. Celarium Expenduntur vi lag. vini de remanentia. Butillaria Expenduntur lxxviii lag. cervisie. Et remanent DCv

110 MS 'eodem'.

111 Omission from MS: 8*d*. worth of ale abated.

112 Totals 72*s*. 9*d*.

lag. cervisie. Coquina Expenduntur i qr. di. bovis i cassa multonis i bacon' i porcus. Item expenduntur xiiii galline iiii auce iiii cuniculi i carcosium vituli i cignus i damus recens de stauro. \ In viii aucis emptis v s. iiii d. In xii caponibus iiii s. i d. / Candelaria Expenduntur vii lib. candelarum de stauro. Stabulum Fenum pro xxvi equis iiii hakeneis de stauro. In avenis pro eisdem i qr. iii bus. avenarum. Item fenum apud Remesbur' pro xx equis iii hakeneis de stauro. In prebenda eorundem vii bus. avenarum.

Probatur Summa empcionum ix s. v d.

Panteria De precomputato. Celarium Vinum de remanentia. Butillaria De precomputato.[113] Coquina Empciones <nichil> ix s. v d. Candelaria De stauro. Stabulum Fenum avene de stauro.

[*f.27r*] *Gentiles xxv Valecti et garciones lx Summa ferculorum iiii*^{xx}*v*

Extranii suffraganus domini se iiii^{o} *Hulcot cum uxore et*[114] *aliis vi Becot se iii*^{o} *Stanes se iii*^{o} *Metford se ii*^{o} *More se ii*^{o} *et alii l*

Die veneris xxxi^{o} Decembris Panteria Expenduntur Clx panes unde pro ferculis iiii^{xx}v trencheris x liberacionibus x coquina iii canibus xxvi et tantum quia Hulcot habuit v leporarios rewardis xxvi panes. Et remanent xlii panes. Celarium Expenduntur viii lag. vini de remanentia. Butillaria Expenduntur lxx lag. cervisie. Et remanent Dxxxv lag. cervisie. Coquina Expenduntur CC allec album C allec rubium vii congri salcii viii stok' de stauro. Item iiC[115] ova de precomputato. Item in lacte iii d. In xvi casiis emptis ii s. iiii d. et expensis. Candelaria Expenduntur viii lib. candelarum de stauro. Stabulum Fenum pro l equis iiii hakeneis de stauro. In avenis pro eisdem i qr. iiii bus. di. avenarum. Item fenum apud Remesbur' pro xx equis iii hakeneis de stauro. In avenis pro eisdem vii bus.

Probatur Summa empcionum ii s. vii d.

Panteria De precomputato. Celarium Vinum de remanentia. Butillaria De precomputato. Coquina Empciones ii s. vii d. Candelaria De stauro. Stabulum Fenum avene de stauro.

Summa empcionum istius mensis xxvi li. ii d. ob.[116]

[*f.27v*] *Poterne Gentiles xliii Valecti garciones* <*l*> *C Summa ferculorum Cxliii*

Extranii <*Summa ferculorum*> *suffraganus domini se iiii*^{o} *Hulcot cum uxore se viii*^{o} *Becot se iii*^{o} *Stanes se ii*^{o} *Metford se ii*^{o} *J.Peres se iii*^{o} *et alii de tenentibus domini lx*

Die sabbati primo Januarii Panteria Furniuntur per i talliam ii qr. iiii bus. frumenti que respondent ad Dviii panes. Et expenduntur CC panes unde

[113] MS 'precompciones'.

[114] MS omits 'et'.

[115] MS 'iiCC'.

[116] Totals £26. 1*s*. 2½*d*.

pro ferculis Cxliii panes trencheris xvi liberacionibus x coquina iiii canibus xx rewardis vii panes. Et remanent CCCl panes. Celarium Expenduntur xvi lag. vini de remanentia. Butillaria Expenduntur C lag. vini de remanentia. <Butillaria> Et remanent CCCCxxxv lag. cervisie. Coquina CC allec rubium CCl allec album xii pisces salcii xviii stok' iii salmones salcii ii pikes ii anguille grosse iiii roches iiii perches CC ova de precomputato. Candelaria Expenduntur ix lib. candelarum de stauro. Stabulum Fenum pro liiii equis iiii hakeneis de stauro. In avenis pro eisdem ii qr. avenarum de stauro. Item fenum apud Remesbur' pro xxiiii equis ii hakeneis de stauro. In prebenda eorundem i qr. i bus. avenarum.

Summa empcionum[117]

Panteria Furniuntur ii qr. iiii bus. frumenti que respondent ad vCviii panes. Celarium Vinum de remanentia. Butillaria De precomputato. Coquina Empciones nichil. Candelaria De stauro. Stabulum Fenum avene[118]

Gentiles <xv> Cxx Valecti garciones iiii^{xx}xv Summa ferculorum CCxv Extranii suffraganus domini se iii^{o} Hulcot' cum uxore et aliis x Metford se iiii^{o} Becot se iii^{o} Stanes se ii^{o} Hunt se ii^{o} magister Simon Best se ii^{o} maior de Vise cum xxiiii burgencibus de eadem et de tenentibus domini de la Vis Grene et Canyng' Cxx vicarius ville cum ii capellanis Johannes Nicolas se iii^{o} Bakhouse se ii^{o} Summa extraniorum Clxvi

Die dominica secundo Januarii Panteria Furniuntur per i talliam ii qr. frumenti que respondent ad CCCCiiii panes. Et expenduntur CCCC panes unde pro ferculis CCxv panes trencheris xx liberacionibus x coquina xvi canibus xvi rewardis Cxxiii panes. Et remanent CCCliiii panes. Celarium Expenduntur xxxiii lag. vini de remanentia. Butillaria Expenduntur CC lag. cervisie. Et remanent CCxxxv lag. cervisie. Coquina Expenduntur i carcosium bovis v casse multonum de precomputato. Item expenduntur ii porci de stauro. Item xii capones xxviii galline de precomputato. Item iiii cigni de stauro xx auce. In x cassis multonum emptis <xviii s. viii d.> \ xvi s. viii d. / et expenduntur v. In ii carcosiis vitulorum emptis et expensis vii s. iiii d. In xxii porcellis emptis viii s. x d. et expenduntur xviii. In vii aucis emptis ii s. iiii d. In iiii caponibus emptis xiii d. In iii gallinis emptis vi d. In ixC ovis emptis iii s. ix d. In lacte x d. et expenso. In ix snites emptis iii d. In vi plovers emptis xii d. In iiii^{xx}xiiii grossis avibus emptis ii s. In xxx parvis avibus emptis iii d. et expensis. Item expenduntur xxxi cuniculi. Item expenduntur iii fasiani de stauro. Item expenduntur ii dami salcii iii dami recentes de stauro. Item iii pulcini de precomputato. Candelaria Expenduntur x lib. candelarum de stauro. Stabulum Fenum pro xxxi equis iii hakeneis de stauro. In avenis pro eisdem i qr. ii bus. avenarum de stauro. Item fenum

[117] Followed by a blank space in MS.
[118] Followed by a blank space in MS.

apud Remesbur' pro xxiii equis ii hakeneis de stauro. In avenis pro eisdem i qr. ii pec.

Probatur   Summa empcionum xliiii s. x d.

Panteria Furniuntur ii qr. frumenti que respondent ad iiiiCiiii panes. Celarium Vinum de remanentia. Butillaria De precomputato. Coquina Empciones xliiii s. x d. Candelaria De stauro. Stabulum Fenum avene de stauro.

[*f.28r*] *Poterne Gentiles xlv Valecti garciones lxx Summa ferculorum Cxv*
Extranii suffraganus <Summa ferculorum> Hulcot se viii^{o} *R.Hunt se iii*^{o} *Becot se ii*^{o} *Metford se ii*^{o} *Johannes Perus se ii*^{o} *ii fratres*[119] *et alii xxx*

Die lune iii^{o} Januarii Panteria Expenduntur Clxxviii panes unde pro ferculis Cxv panes trencheris xiiii liberacionibus vii coquina x canibus xv panes rewardis xvii panes. Et remanent Clxxvi panes. Celarium Expenduntur xii lag. vini de remanentia. Butillaria Expenduntur iiii^{xx} lag. cervisie. Et remanent Clv lag. cervisie. Coquina Expenduntur i qr. di. bovis ii casse di. multonum de precomputato. Item expenduntur ii bacones de stauro. Item expenduntur x cuniculi de precomputato. Item expenduntur x capones viii galline de precomputato. Candelaria Expenduntur vi lib. candelarum de stauro. Stabulum Fenum pro xiiii equis iiii hakeneis de stauro. In avenis pro eisdem i qr. ii bus. avenarum. Item fenum apud Remesbur' pro xxiii equis ii hakeneis de stauro. In prebenda eorundem i qr. i bus. avenarum de stauro.

Panteria De precomputato. Celarium Vinum de remanentia. Butillaria De precomputato. Coquina Empciones nichil. Candelaria De stauro. Stabulum Fenum avene de stauro.

Gentiles iiii^{xx}*x Valecti garciones Cviii Summa ferculorum Ciiii*^{xx}*xviii*
Extranii suffraganus se iii^{o} *magister W.Metford se iii*^{o} *prior de Pokele se vi*^{o} *Hulcot se viii*^{o} *R.Hunt se ii*^{o} *Metford se ii*^{o} *vicarius de Lavingt' se ii*^{o} *vicarius de Roude se ii*^{o} *vicarius de Synde rector de Cheverell' se ii*^{o} *Becot se ii*^{o} *magister Radulphus se vi*^{o} *magister J.Wotton' se iii*^{o} *vicarius ville se iii*^{o} *rector de Poulesholt rector de Brigthton' Johannes Nicholas se ii*^{o} *Lepyat se iii*^{o} *magister T.Thirlewall' et alii de tenentibus domini de Lavyngt' C Latton' se iii*^{o} *Goderich' se ii*^{o}

Die martis iiii^{o} Januarii Panteria Furniuntur per i talliam ii qr. iiii bus. frumenti que respondent ad Diii panes. Et expenduntur CCCC panes unde pro ferculis Ciiii^{xx}xviii panes trencheris xxv liberacionibus vii coquina xvi canibus x rewardis Cxliiii panes. Et remanent CClxxix panes. Celarium Expenduntur xx lag. vini de remanentia. Butillaria Expenduntur Clv lag. <v> cervisie. Et nichil remanet. Coquina Expenduntur iii qr. bovis v casse multonum de precomputato. Item expenditur i porcus de stauro. Item

[119] MS 'frates'.

expenduntur xii capones xx galline x auce iii cigni de stauro. In i carcosio vituli empto iiii s. et expenso. In viii caponibus emptis ii s. viii d. In lx cuniculis emptis xv s. et expenduntur ix porcelli de precomputato. Item expenduntur xxx cuniculi de precomputato. Item expenduntur ii dami recentes de exhennio CCC ova de precomputato. Candelaria[120] Expenduntur x lib. candelarum de stauro. Stabulum Fenum pro xxviii equis iiii hakeneis de stauro. In prebenda eorundem i qr. iiii bus. avenarum de stauro. Item fenum apud Remesbur' pro xxiii equis ii hakeneis de stauro. In prebenda eorundem i qr. i bus. avenarum de stauro.

Probatur Summa empcionum xxi s. viii d.

Panteria Furniuntur ii qr. iiii bus. frumenti que respondent ad[121] vCiii panes. Celarium Vinum de remanentia. Butillaria De precomputato. Coquina Empciones xxi s. viii d. Candelaria De stauro. Stabulum Fenum avene de stauro.

[*f.28v*] *Poterne Gentiles xlvi Valecti garciones lxxii Summa ferculorum Cxviii*

Extranii magister Walterus Metford se vii^{o} *magister Simon Sydenham se v*^{o} *Bonham se iiii*^{o} *Laurencius Dru se vii*^{o} *Wilescoumbe se iiii*^{o} *R.Hunt se iii*^{o} *Becot se ii*^{o} *Hulcote se vii*^{o} *magister J.Wotton' se ii*^{o} *Latton' se ii*^{o} *Metford se ii*^{o} *Goderych' se ii*^{o} *et alii xliii*

Die mercurie v Januarii Panteria Expenduntur CC panes unde pro ferculis Cxviii panes trencheris xv liberacionibus viii coquina viii canibus xii rewardis xxxix panes. Et remanent lxxix panes. Celarium Expenduntur viii lag. vini de remanentia. Butillaria <Ex. . .> In Cxix lag. cervisie emptis de Shepherd' precium lag. i d. ob. deductis inde x lag. de avantagio xiii s. vii d. ob. In xxvi lag. cervisie emptis de eadem[122] precium lag. i d. deductis inde ii lag. de avantagio ii s. In lxxv lag. cervisie emptis de Carlet precium lag. i d. ob. deductis inde vi lag. cervisie de avantagio viii s. vii d. ob. In xxxvi lag. cervisie emptis de eadem[123] precium lag. i d. deductis inde iii lag. de avantagio ii s. x d. In lxii lag. cervisie emptis de Johanne atte Nasshe precium lag. i d. ob. deductis inde v lag. de avantagio vii s. i d. ob. In xiiii lag. cervisie emptis de eodem precium lag. i d. deducta inde i lag. de avantagio xiii d. In iiii^{xx} lag. cervisie emptis de Lang' precium lag. i d. deductis inde vi lag. di. de avantagio ix s. ii d. ob. In xl lag. cervisie emptis de eodem precium lag. i d. deductis inde iii lag. di. de avantagio iii s. ob. In xlvi lag. cervisie emptis de Felicia Aas precium lag. i d. ob. deductis inde iii

[120] MS omits underline.
[121] MS omits 'ad'.
[122] MS 'eodem'.
[123] MS 'eodem'.

lag. di. v s. iii d. ob. In xxx lag. cervisie emptis de eadem[124] precium lag. i d. deductis inde ii lag. di. de avantagio ii s. iii d. ob. In lxxiiii lag. cervisie emptis de Axford precium lag. i d. ob. deductis inde vi lag. de avantagio viii s. vi d. In xxiiii lag. cervisie emptis de eadem[125] precium lag. i d. deductis inde ii lag. xxii d. Et expenduntur iiii^{xx}x lag. cervisie. Et remanent Dxxxvi lag. cervisie. Coquina Expenduntur i qr. di. bovis iii casse di. multonum vi capones iiii galline viii cuniculi de exhennio CCl ova de precomputato. Item expenduntur l allec album l allec rubium ii pisces salcii i congrus salcius i salmon' salcius. In iiii lag. lactis emptis et expensis iiii d. In casio empto iii d. et expenso. In DCCC ovis emptis iii s. iiii d. In i lag. di. i pint olei emptis xx d. et expensis. Candelaria Expenduntur <viii> \ x / lib. candelarum de stauro. Stabulum Fenum pro lxvi equis vii hakeneis de stauro. In prebenda eorundem iii qr. iiii bus. avenarum. Item fenum apud Remesbury pro xxiii equis ii hakeneis de stauro. In avenis pro eisdem i qr. i bus.

Probatur Summa empcionum lxxi s. ob. unde

Panteria De precomputato. Celarium Vinum de remanentia. Butillaria In DCxxvi lag. cervisie lxv s. v d. ob. Coquina Empciones v s. vii d. Candelaria De stauro. Stabulum Fenum avene de stauro.

Gentiles xlv Valecti garciones iiii^{xx}xii Summa ferculorum Cxxxvii

Extranii magister W.Metford ut supra magister Simon Sydenham se v^{o} Bonham se iiii^{o} Laurencius Dru se vi^{o} Hulcot se viii^{o} R.Hunt se ii^{o} Metford se ii^{o} Becot se ii^{o} Latton' se ii^{o} Holgrave se ii^{o} Goderich se ii^{o} et alii xl

Die jovis vi^{o} Januarii Panteria Furniuntur per i talliam i qr. vii bus. frumenti que respondent ad CCCiiii^{xx} panes. Et expenduntur Ciiii^{xx}xviii[126] panes unde pro ferculis Cxxxvii panes trencheris x liberacionibus viii coquina iiii canibus x rewardis. Et remanent CClxi panes. Celarium Expenduntur xv lag. vini de remanentia. Butillaria Expenduntur iiii^{xx}viii lag. cervisie. Et remanent CCCCxlviii lag. cervisie. Coquina Expenduntur i qr. di. bovis ii casse di. multonum ii bacones de stauro. Item expenditur i aper de precomputato. Item expenditur i porcus de precomputato. Item xi capones x galline vi auce ii cigni de precomputato. In vii cassis multonum emptis ix s. vi d. et expenduntur ii. In ii carcosiis vitulorum emptis et expensis viii s. iiii d. In iiii porcellis emptis et expensis xx d. In v aucis emptis xxi d. In \ xl / iiii grossis avibus emptis x d. In ii plovers iiii d. In ii wodecok*es* et iii grossis avibus emptis iii d. et expensis. Item expenduntur xxiiii cuniculi. Item expenduntur iii maulard*i* de rivera ii wodecok*es* de precomputato. Item expenduntur CC ova de precomputato. Candelaria

[124] MS 'eodem'.

[125] MS 'eodem'.

[126] 169 loaves disbursed.

Expenduntur viii lib. candelarum de stauro. Stabulum Fenum pro lx equis v hakeneis de stauro. In avenis pro eisdem iii qr. de stauro. Item fenum apud Remesbury pro xvii equis ii hakeneis de stauro. In avenis pro eisdem vi bus. avenarum.

Probatur Summa empcionum xxii s. viii d.

Panteria Furniuntur i qr. vii bus. frumenti que respondent ad[127] CCCiiii^{xx} panes. Celarium Vinum de remanentia. Butillaria De precomputato. Coquina Empciones xxii s. viii d. Candelaria De stauro. Stabulum Fenum avene[128]

[*f.29r*] *Gentiles xx Valecti garciones xliii Summa ferculorum lxiii*
Extranii magister W. ut supra magister S.Sydenham se vi° Hulcot se viii° R.Hunt se ii° Becot se ii° Metford se ii° magister J.Wotton' se ii° Gore se iii° Johannes Skriveyn se ii° et alii xxx

Die veneris vii° Januarii Panteria Expenduntur iiii^{xx}x panes unde pro ferculis lxiii panes trencheris iiii liberacionibus v coquina iii canibus x rewardis v panes. Et remanent Clxx panes.[129] Celarium Expenduntur v lag. vini de remanentia. Butillaria Expenduntur l lag. cervisie. Coquina Expenduntur CC allec album C allec rubium iii pisces salcii viii stok' ii salmones salcii. Item CC ova de stauro. In MCCC ostriis emptis ii s. iiii d. ob. et expenduntur DC. In CCCCl welkes emptis xi d. <In> et expenduntur CC. In iiii lag. lactis di. et expensis iiii d. ob. In expensis emptoris per ii dies precedentes iii d. Candelaria Expenduntur viii lib. candelarum de stauro. Stabulum Fenum pro xxxiii equis v hakeneis de stauro. In avenis pro eisdem i qr. ii bus. avenarum de stauro. Item fenum apud Remesbur' pro xvii equis ii hakeneis de stauro. In avenis pro eisdem vi bus. di. avenarum de stauro.

Probatur Summa empcionum iii s. xi d.

Panteria De precomputato. Celarium Vinum de remanentia. Butillaria De precomputato. Coquina Empciones iii s. xi d. Candelaria De stauro. Stabulum Fenum avene[130]

Gentiles xxix Valecti garciones xliii Summa ferculorum lxxii
Extranii Hulcot se vi° Hunt se iiii° Becot se ii° Walront se iii° et alii x

Die sabbati viii° Januarii Panteria Expenduntur Cx panes unde pro ferculis lxxii panes trencheris v liberacionibus v coquina iii canibus ix rewardis xvi panes. Et remanent lx panes. Celarium Expenduntur vi lag. vini de stauro remanenti. Butillaria Expenduntur l lag. cervisie. Et remanent CCCxlviii lag. cervisie. Coquina Expenduntur CCl allec album C allec rubium iii

[127] MS omits 'ad'.
[128] Followed by a blank space in MS.
[129] 171 loaves remain.
[130] Followed by a blank space in MS.

pisces salcii ii salmones salcii viii stok' de stauro. In i hake xx gurnard et viii merling emptis et expensis iiii s. vi d. In expensis emptoris de Pot*er*ne usque Wermustr' v d. In lacte i d. et expenduntur viiC<C> ostria de precomputato. Item expenduntur C ova de precomputato. Candelaria Expenduntur viii lib. candelarum de stauro. Stabulum Fenum pro xiiii equis iiii hakeneis de stauro. In prebenda eorundem vii bus. avenarum de stauro. Item fenum apud Remesbury pro xxii equis ii hakeneis de stauro. In prebenda eorundem i qr. i bus. avenarum de stauro.

Probatur Summa empcionum v s.

Panteria De precomputato. Celarium Vinum de remanentia. Butillaria De precomputato. Coquina Empciones v s. Candelaria De stauro. Stabulum Fenum avene de stauro.

In vadiis Thome Ferro*ur* a xi^{o} die Decembris usque viii diem Januarii utroque computato capientis per diem iii d. ii s. vi d.

In vadiis pagetti senescalli apud Remesbur' a xxiiii^{o} die Decembris usque viii diem Januarii utroque computato videlicet per xvi dies capientis per diem i d. ob. ii s.

Item in vadiis pagetti Shupton' ibidem per xvii dies capientis per diem i d. ob. ii s. i d. ob.

Item in vadiis Forey pagetti Cap*er*on' et pagetti Holcot' a xxvi^{o} die Decembris usque viii diem Januarii utroque computato capiencium inter se per diem iiii d. ob. v s. iii d.

Item in vadiis Johannis Lang ibidem per xi dies pagetti Restewold per xi dies et pagetti Tydemerssh' per xii dies quilibet capiens per diem i d. ob. iiii s. iii d.

Item in vadiis Bath' ibidem a xxv^{o} die Decembris usque viii diem Januarii et Thome Norman ibidem per x dies quilibet capiens per diem ii d. iiii s.

In vadiis pagetti cancellarii ibidem per xi dies capientis per diem i d. ob. <ii s. ix d.> \ xxii d. /

Probatur Summa xxi s. xi d. ob.

xxi s. xi d. ob. <xxii s. x d. ob.>[131]

[*f.29v*] *Poterne Gentiles xxix Valecti garciones xlv Summa ferculorum lxxiiii Extranii Hulcot se viii^{o} . . . Hunt se iiii^{o} Becot se ii^{o} Walront se ii^{o} . . . alii xiiii*

Die dominica ix^{o} Januarii Panteria Furniuntur per i talliam ii qr. frumenti que respondent ad CCCCv panes. Et expenduntur Cxx panes unde pro ferculis lxxiiii panes trencheris viii liberacionibus vi coquina iii canibus x rewardis xix panes. Et remanent CCCxlv panes. Celarium Expenduntur viii lag. vini de remanentia. Butillaria Expenduntur liii lag. cervisie. Et remanent CCiiii^{xx}xv lag. cervisie. Coquina Expenditur i qr. di. bovis de stauro. Item expenduntur di. apri i bacon' de stauro. Item di. porcus de

[131] Both sums in the bottom right hand corner in another hand.

stauro. Item expenduntur ii casse multonum de precomputato. Item expenduntur iiii capones vi galline C ova de precomputato. In ii cassis multonum emptis[132] ii s. viii d. In i carcosio vituli empto et expenso iiii s. \ Item expenduntur iii cuniculi. / In iii porcellis emptis xii d. In vi caponibus emptis ii s. In ii gallinis emptis iiii d. In expensis emptoris i d. Candelaria Expenduntur <x> viii <lag.> lib. candelarum de stauro. Stabulum Fenum pro xv equis iiii hakeneis de stauro. In prebenda eorundem v bus. avenarum de stauro. Item fenum apud Remesbur' pro xxiii equis ii hakeneis de stauro. In avenis pro eisdem i qr. i bus. avenarum.

Probatur Summa empcionum x s. i d.

Panteria Furniuntur ii qr. frumenti que respondent ad iiiiCv panes. Celarium Vinum de remanentia. Butillaria De precomputato. Coquina Empciones x s. i d. Candelaria De stauro. Stabulum Fenum avene de stauro.

Gentiles xxxii Valecti garciones <xxxii> \ lv / Summa ferculorum iiii^{xx}vii Extranii Bonham se iii^{o} . . .awein se iii^{o} . . .lcot se viii^{o} . . . Hunt se iii^{o} . . .scoumbe se ii^{o} . . . Ministrall'[133] *se ii^{o} . . . alii xx*

Die lune x^{o} Januarii Panteria Expenduntur Cxx panes unde pro ferculis iiii^{xx}vii panes trencheris x liberacionibus iiii coquina iii canibus x rewardis vi panes. Et remanent CCxxv panes. Celarium Expenduntur vi lag. vini de remanentia. Butillaria Expenduntur l lag. cervisie. Et remanent CCxlv lag. cervisie. Coquina Expenduntur i qr. bovis i bacon' de stauro. Item expenduntur iii casse multonum iiii capones viii galline de precomputato. Item expenduntur xliiii grosse[134] aves ii plovers ii wodecok*es* iii grosse aves de precomputato. Candelaria Expenduntur viii lib. candelarum de stauro. Stabulum Fenum pro xxvi equis iiii hakeneis de stauro. In prebenda eorundem i qr. iii bus. avenarum de stauro. Item fenum apud Remesbur' pro xix equis iii hakeneis de stauro. In avenis pro eisdem i qr. avenarum. Panteria De precomputato. Celarium Vinum de remanentia. Butillaria De precomputato. Coquina Empciones nichil. Candelaria de stauro. Stabulum Fenum avene de stauro.

[f.30r] Poterne Gentiles xx Valecti garciones xxxviii Summa ferculorum lviii Magister Johannes Keteryk' se vi^{o} Robertus Hunte se ii^{o} et alii extranii xii

Die sabbati xv^{o} Januarii Panteria Expenduntur Ciiii panes[135] unde pro ferculis lviii trencheris vi liberacionibus v coquina[136] iiii canibus v rewardis xxxi. Et remanent Cxlix panes. Celarium Expend*un*tur[137] lag. vini de

[132] MS repeats 'empt''.
[133] MS ?'Minustrall''.
[134] Possibly an error for 'minute'.
[135] The arithmetic cannot be followed.
[136] MS 'can''.
[137] Followed by a blank space in MS.

stauro. Butillaria Expenduntur xliiii lag. cervisie. Et remanent xliiii lag. cervisie.[138] Coquina Expenduntur Cl allec album l rubium ii pisces salcii ii salmones salcii ii stok' Cl ova de precomputato. In iiii thornbak*es* Ciiii^{xx} pylch*er*s emptis iii s. iiii d. In i lag. <lag.> lactis empta i d. Item expenduntur D ostria de precomputato. Candelaria Expenduntur vi lib. candelarum de stauro. Stabulum Fenum pro xiiii equis v hakeneis de stauro. In prebenda vi bus. di. avenarum de stauro. Item fenum pro xvii equis iii hakeneis de stauro. In avenis pro eisdem vii bus. pec. avenarum de stauro.

Probatur Summa empcionum iii s. v d.

Panteria De precomputato. Celarium Vinum de remanentia. Butillaria De precomputato. Coquina Empciones iii s. v d. Candelaria De stauro. Stabulum Fenum avene de stauro.

Gentiles xxvii Valecti garciones xlviii Summa ferculorum lxxv

Magister Johannes Chytterne se viii^{o} magister Johannes Keterryk' se viii^{o} vicarius ville et alii extranii xv

Die dominica xvi Januarii Panteria Expenduntur Cxxiiii panes[139] unde pro ferculis lxxv panes trencheris x liberacionibus vi coquine[140] iiii canibus vi rewardis xxiii. Et remanent xxv panes. Celarium Expend*un*tur[141] lag. vini de stauro. Butillaria Expenduntur xliiii lag. cervisie de precomputato. <Candelaria> Coquina Expenduntur i qr. bovis i baco de stauro. Item ii casse di. multonum i caponis vi galline iiii wodecok*es* iiii^{xx}iii grosse aves l ova de precomputato. Item expenduntur di. porcus i cignus de stauro. Item ii porcelli v cuniculi de precomputato. In ii porcellis emptis et expensis viii d. In xlviii grossis avibus emptis vi d. In x cuniculis emptis ii s. vi d. Candelaria Expenduntur vii lib. candelarum de stauro. \ *vii lib.* / Stabulum Fenum pro x equis v hakeneis de stauro. In prebenda eorundem vi bus. avenarum de stauro. Item fenum apud Remesbur' pro xviii equis ii hakeneis de stauro. In avenis pro eisdem vii bus. pec.

Probatur Summa empcionum iii s. viii d.

Panteria De precomputato. Celarium Vinum de remanentia. Butillaria De precomputato. Coquina Empciones iii s. viii d. Candelaria De stauro. Stabulum Fenum avene de stauro.

[*f.30v*] *Poterne Gentiles xxiii Valecti garciones xl <Garciones> Summa ferculorum lxiii*

Rector de Alynton' se ii^{o} et alii extranii xii Magister Johannes Chitterne se viii^{o}

[138] 201 gallons should remain.

[139] MS 'lag. cervisie'.

[140] Underlined in MS.

[141] Followed by a blank space in MS.

Die lune xvii° Januarii Panteria Furniuntur per i talliam i qr. vii bus. frumenti de stauro que respondent de CCCiiii^{xx}i. Et expenduntur Cxx panes unde pro ferculis lxiii trencheris x liberacionibus vi coquine iiii canibus vii rewardis xxx panes. Et remanent CCiiii^{xx}vi panes. Celarium Expend*un*tur[142] lag. vini de stauro. Butillaria In lxix lag. cervisie emptis de Warner precium lag. i d. ob. deductis inde vi lag. cervisie vii s. x d. ob. In xxiiii lag. cervisie emptis de eodem precium lag. i d. deductis inde ii lag. de avantagio xxiii d. In lxx lag. cervisie emptis de Axford precium lag. i d. ob. deductis inde vi lag. cervisie de avantagio viii s. \ i d. ob. / In xvii lag. cervisie emptis de eadem[143] precium lag. i d. deducta inde i lag. de cervisia xv d. ob. In x lag. cervisie emptis de Walssh' de Devys' precium lag. i d. ob. xv d. Et expenduntur xxxviii lag. cervisie. Et remanent Clii lag. cervisie. Coquina Expenduntur i qr. bovis i baco de stauro. Item ii casse multonum i caponis de precomputato. Item ii galline de stauro. Item iii wodecok*es* CC ova de precomputato. Candelaria Expend*un*tur[144] lib. candelarum de stauro. Stabulum Fenum pro vi equis iiii hakeneis de stauro. In prebenda eorundem iii bus. avenarum de stauro. Item fenum apud Remesbur' pro xviii equis ii hakeneis de stauro. In avenis pro eisdem vii bus.

Probatur Summa empcionum xx s. v d. ob.

Panteria Furniuntur i qr. vii bus. frumenti que respondent ad iiiCiiii^{xx}i panes. Celarium Vinum de remanentia. Butillaria In Ciiii^{xx}x lag. cervisie emptis xx s. v d. ob. Coquina Empciones nichil. Candelaria De stauro Stabulum Fenum avene de stauro.

Gentiles xxiii Valecti garciones lx Summa ferculorum iiii^{xx}iii

Extranii rector de Alynton' vicarius ville et de tenentibus domini de Poterne cariantibus buscum xx

Die martis xviii° Januarii Panteria Expenduntur Cxxiiii panes unde pro ferculis iiii^{xx}iii trencheris viii liberacionibus v coquine iiii canibus vi rewardis xviii. Et remanent Clxiii panes.[145] Celarium Expend*un*tur[146] lag. vini de stauro. Butillaria Expenduntur xlviii lag. cervisie. Et remanent Ciiii lag. cervisie. Coquina Expenduntur i qr. bovis i baco di. <de> viii galline di. porcus de stauro. Item ii casse di. multonum v cuniculi l ova de precomputato. In v cassis multonum emptis viii s. iiii d. In ii porcellis emptis et expensis viii d. In ii gallinis emptis et i caponis vii d. In vii pulcinis emptis vi d. Candelaria Expend*un*tur[147] lib. candelarum de stauro. Stabulum Fenum pro xiiii equis iiii hakeneis de stauro. In prebenda eorundem vi bus.

[142] Followed by a blank space in MS.

[143] MS 'eodem'.

[144] Followed by a blank space in MS.

[145] 162 loaves should remain.

[146] Followed by a blank space in MS.

[147] Followed by a blank space in MS.

avenarum de stauro. Item fenum apud Remesbur' pro xviii equis. In prebenda eorundem vii bus. avenarum.

Probatur   Summa empcionum x s. i d.

Panteria De precomputato. Celarium Vinum de remanentia. Butillaria De precomputato. Coquina Empciones x s. i d. Candelaria De stauro. Stabulum Fenum avene[148]

[*f.31r*] *Poterne Gentiles xxiiii Valecti garciones xlviii Summa ferculorum lxxii*

Extranii vicarius ville et alii extranii x

Die mercurie xix Januarii Panteria Expenduntur Cx panes unde pro ferculis lxxii trencheris vii liberacionibus vi coquine[149] iii canibus vi rewardis xvi panes. Et remanent liii panes. Celarium Expenduntur iiii lag. vini de stauro. Butillaria Expenduntur xxxviii lag. cervisie. <de> Et remanent lxvi lag. cervisie. Coquina Expenduntur di. qr. bovis i baco de stauro. Item ii casse multonum l ova de precomputato. Item expenduntur xiii allec rubium xxv album di. piscis salcius di. salmo salsius de precomputato. Item iii lag. lactis emptis et expensis iii d. In DCC ovis emptis ii s. xi d. Candelaria Expenduntur iii lib. candelarum. Stabulum Fenum pro xv equis ii hakeneis de stauro. In prebenda eorundem vi bus. avenarum de stauro. Item fenum apud Remesbur' pro xviii equis iii hakeneis de stauro. In avenis pro eisdem vii bus. avenarum de stauro.

Probatur   Summa empcionum iii s. ii d.

Panteria De precomputato. Celarium Vinum de stauro remanenti. Butillaria De precomputato. Coquina Empciones iii s. ii d. Candelaria De stauro. Stabulum Fenum avene de stauro.

Gentiles xxi Valecti garciones xxxvi Summa ferculorum lvii

Extranii Sotysbrook' se ii^{o} vicarius ville et alii xii

Die jovis xx^{o} Januarii Panteria Furniuntur per i talliam ii qr. frumenti de stauro que respondent de CCCCv panibus. Et expenduntur Cviii panes[150] unde pro ferculis lvii trencheris vi liberacionibus v coquine iiii canibus vi rewardis xxxi panes. Et remanent CCCl panes. Celarium Expenduntur iiii lag. vini de stauro. Butillaria Expenduntur xxxiiii lag. cervisie. Et remanent xxxii lag. cervisie. Coquina Expenduntur i qr. bovis i baco de stauro. Item ii casse di. multonum i caponis i gallina de precomputato. In ii casse multonum emptis iii s. ii d. In ii porcellis emptis et expensis viii d. In ii caponibus emptis viii d. In vii gallinis emptis xiiii d. In Cxlix grossis avibus et ii snyt*es* emptis ii s. vii d. <I> Et expenduntur iiii^{xx}. In expensis emptoris ii d. ob. Candelaria Expenduntur v lib. candelarum de stauro.

[148] Followed by a blank space in MS.

[149] Underlined in MS.

[150] 109 loaves disbursed.

Stabulum Fenum pro ix equis iii hakeneis de stauro. In prebenda eorundem iiii bus. avenarum de stauro. Item fenum apud Remesbury xix° <die> equis ii hakeneis de stauro. In avenis pro eisdem vii bus. di.
In vadiis Thome Ferro*ur* apud Remesbur' a viii° die Januarii usque xx diem eiusdem videlicet per xiiii dies iii s. vi d.
In vadiis garcionis eiusdem ibidem per idem tempus capientis per diem ii d. ii s. iiii d.
In vadiis garcionis cancellarii per idem tempus capientis per diem ii d. ii s. iiii d.
In vadiis Forey pagetti Cap*er*on' et pagetti Shupton' per idem tempus quilibet capiens per diem i d. ob. v s. iii d.
In vadiis Thome Norman' ibidem per vii dies capientis per diem ii d. xiiii d.
In vadiis pagetti Tidemerssh' per x dies pagetti Hulcot per xiii dies capiencium inter se per diem iii d. ii s. x d. ob.
Item in vadiis Galfridi Chariet*er* ibidem per v dies capientis per diem ii d. ob. xii d. ob.
Item in vadiis garcionis eiusdem ibidem per idem tempus capientis per diem ii d. x d.

Probatur unde Summa empcionum \ cum vadiis / xxvii s. ix d. ob.

Panteria Furniuntur ii qr. frumenti que respondent ad iiiiCvi panes. Celarium Vinum de remanentia. Butillaria De precomputato. Coquina Empciones viii s. v d. ob. Candelaria De stauro. Stabulum Fenum avene de stauro. Vadia xix s. iiii d. <ob.>
[*f.31v*] *Poterne Gentiles xiiii Valecti garciones xxvii Summa ferculorum xli Extranii* sire *Johannes Berkle se x et alii viii*
Die veneris xxi Januarii Panteria Expenduntur iiii^{xx}v panes unde pro ferculis xli trencheris vi liberacionibus v coquine ii canibus viii rewardis xxiii. Et remanent CClxv panes. Celarium Expenduntur iiii lag. vini de stauro. Butillaria Expenduntur xxviii lag. cervisie. Et remanent iiii lag. cervisie. Coquina Expenduntur Cl allec album i qr. rubii i piscis salcius et di. de precomputato. \ In CCClx allece albo expensis v s. / In pisce recenti empto videlicet i turbut i leng l merlyng xxiiii gurnard emptis ix s. et expenduntur di. turbut xxv[151] merlyng et xii gurnard. In ii lag. lactis emptis et expensis ii d. Candelaria Expenduntur v lib. candelarum de stauro. Stabulum Fenum pro xxiiii equis ii hakeneis de stauro. In prebenda i qr. ii bus. avenarum de stauro. Item fenum apud Remesbury pro xii equis iii hakeneis de stauro. In prebenda eorundem v bus. avenarum.

Probatur Summa empcionum xiiii s. ii d. <ob>.

Panteria De precomputato. Celarium Vinum de remanentia. Butillaria De

[151] MS 'xxv et merlyng xii gurnard'.

precomputato. Coquina Empciones xiiii s. ii d. <ob.> Candelaria De stauro. Stabulum Fenum avene de stauro.
Gentiles xix Valecti garciones xxxix Summa ferculorum lviii
Extranii vicarius ville et alii xiii
Die sabbati xxii Januarii Panteria Expenduntur Cviii panes[152] unde pro ferculis lviii trencheris iiii liberacionibus v coquine ii canibus viii rewardis xxx. Et remanent Clvii panes. Celarium Expenduntur iiii lag. vini de stauro. Butillaria <Expend*un*tur> In Cxliii lag. cervisie emptis de Shepherd' precium lag. i d. ob. deductis inde xii lag. de avantagio xvi s. iiii d. ob. In xl lag. cervisie emptis de eadem precium lag. i d. deductis inde iii lag. de avantagio iii s. i d. Et expenduntur xxxviii lag. cervisie. Et remanent Cxlix lag. cervisie. Coquina Expenduntur Cl allec album i qr. rubii i piscis salsius et di. di. salmo salcius de stauro. In M ostriis emptis xx d. et expenduntur CCCC ostria. In i lag. lactis empta i d. et expensa. Item expenduntur xii merlyng vi gurnard di. turbut i leng recens l ova de precomputato. Candelaria Expenduntur v lib. candelarum de stauro. Stabulum Fenum pro viii equis ii hakeneis de stauro. In prebenda eorundem iiii bus. di. avenarum de stauro. Item fenum apud Remesbur' pro xii equis de stauro. In prebenda eorundem v bus. avenarum de stauro.
Item in vadiis Galfridi Cato*ur* cum equo suo equitantis London' pro victualibus ibidem emendis per viii dies v s. iiii d.
Item solutum famulo Tidemerssh' pro vadiis suis per x dies capienti per diem i d. ob. xv d.

Probatur Summa empcionum \ cum vadiis / xxvii s. <viii> \ ix / d. ob. unde

Panteria De precomputato. Celarium Vinum de remanentia. Butillaria In Ciiii^{xx}iii lag. cervisie xix s. <iiii> \ v / d. ob. Coquina Empciones xxi d. Candelaria De stauro. Stabulum Fenum avene de stauro. Vadia vi s. vii d.
[*f.32r*] *Poterne Gentiles xxii Valecti garciones xliii Summa ferculorum lxv*
Extranii vicarius ville ii burgences de Devys' et alii xiiii
Die dominica xxiii Januarii Panteria Expenduntur Cxiiii panes unde pro ferculis lxv trencheris v liberacionibus v coquine iiii canibus v rewardis xxx panes. Et remanent xliii panes. Celarium Expenduntur v lag. vini de stauro. Butillaria Expenduntur xliiii lag. cervisie. Et remanent Cv lag. cervisie. Coquina Expenduntur i qr. bovis di. baco de stauro. Item ii casse multonum ii capones l ova de precomputato. Item expenditur di. porcus de stauro. In iii cassis multonum emptis v s. iiii d. In i carcosio vituli empto iii s. iiii d. et expenduntur iii qr. In iiii snyt*es* et iiii grossis avibus emptis et expensis i d. ob. In ii porcellis emptis et expensis xii d. Candelaria Expenduntur v lib. candelarum de stauro. Stabulum Fenum pro vii equis

[152] 107 loaves disbursed.

ii hakeneis de stauro. In prebenda eorundem iii bus. avenarum de precomputato. Item fenum apud Remesbur' pro xvi equis iiii hakeneis de stauro. In prebenda eorundem vii bus. avenarum.

Probatur Summa empcionum ix s. ix d. ob.

Panteria De precomputato. Celarium Vinum de remanentia. Butillaria De precomputato. Coquina Empciones ix s. ix d. ob. Candelaria De stauro. Stabulum Fenum avene de stauro.

Gentiles xxv Valecti garciones xlv Summa ferculorum lxx

Extranii vicarius ville ii capellani Sarum Becot se ii° et alii xii

Die lune xxiiii° Januarii Panteria Furniuntur per i talliam i qr. vii bus. frumenti de stauro que respondent de CCCiiii^{xx}iiii panibus. Et expenduntur C panes unde pro ferculis lxx panes trencheris iiii liberacionibus v coquine ii canibus v rewardis xiiii. Et remanent CCCxxvii panes. Celarium Expenduntur iiii lag. vini de stauro. Butillaria Expenduntur xl lag. cervisie. Et remanent lxv lag. cervisie. Coquina Expenduntur i qr. bovis i baco de stauro. Item ii cuniculi i cassa di. multonum CC ova i perdix de precomputato. Candelaria Expenduntur v lib. candelarum de stauro. Stabulum Fenum pro x equis ii hakeneis de stauro. In prebenda eorundem iiii bus. di. avenarum de stauro. Item fenum apud Remesbur' pro xv equis iiii hakeneis de stauro. In avenis pro eisdem vi bus. di. avenarum de stauro. Panteria Furniuntur i qr. vii bus. frumenti que respondent ad iiiCiiii^{xx} panes. Celarium Vinum de remanentia. Butillaria De precomputato. Coquina Empciones nichil. Candele de stauro. Stabulum Fenum avene de stauro.

[*f.32v*] *Poterne Gentiles xxii Valecti garciones lii Summa ferculorum lxxiiii*

Extranii Bekkote se ii° Foxhangre se ii° Wylmynton' se ii° Menger et carectarii et alii extranii xii

Die martis xxv Januarii Panteria Expenduntur Cxii panes unde pro ferculis lxxiiii trencheris v liberacionibus v coquine iiii canibus v rewardis xix. Et remanent CCxv panes. Celarium Expend*un*tur[153] lag. vini de stauro. Butillaria Expenduntur xxxviii lag. cervisie. Et remanent xxvii lag. cervisie. Coquina Expenduntur i qr. bovis di. baco ii di. porci de stauro. Item i qr. vituli ii casse multonum xii galline[154] ii cuniculi de precomputato. In iii cassis multonum emptis v s. iii d. Candelaria Expenduntur iiii lib. candelarum de stauro. Stabulum[155] Fenum pro xxv equis ii hakeneis de stauro. In prebenda <ii b> i qr. ii bus. avenarum de precomputato. Item fenum apud Remesbur' pro xvi equis iii hakeneis de stauro. In avenis pro eisdem vii bus. avenarum.

Probatur Summa empcionum v s. iii d.

[153] Followed by a blank space in MS.

[154] MS 'gallini'.

[155] MS omits underline.

Panteria De precomputato. Celarium Vinum de remanentia. Butillaria De precomputato. Coquina Empciones v s. iii d. Candelaria De stauro. Stabulum Fenum avene[156]

Gentiles xxvi Valecti garciones xlv Summa ferculorum lxxi

Extranii Littylton' se iii^{o} vicarius ville Flour Johannes Piers et alii extranii xii Foxhangr' se ii^{do}

Die mercurie xxvi Januarii Panteria Expenduntur Cviii panes unde pro ferculis lxxi trencheris vii coquine v canibus x liberacionibus viii rewardis vii. Et remanent Cviii panes.[157] Celarium Expend*un*tur[158] lag. vini de stauro. Butillaria Expenduntur xlvi lag. cervisie.[159] Et remanet nichil. Coquina Expenduntur di. qr. bovis ii casse multonum di. baco de stauro. Item iiii galline de stauro. Item ii cuniculi iii mallard*i* iii tel*es* de precomputato. Item l allec album xl allec rubium di. leng poudrus i piscis salcius vi merlyng iii gurnard de precomputato. In ii lag. lactis emptis et expensis \ ii d. / In M ostriis emptis xx d. et expenduntur CCC ostria.[160] Candelaria Expenduntur vi lib. candelarum de stauro. Stabulum Fenum pro xxvi equis iii hakeneis de stauro. In avenis pro eisdem i qr. iii bus. avenarum de stauro. Item fenum apud Remesbur' pro xv equis iii hakeneis de stauro. In prebenda eorundem vi bus. di. avenarum.

Probatur Summa empcionum xxii d.

Panteria De precomputato. Celarium Vinum de remanentia. Butillaria De precomputato. Coquina Empciones xxii d. Candelaria De stauro. Stabulum Fenum avene[161]

[*f.33r*] *Poterne Gentiles xxx Valecti garciones li Summa ferculorum iiii^{xx}i*

Extranii Lyttylton' se iii^{o} vicarius ville uxor Osbarn' se ii^{o} Foxhangr' se ii^{o} et alii extranii xiiii

Die jovis xxvii Januarii Panteria Expenduntur Cviii panes[162] unde pro ferculis iiii^{xx}i panes trencheris x liberacionibus vii coquine vi canibus[163] x rewardo i panis. Et remanet nichil. Celarium Expenduntur vi lag. vini de stauro. Butillaria In xlviii lag. cervisie emptis de Johanne Nassh' precium lag. i d. ob. deductis inde iiii lag. cervisie de avantagio v s. vi d. In xvii lag. cervisie emptis de eodem precium lag. i d. deductis inde i lag. di. de avantagio xv d. ob. In l lag. cervisie emptis de Roberto Baker precium lag. i d. ob. deductis inde iiii lag. de avantagio v s. ix d. In xl lag. cervisie emptis

[156] Followed by a blank space in MS.
[157] 107 loaves should remain.
[158] Followed by a blank space in MS.
[159] Only 27 gallons left the previous day.
[160] MS repeats 'ostr''.
[161] Followed by a blank space in MS.
[162] 115 loaves disbursed.
[163] MS 'Canyng''.

de eodem precium lag. i d. deductis inde iii lag. di. de avantagio iii s. ob. In Cxl lag. cervisie emptis de Shepherde precium lag. i d. ob. deductis inde xi lag. di. de avantagio xvi s. In xl lag. cervisie de eadem[164] precium lag. i d. deductis inde iii lag. di. de avantagio iii s. ob. Et expenduntur l lag. cervisie. Et remanent CCiiii^{xx}v lag. cervisie. Coquina Expenduntur i qr. bovis i baco xii galline <de> i cignus de stauro. Item iii casse multonum l ova de precomputato. In iii cassis multonum emptis vi s. iii d. In iiii porcellis emptis et expensis xxii d. In v gallinis emptis x d. In ii wodecok*es* iii plovers vi grossis avibus et vi parvis avibus emptis et expensis x d. In expensis emptoris i d. Candelaria Expenduntur vii lib. candelarum de stauro. Stabulum Fenum pro xxviii equis iii hakeneis de stauro. In avenis[165] pro eisdem <iii> i qr. iii bus. avenarum de stauro. Item fenum apud Remesbur' pro xvi equis ii hakeneis de stauro. In prebenda eorundem vi bus. di. avenarum de stauro.

Probatur Summa empcionum xliiii s. vi d. ob.[166] unde

Panteria celarium De precomputato. Butillaria In CCCxxxv lag. cervisie xxxiiii s. vii d. ob. Coquina Empciones ix s. xi d.[167] Candelaria De stauro. Stabulum Fenum avene de stauro.

Gentiles xii Valecti garciones xxvi Summa ferculorum xxxviii
*Extranii xiiii Foxhangr' se ii^{o} vicarius ville dominus Johannes Gardin*er *Adam Axford*

Die veneris xxviii Januarii Panteria Furniuntur per i talliam ii qr. frumenti de stauro que respondent de CCCCx panibus. Et expenduntur iiii^{xx} panes unde pro ferculis xxxviii panes trencheris vi liberacionibus v coquine ii canibus vi rewardis xxiii panes. Et remanent CCCxxx panes. Celarium Expend*un*tur[168] lag. vini de stauro. Butillaria Expenduntur xl lag. cervisie. Et remanent CCxlv lag. cervisie de precomputato. Coquina Expenduntur C allec album l rubium i piscis salcius et di. i salmo salcius CCCC ostria de precomputato. In iii lag. lactis emptis et expensis iii d. Candelaria Expenduntur vi lib. candelarum[169] de stauro. Stabulum Fenum pro xii equis iii hakeneis de stauro. In avenis pro eisdem i qr. avenarum de stauro. Item fenum pro xv equis iii hakeneis de stauro. In avenis pro eisdem vi bus. di. avenarum.

Probatur Summa empcionum iii d.

Panteria Furniuntur ii qr. frumenti que respondent ad iiiiCx panes.

[164] MS 'eodem'.
[165] MS 'avenenis'.
[166] Total should be 1*d*. less.
[167] Total should be 1*d*. less.
[168] MS repeats 'Expen'', followed by a blank space.
[169] MS 'lag. vini'.

Celarium Vinum de remanentia. Butillaria De precomputato. Coquina Empciones iii d. Candelaria De stauro. Stabulum Fenum avene de stauro. [*f.33v*] *Poterne Gentiles xxiii Valecti garciones xliii Summa ferculorum lxvi iii capellani extranii vicarius ville et alii extranii x*

Die sabbati xxix Januarii Panteria Expenduntur Cxiiii panes[170] unde pro ferculis lxvi trencheris vi liberacionibus vi coquine ii canybus viii rewardis xvi. Et remanent CCxvi panes. Celarium Expenduntur iiii lag. vini de stauro. Butillaria Expenduntur xlvi lag. cervisie. Et remanent Ciiii^{xx}xix lag. cervisie. Coquina Expenduntur C allec album C allec rubium i piscis di. salcii de stauro. Item CC ova CCC ostria de precomputato. In xii huss emptis ii s. In iii crabb*es* emptis iii s. ii d. Et expenduntur xii huss et i crabb'. Candelaria Expenduntur iii lib. candelarum de stauro. Stabulum Fenum pro xvii equis iii hakeneis de stauro. In avenis pro eisdem i qr. i bus. avenarum. Item fenum apud Remesbur' pro xv equis iiii hakeneis de stauro. In avenis vi bus.

Item in vadiis Johannis Podich pagetti senescalli apud Remesbur' per i septimanam x d. ob.

Probatur Summa empcionum vi s. ob.

Panteria De precomputato. Celarium Vinum de remanentia. Butillaria De precomputato. Coquina Empciones v s. ii d. Candelaria De stauro. Stabulum Fenum avene de stauro. Vadia x d. ob.

Gentiles xxvi Valecti garciones xlvii Summa ferculorum lxxiii

Extranii Bacon se ii^{o} vicarius ville iii capellani extranii et alii xiii

Die dominica xxx^{o} Januarii Panteria Expenduntur Cxx panes unde pro ferculis lxxiii trencheris vi liberacionibus v coquine iii canibus vii rewardis xxvi. Et remanent iiii^{xx}xvi panes. Celarium Expenduntur v lag. vini de stauro. Butillaria Expenduntur liiii lag. cervisie. Et remanent Cxlv lag. cervisie. Coquina Expenduntur i qr. bovis di. baco di. porcus <x> viii galline de stauro. Item expenduntur iiii capones de precomputato. In iii cassis multonum emptis vi s. \ iii d. / et expenduntur ii. In ii porcellis emptis et expensis x d. In x gallinis emptis xxi d. In i wodecok empto et expenso i d. In viii grossis avibus et l parvis avibus emptis et expensis vi d. In expensis emptoris ob. Candelaria Expenduntur vi lib. candelarum de stauro. Stabulum Fenum pro xvii equis iii hakeneis de stauro. In avenis pro eisdem i qr. i bus. di. Item fenum apud Remesbur' pro xiii equis iiii hakeneis de stauro. In prebenda eorundem vi bus. avenarum de stauro.

Probatur Summa empcionum ix s. v d. ob.

Panteria De precomputato. Celarium Vinum de remanentia. Butillaria De precomputato. Coquina Empciones ix s. v d. ob. Candelaria De stauro. Stabulum Fenum avene de stauro.

[170] 104 loaves disbursed.

[f.34r] Poterne Gentiles xxv Valecti garciones xlvi Summa ferculorum lxxi
Extranii Walrond vicarius ville vicarius de Milkesham et alii xi
Die lune ultimo Januarii Panteria <Expend*un*tur> Furniuntur per i talliam i qr. v bus. frumenti de stauro que respondent de CCCxxxi panibus. Et expenduntur Cxvi panes unde pro ferculis lxxi trencheris vii liberacionibus vi coquine iiii canibus vii rewardis xxi. Et remanent CCCxi panes. Celarium Expend*un*tur[171] lag. vini de stauro. Butillaria Expenduntur xlvi lag. cervisie. Et remanent iiii^{xx}xix lag. cervisie. Coquina Expenduntur di. qr. bovis di. baco v galline[172] de stauro. Item ii casse multonum CC ova de precomputato. Candelaria Expenduntur iiii lib. candelarum de stauro. Stabulum[173] Fenum pro xii equis iii hakeneis de stauro. In avenis vi bus. avenarum de stauro. Item fenum apud Remesbur' pro xiiii equis iii hakeneis de stauro. In avenis pro eisdem vi bus. avenarum.

Summa[174]

Panteria Furniuntur i qr. v bus. frumenti que respondent ad CCCxxxi panes. Celarium Vinum de remanentia. Butillaria De precomputato. Coquina Empciones nichil. Candelaria De stauro. Stabulum Fenum avene de stauro.[175]

[f.34v] Poterne Gentiles xii Valecti garciones xxiiii Summa ferculorum xxxvi
Uxor Willelmi Worston' se viii^{o} et alii <A> extranii viii
Die martis primo Februarii Panteria Expenduntur iiii^{xx}v panes unde pro ferculis xxxvi trencheris v liberacionibus vi coquine iiii canibus viii rewardis xxvi. Et remanent CCxxvi panes. Celarium Expenduntur <v> iii lag. vini de stauro. Butillaria Expenduntur xxviii lag. cervisie. Et remanent lxxi lag. cervisie. Coquina Expenduntur l allec album di. piscis salcius de stauro. Candelaria Expenduntur vi lib. candelarum de stauro. Stabulum Fenum pro xviii equis ii hakeneis de stauro. In avenis pro eisdem i qr. avenarum de stauro. Item fenum apud Remesbur' pro xi equis ii hakeneis de stauro. In avenis pro eisdem v bus.

Summa nichil quia de precomputato

Panteria De precomputato. Celarium Vinum de remanentia. Butillaria De precomputato. Coquina Empciones nichil. Candelaria De stauro. Stabulum Fenum avene de stauro.

Festum Purificacionis Beate Marie Gentiles xxv Valecti garciones xlvi Summa ferculorum lxxi
Extranii uxor Willelmi Worston' se viii^{o} vicarius ville et alii extranii xvi

171 Followed by a blank space in MS.
172 MS 'gallini'.
173 MS omits underline.
174 Followed by a blank space in MS.
175 On a new line, by itself, 'Die'.

Die mercurie secundo Februarii Panteria Expenduntur Cxxx panes unde pro ferculis lxxi trencheris xiiii liberacionibus vi coquine iiii canibus viii rewardis xxvii. Et remanent iiii^{xx}xvi panes. Celarium Expend*un*tur[176] lag. vini de stauro. Butillaria Expenduntur lviii lag. cervisie. Et remanent xiii lag. cervisie. Coquina Expenduntur di. qr. bovis di. baco di. porcus i cignus viii galline de stauro. Item expenduntur l allec album l rubium i piscis salcius i salmo salcius iii anguille grosse salcie de stauro. In l merlyng emptis iii s. Et expenduntur xii. In lxiii gurnard emptis v s. Et expenduntur xvi. In iii cassis multonum emptis vi s. iii d. Et expenduntur ii casse multonum. In iii porcellis emptis et expensis xiiii d. In expensis Huberti ibidem pro dictis victualibus emendis apud Sarum vii d. Item expenditur i fesant de stauro. Item CC ostria de precomputato. Candelaria Expenduntur iiii lib. candelarum de stauro. Stabulum Fenum pro xviii equis iii hakeneis de stauro. In avenis pro eisdem i qr. avenarum i bus. Item fenum apud Remesbur' pro xiiii equis iii hakeneis de stauro. In avenis pro eisdem vi bus.

Probatur Summa empcionum xvi s.

Panteria De precomputato. Celarium Vinum de remanentia. Butillaria De precomputato. Coquina Empciones xvi s. Candelaria De stauro. Stabulum Fenum avene de stauro.

[*f.35r*] *Poterne Gentiles xxiiii Valecti garciones xl Summa ferculorum lxiiii Extranii uxor Willelmi Worston' se viii^{o} vicarius de Milkesham dominus Johannes Wotton' magister Thomas Fisicianus et alii extranii xvi*

Die jovis tercio Februarii Panteria Furniuntur per i talliam ii qr. frumenti de stauro que respondent de CCCCxii panibus. Et expenduntur Cxiiii panes unde pro ferculis lxiiii panes trencheris viii liberacionibus v coquine iii canibus vi rewardis xxviii. Et remanent CCCiiii^{xx}xiiii panes. Celarium Expenduntur iiii lag. vini de stauro. Butillaria <Expend*un*tur> In Clxvii lag. cervisie emptis de Shephe*r*de precium lag. i d. ob. deductis inde xiiii lag. de avantagio xix s. i d. ob. In lxiii lag. cervisie emptis de eadem[177] precium lag. i d. deductis inde v lag. de avantagio iiii s. x d. Et expenduntur xlviii lag. cervisie. Et remanent CCxliii lag. cervisie. Coquina Expenduntur i qr. bovis di. baco vi galline i perdix de stauro. Item ii cuniculi de precomputato. \ Coquina In iii cassis multonum vi s. iii d. In ii porcellis emptis ix d. In iiii plovers i tele emptis et expensis ix d. In ix grossis avibus vi d. In xii caponibus emptis iii s. <i>iii d. In xxix gallinis v s. i d. et expensis. / Candelaria Expenduntur iii lib. candelarum de stauro. Stabulum Fenum pro xviii equis iiii hakeneis de stauro. In prebenda eorundem i qr.

[176] Followed by a blank space in MS.
[177] MS 'eodem'.

avenarum. Item fenum apud Remesbur' pro xxi equis ii hakeneis de stauro. In avenis pro eisdem i qr. avenarum.

Probatur Summa empcionum xl s. vi d. ob.[178] unde

Panteria Furniuntur i qr. frumenti que respondent ad iiiiCxii panes. Celarium Vinum de remanentia. Butillaria In CCxxxi lag. cervisie xxiii s. xi d. ob. Coquina Empciones xvi s. vii d. Candelaria De stauro. Stabulum Fenum avene de stauro.

Gentiles xv Valecti garciones xxxvi Summa ferculorum li

Extranii dominus Johannes Wotton' se ii^{o} *Robertus Gore se ii*^{o} *Petrus Pynforde Bacon' se ii*^{o} *magister Thomas fisic*ianus *domini Johannes Piers cum uxore et alii extranii xii*

Die veneris iiii^{to} Februarii Panteria Expenduntur iiii^{xx}x panes unde pro ferculis li trencheris iiii liberacionibus vi coquine iii canibus viii rewardis xviii. Et remanent CCCiiii panes. Celarium Expenduntur v lag. vini de stauro. Butillaria Expenduntur xxxviii lag. cervisie. Et remanent CCv lag. cervisie. Coquina Expenduntur C allec album C allec rubium i piscis salcius et di. i salmo salcius de stauro. Item expenditur i crabb' de precomputato. In M ostriis emptis xx d. et expenduntur CCCC ostria. In DC welk*es* emptis xv d. et expenduntur CC. In CCClx allece albo empto iiii s. ix d. In iii lag. lactis emptis et expensis iii d. Candelaria[179] Expenduntur vi lib. candelarum de stauro. Stabulum Fenum pro xx equis iii hakeneis de stauro. In avenis pro eisdem i qr. i bus. avenarum de stauro. Item fenum apud Remesbur' pro xxi equis ii hakeneis de stauro. In prebenda eorundem i qr. avenarum de stauro.

Probatur Summa empcionum vii s. xi d.

Panteria De precomputato. Celarium Vinum de remanentia. Butillaria De precomputato. Coquina Empciones vii s. xi d. Candelaria De stauro. Stabulum Fenum avene de stauro.

[*f.35v*] *Poterne Gentiles xxx Valecti garciones xl Summa ferculorum lxx*

Extranii prior de Motesfunte se iiii^{o} *Lamb*ert *se ii*^{o} *Gore se ii*^{o} *Petrus Pynforde se ii*^{o} *Johannes Metford cum fratre vicarius ville se ii*^{o} *Flour se ii*^{o} *magister T. fisic*ianus *domini se ii*^{o} *et alii extranii xvi*

Die sabbati v Februarii Panteria Expenduntur Cxx panes unde pro ferculis lxx trencheris vi liberacionibus vi coquine ii canibus viii rewardis xxviii panes. Et remanent Ciiii^{xx}iiii panes. Celarium Expenduntur v lag. vini de stauro. Butillaria Expenduntur l lag. cervisie. Et remanent Clv lag. cervisie. Coquina Expenduntur C allec album Cl rubium i piscis salcius et di. DC ostria iiiiC welk*es* CC ova de precomputato. In ii lag. <lag.> lactis emptis et expensis ii d. In DCx ovis emptis et expensis ii s. ii d. Candelaria

178 MS 'xlvi s. ob.'

179 MS 'Coquina'.

Expenduntur iiii lib. candelarum de stauro. Stabulum Fenum pro xxi equis iiii hakeneis de stauro. In prebenda eorundem i qr. ii bus. avenarum de stauro. Item fenum apud Remesbur' pro xiiii equis ii hakeneis de stauro. In prebenda eorundem vi bus.

Probatur Summa empcionum ii s. iiii d.

Panteria De precomputato. Celarium Vinum de remanentia. Butillaria De precomputato. Coquina Empciones ii s. iiii d. Candelaria De stauro. Stabulum Fenum avene[180]

Gentiles xxxii Valecti garciones xlii Summa ferculorum lxxiiii

*Extranii prior de Motesfonte se iiii^{o} Gore se ii^{o} Pynforde se ii^{o} vicarius ville se ii^{o} Flour se ii^{o} Johannes Metford se iii^{o} magister T. fisic*ianus *domini se ii^{o} et alii extranii xviii*

Die dominica vi^{o} Februarii Panteria Expenduntur Cxl panes unde pro ferculis lxxiiii panes trencheris xii liberacionibus viii coquine[181] viii canibus x rewardis xxviii panes. Et remanent xliiii panes. Celarium Expenduntur vi lag. vini de stauro. Butillaria Expenduntur lviii lag. cervisie. Et remanent iiii^{xx}xvii lag.[182] cervisie. Coquina Expenduntur i qr. bovis di. baco di. porcus xx galline de stauro. Item expenduntur ii casse di. multonum CC ova de precomputato. In i qr. bovis empto iii s. In iii cassis multonum emptis vi s. In i carcosio vituli empto et expenso iii s. x d. In x cuniculis emptis ii s. iiii d. In i lag. lactis empta et expensa i d. Candelaria Expenduntur vi lib. candelarum de stauro. Stabulum Fenum pro[183] xx equis iiii hakeneis de stauro. In prebenda eorundem i qr. i bus. avenarum de stauro precomputato. Item fenum apud Remesbur' pro xix equis ii hakeneis de stauro. In prebenda eorundem i qr. avenarum

Probatur Summa empcionum xv s. iii d.

Panteria De precomputato. Celarium Vinum de remanentia. Butillaria De precomputato. Coquina Empciones xv s. iii d. Candelaria De stauro. Stabulum Fenum avene[184]

[f.36r] Poterne Gentiles xxv Valecti garciones xli Summa ferculorum lxvi

*Extranii ii fratres predicatores vicarius ville se ii^{o} magister T. fisic*ianus *domini se ii^{o} Johannes Metford cum fratre*

Die lune vii Februarii Panteria Furniuntur per i talliam ii qr. frumenti de stauro que respondent de CCCCxvii panibus. Et expenduntur Cxxviii panes[185] unde pro ferculis lxvi panes trencheris x liberacionibus viii

[180] Followed by a blank space in MS.
[181] Underlined in MS.
[182] MS repeats 'lag.'
[183] MS omits 'Fenum pro'.
[184] Followed by a blank space in MS.
[185] 127 loaves disbursed.

coquine iii canibus x rewardis xxxii panes. Et remanent CCCxxxiii panes. Celarium Expenduntur iii lag. vini de stauro. Butillaria Expenduntur l lag. cervisie. Et remanent xlvii lag. cervisie. Coquina Expenduntur di. qr. bovis i baco de stauro. Item iii casse multonum CCCC ova de precomputato. Item <i> expenduntur iiii mallard*i* et i tel*e* iiii plovers viii parve aves de precomputato. Item expenduntur v cuniculi de precomputato. Candelaria Expenduntur iiii lib. candelarum de stauro. Stabulum Fenum pro xx equis iii hakeneis de stauro. In prebenda eorundem i qr. i bus. avenarum de precomputato. Item fenum apud Remesbur' pro xii equis ii hakeneis de stauro. In avenis pro eisdem v bus.
Panteria Furniuntur ii qr. frumenti que respondent ad iiiiCxvii panes. Celarium Vinum de remanentia. Butillaria De precomputato. Coquina Empciones nichil. Candelaria De stauro. Stabulum Fenum avene de stauro.
Gentiles xxxiii Valecti garciones xlvi Summa ferculorum[186] *lxix*[187]
Extranii magister J.Maydenhith' se vii^{o} Wilmyngton' se ii^{o} magister Thomas Therlownt ii fratres vicarius ville se v^{o} Floure se iii^{o} maior se ii^{o} et alii xx
Die martis viii Februarii Panteria Expenduntur Cxl panes unde pro ferculis lxix panes trencheris x liberacionibus x coquina iiii canibus xii rewardis xxxv panes. Et remanent Ciiii^{xx}xiii panes. Celarium[188] vi lag. vini de remanentia. Butillaria In xxxiiii lag. cervisie emptis de Willelmo Lang' precium lag. i d. ob. deductis inde iii lag. de avantagio iii s. x d. ob. In iiii^{xx}ii lag. cervisie emptis de Axford precium lag. i d. ob. deductis inde vii lag. de avantagio viii s. x d. ob. In xxxiiii lag. cervisie emptis de eadem[189] precium lag. i d. deductis inde iii lag. de avantagio ii s. vii d. In lxi lag. cervisie emptis de Felicia Aas precium lag. i d. ob. deductis inde v lag. vii s. In xxvi lag. cervisie emptis de eadem precium lag. i d. deductis inde ii lag. de avantagio ii s. In iiii^{xx}iiii lag. cervisie emptis de Warener precium lag. i d. \ ob. / deductis inde vii lag. de avantagio ix s. i d. ob. In xx lag. cervisie emptis de eodem precium lag. i d. deductis inde i lag. di. xviii d. ob. In lx lag. cervisie emptis de Axford precium lag. i d. ob. deductis inde v lag. de avantagio vi s. ix d. In xxiiii lag. cervisie emptis de eadem precium lag. i d. deductis inde ii lag. de avantagio xxii d. In lxv lag. cervisie emptis de <eadem> \ Carlet / precium lag. i d. ob. deductis inde v lag. di. de avantagio vii s. v d. ob. qua. In xl lag. cervisie emptis de eadem[190] precium lag. i d. deductis inde iii lag. iii s. i d. Et expenduntur lxiii lag. cervisie. <de> Et remanent CCCClxxiiii

[186] MS repeats 'F''.
[187] Totals 79, but only 69 loaves disbursed for *fercula*. The figures for *gentiles*, *valecti* and *garciones* may be incorrect.
[188] MS omits underline.
[189] MS 'eodem'.
[190] MS 'eodem'.

lag. cervisie. Coquina Expenduntur i qr. bovis di. bacon' di. porcus. <de> In ii edis emptis et expensis xx d. In iii porcellis emptis et expensis xvi d. In vi pulcinis emptis et expensis vi d. In i lag. lactis i d. et expensa. \ In ii cassis multonum emptis et expensis iiii s. ii d. / Item expenduntur xiiii <g> capones xxiii galline iii casse multonum de precomputato. Item expenduntur i fasianus ii perdices i cignus de precomputato. Item expenduntur DCC ova de precomputato. Candelaria Expenduntur iiii lib. candelarum de stauro. Stabulum Fenum pro xxiiii equis[191] iiii hakeneis de stauro. In prebenda eorundem i qr. ii bus. avenarum de stauro. Item fenum apud Remesbur' pro xvi equis ii hakeneis de stauro. In avenis pro eisdem vi bus.

Probatur Summa lxi s. x d. ob. qua. unde

Panteria De precomputato. Celarium Vinum de remanentia. Butillaria In Dxxx lag. cervisie liiii s. i d. ob. qua. Coquina Empciones vii s. ix d. Candelaria De stauro. Stabulum Fenum avene[192]

[f.36v] Poterne Fercula Gentiles xvii Valecti garciones xxvii Summa ferculorum xliiii

Extranii magister J. Maydenhith' se vi^o^ magister J. Wotton' se iiii^o^ Wilmyngton' se ii^o^ rector de Chilton' se ii^o^ et alii xx

Die mercurie ix° Februarii Panteria Expenduntur C panes unde pro ferculis xliiii trencheris viii liberacionibus[193] vi coquina[194] iiii canibus xii rewardis xxvi panes. Et remanent iiii^{xx}xiii panes. Celarium Expenduntur v lag. vini de remanentia. Butillaria Expenduntur xl lag. cervisie. Et remanent CCCCxxxiiii lag. cervisie. Coquina Expenduntur Cl allec album C allec rubium iii pisces salcii i salmon' salcius ix stok' i pecia storjon de stauro. In MCC ostriis emptis ii s. et expenduntur ixC. Item expenditur i lag. olei de stauro precomputato. Candelaria Expenduntur iii lib. candelarum. Stabulum Fenum pro xxvii equis iiii hakeneis de stauro. In avenis pro eisdem i qr. ii bus. avenarum de precomputato. Item fenum apud Remesbur' pro xiii equis iii hakeneis de stauro. In prebenda eorundem v bus. avenarum.

Probatur Summa empcionum ii s.

Panteria De precomputato. Celarium Vinum de remanentia. Butillaria De precomputato. Coquina Empciones ii s. Candelaria De stauro. Stabulum Fenum avene[195]

Gentiles xx Valecti garciones xli Summa ferculorum lxi

Extranii dominus J. Drayton magister J. Maydenhith' se iii^o^ magister Simon Best se ii^o^ Wilmington' se ii^o^ et alii xx

[191] MS omits 'equis'.
[192] Followed by a blank space in MS.
[193] Underlined in MS.
[194] Underlined in MS.
[195] Followed by a blank space in MS.

Die jovis x^{o} Februarii Panteria <Expen> Furniuntur per i talliam i qr. vii bus. frumenti que respondent ad CCCiiii^{xx}iiii panes. Et expenduntur Cxx panes[196] unde pro ferculis lxi trencheris viii liberacionibus x coquina iiii canibus xii rewardis xxiiii panes. Et remanent CCClvii panes. Celarium Expenduntur vi lag. vini de remanentia. Butillaria Expenduntur lviii lag. cervisie. Et remanent CCClxxvi lag. cervisie. Coquina[197] Expenduntur Cl allec rubium l allec album iii pisces salcii i salmon' salcius de stauro. In xxxii merling xl gurnard ii thornebak*es* i haddok et v codeling emptis vii s. <x> \ vi / d. In i qr. porpois recentis empto v s. vi d. In i turbot empto iii s. In ii bus. pisarum viridarum emptis xx d. In <i bus. pisarum viridarum> \ farina / empta xi d. In expensis emptoris ii d. Et expenduntur xx merling xxv gurnard i haddok iii codeling i pecia porpois de precomputato. Item expenduntur xii roches de stauro CCC ostria de precomputato. Candelaria Expenduntur iiii lib. candelarum de stauro. Stabulum Fenum pro xliii equis iiii hakeneis de stauro. In prebenda eorundem i qr. vi bus. avenarum de stauro. Item fenum apud Remesbur' pro xiii equis ii hakeneis de stauro. In avenis pro eisdem v bus.

Probatur Summa empcionum xviii s. ix d.

Panteria Furniuntur i qr. vii bus. frumenti que respondent ad iiiCiiii^{xx}iiii panes. Celarium Vinum de remanentia. Butillaria De precomputato. Coquina Empciones xviii s. ix d. Candelaria De stauro. Stabulum Fenum avene de stauro.

[*f.37r*] *Poterne Gentiles xviii Valecti garciones xxxii Summa ferculorum l Extranii* sire *J. Drayton se magister W. Metford se vii^{o} magister J. Shirbo*urne *se iii^{o} et alii xv*

Die veneris xi Februarii Panteria Expenduntur C panes unde pro ferculis l trencheris vi liberacionibus ix coquina iiii canibus viii rewardis[198] xxiii panes. Et remanent CClvii panes. Celarium Expenduntur iiii lag. vini de remanentia. Butillaria Expenduntur xl \ <iii> / lag. cervisie. Et remanent CCCxxxvi lag. cervisie. Coquina Expenduntur C allec album C allec rubium i piscis salcius i salmon' salcius de stauro. Item expenduntur xii merling xii gurnard de precomputato. Candelaria Expenduntur iiii lib. candelarum de stauro. Stabulum Fenum pro xlv equis iii hakeneis de stauro. In prebenda eorundem i qr. iiii bus. avenarum de stauro. Item fenum apud Remesbur' pro xii equis ii hakeneis de stauro. In avenis pro eisdem iiii bus. di. avenarum.

Summa nichil quia de precomputato

Panteria De precomputato. Celarium Vinum de remanentia. Butillaria De

[196] 119 loaves disbursed.

[197] MS omits underline.

[198] MS 'lib' reward''.

precomputato. Coquina Empciones nichil. Candelaria De stauro. Stabulum Fenum avene de stauro.
Gentiles xviii Valecti garciones xxxii Summa ferculorum l
Extranii dominus J.Drayton' magister W.Metford se vi^{o} *magister J.Shirbourne se ii*^{o} *magister J.Pedwell' se ii*^{o} *J.Latton' se ii*^{o} *et alii xiiii*
Die sabbati xii Februarii Panteria \ Expenduntur / C panes unde pro ferculis l trencheris vii liberacionibus v coquina iiii canibus vi rewardis xxviii panes. Et remanent Clvii panes. Celarium Expenduntur v lag. vini de remanentia. Butillaria Expenduntur xl lag. cervisie. Et remanent CCiiii^{xx}xvi lag. cervisie. Coquina C allec rubium C allec album ii pisces salcii de stauro remanenti. Item expenduntur ii thornebak*es* viii merling x gurnard i haddok et v codeling de precomputato. In x thornebak*es* emptis iii s. vi d. In i qr. porpois empto vi s. i d. Item expenditur i salmon' salcius de stauro. Item expenditur i turbot de precomputato. Candelaria Expenduntur iii lib. candelarum de stauro. Stabulum Fenum pro xlvi equis iiii hakeneis de stauro. In prebenda eorundem i qr. iii bus. avenarum de stauro. Item fenum apud Remesbir' pro xiii equis iii hakeneis de stauro. In avenis v bus.
In vadiis Thome Ferror apud Remesbury a xxi die Januarii usque xiii diem Februarii utroque computato capientis per diem iii d. v s. iii d.
In vadiis garcionis sui ibidem per idem tempus capientis per diem ii d. iii s. vi d.
In vadiis garcionis cancellarii ibidem per idem tempus capientis per diem \ ii d. / iii s. vi d.
In vadiis pagetti Holcot' Forrey et pagetti Cap*er*on' ibidem per idem tempus capiens quilibet per diem i d. ob. vii s. x d. ob.
In vadiis Thome Norman ibidem per xvi dies capientis per diem ii d. ii s. viii d.
In vadiis pagetti senescalli per vii dies pagetti Tydemerssh' per ix dies et pagetti Shupton' ibidem per xii dies capiens quilibet eorum per diem i d. ob. iii s. vi d.
In vadiis Huberti cum somerario de Pot*er*ne usque <Sl> Hampton' eundo et redeundo per iii dies pro pisce et allece ibidem querendis ii s.

Probatur Summa empcionum xxxvii s. x d. ob. unde
Panteria De precomputato. Celarium Vinum de remanentia. Butillaria De precomputato. Coquina Empciones ix s. vii d. Candelaria De stauro. Stabulum Fenum avene[199] Vadia xx<iiii s.> \ <ix> viii s. / iii d. ob.
[*f.37v*] *Poterne Gentiles xviii Valecti garciones xlv Summa ferculorum lxiii*
Extranii magister W.Metford se vii^{o} *magister J.Pedwelle se iii*^{o} *J.Latton' se ii*^{o} *rector extranius se ii*^{o} *magister J.Shirbourne se ii*^{o} *et alii xx*

199 Followed by a blank space in MS.

Die dominica xiii Februarii Panteria Expenduntur Cxl panes[200] unde pro ferculis lxiii panes trencheris x liberacionibus vii coquina vi canibus xv rewardis xxxi panes. Et remanent xvii panes. Celarium Expenduntur vi lag. vini de remanentia. Butillaria Expenduntur lvi lag. cervisie. Et remanent CCii lag. cervisie.[201] Coquina Expenduntur Cl allec album C allec rubium iii pisces salcii ii salmones salcii xii stok' de stauro. Item expenditur i qr. porpois de precomputato. Item expenduntur i pecia storjon i lag. olei de stauro. In di. bus. musculis[202] empto et expenso vi d. Candelaria Expenduntur vi lib. candelarum de stauro. Stabulum Fenum pro xxxii equis iii hakeneis de stauro. In prebenda eorundem i qr. iiii bus. Item fenum apud Remesbur' pro xvii equis ii hakeneis de stauro. In prebenda eorundem vi bus. avenarum.

Probatur Summa empcionum <x d.> vi d.

Panteria De precomputato. Celarium Vinum de remanentia. Butillaria De precomputato. Coquina Empciones <x d.> vi d. Candelaria De stauro. Stabulum Fenum avene de stauro.

Memorandum quod i barellus allecis albi continet DCCCCxxxv i cade DC
Gentiles xii Valecti garciones xxxvii Summa ferculorum xlix
Extranii maior[203] *de Devis' se iii^{o} et alii xiiii*

Die lune xiiii^{o} Februarii Panteria Furniuntur per i talliam i qr. iiii bus. frumenti que respondent ad CCCxii panes. Et expenduntur Cxx panes unde pro ferculis xlix panes trencheris v liberacionibus v coquina iii canibus xv panes rewardis xliii panes. Et remanent CCix panes. Celarium Expenduntur iiii lag. vini de remanentia. Butillaria Expenduntur xxxv lag. cervisie. Et remanent Clxv lag. cervisie.[204] Coquina Expenduntur C allec album C allec rubium ii pisces salcii i salmon' salcius de stauro. \ In di. bus. muscul*is* empto vi d. In C ostriis iiii d. et expensis. / Candelaria Expenduntur vi lib. candelarum de stauro. Stabulum Fenum pro viii equis iii hakeneis de stauro. In avenis pro eisdem iii bus. di. avenarum de stauro. Item fenum apud Pot*er*ne pro xv equis ii hakeneis de stauro. In avenis pro eisdem v bus. pec.

Probatur Summa empcionum x d.

Panteria Furniuntur i qr. iiii bus. frumenti que respondent ad iiiCxii panes. Celarium Vinum de remanentia. Butillaria De precomputato. Coquina Empciones x d. Candelaria De stauro. Stabulum Fenum avene de stauro.

[200] 132 loaves disbursed.
[201] 240 gallons should remain.
[202] MS 'In di. musculis'.
[203] MS 'magor'.
[204] 167 gallons should remain.

[f.38r] Poterne Gentiles xv Valecti garciones xxxv Summa ferculorum xl[205]
Extranii ii clerici ducis Ebor' et alii xiiii
Die martis xv^{mo} Februarii Panteria Expenduntur C<xv> panes[206] unde pro ferculis xl trencheris v liberacionibus vi coquine v canibus xiiii rewardis xxvi. Et remanent Cix panes. Celarium Expend*un*tur[207] lag. vini de remanentia. Butillaria Expenduntur xxxiiii lag. cervisie. Et remanent Cxxxi <panes> lag. cervisie. Coquina Expenduntur C allec album C allec rubium ii pisces salcii x stok' di. lag. olei di. bus. musculis CC ostria de precomputato. Item expenduntur viii roch*es* de stauro. Candelaria Expend*un*tur[208] lib. candelarum de stauro. Stabulum Fenum pro x equis iiii hakeneis de stauro. In prebenda v bus. avenarum de stauro. Item fenum apud Remesbur' pro xv equis ii hakeneis de stauro. In prebenda eorundem v bus. avenarum.

Summa empcionum[209]

Panteria De precomputato. Celarium Vinum de remanentia. Butillaria De precomputato. Coquina Empciones[210] Candelaria De stauro. Stabulum Fenum avene de stauro.
Gentiles x Valecti garciones xxiiii Summa ferculorum xxxiiii
Extranii Gaweyn se iiii^{o} Bowyer' cum socio et alii extranii viii
Die mercurie xvi^{o} Februarii Panteria Expenduntur lxviii panes unde pro ferculis xxxiiii trencheris iiii liberacionibus vi^{o} coquine ii <coquine> canibus xiiii rewardis viii. Et remanent lxiii panes.[211] Celarium Expend*un*tur[212] lag. vini de remanentia. Butillaria Expenduntur xxviii lag. cervisie. Et remanent Ciii lag. cervisie. Coquina Expenduntur C allec album l rubium ii pisces salcii de stauro. In CCC musculis emptis ix d. In di. bus. cokk*les* empto xviii d. et expenditur i pec. In CCC welk*es* emptis xviii d. In i pot piscis recentis empto continenti xvi gurnard et Cxv merlyng emptis xii s. et expenduntur xl merlyng. In i crabb' empto ii s. In i pec. shrymp*es* empto vi d. Candelaria Expend*un*tur[213] lib. candelarum de stauro. Stabulum Fenum pro xvii equis iiii hakeneis de stauro. In prebenda i qr. avenarum de precomputato. Item fenum apud R' pro xii equis i hakeneo de stauro. In avenis pro eisdem iiii bus. di. avenarum.

[205] Totals 50, but only 40 loaves disbursed for *fercula*. The figures for *gentiles*, *valecti* and *garciones* may be incorrect.
[206] 96 loaves disbursed.
[207] Followed by a blank space in MS.
[208] Followed by a blank space in MS.
[209] Followed by a blank space in MS.
[210] Followed by a blank space in MS.
[211] 41 loaves should remain.
[212] Followed by a blank space in MS.
[213] Followed by a blank space in MS.

Probatur Summa empcionum xviii s. ii d.

Panteria De precomputato. Celarium Vinum de remanentia. Butillaria De precomputato. Coquina Empciones xviii s. iii d. Candelaria De stauro. Stabulum Fenum avene de stauro.

[*f.38v*] *Fercula Gentiles xvi Vallecti garciones xxvii Summa ferculorum xliii*
Extranii Gawayn se iiii^o^ Alicia Begot se iiii^o^ et iiii alii

Die jovis xvii° Februarii Panetria \ Furniuntur i qr. vi bus. frumenti que respondent ad iiiClii panes. De quibus / expenduntur <Cxv> \ C / panes unde in trencheris v liberacionibus vi coquina iiii canibus xi ferculis xliii rewardis xxxi panes. Et remanent iiiCxv panes. Celarium Expenduntur iii lag. vini. Buttillaria Expenduntur xxxix lag. cervisie. Et remanent lxv lag. cervisie.[214] Coquina Expenduntur C allec album C allec rubium ii pisces salsi iii pisces duri. In D oistr*es* emptis x d. de quibus expenduntur iiiiC. Et remanent iiiC oistr*es*. Item expenditur i pec. muscul*is* de precomputato. Candelaria Expenduntur iii lib. candelarum. Stabulum[215] In feno pro xiiii equis iii <hakeneis> hakeneis de stauro. In prebenda eorundem i qr. Item fenum apud Remesbur' pro xii equis ii hakeneis de stauro. In avenis pro eisdem v bus.

Probatur Summa empcionum x d.

Panteria Furniuntur i qr. vi bus. frumenti que respondent ad[216] iiiClii panes. Celarium Vinum de remanentia. Butillaria De precomputato. Coquina Empciones x d. Candelaria De stauro. Stabulum Fenum avene de stauro.

Fercula Gentiles x Vallecti garciones xxii Summa xxxii
Extranii magister R. canon se iiii^o^ Alicia Begot se iii^o^ et alii

Die veneris xviii° Februarii Panetria Expenduntur iiii^xx^ panes unde in trencheris iii ferculis xxxii coquina iii liberacionibus v panes canibus xi rewardis xxvi panes. Et remanent CCxxv panes.[217] <Et remanent> Celarium Expenduntur iiii lag. vini. Buttillaria Expenduntur xxviii lag. cervisie de remanentia. Et remanent xxxvii lag. cervisie. Coquina Expenduntur l allec album l allec rubium iii pisces salsi xii gurnard xxiiii welk*es* de precomputato. Candelaria Expenduntur iii lib. candelarum de coton. Stabulum[218] Fenum pro xv equis et ii hakeneis de stauro. In prebenda pro eisdem vii bus. avenarum. Item fenum apud Remesbury pro xii equis i hakeneo de stauro. In prebenda eorundem iiii bus. di.

Summa nichil quia de precomputato

Panteria De precomputato. Celarium Vinum de remanentia. Butillaria De

[214] 64 gallons should remain.
[215] MS omits underline.
[216] MS omits 'ad'.
[217] 235 loaves should remain.
[218] MS omits underline.

precomputato. Coquina Empciones[219] Candelaria De stauro. Stabulum Fenum avene de stauro.

Fercula Gentiles xii Vallecti garciones xxii Summa ferculorum xxxiiii

Die sabbati xix° Februarii Panetria Expenduntur iiii^{xx}v panes[220] unde in trencheris iii ferculis xxxiiii coquina v liberacionibus vi canibus xiiii rewardis xi panes. Et remanent Cl panes.[221] Celarium Expenduntur iii lag. vini. Buttillaria[222] Expenduntur xxix lag. cervisie < . . . > de remanentia. Et remanent viii lag. cervisie. Coquina Expenduntur[223] C allec album l allec rubium ii pisces salsi xl merlyng iiiiC oistr*es* C muscul*is* xxiiii welk*es* de precomputato. \ In MCC ostriis emptis ii s. In viii thornbak*es* iiii^{xx}x merlyng xx rogett*es* et i brem emptis x s. v d. / Candelaria Expenduntur iii lib. candelarum. Stabulum Fenum pro xv equis \ et ii hakeneis / de stauro. In prebenda eorundem vii bus. avenarum. In ferura equorum iii d. Item fenum apud Remesbur' pro xiiii equis i hakeneo de stauro. In avenis pro eisdem v bus. avenarum.

Probatur Summa empcionum xii s. viii d. unde

Panteria De precomputato. Celarium Vinum de remanentia. Butillaria De precomputato. Coquina Empciones xii s. v d. Candelaria De stauro. *Stabulum iii d.* Stabulum Fenum avene de stauro. In ferrura equorum iii d.

[f.39r] Fercula Gentiles xviii Vallecti garciones xxxiiii Summa ferculorum lii Extranii magister Radulphus canonicus se iiii° Alicia Begot se ii° Johannes Perys cum uxore se iiii° et x alii

Die dominica xx° Februarii Panetria Expenduntur Cxx panes de remanentia unde in trencheris vi liberacionibus v coquina vii ferculis lii canibus xii rewardis xxxviii panes. Et remanent xxx panes. Celarium Expenduntur vi lag. vini de remanentia. Buttillaria In Clxxi lag. cervisie emptis de Alicia Schephe*r*de precii lag. i d. ob. deductis inde xiii lag. di. pro avantagio xix s. vii d. ob. qua. Item in xlii lag. cervisie emptis de eadem precii lag. i d. deductis inde pro avantagio iii lag. iii s. iii d. Et expenduntur xlviii lag. cervisie. Et remanent Clxxiii lag. cervisie. Coquina[224] Expenduntur Cl allec album C allec rubium iii pisces salsi i salmo iiii^{xx} merlyng i potel olei i pec. cokl*es* i brem ii gurnard de precomputato. In iii pec. muscul*is* emptis ix d. In viii lag. \ di. / vini acerbi emptis iii s. xi d. ob. Candelaria Expenduntur iiii lib. candelarum de coton. Stabulum Fenum pro xi equis et iii hakeneis de stauro. In prebenda eorundem vi bus. avenarum de

[219] Followed by a blank space in MS.
[220] 73 loaves disbursed.
[221] Correct if the error in the previous day's total is ignored.
[222] MS omits underline.
[223] MS repeats 'Expenduntur'.
[224] MS omits underline.

precomputato. Item fenum apud Remesbur' pro xiiii equis i hakeneo de stauro. In avenis pro eisdem v bus. avenarum de stauro.

Probatur Summa empcionum xxviii s. vii d. qua. unde

Panteria De precomputato. Celarium Vinum de remanentia. Butillaria In CCxiii lag. cervisie xxii s. x d. ob. qua. Coquina Empciones v s. viii d. ob.[225] Candelaria De stauro. Stabulum Fenum avene de stauro.

Fercula Gentiles xvi Wallecti garciones xxviii Summa ferculorum xliiii

Extranii Alicia Begot se ii° Osbern' se ii° Walrond' se ii° et xv alii

Die lune xxi° Februarii Panetria <Expend*un*tur> Furniuntur i qr. frumenti que respondent ad iiiiCxiii panes. Et expenduntur C panes unde in trencheris vi ferculis xliiii liberacionibus vi coquina iiii canibus xii panes rewardis xxviii panes. Et remanent iiiCxliii panes. Celarium Expenduntur iiii lag. vini. Buttillaria Expenduntur xxxvii lag. cervisie de remanentia. Et remanent Cxxxvi lag. cervisie. Coquina Expenduntur C allec album C allec rubium ii pisces salsi viii thornbak*es* iiiiC oistr*es* de precomputato. Candelaria Expenduntur iii lib. candelarum de coton. Stabulum Fenum pro iii equis <ap> et iii hakeneis apud Pot*er*ne de stauro. In prebenda eorundem i bus. di. In diversis medicinis \ pro ii equis domini / emptis per fabrum apud le Vys una cum ferura eorundem et aliorum equorum iii s. iiii d. Item fenum apud Remesbir' pro xx equis iii hakeneis de stauro. In avenis pro eisdem i qr. i bus. avenarum de stauro.

Probatur Summa empcionum iii s. iiii d.

Panteria Furniuntur ii qr. frumenti que respondent ad iiiiCxiii panes. Celarium Vinum de remanentia. Butillaria De precomputato. Coquina De precomputato. Candelaria De stauro. *Stabulum iii s. iiii d.* Stabulum Fenum Avene de stauro. In medicinis iii s. iiii d.

[*f.39v*] *Fercula <Gentiles> Gentiles xv Vallecti garciones xxvii Summa ferculorum xlii*

*Extranii Alicia Begot se ii° Osbern*us *se iii° Dionisia Perys se ii° Walrond vii alii*

Die martis xxii° die Februarii Panetria Expenduntur C panes unde in trencheris v ferculis xlii coquina iii panes liberacionibus v \ rewardis xxxiii / canibus xii. Et remanent CCxliii panes. Celarium[226] Expenduntur iii lag. vini. Buttillaria Expenduntur xxxii lag. cervisie. Et remanent Ciiii lag. cervisie. Coquina Expenduntur C allec album C allec rubium ii pisces salsi ix pisces duris C oistr*es* i potel olei xii gurnard xxxiii merlyng de precomputato i pec. muscul*is*. Candelaria Expenduntur iii lib. candelarum. Stabulum Fenum pro iiii equis et iii hakeneis apud Pot*er*ne de stauro. In

[225] Totals 4*s*. 8½*d*.

[226] MS omits underline.

prebenda eorundem ii bus. avenarum. Item fenum apud Remesbur' pro xix equis ii hakeneis de stauro. In avenis pro eisdem vii bus. di.

Summa nichil quia de precomputato

Panteria De precomputato. Celarium Vinum de remanentia. Butillaria De precomputato. Coquina Empciones nichil. Candelaria De stauro. Stabulum Fenum avene de stauro.

Fercula Gentiles xi Vallecti garciones xix Summa ferculorum xxx
Extranii Alicia Begot se ii° iiii alii

Die mercurie xxiii° die Februarii Panetria[227] lxxvi panes de remanentia unde in trencheris iiii ferculis xxx coquina iii liberacionibus v canibus xii rewardis xxii. Et remanent Clxvii panes. Celarium Expenduntur iii lag. vini. Buttillaria Expenduntur xxix lag. cervisie de remanentia. Et remanent lxxv lag. cervisie. Coquina Expenduntur[228] C allec album et C allec rubium ii pisces salsi i salmo salsus de precomputato. Item in MCC oistr*es* emptis ii s. et expenduntur iiiiC oistr*es*. In iii pec. cok*les* emptis et expensis viii d. Item in iii crabb*es* et iii lobsters emptis ix s. x d. et expenditur i lobster. In DCl welk*es* emptis precii C^{e} v d. ii s. viii d. ob. et expenduntur iiiC welk*es*. Et remanent iiiCl welk*es*. In expensis emptoris viii d. Candelaria Expenduntur iii lib. candelarum. Stabulum Fenum pro iii equis iii hakeneis apud Pot*er*ne \ de / stauro. In prebenda eorundem i bus. ii pec. avenarum de precomputato. Item fenum apud Remesbur' pro[229] xix equis ii hakeneis de stauro. In prebenda eorundem vii bus. di. avenarum de stauro.

Probatur   Summa empcionum xv s. x d. ob.

Panteria De precomputato. Celarium Vinum de remanentia. Butillaria De precomputato. Coquina Empciones xv s. x d. ob. Candelaria De stauro. Stabulum Fenum avene de stauro.

[*f.40r*] *xxxvii Gentiles xiii Vallecti garciones xxiiii Summa ferculorum xxxvii*
Extranii Alicia Begot se ii° Manger se ii° et iiii alii extranii

Die jovis xxiiii° Februarii Panetria Expenduntur iiii^{xx} panes de remanentia unde in trencheris vi panes ferculis <x>xxxvii coquina v liberacionibus v panes canibus xii rewardis xv panes. Et remanent iiii^{xx}vii panes. Celarium Expenduntur iiii lag. vini. Buttillaria Expenduntur xxxii lag. cervisie de remanentia. Et remanent xliii lag. cervisie. Coquina Expenduntur Cxxv allec album C allec rubium ii pisces salsi i salmo salsus iiii pisces duri l merlyng i crabbe i lobster CC welkys. Candelaria Expenduntur iiii lib. candelarum de coton. Stabulum Fenum pro viii equis et iii hakeneis de stauro. In prebenda eorundem iiii bus. ii pec. Item fenum apud Remesbur' pro xix equis ii hakeneis de stauro. In avenis pro eisdem vii bus. di.

227 MS omits underline.
228 MS repeats 'Expenduntur'.
229 MS omits 'pro'.

Summa nichil quia de precomputato

Panteria De precomputato. Celarium Vinum de remanentia. Butillaria De precomputato. Coquina Empciones[230] Candelaria De stauro. Stabulum Fenum avene de stauro.

Fercula Gentiles xi Vallecti garciones xix Summa ferculorum xxx

Extranii Alicia Begot se ii° Manger se ii° et iiii alii

Die veneris xxv° Februarii Panetria Expenduntur lxxii panes unde in trencheris iiii ferculis xxx panes coquina iii panes liberacionibus v panes canibus xii rewardis xviii panes. Et remanent xv panes. Celarium Expenduntur ii lag. vini. Buttillaria Expenduntur xxx lag. cervisie de remanentia. Et remanent <x> xiii lag. cervisie. Coquina Expenduntur C allec rubium C allec album ii pisces salsi C <allec> welk*es* de precomputato. Candelaria iii lib. candelarum. Stabulum Fenum pro ii equis et iii hakeneis de stauro. In prebenda eorundem i bus. ii pec. avenarum de precomputato. Item fenum apud Remesbur' pro xvii equis ii hakeneis de stauro. In avenis pro eisdem vii bus.

Summa nichil quia de precomputato

Panteria De precomputato. Celarium Vinum de remanentia. Butillaria De precomputato. Coquina Empciones[231] Candelaria De stauro. Stabulum Fenum avene de stauro.

[*f.40v*] *Fercula Gentiles xii Vallecti garciones xviii Summa ferculorum xxx*

Extranii Alicia Begot se ii° et vi alii

Die sabbati xxvi° Februarii Panetria Furniuntur ii qr. frumenti que respondent ad iiiiCxvi panes. Et expenduntur lxxiiii panes unde in trencheris iiii ferculis xxx panes coquina iii panes liberacionibus v canibus xv rewardis xvii panes. Et remanent iiiClvii panes. Celarium iii lag. vini. Buttillaria In Cxliiii lag. cervisie emptis de Alicia Scheph*er*de precii lag. i d. ob. deductis inde xi lag. <di.> pro avantagio xvi s. vii d. ob. In l lag. cervisie emptis de eadam per eandem talliam deductis inde iiii lag. cervisie precii lag. i d. iii s. x d. Et expenduntur xxxi lag. cervisie. Et remanent Clxxvi lag. cervisie. Coquina Expenduntur C allec rubium C allec album ii pisces salsi de precomputato. In Cl merlyng x rogett*es* i haddok emptis viii s. vi d. et expenduntur l merlyng i haddok. In i gurnard i bas' emptis vi d. In iiii <gurn> thornbak*es* emptis iii s. iiii d. Item in expensis emptoris apud Wermynst' v d. Item expenduntur DC oistr*es* de precomputato. Candelaria Expenduntur iiii lib. di. candelarum. Stabulum[232] Fenum pro x equis v hakeneis de stauro. In prebenda vii bus. avenarum de precomputato. Item

[230] Followed by a blank space in MS.

[231] Followed by a blank space in MS.

[232] MS omits underline.

fenum apud Remesbur' pro xvii equis i hakeneo de stauro. In prebenda eorundem vii bus. di. avenarum.

Probatur Summa empcionum xxxiii s. ii d. ob. unde

Panteria Furniuntur ii qr. que respondent ad iiiiCxvi panes. Celarium Vinum de remanentia. Butillaria <De p> In Ciiii^{xx}xiiii lag. xx s. v d. ob. Coquina Empciones xii s. ix d. Candelaria De stauro. Stabulum Fenum avene de stauro.

In vadiis Thome Ferro*ur* a xii^{o} die Februarii illo die computato per xiiii dies sequentes capientis per diem iii d. iii s. vi d.

Item in vadiis garcionis sui ibidem a predicto die per xiii dies per diem ii d. ii s. ii d.

Item in vadiis <pagetti> \ garcionis / cancellarii a predicto die per xiiii dies \ capientis per diem ii d. / vadiis Forey pagetti senescalli pagetti Schipton' pagetti Tydm*er*sch' per xiiii dies ut supra cuilibet per diem i d. ob. <viii s. xi d. ob.> \ ix s. vi d. /

Item in vadiis Thome Norman a predicto xii^{o} die usque xxv Februarii utroque computato per xiiii \ dies / ii s. iiii d.

Item in vadiis pagetti Lovell' a xxi^{o} die Februarii illo die computato per v dies per diem i d. ob. vii d. ob.

Item in vadiis Galfridi Chariett*er* a xxii^{o} die Februarii usque xxv diem eiusdem mensis per iiii dies capientis per diem ii d. ob. Thome Charett*er* per idem tempus per diem ii d. xviii d.

Summa xix s. vii d. ob.

Probatur Summa vadiorum xix s. vii d. ob.

[*f.41r*] *Poterne Gentiles xxvi Valecti garciones xl Summa ferculorum lxvi*

Extranii Alicia Becot se iii^{o} rector de Dantesey Johannes Piers se iii^{o} et alii extranii xv

Die dominica xxvii^{o} Februarii Panteria Expenduntur Cxxiiii panes unde pro ferculis lxvi panes trencheris viii liberacionibus vi coquina viii canibus xiiii rewardis xxii. Et remanent CCxxxiii panes. Celarium Expenduntur v lag. vini de remanentia. Butillaria Expenduntur l lag. cervisie. Et remanent Cxxvi lag. cervisie. Coquina Expenduntur Cl allec album Cl rubium iii pisces salcii xiiii stok' i lag. olei ii pecie sto*ur*jon x gurnard l merlyng i bas' CCC welk*es* i lopster de precomputato. Item expenduntur i pikerell xxv anguille parve de stauro de Shirbo*urn*. Candelaria Expenduntur v lib. candelarum de stauro. Stabulum Fenum pro xx equis iiii hakeneis de stauro. In prebenda eorum i qr. avenarum de precomputato. Item fenum apud Remesbur' pro xviii equis iii hakeneis de stauro. In prebenda eorundem vii bus. avenarum de stauro.

Summa nichil quia de precomputato

Panteria De precomputato. Celarium Vinum de remanentia. Butillaria

De precomputato. Coquina Empciones nichil. Candelaria De stauro. Stabulum Fenum avene de stauro.

Gentiles xix Valecti garciones xxxvii Summa ferculorum lvi

Extranii Chytterne se viii^{o} dominus Willelmus Werkman se iii^{o} Alicia Becot se iii^{o} Johannes Piers se iii^{o} et alii extranii x

Die lune xxviii^{o} Februarii Panteria Expenduntur Cxx panes unde pro ferculis lvi trencheris vi liberacionibus v coquina iiii canibus xv rewardis xxxiiii. Et remanent Cxiii panes. Celarium Expenduntur iii lag. vini de remanentia. Butillaria Expenduntur xliiii lag. cervisie. Et remanent iiii^{xx}ii lag. cervisie. Coquina Expenduntur C allec rubium C album ii pisces salcii i salmo salcius iiii stok' i salmo salcius xxv merlyng CC welk*es* de precomputato. Item expenduntur xxv anguille parve de stauro de Shirbo*urn*e. Candelaria Expenduntur iii lib. candelarum de stauro. Stabulum Fenum pro iiii equis v hakeneis de stauro. In prebenda eorundem iii bus. avenarum de precomputato. Item fenum apud Remesbur' pro xx equis i hakeneo de stauro. In prebenda eorundem i qr. avenarum.

Summa nichil quia de precomputato

Panteria De precomputato. Celarium Vinum de remanentia. Butillaria De precomputato. Coquina Empciones nichil. Candelaria De stauro. Stabulum Fenum avene[233]

[*f.41v*] *<Poterne Gentiles xviii Valecti garciones xxxv Summa ferculorum liii*

Extranii Chytterne se viii^{o} dominus Willelmus Workman se iiii^{o} Alicia Becot se iii^{o} et alii extranii viii>

Gentiles xviii Valecti garciones xxxv Summa ferculorum liii

Extranii Chytterne se viii^{o} dominus Willelmus Werkman Alicia Becot se iii^{o} et alii viii

Die martis primo Marcii Panteria Expenduntur Cxiii panes unde pro ferculis liii trencheris vi liberacionibus v coquina v canibus xv rewardis.[234] Et remanet nichil. Celarium Expenduntur iiii lag. vini de stauro. Butillaria Expenduntur xxxviii lag. cervisie. Et remanent xliiii lag. cervisie. Coquina Expenduntur Cl allec rubium C album ii pisces salcii vi stok' xxv merlyng de precomputato. Candelaria Expenduntur iiii lib. candelarum. Stabulum Fenum pro xii equis iiii hakeneis de stauro. In prebenda i qr. avenarum de precomputato. Item fenum apud R' pro xix equis i hakeneo de stauro. In avenis pro eisdem vii bus.

Summa nichil quia de precomputato

Panteria De precomputato. Celarium Vinum de remanentia. Butillaria De

233 Followed by a blank space in MS.

234 Followed by a blank space in MS; 29 loaves unaccounted, presumably disbursed as rewards.

precomputato. Coquina Empciones[235] Candelaria De stauro. Stabulum Fenum avene[236]
[*f.42r*] *Poterne Gentiles xi Valecti garciones xix Summa ferculorum xxx*
Extranii Alicia Becot se et alii extranii viii
Die mercurie secundo Marcii Panteria Furniuntur per i talliam ii qr. frumenti de stauro que respondent ad[237] CCCCxii panes. Et expenduntur iiii^{xx} panes unde pro ferculis xxx trencheris v liberacionibus v coquine iiii canibus xv rewardis xxi. Et remanent CCCxxxii <lag. cervisie> panes. Celarium Expenduntur iii lag. vini de stauro. Butillaria Expenduntur xxviii lag. cervisie. Et remanent xvi lag. cervisie. Coquina Expenduntur Cl allec album C rubium iii pisces salcii ii thornbak*es* de precomputato. Item i pykerell xii roch*es* de stauro de Shirbo*ur*ne. In MCCCC ostriis emptis ii s. iiii d. In xxxii gurnard lxx merlyng i congro recenti emptis viii s. In D welk*es* emptis ii s. vi d. In i bus. pec. cokk*les* emptis vii d. In shrimp*es* emptis iii d. In i haddok empto vii d. In expensis emptoris per iii dies xvi d. Et expenduntur xx merlyng i congrus recens i haddok i bus. cokk*les* de precomputato. Candelaria Expenduntur iiii lib. candelarum de stauro. Stabulum Fenum pro vii equis iiii hakeneis de stauro. In prebenda eorundem iiii bus. avenarum de precomputato. Item fenum apud Remesbur' pro xix equis ii hakeneis de stauro. In avenis pro eisdem vii bus. di.

Probatur Summa empcionum xv s. vii d.

Panteria Furniuntur ii qr. frumenti que respondent ad iiiiCxii panes. Celarium Vinum de remanentia. Butillaria De precomputato. Coquina Empciones xv s. vii d. Candelaria De stauro. Stabulum Fenum avene de stauro.
Gentiles xxi Valecti garciones xlv Summa ferculorum lxvi
*Extranii decanus Sarum se x^{o} magister R.Harwell' se iiii^{o} magister Sim*on *Sydenham se iiii^{o} magister R. canon*icus *se iii Alicia Becot se iii^{o} rector de Dauntesey priorissa de Bromhale et alii extranii x*
Die jovis tercio Marcii Panteria Expenduntur Cxxxiiii panes unde pro ferculis lxvi trencheris ix liberacionibus viii coquine iiii canibus xvii rewardis xxx. Et remanent Cxviii panes.[238] Celarium Expenduntur vii lag. vini de remanentia. Butillaria In iiii^{xx}iiii lag. cervisie emptis de Warner precium lag. i d. ob. deductis inde vi lag. di. cervisie ix s. viii d. In xv lag. cervisie emptis de eodem deducta inde i lag. de avantagio xiiii d. In l lag. cervisie emptis de Axford precium lag. i d. ob. deductis inde iiii lag. cervisie de avantagio v s. v d. Et expenduntur lvii lag. cervisie. Et

[235] Followed by a blank space in MS.
[236] Followed by a blank space in MS.
[237] MS omits 'ad'.
[238] 198 loaves should remain.

remanent Cviii lag. cervisie. Coquina Expenduntur Cl allec rubium Cl allec album iii pisces salcii vi stok' CCC ostria de precomputato. Item expenduntur i pik' i tench de stauro de Shirbo*urn*e. Item expenduntur ii crabb*es* CC welk*es* i lag. olei xxxiiii rogett*es* l merlyng de precomputato. Item expenduntur ii anguille grosse de stauro de Shirbo*urn*. In C merlyng emptis iii s. iiii d. In ii thornbak*es* <emptis> vi gurnard et ii brem*es* emptis iiii s. Candelaria Expenduntur v lib. di. candelarum de stauro. Stabulum Fenum pro v equis iiii hakeneis de stauro. In prebenda iii bus. di. avenarum de precomputato. Item fenum apud Remesbur' pro xxi equis i hakeneo de stauro. In prebenda eorundem i qr. i bus.

Probatur Summa empcionum xxiii s. vii d. unde

Panteria De precomputato. Celarium Vinum de remanentia. Butillaria In Cxlix lag. cervisie xvi s. iii d. Coquina Empciones vii s. iiii d. Candelaria De stauro. Stabulum Fenum avene[239]

[*f.42v*] *Poterne Gentiles xvi Valecti garciones xxxiiii Summa ferculorum l*
*Extranii magister Roger*us *Harwell' se iiii*^{o} *magister Simo*n *Sydenham se iiii*^{to} *magister R. canon*icus *se iii*^{o} *magister Johannes Stone se ii*^{o} *rector de Dauntesey se ii*^{o} *rector de Fromq*uintyn *se ii*^{o} *priorissa de Bromhale se iiii*^{to} *Alicia Becote se ii*^{o} *et alii extranii viii*

Die veneris iiii^{to} Marcii Panteria Expenduntur Cxviii panes de remanentia unde pro ferculis l trencheris vii liberacionibus vi coquine v canibus xv rewardis xxxv de remanentia. Celarium Expenduntur v lag. vini de precomputato. Butillaria Expenduntur xliiii lag. cervisie. Et remanent lxvii lag. cervisie.[240] Coquina Expenduntur Cl allec rubium Cl allec album iii pisces salcii i salmo salcius de precomputato. Item expenduntur l merlyng ii thornbak*es* vi gurnard ii brem*es* de precomputato. Candelaria Expenduntur iiii lib. candelarum de stauro. Stabulum Fenum pro iiii equis iiii hakeneis de stauro. In prebenda ii bus. avenarum de precomputato. Item fenum apud Remesbur' pro xx equis i hakeneo de stauro. In prebenda eorundem i qr. avenarum de stauro.

Summa empcionum nichil quia de precomputato

Panteria De precomputato. Celarium Vinum de remanentia. Butillaria De precomputato. Coquina Empciones nichil. Candelaria De stauro. Stabulum Fenum avene de stauro.

Gentiles xii Valecti garciones xxviii Summa ferculorum xl
Extranii priorissa de Bromhale se iiii^{o} *Alicia Becote se ii*^{o} *et alii extranii vi*

Die sabbati v^{to} Marcii Panteria Furniuntur per i talliam ii qr. frumenti de stauro que respondent de CCCCxii panibus. Et expenduntur iiii^{xx}x panes unde pro ferculis xl trencheris v liberacionibus v coquine iiii canibus xvi

[239] Followed by a blank space in MS.
[240] 64 gallons should remain.

rewardis xx. Et remanent CCCxxii panes. Celarium Expenduntur iii lag. vini de <stauro> precomputato. Butillaria Expenduntur xxx lag. cervisie. Et remanent xxxvii lag. cervisie. Coquina Expenduntur C allec rubium C allec album ii pisces salcii de stauro. In i pot de merlyng gurnard et plais brem*es* empto viii s. xi d. et expenduntur xx gurnard l merlyng ii brem*es*. Item expenduntur ii crabb*es* CC welk*es* i lag. olei de precomputato. Candelaria Expenduntur iii lib. candelarum de stauro. Stabulum Fenum pro vii equis vi hakeneis de stauro. In prebenda v bus. avenarum de precomputato. Item fenum apud Remesbur' pro xxi equis ii hakeneis de stauro. In avenis pro eisdem i qr. i bus.

Probatur   Summa empcionum viii s. xi d.

Panteria Furniuntur ii qr. frumenti que respondent ad iiiiCxii panes. Celarium Vinum de remanentia. Butillaria De precomputato. Coquina Empciones viii s. xi d. Candelaria De stauro. Stabulum Fenum avene[241]

[*f.43r*] *Poterne Gentiles xxiii Valecti garciones xlv Summa ferculorum lxviii*
Extranii Alicia Becot se ii^{o} *Johannes Perys cum uxore et alii extranii xiiii*

Die dominica vi^{o} Marcii Panteria Expenduntur Cxxxii panes unde pro ferculis lxviii trencheris ix liberacionibus vi coquine viii canibus xvi rewardis xxv. Et remanent Ciiii^{xx}x panes. Celarium Expenduntur iiii lag. vini de stauro. Butillaria Expenduntur in Ciiii^{xx}xvii lag. cervisie emptis de Shepherde precium lag. i d. ob. deductis inde xvi lag. di. cervisie de avantagio xxii s. vii d. In xxv lag. cervisie emptis de eadem precium lag. i d. deductis inde ii lag. de avantagio xxiii d. In iiii^{xx}viii lag. cervisie emptis de Warn*er* precium lag. i d. ob. deductis inde vii lag. de avantagio x s. i d. ob. In xv lag. cervisie emptis de eodem precium lag. i d. deducta inde i lag. de avantagio xiiii d. Et expenduntur liiii lag. cervisie. Et remanent CCCviii lag. cervisie. Coquina Expenduntur Cl allec rubium Cl allec album iii pisces salcii xii stok' i salmo salcius. Item expenduntur xii plais xxv gurnard l merlyng C welk*es* i lag. olei de precomputato. Candelaria Expenduntur iiii lib. candelarum de stauro. Stabulum Fenum pro iiii equis vi hakeneis de stauro. In prebenda ii bus. di. avenarum de precomputato. Item fenum apud Remesbur' pro xviii equis ii hakeneis de stauro. In prebenda eorundem vii bus. avenarum.

Probatur   Summa empcionum xxxv s. ix d. ob.

Panteria De precomputato. Celarium Vinum de remanentia. Butillaria In CCCxxxv lag. cervisie xxxv s. ix d. ob. Coquina Empciones Candelaria De stauro. Stabulum Fenum avene de stauro.

Gentiles xx Valecti garciones xxxvii Summa ferculorum lvii
Extranii Alicia Becot se ii^{o} *Johannes Piers cum uxore et alii extranii viii*

Die lune vii^{o} Marcii Panteria Expenduntur Cxxv panes unde pro ferculis

[241] Followed by a blank space in MS.

lvii panes trencheris viii liberacionibus vi coquine v canibus xviii rewardis xxxi. Et remanent lxv panes. Celarium Expenduntur ii lag. vini de stauro. Butillaria Expenduntur xliiii lag. cervisie. Et remanent CClxiiii <p> lag. cervisie. Coquina Expenduntur Cl allec rubium Cl allec album ii pisces salcii iiii stok' xx gurnard CCC welk*es* CCCC ostria de precomputato. <E> In vi bus. pisarum viridum emptis iiii s. ii d. In M ostriis emptis xx d. In DCCClxxv welk*es* emptis iii s. vii d. ob. Candelaria Expenduntur iii lib. candelarum de stauro. Stabulum Fenum pro x equis iiii hakeneis de stauro. In prebenda vii bus. avenarum de precomputato. Item fenum apud Remesbur' pro xix equis ii hakeneis de stauro. In avenis pro eisdem vii bus. avenarum de stauro.

Probatur Summa empcionum ix s. v d.[242]

Panteria De precomputato. Celarium Vinum de remanentia. Butillaria De precomputato. Coquina Empciones ix s. v d.[243] Candelaria De stauro. Stabulum Fenum avene de stauro.

[*f.43v*] *Poterne Gentiles xvii Valecti garciones xxxvii Summa ferculorum liiii Extranii Alicia Becot se ii^o^ magister J.Rowbourne se ii^o^ et alii extranii viii*

Die martis viii° Marcii Panteria Furniuntur per i talliam i qr. vii bus. frumenti de stauro que respondent de CCCiiii^xx^ii. Et expenduntur Cvii panes unde pro ferculis liiii panes trencheris vi liberacionibus vi coquine v canibus xviii rewardis xviii. Et remanent CCxl panes.[244] Celarium Expenduntur iii lag. vini de stauro. Butillaria Expenduntur xlii lag. cervisie. Et remanent CCxxii <panes> lag. cervisie. Coquina Expenduntur Cl allec rubium Cl album ii pisces[245] salcii iiii stok' i salmo salcius. Item iiii brem*es* xviii merlyng CC welk*es* de precomputato. Item viii roch*es* de stauro. Candelaria Expenduntur iiii lib. candelarum de stauro. Stabulum Fenum pro xx equis iiii hakeneis de stauro. In prebenda i qr. iii bus. avenarum de precomputato. Item fenum apud Remesbur' pro xx equis i hakeneo de stauro. In avenis pro eisdem i qr. i bus. avenarum.

Summa nichil quia de precomputato

Panteria Furniuntur i qr. vii bus. frumenti iiiCiiii^xx^ii panes. Celarium Vinum de remanentia. Butillaria De precomputato. Coquina Empciones nichil. Candelaria De stauro. Stabulum Fenum avene de stauro.

Gentiles xvii Valecti garciones xxviii Summa ferculorum xlv

*Extranii prior de Motesfonte Leycestr' heraud' se ii^o^* sire *Willelmus Frank' se ii^o^ Alicia Becote se ii^o^ Johannes Perys et alii extranii xiiii*

Die mercurie ix° Marcii Panteria Expenduntur Cviii panes unde pro

242 Total should be ½*d*. more.

243 Total should be ½*d*. more.

244 340 loaves should remain.

245 MS 'pesces'.

ferculis xlv trencheris vi liberacionibus vi coquine iii canibus xviii rewardis xxx. Et remanent Cxxxii panes. Celarium Expenduntur iiii lag. vini de remanentia. Butillaria Expenduntur xxxii lag. cervisie. Et remanent Ciiii^{xx}x lag. cervisie. Coquina Expenduntur C allec album l rubium ii pisces salcii i salmo salcius de stauro. Item expenduntur D welk*es* de precomputato. In i pot piscis recentis empto continenti xlviii gurnard lxx merlyng ii plais et i turbut vii s. In xxv bas*is* emptis viii s. In i sol*e* empto ii d. In v lopsters emptis ii s. In expensis <expen'> emptoris apud Sarum cum somerario viii d. Et expenduntur xxviii gurnard xxv merlyng ii plais. Item expenduntur v bas*is* et i sol*e* CCCC ostria de precomputato. Candelaria Expend*un*tur[246] lib. candelarum de <de> stauro. Stabulum Fenum pro xxi equis iiii hakeneis de stauro. In prebenda xii bus. avenarum de precomputato. Item fenum apud Remesbur' pro xxi equis i hakeneo de stauro. In prebenda eorundem i qr. avenarum.

Probatur Summa empcionum xvii s. x d.

Panteria De precomputato. Celarium Vinum de remanentia. Butillaria De precomputato. Coquina Empciones xvii s. x d. Candelaria De stauro. Stabulum Fenum avene[247]

[f.44r][248] *Poterne Fercula Gentiles xviii Valecti garciones xxxi Summa ferculorum xlix*

Extranii dominus Robertus Bussh' se iii^{o} et alii xiiii

Die jovis xvii^{o} Marcii Panteria Expenduntur Cxviii panes unde pro ferculis xlix panes trencheris v liberacionibus v coquina iiii canibus xvi panes rewardis xxxix panes. Et remanent Cx panes. Celarium Expenduntur iii lag. vini de remanentia. Butillaria Expenduntur xxxv lag. cervisie. Et remanent lxvii lag. cervisie. Coquina Expenduntur CC allec album C allec rubium iiii pisces salcii vi stok' de stauro. Item expenduntur vi mullett*es* de stauro precomputato. In iiii piscibus salciis iiii s. In v thornebak*es* emptis iii s. iiii d. et expenduntur ii thornebak*es* de precomputato. Candelaria Expenduntur iii lib. candelarum de stauro. Stabulum Fenum pro ix equis ii hakeneis de stauro. In prebenda eorundem iiii bus. avenarum de stauro. Item fenum apud Remesbur' pro viii equis ii hakeneis de stauro. In prebenda eorundem iiii bus. avenarum.

Probatur Summa empcionum vii s. iiii d.

Panteria De precomputato. Celarium Vinum de remanentia. Butillaria De precomputato. Coquina Empciones vii s. iiii d. Candelaria De stauro. Stabulum Fenum avene de stauro.

[246] Followed by a blank space in MS.
[247] Followed by a blank space in MS.
[248] The folios with the entries for 10–16 March are now missing.

Gentiles xi Valecti garciones xxii Summa ferculorum xxxiii
Extranii rector de Dauntesay se ii^{o} Wynslow se ii^{o} et alii viii
Die veneris xviii^{o} Marcii Panteria Expenduntur iiii^{xx} panes unde pro ferculis xxxiii panes trencheris iiii liberacionibus vi coquina iiii canibus xv rewardis xviii panes. Et remanent xxx panes. Celarium Expenduntur ii lag. vini de remanentia. Butillaria Expenduntur xxxii lag. cervisie. Et remanent xxxv lag. cervisie. Coquina Expenduntur C allec album l allec rubium ii pisces salcii de stauro. Item ii pisces salsii de precomputato iii stok' de stauro. Item expenditur i salmon' salcius de stauro. Candelaria Expenduntur ii lib. candelarum de stauro. Stabulum Fenum pro xx equis iiii hakeneis de stauro. In avenis pro eisdem i qr. iiii bus. Item fenum apud Remesbur' pro ix equis iii hakeneis de stauro. In prebenda eorundem iiii bus. avenarum.

Summa empcionum nichil quia de precomputato

Panteria De precomputato. Celarium Vinum de remanentia. Butillaria De precomputato. Coquina Empciones nichil. Candelaria De stauro. Stabulum Fenum avene[249]

[*f.44v*] *Poterne Fercula Gentiles vii Valecti garciones xv Summa ferculorum xxii*
Extranii viii
Die sabbati xix^{o} Marcii Panteria Furniuntur per i talliam ii qr. frumenti que respondent ad CCCCxiiii panes. Et expenduntur lxx[250] unde pro ferculis xxii panes trencheris vii liberacionibus vii coquina viii canibus xvii panes rewardis \ x. / Et remanent CCClxxiiii panes. Celarium Expenduntur iii lag. vini de stauro. Butillaria Expenduntur xxx lag. cervisie. Et remanent v lag. cervisie. Coquina Expenduntur Cl allec album C allec rubium iii pisces salsii iiii stok' de stauro. Item expenduntur iii pecie storjon'. In i pot piscis recentis empto x s. In ix plais emptis et expensis iii s. In expensis emptoris v d. In M ostriis emptis xx d. et expenduntur D. Item expenditur di. pot piscis de precomputato. Candelaria Expenduntur ii lib. candelarum de stauro. Stabulum Fenum pro xx equis iii hakeneis de stauro. In prebenda eorundem i qr. i bus. avenarum de stauro. Item fenum apud Remesbur' pro ix equis iii hakeneis de stauro. In prebenda eorundem iii bus. di. avenarum de stauro.

Probatur Summa empcionum xv s. i d.

Panteria Furniuntur ii qr. frumenti que respondent ad iiiiCxiiii panes. Celarium Vinum de remanentia. Butillaria De precomputato. Coquina Empciones xv s. i d. Candelaria De stauro. Stabulum Fenum avene de stauro.

[249] Followed by a blank space in MS.
[250] 71 loaves disbursed.

In vadiis pagetti senescalli apud Remesbur' a xiii^{o} die Marcii usque xix diem eiusdem primo et ultimo computatis capientis per diem i d. ob. x d. ob.
In vadiis Roberti Baker' equitantis in negociis domini per iii dies mense Marcii videlicet usque Bedewynde Sarum et alibi xii d.
Fercula Gentiles xxiiii Valecti garciones xxxix Summa ferculorum lxiii
Extranii magister J. Wotton' se iii^{o} vicarius ville se ii^{o} et alii xv
Die dominica xx Marcii Panteria Expenduntur Cxx panes[251] unde pro ferculis lxiii panes trencheris vii liberacionibus vii coquina viii canibus xvii rewardis ix panes. Et remanent CCliiii panes. Celarium Expenduntur iiii lag. vini de stauro. Butillaria In Clxvii lag. cervisie emptis de Shepherd' precium lag. i d. ob. deductis inde xiiii lag. de avantagio xix s. i d. ob. In l lag. cervisie emptis de eadem[252] precium lag. i d. deductis inde iiii lag. di. iii s. ix d. In Clxxiii lag. cervisie emptis de eadem[253] precium lag. i d. ob. deductis inde xv lag. de avantagio <xxii s. iii d.> \ xix s. ix d. / In xxv lag. cervisie emptis de eadem[254] precium lag. i d. deductis inde ii lag. de avantagio xxiii d. In Cxxi lag. cervisie emptis de Barlich' precium lag. i d. ob. deductis inde ix lag. de avantagio xiiii s. In iiii^{xx}xviii lag. cervisie emptis de Warener precium lag. i d. ob. deductis inde viii lag. di. xi s. iii d. Et expenduntur xlviii lag. cervisie. Et remanent Diiii^{xx}xi lag. cervisie. Coquina Expenduntur CC allec album Cl allec rubium iiii pisces salcii ii salmones i qr. storjon' x stok' de stauro. Item expenduntur D ostres de precomputato. Item expenditur di. piscis recentis de precomputato. Candelaria Expenduntur iii lib. candelarum de stauro. Stabulum Fenum pro xxiiii equis ii hakeneis de stauro. In avenis pro eisdem i qr. ii bus. avenarum. Item fenum apud Remesbur' pro ix equis ii hakeneis de stauro. In avenis pro eisdem iii bus. di. avenarum.

Probatur Summa empcionum lxxi s. <ix> \ vii[255] / d. unde Panteria De precomputato. Celarium Vinum de remanentia. Butillaria In viCxxxiiii lag. cervisie emptis lxix s. ix d. ob. Coquina Empciones[256] Candelaria De stauro. Stabulum Fenum avene de stauro. Vadia xxii d. ob.
[*f.45r*] *Poterne Fercula Gentiles xviii Valecti garciones xxxiii Summa ferculorum li*
Extranii magister J. Wotton' se iii^{o} vicarius ville et alii x
Die lune xxi Marcii Panteria Expenduntur Cviii panes unde pro ferculis li

[251] 111 loaves disbursed.
[252] MS 'eodem'.
[253] MS 'eodem'.
[254] MS 'eodem'.
[255] Total should be 1*d.* more.
[256] Followed by a blank space in MS.

panes trencheris v liberacionibus v coquina iiii canibus xv rewardis xxviii panes. Et remanent Cxlvi panes. Celarium[257] Expenduntur ii lag. vini de remanentia. Butillaria Expenduntur xxxviii lag. cervisie. Et remanent Dxliii[258] lag. cervisie.[259] Coquina Expenduntur Cl allec album C allec rubium iiii pisces salsii iiii stok' de stauro. Candelaria Expenduntur ii lib. candelarum. Stabulum Fenum pro xvi equis iii hakeneis de stauro. In avenis pro eisdem[260] vi bus. Item fenum apud Remesbur' pro xxiii equis iii hakeneis de stauro. In avenis pro eisdem i qr. i bus. di. avenarum.

Summa nichil quia de precomputato

Panteria De precomputato. Celarium Vinum de remanentia. Butillaria De precomputato. Coquina Empciones nichil. Candelaria De stauro. Stabulum Fenum avene de stauro.

Fercula Gentiles xv Valecti garciones xxx Summa ferculorum xlv

Extranii suffraganus domini se iiii° magister Simon Sidenham et alii xiiii

Die martis xxii Marcii Panteria Expenduntur Cv unde pro ferculis xlv panes trencheris v liberacionibus vi coquina iiii canibus xvi panes rewardis xxix panes. Et remanent xli panes. Celarium Expenduntur iii lag. vini de remanentia. Butillaria Expenduntur xxxvii lag. cervisie. Et remanent Dvi lag. cervisie. Coquina Expenduntur Cl allec album C allec rubium i salmon' salcius vi stok' i pecia storjon' de stauro. In muscul*is* emptis et expensis iiii d. Candelaria Expenduntur ii lib. candelarum de stauro. Stabulum Fenum pro[261] xix equis iii hakeneis de stauro. In prebenda eorundem i qr. avenarum de stauro. Item fenum apud Remesbur' pro xxix equis ii hakeneis de stauro. In prebenda eorundem i qr. iii bus. avenarum.

Probatur Summa empcionum iiii d.

Panteria De precomputato. Celarium Vinum de remanentia. Butillaria De precomputato. Coquina Empciones iiii d. Candelaria De stauro. Stabulum Fenum avene de stauro.

[*f.45v*] *Poterne Fercula Gentiles x Valecti garciones xxxii Summa ferculorum xlii*

Extranii suffraganus domini se iiii° magister Simon Sydenham se iii° et alii viii

Die mercurie xxiii Marcii Panteria Furniuntur per i talliam i qr. vi bus. frumenti que respondent ad CCCxlviii panes. Et expenduntur Cx<x> panes unde pro ferculis xlii panes trencheris iiii liberacionibus viii coquina v canibus xvii panes rewardis xxxiiii panes. Et remanent CClxxix panes.

257 MS omits underline.
258 553 gallons should remain.
259 MS 'panes'.
260 MS repeats 'in avenis pro eisdem'.
261 MS omits 'pro'.

Celarium Expenduntur iii lag. vini de remanentia. Butillaria Expenduntur xxxv lag. cervisie. Et remanent CCCClxxi lag. cervisie. Coquina Expenduntur CC allec album C allec rubium ii pisces salsii i pecia storjon' de stauro. In i pot piscis recentis continenti lvi gurnard lvi merlyng i thornebak[262] xi s. viii d. In i turbot empto ii s. In iiii lopsters emptis ii s. In xxviii lib. dat*es* emptis viii s. x d. In iiii lag. aceti emptis xii d. In expensis emptoris iiii d. et expenduntur xv gurnard xxvi merlyng i lopster iiii lag. aceti de precomputato. \ In MCCCC ostriis emptis ii s. iiii d. et expenduntur iiiiC. / Candelaria Expenduntur ii lib. candelarum de stauro. Stabulum Fenum pro xxvii equis vi hakeneis de stauro. In avenis pro eisdem i qr. iiii bus. avenarum de stauro. Item fenum apud R' pro xxv equis i hakeneo de stauro. In prebenda eorundem i qr. i bus. avenarum de stauro.

Probatur Summa empcionum xxviii s. ii d.

Panteria Furniuntur i qr. vi bus. frumenti que respondent ad iiiCxlviii. Celarium Vinum de remanentia. Butillaria De precomputato. Coquina Empciones xxviii s. ii d. Candelaria De stauro. Stabulum Fenum avene de stauro.

Fercula Gentiles xvii Valecti garciones xxiii Summa ferculorum xli[263]

Extranii suffraganus[264] *domini magister Simon Sidenham se vi*^{o} *et alii xiiii*

Die jovis xxiiii^{o} Marcii Panteria Expenduntur C panes unde pro ferculis xli panes trencheris vi liberacionibus vii coquina vi canibus xvi panes rewardis xxiiii panes. Et remanent Clxxix panes. Celarium Expenduntur ii lag. vini de remanentia. Butillaria Expenduntur xxxvi lag. cervisie. Et remanent CCCCxxxv lag. cervisie. Coquina Expenduntur C allec album C allec rubium ii pisces salsii i salmon' salsius de stauro. Item expenduntur vi gurnard de precomputato xxvi merling de precomputato. \ Item iiiC ostria. / Candelaria Expenduntur ii lib. candelarum de stauro. Stabulum Fenum pro <i> xv equis iiii hakeneis de stauro. In prebenda eorundem i qr. avenarum. Item fenum apud Remesbur' pro xxiiii equis ii hakeneis de stauro. In[265] prebenda eorundem i qr. ii pec. avenarum de stauro.

Summa nichil quia de precomputato

Panteria De precomputato. Celarium Vinum de remanentia. Butillaria De precomputato. Coquina Empciones nichil. Candelaria De stauro. Stabulum Fenum avene de stauro.

[*f.46r*] *Poterne Fercula Gentiles xi Valecti garciones xxii Summa ferculorum xxxiii*

[262] MS 'tohornebak''.

[263] Totals 40, but 41 loaves disbursed for *fercula*. The figures for *gentiles*, *valecti* and *garciones* may be incorrect.

[264] MS 'suffragamus'.

[265] MS repeats 'in'.

Extranii suffraganus se iii^{o} magister S.Sydenham se vi^{o} unus valectus domini regis et alii x

Die veneris xxv Marcii Panteria Expenduntur iiii^{xx}[266] panes unde pro ferculis xxxiiii trencheris iii liberacionibus vii coquina viii canibus xvi panes rewardis xx panes. Et remanent iiii^{xx}xix panes. Celarium Expenditur i lag. vini. Butillaria Expenduntur xxiiii lag. cervisie. Et remanent CCCCxi lag. cervisie.[267] Coquina Expenditur nichil quia in die Parasceves. Candelaria Expenduntur iii lib. candelarum de stauro. Stabulum Fenum pro xii equis vi hakeneis de stauro. In avenis pro eisdem vi bus. de stauro. Item fenum apud Remesbur' pro xxvi equis ii hakeneis de stauro. In prebenda eorundem i qr. ii bus. avenarum de stauro.

Summa nichil quia de precomputato

Panteria De precomputato. Celarium Vinum de remanentia. Butillaria De precomputato. Coquina Empciones nichil. Candelaria De stauro. Stabulum Fenum avene de stauro.

Gentiles xvii Valecti garciones xxviii Summa ferculorum xlv

Extranii suffraganus se iii^{o} magister Simon Sidenham se iii^{o} Notyngham se iii^{o} Becot se iiii^{o} et alii xiiii

Die sabbati xxvi^{o} Marcii Panteria Furniuntur per i talliam ii qr. frumenti que respondent ad CCCCxi panes. \ Expenduntur Cx panes / unde pro ferculis xlv trencheris vi liberacionibus viii coquina vi canibus xvi panes rewardis xxix panes. Et remanent CCCC panes. Celarium Expenduntur iiii lag. vini de remanentia. Butillaria Expenduntur xxxix lag. cervisie. Et remanent CCClxxii <pe> lag. cervisie. Coquina Expenduntur Cl allec rubium Cl allec album iii pisces salsii i salmon' salsius ii pikes de stauro ii peces storjon' de stauro. Item expenduntur DC ostria de precomputato. In xxvii gurnard vii merling et iii bremes emptis et expensis v s. iiii d. In expensis emptoris de Poterne usque Werminstr' pro dictis victualibus ibidem emendis v d. In ii crevis emptis[268] et expensis. Candelaria Expenduntur iii lib. candelarum de stauro. Stabulum Fenum pro[269] xii equis vii hakeneis de stauro. In avenis pro eisdem vii bus. avenarum. Item fenum apud Remesbur' pro xxvii equis i hakeneo de stauro. In avenis pro eisdem i qr. ii bus.

Probatur Summa empcionum v s. ix d.

Panteria Furniuntur ii qr. frumenti que respondent ad iiiiCxi panes. Celarium Vinum de remanentia. Butillaria De precomputato. Coquina Empciones v s. ix d. Candelaria De stauro. Stabulum Fenum avene de stauro.

266 88 loaves disbursed.

267 MS 'panes'.

268 Followed by a blank space in MS.

269 MS omits 'pro'.

[*f.46v*] *Poterne*

Festum Pasche

Gentiles xxxvi Valecti garciones xlviii Summa ferculorum iiii^{xx}iiii
Extranii suffraganus se iii^{o} magister Simon[270] *Sidenham se iii^{o} Becot cum uxore se iii^{o} Notingham se iii^{o} et alii xxiiii. Necantur i bos i porcus.*[271]
Die dominica xxvii^{o} Marcii Panteria Expenduntur Clx panes unde pro ferculis iiii^{xx}iiii panes trencheris xiiii liberacionibus x coquina xiiii canibus xvi panes rewardis xxii panes. Et remanent CCxl panes. Celarium Expenduntur x lag. vini de remanentia. Butillaria Expenduntur lxiiii lag. cervisie. Et remanent CCCviii lag. cervisie. Coquina Expenduntur i qr. bovis di. bacon' de stauro. In iii cassis multonum emptis vi s. vi d. et expenduntur i cassa di. In iii carcosiis vitulorum emptis x s. et expenduntur ii. Item expenditur di. porcus de stauro. In ii cassis agninis emptis ii s. iiii d. et expenduntur. In ii edis emptis ii s. v d. et expenditur i. In vi porcellis emptis iii s. et expenduntur iiii. In xx caponibus emptis v s. ii d. et expenduntur x. In xlviii pulcinis emptis iiii s. iii d. et expenduntur xxii. In M ovis emptis iii s. ix d. et expenduntur vC. <ii> Item expenditur i dama recens de stauro. Candelaria Expenduntur ii lib. candelarum de stauro. Stabulum Fenum pro xii equis iiii hakeneis de stauro. In prebenda eorundem v bus. di. avenarum de stauro. Item fenum apud Remesbur' pro xxvi equis iii hakeneis de stauro. In avenis pro eisdem i qr. ii bus. avenarum.

Probatur   Summa empcionum xxxvii s. v d.

Panteria De precomputato. Celarium Vinum de remanentia. Butillaria De precomputato. Coquina Empciones xxxvii s. v d. Candelaria De stauro. Stabulum Fenum avene[272]

Gentiles xxxv Valecti garciones xlii Summa ferculorum lxxvii
Extranii suffraganus se iii^{o} magister S.Sidenham se iii^{o} Notyngham se iii^{o} Becot cum uxore se iii^{o} uxor J.Perys se iii^{o} vicarius ville se iii^{o} et alii xv
Die lune xxviii^{o} Marcii Panteria Expenduntur Cxxx panes[273] unde pro ferculis lxxvii panes trencheris xiiii liberacionibus viii coquina x canibus xvi panes rewardis xv panes. Et remanent Cx panes. Celarium Expenduntur vi lag. vini de stauro remanenti. Butillaria Expenduntur lxii lag. cervisie. Et remanent CCxlvi lag. cervisie. Coquina Expenduntur i qr. bovis i cassa multonis i bacon'. Item expenduntur i caponis iiii pulcini i carcosium vituli ii porcelli i damus salcius. Item Cl ova de precomputato.[274] Candelaria

[270] MS 'Sinom'.
[271] 'Necantur' etc. in right margin.
[272] Followed by a blank space in MS.
[273] 140 loaves disbursed.
[274] MS repeats 'de precomputato'.

Expenduntur ii lib. candelarum de stauro. Stabulum Fenum pro xi equis iii hakeneis de stauro. In prebenda eorundem v bus. de stauro. Item fenum apud Remesbur' pro xxiiii equis. In prebenda eorundem i qr. i bus. avenarum de stauro.

Summa nichil quia de precomputato

Panteria De precomputato. Celarium Vinum de remanentia. Butillaria De precomputato. Coquina Empciones nichil. Candelaria De stauro. Stabulum Fenum avene de stauro.

[*f.47r*] *Fercula Gentiles xxviii Valecti garciones xxxvi Summa ferculorum lxiiii*

Extranii suffragannus Dionisia Peris se ii^{o} Becot cum uxore se iii^{o} vicarius ville se ii^{o} rector de Pouleshomll' et alii xviii

Die martis xxix^{o} Marcii Panteria Furniuntur[275] per i talliam ii qr. iiii bus. frumenti que respondent ad Dxvi panes. Expenduntur Cxxxiii panes[276] unde pro ferculis lxiii panes trencheris x liberacionibus viii coquina vi canibus xvi rewardis xx panes. Et remanent CCCCiiii^{xx}iii panes.[277] Celarium Expenduntur iii lag. vini de remanentia. Butillaria Expenduntur liiii lag. cervisie. Et remanent Ciiii^{xx}xii lag. cervisie. Coquina Expenditur i qr. bovis. Item i bacon' de stauro i cassa i qr. multonum iii capones de precomputato. In i cassa multonis empta ii s. iiii d. In i carcosio vituli empto et expenso iii s. iiii d. In i agno empto et expenso xii d. In iii porcellis emptis et expensis xviii d. Item expenditur i qr. edi de precomputato. Candelaria Expenduntur ii lib. candelarum de stauro. Stabulum Fenum pro viii equis iiii hakeneis de stauro. In prebenda eorundem iiii bus. avenarum de stauro. Item fenum apud Remesbur' pro xx equis ii hakeneis de stauro. In prebenda eorundem i qr. avenarum de stauro.

Probatur Summa empcionum viii s. ii d.

Panteria Furniuntur ii qr. iiii bus. frumenti que respondent ad vCxvi panes. Celarium Vinum de remanentia. Butillaria De precomputato. Coquina Empciones viii s. ii d. Candelaria De stauro. Stabulum Fenum avene de stauro.

Fercula Gentiles xxiii Valecti garciones xxxviii Summa ferculorum lxi

Extranii suffraganus se iiii^{o} Becot cum uxore se iii^{o} et alii xiiii

Die mercurie xxx Marcii Panteria Expenduntur Cxxxiii panes unde pro ferculis lxi panes trencheris viii liberacionibus vii coquina vi canibus xvi panes rewardis xxxv panes. Et remanent CCCl panes. Celarium Expenduntur iiii lag. vini de remanentia. Butillaria Expenduntur li lag. cervisie. Et remanent Cxli lag. cervisie. Coquina Expenduntur di. qr. bovis

[275] Preceded by 'Expenduntur' in MS.
[276] 123 loaves disbursed.
[277] 493 loaves should remain.

di. bacon' de stauro. Item expenduntur i caponis di. edi de precomputato. Item expenduntur CC ova de precomputato. Item C allec album l allec rubium i piscis salsius i salmon' salcius. Item expenditur i tenche de stauro. Candelaria Expenduntur ii lib. candelarum de stauro. Stabulum Fenum pro xii equis iiii hakeneis de stauro. In prebenda eorundem v bus. avenarum de stauro. Item fenum apud Remesbur' pro xxii equis de stauro. In avenis pro eisdem i qr. de stauro.

Summa nichil quia de precomputato

Panteria De precomputato. Celarium Vinum de remanentia. Butillaria De precomputato. Coquina Empciones nichil. Candelaria De stauro. Stabulum Fenum avene[278]

[*f.47v*] *Poterne Fercula Gentiles xix Valecti garciones xxx Summa ferculorum xlix*

Extranii Becot cum uxore et alii xv

Die jovis ultimo Marcii Panteria Expenduntur Cxii panes[279] unde pro ferculis xlix panes trencheris vii liberacionibus vi coquina vi canibus xv panes rewardis xlix panes. Et remanent CCxxxviii panes. Celarium Expenduntur iii lag. vini de remanentia. Butillaria Expenduntur xxxv lag. cervisie. Et remanent Cvi lag. cervisie. Coquina Expenduntur di. qr. bovis di. bacon' de stauro. Item expenduntur qr. multonis de precomputato ii capones iiii pulcini. In i cassa di. multonum iii s. vi d. et expenditur di. In i carcosio vituli empto iii s. et expenso. In ii porcellis emptis et expensis xiiii d. In i bus. ceparum xii d. In i bus. farine avenarum x d. In expensis emptoris ii d. Item expenduntur C ova de precomputato. Candelaria Expenduntur ii lib. candelarum de stauro. Stabulum Fenum pro x equis iii hakeneis de stauro. In avenis pro eisdem iiii bus. di. de stauro. Item fenum apud R' pro xxiiii equis iii hakeneis de stauro. In avenis pro eisdem i qr. i bus. avenarum.

Probatur Summa empcionum ix s. viii d.

Panteria De precomputato. Celarium Vinum de remanentia. Butillaria De precomputato. Coquina Empciones ix s. viii d. Candelaria De stauro. Stabulum Fenum avene de stauro.[280]

[*f.48r*] *Poterne Fercula Gentiles ix Valecti garciones xix Summa ferculorum xxviii*

Extranii Becot cum uxore se iii^{o} et alii vi

Die veneris primo Aprilis Panteria Expenduntur iiii^{xx}x panes[281] unde pro ferculis xxviii panes trencheris v liberacionibus vii coquina iiii canibus

[278] Followed by a blank space in MS.
[279] 132 loaves disbursed.
[280] Further down the page, by itself, 'Die veneris'.
[281] 87 loaves disbursed.

xv panes rewardis xxviii panes. Et remanent Cxlviii panes. Celarium Expenduntur ii lag. vini de remanentia. Butillaria Expenduntur xx<x>\ v / lag. cervisie. Et remanent iiii^{xx}i lag. cervisie. Coquina Expenduntur lxxv allec album lxxv allec rubium ii pisces salsii iiii stok' de stauro. \ Item expenditur i lopster. In lacte iiii d. / Candelaria Expenduntur ii lib. candelarum de stauro. Stabulum Fenum pro x equis iii hakeneis de stauro. In avenis pro eisdem iiii bus. di. Item fenum apud Remesbur' pro xx equis ii hakeneis de stauro. In prebenda eorundem i qr. avenarum.

Probatur Summa empcionum iiii d.

Panteria De precomputato. Celarium Vinum de remanentia. Butillaria De precomputato. Coquina Empciones iiii d. Candelaria De stauro. Stabulum Fenum avene de stauro.

Fercula Gentiles xix Valecti garciones xxxix Summa ferculorum lviii

Extranii unus episcopus Hibernie se vii^{o} Becot cum uxore se iii^{o} Wilmyngton' se ii^{o} Gore se ii^{o} et alii x

Die sabbati secundo Aprilis Panteria Expenduntur Cxl panes unde pro ferculis lviii panes trencheris vi liberacionibus viii coquina iii canibus xvi panes rewardis xlix panes. Et remanent viii panes. Celarium Expenduntur iii lag. vini de remanentia. Butillaria Expenduntur xliii lag. cervisie. Et remanent xxxviii lag. cervisie. Coquina Expenduntur C allec rubium C allec album ii pisces salsii iiii stok' i salmon' salcius. Item expenduntur iii pecie storjon'. Item expenduntur Cl ova de precomputato. In iii thornebak*es* emptis et ix gurnard et ii crabbes emptis v s. x d. et expenduntur iii thornebak*es* ix gurnard de precomputato. Candelaria Expenduntur ii lib. candelarum de stauro. Stabulum Fenum pro xv equis iii hakeneis de stauro. In avenis vii bus. de stauro. Item fenum apud Remesbur' pro xxii equis iii hakeneis de stauro. In avenis pro eisdem i qr. de stauro.

In vadiis Forey pagetti domini apud Remesbury a xiii^{o} die Marcii usque secundum diem Aprilis utroque computato capiens per diem i d. ob. ii s. vii d. ob. Item in vadiis pagetti senescalli ibidem per vi die*s* capientis per diem i d. ob. ix d.

<Summa vadiorum iii s. iiii d. ob.>

Probatur Summa empcionum ix s. ii d. ob. unde

Panteria De precomputato. Celarium Vinum de remanentia. Butillaria De precomputato. Coquina Empciones v s. x d. Candelaria De stauro. Stabulum Fenum avene de stauro. Vadia iii s. iiii d. ob.

[*f.48v*] *Poterne Fercula Gentiles xxvii Valecti garciones xl Summa ferculorum lxvii*

Extranii unus episcopus Hibernie se vi^{o} Becot cum uxore se iii^{o} Wilmyngton' se ii^{o} Gore se ii^{o} Walrond se ii^{o} magister Thomas Thirlewall' se ii^{o}. Necatur i bos.[282]

282 'Necatur' etc. in right margin.

Die dominica tercio Aprilis Panteria Furniuntur per i talliam i qr. vii bus. <av> frumenti que respondent ad CCClxxiiii panes. Et expenduntur Cxlviii panes unde pro ferculis lxvii panes trencheris vi liberacionibus viii coquina x <l> canibus xvi panes rewardis xli panes. Et remanent CCxxxiiii panes. Celarium Expenduntur iiii lag. vini de remanentia. Butillaria In Cxlvii lag. cervisie emptis de Shepherd deductis inde xii lag. de avantagio precium lag. i d. ob. xvi s. x d. ob. In xxv lag. cervisie emptis de eadem[283] precium lag. i d. deductis inde ii lag. de avantagio xxiii d. In Cxxvi lag. cervisie emptis de Shepherd precium lag. i d. ob. deductis inde x lag. di. de avantagio xiiii s. iiii d. ob. In xxv lag. cervisie emptis de eadem[284] precium lag. i d. deductis inde ii lag. de avantagio xxiii d. Et expenduntur xlviii lag. cervisie. Et remanent CClxxiiii lag. cervisie. Coquina Expenduntur i qr. bovis i cassa multonis de precomputato. Item expenduntur i bacon' di. porcii vi capones vi pulcini de precomputato. In ii cassis multonum emptis iiii s. x d. et expenditur i. In i carcosio vituli empto et expenso ii s. xi d. In i agno empto xv d. et expenditur di. In iii porcellis emptis et expensis xix d. In xii caponibus emptis iii s. x d. In xi pulcinis emptis xi d. In M ovis emptis iii s. ix d. In iii lag. aceti emptis vii d. ob. In di. bus. seminis cenapii empto xii d. In expensis emptoris ii d. Candelaria Expenduntur ii lib. candelarum de stauro. Stabulum Fenum pro xxvi equis v hakeneis de precomputato. In avenis i qr. v bus. avenarum de precomputato. Item fenum apud Remesbur' pro xxii equis et iiii hakeneis de stauro. In prebenda eorundem i qr. i bus. avenarum.

Probatur Summa empcionum lv s. xi d. ob. unde
Panteria Furniuntur i qr. vii bus. frumenti que respondent ad iiiClxxiiii panes. Celarium Vinum de remanentia. Butillaria In CCC<lxxi>\ xxiiii / lag. cervisie xxxv s. i d. Coquina Empciones xx s. x d. ob. Candelaria De stauro. Stabulum Fenum avene de stauro.

Fercula Gentiles xxiiii Valecti garciones xliii Summa ferculorum lxvii

Extranii suffraganus extranius se vi^{o} *Becot cum uxore se iii*^{o} *magister T. Thirlewall rector de Alyngton' se ii*^{o} *Gore se ii*^{o} *Osberne se ii*^{o} *Walrond' se ii*^{o} *et alii xv*

Die lune iiii Aprilis Panteria Expenduntur C\x/lviii panes unde pro ferculis lxvii trencheris x liberacionibus viii coquina vi canibus xvi rewardis xli panes. Et remanent iiii^{xx}v panes.[285] Celarium Expenduntur iiii lag. vini de remanentia. Butillaria Expenduntur xlviii lag. cervisie. Et remanent CCxxiii lag. cervisie.[286] Coquina Expenduntur i qr. bovis i cassa multonis

[283] MS 'eodem'.

[284] MS 'eodem'.

[285] 86 loaves should remain.

[286] 226 gallons should remain.

de precomputato. Item expenditur i bacon' de stauro. Item expenduntur iii capones vi pulcini de precomputato. Item expenduntur C ova de precomputato. Candelaria Expenduntur iii lib. candelarum de stauro. Stabulum Fenum pro xii equis iiii hakeneis de precomputato. In avenis vii bus. avenarum de precomputato. Item fenum apud Remesbur' pro xvi equis ii hakeneis de stauro. In avenis pro eisdem i qr. i pec.

Summa nichil quia de precomputato

Panteria De precomputato. Celarium Vinum de remanentia. Butillaria De precomputato. Coquina Empciones nichil. Candelaria De stauro. Stabulum Fenum avene de stauro.

[*f.*49r] *Poterne Gentiles xxiii Valecti garciones xxxix Summa ferculorum lxii*
Extranii Becot cum uxore se iii^{o} *rector de Alyngton' magister T. Thirlewall' se iii*^{o} *et alii xv*

Die martis v^{o} Aprilis Panteria Expenduntur iiii^{xx}v panes[287] unde pro ferculis lxii panes trencheris viii liberacionibus x coquina vi canibus xvi panes rewardis <xxxviii> panes. Et \ nichil / remanet. Celarium Expenduntur iiii lag. vini de remanentia. Butillaria Expenduntur xlviii lag. cervisie. Et remanent Clxxv lag. cervisie. Coquina Expenduntur di. qr. bovis iii qr. multonis de precomputato iii qr. baconis de stauro ii capones ii pulletti de precomputato. Item expenditur di. agni de precomputato. In i carcosio vituli empto et expenso iii s. iiii d. In ii cassis multonum emptis iiii s. x d. In ii porcellis emptis et expensis xiiii d. In ii gallinis emptis iiii d. In ii caponibus emptis vii d. In xi pulcinis emptis xi d. Candelaria Expend*un*tur[288] lib. candelarum de stauro. Stabulum Fenum pro xii equis iii hakeneis de precomputato. In avenis vi bus. avenarum de precomputato. Item fenum apud Remesbur' pro xvii equis ii hakeneis de stauro. In prebenda eorundem vii bus. avenarum de stauro.

Probatur Summa empcionum xi s. ii d.

Panteria De precomputato. Celarium Vinum de remanentia. Butillaria De precomputato. Coquina Empciones xi s. ii d. <ob.> Candelaria De stauro. Stabulum Fenum avene de stauro.

Gentiles xxii Valecti garciones xxxvi Summa ferculorum lviii
Extranii Alicia Becot se iii^{o} *et aliorum extraniorum xi*

Die mercurie vi^{to} Aprilis Panteria Furniuntur per i talliam ii qr. frumenti de stauro que respondent de CCCCxviii panibus. Et expenduntur Cx panes unde pro ferculis lviii trencheris vi liberacionibus v coquine ii canibus vii rewardis xxxii panes. Et remanent CCCviii panes. Celarium Expend*un*tur[289] lag. vini de remanentia. Butillaria Expenduntur xxxviii lag. cervisie. Et

[287] 140 loaves disbursed, although only 85 remained from the previous day.
[288] Followed by a blank space in MS.
[289] Followed by a blank space in MS.

remanent Cxxxvii lag. cervisie. Coquina Expenduntur di. qr. bovis di. baco i exitus bovis de stauro. Item expenduntur i caponis ii pulcini de precomputato. Item expenduntur l allec rubium l album i piscis salcius iiii stok' C ova de precomputato. In v lag. lactis emptis v d. In butiro i d. Candelaria Expend*un*tur[290] lib. candelarum de stauro. Stabulum Fenum pro xii equis iii hakeneis de precomputato. In avenis vi bus. avenarum de precomputato. Item fenum apud Remesbur' pro xi equis ii hakeneis de stauro. In avenis iii bus. di.

Probatur Summa empcionum vi d.

Panteria Furniuntur ii qr. frumenti que respondent ad iiiiCxviii panes. Celarium Vinum de remanentia. Butillaria De precomputato. Coquina Empciones vi d. Candelaria De stauro. Stabulum Fenum avene de stauro.

[f.49v] Gentiles xx Valecti garciones xxxiiii Summa ferculorum liiii

Extranii Alicia Becot se iii^{o} uxor Bysle se iii^{o} et aliorum extraniorum x

Die jovis vii^{o} Aprilis Panteria Expenduntur C panes unde pro ferculis liiii trencheris x liberacionibus vii coquine iii canibus viii rewardis xviii. Et remanent CCviii panes. Celarium Expend*un*tur[291] lag. vini[292] de stauro. Butillaria Expenduntur xl lag. cervisie de precomputato. Et remanent iiii^{xx}xvii lag. cervisie. Coquina Expenduntur i qr. bovis iii qr. baconis de stauro. Item i cassa multonis iii capones vi pulcini C ova de precomputato. In i carcosio vituli empto iii s. vi d. In ii porcellis emptis xiiii d. et expensis. In xiii caponibus emptis iiii s. ii d. In iii gallinis emptis vi d. In vi pulcinis emptis vi d. In expensis emptoris ii d. ob. Candelaria Expend*un*tur[293] lib. candelarum de stauro. Stabulum Fenum pro xiiii equis iii hakeneis de precomputato. In avenis vii bus. Item fenum apud Remesbur' pro xii equis ii hakeneis de stauro. In avenis pro eisdem iiii bus. di.

Probatur Summa empcionum x s. ob.

Panteria De precomputato. Celarium Vinum de remanentia. Butillaria De precomputato. Coquina Empciones x s. ob. Candelaria De stauro. Stabulum Fenum avene de stauro.

Gentiles xii Valecti garciones xxx Summa ferculorum xlii

Extranii Alicia Becot se iii^{o} uxor Bysle se iii^{o} vicarius ville et alii extranii xii

Die veneris viii Aprilis Panteria Expenduntur iiii^{xx}iiii panes unde pro ferculis xlii trencheris iiii liberacionibus v coquine iii canibus vii rewardis xxiii panes. Et remanent Cxxiiii panes. Celarium Expend*un*tur[294] lag. vini de stauro. Butillaria Expenduntur xxxii lag. cervisie de precomputato. Et

[290] Followed by a blank space in MS.

[291] Followed by a blank space in MS.

[292] MS 'cervisie'.

[293] Followed by a blank space in MS.

[294] Followed by a blank space in MS.

remanent lxv lag. cervisie de precomputato. Coquina Expenduntur iii qr. allecis albi iii qr. allecis rubii ii pisces salsii et di. vii stok' de stauro. Item expenduntur ii crabb*es* de precomputato. In iii lag. lactis emptis iii d. Candelaria Expend*un*tur[295] lib. candelarum de stauro. Stabulum Fenum pro xii equis iiii hakeneis de precomputato. In prebenda eorundem vi bus. avenarum de precomputato. Item fenum apud Remesbur' pro xiii equis ii hakeneis de stauro. In avenis pro eisdem iiii bus. di.

Probatur Summa empcionum iii d.

Panteria De precomputato. Celarium Vinum de remanentia. Butillaria De precomputato. Coquina Empciones iii d. Candelaria De stauro. Stabulum Fenum avene de stauro.

[*f.50r*] *Poterne Gentiles xx Valecti garciones xxxv Summa ferculorum lv Extranii Alicia Becot se iii*^{o} *uxor Bysle se iii*^{o} *et alii extranii x Calston' se iiii*^{o}

Die sabbati ix Aprilis Panteria Expenduntur C panes unde pro ferculis lv trencheris v liberacionibus vii coquine iii canibus viii rewardis xxii. Et remanent xxiiii panes. Celarium Expend*un*tur[296] lag. vini de stauro. Butillaria Expenduntur xliiii lag. cervisie. Et remanent xxi lag. cervisie de precomputato. Coquina Expenduntur iii qr. allecis albi iii qr. allecis rubii ii pisces salcii et di. ii troughtes de stauro. In xxvii brem*es* xvi merlyng ii gurnard et i thornbak emptis v s. viii d. et expensis. In expensis emptoris apud Wermystr' cum ii equis viii d. ob. Candelaria Expend*un*tur[297] lib. candelarum de stauro. Stabulum Fenum pro x equis iii hakeneis de precomputato. In avenis vi bus. avenarum de precomputato. Item fenum apud Remesbur' pro xv equis i hakeneo de stauro. In avenis vi bus. di.

Probatur Summa empcionum vi s. iiii d. ob.

Panteria De precomputato. Celarium Vinum de remanentia. Butillaria De precomputato. Coquina Empciones vi s. iiii d. ob. Candelaria De stauro. Stabulum Fenum avene de stauro.

In vadiis Thome Ferour apud Remesbury a xiii^{o} die Marcii usque ix diem Aprilis illo die computato vii s.

In vadiis garcionis forgii ibidem per idem tempus capientis per diem ii d. iiii s. viii d.

In vadiis Galfridi Char' et garcionis sui ibidem per ii septimanas Galfridi capientis per septimanam xviii d. et garcionis capientis per septimanam xiiii d. v s. iiii d.

In vadiis Thome Norman ibidem per iii septimanas capientis per septimanam xiiii d. iii s. vi d.

[295] Followed by a blank space in MS.
[296] Followed by a blank space in MS.
[297] Followed by a blank space in MS.

In vadiis Forrey ibidem per iii septimanas et ii dies capientis per septimanam x d. ob. ii s. x d. ob.
In vadiis Lang' ibidem per ii septimanas capientis per septimanam x d. ob. xxi d.
In vadiis ii pagettorum Shypton' et Holcote ibidem per ii septimanas et iii dies utroque capienti per septimanam x d. ob. iiii s.
In vadiis pagetti senescalli ibidem per ix dies pagetti Cap*er*on' per vi dies et valecti Gyrkyn ibidem per ii dies ii s. ii d. ob.
Gentiles xxviii Valecti garciones lxi Summa ferculorum iiii^{xx}*ix*
Extranii Alicia Becot se iii^{o} *uxor Bysle se iii*^{o} *Willelmus Covyntr' Fraunceys uxor Johannis Perys et alii extranii xxii*
Die dominica x^{o} Aprilis Panteria Furniuntur per i talliam ii qr. frumenti de stauro que respondent de CCCCxiiii panes. Et expenduntur Cxl panes unde pro ferculis iiii^{xx}ix panes trencheris x liberacionibus vi coquine vi canibus vii rewardis xxii. Et remanent CCiiii^{xx}xviii panes. Celarium Expend*un*tur[298] lag. vini de stauro. Butillaria In Cxl lag. cervisie emptis de Shephe*r*de precium lag. i d. ob. deductis inde xi lag. di. de avantagio xvi s. In lxi lag. cervisie emptis de eadem[299] precium lag. i d. deductis inde v lag. cervisie de avantagio iiii s. viii d. In iiii^{xx}i lag. cervisie emptis de Warner precium lag. i d. ob. deductis inde vi lag. di. cervisie de avantagio <iii> \ x / s. iii d. ob. In xxvi lag. cervisie emptis de eodem precium lag. i d. deductis inde ii lag. de avantagio ii s. Et expenduntur lx lag. cervisie. Et remanent CClxix lag. cervisie. Coquina Expenduntur i qr. bovis iii qr. baconis de stauro. Item i cassa multonis iii capones viii pulcini CC ova de precomputato. Item expenditur i fesant de stauro. In ii cassis multonum emptis iiii s. vi d. In i carcosio vituli empto et expenso iii s. iiii d. In iii porcellis emptis et expensis xxi d. In MD ovis emptis precium C^{e} iiii d. ob. v s. vii d. ob. Candelaria Expend*un*tur[300] lib. candelarum de stauro. Stabulum Fenum pro x equis iii hakeneis de precomputato. In prebenda eorundem v bus. avenarum de precomputato. Item fenum apud Remesbur' pro xii equis. In avenis pro eisdem iiii bus. di.

Probatur Summa empcionum lx<xviii>\xix/ s. vi d. unde Panteria Furniuntur ii qr. frumenti que respondent ad iiiiCxiiii panes. Celarium Vinum de remanentia. Butillaria In CCCviii lag. cervisie xxxii s. xi d. ob. Coquina Empciones xv s. ii d. ob. Candelaria De stauro. Stabulum Fenum avene de stauro. Vadia xxxi s. iiii d.
[*f.50v*] *Poterne Gentiles xxiiii Valecti garciones xxxviii Summa ferculorum lxii*

[298] Followed by a blank space in MS.
[299] MS 'eodem'.
[300] Followed by a blank space in MS.

Extranii Alicia Becot se ii° uxor Bysle se iii° uxor Johannis Peris et alii extranii xvi
Die lune xi° Aprilis Panteria Expenduntur Cx panes unde pro ferculis lxii trencheris vi liberacionibus \ vi / coquine iiii canibus ix rewardis xxiii panes. Et remanent Ciiii^xx^viii panes. Celarium Expenduntur iii lag. vini de stauro. Butillaria Expenduntur xliii lag. cervisie. Et remanent CCxxvi lag.[301] cervisie. Coquina Expenduntur di. qr. bovis iii qr. baconis de stauro. Item i cassa multonis i caponis ii pulcini C ova de precomputato. Candelaria Expend*un*tur[302] lib. candelarum de stauro. Stabulum Fenum pro xi equis iiii hakeneis de stauro. In avenis pro eisdem viii bus. avenarum. Item fenum apud Remesbur' pro xxii equis ii hakeneis de stauro. In avenis pro eisdem i qr. iii bus. avenarum.

Summa empcionum[303]

Panteria De precomputato. Celarium Vinum de remanentia. Butillaria De precomputato. Coquina Empciones nichil. Candelaria De stauro. Stabulum Fenum avene[304]
Gentiles xxviii Valecti garciones xl Summa ferculorum lxviii
*Extranii Alicia Becot se ii° Rouse se iii° vicarius de Po*terne *Flour Wilmynton* ii *capellani extranii uxor Johannis Peris se iii° et alii extranii viii*
Die martis xii Aprilis Panteria Expenduntur Cxxiiii panes unde pro ferculis lxviii panes trencheris viii liberacionibus vi coquine iiii canibus viii rewardis xxx panes. Et remanent lxiiii panes. Celarium Expenduntur iiii lag. vini de stauro. Butillaria Expenduntur xlviii lag. cervisie. Et remanent Clxxviii lag. cervisie. Coquina Expenduntur i qr. bovis di. baco de stauro. Item i cassa multonis iii capones vi pulcini Cl ova de precomputato. In i carcosio vituli empto et expenso iii s. In ii porcellis emptis et expensis xii d. \ In vi pulcinis vi d. / Candelaria Expend*un*tur[305] lib. candelarum de stauro. Stabulum Fenum pro xii equis iiii hakeneis de stauro. In avenis pro eisdem <i qr.> \ vi bus. / avenarum. Item fenum apud Remesbur' pro xxii equis i hakeneo de stauro. In avenis pro eisdem i qr. ii bus.

Probatur Summa empcionum iiii s. vi d.

Panteria De precomputato. Celarium Vinum de stauro. Butillaria De precomputato. Coquina Empciones iiii s. vi d. Candelaria De stauro. Stabulum Fenum avene de stauro.
[f.51r] Poterne Gentiles xx Valecti garciones xxiiii Summa ferculorum xliiii
Extranii Alicia Becot se iii° vicarius ville et alii extranii viii

301 MS repeats 'lag.'
302 Followed by a blank space in MS.
303 Followed by a blank space in MS.
304 Followed by a blank space in MS.
305 Followed by a blank space in MS.

Die mercurie xiii Aprilis Panteria Furniuntur per i talliam i qr. iiii bus. frumenti de stauro que respondent de CCCxviii panibus. Et expenduntur iiii^{xx}iii panes[306] unde pro ferculis xliiii panes trencheris vi liberacionibus v coquine ii canibus viii rewardis nichil. Et remanent CCiiii^{xx}xix panes. Celarium Expenduntur ii lag. vini de stauro. Butillaria Expenduntur xxxvi lag. cervisie. Et remanent Cxlii lag. cervisie. Coquina Expenduntur di. qr. bovis di. baco de stauro. Item expenduntur iii qr. multonis i caponis ii pulcini de precomputato. Item expenduntur l allec album l allec rubium i piscis salcius ii trouth*es* de stauro. Item expenduntur CC ova de precomputato. In iiii lag. lactis emptis iiii d. In casio et butiro emptis iii d. ob. Candelaria Expend*un*tur[307] lib. candelarum de stauro. Stabulum Fenum pro xiiii equis iiii hakeneis de stauro. In avenis vii bus. avenarum de stauro. Item fenum apud Remesbur' pro xxii equis. In avenis i qr. ii bus.

Probatur Summa empcionum vii d. ob.

Panteria Furniuntur i qr. iiii bus. frumenti que respondent ad CCCxviii. Celarium Vinum de remanentia. Butillaria De precomputato. Coquina Empciones vii d. ob. Candelaria De stauro. Stabulum Fenum avene de stauro.

Gentiles xxii Valecti garciones xxx Summa ferculorum lii

Extranii Alicia Becot se iii^{o} et alii extranii viii

Die jovis xiiii^{o} Aprilis Panteria Expenduntur C panes unde pro ferculis lii trencheris vi liberacionibus v coquine iiii canibus ix rewardis xxiiii panes. Et remanent Ciiii^{xx}xix panes. Celarium Expenduntur ii lag. vini de stauro. Butillaria Expenduntur xxxviii lag. cervisie. Et remanent Ciiii lag. cervisie. Coquina Expenditur di. qr. bovis de stauro. Item i porcus de stauro. Item expenduntur i caponis vi pulcini C ova de precomputato. Item expenditur i cassa multonis de precomputato. In ii cassis multonum emptis iiii s. x d. In xviii pulcinis emptis xx d. In di. carcosio vituli < . . . . . > empto et expenso xv d. In expensis apud le Devys' ii d. Candelaria Expend*un*tur[308] lib. candelarum de stauro. Stabulum Fenum pro xv equis iii hakeneis de stauro. In avenis i qr. avenarum de stauro. Item fenum apud Remesbur' pro xxii equis ii hakeneis de stauro. In avenis i qr. ii bus.

Probatur Summa empcionium vii s. xi d.

Panteria De precomputato. Celarium Vinum de remanentia. Butillaria De precomputato. Coquina Empciones vii s. xi d. Candelaria De stauro. Stabulum[309]

[*f.51v*] *Poterne Gentiles xii Valecti garciones xxviii Summa ferculorum xl*

[306] 65 loaves disbursed.

[307] Followed by a blank space in MS.

[308] Followed by a blank space in MS.

[309] Followed by a blank space in MS.

Extranii Alicia Becot se ii^{o} *vicarius de Froxfeld' vicarius de Pot*e*rne et alii extranii viii*

Die veneris xv Aprilis Panteria Expenduntur iiii^{xx} panes unde pro ferculis xl trencheris iiii liberacionibus vi coquine iiii canibus ix rewardis xvii. Et remanent Cxix panes. Celarium Expend*un*tur[310] lag. vini de stauro. Butillaria Expenduntur xxx lag. cervisie. Et remanent <lag.> lxix lag. cervisie.[311] Coquina Expenduntur iii qr. allecis albi l allec rubium ii pisces salcii de stauro. In xxvi piscibus salciis emptis xx s. i d. In iii baas iii lopsters et i crabb' emptis ii s. vi d. et expenduntur iii baas et i lopster. In expensis Huberti cum somerario de Pot*er*ne usque Sarum pro[312] pisce emendo viii d. In ii lag. lactis emptis et expensis ii d. In xl roch*es* emptis et expensis xiiii d. Candelaria Expenduntur iii lib. candelarum de stauro. Stabulum Fenum pro xii equis iii hakeneis de stauro. In avenis vi bus. avenarum. Item fenum apud Remesbur' pro xx equis. In avenis i qr. avenarum.

Probatur Summa empcionum xxiiii s. vii d.

Panteria De precomputato. Celarium Vinum de remanentia. Butillaria De precomputato. Coquina Empciones xxiiii s. vii d. Candelaria De stauro. Stabulum Fenum avene de stauro.

Gentiles xx Valecti garciones xxxiii Summa ferculorum liii

Extranii Alicia Becot se ii^{o} *vicarius ville Wall' i capellanus extran*ius *Godefrey Forestarius et alii extranii viii*

Die sabbati xvi Aprilis Panteria Expenduntur C panes unde pro ferculis liii trencheris vi liberacionibus vi coquine iiii canibus ix rewardis xxii. Et remanent xix panes. Celarium Expend*un*tur[313] lag. vini de stauro. Butillaria Expenduntur xxxviii lag. cervisie. Et remanent xxxi lag. cervisie. Coquina Expenduntur C allec album iii pisces salcii ii stok' de stauro. In xii brem*es* iiii merlyng i gurnard i thornbak et vi mulett*es* emptis et expensis vi s. iiii d. In expensis emptoris cum somerario apud Wermystr' pro pisce emendo v d. In menusis emptis et expensis iii d. In i lag. lactis empta i d. In i pik' empto et expenso ii s. iiii d. Candelaria Expend*un*tur[314] lib. candelarum de stauro. Stabulum Fenum pro[315] xii equis iii hakeneis de stauro. In avenis pro eisdem vi bus. Item fenum apud Remesbur' pro xix equis. In avenis i qr.

Probatur Summa empcionum ix s. v d.

Panteria De precomputato. Celarium Vinum de remanentia. Butillaria De

[310] Followed by a blank space in MS.
[311] 74 gallons should remain.
[312] MS omits 'pro'.
[313] Followed by a blank space in MS.
[314] Followed by a blank space in MS.
[315] MS adds 'Item fenum apud pro'.

precomputato. Coquina Empciones ix s. v d. Candelaria De stauro. Stabulum[316]
[*f.52r*] *Poterne Gentiles xxiii Valecti garciones xliii Summa ferculorum lxvi Extranii Alicia Becot se ii*^{o} *uxor Ricardi Osbern' se iii*^{o} *Johannes Perys vicarius ville et alii extranii xvi*
Die dominica xvii Aprilis Panteria Furniuntur per i talliam i qr. vi bus. frumenti de stauro que respondent de CCClii panibus et expenduntur Cxx panes unde pro ferculis lxvi trencheris vi liberacionibus v coquine iiii canibus viii rewardis xxxi panes. Et remanent CCli panes. Celarium Expenduntur iiii lag. vini de stauro. Butillaria In Cxxiii lag. cervisie emptis de Shepherde precium lag. i d. ob. deductis inde x lag. de avantagio xiiii s. i d. ob. In \ lxx / lag. cervisie emptis de eadem precium lag. i d. deductis inde v lag. di. cervisie de avantagio vii s. xi d. In xiii lag. cervisie emptis de Carlett' precium lag. i d. ob. deducta inde i lag. de avantagio xii d. Et expenduntur liiii lag. cervisie. Et remanent Ciiii^{xx}iii lag. cervisie. Coquina Expenduntur i qr. bovis di. baco de stauro. Item expenduntur i cassa multonis iii capones vi pulcini CC ova de precomputato. In i qr. bovis empto iii s. iiii d. In ii cassis multonum emptis iiii s. iiii d. In carcosio vituli empto et expenso iii s. vi d. In ii porcellis emptis et expensis xii d. In di. porco empto xxii d. et expenditur i qr. Candelaria Expend*un*tur[317] lib. candelarum de stauro. Stabulum Fenum pro xii equis iii hakeneis de stauro. In avenis pro eisdem vi bus. Item fenum apud Remesbur' pro xvii equis i hakeneo. In avenis i qr. i bus.

Probatur Summa empcionum xxxvii s. ob. unde
Panteria Furniuntur i qr. vi bus. frumenti que respondent ad iiiClii panes. Celarium Vinum de remanentia. Butillaria De precomputato. In CCvi lag. xxiii s. ob. Coquina Empciones xiiii s. Candelaria De stauro. Stabulum Fenum avene de stauro.
Fercula Gentiles xxv Valecti garciones xxxvii Summa ferculorum lxii Extranii Alicia Becot se iii^{o} *Johannes Perys se ii*^{o} *vicarius ville et alii xiiii*
Die lune xviii^{o} Aprilis Panteria Expenduntur Cxxii panes unde pro ferculis lxv panes trencheris vi liberacionibus vi coquina iiii canibus xx panes rewardis xxi panes. Et remanent Cxxix panes. Celarium Expenduntur iii lag. vini de remanentia. Butillaria Expenduntur lii lag. cervisie. Et remanent Cxxxi lag. cervisie. Coquina Expenduntur di. qr. bovis i bacon' de stauro. Item expenduntur i cassa di. multonum de precomputato i caponis iiii pulcini de precomputato. Item CC ova de precomputato. Candelaria Expenditur i lib. candelarum de stauro. Stabulum Fenum pro

[316] Followed by a blank space in MS.
[317] Followed by a blank space in MS.

xiii equis iii hakeneis de stauro. In avenis pro eisdem i qr. Item fenum apud Remesbur' pro xvii equis i hakeneo. In avenis pro eisdem i qr.

Summa[318]

Panteria De precomputato. Celarium Vinum de remanentia. Butillaria De precomputato. Coquina Empciones[319] Candelaria De stauro. Stabulum Fenum avene de stauro.

[*f.52v*] *Poterne Gentiles xxvi Valecti garciones xxxiii Summa ferculorum lix Extranii Alicia Becot se iii° vicarius ville se ii° i capellannus extranius et alii xiiii*

Die martis xix° Aprilis Panteria Expenduntur Cxviii panes unde pro ferculis lix panes trencheris viii liberacionibus vi coquina vi canibus xiiii panes rewardis xxv panes. Et remanent xi panes. Celarium Expenduntur iii lag. vini de remanentia. Butillaria Expenduntur l lag. cervisie. Et remanent iiii^xx^i lag. cervisie. Coquina Expenduntur di. qr. bovis i bacon' de stauro. Item expenduntur iii capones iiii pulcini de stauro precomputato. In i qr. bovis empto iii s. iiii d. In i carcosio vituli empto iii s. iiii d. et expenditur di. In i porcello empto et expenso vi d. In iiii caponibus emptis xvi d. In vii pulcinis emptis vii d. ob. Item expenduntur i cassa multonis i qr. porci de precomputato. Item expenduntur C ova de precomputato. Candelaria Expenduntur ii lib. candelarum de stauro. Stabulum Fenum pro ix equis v hakeneis de stauro. In avenis pro eisdem v bus. avenarum. Item fenum pro xvii equis i hakeneo de stauro. In avenis pro eisdem i qr.

Probatur Summa empcionum ix s. i d. ob.

Panteria De precomputato. Celarium Vinum de remanentia. Butillaria De precomputato. Coquina Empciones ix s. i d. ob. Candelaria De stauro. Stabulum Fenum avene de stauro.

Gentiles xxviii Valecti garciones l Summa ferculorum lxxviii

Extranii prior de Moteshunt se vi° Alicia Becot se iii° magister J. Malverne se vi magister T. Thirwall' se ii° vicarius ville se ii° et alii xiiii

Die mercurie xx Aprilis Panteria Furniuntur per i talliam ii qr. frumenti que respondent ad CCCCxix panes. Et expenduntur Cxl panes unde pro ferculis lxxviii panes trencheris x liberacionibus x coquina iiii canibus xiiii panes rewardis xxiiii panes. Et remanent CCiiii^xx^x panes. Celarium Expenduntur vi lag. vini de remanentia. Butillaria Expenduntur lviii lag. cervisie. Et remanent xxiii lag. cervisie. Coquina Di. qr. bovis di. bacon' di. carcosium vituli viii pulcini de precomputato. In iiii mulett*es* emptis et expensis xvi d. In lacte iii d. In butiro ob. In expensis emptoris usque Sarum viii d. In M ovis emptis iiii s. ii d. \ In viii lag. di. vini acerbi iiii s. ix d. ob. / Item expenduntur l allec album l allec rubium i piscis salcius di. ii

[318] Followed by a blank space in MS.
[319] Followed by a blank space in MS.

stok' i pecia storjon' de stauro. Item expenduntur CCC ova de precomputato. Candelaria Expenduntur iii lib. candelarum de stauro. Stabulum Fenum pro xxii equis v hakeneis de stauro. In avenis pro eisdem i qr. iiii bus. avenarum. Item fenum apud Remesbur' pro xvii equis. In avenis vi bus. avenarum.

Probatur Summa empcionum xi s. v d.

Panteria Furniuntur ii qr. frumenti que respondent ad iiiiCxix panes. Celarium Vinum de remanentia. Butillaria De precomputato. Coquina Empciones xi s. v d. Candelaria De stauro. Stabulum Fenum avene de stauro.

[*f.53r*] *Poterne Gentiles xxxviii Valecti garciones lviii Summa ferculorum iiii*^{xx}*xvi*

Extranii prior de Motteshunt se vii^{o} *magister J.Malverne se vi*^{o} *magister T.Thirlewal se iii*^{o} *Alicia Becot se iii*^{o} *vicarius ville se ii*^{o} *et alii xxiiii*

Die jovis xxi Aprilis[320] Panteria Expenduntur Cl panes[321] unde pro ferculis iiii^{xx}xvi panes trencheris xii liberacionibus vii coquina v canibus xiiii panes rewardis xxv panes. Et remanent <Cii> Cxl panes. Celarium Expenduntur vi lag. vini de remanentia. Butillaria In lxviii lag. cervisie emptis de Axford precium lag. i d. ob. deductis inde v lag. di. de avantagio vii s. ix d. ob. In xl lag. cervisie emptis de eadem[322] precium lag. i d. deductis inde iii lag. de avantagio iii s. i d. Et expenduntur liii lag. cervisie. Et remanent lxxviii lag. cervisie. Coquina Expenduntur i qr. bovis i bacon' di. de stauro. Item expenduntur vi capones vi pulcini de precomputato. Item expenduntur CCCC ova de precomputato. In carnibus bovinis emptis et expensis ii s. In ii cassis multonum emptis et expensis iiii s. x d. In i carcosio vituli empto et expenso iii s. iiii d. In di. porco empto xxii d. et expenso. In ii porcellis emptis xiii d. In xvii caponibus emptis v s. vi d. In xxii pulcinis emptis ii s. In expensis emptoris ii d. ob. Item expenduntur i fasianus iii herons de stauro. Candelaria Expenduntur iii lib. candelarum de stauro. Stabulum Fenum pro xxx equis iii hakeneis de stauro. In avenis pro eisdem i qr. vi bus. avenarum. Item fenum apud Remesbur' pro xvi equis ii hakeneis de stauro. In avenis i qr.

Probatur Summa empcionum xxxi s. viii d. unde

Panteria De precomputato. Celarium Vinum de remanentia. Butillaria <De> In Cviii lag. cervisie[323] x s. x d. ob. Coquina Empciones xx s. ix d. ob. Candelaria De stauro. Stabulum Fenum avene de stauro.

Gentiles xvii Valecti garciones xxviii Summa ferculorum xlv

[320] MS omits 'Aprilis'.
[321] 159 loaves disbursed.
[322] MS 'eodem'.
[323] MS omits 'lag. cervisie'.

Extranii prior de Moteshunt se iiii^{o} magister J.Malverne se iii^{o} magister T.Thirlewall' se iii^{o} uxor Becot se iii^{o} vicarius ville se ii^{o} iii presbiteri extranii se iii^{o} Best et alii xii

Die veneris xxii Aprilis Panteria Expenduntur iiii^{xx} panes[324] unde pro ferculis xlv panes trencheris x liberacionibus vii coquina iiii canibus xvi panes rewardis.[325] Et remanent lx panes. Celarium Expenduntur iiii lag. vini de remanentia. Butillaria Expenduntur xl lag. cervisie. Et remanent xxxviii lag. cervisie. Coquina Expenduntur l allec album iii pisces salcii de stauro. Item expenduntur lx makerell de precomputato i salmon' salcius. In lx makerell recentibus emptis v s. iiii d. et expenduntur l. In i crabb' empto iiii d. In lacte ii d. In viii perches emptis vi d. et expensis. Candelaria Expenduntur iii lib. candelarum de stauro. Stabulum Fenum pro xx equis v hakeneis de stauro. In avenis pro eisdem i qr. iii bus. avenarum. Item fenum apud Remesbir' pro xix equis ii hakeneis de stauro. In avenis pro eisdem i qr.

Probatur Summa empcionum vi s. iiii d.

Panteria De precomputato. Celarium De remanentia. Butillaria De precomputato. Coquina Empciones vi s. iiii d. Candelaria De stauro. Stabulum Fenum avene de stauro.

[*f.53v*] *Poterne Gentiles xxiiii Valecti garciones xxxviii Summa ferculorum lxii*

Extranii magister J.Malverne se ii^{o} magister T.Thirlewall' se ii^{o} Spersholt se vi^{o} magister S.Best se iii^{o} iii capellanni extranii se ii^{o} et alii xiiii

Die sabbati xxiii Aprilis Panteria Furniuntur per i talliam ii qr. frumenti que respondent ad CCCCxvii panes. <unde> Et expenduntur Cxx panes unde pro ferculis lxii panes trencheris x liberacionibus viii coquina iiii canibus x rewardis xxvi panes. Et remanent CCClvii panes. Celarium Expenduntur vi lag. vini de remanentia. Butillaria In xxxvi lag. cervisie emptis de Felicia Aas precium lag. i d. ob. deductis inde iii lag. de avantagio iiii s. i d. ob. In xvi lag. cervisie emptis de eadem[326] precium lag. i d. deducta inde i lag. de avantagio xv d. In xl lag. cervisie emptis de Willelmo Lang' precium lag. i d. ob. deductis inde iii lag. de avantagio iiii s. vi d. In xl\iii/ lag. cervisie emptis de eodem precium lag. i d. deductis inde iii lag. di. de avantagio iii s. iii d. ob. In Cl lag. cervisie emptis de Barlich' precium lag. i d. ob. deductis inde xii lag. de avantagio xvii s. ii d. In xliii lag. cervisie emptis[327] de eodem precium lag. i d. deductis inde iii lag. di. de avantagio iii s. iii d. ob. Et expenduntur l lag. cervisie. Et

[324] 82 loaves disbursed without rewards.

[325] Followed by a blank space in MS.

[326] MS 'eodem'.

[327] MS repeats 'empt''.

remanent CClxxviii lag. cervisie. Coquina Expenduntur C allec rubium C allec album iii pisces salcii de stauro. Item xl makerell de precomputato. In xii bremes ii merling et i mulett emptis et expensis iii s. vi d. In iii thornebak*es* emptis ii s. In di. salmone recenti empto xviii d. \ In expensis emptoris v d. / Candelaria Expenduntur iii lib. candelarum de stauro. Stabulum Fenum pro xxi equis iiii hakeneis de stauro. In avenis pro eisdem i qr. ii bus. avenarum. Item fenum apud Remesbur' pro xix equis ii hakeneis de stauro. In avenis[328] pro eisdem i qr. avenarum.
In vadiis Thome Ferro*ur* apud Remesbur' a x^{o} die Aprilis usque xxiii diem eiusdem utroque computato capientis per diem iii d. iii s. vi d.
Item in vadiis Forrey pagetti domini pagetti Hulcot pagetti Cap*er*on' per idem tempus et pagetti senescalli per xiii dies quilibet capiens per diem i d. ob. vi s. x d. ob.
Item in vadiis Thome Norman ibidem per viii dies capientis per diem ii d. xvi d.
In vadiis pagetti magistri Walteri Medford apud Remesbury cum equ*o* magistri sui per i septimanam x d. ob.
In vadiis Bathe[329] ibidem per xiiii dies capientis per diem ii d. ii s. iiii d.
Probatur Summa empcionum lv s. xi d. ob. unde
Panteria Furniuntur ii qr. frumenti que respondent ad iiiiCxvii panes. Celarium Vinum de remanentia. Butillaria In CCCxxviii lag. cervisie xxxiii s. vii d. ob. Coquina Empciones vii s. v d. Candelaria De stauro. Stabulum Fenum avene[330] Vadia xiiii s. xi d.
Gentiles xxvi Valecti garciones xl Summa ferculorum lxvi
Extranii magister J.Malverne se ii^{o} magister T.Thirlewal se ii^{o} Spersholt se iiii^{o} uxor Becot se iii^{o} vicarius ville se iii^{o} et alii xxvi
Die dominica xxiiii Aprilis Panteria Expenduntur Cxxx panes unde pro ferculis lxvi panes trencheris xii liberacionibus viii coquina vii canibus xii panes rewardis xxv panes. Et remanent CCxxvii panes. Celarium Expenduntur iiii lag. vini de remanentia. Butillaria Expenduntur l lag. cervisie. Et remanent CCxxviii lag. cervisie. Coquina Expenduntur i qr. bovis i bacon' de stauro. Item expenduntur iiii capones iiii pulcini i cassa multonis de precomputato. In ii cassis multonum iiii s. viii d. In i carcosio vituli empto et expenso ii s. vi d. In iii porcellis emptis et expensis xv d. In xxiiii columbellis emptis viii d. et expenduntur xvii. Item expenduntur CCC ova de precomputato. \ Item ii herons i fasianus. / Candelaria Expenduntur iii lib. candelarum de stauro. Stabulum Fenum pro xx equis iiii hakeneis de stauro. In avenis i qr. <iii> \ ii / bus. avenarum de stauro.

[328] MS repeats 'In avenis'.
[329] MS possibly 'Rathe'.
[330] Followed by a blank space in MS.

Item fenum apud Remesbur' pro xviii equis i hakeneo de stauro. In avenis i qr. ii bus. avenarum.

Probatur Summa empcionum ix s. i d.

Panteria De precomputato. Celarium Vinum de remanentia. Butillaria De precomputato. Coquina Empciones ix s. i d. Candelaria De stauro. Stabulum Fenum avene[331]

[*f.54r*] *Poterne Gentiles xxx Valecti garciones xxxix Summa ferculorum lxix Extranii Calston' se v° Holcot se vii° Becot se v° magister J.Malverne se v° magister T.Thirlewall' Best se iii° Coventr' se iii° Metford se ii° Walront se ii° J.Peris se ii° et alii x*

Die lune xxv° Aprilis Panteria Expenduntur Cxx\x[332]/ panes unde pro ferculis lxix panes trencheris xii liberacionibus x coquina v canibus xvi panes rewardis xvii panes. Et remanent iiii^{xx}xvii panes. Celarium Expenduntur iiii lag. vini de remanentia. Butillaria Expenduntur lv lag. cervisie. Et remanent Clxxiii lag. cervisie. Coquina Expenduntur C allec album l makerell ii pisces salcii de precomputato. Item expenduntur \C/l ova de precomputato. In menues emptis et expensis x d. In butiro iii d. In lacte iiii d. Candelaria Expenduntur iii lib. candelarum de stauro. Stabulum Fenum pro xxx equis v hakeneis de stauro. In prebenda eorundem i qr. iiii bus. avenarum. Item fenum apud Remesbur' pro xviii equis i hakeneo de stauro. i qr. avenarum.

Probatur Summa empcionum xvii d.

Panteria De precomputato. Celarium Vinum de remanentia. Butillaria De precomputato. Coquina Empciones xvii d. Candelaria De stauro. Stabulum Fenum avene de stauro.

Gentiles xxxi Valecti garciones xlv Summa ferculorum lxxvi Extranii Holcot se vii° Becot se v° magister J.Malverne se iii° magister T.Thirlewal magister S.Best se iii° Walront se ii° J.Peris se ii° Wilmyngton' se ii° et alii

Die martis xxvi Aprilis Panteria \ Furniuntur per i talliam ii qr. iii bus. frumenti que respondent ad CCCClxxiii. / Expenduntur Cxl panes unde pro ferculis lxxvi panes trencheris xii liberacionibus x coquina ix canibus xvi rewardis xvii panes. Et remanent CCCCxxx panes. <unde> Celarium Expenduntur vii lag. vini de remanentia. Butillaria Expenduntur lxx lag. cervisie. Et remanent Ciii lag. cervisie. Coquina Expenduntur i qr. bovis i bacon' de stauro. Item expenditur i cassa multonis de precomputato. Item C ova de precomputato. In ii cassis multonum emptis[333] iiii s. viii d. et expenditur i. In i carcosio vituli empto et expenso ii s. vi d. In vi caponibus

331 Followed by a blank space in MS.

332 129 loaves disbursed.

333 MS repeats 'empt''.

emptis xxii d. In viii pulcinis emptis x d. In xxxvi columbellis emptis et expensis xii d. In iii porcellis emptis et expensis xix d. Item expenduntur iii capones iiii pulcini de precomputato. Candelaria Expenduntur ii lib. candelarum de stauro. Stabulum Fenum pro xxx equis v hakeneis de stauro. In avenis pro eisdem i qr. vi bus. avenarum de stauro. Item fenum apud Remesbur' pro xix equis i hakeneo de stauro. In avenis i qr. i bus.

Probatur Summa empcionum xii s. v d.

Panteria Furniuntur ii qr. \ iii bus. / frumenti que respondent ad iiiiClxxiii panes. Celarium Vinum de remanentia. Butillaria De precomputato. Coquina Empciones xii s. v d. Candelaria De stauro. Stabulum Fenum avene[334]

[*f.54v*] *Poterne Gentiles xxvii Valecti garciones xxxvi Summa ferculorum lxiii*

Extranii Halcot se vi^o Becot se iii^o et alii xiiii

Die mercurie xxvii° Aprilis Panteria Expenduntur Cxx panes[335] unde pro ferculis lxiii trencheris x liberacionibus x coquina vi canibus xvi rewardis xviii panes. Et remanent CCCx panes. Celarium Expenduntur vi lag. vini de remanentia. Butillaria Expenduntur liiii lag. cervisie. Et remanent l lag. cervisie.[336] Coquina Expenduntur di. qr. bovis di. cassa multonis i bacon' de stauro. Item expenduntur Cl ova de precomputato. Item iiii pulcini. Item expenduntur C allec album i piscis salcius i salmon' salcius de stauro. In iiii lag. lactis emptis iiii d. Butiro i d. In menues ii d. In ii bus. pisarum emptis pro potagio xx d. In i bus. farine avenarum xi d. et expenso. Candelaria Expenduntur iii lib. candelarum de stauro. Stabulum Fenum pro xxiii equis vi hakeneis de stauro. In avenis pro eisdem i qr. iii bus. avenarum. Item fenum apud Remesbur' pro xx equis iii hakeneis de stauro. In avenis i qr. i bus.

Probatur Summa empcionum iii s. ii d.

Panteria De precomputato. Celarium[337] Butillaria De precomputato. Coquina Empciones iii s. ii d. Candelaria De stauro. Stabulum Fenum avene de stauro.

Gentiles xxvii Valecti garciones xxxviii Summa ferculorum lxv

Extranii Hulcot se vi^o Becot se iii^o iii rectores extranii cum iiii capellanis extraniis et alii x

Die jovis xxviii° Aprilis Panteria Expenduntur Cxx panes unde pro ferculis lxv trencheris x liberacionibus x coquina viii canibus xvi panes rewardis xi panes. Et remanent Ciiii^{xx}x panes. Celarium Expenduntur iiii lag. vini de

[334] Followed by a blank space in MS.

[335] 123 loaves disbursed.

[336] 49 gallons should remain.

[337] MS repeats 'Celarium', followed by a blank space.

remanentia. Butillaria Expenduntur l lag. cervisie. Coquina Expenduntur i qr. bovis i bacon' de stauro. Item di. cassa multonis de precomputato. Item expenduntur iiii capones vi pulcini ii herons de precomputato. In ii cassis multonum emptis iiii s. vi d. et expenditur i. In i carcosio vituli empto et expenso ii s. vii d. In ii porcellis emptis et expensis xii d. In xvii pulcinis emptis xx d. In xxxix columbellis emptis et expensis xiii d. In expensis emptoris iii d. In M ovis emptis et expensis iiii s. ii d. et expenduntur[338] Cl ova de precomputato. Candelaria Expenduntur iii lib. candelarum de stauro. Stabulum Fenum pro xiiii equis iiii hakeneis de stauro. In avenis pro eisdem viii bus. avenarum de stauro. Item fenum apud Remesbur' pro xxiiii equis ii hakeneis de stauro. In avenis pro eisdem i qr. v bus.

Probatur Summa empcionum xv s.[339] <v d.> \ iii d. /

Panteria De precomputato. Celarium Vinum de remanentia. Butillaria De precomputato. Coquina Empciones xv s.[340] <v d.> \ iii d. / Candelaria De stauro. Stabulum Fenum avene de stauro.

[*f.55r*] *Poterne Gentiles xii Valecti garciones xxv Summa ferculorum xxxvii Extranii viii*

Die veneris xxix^{o} Aprilis Panteria Expenduntur iiii^{xx} panes unde pro ferculis xxxvii panes trencheris iiii liberacionibus vi coquina iiii canibus xvi panes rewardis xiii panes. Et remanent C panes.[341] Celarium Expenduntur iiii lag. vini de remanentia. Butillaria In Cix lag. cervisie emptis de Warener precium lag. i d. ob. deductis inde ix lag. de avantagio xii s. vi d. In xxviii lag. cervisie emptis de eodem precium lag. i d. deductis inde ii lag. de avantagio ii s. ii d. In Ciiii^{xx}x lag. cervisie emptis de Shepherd precium lag. i d. ob. deductis inde xv lag. di. de avantagio <precium lag. i d.> xxi s. ix d. ob. In l lag. cervisie emptis de eadem[342] precium lag. i d. deductis inde iiii lag. de avantagio iii s. x d. Et expenduntur xxx lag. cervisie. Coquina Expenduntur C allec album iiii pisces salcii iiii stok' de stauro. Item di. salmon' de stauro. In xii piscibus salciis emptis xiii s. i d. In menues emptis et expensis ii d. In lacte iiii d. In butiro i d. Candelaria Expenduntur iii lib. candelarum de stauro. Stabulum Fenum pro xxvi equis vii hakeneis de stauro. In avenis pro eisdem i qr. ii bus. avenarum. Item fenum apud Remesbur' pro xvii equis ii hakeneis de stauro. In avenis pro eisdem vii bus. di.

Probatur Summa empcionum liii s. xi d.[343] unde

[338] MS repeats 'et expenduntur'.
[339] Altered from 'xii s.'
[340] Altered from 'xii s.'
[341] 110 loaves should remain.
[342] MS 'eodem'.
[343] Total should be ½*d.* more.

Panteria De precomputato. Celarium Vinum de remanentia. Butillaria In CCClxxvii lag. cervisie xl s. iii d.[344] Coquina Empciones xiii s. viii d. Candelaria De stauro. Stabulum Fenum avene de stauro.

Gentiles xxxiii Valecti garciones xlviii Summa ferculorum iiii^{xx}*i*

Extranii dominus Ivo Fitzwaryn se xii^{o} *soror domini se viii*^{o} *magister R.Harwell' se vii*^{o} *et alii xv*

Die sabbati xxx^{o} Aprilis Panteria Furniuntur per i talliam i qr. vii bus. frumenti que respondent ad CCClxxii panes. Et expenduntur Cxl panes unde pro ferculis iiii^{xx}i panes trencheris xii liberacionibus xi coquina vi canibus xii rewardis xviii panes. Et remanent CCCxxxii panes. Celarium Expenduntur iiii lag. vini de remanentia. Butillaria Expenduntur lx lag. cervisie. Et remanent CCiiii^{xx}vii lag. cervisie. Coquina Expenduntur C allec album iiii pisces salcii viii stok' di. salmon' salcius de stauro iii pecie storjon'. Item expenduntur CCC ova de precomputato. In xiii gurnard xiii merling vii bremes et ii thornebak*es* emptis et expensis vi s. vii d. In expensis emptoris v d. In menues emptis et expensis i d. Candelaria Expenduntur ii lib. candelarum de stauro. Stabulum Fenum pro xxiiii equis vii hakeneis de stauro. In avenis pro eisdem i qr. iii bus. avenarum. Item fenum apud Remesbur' pro xvii equis ii hakeneis de stauro. In avenis pro eisdem vii bus. di.

Probatur Summa empcionum vii s. i d.

Panteria Furniuntur i qr. vii bus. frumenti que respondent ad iiiClxxii panes. Celarium Vinum de remanentia. Butillaria De precomputato. Coquina Empciones vii s. i d. Candelaria De stauro. Stabulum Fenum avene de stauro.

[*f.55v*] *Poterne*

<Die dominica>

[*f.56r*] *Gentiles xlvi Valecti garciones lx Summa ferculorum Cvi*

Extranii dominus Ivo Fitzwar' se xii^{o} *soror domini se viii*^{o} *magister R.Harwell' se iii*^{o} *J.Peris se ii*^{o} *Walront se ii*^{o} *Wilmyngton' se ii*^{o} *et alii xxx*

Die dominica primo Maii Panteria Expenduntur Clxvi panes[345] unde pro ferculis Cvi panes trencheris xii liberacionibus x coquina xii canibus xv rewardis x panes. Et remanent Clxvi panes. Celarium Expenduntur viii lag. vini de remanentia. Butillaria Expenduntur iiii^{xx} lag. cervisie. Et remanent CCvii lag. cervisie. Coquina Expenduntur i qr. bovis i bacon' de stauro. Item expenditur i cassa multonis de precomputato. In carnibus bovinis emptis et expensis ii s. In i cassa multonis empta ii s. iiii d. et expensa. In i agno empto et expenso xvi d. In i carcosio di. vitulorum emptis iii s. x d. In iii porcellis emptis et expensis xvi d. In iiii^{xx}xvi columbellis emptis et

[344] Total should be ½*d*. more.

[345] 165 loaves disbursed.

expensis ii s. viii d. In xxii pulcinis emptis ii s. ii d. In lacte iii d. et expenso. In di. porco empto et expenso xviii d. Item expenduntur CC ova de precomputato. Item expenduntur x capones vi pulcini iiii ardei de precomputato. Candelaria Expenduntur iii lib. candelarum de stauro. Stabulum Fenum pro xxii equis vii hakeneis de stauro. In prebenda eorundem i qr. ii bus. avenarum de stauro. Item fenum apud Remesbur' pro xvi equis ii hakeneis de stauro. In avenis pro eisdem i qr.

Probatur Summa empcionum xvii s. v d.

Panteria De precomputato. Celarium Vinum de remanentia. Butillaria De precomputato. Coquina Empciones xvii s. v d. Candelaria De stauro. Stabulum Fenum avene de stauro.

Gentiles xvi Valecti garciones xxvii Summa ferculorum xliii
Extranii soror domini se iii^{o} magister R.Harwell' se vi^{o} et alii viii

Die lune secundo Maii Panteria Expenduntur iiii^{xx} panes unde pro ferculis xliii panes trencheris vi liberacionibus vii coquina iii canibus x rewardis xi panes. Et remanent iiii^{xx}vi panes. Celarium Expenduntur vi lag. vini de remanentia. Butillaria In v lag. cervisie emptis de i homine de la Vise x d. Et expenduntur xl lag. cervisie. Et remanent Clxvii lag. cervisie. Coquina Expenduntur C ova de precomputato. Item expenduntur iiii pisces salcii i salmon' salcius iii pecie storjon' iiii stok' CCC ova de precomputato. In v lag. lactis emptis v d. In viii casiis emptis ii s. In menues emptis ii d. Candelaria Expenduntur iii lib. candelarum de stauro. Stabulum Fenum pro xxiii equis iiii hakeneis de stauro. In prebenda eorundem i qr. iii bus. avenarum. Item fenum apud Remesbur' pro xiii equis ii hakeneis de stauro. In avenis pro eisdem i qr.

Probatur Summa empcionum iii s. v d. unde

Panteria De precomputato. Celarium De precomputato. Butillaria In v lag. cervisie x d. Coquina Empciones ii s. vii d. Candelaria De stauro. Stabulum Fenum avene de stauro.

[*f.56v*] *Poterne Gentiles xxv Valecti garciones xliiii Summa ferculorum lxix Extranii soror domini se vi^{o} R.Hunt se iii^{o} uxor Becot se iii^{o} magister Thomas Thirlewall' et alii xii*

Die martis iii^{o} Maii Panteria Expenduntur iiii^{xx}vi panes[346] unde pro ferculis lxix panes trencheris iii liberacionibus coquina ii canibus v rewardis iii panes. Et \ nichil / remanet. Celarium Expenduntur iiii lag. vini de remanentia. Butillaria Expenduntur liiii lag. cervisie. Et remanent Cxiii lag. cervisie. Coquina Expenduntur iiii pisces salcii i salmon' salcius x stok' CCCC ova de stauro. In v lag. lactis emptis v d. In butiro v d. In menues ii d. In DC ovis emptis ii s. vi d. Candelaria Expenduntur ii lib. candelarum de stauro. Stabulum Fenum pro xlv equis iiii hakeneis de stauro. In

346 82 loaves disbursed.

prebenda eorundem i qr.[347] ii bus. avenarum. Item fenum apud Remesbur' pro xii equis ii hakeneis de stauro. In avenis pro eisdem vi bus. avenarum de stauro.

Probatur Summa empcionum iii s. vi d.

Panteria De precomputato. Celarium Vinum de remanentia. Butillaria De precomputato. Coquina Empciones iii s. vi d. Candelaria De stauro. Stabulum Fenum avene[348]

In vadiis Thome Ferro*ur* apud Remesbur' a xxiiii^{o} die Aprilis usque iii diem Maii utroque computato capientis per diem iii d. ii s. vi d.

In vadiis Thome Norman ibidem per idem tempus capientis per diem ii d. xx\ii/ d.

In vadiis Bathe ibidem per <idem tempus> ii dies iiii d.

In vadiis Forey pagetti domini pagetti senescalli pagetti Cap*er*on' pagetti Tydemerssh' per xi dies quilibet capiens per diem i d. ob. v s. vi d.

In vadiis pagetti magistri Walteri Metford per vii dies capientis per diem i d. ob. x d. ob.

In vadiis pagetti Hulcot ibidem per <x> viii dies capientis per diem i d. ob. xii d.

Gentiles xiiii Valecti garciones xxxiii Summa ferculorum xlvii

Extranii soror domini se vii^{o} R.Hunt se iii^{o} uxor Becot se iii^{o} Harwell' se iii^{o} et alii xiiii

Die mercurie iiii die Maii Panteria Furniuntur per i talliam ii qr. frumenti que respondent ad CCCCxvi panes. Et expenduntur C panes[349] unde pro ferculis xlviii trencheris v liberacionibus x coquina v canibus xii rewardis xix panes. Et remanent CCCxvi panes. Celarium Expenduntur vi lag. vini de remanentia. Butillaria Expenduntur xliiii lag. cervisie. Et remanent lxix lag. cervisie. Coquina Expenduntur iiii pisces salcii i salmon' salsius viii stok' CCC ova iii casia de precomputato. In vi lag. di. lactis emptis vi d. ob. In but*i*ro empto vi d. In i perche empto viii d. In menues emptis i d. et expensis. Item expenduntur ii trught*es* de exhennio. Candelaria Expenduntur ii lib. candelarum de stauro. Stabulum Fenum pro lii equis v hakeneis de stauro. In prebenda eorundem iii qr. avenarum. Item fenum apud Remesbur' pro xiiii equis ii hakeneis de stauro. In avenis pro eisdem vii bus.

Probatur Summa empcionum xiii s. x d. <ob.>

Panteria Furniuntur ii qr. frumenti que respondent ad iiiiCxvi panes. Celarium Vinum de remanentia. Butillaria De precomputato. Coquina

[347] Possibly 'ii qr.'

[348] Followed by a blank space in MS.

[349] 99 loaves disbursed.

Empciones xxi d. ob. Candelaria De stauro. Stabulum Fenum avene de stauro. Vadia xii s. ob.

[*f.57r*] *Poterne Gentiles xxxviii Valecti garciones lv Summa ferculorum iiii^{xx}xiii*

Extranii soror domini se viii^{o} Harwelle se v^{o} Bonham se iii^{o} Gawein se iiii^{o} Metford se iii^{o} J.Peris se iii^{o} Wilmyngton' se iii^{o} et alii xxxv

Die jovis v Maii Panteria Expenduntur Clx panes unde pro ferculis iiii^{xx}xiii panes trencheris xii liberacionibus xiiii coquina v canibus xv panes rewardis xxi panes. Et remanent Clvi panes. Celarium Expenduntur x lag. vini de remanentia. Butillaria Expenduntur lxix lag. cervisie.[350] Et nichil remanet. Coquina Expenduntur i qr. bovis i bacon' de stauro. Item expenduntur i cassa di. multonum de precomputato. Item expenduntur vi capones iiii pulcini CC ova de precomputato. In i qr. bovis empto v s. ix d. et expenditur di. In iiii cassis multonum emptis vi s. x d. et expenduntur ii. In ii porcellis emptis xiiii d. et expensis. In xx caponibus emptis vi s. vi d. In iiii^{xx}vi columbellis emptis et expensis ii s. viii d. In expensis emptoris iii d. ob. \ In i carcosio vituli ii s. iiii d. / Candelaria Expenduntur ii lib. candelarum. Stabulum Fenum pro xxx equis v hakeneis de stauro. In avenis pro eisdem ii qr. de stauro. Item fenum apud Remesbur' pro xiiii equis iii hakeneis de stauro. In avenis pro eisdem vii bus.

Probatur Summa empcionum xxv s. x d. ob.[351]

Panteria De precomputato. Celarium Vinum de remanentia. Butillaria De precomputato. Coquina Empciones xxv s. x d. ob.[352] Candelaria De stauro. Stabulum Fenum avene de stauro.

Gentiles xx Valecti garciones xxxv Summa ferculorum lv

Extranii soror domini se vi^{o} dominus J.Drayton' se x^{o} magister R.Harwell' se vi^{o} R.Hunt se iii^{o} magister J.Pedwelle se iii^{o} et alii xiiii

Die veneris vi^{o} Maii Panteria Expenduntur iiii^{xx}x panes unde pro ferculis lv panes trencheris iiii liberacionibus vi canibus x coquina iii rewardis xii panes. Et remanent lxvi panes. Celarium Expenduntur v lag. vini de remanentia. Butillaria In Ci lag. cervisie emptis de Warener precium lag. i d. ob. deductis inde viii lag. de avantagio xi s. vii d. ob. In xxvii lag. cervisie emptis de eodem precium lag. i d. deductis inde ii lag. de avantagio ii s. i d. In Cv lag. cervisie emptis de Shepherd precium lag. i d. ob. deductis inde viii lag. di. de avantagio xii s. ob. In xli lag. cervisie emptis de eadem[353] precium lag. i d. deductis inde iii lag. de avantagio iii s. i d. In xxviii lag. cervisie emptis de Axford precium lag. i d. ob. deductis inde ii lag. de

350 MS 'panes'.

351 Totals 25*s*. 6½*d*.

352 Totals 25*s*. 6½*d*.

353 MS 'eodem'.

avantagio iii s. iii d. In xiiii lag. cervisie emptis de Willelmo Porter precium lag. i d. ob. deducta inde i lag. de avantagio xix d. ob. In xxvii lag. cervisie emptis de Nassh' precium lag. i d. ob. deductis inde ii lag. de avantagio iii s. i d. ob. Et expenduntur xliiii lag. cervisie. Et remanent CCC lag. cervisie. Coquina Expenduntur vi pisces salcii vii stok' ii salmones salcii de stauro. Item expenduntur ii tenchis xii roches de stauro. In v lag. lactis v d. et expensis.[354] In i casio empto ix d. In butiro iiii d. et expenso. Candelaria Expenduntur ii lib. candelarum de stauro. Stabulum Fenum pro xx equis v hakeneis de stauro. In avenis pro eisdem i qr. ii bus. avenarum de stauro. Item fenum apud Remesbur' pro xiiii equis ii hakeneis de stauro. In avenis pro eisdem vi bus.

Probatur Summa empcionum xxxviii s. iiii d. unde
Panteria De precomputato. Celarium Vinum de remanentia. Butillaria In CCCxliii lag. cervisie[355] xxxvi s. x d. Coquina Empciones xviii d. Candelaria De stauro. Stabulum Fenum avene de stauro.

[*f.57v*] *Gentiles xxii Valecti garciones xxxv Summa ferculorum lvii*
*Extranii soror domini se vi° magister R.Harwell' se iiii° rector de Pouleshol*t
*vicarius ville se iii° i armig*er *se ii° J.Peris se iii°*

Die sabbati vii° die Maii Panteria \ Furniuntur per i talliam ii qr. frumenti que respondent ad CCCCxii panes. / Expenduntur Cx panes unde pro ferculis lvii panes trencheris v liberacionibus viii coquina iii canibus xii rewardis xxv panes. Et remanent CCClxviii panes. Celarium Expenduntur v lag. vini de remanentia. Butillaria Expenduntur liii lag. cervisie. Et remanent CCxlvii lag. cervisie. Coquina Expenduntur v pisces salsii ii salmones salsii de stauro. Item expenduntur \ l / iiii roches de stauro. Item CC ova de precomputato. In iii lag. lactis iii d. In menues ii d. et expensis. In iii thornebak*es* emptis et expensis v s. Candelaria Expenduntur ii lib. candelarum de stauro. Stabulum Fenum pro xxix equis v hakeneis de stauro. In avenis pro eisdem ii qr. avenarum. Item fenum apud Remesebur' pro x equis i hakeneo de stauro. In avenis iiii bus.

Probatur Summa empcionum v s. v d.
Panteria Furniuntur ii qr. frumenti que respondent ad iiiiCxii panes. Celarium Vinum de remanentia. Butillaria De precomputato. Coquina Empciones v s. v d. Candelaria De stauro. Stabulum Fenum avene de stauro.

Gentiles xxviii Valecti garciones lvi Summa ferculorum iiii^{xx}iiii
Extranii soror domini se vi° magister Rogerus Harwell' se vii° R.Hunt se iii°
J.Peris se iii° vicarius ville se ii° . . . Horne se ii° . . . alii xxiiii

[354] MS adds 'v d.'
[355] MS omits 'lag. cervisie.'

Die dominica viii° Maii Panteria Expenduntur Clx panes[356] unde pro ferculis iiii^{xx}iiii panes trencheris viii liberacionibus x coquina xii rewardis xxxi panes. Et remanent CCviii panes. Celarium Expenduntur viii lag. vini de remanentia. Butillaria Expenduntur lxiiii lag. cervisie. Et remanent Ciiii^{xx}iiii lag. cervisie.[357] Coquina Expenduntur i qr. bovis di. bacon' ii casse multonum de precomputato. In ii cassis multonum emptis iiii s. viii d. et expenduntur i et di. In i carcosio vituli empto et expenso iiii s. In ii porcellis emptis xii d. et expensis. In vi caponibus emptis ii s. In ii gallinis emptis iiii d. In iiii^{xx}vii columbellis emptis et expensis ii s. v d. In D ovis emptis ii s. i d. In xvii aucis emptis iii s. viii d. ob. Item expenduntur iiii capones ii galline vi pulcini CCC ova de precomputato. Item expenditur di. porcus de stauro. Candelaria Expenduntur ii lib. candelarum de stauro. Stabulum Fenum pro xx equis v hakeneis de stauro. In avenis pro eisdem i qr. iiii bus. avenarum. Item fenum apud Remesbur' pro viii equis ii hakeneis de stauro. In avenis pro eisdem iii bus.

Probatur Summa empcionum xx s. ii d. ob.

Panteria De precomputato. Celarium Vinum de remanentia. Butillaria De precomputato. Coquina Empciones xx s. ii d. ob. Candelaria De stauro. Stabulum Fenum avene[358]

[*f.58r*] *Poterne Gentiles xvi Valecti garciones xxxviii Summa ferculorum liiii Extranii soror domini se vi° R.Hunt se iii° magister R.Harwell' se iiii° et alii x*

Die lune ix° Maii Panteria Expenduntur Cx panes unde pro ferculis liiii panes trencheris v liberacionibus viii coquina iii canibus xii rewardis xxviii panes. Et remanent iiii^{xx}xviii panes. Celarium Expenduntur iiii lag. vini de remanentia. Butillaria Expenduntur xliiii lag. cervisie. Et remanent Cxl lag. cervisie. Coquina Expenduntur i qr. bovis i cassa di. multonis de stauro. Item i bacon' de stauro. Item expenduntur vi pulcini xxiiii columbelle de precomputato. Candelaria Expenduntur ii lib. candelarum de stauro. Stabulum Fenum pro xx equis vi hakeneis de stauro. In avenis pro eisdem i qr. ii bus. avenarum. Item fenum apud Remesbur' pro x equis i hakeneo de stauro. In avenis iiii bus.

Summa nichil quia de precomputato

Panteria De precomputato. Celarium Vinum de remanentia. Butillaria De precomputato. Coquina Empciones nichil. Candelaria De stauro. Stabulum Fenum avene[359]

356 145 loaves disbursed.
357 183 gallons should remain.
358 Followed by a blank space in MS.
359 Followed by a blank space in MS.

Gentiles xxv Valecti garciones xxxi Summa ferculorum lvi
Extranii soror domini se vi^{o} R.Hunt se v^{o} magister R.Harwell' se vi^{o} et alii xiiii
Die martis x^{o} Maii Panteria Furniuntur per i talliam i qr. vii bus. frumenti que respondent ad CCClxx panes. Et expenduntur Cxl panes unde pro ferculis lvi panes trencheris viii liberacionibus x coquina ix canibus xii rewardis xlv panes. Et remanent CCCxxviii panes. Celarium Expenduntur v lag. vini de remanentia. Butillaria Expenduntur l lag. cervisie. Et remanent iiii^{xx}x lag. cervisie. Coquina Expenduntur i qr. bovis de stauro i bacon' de stauro. Item expenditur di. porci recentis. Item expenduntur iii capones vi pulcini de precomputato. In ii cassis multonum emptis iiii s. vi d. et expenditur i. In i carcosio vituli empto ii s. viii d. et expenso. In ii porcellis emptis xii d. et expensis. Item expenduntur CCC ova de precomputato. Candelaria Expenduntur iii lib. candelarum de stauro. Stabulum Fenum pro xii equis vi hakeneis de stauro. In avenis pro eisdem vi bus. avenarum. Item fenum apud Remesbur' pro ix equis i hakeneo de stauro. In avenarum iii bus.

Probatur Summa viii s. ii d.

Panteria Furniuntur i qr. vii bus. frumenti que respondent ad iiiClxx panes. Celarium Vinum de remanentia. Butillaria De precomputato. Coquina Empciones viii s. ii d. Candelaria De stauro. Stabulum Fenum avene de stauro.
[*f.58v*] *Poterne Gentiles xxvii Valecti garciones xlv Summa ferculorum lxxii*
Extranii soror domini se vi^{o} R.Hunt se iii^{o} magister R.Harwell' se iii^{o} Laurencius Dru se vi^{o} et alii xiiii
Die mercurie xi Maii Panteria Expenduntur Cxlv panes unde pro ferculis lxxii panes trencheris x liberacionibus xi coquina x canibus xii rewardis xxx panes. Et remanent Ciiii^{xx}iii panes. Celarium Expenduntur viii lag. vini de remanentia. Butillaria Expenduntur lv lag. cervisie. Et remanent xxxv lag. cervisie. Coquina Expenduntur di. qr. bovis i cassa multonis i bacon' de stauro. Item expenduntur iii capones vi pulcini de precomputato. Item expenduntur ii pisces salcii i salmon'[360] salsius de stauro C makerell de precomputato. Item expenditur i lampreda de exhenio. Item expenduntur xxiiii roches de stauro. Item expenduntur CCC ova de precomputato. In i pot makerell recenti empto iii s. iiii d. et expenditur di. In lacte v d. In butiro iiii d. et expenso. Candelaria Expenduntur ii lib. candelarum de stauro. Stabulum Fenum pro \x/xii equis vi hakeneis de stauro. In avenis pro eisdem i qr. iii bus. < . . . > avenarum. Item fenum apud Remesbur' pro ix equis ii hakeneis de stauro. In avenis iii bus. di.

Probatur Summa empcionum iiii s. i d.

[360] MS repeats 'salmon''.

Panteria De precomputato. Celarium Vinum de remanentia. Butillaria De precomputato. Coquina Empciones iiii s. i d. Candelaria De stauro. Stabulum Fenum avene de stauro.

Gentiles xx Valecti garciones xl Summa ferculorum lx

Extranii soror domini se vi^{o} R.Hunt se iiii^{o} magister R.Harwell' se iii^{o} Laurencius Dru se iiii^{o} . . . alii xxiiii

Die jovis xii^{o} Maii Panteria Expenduntur Cxx panes unde pro ferculis lx panes trencheris viii liberacionibus viii coquina x canibus xiiii panes rewardis xx panes. Et remanent lxiii panes. Celarium Expenduntur viii lag. vini de remanentia. Butillaria <Expend*un*tur> In xlv lag. cervisie emptis de Warner precium lag. i d. ob. deductis inde iii lag. di. cervisie <p'> v s. ii d. In xxix lag. cervisie emptis de eodem precium lag. i d. deductis inde ii lag. di. cervisie ii s. ii d. ob. In C lag. cervisie emptis de Shiph*er*de precium lag. i d. ob. deductis inde viii lag. di. cervisie xi s. iiii d. ob. In xxvi lag. cervisie emptis de eadem[361] precium lag. i d. deductis inde ii lag. de avantagio ii s. In xx lag. cervisie emptis de Johanna Godefray precium lag. i d. ob. deductis inde i lag. di. de avantagio <xvii d. ob.> ii s. iii d. ob. Et expenduntur xxxviii lag. cervisie. Et remanent CCxii lag. cervisie. Coquina Expenduntur i qr. bovis i baco ii casse multonum de stauro. Item vi capones xii pulcini de precomputato. In i cassa multonis empta[362] ii s. ii d. In i carcosio vituli empto ii s. vi d. et expenso. In carnibus bovinis emptis pro potagio xii d. In xxvii caponibus emptis viii s. viii d. In xxi columbellis emptis et expensis vii d. In M ovis emptis iiii s. ii d. Candelaria Expend*un*tur[363] lib. candelarum de stauro. Stabulum Fenum pro xxii equis viii hakeneis de stauro. In prebenda eorundem i qr. ii bus. avenarum de precomputato. Item fenum apud Remesbur' pro xii equis i hakeneo de stauro. In avenis pro eisdem iiii bus. di. avenarum.

Probatur Summa empcionum <xx> xlii s. i d. ob. unde Panteria <In> De precomputato. Celarium Vinum de remanentia. Butillaria In CCxx lag. cervisie xxiii s. ob. Coquina Empciones xix s. i d. Candelaria De stauro. Stabulum Fenum avene de stauro.

[*f.59r*] *Poterne Gentiles xiiii Valecti garciones xx Summa ferculorum xxxiiii*

Extranii soror domini se vi Robertus Hunte se ii^{o} uxor Holcote se iiii^{o} uxor Becot magister Rogerus Harwell' et alii extranii viii

Die veneris xiii Maii Panteria Furniuntur[364] per i talliam i qr. iiii bus. frumenti de stauro que respondent de CCCx panibus. Et expenduntur

[361] MS 'eodem'.

[362] MS repeats 'emp".

[363] Followed by a blank space in MS.

[364] Preceded by 'Expend*un*tur' in MS.

iiii^{xx}v panes[365] unde pro ferculis xxxiiii trencheris iii liberacionibus vii coquine iii canibus xii rewardis xxii panes. Et remanent CCiiii^{xx}viii panes. Celarium Expenduntur iiii lag. vini de stauro. Butillaria Expenduntur xxviii lag. cervisie. Et remanent Ciiii^{xx}iiii lag. cervisie. Coquina[366] Expenduntur iii pisces salcii i salmo salcius de stauro. In di. salmone recenti i lampreda salcia C makerell poudris de precomputato. In vi piscibus salciis emptis vi s. ix d. In lacte empto et expenso iii d. Candelaria Expend*un*tur[367] lib. candelarum de stauro. Stabulum Fenum pro xxx equis x hakeneis de stauro. In prebenda eorundem ii qr. avenarum de precomputato. Item fenum apud Remesbur' pro viii equis ii hakeneis de stauro. In avenis pro eisdem ii bus. di.

Probatur Summa empcionum vii s.

Panteria Furniuntur i qr. iiii bus. frumenti que respondent ad iiiCx panes. Celarium Vinum de remanentia. Butillaria De precomputato. Coquina Empciones vii s. Candelaria De stauro. Stabulum Fenum avene de stauro.

Gentiles xiiii Valecti garciones xxiiii Summa ferculorum xxxviii

Extranii soror domini se v magister Simon Sydenham uxor Holcote se iiii^{o} uxor Becot[368] *magister R.Harwell' magister J.Wotton' se ii^{o} vicarius ville et alii extranii x*

Die sabbati xiiii^{o} Maii Panteria Expenduntur iiii^{xx}v panes unde pro ferculis xxxviii trencheris iiii liberacionibus ix coquine ii canibus xiii rewardis xix. Et remanent CCiii panes. Celarium Expenduntur vi lag. vini de stauro. Butillaria Expenduntur xxx lag. cervisie. Et remanent Cliiii lag. cervisie de precomputato. Coquina Expenduntur iiii pisces salcii i salmo salcius de stauro. Item i lampreda salcia de precomputato. In l brem*es* i mulet vi <mu. . .> gurnard et ii merlyng emptis vii s. vi d. Et expenduntur xxxiiii brem*es* vi gurnard et ii merlyng. In i crabb' empto vi d. Candelaria Expend*un*tur[369] lib. candelarum de stauro. Stabulum Fenum pro xxx equis vii hakeneis de precomputato. In prebenda eorundem i qr. iiii bus. avenarum de precomputato. Item fenum apud Remesbur' pro ix equis i hakeneo de stauro. In avenis pro eisdem iii bus.

Probatur Summa empcionum viii s.

Panteria De precomputato. Celarium Vinum de remanentia. Butillaria De precomputato. Coquina Empciones viii s. Candelaria De stauro. Stabulum Fenum avene de stauro.

[365] 81 loaves disbursed.
[366] MS 'Caquina'.
[367] Followed by a blank space in MS.
[368] MS 'Becocot'.
[369] Followed by a blank space in MS.

[*f.59v*] *Poterne Gentiles xxx Valecti garciones lxv Summa ferculorum iiii*^{xx}*xv*
Extranii soror domini se v^{to} *magister Simon Sydenham se iiii*^{o} *uxor Holcote se iiii*^{o} *uxor Becot Robertus Hunte magister Johannes Wotton' Ricardus Osbern' se iii*^{o} *Walrond' vicarius ville magister Rogerus Harwell' se v*^{to} *et alii extranii xxvi*
Die dominica xv^{o} Maii Panteria Expenduntur Cxliiii panes[370] unde pro ferculis iiii^{xx}xv trencheris x liberacionibus x coquine vi canibus xiii rewardis vi. Et remanent lxiii panes.[371] Celarium Expenduntur viii lag. vini de stauro. Butillaria Expenduntur xliiii lag. cervisie. Et remanent Cx lag. cervisie de precomputato. Coquina Expenduntur[372] i qr. bovis i baco de stauro. Item expenduntur vi capones <iiii> \ x / pulcini de precomputato. Item expenduntur vi auce de precomputato. In iii cassis multonum emptis iii s. vi d. et expenduntur ii cassis di. multonum. In i porco empto ii s. x d. et expenditur di. In ii porcellis emptis et expensis ix d. In xiiii pulcinis emptis xvi d. In i carcosio vituli empto et expenso ii s. iiii d. Item expenduntur CC ova de precomputato. \ In lacte iiii d. / Candelaria Expend*un*tur[373] lib. candelarum de stauro. Stabulum Fenum pro xxii equis vii hakeneis de precomputato. In prebenda eorundem i qr. iii bus. avenarum de precomputato. Item fenum apud Remesbur' pro xi equis ii hakeneis de stauro. In avenis iiii bus.

Probatur Summa empcionum xi s. i d.

Panteria De precomputato. Celarium Vinum de remanentia. Butillaria De precomputato. Coquina Empciones xi s. i d. Candelaria De stauro. Stabulum Fenum avene de stauro.
Gentiles xxxi Valecti garciones lv Summa ferculorum iiii^{xx}*vi*
Extranii soror domini se v magister Simon Sydenham se iiii Calston' se iii^{o} *uxor Holcote se iiii*^{o} *uxor Becote se Latton' se ii*^{o} *Metford cum fratre Ricardus Osbern' se ii*^{o} *magister Johannes Wotton' se ii*^{o} *. . . alii extranii xv*
Die lune xvi^{o} Maii Panteria <Expen> Furniuntur per i talliam ii qr. i bus. frumenti de stauro que respondent de CCCCxxx panibus. \ Et expenduntur Cxxxv / unde pro ferculis iiii^{xx}vi trencheris x liberacionibus x coquine iii canibus xiii rewardis xiii. Et remanent CCClviii panes. Celarium Expenduntur vi lag. vini de stauro. Butillaria Expenduntur xxxii lag. cervisie. Et remanent lxxviii lag. cervisie. Coquina Expenduntur i qr. bovis i baco de stauro. Item i cassa multonis et di. viii capones viii pulcini de precomputato. In xii columbellis emptis et expensis iiii d. \ In i carrcosio

370 140 loaves disbursed.
371 59 loaves should remain.
372 MS repeats 'Expen''.
373 Followed by a blank space in MS.

vituli ii s. In ii porcellis x d. / Candelaria Expend*un*tur[374] lib. candelarum de stauro. Stabulum Fenum pro xvi equis vii hakeneis de precomputato. In prebenda eorundem i qr. i bus. avenarum de precomputato. Item fenum apud Remesbur' pro x equis ii hakeneis de stauro. In avenis iii bus. di.

Probatur Summa empcionum iii s. iiii d.[375]

Panteria Furniuntur ii qr. i bus. frumenti que respondent ad CCCCxxx. Celarium Vinum de remanentia. Butillaria De precomputato. Coquina Empciones iii s. iiii d.[376] Candelaria De stauro. Stabulum Fenum avene de stauro.

[*f.60r*] *Poterne Gentiles xiii Valecti garciones xxxv Summa ferculorum xlviii*
Extranii soror domini se iiii^{o} magister Simon Sydynham uxor Becote R.Hunte Latton' vicarius ville Medford de Genge cum fratre et alii extranii viii

Die martis xvii Maii Panteria Expenduntur C<xx> panes unde pro ferculis xlviii trencheris v liberacionibus vii coquine iii canibus xiii rewardis xxiiii. Et remanent CClviii panes. Celarium Expenduntur vi lag. vini de stauro. Butillaria Expenduntur xxx lag. cervisie. Et remanent xlviii lag. cervisie. Coquina Expenduntur di. qr. bovis di. baco de stauro. Item i cassa di. multonum de precomputato. Item i caponis iiii pulcini de precomputato. In i cassa multonis empta ii s. In i carcosio vituli empto et expenso ii s. iiii d. In iiii pulcinis vi d. In ii porcellis emptis et expensis x d. Candelaria Expend*un*tur[377] lib. candelarum de precomputato. Stabulum Fenum pro ix equis vi hakeneis de precomputato. In prebenda eorundem v bus. avenarum de precomputato. Item fenum apud Remesbur' pro xvi equis iii hakeneis de stauro. In avenis pro eisdem i qr.

Probatur Summa empcionum v s. viii d.

Panteria De precomputato. Celarium Vinum de remanentia. Butillaria De precomputato. Coquina Empciones v s. viii d. Candelaria De stauro. Stabulum Fenum avene de stauro.

Gentiles vii Valecti garciones xx Summa ferculorum xxvii
Extranii soror domini se iii^{o} Robertus Hunte se ii^{o} uxor Becot Stokke se ii^{o} et alii extranii viii

Die mercurie xviii Maii Panteria Expenduntur lx panes unde pro ferculis xxvii trencheris ii liberacionibus v coquine ii canibus xii rewardis xii. Et remanent Ciiii^{xx}xviii panes. Celarium Expenduntur ii lag. vini de stauro. Butillaria Expenduntur xx lag. cervisie. Et remanent xxviii lag. cervisie. Coquina Expenduntur iiii pisces salcii i salmo salcius et di. de stauro. Item

[374] Followed by a blank space in MS.
[375] Totals 2*d*. less.
[376] Totals 2*d*. less.
[377] Followed by a blank space in MS.

expenduntur x brem*es* de precomputato. In xlviii makerell recentibus emptis xix d. In ii lag. lactis emptis et expensis ii d. In butiro empto et expenso iiii d. ob. <u>Candelaria</u> Expend*un*tur[378] lib. candelarum de stauro. <u>Stabulum</u> Fenum pro xv equis vi hakeneis de precomputato. In prebenda eorundem i qr. i bus. avenarum de precomputato. Item fenum apud Remesbur' pro xvii equis ii hakeneis de stauro. In avenis pro eisdem i qr. i bus.

In vadiis <Thom. . .> \ famuli / Ferour apud Remesbury a iiii° die Maii usque xviii eiusdem utroque computato capientis per diem ii d. ii s. vi d.

In vadiis pagetti Tydem*er*ssh' et pagetti Hunte ibidem per ii septimanas utroque capienti per diem i d. ob. iii s. . . .

In vadiis Thome Ferrour ibidem per x dies capientis per diem iii d. ii s. . . .

In vadiis Thome Norman ibidem per idem tempus capientis per diem <u>ii d.</u> . . .

In vadiis paget*ti* seneschalli ibidem per ii septimanas capientis per diem i d. ob. . . .

Probatur Summa empcionum xiiii s. ob. unde

Panteria De precomputato. Celarium Vinum de remanentia. Butillaria De precomputato. Coquina Empciones . . . . . Candelaria De stauro. Stabulum Fenum avene de stauro. Vadia xi s. x. . .

[*f.60v*] *. . .entiles xiiii Valecti garciones xxxv Summa ferculorum xlix Extranii soror domini se iiii° R.Hunte se ii° magister J.Metford se iii° <vill'> vicarius ville et alii extranii v*

Die jovis xix Maii <u>Panteria</u> Expenduntur Ciiii panes[379] unde pro ferculis xlix trencheris v liberacionibus iiii coquine vii canibus xii rewardis xxxvi. Et remanent iiii^{xx}xiiii panes. <u>Celarium</u> Expenduntur iii lag. vini de stauro. <u>Butillaria</u> Expenduntur xxviii lag. cervisie de precomputato. <u>Coquina</u> Expenduntur di. qr. bovis di. baco de stauro. Item i cassa multonis ii capones iiii pulcini CC ova de precomputato. In i cassa multonis empta ii s. iiii d. In i carcosio vituli empto et expenso ii s. viii d. In ii porcellis emptis et expensis x d. Item expenduntur ii auce de precomputato. <u>Candelaria</u> Expend*un*tur[380] lib. candelarum de stauro. <u>Stabulum</u> Fenum pro xiiii equis vi hakeneis de precomputato viii bus. avenarum de precomputato. Item fenum apud Remesbur' pro xvii equis ii hakeneis de stauro. In avenis i qr. avenarum.

Probatur Summa empcionum v s. x d.

Panteria De precomputato. Celarium Vinum de remanentia. Butillaria De

[378] Followed by a blank space in MS.

[379] 113 loaves disbursed.

[380] Followed by a blank space in MS.

precomputato. Coquina Empciones v s. x d. Candelaria De stauro. Stabulum Fenum avene de stauro.
. . . . . vii . . . . . xx . . . . .erculorum xxvii
. . . . .or domini se iiii^{to} *. . . . . extranii vi*
Die veneris xx Maii Panteria Expenduntur lxx panes unde pro ferculis xxvii trencheris ii liberacionibus vii coquine iii canibus[381] x rewardis xxi panes. Et remanent xxiiii panes. Celarium Expenduntur iii lag. vini de stauro. Butillaria <Expend*un*tur> In Cix lag. cervisie emptis de Sheph*er*de precium lag. i d. ob. deductis inde ix lag. de avantagio xii s. vi d. In xxxii lag. cervisie emptis de eadem[382] deductis inde ii lag. di. cervisie de avantagio ii s. v d. ob. In xxxv lag. cervisie emptis de Carlet' precium lag. i d. ob. deductis inde iii lag. de avantagio <ii s. viii d.> iiii s. In xv lag. cervisie emptis de eadem[383] precium lag. i d. xiiii d. In vi lag. cervisie emptis de Warn*er* precium lag. i d. ob. ix d. Et expenduntur xxiiii lag. cervisie. Et remanent Clxxiii lag. cervisie. Coquina Expenduntur iiii pisces salcii i salmo salcius de stauro. In butiro et lacte emptis iiii d. \ In i bus. farine xi d. In i bus. salis x d. / In crem' empto ii d. Candelaria Expend*un*tur[384] lib. candelarum de stauro. Stabulum Fenum pro xii equis v hakeneis de precomputato. In prebenda eorundem i qr. avenarum de precomputato. Item fenum apud Remesbur' pro xvi equis ii hakeneis de stauro. In avenis pro eisdem i qr.

Probatur Summa empcionum xxiii s. i d.[385] unde
Panteria De precomputato. Celarium Vinum de remanentia. Butillaria De precomputato. In $Ciiii^{xx}xvii$ lag. xx s. x d.[386] Coquina Empciones[387] ii s. iii d. Candelaria De stauro. Stabulum Fenum avene de stauro.
[*f.61r*] *Poterne Gentiles xiiii Valecti garciones xxx Summa ferculorum xliiii Extranii soror domini se* iiii^{o} *rector de Henreth' se* ii^{o} *magister Johannes Metford se* ii^{o} *magister Johannes Wotton' se* ii^{o} *et alii extranii xv*
Die sabbati xxi Maii Panteria Furniuntur per i talliam ii qr. frumenti de stauro que respondent de CCCCvi panibus. Et expenduntur $iiii^{xx}xv$ panes[388] unde pro ferculis xliiii trencheris iii liberacionibus v coquine iii canibus x rewardis xxxiii panes. Et remanent CCCCxxx panes.[389] Celarium Expenduntur iiii lag. vini de stauro. Butillaria Expenduntur xxxiiii lag.

[381] MS 'cany*ng*'.
[382] MS 'eodem'.
[383] MS 'eodem'.
[384] Followed by a blank space in MS.
[385] Total is ½*d*. more.
[386] Total is ½*d*. more.
[387] MS repeats 'empciones'.
[388] 98 loaves disbursed.
[389] 335 loaves should remain.

cervisie. Et remanent Cxxxix lag. cervisie. Coquina Expenduntur vi pisces salcii de stauro. In i thornbak et C makerell recentibus emptis et expensis ii s. ii d. Candelaria Expend*un*tur[390] lib. candelarum de stauro. Stabulum Fenum pro xiiii equis v hakeneis de precomputato. In prebenda eorundem i qr. i bus. avenarum de precomputato. Item fenum apud Remesbur' pro xvi equis ii hakeneis de stauro. In avenis i qr.

Probatur Summa empcionum ii s. ii d.

Panteria Furniuntur ii qr. frumenti de stauro que respondent ad[391] iiiiCvi panes. Celarium Vinum de remanentia. Butillaria De precomputato. Coquina Empciones ii s. ii d. Candelaria De stauro. Stabulum Fenum avene[392]

Gentiles xxv Valecti garciones xl Summa ferculorum lxv

Extranii soror domini se iiii^{o} *magister Johannes Metford rector de Henreth' vicarius de Poterne Flour magister Johannes Wotton' Covyntr' Ricardus Osbern' Johannes Walrond et alii extranii xxx*

Die dominica xxii Maii Panteria Expenduntur Cxxv panes unde pro ferculis lxv trencheris v liberacionibus iiii coquine v canibus xii rewardis xxxiiii. Et remanent CCCv <lag.> panes. Celarium Expenduntur vi lag. vini de stauro. Butillaria Expenduntur xxxviii lag. cervisie. Et remanent Ci lag. cervisie. Coquina Expenduntur i qr. bovis i baco de stauro. Item iiii capones vi pulcini v auce C ova de precomputato. In ii cassis multonum emptis et expensis iiii s. x d. In i porco empto ii s. vi d. et expenditur di. porcus. In i carcosio vituli empto et expenso iii s. In iii lag. lactis emptis iii d. In ix pulcinis emptis x d. In ii porcellis emptis et expensis x d. Candelaria Expend*un*tur[393] lib. candelarum de stauro. Stabulum Fenum pro x equis iiii hakeneis de precomputato. In prebenda eorundem vii bus. avenarum de precomputato. Item fenum apud Remesbur' pro xvi equis ii hakeneis de stauro. In avenis pro eisdem i qr.

Probatur Summa empcionum xii s. iii d.

Panteria De precomputato. Celarium Vinum de remanentia. Butillaria De precomputato. Coquina Empciones . . . . . Candelaria De s. . . . . Stabulum Fenu. . . av. . . . .

[f.61v] Gentiles xv Valecti garciones xxx Summa ferculorum xlv

Extranii soror domini se iiii^{o} *R.Osbern' se iii*^{o} *Walrond se ii*^{o} *et alii xii*

Die lune xxiii Maii Panteria Expenduntur iiii^{xx}iiii panes unde pro ferculis xlv trencheris iii liberacionibus v coquine iii canibus xii rewardis xvi. Et remanent CCxxi panes. Celarium Expenduntur iiii lag. vini de stauro.

390 Followed by a blank space in MS.
391 MS omits 'ad'.
392 Followed by a blank space in MS.
393 Followed by a blank space in MS.

Butillaria Expenduntur xxviii lag. cervisie. Et remanent lxxiii lag. cervisie. Coquina Expenduntur di. qr. bovis iii qr. baconis de stauro. Item i cassa di. multonum ii capones iiii pulcini de precomputato. Candelaria Expend*un*tur[394] lib. candelarum de stauro. Stabulum Fenum pro xvi equis v hakeneis de precomputato. In prebenda eorundem i qr. ii bus. avenarum de precomputato. Item fenum apud Remesbur' pro xvi equis ii hakeneis de stauro. In avenis pro eisdem vii bus.

Summa nichil quia de precomputato

Panteria De precomputato. Celarium Vinum de remanentia. Butillaria De precomputato. Coquina Empciones nichil. Candelaria De stauro. Stabulum Fenum avene de stauro.

..... xix ..... xxxvii .....culorum lvi

.....ror domini se iiii^to^ ..... se iiii^to^ ...imon canonicus Sarum se iiii^to^ ... Wylmynton' se ii^o^ .....bern' se ii^o^ ..... extranii x

Die martis xxiiii Maii Panteria Expenduntur Ciiii panes unde pro ferculis lvi trencheris vi liberacionibus x coquine vi canibus xv rewardis xi. Et remanent Cxv panes.[395] Celarium Expenduntur vi lag. vini de stauro. Butillaria Expenduntur xliiii lag. cervisie. Et remanent xxix lag. cervisie. Coquina Expenduntur i qr. bovis i baco de stauro. Item expenduntur ii capones iiii pulcini de precomputato. In i carcosio vituli empto et expenso ii s. ii d. In ii cassis multonum emptis et expensis iiii s. viii d. In ii porcellis emptis et expensis xii d. In xxiiii columbellis emptis et expensis viii d. Candelaria Expend*un*tur[396] lib. candelarum de stauro. Stabulum Fenum pro xxx equis xi hakeneis de precomputato. In prebenda eorundem ii qr. ii bus. avenarum de precomputato. Item fenum apud Remesbur' pro xvi equis ii hakeneis de stauro. In avenis vii bus.

Probatur Summa empcionum viii s. vi d.

Panteria De precomputato. Celarium Vinum de remanentia. Butillaria De precomputato. Coquina Empciones viii s. vi d. Candelaria De stauro. Stabulum Fenum avene de stauro.

[*f.62r*] *Poterne Gentiles xx Valecti garciones xliii Summa ferculorum lxiii Extranii magister Johannes Frank' se iiii^to^ magister Simon Yarty se iiii^to^ Wilmynton' se ii^o^ Ricardus Osbern' se ii^o^ vicarius ville Flour Thomas Edward Ryle Axford et alii extranii xxiiii*

Die mercurie xxv^to^ Maii Panteria Furniuntur per i talliam ii qr. iiii bus. frumenti de stauro que respondent de Dxi panibus. Et expenduntur Cxliiii panes unde pro ferculis lxiii trencheris vi liberacionibus viii coquine iii canibus xiiii rewardis l panes. Et remanent CCCCiiii^xx^ii panes. Celarium

[394] Followed by a blank space in MS.
[395] 117 loaves should remain.
[396] Followed by a blank space in MS.

Expenduntur viii lag. vini de stauro. Butillaria <Expend*un*tur> In li lag. cervisie emptis de Willelmo Blake precium lag. i d. ob. deductis inde iiii lag. de avantagio vi s. iii d. In xxi lag. cervisie emptis de eodem precium lag. i d. deductis inde i lag. di. de avantagio xix d. ob. In xxxvi lag. cervisie emptis de Johanne Enge precium lag. i d. ob. deductis inde iii lag. de avantagio iiii s. i d. ob. Et expenduntur xlviii lag. cervisie. Et remanent iiii^{xx}ix lag. cervisie. Coquina Expenduntur di. qr. bovis i cassa di. multonum ii capones iiii pulcini xii columbelle de precomputato. Item expenduntur iii pisces salcii i salmo salcius l makerell de stauro. In i pot makerell poudrorum empto iii s. iiii d. In iii lag. lactis emptis iii d. <In i carcosio vituli empto> In butiro iii d. In CC ovis emptis x d. \ In i cassa multonis ii s. iiii d.[397] / Candelaria Expend*un*tur[398] lib. candelarum de precomputato. Stabulum Fenum pro x equis v hakeneis de precomputato. In prebenda eorundem <i> iiii bus. di. avenarum de precomputato. Item fenum apud Remesbur' pro xvi equis ii hakeneis de stauro. In avenis vii bus.

Probatur Summa empcionum xix s. unde

Panteria Furniuntur ii qr. iiii bus. frumenti que respondent ad[399] vCxi panes. Celarium Vinum de remanentia. Butillaria In Cviii lag. xii s. Coquina Empciones vii s. Candelaria De stauro. Stabulum Fenum avene de stauro.

Gentiles xiiii Valecti garciones xl Summa ferculorum liiii

Extranii magister R.Harwell' se iiii^{o} vicarius ville Flour' et alii tam carectarii quam extranii Sar' h. . . . .d' [400] *xxx*

Die jovis xxvi^{to} Maii Panteria Expenduntur Ciiii^{xx}ii panes[401] unde pro ferculis liiii trencheris iii liberacionibus v coquine iiii canibus viii rewardis Cvi. Et remanent CCC panes. Celarium Expenduntur vi lag. vini de precomputato. Butillaria Expenduntur xliiii lag. cervisie. Et remanent xlv lag. cervisie. Coquina Expenduntur di. qr. bovis di. baco de stauro. Item ii casse multonum ii capones iiii pulcini C ova de precomputato. In carnibus bovinis emptis pro potagio viii d. In i cassa multonis empta et expensa ii s. ii d. In i qr. porci empto et expenso xii d. In i porcello empto et expenso vii d. In xii columbellis emptis et expensis iiii d. In iii lag. lactis emptis iii d. In i carcosio vituli empto et expenso ii s. iiii d. Candelaria Expend*un*tur[402] lib. candelarum de stauro. Stabulum Fenum pro xxxv equis et viii hakeneis de precomputato. In prebenda eorundem ii qr. vi bus. de precomputato cum

[397] MS adds 'in'.
[398] Followed by a blank space in MS.
[399] MS omits 'ad'.
[400] MS obscure, possibly 'h' followed by 3 minims and 'd''.
[401] 180 loaves disbursed.
[402] Followed by a blank space in MS.

rewardis factis carectariis. Item fenum apud Remesbur' pro xvi equis ii hakeneis de stauro. In avenis vii bus.

Probatur Summa empcionum vii s. iiii d.

Panteria De precomputato. Celarium Vinum de remanentia. Butillaria De precomputato. Coquina Empciones vii s. iiii d. Candelaria De stauro. Stabulum Fenum avene de stauro.

[*f.62v*] *Poterne*

Familia domini apud Pot*er*ne in prandio Sarum in cero

Gentiles x Valecti garciones xxviii Summa ferculorum xxxviii

Extranii magister R.Harwell' vicarius ville Johannes Mone Flour' et alii xviii

Die veneris xxvii Maii Panteria Expenduntur C panes unde pro ferculis xxxviii trencheris ii liberacionibus nichil coquine iiii canibus viii rewardis xlviii. Et remanent CC panes. Celarium Expenduntur viii lag. vini de precomputato. Butillaria In xxi couveles cervisie emptis de Waltero Cooke continentibus CCiiii^{xx}xiiii lag. cervisie precium couvele xviii d. ultra avantagium xxxi s. vi d. In viii couveles cervisie emptis de eodem continentibus Cxii lag. cervisie precium couvele xii d. ultra avantagium viii s. In xvi couveles cervisie emptis de Byston' continentibus Ciiii^{xx}xii lag. cervisie precium couvele xviii d. xxiiii s. In iii couveles cervisie emptis de eodem continentibus xlii lag. cervisie precium couvele xii d. ultra avantagium iii s. In viii couveles cervisie emptis de Levessham continentibus Cxii lag. cervisie precium couvel*e* xviii d. ultra avantagium xii s. Et expenduntur l lag. cervisie. Et remanent DCCii lag. cervisie. Coquina Expenduntur v pisces salcii C makerell i salmo salcius de precomputato. In ii piscibus salciis emptis et expensis ii s. ii d. In ii lag. lactis ii d. In casio empto iiii d. et expenso. Candelaria Expenduntur ii lib. candelarum de stauro. Stabulum Fenum pro xl equis x hakeneis de stauro. In avenis pro eisdem ii qr. iiii bus.

Probatur Summa empcionum <xi> iiii li. xiiii d.[403] unde

Panteria De precomputato. Celarium Vinum de remanentia. Butillaria In viiClii lag. cervisie lxxviii s. vi d. Coquina Empciones ii s. viii d. Candelaria De stauro. Stabulum Fenum avene de stauro.

Preteria in pane cervisia carnibus piscibus et aliis victualibus emptis pro magistro Waltero Metford magistro Simon Sydenham Johanne Gaweyn Thoma Bonham Georgio Louthorp Thoma Wysebech' et pluribus aliis de famulia domini existentibus apud Sarum ad diversas vices per xii dies in absencia hospicii pro ordinacione facienda p*ur* lent*er*ment ut patet per parcellas iiii li. iii s. ii d. ob.

Gentiles xxiiii Valecti garciones lxxv Summa ferculorum iiii^{xx}xix

Extranii xxxviii

403 MS 'xiiiii d.': total is £4. 14*d*.

Die sabbati xxviii Maii Panteria Expenduntur Cxlviii panes[404] unde pro ferculis iiii^{xx}xix trencheris iii liberacionibus iiii coquine xv canibus vii rewardis xviii. Et remanent lii panes. Celarium Expenduntur vi lag. vini de precomputato. Butillaria Expenduntur lviii lag. cervisie. Et remanent DCxliiii lag. cervisie. Coquina Expenduntur ii pisces salsii de stauro. In v piscibus salciis emptis vi s. iii d. In ii congris salciis iii s. iiii d. In C makerell emptis ii s. In i thornebak empto xii d. In xii mulett*es* emptis v s. vi d. In i baas empto ix d. In shrimp x d. In cokkes iiii d. In portagio iii d. In iiii lopsters ii s. et expensis. Candelaria Expenduntur ii lib. candelarum de stauro. Stabulum Fenum pro xl equis iiii hakeneis de stauro. In avenis pro eisdem ii qr. iiii bus.
In vadiis Thome Ferro*ur* apud Remesbur' et alibi tam pro se quam pro equo suo in negociis domini vi s.
In vadiis Bathe ibidem per x dies capientis per diem ii d. xx d.
In vadiis pagetti Tidemerssh' ibidem per idem tempus xv d.
In vadiis pagetti Restewold ibidem per idem tempus xv d.
In vadiis pagetti Hulcot ibidem per idem tempus xv d.
In vadiis pagetti Faucon*er* ibidem per iiii dies vi d.
In vadiis pagetti Lovell' ibidem per xviii dies ii s. iiii d.
In vadiis Forrey ibidem per iii die*s* capientis per diem i d. ob. iiii d. ob.
Probatur Summa empcionum vi li. i d. unde
Panteria De precomputato. Celarium Vinum de remanentia. Butillaria <In> De precomputato. Coquina Empciones xxii s. iii d. Candelaria De stauro. Stabulum Fenum avene de stauro. Preteria iiii li. iii s. ii d. ob. Vadia xiiii s. vii d. ob.
[*f.63r*] *Sarum Gentiles xxxvi Valecti garciones iiii^{xx}x Summa ferculorum Cxxvi*
Extranii Covyntr' se ii^{o} et alii xliiii. Episcopus Wynton' cum familia in potacione
Die dominica xxix Maii Panteria Furniuntur per ii tallias iii qr. iii bus. frumenti de stauro que respondent de DCiiii^{xx}ix panibus. Et expenduntur CCxx panes unde pro ferculis Cxxvi panes trencheris vi liberacionibus v coquine xxviii canibus vii rewardis xlviii panes. Et remanent Dxxi panes. Celarium Expenduntur xii lag. vini de precomputato. Butillaria Expenduntur iiii^{xx}iiii lag. cervisie. Et remanent Dlx lag. cervisie. Coquina Expenduntur <di. bovis v casse multonum de precomputato.> In i carcosio bovis empto xx s. et expenditur di. In vi cassis multonum emptis xii s. vi d. et expenduntur v. In i carcosio vituli empto et expenso iii s. In di. porco empto et expenso ii s. In iiii porcellis emptis et expensis ii s. iiii d. In iiii duodenis columbarum emptis ii s. In xii pulcinis xx d. In portagio iiii d.

404 146 loaves disbursed.

\ Item iiii capones. / In vi lag. lactis vi d. et expensis. Candelaria Expenduntur ii lib. candelarum de stauro. Stabulum Fenum pro xl equis iiii hakeneis de stauro. In avenis pro eisdem ii qr. iiii bus. avenarum.

Probatur Summa empcionum xliiii s. iiii d.

Panteria Furniuntur iii qr. \ iii bus. / frumenti que respondent ad viCiiii^{xx}ix panes. Celarium Vinum de remanentia. Butillaria De precomputato. Coquina Empciones xliiii s. iiii d. Candelaria De stauro. Stabulum Fenum avene de stauro.

Gentiles xxxii Valecti garciones iiii^{xx} *Summa ferculorum Cxii*

Extranii dominus Robertus Bussh' se iiii^{to} *Beckote se ii*^{o} *Metford se ii*^{o} *et alii lv*

Die lune xxx^{mo} Maii Panteria Expenduntur CCx panes unde pro ferculis Cxii trencheris viii liberacionibus v coquine xvi canibus vii rewardis lxii. Et remanent CCCCi panes.[405] Celarium Expenduntur viii lag. vini de precomputato. Butillaria Expenduntur lxviii lag. cervisie. Et remanent CCCCxxxv lag. cervisie.[406] Coquina Expenduntur di. carcosium bovis i bacon' iiii capones vi pulcini de empto. Item i cassa multonis de precomputato. Item in iii cassis multonum emptis et expensis vi s. vi d. Candelaria Expenduntur ii lib. candelarum de stauro. Stabulum Fenum pro xl equis iii hakeneis de stauro. In avenis ii qr. iiii bus. avenarum.

Probatur Summa empcionum vi s. vi d.

Panteria De precomputato. Celarium Vinum de stauro. Butillaria De precomputato. Coquina Empciones vi s. vi d. Candelaria De stauro. Stabulum Fenum avene de stauro.

[*f.63v*] *Sarum Gentiles xxx Valecti garciones lxv Summa ferculorum iiii*^{xx}*xv*

Extranii soror domini se iiii^{to} *Robertus Hunte se ii*^{o} *Thomas Germayn se ii*^{o} *Becok' Metford Robertus Bussh' se iii*^{o} *ii fratres et alii extranii xxxii*

Die martis ultimo Maii Panteria Expenduntur Cxliiii panes unde pro ferculis iiii^{xx}xv trencheris vi liberacionibus v coquine xxi canibus vii rewardis x. Et remanent CClvii panes. Celarium Expenduntur iiii lag. vini de precomputato. Butillaria Expenduntur lviii lag. cervisie. Et remanent CCClxxvii lag. cervisie. Coquina Expenduntur in carnibus bovinis xix s. In v cassis multonum xi s. ii d. In i carcosio di. vitulorum iiii s. viii d. In iiii porcellis emptis ii s. vi d. In xii pulcinis emptis ii s. In ii lag. <lactis ii d.> diversorum sals*ament*orum emptis xiiii d. et expensis. Candelaria Expenduntur ii lib. candelarum de stauro. Stabulum Fenum pro xliiii equis ii hakeneis de stauro. In avenis pro eisdem ii qr. iiii bus.

Probatur Summa empcionum xl s. vi d.

Panteria De precomputato. Celarium Vinum de remanentia. Butillaria De

[405] 311 loaves should remain.

[406] 492 gallons should remain.

precomputato. Coquina Empciones xl s. vi d. Candelaria De stauro. Stabulum Fenum avene de stauro.

[*f.64r*] *Sarum Gentiles xxxi Valecti garciones iiii*^{xx}*x Summa ferculorum Cxxi*
Extranii soror domini se iiii^{o} *Robertus Hunte se ii*^{o} *Thomas Germayn' se ii*^{o}
Metford Beckot et alii extranii xlv

Die mercurie primo <Julii> \ Junii / Panteria Expenduntur CClvii panes unde pro ferculis Cxxi trencheris vi liberacionibus v coquine xviii canibus vii rewardis C panes. Et remanent nichil. Celarium Expenduntur vi lag. vini de precomputato. Butillaria Expenduntur lxiiii lag. cervisie. Et remanent CCCxiii lag. cervisie. Coquina <Expend*un*tur> In v piscibus salsiis v s. x d. In i congro salsio empto xii d. In C makerell <salsiis emptis xii d.> In C makerell salciis ii s. In v mulett*es* <emptis> et i baas emptis iii s. In i congro recenti empto iii s. In xiii plais emptis xvi d. In iii crabbes emptis xviii d. In di. salmone recenti empto iii s. In iii lag. lactis iii d. In butiro ii d. In portagio iii d. Candelaria Expenduntur ii lib. candelarum. Stabulum Fenum pro xlviii equis ii hakeneis de stauro. In avenis pro eisdem ii qr. avenarum.

Probatur Summa empcionum xxi s. iiii d.

Panteria De precomputato. Celarium Vinum de stauro. Butillaria De precomputato. Coquina Empciones xxi s. iiii d. Candelaria De stauro. Stabulum Fenum avene de stauro.

Gentiles xl Valecti garciones lxxv Summa ferculorum Cxv
Extranii lxx

Die jovis secundo <Julii> \ Junii / Panteria Furniuntur per iii tallias vii qr. frumenti de stauro que respondent de MCCCCxiiii panibus. Et expenduntur Clx panes unde pro ferculis Cxv panes trencheris x liberacionibus iiii coquina viii canibus x rewardis xiii panes. Et remanent MDlxvi panes.[407] Celarium Expenduntur x lag. vini de remanentia. Butillaria Expenduntur iiii^{xx} lag. cervisie. Et remanent CCxxxiii lag. cervisie. Coquina[408] Expenduntur i bacon' de stauro i qr. di. bovis vii casse multonum. In i carcosio vituli empto iii s. ii d. In iii porcellis xviii d. In xii pulcinis xxi d. In albo pinguedine ii s. ii d. In di. porco empto xxii d. In xvi rabettis emptis ii s. iiii d. \ et expensis. / In C caponibus emptis xxxvii s. vi d. et expenduntur xxiiii. Candelaria Expenduntur iiii <lag.> lib. Stabulum Fenum pro xlix equis. In avenis iii qr. vii bus.

Probatur Summa empcionum l s. iii d.

Panteria Furniuntur vii qr. frumenti que respondent . . . . . Celarium Vinum de remanentia. Butillaria De precomputato. Coquina Empciones . . . . . Candelaria De stauro. Stabulum Fenum avene . . . . .

[407] 1254 loaves should remain.
[408] MS omits underline.

[*f.64v*] *Sarum Gentiles xxxi Valecti garciones iiii*^{xx} *Summa ferculorum Cxi*
Extranii lxx
Die veneris tercio Junii Panteria Expenduntur Clx panes[409] unde pro ferculis Cxi panes trencheris viii liberacionibus vi coquina iiii canibus v rewardis xxxvi panes. Et remanent Miiii^{xx}xiii panes.[410] Celarium Expenduntur viii lag. vini de stauro. Butillaria Expenduntur lxxiiii lag. cervisie. Et remanent Clvii lag. cervisie. Coquina <Exp> In vi piscibus salsiis emptis vii s. In C makerell salsiis ii s. ii d. In xi congris poudris ix s. In vi bremes ix makerell emptis ii s. viii d. In v mulett*es* ii baas iii s. v d. In vi lag. lactis vi d. In butiro iii d. In crem iii d. In i lag. aceti vii d. In di. lag. cenapii iii d. ob. et expensa. Candelaria Expenduntur vii lib. candelarum de stauro. Stabulum[411] Fenum pro xlii[412] equis. In avenis ii qr. iiii bus.
Probatur Summa empcionum xxvi s. i d. ob.
Panteria De precomputato. Celarium De stauro. Butillaria De precomputato. Coquina Empciones xxvi s. i d. ob. Candelaria De stauro. Stabulum Fenum avene de stauro.
Gentiles li Valecti garciones iiii^{xx}*xii Summa Cxliii*
Extranii lxx
Die sabbati iiii^{o} Junii Panteria Expenduntur CCxx panes unde pro ferculis Cxliii panes trencheris xvi liberacionibus viii coquina vi canibus v rewardis xlii panes. Et remanent DCCClxxiii panes. Celarium Expenduntur xx lag. vini de stauro. Butillaria Expenduntur C lag. cervisie. Et remanent lvii lag. cervisie. Coquina <Expend*un*tur> In vi piscibus salsiis emptis vii s. In C makerell salsiis ii s. In i congro salcio xxii d. In i congro recenti iii s. viii d. In iiii mulett*es* iii baas emptis iiii s. \ et expensis. / In viii crabb*es* emptis iiii s. x d. In i trught empto xi d. In menues emptis xii d. In scrimpes viii d. In cocules viii d. In lacte iii d. In portagio iii d. In iii congris di. salciis emptis vi s. iii d. In iii congris recentibus v s. In portagio i d. Et expenduntur preter iiii crabbes. Candelaria Expenduntur iiii lib. candelarum. Stabulum Fenum pro iiii^{xx}vi equis ii hakeneis de stauro. In avenis iiii qr. ii bus.
Probatur Summa empcionum xxxviii s. v d.
Panteria De precomputato. Celarium Vinum de stauro. Butillaria De precomputato. Coquina Empciones xxxviii s. v d. Candelaria De stauro. Stabulum Fenum avene de stauro.
[*f.65r*] *Sarum Gentiles lxviii Valecti garciones iiii*^{xx}*xix Summa ferculorum Clxvii*
Extranii C

409 170 loaves disbursed.
410 If the previous figure for the remainder is discounted, 1094 loaves should remain.
411 MS omits underline.
412 MS ‘xlxii’.

Die dominica v^{o} Junii Panteria Expenduntur CCC panes unde pro ferculis Clxvii panes trencheris xvi liberacionibus viii coquina v canibus v rewardis iiii^{xx}xix panes. Et remanent Dlxxiii panes. Celarium Expenduntur xx lag. vini.[413] Butillaria In xxvii coules cervisie et vii lag. emptis de Furbo*ur* per ii tallias continentibus CCC<lxxviii>\ iiii^{xx}v / lag. cervisie precium cuiuslibet coule xviii d. xli s. v d. ob. In Diiii lag. cervisie emptis de Longbruer per ii tallias continentibus xxxvi coules precium coule xviii d. liiii s. In ii cole cervisie emptis de eodem ii s. Et expenduntur Cxx lag. cervisie. Et remanent DCCCxxvi lag. cervisie. Coquina In carnibus bovinis emptis et expensis ix s. In iiii carcosiis vitulorum emptis et expensis xii s. In xxiiii pulcinis emptis iii s. x d. In xx rabettis emptis et expensis iii s. ix d. In vi lag. lactis vi d. In xxxvi columbellis emptis xviii d. In portagio iii d. Item expenduntur xxiiii capones de stauro. Stabulum[414] Fenum pro iiii^{xx} et xiiii equis. In avenis iiii qr. vi bus.

Probatur Summa empcionum vi li. viii s. iii d. ob.

Panteria De precomputato. Celarium Vinum de remanentia. Butillaria In ixCxvii lag. cervisie iiii li. xvii s. v d. ob. Coquina Empciones xxx s. x d. Candelaria[415] Stabulum[416]

Gentiles CC Valecti garciones CCx Summa ferculorum CCCCx

Die lune vi^{o} Junii Panteria Furniuntur per iii tallias viii qr. di. frumenti que respondent ad MDCCxxxv panes. Et expenduntur DCCCC[417] panes unde pro ferculis CCCCx panes trencheris xl liberacionibus xl coquina Clx canibus x rewardis CCxl[418] panes. Et remanent MDCCCviii panes. Celarium Expenduntur xl lag. vini.[419] Butillaria Expenduntur CCC lag. cervisie. Et remanent D <lag.> xxvi lag. cervisie. Coquina Expenduntur iii qr. bovis de stauro emptis die sequenti. Item expenduntur de precomputato lx capones xxiiii pulcini de precomputato. Item expenduntur x casse multonum de stauro. Candelaria Expenduntur vi lib. candelarum de stauro. Stabulum Fenum pro Cxx equis. In avenis vi qr. avenarum.

Summa nichil quia de precomputato

Panteria Furniuntur viii qr. di. . . . . . Celarium Vinum de stauro. Butillaria De precomputato. Coquina Empciones nichil. Candelaria De stauro. Stabulum Fenum avene . . . . .

413 MS 'cervisie', followed by 'E'.

414 MS omits underline.

415 Followed by a blank space in MS.

416 Followed by a blank space in MS.

417 MS 'CCCCC'.

418 This figure possibly deleted in MS.

419 MS 'cervisie'.

[*f.65v*] *Sarum*

P*ur* lent*er*ment

Fercula Gentiles MCCC Valecti garciones Cl Summa ferculorum MCCCCl Extranii episcopus Norwyc' se xxiiii° *J.suffraganus se vi° dominus Johannes Drayton' se xii° Henricus Popham se xii° prior de Motfont se x° soror domini se xii° domina de Cary se xii° Wroghton' se xii° Edmundus Spersholt Item decanus Sarum cum xiii canonicis vicariis omnibus aliis officiariis ecclesie Sarum Dominus Ivo Fitzwarin Item maior Sarum cum omnibus burgencibus ibidem Rous se iiii° Calston' se vi° Hulcot se vi° Becot se iiii° Becot junior se iiii° R.Hunt se iiii° dominus de Wyke se iii° dominus de Larkestok se iii° magister del hospital Latton se iiii° ..... se iiii° ..... se iiii° ..... se iiii° ..... iiii° ..... domini*

Die martis vii° Junii Panteria Furniuntur per vi tallias xii qr. frumenti que respondent ad MMCCCCxlvi panes. Et expenduntur MMDCCxlvi panes unde pro ferculis MCCCCl panes trencheris iiii^{xx} liberacionibus xx coquina C canibus v panes rewardis Miiii^{xx}xi panes. Et remanent MDviii panes. Celarium[420] Expend*un*tur[421] vini de stauro. Butillaria In lxxv lag. cervisie de Waltero Cooke per i talliam continentibus v coules precium coule xviii d. vii s. vi d. In lvi lag. cervisie emptis de eodem per dictam talliam continentibus iiii coules precium coule xii d. iiii s. Item in iiii^{xx}iiii lag. cervisie emptis de Thoma Holme per i talliam continentibus vi coules precium coule xviii d. ix s. In iii coles emptis de eodem continentibus xlii lag. iii s. In Cxv lag. cervisie emptis de Roberto Galon' per i talliam continentibus viii coules et iii lag. precium coule xviii d. xii s. iiii d. ob. Et expenduntur viiCi lag. cervisie. Et remanent Ciiii^{xx}iii lag. cervisie. Coquina In x carcossiis boum emptis precium pecie xix s. ix li. x s. et expenduntur viii carcosia di. In \iiii^{xx}/xii cassis multonum emptis et expensis ix li. xi s. viii d. In xxxv carcosiis vitulorum emptis precium pecie iii s. Cv s. et expensis. Item expenduntur xliii casse multonum de stauro. Item expenduntur lxi porci de stauro. In CCCxli aucis emptis precium capitis ii d. ob. lxxi s. ob. In xxx aucis emptis precium pecie iii d. vii s. vi d. In CCx aucis emptis per prepositum de Canyng' nichil hic quia per dictum prepositum et expenduntur CCCCiiii^{xx}i auce.[422] In CCC caponibus emptis precium capitis v d. vi li. v s. In CCCC caponibus emptis precium capitis vi d. x li. In xliiii caponibus precium capitis vi d. xxii s. In lx caponibus emptis precium pecie vii d. xxxv s. In viii caponibus emptis precium pecie viii d. v s. iiii d. In xxx caponibus emptis[423] apud Shirbo*ur*ne xxvi s. In xl gallinis

[420] MS omits underline.
[421] Followed by a blank space in MS.
[422] MS 'auci'.
[423] MS repeats 'empt''.

emptis precium pecie ii d. ob. viii s. iiii d. In xxxix gallinis emptis precium pecie ii d. vi s. vi d. In vii ardeis emptis apud Remesbur' precium pecie ix d. cum ii s. pro cariagio vii s. iii d. In xx ardeis emptis apud Wymbo*ur*ne precium cuiuslibet viii d. xiii s. iiii d. In viii egerett*es* emptis precium capitis v d. iii s. iiii d. In sustentacione eorundem ibidem per vii dies <una cum expensis> una cum expensis Radulphi de Butery equitantis per ii vices pro cariagio eorum de ibidem usque Sarum iiii s. v d. In Cxxvi rabettis precium cuiuslibet iii d. xxxi s. vi d. In CCxlii porcellis emptis ad diversa precia ut patet in parvo papiro de empcionibus vi li. ix s. vii d. In viiiMDCCxl ovis emptis precium <CC> C^{ne} v d. ob. xxxix s. iiii d. ob. et expensis. In lxii casiis emptis xxi s. In Cxl lag. lactis xi s. viii d. In xvii lag. creme emptis xvii s. In iiii qr. ii bus. salis xxiii s. iiii d. In di. bus. farine avenarum emptis vi d. In xvii lag. verjuc*e* iiii s. i d. In viii lag. cenapii iiii s. viii d. In allio iiii d. Item in xxix lag. lactis emptis ii s. v d. In xxvi lib. albi pinguedinis ii s. ii d. In expensis Galfridi equitantis in patria pro dictis victualibus emendis xi s. In iii bus. pisarum viridum emptis London' per R.Cooke cum xx d. pro cariagio v s. viii d. In lxiii columbellis <iii>\ xx / s. i d. In iii qr. brasii emptis pro pullettria sustinenda xii s. Et expenduntur preter Cx capones C auce lxvii porcelli. Candelaria Expenduntur viii lib. candelarum. Stabulum Fenum pro Cxl equis de stauro. In avenis vii qr.

Probatur Summa empcionum lxviii li. xv s. vii d. ob.

Panteria Furniuntur xii qr. frumenti que respondent ad MMiiiiCxlvi panes. Celarium Vinum de stauro. Butillaria In CCClxxii lag. cervisie xxxv s. x d. ob. Coquina Empciones lxvi li. xix s. ix d. Candelaria De stauro. Stabulum Fenum avene de stauro.

[*f.66r*][424] *Sarum Gentiles Ciii Valecti garciones CCl Summa ferculorum CCCliii*

Extranii CClx

Die mercurie viii° Junii Panteria Expenduntur D panes unde pro ferculis CCCliii trencheris xx liberacionibus xiiii coquina vi canibus iiii rewardis Ciii panes. Et remanent Mviii panes. Celarium Expenduntur xii lag. vini de stauro. Butillaria In lxx lag. cervisie emptis de Waltero Or*um* per i talliam continentibus v coules precium coule xviii d. vii s. vi d. In i coule cervisie empto de eodem xii d. In Cxx lag. cervisie emptis de Foystour per i talliam continentibus viii coules et viii lag. precium coule xviii d. xiii s. Et expenduntur Clviii lag. cervisie. <Coquina> Et remanent CCxxviii lag. cervisie. *De empcione Clviii s.*[425] Coquina Expenduntur <E> iii qr. bovis viii casse multonum xx capones xxxiiii auce x porcelli de precomputato. In

[424] At the top of the page, towards the right, in a small hand, '$Ciiii^{xx}xv$'.
[425] In right margin.

vi piscibus salciis emptis[426] et expensis vii s. In vii congris salciis emptis et expensis ix s. ix d. In C makerell salciis emptis ii s. In v mullett*es* i baas recentibus emptis et expensis iii s. iiii d. In i thornebak empto viii d. In i congro recenti ii s. In iii <th> trught*es* xii d. In viii baas et mulett*es* xiiii d. In menues xvi d. In vi lopsters ii s. In lacte xvi d. In butiro iiii d. In portagio iii d. et expenduntur. Candelaria[427] Expenduntur iiii lib. candelarum. Stabulum Fenum pro lx equis. In avenis iii qr.

Probatur Summa empcionum liii s. viii d. unde

Panteria De precomputato. Celarium De <remanentia> stauro. Butillaria In CCiiii lag. cervisie. xxi s. vi d. *iii s.*[428] Coquina Empciones xxxii s. ii d. Candelaria De stauro. Stabulum Fenum avene de stauro.

Gentiles lxxiiii Valecti garciones Cl Summa ferculorum CCxxiiii
Extranii Cxiiii

Die jovis ix^{o} Junii Panteria Expenduntur CCC panes unde pro ferculis CCxxiiii trencheris x liberacionibus v coquina iii canibus v rewardis liii panes. Et remanent DCCiiii^{xx}iiii panes.[429] Celarium Expenduntur xxiiii lag. vini. Butillaria Expenduntur Cxx lag. cervisie. Et remanent Cviii lag. cervisie. Coquina Expenduntur iii qr. bovis viii casse multonum xxvi capones xxxix auce xv porcelli de precomputato. In carnibus bovinis emptis xviii d. In ii cassis multonum emptis iiii s. iiii d. In ii carcossiis vitulorum emptis vii s. In portagio ii d. Et expenduntur. *Cxx s.*[430] Candelaria Expenduntur ii lib. candelarum de stauro. Stabulum Fenum pro xxx equis v hakeneis. In avenis ii qr. avenarum.

Probatur Summa empcionum xiii s.

Panteria De precomputato. Celarium Vinum de stauro. Butillaria De precomputato. Coquina Empciones xiii . . . Candelaria De stauro. Stabulum Fenum avene de stauro.

[*f.66v*] *Sarum Gentiles l Valecti garciones iiii^{xx} Summa ferculorum Cxxx*
Extranii [431]

Die veneris x^{o} Junii Panteria Expenduntur CCxl panes unde pro ferculis Cxxx panes trencheris x liberacionibus iiii coquina v canibus v rewardis iiii^{xx}vi panes. Et remanent Dxliiii panes \ qui liberantur magistro Waltero M. per manus H.Buteler. / Celarium Expenduntur xxx lag. vini de stauro. Butillaria Expenduntur lxx lag. cervisie. Et remanent xxxviii lag. cervisie \ que liberantur magistro W.M. per H.Buteler. / Coquina <Expend*un*tur>[432]

[426] MS adds 'et empt''.
[427] MS omits underline.
[428] In right margin.
[429] 708 loaves should remain.
[430] In right margin.
[431] Followed by a blank space in MS.
[432] In right margin: 'CC'.

In vi piscibus salciis emptis vii s. vi d. In iiii congris salsiis vi s. In xiiii plais iii s. viii d. In i congro recenti iii s. iiii d. In v mullett*es* v baas emptis v s. In ii thornebak*es* emptis xx d. In iii crabb*es* xx d. In Cl makerell iii s. In lacte vi d. In butiro iiii d. <In> Et expenduntur. In portagio iii d. In i baas empto et expenso xii d. *lxxv s.*[433]

Probatur Summa xxxiii s. xi d.

Panteria De precomputato. Celarium De precomputato. Butillaria De precomputato. Coquina Empciones xxxiii s. xi d. Candelaria De stauro. Stabulum[434]

Die sabbati xi^{o} Junii in victualibus emptis ut patet in parvo papiro pro magistro Waltero Metford et aliis in hospicio suo apud Sarum xxi s. iii d.

Probatur Summa xxi s. iii d.

In vadiis Thome Ferro*ur* apud Remesbur' per iii dies mense Junii capientis per diem iii d. ix d.

In vadiis Bath' ibidem a primo die Junii usque xi diem eiusdem utroque computato xxii d.

In vadiis pagetti sororis domini ibidem per idem tempus pagetti Tydemerssh' et pagetti senescalli per idem tempus quilibet capiens per diem i d. ob. iiii s. i d. ob.

In vadiis Roberti Baker apud Wodeford pro[435] pane furniendo tam pro hospicio quam p*ur* lent*er*ment per ix dies capientis per diem iii d. ii s. iii d.

In vadiis Rogeri Swayne ibidem per xx dies videlicet toto tempore quo hospicium erat apud Sarum iii s. iiii d.

In vadiis Prior ibidem per x dies adiuvantis eisdem Rogero et Roberto ibidem capientis per diem ii d. xx d.

Probatur Summa vadiorum xiii s. xi d. ob.

[*f.67r*] *Pret*eri*a* In diversis expensis factis p*ur* lent*er*ment et aliis neccessariis ultra expensas factas[436] die martis proximo precedenti et alibi

In primis solutum xxxix cocis conductis p*ur* lenterment laborantibus per iii dies circa diversa officia in coquina ad diversa saliria ut patet per billam parcellarum lix s. vi d.

Item pro meiremio et cordis p*ur* lez hales videlicet pur le hastr' p*ur* lez dresso*urs* et p*ur* le squilery conductis vi s. viii d.

Item in viii schroudes conductis de Pynok' et Chipenham pro coopertura eorundem viii s.

Item in i shroude de canevas perdit*o* continenti xxx ulnas empt*o* de Pinok' x s.

433 In right margin.

434 Followed by a blank space in MS. No stable account this day.

435 MS 'per'.

436 MS 'faac''.

Item in xviii fates xxiiii cuvis conductis pro coquina per Walterum Cooke vi s.
Item in xxx spites ferri et i magno plumbo conductis per eundem vii s. iiii d.
Item in iii hominibus conductis pro spites et vasis mundandis in coquina per iiii dies xvi d.
In iii novis scoupes emptis pro coquina xvi d.
In x pipis vacuis emptis de Sherley pro cervisia imponenda una cum circulis ligneis emptis pro emendacione eorundem per Henricum Buteler xvii s. iiii d.
Item CCiiii^{xx}vii ollis luteis emptis pro butillaria et celario per Henricum Buteler cum vi d. pro expensis eiusdem equitantis pro eisdem xiii s. iii d.
Item in CCC ciphis fraxini emptis xv s.
Item in CC ciphis fraxini emptis ix s.
Item in expensis dicti Henrici existentis apud Sarum pro ordinacione facienda tam pro hospicio quam p*ur* lent*er*ment per ii septimanas cum equo suo iiii s. ii d.
In stipendiis i hominis adiuvantis eidem Henrico in butillaria per ii dies iiii d.
Item in expensis equ*orum* Rogeri Cooke Roberti de Camera Henrici Buteler et Willelmi Shirwode existentium in villa per vii dies causa multidudinis extraniorum in palacio domini v s. iiii d.
In iiiiMCC platellis discis et sauceriis conductis de Johanne Mate dando pro tribus C^{nis} ii s. xxviii s.
Item solutum pro CCC discis platellis et sauceriis perditis videlicet per iii pecias i d. viii s. iiii d.
Item in xxvi treis conductis de eodem pro coquina ii s. vi d.
Item solutum Johanni Ferro*ur* pro lxv ferris equinis et xlv remosionibus dando pro xx peciis iii s. iiii d. quolibet remocione ob. xii s. x d.
Item solutum Hindon' de Sarum pro cariagio DCxiiii lib. diversorum neccessariorum videlicet specierum panni linei et aliorum dando pro C^{na} xx d. x s. ii d.
Item in expensis equorum Nicholai Cap*er*on' apud Sarum ut in feno empto pro eisdem in villa ibidem ii s. v. . . . .
Item in rewardo facto servienti manerii de Wodeford pro eorum labore adiuvantium Roberto Baker in pistrina ibidem et cariancium panem usque Sarum p*ur* lent*er*ment . . . . .
In lect*is* conduct*is* ibidem pro Roberto Baker Rogero Swayne et Willelmo Prior ibidem ut patet \ supra / in vadiis . . . . .
In expensis Radulphi de Butery equitantis in patria per iiii dies pro providencia facienda p*ur* lent*er*ment una cum expensis equi eiusdem in villa per vi dies causa extraniorum in palacio . . . . .
In expensis Galfridi <Ca> Chariet*er* et garcionis sui cum chariett*e* et vii

equis per vices pro vino cariando de Pot*er*ne usque Sarum una cum expensis carect*arum* de Pot*er*ne Canyng' ..... cariancium harnesium famulie hospicii usque Sarum eundo et rediundo per x dies .....
Item in[437] emendacione cerure domus pullettrie per Clav*er*ing' .....
Item solutum ii hominbus de Pot*er*ne adiuvantibus eidem in le squiler' .....
Item in i patella conducta per Clav*er*ing' p*ur* le squiler' .....
Item solutum cuidam homini de Vise per G.[438] custodienti pullettriam vi d.
[*f.67v*] Item solutum Foxton' et Thome Botuler ut de rewardo facto eisdem pro eorum expensis de London usque Sarum v s. iiii d.
In expensis ii carectariorum cum carect*is* manerii de Shirbo*ur*ne usque Sarum cum vicualibus ii s. vi d.
In ii carectariis de Pot*er*ne cariantibus aucas de ibidem usque Sarum xii d.
In expensis i carectarii de <ca> Canyng' cum carect*a* et iiii equis de ibidem usque Sarum cum caponibus et aliis victualibus una cum stipendiis i hominis et iii equorum per iiii dies vii s. ob.
Item in expensis ii carectariorum de Berdon' cum carect*is* manerii et vii equis cariancium dam*os* rabettos et heronsues de ibidem usque Sarum ii s.
xii li. vii s. vi d.
iii li. ob.
[*f.9r*][439]

Empciones cere cum factura

In primis in CCiii qr. iii lib. cere emptis London' per Nicholaum Cap*er*on' precium C^{e} xlviii s. iiii d. vi li. xiiii s. ii d.
In xliii lib. lichini emptis[440] pro torches tortis tortis de <brok> broch' precium lib. ii d. vii s. ii d.
Item in vi lib. lichini emptis pro parvis candelis inde faciendis precium lib. iii d. xviii d.
Item solutum Johanni Paynto*ur* de la Vise pro CCxxxviii lib. cere factis ut in viii torches xii tortys xxiiii tortis de broch' xl preket*es* vi bundellis de perchers xvii bundellis parvarum candelarum pro capella et xii tapers danti pro factura lib. ob. ix s. xi d.
Item in vii lib. di. de weke emptis per Galfridum pro candelis de coton inde faciendis mense Novembris ii s. v d.
Pro festo Purificacionis et Pasche In xxxi lib. lichini emptis de Johanne

437 MS omits 'in'.
438 Possibly 'C.'
439 f. 9 is a singleton, bound out of place, which originally formed a part of the section (and possibly separate book) for bulk purchases, now ff. 68–80. Its exact original position is unclear; to judge by the conservation work to the outer edge, it may originally have been bound the other way round, with f. 9^{v} preceding f. 9^{r}.
440 MS 'emt''.

Peynto*ur* de le Vyse unde xxviii lib. precii lib. ii d. et iii lib. precii lib. iii d. pro torch*es* tortys et parvis candelis et tapers v s. v d.
Item solutum eidem Johanni pro vi torch*es* iiii tortys uno pascall' viii tortys de broche Cxxviii tapers vi bundellis perch*ers* faciendis de cera domini ponderanti Ciiii^{xx}i lib. pro lib. ob. vii s. vii d. ob.
[*f.9v*]

Empciones specierum

In primis in xviii lib. piperis emptis precium lib. xi d. xvi s. vi d. In ii lib. saffran emptis precium lib. xii s. iiii d. xxiiii s. viii d. In ii xii lib. zinzeberis emptis precium lib. xviii d. xviii s. vi d. In xiii lib. canelle emptis precium lib. xiii d. xiiii s. i d. In ii lib. cloves emptis v s. iiii d. In xii lib. resing*es* de Cor' iiii s. vi d. In xii lib. dat*es* emptis ii s. vi d. In ii lib. saundres emptis[441] ii s. ii d. In C lib. amigdolarum emptis xxii s. In xii lib. ris vi d. In ii lib. anis emptis vi d. In iii lib. comyn ix d. In ii lib. liquoris emptis ii d. In xii lib. sugr*e* emptis xvii s. In i lib. maces empta vi s. In i qr. almondes empto de Castelton' vi s. In i lib. di. saundres emptis de eodem ii s. iiii d. Item C lib. amigdolarum Jardein emptis London' per Galfridum Cato*ur* xxv s. Item in C lib. amigdolarum Valenc' emptis ibidem per eundem xviii s. Item in xii lib. piperis emptis ibidem per eundem xii s. In x lib. ging*eberis* emptis ibidem per eundem xviii s. vi d. In xl lib. dat*es* emptis ibidem per eundem precium lib. ii d. iii qua. ix s. ii d. In xx lib. sugr*e* emptis xl s. In ii lib. saundres emptis ibidem per eundem ii s. vi d. In ii lib. clowes emptis ibidem per eundem v s. iiii d. In[442] i lib. <dat*es*> \ di. mac*es* / emptis apud Pot*er*ne per Nicholaum ix s. Item solutum Johanni Colyn pro notemuk' et aliis per ipsum emptis apud Sarum pro domino x d. In iii lib. licoris emptis apud Vise per Nicholaum vi d. In iiii lib. i qr. sugr*e* emptis apud Hampton per Hubertum precium lib. ii s. viii s. vi d. In ii lib. licor*is* emptis[443] apud Hampton' per eundem iii d. In di. lib. pulveris zinziberis empta xii d. In i lib. piperis empta xi d. ob. In C di. et vii lib. amigdolarum Jardein emptis xxxvii s. vi d. In lxvi lib. reys*ins* de Malik' emptis precium lib. ii d. xi s. In i lib. i qr. anis comfit xx d.
Pur lenterment per N.C. Summa lii s. i d. ob.
Quia per Johannem Wotton <In xvi lib. pep*er* emptis London' per Johannem Wotton' precium lib. xi d. ob. xv s. iiii d. In viii lib. ging*eberis* emptis ibidem precium lib. ii s. xvi s. In iiii lib. saffran emptis ibidem precium lib. xv s. lx s. In xii lib. canelle emptis ibidem precium lib. xiiii d. xiiii s. In vi lib. clows precium lib. ii s. vii d. xv s. vi d. In xii lib. saunders precium lib. xiiii d. xiiii s. In iiii lib. maces precium lib. vi s. xxiiii s. In iiii^{xx}

[441] MS repeats 'empt''.
[442] MS repeats 'In'.
[443] MS repeats 'emp''.

lib. reys*ins* de Cor' precium lib. iiii d. xxvi s. viii d. In CC lib. dat*es* precium C^{e} xviii s. xxxvi s. In \ iiii lib. / pruns[444] emptis precium lib. xvi d. v s. iiii d. In \ Cl lib. / prunes precium lib. vi d. lxxv s. In vii lib. qr. sugr*e* precium lib. ii s. xiiii s. vi d. In vi lib. sugr*e* plate precium lib. xiiii d. vii s. In C de foil' auri iii s. iiii d.>

Quia supra <per N.C.> <In C di. et vii lib. amigdolarum emptis apud Sarum per N.Cap*er*on' xxxvii s. vi d. In lxvi lib. rei*sins* de Malek' precium lib. ii d. xi s. In i lib. i qr. anis confect*is* xx d. In i lib. ging*eberis* empta ii s.>

Item in una pec. fic*orum* empta apud Sarum per Hubertum prima septimana xlme vi s.

In xii lib. dat*es* emptis ibidem per eundem eodem tempore

Item in xii lib. resyns emptis ibidem per eundem

[*f.68r*]

Empciones Frumenti

In primis[445]

[*f.68v*]

Empciones vini

In primis in v pipis vini rubii et i pipa vini <rubii> albi emptis apud Hampton' precium dolii ix li. xiii s. iiii d. xxix li.

In xxxii lag. \ di. / vini emptis per[446] Russell' pro una pipa vini in cariagio inter Pot*er*ne et Sarum defracta inplenda cum viii d. pro circulacione et imposicione capitis eiusdem xxxiii s. iiii d.

Item in vi lag. vini dulcis emptis per eundem die cepulture domini viii s.

Cariagium vini In predictis pipis onerandis in carect*is* cum xii barrys pro capitibus eorundem affirmandis xviii d.

In expensis vi carectariis cum iii carectis et xviii equis de Hampton' usque Pot*er*ne pro predictis vi pipis vini cariandis pro Russell' mense Aprilis cum expensis eiusdem equitantis pro dicto vino emendo ibidem per x dies ad ii vices una cum \ vii s. iiii d. pro / rewardis factis \ vi / carectariis prioris de Motysfonte carentibus dictum vinum de prece xxiiii s. x d.

[*f.69r*]

Empciones boum

In primis in i bove empto de preposito de Lavyngton' per senescallum mense Octobris xvi s.

Item in i bove empto de Johanne Florisse de Pot*er*ne per manus Johannis Carlett' nuper prepositi ibidem xviii s.

In iii bobus emptis de preposito de Shirbo*ur*ne xl s.

[444] MS 'puns'.

[445] The rest of the page is blank. The folio has been cut away, but was probably originally the same size as the rest of the MS.

[446] MS 'pro'.

In ii bobus emptis de preposito de Caundell' precium capitis xxx s. lx s.
*Remanent in custodia dicti Willelmi unde r*espondebit
Item in ii geet*es* emptis <apud> de Willelmo Bower' <pro> apud Westasschton' pro lacte de eisdem habendo pro domino iiii s. viii d.
Empcio ardearum
In viii ardeis emptis de preposito de Caundell' . . . . .
[*f.69v*]

Empciones multonum

In lxiiii multonibus emptis apud Shirbo*ur*ne de preposito ibidem lxiiii s.
[*f.70r*]

Empciones porcorum

In primis in[447]
[*f.70v*] Empciones piscium London' et alibi
In primis in vi^{xx}vi piscibus salc*i*is emptis London' per Nicholaum Cap*er*on' <m> mense Octobris vii li. xviii s. iiii d.
Item in i pipa salmonum salciorum empta apud Bristolliam per Galfridum Catour mense predicto iiii li. xiii s. iiii d.
Item in ii barellis allecis albi emptis London' per Thomam Croxby mense Novembris precium barelli xi s. viii d. xxiii s. iiii d.
Item in iiii cades allecis rubii emptis ibidem per eundem precium cad*e* vii s. viii d. xxx s. viii d.
Item in Cvi stok' emptis ibidem per eundem xxvi s. vi d.
Item in v^{xx}ii piscibus salciis emptis London' per Galfridum Cato*ur* mense Januarii vi li. xiii s. iiii d.
Item in iii barellis allecis albi emptis ibidem precium barelli ix s. vii d. xxviii s. ix d.
Item in iiii cades allecis rubii emptis ibidem per eundem precium cade vi s. viii d. xxvi s. viii d.
Item in CCxl stok' emptis precium C^{ne} xxx s. lx s.
Item in ii ferdekyns de storjon' emptis ibidem per eundem xx<iiii>\ v / s. xi d.
Item in ii cades allecis rubii emptis apud Hampton' per Hubertum xiiii s.
Item in <iii> \ ii / barellis allecis emptis apud Sarum per Hubertum prima septimana xlme xxvi s.
Item in iii cad*es* allecis rubii emptis ibidem per eundem eodem tempore xxiii s.
Item in i barello allecis albi empto per Hubertum apud le Vys xiiii^{o} die Marcii xii s. vi d.
Item in i barello allecis albi empto per Hubertum apud le Vis de Rogero Barbo*ur* xxiiii die Marcii xii s. x d.

[447] The remainder of the page is blank.

Item in ii bunches allii emptis London' per Thomam Croxby mense Novembris x d.
In[448] ii bus. separum emptis ibidem per eundem eodem tempore xx d.
Item in ii bunches allii emptis London' per Galf*ri*dum Cato*ur* mense Januarii viii d.
Item in ii bus. separum emptis ibidem per eundem ii s.
Item in portagio dictorum victualium ibidem emptorum per Galfridum xiii d.
Item in x lag. di. olei emptis London' cum x d. pro i barello ad idem xi s. iiii d.
[*f.71r*] Empciones focalis cum cariagio
In primis in xxviii qr. carbonum emptis apud Wodeford per prepositum ibidem erga[449] adventum domini xxviii s.
Item solutum pro cariagio eorundem de Sarum usque Wodeford per prepositum ibidem ii s. ii d.
Item in factura xi qr. carbonum apud Chetu de meiremio domini dando pro qr. iiii d. iii s. viii d.
Item iii qr. carbonum empta de Willelmo Lacy de Remesbur' de busco suo preposito empt*o* apud Chitue ii s.
Item in i homine conducto cum ii equis pro busco cariando auxilianti carect*as* de Canyng' apud Pot*er*ne pro hospicio per ix dies di. capienti per diem pro se et ii equis predictis vi d. mensibus Februarii et Marcii iiii s. ix d.
In stipendiis ii hominum conductorum per xx dies di. ad <taxham> pro focali prosternendo pro hospicio domini in Pot*er*ne Wode capiencium inter se per diem viii d. ad taxham videlicet usque xix die Aprilis xiii s. viii d.
In stipendiis unius hominis per sex dies pro focali prosternendo apud Larkeborgh' per diem iiii d. ii s.
In stipendiis i hominis pro xvii dies pro focali talliando pro cameris[450] domini ad mensam capientis per diem ii d. ii s. x d.
In ii equis conductis apud Pot*er*ne ad auxiliandum carect*as* manerii cariant*es* buscum pro hospicio per xxi dies capientibus per diem ii d. vii s.
In stipendiis diversis hominum prosternencium boscum \ cariancium[451] / et talliancium pro hospicio ut patet per parcellas in parvo papiro per manus Barlich' prepositi de Pot*er*ne xxxiii s. x d. ob.
Item in stipendiis ii hominum conductorum pro bosco findendo pro camera domini \ per v dies / capiencium per diem iiii d. xx d.

[448] MS repeats 'In'.
[449] MS 'arga'.
[450] MS possibly 'cam'io'.
[451] MS obscure, possibly 'canc''.

Item in stipendiis iii hominum per v dies ii hominum per i diem prosternencium subboscum apud Pot*er*ne capiens quilibet eorum iii d. ob. per diem ad taxham iiii s. xi d. ob.

Empciones carbonum cum factura In primis in factura xv qr. carbonum apud Chitue per Martyn Colier v s.

<In iii qr. carbonum emptis de Willelmo Lacy apud Pot*er*ne ii s.>

Item solutum Johanni Baker de Vise pro factura xx qr. carbonum de bosco domini apud Pot*er*ne vi s. viii d.

Item solutum Martin*o* Colier pro vi qr. carbonum faciendis apud Chitue capienti pro qr. iiii d. ii s.

Item in factura xx qr. carbonum[452] apud Chetue v s.

Item in factura vii qr. iiii bus. carbonum per Martin apud Chetue ii. . . . .

Item solutum eidem pro factura vi qr. iiii bus. apud Pot*er*ne Wode . . . . .

Item solutum Johanni Hull' pro factura xix qr. carbonum <dando> apud Chytew dando pro factura qr. iiii d. . . . . .

Item solutum Johanni Hull' pro factura xxv qr. carbonum apud Chytew pro qr. iiii d. . . . . .

[*f.71v*] Empciones avenarum

In primis in xvi qr. avenarum emptis apud Wodeford per prepositum ibidem precium qr. ii s. iiii d. xxxvii s. iiii d.

In xx qr. avenarum emptis de vicario de Froxfeld precium qr. xxii d. xxxvi s. viii d.

In lx qr. avenarum de Thoma Herry apud Pot*er*ne precii qr. ii s. <lx s.> vi li.

In i qr. vi bus. avenarum emptis apud Vise per Thomam Ferro*ur* ii s. ix d.

<*Memorandum quod debentur cuidam Blakgrove pro avenis \ xx qr. / de eodem emptis xxxiii s. iiii d. De quibus soluti eidem xx s.*>

In lxxiiii qr. vi bus. avenarum emptis apud Remesbur' per Thomam Ferro*ur* vi li. iiii s. vii d.

In ix qr. iiii bus. avenarum emptis per Barlich' xix^{o} die Aprilis per i talliam contra Robertum Baker precium qr. xx d. xv s. x d.

In xvi qr. avenarum emptis per Johannem Barliche precium qr. xx d. xxvi s. viii d.

In xx qr. avenarum emptis per senescallum de Thoma Herreys precium qr. xx d. xxxiii s. iiii d.

In xx qr. avenarum emptis per Johannem Barlich' apud Pot*er*ne precium qr. xx d. xxxiii s. iiii d.

In Cxii qr. i bus. avenarum emptis[453] ad diversa precia in patria ix li. xvi s. i d.

[452] MS 'frum''.
[453] MS repeats 'empt''.

In stramine empto apud Remesbur' per Thomam Ferro*ur* pro litera[454] equorum domini ibidem viii s. iiii d.

[*f.72r*] Empciones feni

In vi carectatis feni emptis per Barlich' ad diversa precia xix die Aprilis xxii s. viii d.

In xiii carectatis feni emptis per Barlich' tempore quo hospicium erat ibidem l s. iii d.

In feno empto per Johannem Barlich prepositum de Pot*er*ne xxi s. vi d.

[*f.72v*] Empciones ferri

In primis in xxx ferris equinis emptis apud Sarum de Johanne Ferrour cum imposicione eorundem et viii removiges mense Octobris v s.

Item in xvi ferri*s* equinis ibidem per Thomam Ferror ii s.

Item in xxiiii ferris equinis emptis ad diversa precia per eundem Thomam xxii d.

Item in DC clavis ferri emptis ibidem per dictum Thomam pro dictis ferris imponendis ii s. ii d.

In MCC lib. ferri emptis apud Bristolliam per Galfridum Cato*ur* xxiiii^{o} die Octobris lvi s.

In ferrura equorum domini et famulie apud Pot*er*ne in absencia Thome Ferour mense Novembris x d.

In i lagamine ferri empta pro i patella magna una cum i skym*er* magno empto pro coquina v s.

Item in ferrura equorum domini in absencia Thome Ferro*ur* xii d.

Item in ferrura equorum domini apud Pot*er*ne et a le Vise in absencia Thome Ferro*ur* ii s. vii d. ob.

Item in ferrura rubii cursarii existentis apud dominium domini Johannis Drayton' una cum medicinis emptis ibidem pro sanacione eiusdem per Forrey ii s. ii d.

Item in cepo empto pro equis domini apud Remesbur' per Thomam Ferro*ur* iiii d.

Item in di. lag. mellis empta ibidem pro eisdem iiii d.

In i lib. elene campane empta ibidem per eundem vi d.

In i lib. ernement empta ibidem cum i lib. vincreke vi d.

In ii qr. carbonum maritimorum emptis de Willelmo Lang' apud Pot*er*ne per Nicholaum v s. iiii d.

In ii qr. ii bus. carbonum maritimorum emptis <ib> apud Remesbur' per T.Ferro*ur* vii s. vi d.

In ii qr. v bus. carbonum maritimorum emptis ibidem per eundem viii s. ix d.

[454] MS 'lite'.

[*f.73r*] Neccessaria

In primis in ii quaternis papiri emptis London' per Nicholaum Cap*er*on' mense Octobris viii d.
Item in i magno papiro et i parvo papiro pro compot*is* hospicii domini ibidem scribendis v s. vi d.
Item in i quaterna papiri empta apud Sarum per Thomam Croxby et iii pellibus pergameni xiii d.
In stipendiis unius cuparii de Sene per unum diem apud Pot*er*ne cum xv circulis ligneis ab eodem emptis pro iii fatys circulandis una cum emendacione aliorum vasorum xx d.
In i nov*o* paille de ligno empt*o* pro pistrina per Robertum Baker' apud Pot*er*ne viii d.
In ii dolobris[455] emptis pro aula per Willelmum Porter mense Novembris viii d.
In viii lib. coton emptis London' per Thomam Croxby pro candelis inde faciendis precium lib. xiii d. viii s. viii d.
Item in xi quarternis papiri emptis ibidem per eundem pro interludiis tempore Natalis Domini inde faciendis ii s. ix d. ob.
Item in i sacco empto ibidem per eundem pro predictis imponendis et in eodem cariandis xii d.
Item in portagio predictorum et piscium ibidem per ipsum emptorum de diversis locis usque ad hospicium chariett*er* vi d.
In ii mattis \ longis / emptis pro aula domini apud Pot*er*ne viii d.
Item in i novo ret*e* empto apud Shirbo*ur*ne \ i sacco continenti in lo*ngitudine* viii teis / per Bertelot pro piscaria de Pot*er*ne cum coco apparato ad idem ix s. vi d.
In cirpis emptis apud Pot*er*ne a festo Omnium Sanctorum usque festum Epiphanie Domini per Blake messorem ibidem vii s. vii d.
Item solutum cuidam peuterer de Salesbur' pro xlix lib. i qr. peltri ab eo emptis pro xxvi discis et xii saucers inde faciendis ultra xlviii lib. de peltro domini precium lib. ii d. iiii s. iiii d.
Item solutum pro fimbr*acione* vi sanapp*es* ii copbordclothes ii peciarum mapparum pro hostiaria et xv napkyns ii s.
Item in smigmata empta pro pannis inde lavandis xiii d.
Item in i nova corda empta pro fonte de Pot*er*ne et ii novis cordis emptis pro ii wambties xi d.
Item in pakthrede empt*o* pro emendacione i ret*is* per Galfridum[456] Cato*ur* iiii d.
In CCxiiii peciis mapparum et tuellarum de panteria et Cxx peciis de

[455] MS obscure.
[456] MS 'pro Galfrid''.

camera domini et iiii^{xx}xiiii peciis <p> del <euer> ewery lavandis dando pro vi peciis i d. vi s. ii d. ob.
Item in CC napekyns lavandis dando pro xii i d. a xxvi° die Octobris usque xiii diem Januarii xvi d. ob.
Item in i barhide empto London' per Galfridum pro somerario coquine mense Januarii v s.
Item in xii virgis de sakclothe emptis de Castelton' per Nicholaum iii s. viii d.
Item solutum pro fimbr*acione* iiii sanap*es* et xii napkins per Radulphum Pant' x d.
Item in l ciphis fraxini emptis apud le Devys per Hubertum mense Decembris ii s. vi d.
Item in x virgis de bultello emptis per Robertum Baker de Castleton' precium virge ii d. xx d.
Item in i stillatorio vitrio empto pro domino pro medicin*is* domini inde stillandis per Nicholaum Cap*er*on' iii die mensis Aprilis xii d. . . .
In CCCCiiii^{xx} peciis mapparum et tuellarum de panteria linthiamentis de camera tuellis del ewrye cum lx peciis coquine lavandis dando pro vi peciis i d. cum locacione CC peciarum de napkyns danti pro xii peciis i d. . . . . .
In diversis seminibus emptis apud Remesbury per Thomam Norma*n* ad seminandum in gardino ibidem . . . . .
In captura de trught ibidem per Nicholaum Cap*er*on' . . . . .
In cirpis emptis apud Pot*er*ne per Willelmum Blake a primo die Marcii usque viii die*m* Maii . . . . .
Item solutum cuidam sissori de Pot*er*ne pro factura i toge pro Jak nape. . . . .
In cirpis emptis pro hospicio domini per Blake apud Pot*er*ne . . . . .
Item solutum lotrici apud Pot*er*ne per manus Nicholai Cap*er*on' tempore rec. . . . . de Pot*er*ne usque Sarum . . . . .
. . . . . *iii d.*
[*f.74r*][457] *Pur lez haukes* In primis solutum Johanni Edwyn pro columbellis et aliis neccessariis emptis p*ur* le goshauke ii s. ii d.
In vadiis Petri Faucon*er* existentis in patria cum nisibus[458] domini videlicet apud Huphaven' Wilsford et M*er*den per iii septimanas \ et iiii dies / capientis per septimanam ii s. iiii d. x s. viii d.
Item in vadiis pagetti eiusdem per idem tempus capientis per septimanam x d. ob. iii s. xi d. ob.
Item in xvii gallinis emptis[459] pro dictis nisibus susten*endis*[460] a festo Sancti Michaelis usque xiiii diem Februarii precium capitis ii d. ii s. x. . . . .

[457] f. 73^{v} blank.
[458] MS 'nus''.
[459] MS repeats 'empt''.
[460] MS 'sustenc''.

Item in ferrura equi eiusdem Petri per dictum tempus . . . . .
Item in expensis eiusdem Petri equitantis London' differentis ii nisus de exhenio domini Scokeyn baroni de scaccario eundo et rediundo per iiii dies . . . . .
Item solutum Johanni Edwyn pro gallinis columbellis et aliis neccessariis emptis p*ur* le goshauk' in Passione . . . . .
Item in i ciroteca empta per Johannem Edwyn . . . . .
In i <bak> bage de carde empt*o* per eundem . . . . .
In vadiis Petri Fauconer cum nisibus domini apud Patney Merden et alibi . . . . . capientis per septimanam tam pro se quam pro equo suo ii s. iiii d. . . .
Item in vadiis pagetti eiusdem per idem tempus capientis per septimanam x d. ob. . . . . .
Item in prandio empto pro eisdem ut in carnibus bovinis et porcorum a xiiii . . . . . usque festum Pent*ecoste* . . . . .

[*f.74v*] Custus venatoris

In primis in vadiis Johannis Asshemer a primo die Octobris usque vi diem Novembris utroque computato videlicet per v septimanas et ii dies capientis per diem ii d. vi s. ii d.
Item in vadiis pagetti per idem tempus capientis per diem i d. ob. iiii s. vii d. ob.
In vadiis Thome Feutrer apud Pot*er*ne et Remesbury a primo die Octobris usque x^m diem Novembris videlicet per v<i> septimanas et vi dies capientis per diem ii d. vi s. x d.
In pane empto pro canibus domini apud Remesbury per i noctem iiii d.
In vadiis Johannis Assh*e*mer ibidem a vi die Novembris usque x^m eiusdem utroque computato capientis per diem ii d. viii d.
In vadiis pagetti eiusdem ibidem per idem tempus capientis per diem i d. ob. vi d.
In vadiis Johannis Asshmer ibidem \ per <d> xix dies / a x die Novembris usque x<xiii> eiusdem capientis per diem ii d. iii s. ii d.
In vadiis Thome Feutrer ibidem per idem tempus capientis per diem ii d. iii s. ii d.
In vadiis pagetti venatoris ibidem per iii septimanas ii dies videlicet usque xxv diem Novembris ii s. x d. ob.
In vadiis dicti pagetti ibidem a xxv die <Januarii> Decembris usque xxii diem Januarii illo die computato videlicet per iii septimanas capientis per septimanam x d. ob. iii s. vi d.
In vadiis Johannis Asshm*er* per iii dies in fine Decembris xxxi dies mensis <Februarii> Januarii et x primos dies mensis Februarii capientis per diem ii d. vii s. iiii d.
In vadiis pagetti Asshm*ere* a xxiii^o die Januarii illo die computato per ix

dies sequentes et per xii dies in principio Februarii capientis per diem i d. ob. in universo per xxi dies per diem i d. ob. ii s. vii d. ob.
Item in vadiis Thome Feutrer' a v° die Januarii illo die computato per xxvi dies eiusdem mensis et per xii dies in principio Februarii capientis per diem ii d. in universo per xxxviii dies vi s. iiii d.
In vadiis Thome Feuterer apud Remesbur' per xiii dies capientis per diem ii d. ii s. ii d.
In pane empto ibidem pro canibus domini per eundem xx d.

[*f.75r*] Custus chariette

In primis in ii paribus tractuum emptis pro charietta ponderantibus xiii lib. xiii d.
Item solutum cuidam homine de Devise pro emendacione coleriorum et aliorum ad chariettam domini tam pro corio quam pro aliis neccessariis pertinentibus ad idem xii° die Januarii per G.Catour ii s. vii d.
Item in ii paribus tractuum[461] emptis per Galfridum Charieter ix d.
Item in xii takkes emptis per eundem Thomam Ferrour ii s.
Item in C clavis emptis per eundem cum xviii grossis clavibus emptis pro charietta ix d. ob.
In xii cloutis ferri emptis apud le Devys' per Barlich' pro charietta domini ii s.
Item in iiii paribus tractuum emptis apud Vise per G.Charieter iii s. vi d.
Item in v takkes emptis ibidem per eundem cum clavibus ad idem xiii d.
xiii s. ix d. ob.

[*f.75v*] Custus cellarum et frenorum

In ii cingulis emptis pro somarariis coquine per Hubertum iiii d.
In iii novis capistris duplicatis emptis pro equis domini cum vi novis reyns pro eisdem per Thomam Norman v s.
Item in emendacione cellarum litere apud Sarum tempore quo dominus erat apud Wodeford una cum emendacione aliarum cellarum domini xx d.
v s.

[*f.76r*] Dona anno octavo

In primis datum Agneti de Comberk apud Wodeford iiii° die Octobris precepto domini iii s. iiii d.
Item datum cuidam presbitero phisico inspicienti urinam domini apud Wodeford xiiii die Octobris vi s. viii d.
Item datum cuidam valecto maioris Sarum differenti domino ii lag. malvesy et diversos pisces recentes xvi die Octobris precepto domini iii s. iiii d.
Item datum cuidam garcioni abbatisse de Wilton' differenti ii fesantes xii perdices de exhenio xvi° die Octobris precepto domini xii d.

[461] MS 'tactuu''.

Item datum cuidam presbitero phisico pro medicinis emptis per eundem apud Bristoll' xviii^{o} die Octobris x s.
Item datum Alicie Shepherd de Pot*er*ne et filie sue differentibus domino de exhenio poma et pira ultimo die Octobris apud Pot*er*ne precepto domini xx d.
Item datum famulo Ricardi Osberne differenti domino de exhenio vi capones tercio die Novembris precepto domini viii d.
Item datum famulis domini apud Sarum precepto domini quarto die Novembris xii d.
Item datum \ cuidam paupero / armigero de comitatu Lancaustr' venienti domino usque Pot*er*ne de elemosina vi die Novembris precepto domini iii s. iiii d.
Item datum Hauberk locumtenenti de Pe*v*esham viii die Novembris precepto domini vi s. viii d.
Item datum Willelmo Gardiner de Pot*er*ne et uxori eius presentibus domino poma ibidem x^{o} die Novembris ii s. viii d.
Item datum domini Johanni Bray et Colwyn pro diversis neccessariis per eosdem emptis pro diversis interludiis erga[462] <ad> festum Natalis Domini iii s. iiii d.
Item datum Willelmo Gardyner et uxori sue differentibus domino poma de exhenio precepto domini ii s. viii d.
Item datum Thome Metford xxv die Novembris precepto domini vi s. viii d.
Item datum famulo magistri Johannis Maydenhith' differenti domino de exhenio i aprum precepto domini iiii s. iiii d.
Item datum episcopo Sancti Nicholai apud Pot*er*ne in nocte eiusdem Sancti Nicholai precepto domini iii s. iiii d.
Item datum cuidam hostillario de Hungerford differenti domino de exhenio i trught xx d.
Item datum famulo capellani[463] de Hornesham differenti domino medicinas ex parte magistri sui xii d.
Item datum famulo magistri Symonis Unwyn differenti domino vi capones de exhenio precepto domini xii d.
Item datum Thome Carter de Shirbo*ur*ne venienti de ibidem usque Pot*er*ne cum dam*is* eundo et rediundo per ii dies \ precepto domini / xvi d.
Item datum vii hominibus de Synde ludentibus coram domino in die Sancti Johannis precepto domini v s.
Item datum iii tenentibus domini de Pot*er*ne ludentibus coram domino et

[462] MS 'arga'.
[463] MS 'capellane'.

iii tenentibus domini episcopi Wyncestr' ludentibus coram domino i interludium in die Sanctorum Innocencium precepto domini iiii s.
Item datum cuidam ministrallo de Lavington' existenti apud Pot*er*ne tempore Natalis Domini precepto domini xx. . . . .
Item datum nutrici Osberne existenti apud Pot*er*ne precepto domini . . . . .
Item datum diversis hominibus ludentibus coram domino iiii^{o} die Januarii precepto domini . . . . .
Item datum Rogero Burwassh' custodi chaciam de Houghton' vii^{o} die Januarii precepto domini . . . . .
Item datum famulo Bisle existenti apud Pot*er*ne cum i litera magistri sui \ x^{o} Januarii / . . . . .
Item datum domini Johanni Stokes per Nicholaum Cap*er*on' iiii^{o} die Januarii precepto domini . . . . .
Item datum iiii ministrallis domini de Lovell' existentibus apud Pot*er*ne die Epiphanie . . . . .
Item datum ii ministrallis ducis Ebor' existentibus ibidem xii die Januarii . . . . .
Item datum diversis pauperibus venientibus usque Pot*er*ne per manus Johannis Wither . . . . . apud Schaftesbury . . . . .
Item in elimosina data ibidem alia vice per eundem precepto domini . . . . .
Per senescallum[464] Item datum cuidam clerico et garcioni abbatis de Malmesbur' differen. . . . . xxiiii capones xxiiii cuniculos ii cignos et ii damas de fermes. . . . .
Item datum iiii hominibus de Shirbo*ur*ne ludentibus ii interludia coram domino . . . . .
Item datum cuidam ficholer existenti apud Pot*er*ne die predicto . . . . .
Item datum Thome Carter de Shirbo*urne* venienti usque Pot*er*ne cum ii damis . . . . .
Item iiii hominibus del Vise ludentibus i interludium coram domino <iiii d> de Redy. . . . . Tynker iiii die Januarii . . . . .
Item datum cuidam mulieri de Sarum pro colloquio habendo cum domino pro materia tan. . . . . Hulcot pro filia sua nuper in custodia dicte mulieris die predicto precepto domini . . . . .
[*f.76v*] Item datum iiii hominibus de Erchesfont ludentibus coram domino i interludium vi^{o} die Januarii precepto domini ii s.
Item datum cuidam falconario domini Willelmi Stormy differenti domino die predicto vi herons et iiii maurald*os* de rivera precepto domini iii s. iiii d.
Item datum Ricardo Neubery nakerner existenti apud Pot*er*ne cum domino per x dies infra Natale Domini precium domini cum v d. solut*is* Felicie Aas pro lecto suo iii s. ix d.

[464] Bracketed against the remaining items on this page.

Item datum cuidam giterner existenti ibidem die Epiphanie precepto domini xii d.
Item datum iiii famulis Hulcot existentibus apud Pot*er*ne cum magistro suo viii^{o} die Januarii precepto domini vi s. viii d.
Item datum servienti Calston' armigerii differenti domino de exhennio ii capras xii die Februarii precepto domini xx d.
Item datum famulo wodewardi de Chetu differenti domino i damam iiii d.
Item datum Thome Carter de Shirbo*ur*ne venienti de ibidem usque Pot*er*ne cum ii equis auxiliantibus charet*e* domini venienti cum i dolio vini de ibidem usque Pot*er*ne mense Januarii precepto domini x d.
Item datum famulo domine de Cary differenti domino i literam xii^{o} die Januarii precepto domini ii s.
Item datum famulo domini Georgii Louthorp venienti in negociis domini de Sarum usque Pot' precepto domini viii d.
Item datum Stephano de Coquina Forrey pagetto venatoris Parstok pagetto Faucon*er* et aliis pagettis in hospicio pro eorum annidonis primo die Januarii precepto domini cuilibet eorum iiii d. ii s.
Item datum ii valectis ii garcionibus et i pagetto uxoris Willelmi Worston' existentibus cum domino apud Pot*er*ne in fine Januarii precepto domini ix s. iiii d.
Item datum ii valectis prisonar*iis* venientibus de Wallia usque Pot*er*ne xvi^{o} die Februarii xii d.
Item datum iii pueris ludentibus coram domino in presencia uxoris Willelmi Worston' xii d.
Item datum cuidam mulieri <de> Indee nuper converse ad Christianum cultum xx^{o} die Februarii xii d.
Item datum cuidam valecto domini Lovell' differenti domino unum instrumentum de argento pro virga virili xx^{o} die Februarii precepto domini iii s. iiii d.
Item datum Bertlot venienti de Shirbo*ur*ne usque Pot*er*ne cum pyk*es* et anguillis xxvi^{o} Februarii ii s.
Item datum Roberto famulo Bertlot venienti de Shirbo*ur*ne usque Pot*er*ne cum ii pik*es* x^{o} die Marcii cum conduct*o* unius equi per viam xx d.
Item datum Radulpho Parker de Sonnyng' defferenti domino literam de Laurencio Drew xx^{o} die Marcii xx d.
Item datum Rogero Cooke et sociis suis in coquina p*ur* le wythe in die Pasche precepto domini xiii s. iiii d.
Item datum cuidam heraude vocato Notyngham existenti apud Pot*er*ne xxviii^{o} die Marcii precepto domini vi s. viii d.
Item datum iiii hominibus ludentibus i interludium de Lent <in> apud Pot*er*ne iii die Aprilis precepto domini iii s. iiii d.
Item datum cuidam episcopo de Hibernia venienti domino usque Pot*er*ne dominica in albis precepto domini xx s.

Item in elemosina data diversis pauperibus per manus domini Johannis Stokes elemosinarii ii s. ii d.
Item datum cuidam heremit*o* de Farle apud Pot*er*ne precepto domini viii d.
Item datum i servienti Ricardi Osb*er*n' differenti domino de Horyton usque Pot*er*ne i ollam cervisie de exhennio vi d.
Item datum famulo Foxhangr' venienti usque Pot*er*ne de Wherwell' in negociis domini precepto domini xii d.
Item datum prisonariis in banco regis per manus attorn*ati* eorum apud Pot*er*ne xx° die Aprilis xii d.
Item datum cuidam homini apud Pot*er*ne capienti fasianos et perdices xxiiii die Aprilis precepto domini xii d.
. . . . . in i magna olla enia emendanda cum emendacione i candelabr*e* de laton per . . . . . Colyn junior' mense Januarii xviii d.
. . . . . servient*i* Johannis Foxhaner different*i* sorori domini iiii trughtes iiii° die Maii xii d.
. . . . . cuidam homini[465] Gloucestr' differenti sorori domini de exhenio Johannis Clifford . . . . . et i salmonem recentem vii° die Maii precepto eiusdem sororis iii s. iiii d.
. . . . .is parochii Sancti Edmundi apud Sarum tripudant*ibus* coram magistro Waltero . . . . . x° die Maii precepto eiusdem magistri Walteri xii d.
. . . . .r' in grangia domini apud Sarum die predicto precepto eiusdem iiii d.
Cii s. i d.

[*f.77r*] Stipendia famulorum domini in hospicio

In stipendiis famulorum existencium in hospicio pro termino Natalis Domini ut patet in cedula de nominibus eorundem et de certo cuiuslibet eorum pro quartario xv li. xviii s.
In stipendiis famulorum domini in hospicio pro termino Pasche ut patet in dicta cedula de nominibus eorundem de certo cuiuslibet eorundem pro quartario xv li. v s. vi d.
Item in stipendiis famulorum in hospicio ut patet in parcellis pro termino Nat*ivitatis* Sancti Johannis Baptiste xv li. vi s. iiii d.
In stipendiis domini Johannis Stokis decani capelle superius non computatis xli s. viii d.
Item in stipendiis Michaelis de Coquina pro termino Natalis Domini xviii d.

[*f.77v*] Gardroba

In primis in vi lib. coton emptis London' per Nicholaum Cap*er*on' mense Octobris v s. vi d.
Item in xvi lib. di. sope emptis ibidem per eundem ii s. iiii d.
Item in i pari de corkes empto ibidem pro domino per eundem xiiii d.

[465] MS 'homine'.

Item in ii nithecap emptis ibidem per eundem ii s. viii d.
Item in i hure empt*o* ibidem pro domino per eundem vi d.
Medicina pro domino [466] Item in ii lib. di. oximell' emptis pro domino de uno presbitero phisico in fine mensis Octobris xvi s. viii d.
Item in ii unciis poudr*i* de traiell' emptis apud Pot*er*ne de eodem ad idem tempus xiii s. iiii d.
Item in di. lib. olei benedicti empta ibidem de eodem vi s. viii d.
Item in xi pat*er*nostres de auro emptis de quodam homine de Bristoll' apud Pot*er*ne ponderandis xxv s. x d. vi die Novembris xxvi s. viii d.
In i broche aureo empto de eodem cum iii tal*eis* vi anulis cum lapidibus emptis ibidem de eodem die predicto xvii s.
In xii ulnis panni de Wilton' emptis de Castelton' precium ulne <viii d. ob.> ix d. ix s.
Item in xxviii ulnis panni linei emptis de eodem precium ulne viii d. plus in toto vi d. xix s. ii d.
Annidona empta London' per Thomam Croxby [467] Item in xxiiii anulis de auro emptis London per Thomam Croxby mense Novembris precium pecie xvii d. ob. xxxv s.
Item in xii anulis de auro emptis ibidem per eundem precium pecie iii s. ix d. ob. plus in toto ii d. xlv s. viii d.
Item in xii anulis de auro emptis ibidem per eundem precium pecie xxiii d. ob. xxiii s. vi d.
Item in xxiiii anulis de argento et deauratis emptis ibidem per eundem unde xvi precium pecie viii d. et viii precium pecie ix d. xvi s. viii d.
Item in i pari de bedys de auro empto ibidem cum i parvo broch' de auro pro eisdem xxxiii s. iiii d.
Item in uno alio broche de auro empto ibidem per dictum Thomam xii s. viii d.
Item in vi paribus bedys de get cum pat*er*nostr*e*s de argento et deauratis precium pecie iii s. xviii s.
Item in viii paribus bedis de get cum pat*er*nostr*es* ut supra precium pecie ii s. xvi s.
Item in i electuario empto pro domino apud Wodeford per rectorem de Alyngton' mense Octobris ii s. viii d.
Item in i alio electuario empto apud Sarum per eundem in fine mensis Novembris ii s. x d.
Item in i pari bedis de auro empto apud Pot*er*ne de quodam jocal*ario* ix Decembris xviii s. iiii d.
Item in x anulis auri emptis de eodem ibidem xii s.

[466] Bracketed against the next 3 items.
[467] Bracketed against the next 8 items.

Item in <medicinis emptis pro domino \ T. /Thirlewall' de> \ dat*um* <T.> / magistro Thome Thirlewall' fesic*o* domini per manus Nicholai Cap*er*on' xxii die Decembris xiii s. iiii d.
Item in medicinis emptis de eodem pro domino in fine mensis Decembris iiii s.
Item solutum eidem pro expensis suis de Pot*er*ne usque London' pro medicinis ibidem emendis pro domino in eundo et rediundo per viii dies mense predicto x s.
Item datum eidem pro occupacione sua circa dominum per <xiiii> \ vii / dies in fine Decembris \ et / vii primos dies mensis Januarii apud Pot*er*ne precepto domini xx s.
In medicinis emptis pro domino per Georgium Cresy mense Decembris xiiii s.
Item in viii cultellis emptis per Nicholaum Cap*er*on' pro annidonis puerorum et aliorum de capella precepto domini ii s. x d.
Item in xxiiii bursis emptis pro annidonis domini per Johannem clericum cancellarii xxxiiii s.
Item in xx lib. licoreis emptis London' per Galfridum ii s. vi d.
. . . . . in nutmyg' empt*o* ibidem i lib. ii s. In xii lib. sope emptis ibidem ii s.
Item in i pipa vocata squirte empta vii s. iiii d.
. . . . . in medicinis emptis London pro domino per T.Croxby cum xiiii d. pro i votell' de peltro pro eisdem imponiendis vii s. ii d.
. . . . . diversis medicinis emptis London' per magistrum Thomam Thirlewall' pro domino xiiii s.
. . . . . magistro Thome Therlewall' xiii die Februarii xxvi s. viii d.
. . . . . caumfur' empt*o* pro domino apud Oxon' per magistrum T. fisic*um* domini xvi^{o} Februarii vi s. viii d.
. . . . . vii ulnis panni linii emptis de Castelton' precium ulne viii d. ob. xxvi s. vi d.
. . . . .is panni linii emptis de eodem ii s. iiii d.
. . . . . panni linei empt*is* pro domino apud Pot*er*ne xxvi^{o} die Februarii . . . . . xvi s.
. . . . . de rubio mell*eto* empto per Robertum de Camera pro Wylton' hostiario domini pro liberat*ura* . . . . . domini iiii s. ii d.
. . . . . de argento empto London per Thomam Croxby pro domino mense <Januarii> Marcii x s.
. . . . . medicinis empt*is* Oxonie pro domino per Nicholaum Sy cum xx d. pro expensis eiusdem de . . . . . usque ibidem eundo et rediuno per ii dies in fine mensis Marcii xii s.
. . . . .butter empt*o* pro d. . . . . apud Pot*er*ne iiii d. ob.

[*f.78r*] Custus capelle

In iii longis mattis emptis pro capella et ii curtis et vii <long> rotundis <em> ii s. iiii d.

Item in iii cordulis emptis per Johannem Stokes apud Pot*er*ne pro campanis ibidem ii s.
Item in i claper empt*o* pro i campana ibidem xii d.
In M panibus emptis per Johannem Stok' ad celebrandum xxii d.
In locacione panni per eundem apud Pot*er*ne et alibi ii s. iiii d.
In di. lib. thuris empta per eundem xii d.
In vestimentis emendis per eundem iiii d.
Item solutum cuidam pictori de la Vise pro pictacione i baculi crucis in capella una cum deauracione eiusdem ad ii vices xviii d.

Item gardroba

Item solutum magistro Thome Thirwall' tam pro medicinis quam pro rewardis et labore suo circa dominum apud Pot*er*ne xi die Aprilis liii s. iiii d.
In medicinis emptis pro domino apud Sarum per dictum T. in septimana Pasche xiii s. iiii d.
Item solutum magistro Johanni Malverne pro labore suo existenti cum domino apud Pot*er*ne xxviii die Aprilis liii s. iiii d.
In[468] diversis medicinis emptis apud Sarum pro domino per Nicholaum Cap*er*on' die predicto vi s. x d.
In expensis magistri Johannis Malverne cum ii hominibus et iii equis de Pot*er*ne usque Oxon' v s. vi. . . . .
Item datum magistro Thome Thirlewall' pro rewardo facto eidem ultimo die Aprilis xl. . . . .
Lentierment xliii s. iiii d.[469] Item in iiii^{xx}xvi ulnis panni linii vocato spinol' emptis precium ulne iii d. ob. . . . . .
Item in vi crestes panni linii emptis precium del cres' xxi d. . . . . .
Item in iiii ulnis panni de Braban emptis precium ulne vi d. ob. . . . . .
Item in ix ulnis <d. . . > \ di. / emptis pro discis mundandis precium ulne iii d. ob. . . . . .
Item in panno nigro empto apud Vise per Barlich' pro litera et cista cooperiendis . . . . .
Item in ii virgis panni de medle de secta valecti emptis pro i homine de Sh. . . . . colligenti le croukepeny precium virge ii s. . . . . .
. . . li. . . . s. v d.

[f.78v] Expense forinsece

In primis in expensis Huberti de Wodeford' usque Shirb*our*ne pro iiii^{xx} multonibus et ii bobus ibidem querendis et fugandis usque Pot*er*ne cum iii hominibus conductis axiliantibus eidem Huberto eundo et rediundo per v dies v s. iii d.

468 MS repeats 'in'.
469 Bracketed against all remaining items on the page except the last.

Item in i equo conducto pro dicto Huberto per idem tempus xv d.
Item in expensis Nicholai Cap*er*on per xi dies London' pro piscibus salciis speciebus et aliis ibidem pro hospicio domini ibidem emendis mense Octobris xii s. v d.
Item in v equis conductis pro quibusdam de famulia domini equitantibus cum domino de Wodeford usque Pot*er*ne per iii dies mense Octobris capiens quilibet eorum per diem iii d. iii s. ix d.
In i homine conducto pro eisdem equis reducendis usque Wodeford' vi d.
Item in expensis Thome Croxby de Shirborne usque Wodeford pro libro de registro domini ibidem querendo eundo et rediundo per iii dies mense Octobris xiiii d.
Item in expensis eiusdem de Wodeford' usque London' in negociis domini <xvi> \ iiii / dies mensibus Octobris et Novembris xx d.
Item in expensis ii carectariorum de Shirbo*ur*ne[470] cum carecta et vii equis de Shirbo*ur*ne usque Pot*er*ne cariancium ii pipas vini eundo et redeundo per iiii dies mense Novembris unde per manus Bertlat iii s. iiii d. v s. viii d.
Item in expensis ii carectariorum de Lavyngton' cum carectis et vi equis de Pot*er*ne usque Sarum pro panno de liberatura estivali domini ibidem querendo mense Novembris viii d.
Item in expensis Johannis Brewere equitantis in negociis per xvi dies videlicet una vice de Shirbo*ur*n usque domum Sparwe alia vice de Wodeford usque Berfeld' cum i litera magistro Waltero Metford alia vice de Wodeford usque Sonnyng' pro colloquio habendo ex parte domini cum dicto magistro W. et alia de Shirbo*ur*ne usque Sarum et rectorem de Alynton' mense Septembris v s. x d.
In i equo conducto per eundem Johannem per tempus predictum iiii s. viii d.
Item in expensis Thome Croxby London' tam pro jocalibus piscibus et aliis ibidem emendis quam pro aliis negociis domini ibidem faciendis per xi dies mense Novembris vii s. iii d.
Item[471] in expensis ii carectariorum de Sarum et Wodeford' veniencium cum carect*is* usque Pot*er*ne cariancium i pipam salis albi viii d.
Item in expensis Johannis Russell' de Shirbo*ur*ne usque Wodeford pro[472] ordinacione facienda erga[473] adventum domini ibidem per iii dies mense Octobris xviii d.
Item in expensis eiusdem[474] equitantis de Pot*er*ne usque Shirbo*urne* pro

[470] MS 'Shirbone'.
[471] A note in the left margin, possibly 'per M.'
[472] MS 'per'.
[473] MS 'arga'.
[474] MS 'eusd''.

vasa argentia et vino ibidem <emendis> querendis eundo et rediundo per iii dies mense Octobris xii d.
Item in expensis eiusdem equitantis de Pot*er*ne usque Sarum in negociis domini et deinde usque Welles pro i plastirer ibidem querendo eundo et rediundo per iiii \ ultimos / dies mensis Novembris xv d.
Item in expensis eiusdem usque Chitew pro damis ibidem querendis una cum expensis aliorum de hospicio ibidem xiiii d.
Item in expensis Thome Normam <pro> de Pot*er*ne usque Hornesham cum ii equis pro J.Medico ibidem querendo ad ii vices mense Octobris xi d.
Item in expensis eiusdem de Pot*er*ne usque Sonnyng' pro perdicibus fasianis et aliis ibidem querendis . . . . . festum Epiphanie Domini eundo et rediundo per iii dies xii d. ob.
. . . . . ii talliatoribus conductis talliantibus boscum pro hospicio per xx dies et di. ad taxham capientibus inter se . . . . .i d. ob. xii s. ob.
. . . . . Willelmo Port*er* pro i dolebro empto pro aula viii d.
. . . . . Nicholai Cap*er*on' et aliorum existencium apud Chitue pro dam*is* querend*is* etc. xii d.
. . . . . Benedicti clerici registerarii de Pot*er*ne usque Geinge in negociis domini xii d.
. . . . . rubio plumbo et aliis picturis emptis per Henricum Buteler pro <iii> disgisinges . . . . . fac*tis* tempore Natalis Domini cum iii s. iiii d. de rewardo facto eidem pro labore suo precepto domini ix s. ii d.
. . . . . Buteler Nicholai Sy Thome Clav*er*yng' et aliorum apud Sarum Aumesbury et alibi . . . . . mens*e* Octobris ii s. iiii d.
. . . . . pro i bove vi multonibus et xxiiii porcis necandis pro hospicio per G.Cato*ur* mense Novembris viii d.
. . . . . famulo fabri de Vise venient*i* usque Pot*er*ne cum medicinis pro equis domini iiii d.
. . . . . i homine conducto tam pro baconibus necandis quam pro candelis faciendis per v dies mense Novembris x d.
. . . . . Johannis Bruer equitant*is* de Pot*er*ne usque London' una vice in negociis . . . . . Novembr*is* et per ii alias vices versus Shirbo*ur*ne et alibi per xx dies in toto x s.

iiii li. xv s. viii d.

[*f.79r*] Item in expensis carectariorum maneriorum domini cariancium harnesia domini ad diversos locos per manus J.C. iii s. iiii d.
Item in expensis Galfridi Cato*ur* de Pot*er*ne usque Remesbur' per ii dies pro bobus ibidem querendis mense Novembris x d.
Item in i homine conducto pro dictis bobus fugandis de Remesbur' usque Pot*er*ne xii d.
Item solutum magistro Willelmo Ferro*ur* de Devis' pro medicinis emptis de eodem pro equis domini per G. . . .to*ur* iiii s. iiii d.

Item in expensis domini Thome Wysebech' senescalli hospicii London' tam pro negociis tangentibus Wilmyngton' quam pro medicinis ibidem ordinandis pro domino per iiii dies in fine mensis Januarii cum vi d. pro batulagio ibidem xv s. ii d.
In expensis diversorum hominum existencium apud domum Felicie Aas tempore Natalis Domini iii s. v d.
In expensis Johannis Bruer London' in negociis domini eundo et rediundo per ix dies in fine mensis Decembris cum ferrura equi eiusdem per viam v s. ix d. ob.
Item in expensis eiusdem de Pot*er*ne usque Hornesham pro medicinis ibidem querendis pro domino xvi d.
Item in i equo conducto per dictum tempus per eundem Johannem viii d.
Item in expensis eiusdem alia vice apud Chetu pro dam*is* ibidem querend*is* ix d.
Item in expensis Galfridi <Catour> \ Charietter / de Pot*er*ne usque Shirborn' cum chariett*a* et vii equis per ii vices pro ii doliis vini ibidem querendis eundo et rediundo per viii dies mense Januarii xiiii s.
Item in ferrura equorum chariett*e* per viam xvi d.
Item solutum Ryle pro expensis equorum Laurencii Drue Roberti Gore et aliorum existencium apud domum suam per iiii dies tempore Natalis Domini v s. i d.
In i homine conducto cum ii equis axiliantibus carect*am* de Canyng' carian*tem* boscum pro hospicio per[475] vii dies mense Februarii capienti per diem pro se et equis suis vi d. iii s. x d.
Item in expensis Nicholai Sy de Pot*er*ne usque Sarum pro medicinis ibidem querendis mense Januarii ix d.
Item in expensis Henrici de Coquina de Pot*er*ne usque Remesbury pro cignis ibidem querendis iiii d.
In expensis \ Huberti et / ii carectariorum cum carect*is* et viii equis de Pot*er*ne usque Bristoll' pro i but' salmonum et xiiC ferri ibidem querendis eundo et rediundo per iii dies cum ii jugis boum conductis pro dict*is* carect*is* auxiliand*is* per viam viii s.
In expensis eiusdem Huberti et ii carectariorum cum carect*is* et vii equis de Pot*er*ne usque Sarum pro liberatura yemali ibidem cum iiii sig*nis* cariand*a* de Wodeford' eundo et rediundo per ii dies ii s. vi d.
Item in expensis eiusdem cum somerari*o* de Pot*er*ne usque Remesbury pro cignis ibidem querendis erga festum Natalis Domini vi d.
Item in expensis Cauntelowe equitantis de Pot*er*ne usque Sarum per iii vices pro medicinis querendis pro domino eundo et rediundo per v dies mensibus Januarii et Februarii ii s. . . . . .

[475] MS 'pro'.

In expensis Roberti Baker' equitantis de Pot*er*ne usque Sarum defferentis literam magistro Henrico H*ar*borgh' precepto domini . . . . .
In ii ceruris emptis per Randulphum de Panteria pro i almary in panteria pro diversis neccessariis in eadem custodien. . . . .
In expensis vi equorum magistri Radulphi canonici existencium apud Pot*er*ne xix^{o} die Februarii . . . . .
In expensis Willelmi M*er*sch' equitantis de Pot*er*ne usque Schirbo*ur*ne in fine mensis Novembris . . . . . pro rotulis compotorum ibidem querendis et ducendis usque Sarum per iiii dies eundo et redeundo . . . . .
Item solutum Johanni Leche de Pot*er*ne pro sanacione capitis Stephani pagetti coquine . . . . .
In expensis famulie et equorum priorisse de Bromhal' apud Pot*er*ne apud domum fili. . . . . Johann*is* Foxhangr' ibidem videlicet per iii dies mense Marcii precepto domini . . . . .
In expensis Perye et Drewery de Oxon' usque Pot*er*ne cum expensis Forrey cum iii equis . . . . . et Oxon' pro eisdem <viii d' per> eundo et rediundo per iii dies mense Marcii . . . . .
In expensis Nicholai Cap*er*on' de Pot*er*ne usque Remesbury in negociis domini tangentibus ecclesiam . . . . . mens*e* Februarii precepto domini . . . . .
In expensis Shipton' Nicholai Cap*er*on' Holcote Johannis Warn*er* et viii aliorum de fam. . . . . Chitue pro dam*is* capiend*is* erga festum Pasche . . . . .
[*f.79v*] In expensis Roberti servientis Bertelot cum equo suo de Shirbo*ur*ne usque Pot*er*ne in vigilia Pasche pro pikes cariandis pro hospicio eundo et rediundo per ii dies xii d.
Item in expensis equorum Nicholai Port*er* et Notyngham heraud' existencium apud domum Ryle per ii dies et ii hakeneorum in fine mensis Marcii xiiii d.
Item in expensis Henrici Buteler de Pot*er*ne usque Wermynstr' et alibi in negociis domini dominica in Pas. . . . . Domini xviii d.
Item in expensis Huberti equitantis de Pot*er*ne usque Sarum pro xviii <v> togis <pauperum> ibidem querendis dando pauperibus per dominum in Cena Domini viii d.
Item in expensis Nicholai Cap*er*on' equitantis de Pot*er*ne usque Sonnyng' et Wokingham pro pecuniis ibidem querendis et pro colloquio habendo cum Laurencio Dru una cum expensis clerici manerii ibidem et parcarii equitancium[476] cum eodem usque Wokingham eundo et rediundo per vi dies v s.
In uno equo[477] accomodato magistro Thome <Rodi> phisico per abbatem de Schirbo*ur*ne reducendo de Pot*er*ne usque ibidem ix^{o} die Aprilis viii d.
Item in expensis Galfridi Chariet*er* cum chariett*a* domini et vii equis de

[476] MS 'equitencium'.
[477] MS omits 'equo'.

Pot*er*ne usque London pro piscibus salsiis speciebus et aliis victualibus ibidem querendis eundo et red*i*undo per vii dies mense Januarii xv s. ob.
Item in expensis eiusdem et garcionis sui[478] cum chariett*a* domini et vii equis de Pot*er*ne usque Bristoll' pro ii pipis vini querendis ibidem eundo et rediundo per iii die*s* mense Aprilis vii s. i d.
Item in expensis Russell' equitantis de Pot*er*ne usque Bristoll' pro vino ibidem querendo eundo et rediundo per iii dies mense Aprilis una cum portagio et aliis expensis factis ibidem circa eundem iii s. xi d.
In expensis cuiusdam hominis de Hybernia venientis domino usque Pot*er*ne xxviii die mensis Marcii precepto domini ii s. iiii d.
Item in i homine conducto per ii die*s* capienti fasianos et perdices in fine mensis Aprilis xvi d.
In i equo conducto de Adam Axford auxilianti carect*am* domini inter Pot*er*ne et Shirbo*ur*ne xii d.
In expensis Johannis Russell' equitantis de Pot*er*ne usque Bristoll' pro vino ibidem emendo xxiii d.
In i homine conducto per xii dies di. pro bosco prosternendo et talliando capienti per diem iiii d. per Barlich' prepositum de Pot*er*ne iiii s. ii d.
In i homine conducto per iii dies pro bosco talliando in hospicio ad mensam capienti per diem ii d. vi d.
In i \ homine / conducto per i septimanam capienti fasianos et perdices ultra denarios sibi perantea solutos mense Maii xx d.
Item in expensis Galfridi Chariet*er* et garcionis sui cum chariett*a* domini de Pot*er*ne pro vino[479] cariando ad ii vices usque Sarum eundo et rediundo per iiii dies iiii s. ix d.
In expensis Radulphi de Butery equitantis de Sarum usque Wymbo*ur*ne Mynstr' pro ardeis populers et egerett*es* ibidem emendis eundo et rediundo per ii dies in fine mensis Maii xii d.
Item in rewardo facto Willelmo Helier fratri suo existenti apud Sarum die sepulture domini xvi d.
Item solutum Thome Buteler de rewardo facto eidem iii s. iiii d.
Item solutum iii pagettis in coquina ut in rewardis factis eisdem vi d.
. . . . . solutum cuidam moniali de Wilton' pro expensis sororis domini ibidem iii s. iiii d.
. . . . . expensis baronis de Caru apud Pot*er*ne in domo Ryle mense Maii xii d.
. . . . . conduct*o* pro fasianis et perdicibus capiendis apud Pot*er*ne ii s.
. . . . . Thome Clav*er*ing' de Pot*er*ne usque domum domini Johannis Drayton' cum ii cursariis . . . . . rediundo per iii dies xii d.

[478] MS 'suis'.
[479] MS 'vimo'.

. . . . . Sy equitant*is* de Pot*er*ne xxii die Februarii pro i litera[480] differenda
. . . . . Stafford alia vice usque Reding' pro magistro Thoma Thirlewall'
. . . . . pro domino iiii s.
. . . . . de Shirbo*ur*ne eunt*is* versus Wodeford cum iiii equis et carect*a* domini . . . . . victual*ibus* ac eunt*is* per ii vices cum dictis equis et carect*a* de ibidem usque Pot*er*ne . . . . . illuc cariand*is* per ii vices capien*tis* pro qualibet vice vi s. viii d. xx s.
. . . . .huberd et ii hominum fugancium iii boves et iiii^{xx} bidentes de Shirbo*ur*ne . . . . . ii s. vi d.
. . . . . dol*ium* vini de ibidem usque Pot*er*ne iiii s.
[*f.80r*] *<Forin> Forincece liberaciones*
In denariis accomodatis Ricardo Restewold per quoddam scriptum obligat. . . . . remanens penes dominum xiii li. vi s. viii d.
In denariis liberatis domino ad iii vices per manus computan*tis* ut patet per indenturam de dato xx die Decembris Cvi li. xiii s. iiii d.
In primis liberatum domino Georgio Louthorp' in presencia magistri Walteri Metford apud Sarum in domo eiusdem domini Georgii in partem solucionis panni nigri de liberatura domini pro lent*er*ment xxix^{o} die Maii xl li.
Item liberatum eidem in presencia magistri Rogeri Harwell' in < . . . > camera apud Lendenhalle super solucione*m* Johannis Chaundeler xiiii^{o} die Junii x. . . . .
Item accomodatum Johanni Metford cognato domini xxix^{o} die Decembris precepto magistri <R.> \ W. / M. . . . . .
Item accomodatum magistro Waltero Metford' per manus Johannis Wotton' iiii^{o} die Januarii apud Pot*er*ne . . . . .
Item Johanni Metford' de Geinge primo die Januarii pro expensis suis versus s. . . . .
Item in denariis perdonatis Johanni <Cl> Walront et uxori sue precepto domini . . . . .[481]

[480] MS 'l'ria'.
[481] The bottom of the folio has been cut away. f. 80^{v} is blank.

www.ingramcontent.com/pod-product-compliance
Lightning Source LLC
Chambersburg PA
CBHW071306180926
51613CB00001B/141
* 9 7 8 0 1 9 7 2 6 1 1 2 5 *